FILM
AN INTRODUCTION

FILM

AN INTRODUCTION

FOURTH EDITION

William H. Phillips

University of Wisconsin–Eau Claire

BEDFORD/ST. MARTIN'S   Boston ◆ New York

For Bedford/St. Martin's

Executive Editor for Communication: Erika Gutierrez
Developmental Editor: Margaret Manos
Editorial Assistant: Mae Klinger
Production Editor: Ryan Sullivan
Production Supervisor: Jennifer Peterson
Marketing Manager: Adrienne Petsick
Art Director: Lucy Krikorian
Text Design: Wanda Kossak, Linda Robertson
Copy Editor: Patricia Herbst
Cover Design: Billy Boardman
Composition and Layout: Jan Ewing/Ewing Systems
Printing and Binding: RR Donnelley and Sons

President: Joan E. Feinberg
Editorial Director: Denise B. Wydra
Director of Development: Erica T. Appel
Director of Marketing: Karen R. Soeltz
Director of Editing, Design, and Production: Marcia Cohen
Assistant Director of Editing, Design, and Production: Elise S. Kaiser
Managing Editor: Shuli Traub

Library of Congress Catalog Card Number: 2008931067

Copyright © 2009 by Bedford/St. Martin's

Manufactured in the United States of America.

5 4
f

For information, write: Bedford/St. Martin's, 75 Arlington Street, Boston, MA 02116
(617-399-4000)

ISBN-10: 0-312-48725-8
ISBN-13: 978-0-312-48725-6

Acknowledgments
Acknowledgments and copyrights appear at the back of the book on page 703, which constitutes an extension of the copyright page.

Published and distributed outside North America by
PALGRAVE MACMILLAN
Houndmills, Basingstoke, Hampshire RG21 2XS
Companies and representatives throughout the world.

ISBN-10: 0-230-22332-X; ISBN-13: 978-0-230-22332-5

A catalog record for this book is available from the British Library.

Preface to the Fourth Edition

THE BOOK BEFORE YOU REPRESENTS close to thirty years of research, experimentation in teaching, and writing. I developed and wrote *Film: An Introduction* in the twofold hope that its readers will better understand and appreciate individual films and gain a fuller understanding of the film medium's variety, achievements, and possibilities. It is gratifying that the book has been used as a major text in an immense variety of courses, including Introduction to Film, Writing about Film, Women in Film, Religion and Film, Race in U.S. Cinema, Film and Literature, Introduction to Video Art, The Art of Digital Filmmaking, and many others. *Film: An Introduction* has been used at community colleges, liberal arts colleges, state universities, and private universities throughout the United States, and in Canada, Australia, Ireland, and England. Such wide-ranging adoptions have helped motivate me to undertake the considerable task of doing a fourth edition. So, too, have the positive responses from film instructors. Their suggestions and the responses of my own students have helped shape this major revision.

FEATURES

THE MOST COMPREHENSIVE INTRODUCTION TO FILM *Film: An Introduction* includes a wider array of films, more help for students, and a broader selection of images than any other introductory film book. In addition to introducing students to the technical, aesthetic, theoretical, historical, and cultural aspects of film, every chapter offers an incomparably broad discussion of film, from the silent classics of D. W. Griffith and Sergei Eisenstein to the Hong Kong cinema of John Woo, the documentaries of Errol Morris, and classic and contemporary experimental films.

EXTENSIVE STUDY AIDS ENHANCE THE TEXT'S ACCESSIBILITY A wealth of study aids reinforce key concepts and make review easier: class-tested figures and tables; features that showcase a variety of supplementary information, such as excerpts from the U.S. Production Code; chapter summaries; a chapter that includes helpful tips on writing about films; and a comprehensive four-column chronology detailing major historical and artistic events.

DETAILED, COMPREHENSIVE CAPTIONS ENHANCE LEARNING   In-depth captions explain the important aspects of each image, providing coverage beyond the main text. So extensive are the book's photos and captions that they could function alone as a brief introduction to or review of the book's scope and content and, indeed, the major aspects of the film medium.

***FILM*'S STRUCTURE ALLOWS INSTRUCTORS TO TAILOR THE TEXT TO THEIR CLASSROOM NEEDS**   The structure of *Film* leads its readers from the most familiar and accessible material (the expressiveness of film techniques) to increasingly unfamiliar and somewhat more demanding subjects. Part One considers many of the techniques used in making a film and, more importantly, the consequences for viewers of the filmmakers' choices. Because fictional films have so dominated film viewing and film studies, Part Two explores the sources, components, and types of fictional films. Part Three considers the alternatives to live-action fictional films (including documentaries, animation, and experimental films). Part Four examines ways to understand a film: how viewers can better understand a film when they consider its contexts, how their changing expectations influence their responses to the film, and how viewers learn or formulate meanings. Part Five encourages students to apply their new knowledge of film concepts through reading and writing about films and understanding film analysis. Many instructors will find that the arrangement of chapters reflects the order of the topics they cover in the course. Others may want to teach the chapters or parts of chapters in a different order. Because of the chapter headings and subheadings and the brief marginal definitions of important terms, they may easily do so.

THOROUGH ATTENTION TO FILM LANGUAGE PROVIDES ADDITIONAL SUPPORT   Brief marginal glosses put film definitions at students' fingertips, and an illustrated glossary defines each term more fully and provides examples. To help students identify and understand major concepts, key terms in each chapter are set in boldface and further defined in the glossary, which now includes forty new terms. In addition, a new list of major terms at the end of each chapter helps students review the concepts essential to understanding the chapter.

FILM CITATIONS THROUGHOUT THE BOOK MAKE VIEWING CONCEPTS EFFORTLESS   The fourth edition of *Film* makes it easy for faculty and students to view video or DVD excerpts for many of the examples discussed in the book, with the approximate time into the film often supplied. For example, instead of "early in *Citizen Kane*," readers are now informed "16 1/4 minutes into *Citizen Kane*."

NEW TO THE FOURTH EDITION

EXTENDED EXAMPLES AND CAPTIONS BRING FILM CONCEPTS TO LIFE Throughout the text, new examples and captions provide in-depth context and background to help students who have not seen a wide variety of films better understand the points being made.

A NEW CHAPTER ON WRITING ABOUT FILM Chapter 12 provides valuable class-tested techniques for helping students write successful papers about film. In addition, the number of sample student essays in the book has been expanded from three to seven.

MORE COVERAGE OF HISTORICAL AND CULTURAL CONTEXTS OF FILMS More explanations of contexts help readers more fully understand the descriptions and analyses of films. For example, the discussion of *The Lives of Others* includes background on relevant German history and the role of the Stasi, and *The Motorcycle Diaries* is discussed against the context of related South American history.

EXPANDED COVERAGE OF DOCUMENTARIES AND ANIMATION As documentary and animation have grown in importance and popularity, *Film* has responded with greater coverage in these areas. This edition includes a new Chapter 8 on documentary films, broader coverage of animation in Chapter 9, and more than twice as many color plates devoted to animated films.

EXCITING NEW MATERIAL ON GENDER AND ON SEXUAL ORIENTATION IN FILM Gender and sexuality have always played key roles in film and in our reactions to them. The fourth edition's coverage has been extensively rethought and expanded, with discussions of *Brokeback Mountain*, *Angels in America*, *Fried Green Tomatoes*, *Kissing Jessica Stein*, *Some Like It Hot*, and *Morocco*, among others.

A WIDER VARIETY OF INTERNATIONAL FILM The fourth edition has expanded its emphasis on world cinema with more discussions of German cinema, Asian cinema, and films across the Americas, including films from Mexico, Venezuela, Chile, and Canada.

A FULLY REVISED AND EXPANDED VISUAL PROGRAM With better-quality frame enlargements throughout plus double the previous number of color plates—now two 8-page color inserts for a total of sixty-four plates—the fourth edition's visual program has gotten even better. More than ever, the frames used exactly illustrate the points being discussed. This edition includes new frame enlargements from frequently taught classic films such as *Citizen Kane*, *The Bicycle Thief*, *Touch of Evil*, and *The Godfather*. It also features images from such recent movies as *Ray*, *Pan's Labyrinth*, *8 Mile*, *Sin City*, *The Passion of the Christ*, and *The Lives of Others*.

NEW MATERIAL SHOWS FILM CONCEPTS APPLIED TO A SINGLE FILM A new Chapter 13 utilizes text and full-color images to walk students through a close analysis of Robert Altman's *The Player*, illustrating how many concepts and points from the book can come together and be used to analyze a single film.

OTHER REVISIONS Throughout the text, numerous other revisions have been made to make *Film* the best possible teaching and learning tool for both instructors and students. Revisions include a new postscript at the end of Part One discussing the subtle versus the obvious use of film techniques; new tables to highlight key information; new material on the importance of a film's last shot; a look inside a movie palace in the late 1920s; more in-depth coverage on ambiguity; filmmakers' interpretations of their own films; and many other topics. New icons direct students to *Film*'s companion Web site for links to a variety of supplementary materials like readings, short films, and clips.

INSTRUCTOR'S MANUAL AND WEB SITE

THE INSTRUCTOR'S MANUAL HAS BEEN UPDATED AND REVISED The Instructor's Manual includes teaching strategies for each chapter, revised test questions and an answer key to accompany each chapter, sample syllabi, and assignments for essays, writing exercises, journals, group presentations, a sample quiz, and two types of final examinations. There are also sections on how to help students write more effectively about film and on the course review, as well as useful sources for film teachers: film and video distributors, books, and articles.

THE WEB SITE HAS BEEN MADE EVEN MORE USEFUL The Web site for the fourth edition focuses on supplementary resources for both instructors and students. Students will find chapter summaries and quizzes; an extensive array of Web links to various short films (some of which are discussed in the book); photographs; essays; reviews; materials from previous editions, such as the chapter on the expressiveness of film techniques in *The Third Man* from the second edition; and sample student essays. Instructors can access an electronic version of the Instructor's Manual that they can modify to more closely fit their individual needs. The Web site also includes information about how to contact the author. The site is located at <bedfordstmartins.com/phillips-film>.

ACKNOWLEDGMENTS

Many people have made significant contributions to this edition. Professor Corey Creekmur, University of Iowa, helped update and expand the sections on Bollywood and Hong Kong cinema. Colleague Patti See made a major contribution to the sections on representations of gender and lesbians in film. Adam Oster made test prints of some photo files, and he made the print to illustrate a negative image in Plate 43. Seven of my former students, from California and from Wisconsin, contributed essays that illustrate both the applicability of the book's concepts and what a student essay might be like. Amélie Strohschänk contributed detailed feedback on the drafts of two of the most altered chapters and once again proved invaluable in proofreading. And Professor Eva Santos-Phillips sometimes helped with proofreading and was once again an attentive listener and valued adviser.

The following libraries and archives have aided me in my research: McIntyre Library, University of Wisconsin–Eau Claire; L. E. Phillips Memorial Public Library, Eau Claire, Wisconsin; Pacific Film Archive, Berkeley; Library and Film Center, Museum of Modern Art; and Motion Pictures, Broadcasting, and Recorded Sound Division, U.S. Library of Congress. The following film distributors have also cooperated: Anthology Film Archives, California Newsreel, Canyon Cinema, Chicago Filmmakers, Creative Thinking International, Film-Makers' Cooperative, Flower Films, International Film Bureau, Kino International, Michael Wiese Productions, National Film Board of Canada, New Line Productions, New Video Group, New Yorker Films, Pyramid Film and Video, and Women Make Movies.

REVIEWERS   Over the many years that I wrote and rewrote this book, I have consulted scores of professional filmmakers and film scholars about the accuracy and clarity of various sections of the book. The following people, generous professionals all, gave of their precious allotment of time and provided feedback appropriate for my introductory audience: Les Blank, Flower Films, El Cerrito, California; Rose Bond, Gaea Graphics, Portland, Oregon; Stan Brakhage, University of Colorado–Boulder; Jim Gardner, Sound One, New York; Cecelia Hall, executive sound director, Paramount Pictures; Michael B. Hoggan, past president, American Cinema Editors, and now adjunct professor of filmmaking at University of Southern California and California State University, Northridge; Ken Jacobs, independent filmmaker, New York; George Kuchar, independent filmmaker, San Francisco, California; Tak Miyagishima, Panavision International, L.P.; Errol Morris, Fourth Floor Productions, Cambridge, Massachusetts; J. J. Murphy, University of Wisconsin–Madison; Robert Orlando, Coppola Pictures, New York; Lee Parker, Daedalus Corporation, Turlock, California; Jeff Wall, University of British Columbia; and technical representatives of the IMAX Corporation, Toronto. These professional filmmakers supplied information or photographs (or both), or corrections, suggestions, and encouragement about different sections of the manuscript.

Many people have read the entire manuscript or parts of it for different editions and have made helpful suggestions and corrections: Barbara L. Baker, Central Missouri State University; Bob Baron, Mesa Community College; Frank Beaver, University of Michigan; Peter Bondanella, Indiana University; Christine Catanzarite, Illinois State University; Jeffrey Chown, Northern Illinois State University; Marshall Deutelbaum, Purdue University; Carol Dole, Ursinus College; Bernard Duyfhuizen, University of Wisconsin–Eau Claire; Charles Eidsvik, University of Georgia; Jack Ellis, Northwestern University; Douglas Gomery, University of Maryland; Charles Harpole, University of Central Florida; Ken Harrow, Michigan State University; William H. Hayes, professor emeritus of philosophy, California State University, Stanislaus; Ron Heiss, Spokane Community College; Nel Hellenberg, Spokane Falls Community College; Tim Hirsch, University of Wisconsin–Eau Claire; Deborah Holdstein, Governors State University; Barbara Klinger, Indiana University; Ira Konigsberg, University of Michigan; Don Kunz, University of Rhode Island; Scott MacDonald, Utica College; Karen Mann, Western Illinois University; Mike McBrine, Amherst College; Dale Melgaard, University of Nevada, Las Vegas; Avis Meyer, St. Louis University; Wayne Miller, Franklin University; James Naremore, Indiana University; David Natharius, Arizona State University; Marty Norden, University of Massachusetts–Amherst; Samuel Oppenheim, California State University, Stanislaus; Kimberly M. Radek, Illinois Valley Community College; August Rubrecht, University of Wisconsin–Eau Claire; Eva L. Santos-Phillips, University of Wisconsin–Eau Claire; Paul Scherer, Indiana University, South Bend; Carol Schrepfer, Waubonsee Community College; John Schultheiss, California State University, Northridge; John W. Spalding, Wayne State University; Terry Steiner, Spokane Falls Community College; Sonja Swenson, Taft College; Kristin Thompson, University of Wisconsin–Madison; Frank Tomasulo, Southern Methodist University; and Tricia Welsch, Bowdoin College.

QUESTIONNAIRE RESPONDENTS The following instructors of an introduction to film course responded to Bedford/St. Martin's questionnaires, sharing strategies for teaching the course and their requirements for a textbook: Richard Abel, Drake University; Ernesto Acevedo-Muñoz, University of Colorado–Boulder; Marilyn K. Ackerman, Foothill College; Dr. Robert Adubato, Essex County College; William A. Allman, Baldwin-Wallace College; Ann Alter, Humboldt State University; Bob Alto, University of San Francisco; Victoria Amador, Western New Mexico University; Lauri Anderson, Suomi College; Robert Arnett, Mississippi State University; Bob Arnold, University of Toledo; Paul Arthur, Montclair State University; Dr. Maureen Asten, Worcester State College; Ray Barcia, Goucher College; Dr. Bob Baron, Mesa Community College; Karen Becker, Richland Community

College; Edward I. Benintende, County College of Morris; John Bernstein, Macalester College; Robin Blaetz, Emory University; Alex Blazer, Ohio State University; James Bozan, University of Missouri–Rolla; Bruce C. Browne, University of Wisconsin–Sheboygan; Carolyn R. Bruder, University of Southwestern Louisiana; Lawrence Budner, Rhode Island College; Ken Burke, Mills College; George Butte, Colorado College; Jim Carmody, University of California, San Diego; Ray Carney, Boston University; Lisa Cartwright, University of Rochester; Harold Case, Allan Hancock College; Dr. Christine J. Catanzarite, Illinois State University; Rick Chapman, Des Moines Area Community College; Rick Clemons, Western Illinois University; Jay Cofield, University of Montevallo; Lois Cole, Mt. San Antonio College; David Crosby, Alcorn State University; Rita Csapó Sweete, University of Missouri–St. Louis; Ramona Curry, University of Illinois; Joan Dagle, Rhode Island College; Dr. Kathryn D'Alessandro, Jersey City State College; Mary Jayne Davis, Salt Lake Community College; Margarita De la Vega-Hurtado, University of Michigan–Ann Arbor; Larry R. Dennis, Clarion University; Carol M. Dole, Ursinus College; Fredric Dolezal, University of Georgia; Gus Edwards, Arizona State University; John Ernst, Heartland College; Thomas L. Erskine, Salisbury State University; Jim Everett, Mississippi College; Patty Felkner, Cosumnes River College; Peter Feng, University of Delaware; Jody Flynn, Owensboro Community College; Mike Frank, Bentley College; Arthur M. Fried, Plymouth State College; Don Fredericksen, Cornell University; Linda Fuller, Worcester State College; Keya Ganguly, Carnegie Mellon University; Dr. Joseph E. Gelsi, Central Methodist College; Jerry Girton, Riverland Community College; Joseph A. Gomez, North Carolina State University; John M. Gourlie, Quinnipiac College; William J. Hagerty, Xavier University; Mickey Hall, Volunteer State Community College; James Hallemann, Oakland Community College; Ken Harrow, Michigan State University; Rolland L. Heiss, Spokane Community College; Thomas Hemmetier, Beaver College; Bruce Hinricks, Century College; Allan Hirsch, Central Connecticut State University; Tim Hirsch, University of Wisconsin–Eau Claire; Rosemary Horowitz, Appalachian State University; Sandra Hybels, Lock Haven University; Frank E. Jackson, Lander University; Susan Jhirad, North Shore Community College; Kimberlie A. Johnson, Seminole Community College; Edward T. Jones, York College of Pennsylvania; Leandro Katz, William Paterson College; Thomas K. Kegel, Oakland Community College; Harry Keyishian, Fairleigh Dickinson University; Les Keyser, College of Staten Island; Helmut Kremling, Ohio Wesleyan University; Barry Laga, Mesa State College; Al LaValley, Dartmouth College; Don S. Lawson, Lander University; Carol S. Layne, Jefferson Community College; Paul Lazarus, University of Miami; Peter Lev, Towson State University; Danny Linton, University of Memphis; Susan E. Linville, University of Colorado–Denver; Dr. Cathleen Londino, Keans College of New Jersey; Frances Lozano, Gavilan College; Jean D. Lynch, Villanova University; Karen B. Mann, Western Illinois University;

Walter McCallum, Santa Rosa Junior College; James McGonigle, Madison Area Technical College; Jay McRoy, University of Wisconsin–Parkside; Marilyn Middendorf, Embry Riddle Aeronautical University; Joseph Milicia, University of Wisconsin–Sheboygan; Mark S. Miller, Pikes Peak Community College; Mary Alice Molgard, College of Saint Rose; James Morrison, North Carolina State University; Charles Musser, Yale University; Marty Norden, University of Massachusetts–Amherst; Barry H. Novick, College of New Jersey; Kevin O'Brien, University of Nevada, Las Vegas; Brian O'Leary, Pennsylvania State University–Erie; Jan Ostrow, College of the Redwoods; Richard Peacock, Palomar College; Richard Pearce, Wheaton College; Ruth Perlmutter, University of the Arts; David Popowski, Mankato State University; Joyce Porter, Moraine Valley Community College; Maria Pramaggiore, North Carolina State University; Cynthia Prochaska, Mt. San Antonio College; Leonard Quart, College of Staten Island; Clay Randolph, Oklahoma City Community College; Maurice Rapf, Dartmouth College; Jere Real, Lynchburg College; Gary Reynolds, Minneapolis Community & Technical College; David Robinson, Winona State University; James Rupport, University of Alaska–Fairbanks; Kristine Samuelson, Stanford University; Jaime Sanchez, Volunteer State Community College; Richard Schwartz, Florida International University; Richard Sears, Berea College; Eli Segal, Governors State University; Dr. Rick Shale, Youngstown State University; Craig Shurtleff, Illinois Central College; Charles L. P. Silev, Iowa State University; Joseph Evans Slate, University of Texas–Austin; Thomas J. Slater, Indiana University of Pennsylvania; Claude Smith, Florida Community College at Jacksonville; Elana Starr, Villanova University; Terry J. Steiner, Spokane Falls Community College; Kevin M. Stemmler, Clarion University; Ellen Strain, Georgia Institute of Technology; Judith A. Switzer, Bucks County Community College; Julie Tharp, University of Wisconsin–Marshfield; John Tibbetts, University of Kansas; Marie Travis, George Washington University; Robert Vales, Gannon University; Jonathan Walters, Norwich University; Shujen Wang, Westfield State College; Dr. Rosanne Wasserman, U.S. Merchant Marine Academy; J. R. Welsch, Western Illinois University; Tricia Welsch, Bowdoin College; Bernard Welt, the Corcoran School of Art; Robert D. West, Kent State University; Mary Beth Wilk, Des Moines Area Community College; Deborah Wilson, Arkansas Tech University; and Gerald C. Wood, Carson-Newman College.

QUESTIONNAIRE RESPONDENTS FOR THE FOURTH EDITION The following instructors provided valuable feedback regarding the revision plan for the fourth edition: Barbara L. Baker, University of Central Missouri; Christopher Bates, University College of Bangor, University of Maine at Augusta; John Beatty, Brooklyn College, City University of New York; Joe Benson, North Carolina Agricultural and Technical State University; Sean Benson, Malone College; Jeannie Berg, Glendale Community College; Willard

Bohn, Illinois State University; Shelley L. Brulotte, College of Southern Idaho; Diane Carson, St. Louis Community College at Meramec; Tim Case, University of South Dakota; Jay Cofield, University of Montevallo; Joseph Colavito, Northwestern State University; Cesar Daniel Diaz, University of Turabo; Mark Eaton, Azusa Pacific University; Leigh H. Edwards, Florida State University; Ernest J. Enchelmayer, Arkansas Tech University; Michael Fabrizio, Rockhurst University; Eric Fernandez Santiago, University of Turabo; Daniel J. Fitzstephens, University of Colorado, Boulder; Lynda Goldstein, Pennsylvania State University, Wilkes-Barre; Catherine Hardy, Art Academy of Cincinnati; Nicole Hinrichs-Bideau, Century College; Daniel Humphrey, Keene State College; Philip Hutcheon, San Joaquin Delta College; Jon Inglett, Oklahoma City Community College; Tammy A. Kinsey, University of Toledo; Chris Lippard, University of Utah; Tara Lockhart, University of Pittsburgh; Robert Matorin, Middlesex Community College; Philip Mayfield, Fullerton College; Scott Mazak, Solano College; Brian McCuskey, Utah State University; Mark David McGregor, Santa Clara University; Michael V. Montgomery, Life University; Geoffrey Peterson, University of Wisconsin–Eau Claire; Douglas W. Reitinger, Sheridan College; Marie Rofhok, The College of New Rochelle; Len Rotondaro, Manchester Community College; Gregory Taylor, Purchase College, State University of New York; Steve Vrooman, Texas Lutheran University; Rita Buscher Weeks, Spartanburg Community College; and Yang Ye, University of California, Riverside.

In years past, at the Museum of Modern Art/Film Stills Archive, Terry Geesken and Mary Corliss helped me secure many invaluable historical photographs used in the book. For help in securing photos thanks are also due to the Academy Foundation of the Academy of Motion Picture Arts and Sciences; Barbara Gladstone Gallery (New York); 303 Gallery (New York); California Newsreel (San Francisco/South Burlington, Vermont); Marc Wanamaker, Bison Archives (Hollywood, California); and the British Film Institute Stills, Posters and Designs (London). Photofest in New York provided a copy of the fascinating 1929 program for the largest of the U.S. movie palaces, the Roxy.

Finally, I want to thank the dedicated, hardworking, and skillful people at the New York office of Bedford/St. Martin's who did an enormous amount of work in producing this fourth edition. Making a new edition of this book is an unusually long, complicated, and costly endeavor. Nothing in the third edition and in the new material for this edition escaped an initial skeptical examination. Every word and image underwent repeated scrutiny and sometimes multiple revisions. There were not only the words to be written and rewritten (and rewritten), edited, later copyedited, and proofread but also photographs to be secured and reproduced in an appropriate size and shape and with the right amount of contrast. A few publicity stills needed to be cropped to help more clearly make the desired points. Some photos had imperfections that needed to be digitally minimized. There were also figures, tables, marginal glosses, footnotes, and features to round up and corral into the page. The people whose responsibility it was to see that all these tasks and more got done and done well are listed in the top grouping of page iv. To all I am grateful for their knowledge, skills, counsel, attention to detail, and tolerance of my many directives and requests. To the five people I worked with most closely during the production—Margaret Manos, Jennifer Peterson, Ryan Sullivan, Pat Herbst, and Jan Ewing of Ewing Systems—I am particularly indebted. They are the most talented, most professional group I have had the pleasure of working with during my many years in making books.

ABOUT THE AUTHOR

William H. Phillips received his BA from Purdue University, his MA from Rutgers University, and his PhD (in dramatic literature and film studies) from Indiana University. His postdoctoral studies in film include three sabbaticals to write and to do research at major film archives, libraries, and film distributors in the United States and Europe; participation in an eight-week National Endowment for the Humanities Summer Seminar for College Teachers on the history of film at Northwestern University; and attendance at the first (two-week) American Film Institute Center for Advanced Film Studies Symposium for College Film Teachers. He has also taught short scriptwriting many times and served as producer of readings of original short film scripts for live performance then rebroadcast on cable TV.

Phillips has taught introductory film courses at the University of Illinois–Urbana; Indiana University–South Bend; California State University, Stanislaus; and the University of Wisconsin–Eau Claire. His publications include the books *Analyzing Films* (1985), *Writing Short Scripts* (2nd ed., 1999), and *Writing Short Stories: The Most Practical Guide* (2002).

REPLAYS

For Howard D. Phillips II, Howdy, Bro (1934–2007),
who at seventeen raced away from home the last time
and rushed into marriage and his own life

who shot from behind overturned couch
as brother ducked then returned fire
and sons retrieved their Christmas plastic bullets

and who in the closing seconds waved for time-out
trying to scoop air into smoked-out lungs
trying to suspend the game clock
waving instead good-bye to all.

Brief Contents

Contents

Introduction

GOING TO THE MOVIES is an act that takes many forms. We go to the movies in adolescent packs, on timid first dates, with minivan-loads of children or busloads of friends from the senior center and also alone, on foot, in the middle of the day. We talk back to the characters on the screen, or shush the people behind us who are doing it; we walk out in disgust, or come back the next night, or buy each successive DVD release of something we didn't much care for in the first place. We weep, we rage, we snore, we aspirate our popcorn in bursts of helpless laughter. (Scott)

The lines at the movie theater stretch down the block. At the neighborhood video store, all the copies of the latest hit movie are rented out. Your Netflix queue says that for a recent popular film that you want to see you are in for a very long wait. Some U.S. cities have Movieoke, a movie variation of karaoke, where one or more fans, perhaps well-lubricated devotees, sway before a screen showing scenes from a movie and voice lines and act out some of the action (Kennedy). Immigrant children watch a movie and are captivated by it and united in pleasure (Figure I.1). As a group of people in a remote Cuban village see their first film, their faces radiate joy and wonder, and the short documentary Cuban film "For the First Time" records the event. A young American filmmaker born in Vietnam returns there to make a documentary and interviews former Vietnamese leaders, who ask her "a lot of questions about American film stars." In a scene from the 1988 Senegalese film *Saaraba*, alienated youths in Dakar are seen in the foreground smoking drugs, and in the background hangs a poster for *Apocalypse Now*. Audiences watching the 1995 Academy Award–winning documentary *Anne Frank Remembered* glimpse photos of movie stars on Anne Frank's bedroom wall (Figure I.2). Here was the scene at an Afghan movie theater late in 2001:

> The usher carried a rubber whip and the policeman on duty toted a submachine gun. Patrons had to check their knives, brass knuckles, and other weapons at the door. And audience members had enough combat experience to criticize the film's climactic shootout scene as unrealistic.
>
> On Friday, hundreds of teenage boys enjoyed an afternoon at the movies in Kabul, something they could not do for the past six years. The object of their

FIGURE I.1 The joy of movies
Immigrant children from different countries and ethnic groups are mesmerized by "The Immigrant," a 1917 silent film starring Charlie Chaplin. *Courtesy of Rebecca Cooney and New York Times Pictures*

FIGURE I.2 Photographs of movie stars
Anne Frank—a girl who with her family hid in a secret apartment in an Amsterdam house during the Nazi occupation—is the subject of the documentary film *Anne Frank Remembered* (1995). At several points in the film, audiences see her bedroom wall, on which are hung photographs of movie stars (at the top of the image shown here)—yet another indication of the widespread influence of movies on modern lives. *Sony Pictures Classics*

curiosity—*Elan*, an Indian action movie—was outdated, blurry, and damaged. None of them could understand the dialogue. And the smell of the overcrowded theater they fought to enter was revolting. But no one seemed to care. (Rohde)

In 2007, the *Japan Times* newspaper reported that an Australian state premier compared police who botched an investigation with the Keystone Cops (often spelled *Keystone Kops*)—bumbling police officers in short farcical U.S. films first seen in 1912. At various times in history, Mickey Mouse, Charlie Chaplin, Rudolph Valentino, Marilyn Monroe, John Wayne, Arnold Schwarzenegger, and other stars have been more widely known throughout the world than presidents, popes, and athletes. These examples attest to the power and pervasiveness of film, especially American commercial cinema. (For a variety of accounts by filmmakers, film critics, and film scholars about how they "first fell in love with film," see the *Film Quarterly* article titled "Filmic Memories.")

No one questions the entertainment value of movies: the proof is in the huge number of people who watch them. Many people, though, disagree about whether films have any additional value. To some viewers, movies' ability and proclivity to show sex and violence have made them seem unworthy of study. Movies have been dismissed as "ribbons of dreams" and Hollywood as a "dream factory." Nonetheless, films can be more than commercial entertainment, and studying them and the film medium brings many benefits.

STUDYING FILMS AND THE FILM MEDIUM

Some people fear that studying films will spoil their enjoyment of them. But with guidance and a chance to reach their own conclusions, nearly all viewers find that studying films *increases* their enjoyment and often their appreciation of the effort and creativity involved in filmmaking. Many people find, too, that they enjoy a wider variety of films for more reasons than they did before studying films.

Film study helps viewers understand how different filmmakers have used the medium. It also reveals the medium's possibilities and limitations. For example, considered together, the films *Citizen Kane* and *Pulp Fiction* suggest how complex and varied the structure of a nonchronological film story may be. The experimental "Un chien andalou" shows how a film may be used not to show a story or present facts but to suggest something of the bizarre, irrational, yet sometimes striking images and situations of dreams.

Film study also helps viewers understand and appreciate the wide variety of films, including long films and short ones, fictional films, documentary films, experimental films, and combinations of those films. Film study helps viewers understand and appreciate various groupings of fictional films, such as Italian neorealistic films, Bollywood movies and other musicals, and combinations of fictional types, such as a film that combines elements of horror and science fiction. Film study also helps viewers understand the indebtedness of later films to earlier ones. Studying films will help you understand familiar films in new ways. For example, examining the stories of many popular U.S. movies can reveal how they celebrate individualism and the potential of one person to make a major difference in the course of major events.

Viewers trained in film studies tend to notice more significant details while viewing a film. They are more likely to appreciate the expressiveness of the lighting, composition, camera angles, camera distances from the subjects, and other filmmaking techniques.

Studying films can make you more aware of how contexts influence the making of films. As illustrated in this book, when and where a film is made and which sources it draws on influence what the film will end up being like. A film made under a third world dictatorship, for example, will differ fundamentally from any film made in modern Japan. A musical will be influenced by earlier musical films: it will accept some conventions or traditions of musicals and may reject others.

People who have studied films and the responses they bring forth tend to understand films' meanings in greater depth and to be more aware of how and why others might interpret the same film differently. They also are more likely to be aware of how the viewer's situation—where and when the viewer lives, for example—influences his or her responses to a film.

Finally, films can help us understand different places, people, and cultures—whether a foreign country or a region of the viewer's own country. However, as Chapter 8 explains, films, even documentary films, should never be accepted as objective accounts. Films' subjects must be considered in light of the film medium's inherent properties and the filmmakers' motives, methods, and skills. In the case of experimental films, the worlds glimpsed are likely to exist only in the filmmakers' fertile imaginations.

ABOUT THIS BOOK

Film: An Introduction, Fourth Edition, attempts to help readers understand the film medium more completely. Consequently, the book offers discussions of a wide array of films, including some that have received less than glowing reviews—or have scarcely been reviewed at all. My intention here, however, is not to evaluate films or to focus only on critically acclaimed ones but to advance readers' understanding of films and the film medium itself. When a colleague who does not teach film courses expressed horror and then sympathy for my having "had" to see *Natural Born Killers*, I explained that I see a huge variety of films and enjoy nearly all of them in some way or other. I said that I do not so much try to judge them by some aesthetic standards (after all, my background and assumptions may not be the same as hers) but to see them in some sort of context (for example, a variation of a genre, or type of movies). I also told her that I may enjoy a film for its structure or editing or something else and that all films, on one level, are an exercise in and celebration of human creativity.

To help readers understand unfamiliar terminology, many terms in this book are explained within the paragraph or in the margin. The marginal definitions allow readers to read the chapters in any order without stopping for trips to the glossary. Because of this feature, many terms, such as *genre*, are defined in multiple chapters.

This book includes many other features for the beginning film student:

- Links, on the book's Web site, to a variety of sources, including some of the short films discussed in the text
- Close-Up sections, at the end of most chapters, that apply concepts from the chapter at hand to one or two films
- A summary of the major points of each chapter

- Annotated suggestions for further reading
- A chapter on reading and writing about films
- A sample description and analysis of one film
- An extensive chronology that relates films to history, the arts, and other media and helps readers find dates and check spellings
- An illustrated glossary that includes over fifty drawings and photos
- In the body of the book, more than six hundred illustrations (photographs, tables, and drawings), sixty-four color plates, and many extensive informative captions

In many cases, I provide more than one example or I provide an extended description and analysis along with a photograph, drawing, or table so that students who have not seen the film being discussed will understand the points being made.

Throughout the text, the titles of short films (those less than sixty minutes long) are enclosed in quotation marks, and the titles of films that last sixty or more minutes are set in italic type.

CREDIT WHERE CREDIT IS DUE

As we discuss a film and our responses to it, to whom should we give credit? If the film required only modest resources to make it—as in the case of many experimental films—often one person deserves most or even all of the credit. But what one person could create a full-length movie? To write, costume, direct, light, perform, film, edit, and score a movie is beyond the powers of one mortal. Nonetheless, many film reviewers and critics credit and blame a single person for a movie, usually the director.

In the case of a novel or painting, assigning responsibility to one person is reasonable enough. With films made by many people, however, it is often difficult to know which contributor affected which aspect of the finished film, and in most cases the director is unlikely to be responsible for the creativity of every aspect. For instance, did the writers, director, or actors reword crucial lines of dialogue? Did the writers, director, editors, actors, or producer insist that certain scenes be dropped? Examining the film or film publications usually yields no reliable answers to these and many other questions about creative contributions. To compound the problem, screen credits often inaccurately report who did what on a film. Many questions about specific contributions to the finished film remain unanswerable.

For compactness and as an aid to identification, this book often identifies films by director, but readers should remember that the director alone is not responsible for all the film's creativity. Consider the original *Psycho*, which was directed by Alfred Hitchcock and was first shown in 1960. A reading of the source novel and the script that describes the finished film reveals that author Robert Bloch and scriptwriter Joseph Stefano deserve a major credit for the shape and texture of the finished film. Many of the performers—especially Anthony Perkins, Vera Miles, and Martin Balsam—do more than adequate work. Bernard Herrmann's music contributes to every scene in which it is employed: when any section is viewed without it, its absence is pronounced. The title work by Saul Bass at the beginning and the end of the film is unusually imaginative and appropriate. Hitchcock does deserve much credit for supervising and coordinating all these and other efforts, and various filmmaking strategies that Hitchcock favored reveal his influence on *Psycho*. Nonetheless, thinking of *Psycho* as "Hitchcock's *Psycho*" glosses over the contributions of many others. (For details on the creation of this film, see Stephen Rebello's *Alfred Hitchcock and the Making of* Psycho.)

When someone gives the director full credit or blame for a film that many people helped make, I sometimes am reminded of an account, apocryphal though it may be, of the American director Frank Capra and his frequent collaborator, scriptwriter Robert Riskin. According to Richard Walter's version of the story, Capra expounded on "the Capra touch" in a lengthy interview but did not once mention Riskin. After the interview was published, Riskin sent Capra a manuscript with this note: "'Frank, let's see you put the Capra touch on this.' Inside were blank pages" (4).

WORKS CITED

"Filmic Memories." *Film Quarterly* 52.1 (Fall 1998): 54–71.

Kennedy, Randy. "Oughta Be in Pictures? So Just Drink Up!; Amateur Celebrities Pick a Movie and Join In." nytimes.com 10 Mar. 2004.

"'Keystone Cops' Slur Enrages Australia." *Japan Times* 24 July 2007: 4.

Rebello, Stephen. *Alfred Hitchcock and the Making of* Psycho. New York: Dembner, 1990.

Rohde, David. "Film Critics with a Keen Eye for Violence." *New York Times* 26 Nov. 2001, late ed., final: B5.

Scott, A. O. "The Lasting Picture Show." *New York Times* 3 Nov. 2002, late ed., final: sec. 6: 41.

Walter, Richard. *Screenwriting: The Art, Craft, and Business of Film and Television Writing*. New York: NAL, 1988.

THE EXPRESSIVENESS OF FILM TECHNIQUES

W HAT ARE THE CONSEQUENCES for viewers of the innumerable decisions filmmakers make while creating films? Some answers are explored in this, the first and largest, part of the book.

Part One, "The Expressiveness of Film Techniques," discusses such issues as what settings, subjects, and composition may contribute to a film; how film stock, lighting, and camera can be used to create certain effects; how the resulting footage might be edited and with what consequences; and what the soundtrack can contribute to viewers' experience

◄ In *Secrets & Lies* (1996), a woman (on the right) is starting to realize that the woman on the left is her daughter, the result of a brief liaison. The entire scene consists of only two shots, the second one more than 7½ minutes long. In this publicity still, which closely approximates a frame from the second shot (a little more than 72 minutes into the film), the two subjects are pretty much centered in the frame and are the same height in the image. They are the main objects of interest and are of equal importance. The camera distance and lens make the subjects large enough that viewers can see the many shifting, complex feelings suggested by the actors' expressive faces. The background, a restaurant, is slightly out of focus and empty, so there are no distractions or competing visual information there. The filmmakers illuminated the subjects and setting clearly and evenly.

The scene conveys many contrasts: the two women are of different races, social classes, and temperaments. The woman on the left is dressed professionally, holds briefcase and papers, and does not smoke. The woman on the right is casually dressed, disheveled, and smokes. The woman on the left has an enunciation and accent of an educated person; the woman on the right does not. The woman on the left largely reins in her emotions; the woman on the right gets extremely emotional. Although the two subjects are quite unlike, they share and help communicate a complicated, difficult emotional situation.

Change the arrangement of the subjects within the frame, background, camera distance, camera lens, focus, clothing, lighting, editing, or actors, and the scene and the audience's response to them would be altered. *October Films*

9

of a film. It focuses on the impact of the many choices filmmakers make.

To create a desired effect, a technique such as lighting or camera lenses or camera angles may change as the film progresses — for example, to give a sense of the walls and ceiling closing in on the characters. Usually during film showings, such changes are gradual and imperceptible, especially in mainstream movies.

A particular technique, such as a camera angle, may have one effect in one part of a film and a different effect elsewhere in the same film or in a different film. Often a low camera angle reinforces the sense that the subject is large, dominant, imposing, or powerful, but not always. Sometimes, for example, the filmmakers simply want viewers to notice the relationship of the subject in the foreground to a tall object in the background. Similarly, a high camera angle does not always make the subject seem small, vulnerable, or weak, although in many contexts it does. It depends on the contexts and on other techniques used at the same time.

Finally, several techniques used together create a particular effect. For example, in some desert shots in *Lawrence of Arabia* (Figure 1.10a), viewers may be struck by how much the characters are engulfed by an inhospitable environment. But it's not just the camera distance and smallness of the subjects in the image that create that effect: the slight high angle somewhat further diminishes the size of the subjects and the (hot) color is unvarying and inhospitable. To illustrate the expressiveness of various cinematic techniques, the first four chapters focus on them one at a time, although they never function in isolation.

Links to a variety of sources, including supplementary readings and short films, are available for each chapter on the Web site for this book at <bedfordstmartins.com/phillips-film>.

CHAPTER 1

Mise en Scène

M ISE EN SCÈNE — pronounced "meez ahn sen," with a nasalized second syllable — originally meant a director's staging of a play. Often in film studies the term refers to everything put before the camera in preparation for filming. As used in this book, **mise en scène** consists of the three major aspects of filmmaking that are also components of staging a play: the **settings**; the subject(s) being filmed, usually actors or people as themselves; and the **composition**, the arrangement of the settings, lighting, and subjects. In French, *mise en scène* means "staging." The phrase is used in the opening credits for some French films where English-language films would use "direction," as in "Mise en scène de Luis Buñuel," meaning "Direction by Luis Buñuel."

As the 2004 TV **documentary film** "The Hidden Art of Hollywood" explains, a film's **designer** might point out that the script could be most effectively visualized if the film had a certain type of lighting and a particular color palette throughout. Or the designer might suggest that the film should have one type of look for one character and an opposing look for an opposing character, as in *Amadeus* (1984; see Plates 17–18 in Chapter 2). A film's **cinematographer** may be deeply involved in matters of mise en scène, too, but in large productions of movies, the director usually makes the final decisions about mise en scène.

So expressive can mise en scène be that a movie may begin with carefully selected wordless **scenes**. For a little more than 7½ minutes after the opening credits of Sergio Leone's Italian (**spaghetti**) **western** *The Good, the Bad, and the Ugly* (1966), wordless mise en scène (with some assistance from music and occasional, mostly faint animal sounds) conveys settings, moods, plot, and characters (Figure 1.1). Finally, we viewers hear the film's first dialogue, a question the family man puts to the uninvited visitor, "You're from Baker?" The film's opening mise en scène offers something more, though viewers may not appreciate it in the early minutes of the film or even later. The initial mise en scène also includes a torn Reward poster just outside those swinging doors (Figure 1.1a). Perhaps the reward poster

Terms in **boldface** are defined in the Illustrated Glossary beginning on page 667.

designer: The person responsible for the appearance of much of what is photographed in a movie, including locations, costumes, and hairstyles.

scene: A section of a narrative that gives the impression of continuous action taking place in continuous time and space.

spaghetti westerns: A film movement consisting of hundreds of westerns filmed from 1964 to the mid-1970s mostly in Italian studios and often on barren locations.

11

a)

b)

FIGURE 1.1 A film's expressive initial mise en scène
The initial wordless scenes of the 161-minute version of *The Good, the Bad, and the Ugly* (1966) show the dry, largely barren western settings; convey the moods (threatening, humorous, and then threatening again); and surprise viewers with the plot developments. The first three men that viewers see (a) meet not to have a shootout, as most viewers probably initially expect, but to rush through the swinging doors of what is probably a saloon in hopes of capturing an out-law. The film's opening also introduces two of the film's three major characters. Viewers see Ugly (bursting through the saloon's large plate-glass window while holding a humongous leg of cooked meat and a bottle of wine in one hand and a gun in the other). In a later scene, Bad (b), who approaches and enters a remote ranch home, sits at the family man's table, and begins eat-ing with him. After a while, viewers then hear the film's first words. *Produzioni Europee Associati and others; MGM Home Entertainment DVD*

included a photo of "the Ugly," but on his way into the saloon, he tore off most of it. The film rewards viewers attentive to its mise en scène with this probable subtlety. Similarly, the beginning of Gus Van Sant's *Last Days* (2005), which is based on Kurt Cobain's last days, relies entirely on visuals and sound effects. Viewers see the film's central character, a troubled young musician, walking through woods, briefly wading in a river and diving near a waterfall, drying off by a campfire, approaching a largely empty greenhouse and entering it briefly, using a shovel to dig up some-thing, and much more. Viewers can hear no distinct words of any conse-quence until about sixteen minutes into the film. Most of the remainder of the film is also highly visual and mostly wordless as the main character putters around and stumbles around and tries to remain conscious and evade people.

Visuals may be used throughout a film to intrigue viewers, to stimu-late them to consider what is going on and why. *Paradise Now* (2005) is set in modern-day Palestine and Israel and focuses on two young men, Said and Khaled, who are close friends considering becoming suicide bombers. The film includes many examples of characters looking at someone or something and presumably thinking about something, but no dialogue, ti-tle cards, or narration tells us what they are thinking. Almost 66½ min-utes into the film, Khaled takes a break from his frantic search for Said when he sees two boys playing with a kite. Khaled watches them, and the filmmakers dwell on the sight long enough to suggest it is of some importance. Perhaps Khaled is thinking of when he and Said played together as boys. Perhaps not. Various **shots** of Said's mother show her looking at him, thinking something but saying nothing. Given her facial expressions, she seems to be deeply concerned about her son's welfare. Another example of a character watching but not talking occurs when Suha, the young woman attracted to Said, watches him as he works under the hood of her car. By this point in the story, he has agreed to be a suicide bomber, has allowed his hair to be cut, has dressed in a black suit, and has been instructed to tell others, if he must, that he is going to a wedding. In this scene, Suha is once again looking at Said, trying to understand his changed appearance and manner. The film was made by filmmakers who created their images carefully and then trusted them to involve viewers.

Mise en scène can be so expressive that sometimes a single image can convey the essence of an entire movie, as in Figure 1.2.

SETTINGS

The setting is the place where filmed action occurs. It may be a **set**, a constructed place used for filming (Figure 1.3). Or a setting may be a **location**, a real place that is not built expressly for the filmmakers, though filmmakers often modify certain of its details before filming (Figure 1.4). Filmmakers have many options in selecting and creating settings. In recent years, settings for certain movies, especially science fiction and action films, have been created in computers and then eventually transferred to film for showings in theaters. Usually, though, most of a film's scenes are shot on a set or on location. Many films combine shots made on a set with those made on location. A film's setting—such as the wide-open spaces of a western or the cramped confines of a prison, submarine, or other workspace—can have tremendous impact

shot (noun): An uninterrupted strip of exposed motion-picture film or videotape that represents a subject during an uninterrupted segment of time.

FIGURE 1.2 Mise en scène of one image conveying the essence of a story
The setting, subjects, and composition of this carefully selected image reveal much of the story of *The Syrian Bride* (2004). The film is set in the Golan Heights, a disputed area between Israel and Syria that has been under Israeli control since the 1967 Six-Day War. The film concerns events on the day a young Druze woman from the Golan Heights (seen above) is to marry a man who lives and works in Syria. Bureaucratic complications fueled in part by ill will repeatedly delay the wedding at the border of the two countries. Here, nearly 75 1/2 minutes into the film, the bride-to-be appears on the Golan Heights side, a UN vehicle on one side in the background and an Israeli soldier behind her and on the other side. She looks toward her groom-to-be, who is within her view, just beyond the no-man's land under UN control. The UN vehicle in the background is a reminder of the UN presence. The film's one UN representative, a European, tries to solve the impasse but ultimately cannot—a situation that many in the Middle East could see as symptomatic of outsiders' ineffective presence in the region. The soldier in this image suggests a show of potential force and the possibility for violence. Most significantly, the shot suggests the woman's entrapment; she is a prisoner in an exasperating situation. The incongruity of the situation is conveyed by this image of a concerned, young woman in her wedding dress, not at her wedding, not on her way to her wedding, but behind bars and impeded from moving forward—an image the filmmakers use a number of times as the film nears its ending. *Neue Impuls Film, Eran Riklis Productions, and MACT Productions; Mongrel Media DVD*

FIGURE 1.3 Early film set
Interior of filmmaker Georges Méliès's glassed-in film studio, one of the world's first sets, which was built in France in 1897. Many windows were necessary because early films were made without artificial light. This studio was used for preparations for filming—for instance, for painting scenery—and for filming Méliès's early, very short films. Méliès himself is seen on the left. *The Museum of Modern Art/Film Stills Archive*

FIGURE 1.4 Filming on location
In the 1890s, the (two) Lumière Brothers of France took a camera outside and recorded brief actions as separate silent films, such as a train arriving at a station, workers leaving a factory, children digging for clams, and a family having a meal. The film illustrated here—"Childish Quarrel" (aka "Babies Quarrel," 1896)—runs about 45 seconds at 24 frames per second and is one of the earliest home movies. It is also one of the most fascinating of the many Lumière short films. The baby on the right (the one with the little lamb before it) is the unruffled aggressor who looks at the camera from time to time, and the baby on the left is shown to be helpless at defense and at counterattacking and is oblivious to the camera. *Lumière Brothers; Image Entertainment DVD*

on the viewer's experience. As is shown below, the setting implies a time and place and reveals or enhances character, mood, and meaning.

Types of Settings

A setting may draw no attention to itself—for example, it may be blank (**limbo**) or out of focus (Figure 1.5). Besides limbo sets, two other main types of settings are used by filmmakers: realistic settings and nonrealistic settings.

Realistic settings are used in most movies to try to convince viewers that what they are seeing could exist—and thus to help viewers get caught up in the world and action of the film. In *American Beauty* (1999), for example, the cubicle where the man works and the home of the wealthy couple look as one would imagine for such a couple in modern-day America (Figure 1.6).

FIGURE 1.5 Limbo set
An indistinct background, sometimes called a *limbo* or *limbo set*, sets off Gene Kelly and Cyd Charisse in one of the dance numbers from 85 or so minutes into the classic MGM musical *Singin' in the Rain* (1952). With such an indistinct background, viewers have no choice but to give full attention to the two dancers. There is nothing else to look at. *Arthur Freed, Loew's, Metro-Goldwyn-Mayer; Warner Home Video DVD*

a)

b)

FIGURE 1.6 Realistic settings revealing character
At the beginning of *American Beauty* (1999), the Kevin Spacey character, Lester Burnham, is a middle-aged man bored with his job and unengaged in his home life. He is cynical, lethargic, and unassuming. Appropriately, the film's settings quickly convince viewers of their authenticity and help reveal the character's situation and character. (a) About 5 minutes into the film, viewers can see that Lester's work environment is not very individualized: it's mainly crammed with the things he needs to do his job. An earlier shot reveals that his work area is much like all the others in the large room that is bathed in artificial light and shades of gray. Here he is flashing an insincere smile at his supervisor. (b) Nearly 75 minutes into the film, Lester uses a remote-controlled toy vehicle to attack his wife, action suggesting Lester's rebellious return to childhood and its sometimes aggressive play. Realistic clutter has begun to appear in the previously immaculate room. On the coffee table are Lester's bare feet, an open beer bottle, and a banana peel. Later in the scene, his wife is so concerned that Lester will spill beer on the $4,000 couch that the mood changes, he gives up his attempt to seduce her, and he never again tries to approach her intimately. *Jinks/Cohen Production and Dream-Works; DreamWorks Home Entertainment DVD*

Sometimes settings are deliberately nonrealistic: they may be exaggerated or lack the right details to convince audiences that they closely represent the world that viewers know. Nonrealistic settings may include unexpected colors. They may look misshapen or contain abstract shapes. Such settings may be enjoyed for their creativity or whimsy, as in a number of scenes from the musical *The Band Wagon* (1953, Figure 1.7). Nonrealistic settings may be used to reveal the main character's state of mind, as in the classic German film *The Cabinet of Dr. Caligari* (1919, Figure 1.8). Nonrealistic settings also appear in many animated films, as in *Tim Burton's The Nightmare before Christmas* (1993) and his *Corpse Bride* (2005), and in symbolic or allegorical stories, such as "Neighbours" (1952; see Figure 9.18 on p. 425). In "Neighbours," a detailed, realistic setting would serve no purpose: the film focuses not on setting or the characters' relationship to the setting but on the symbolic significance

FIGURE 1.7 Nonrealistic set helping to establish a scene's location and mood
An imaginative, playful, childlike setting for "Triplets," a whimsical and satirical song-and-dance number that begins 91¼ minutes into the musical *The Band Wagon* (1953). The scene initially shows only the background painting; then the camera reveals the triplets seated before part of it. As in many musical numbers, the set is nonrealistic; the designers made no attempt to re-create a background that viewers would accept as true to life. None is needed. *Arthur Freed, MGM; Warner Home Video DVD*

FIGURE 1.8 Nonrealistic sets reflecting a character's mental state
In *The Cabinet of Dr. Caligari* (1919), viewers see a story told by an insane narrator, and the sets of his story are done in an expressionistic style complete with many irregular, unexpected shapes. In the scene represented here, about 46½ minutes into this version of the film, the man carrying the woman has kidnapped her and carried her over an irregularly shaped footbridge. Pointy, barren trees or bushes frame him and his victim. Note, too, the irregular white shapes on the ground that seem to climb onto the top of the nearby short wall. As in many scenes in *Caligari*, part of the image was also blocked out, or masked, here on both sides of the frame. *Decla-Bioscop; Kino Video DVD Restored Authorized Edition*

of two neighbors' actions. Sometimes filmmakers on a tight budget use nonrealistic sets because it may be cheaper and faster to construct them than detailed realistic ones.

Functions of Settings

Occasionally a setting may be the main subject of a scene, as in a famous scene in the classic German film *Metropolis* (1927, Figure 1.9). But more often, settings are subordinate to other aspects of the film, such as characterization.

Settings often indicate place and time. When the action shifts to Cuba in *The Godfather Part II* (1974), we can see that the location has a warm, humid climate (a long shoreline, palm trees, men dressed in short-sleeved shirts and lightweight hats, most people dressed in white or light-colored clothes). From the variety of skin tones of the many people on the side-walks and from the uniforms of the police or military authorities, we can infer that the story has shifted to a country with a tropical climate, proba-bly somewhere in the Caribbean. From the car Michael is riding in, a 1950s Chevrolet we see earlier in the movie, another 1950s car parked by the curb, and the ankle-length skirts on the women, many viewers can in-fer that the time is the late 1950s or so. We scarcely need the soundtrack to reveal that the action shifts to Cuba.

In action movies set in nature or outer space, the filmmakers may dwell on the settings by using frequent shots of them without people or with people seen only from a distance. They may use shots of the setting that do not advance the story or that last longer than the **narrative** re-quires. Such shots often stress the beauty, wonder, and vastness of nature (see Plate 19 in Chapter 2). When a shot presents the main subject with abundant space around it, the framing is called **loose framing** (Figure 1.10a). At the opposite extreme, **tight framing** leaves little space around

narrative: A representation of unified events (happenings and actions) situated in one or more settings.

a)   b)

FIGURE 1.9 Setting as subject
Metropolis (1927) shows the story of two major classes in a futuristic city: those with power, wealth, and leisure time and those without. The latter include men who march to work lethargi-cally and then labor on huge machines deep under the city. The machine seen here is the main subject of this and other shots: it dominates the frame, and in comparison, the human subjects seem small and inconsequential. The workers are in service to the machine, not vice versa. Image (a), which appears approximately 13 1/2 minutes into the Kino Restored Authorized Version, shows the setting as it is. Image (b), which appears a little over 15 minutes into the restored ver-sion, shows the setting from the point of view of a powerful capitalist's son as he comes to realize that the machine is akin to Moloch, a god of the Canaanites and Phoenicians to whom children were sacrificed. From the young man's point of view, the machine has an enormous mouth that devours the workers marching in formation up the stairs to their doom. (Perhaps the makers of *Pink Floyd The Wall* [1982] borrowed from or were inspired by this imagery in that film's "We Don't Need No Education" number.) *Giorgio Moroder and Erich Pommer; Kino Video DVD*

the subject, and such settings often convey a sense of confinement and stress (Figure 1.10b). Occasionally, tight framing is used until someone abruptly intrudes into the image. For example, a hand may quickly emerge from offscreen and grab a character, as often happens in eerie, frightening scenes (memorably in *Night of the Living Dead*, 1968). Sometimes this **film technique** is used to frighten a character and viewers, but then both quickly realize that the intruder is not a threat. In *Fatal Attraction* (1987), the Michael Douglas character is seen near an edge of the **frame**, listening to a menacing tape from his former lover; then his wife's hands quickly enter the frame to give his shoulders a massage. He and the viewers jump and then are relieved, and perhaps viewers are a little amused.

Settings are often used to help reveal what a character is like or to create or intensify moods. In the Iranian *Taste of Cherry* (1997), most of the film is given over to a middle-aged man, Badii, driving around Tehran and vicinity looking for someone to cover up his body if he commits suicide, which he intends to do. "Instead of talking about his suicidal feelings, Badii passes over and over through a hellish stretch of industrial debris, abandoned machinery, and brown, dry, or dying vegetation. The land itself looks ready to give up. It's an emblematic use of landscape . . . simultaneously a real landscape and a projection of Badii's mental state" (Erickson

frame: The borders of the projected film, TV set, or monitor.

a)   b)

FIGURE 1.10 Loose framing and tight framing
Framing is positioning the camera so that the image is composed in a certain way. (a) In loose framing, the main subject of the shot has ample space for possible movement and does not seem hemmed in by the edges of the frame and the background. Such is very much the case in this image from nearly 20 minutes into *Lawrence of Arabia* (1962, 1989). (b) In tight framing, there is little visible space around the main subject. As a consequence, the subject usually seems to be trapped or at least confined somewhat, as in this frame from about 74¼ minutes into *The Bicycle Thief* (1948), which shows the main character hemmed in by the wall behind him and the crowd of hostile men before him and on both sides. (a) *Horizon and Columbia; Columbia TriStar DVD.* (b) *Giuseppe Amato and Vittorio De Sica; Criterion DVD*

53). Near the end of the Japanese film *Gate of Hell* (1953), the agitated setting mirrors the feelings of the samurai who intends to kill the husband of the woman with whom the samurai has become obsessed. The first, brief shot of the samurai's approach to the couple's house is of plants buffeted by wind. The next shot is of plants in the foreground blowing in a strong wind and then the appearance of the samurai far in the background, waist-high in vegetation. As he approaches the house (and camera), the wind agitates the plants that surround him. Toward the end of the shot, he disappears off to the right of the frame; only the plants and the sky remain briefly in the background. In the next, very brief shot, a few plants blow in the wind. The message conveyed by the setting is that the samurai is like the wind: his agitated presence powerfully affects what is around him.

Where characters live or work, which objects surround them, and how they arrange those objects can also tell us much about the characters. The **expressionistic** castle of Dr. Frankenstein in *Frankenstein* (1931) seems entirely appropriate for its occupant (Figure 1.11).

Sometimes a film's initial setting establishes mood and perhaps even characterization and meaning, as in *Blood Simple* (1984, 2000, Figure 1.12). Settings can also be used throughout a film to mirror changes in situation and moods, as in *American Beauty* (Figure 1.6b).

FIGURE 1.11 Setting reflecting character
In *Frankenstein* (1931), Dr. Frankenstein's castle is made up of massive, roughly hewn stone blocks suggesting a fortress. The building's few, small windows and relative absence of natural light reinforce the sense of Dr. Frankenstein's illegal and immoral deeds away from the light of the world. The steep, wet, and uneven stairs, which lead up to the laboratory, are dangerous and uninviting. The outer door is massive and contains a small, heavily barred window similar to the one seen here in the background. Frankenstein's workplace is a lot like a prison. The building is largely given over to its upstairs laboratory, with its opening to the sky and the lightning that vitalizes the corpse Dr. Frankenstein steals from a grave in the film's opening scene. Frankenstein's building contains nothing to beautify or soften the interiors: no plants, no artworks, no fabrics, just barren surfaces of stone blocks and the equipment Dr. Frankenstein needs in his obsessive work. With its shadows, odd angles in its corners and wooden beams, and irregularly shaped windows, the setting is strongly reminiscent of expressionism. The castle of *Frankenstein* is appropriate for a scientist who has twisted out of line in daring to play god and create life. *Publicity still. Carl Laemmle; Universal*

Fleeting visual jokes may be part of a setting. They may not be terribly significant but they can be fun, as in *Airplane!* (1980). Approximately 11 1/2 minutes into the film, alert viewers can glimpse this sign inside a plane in flight:

NO SMOKING
EL NO A YOU SMOKO
FASTEN SEATBELTS
PUTANA DA SEATBELTZ

a)

b)

FIGURE 1.12 Setting helping to establish mood and meaning
During the initial shots of the Coen Brothers' first film *Blood Simple* (1984, reissued slightly re-vised in 2000), a narrator says that no matter who you are, "something can all go wrong," that what he knows about is Texas, and that "down here you are on your own." Seen here are frames from two of the film's opening seven shots. All seven are extreme long shots of dry, flat Texas landscape. In all seven shots, the only movement is of oil pumps, and the lighting is subdued or darkish. (a) The film's first shot is of a blown-out tire on a highway that fills nearly all the frame. (b) The fifth shot is mostly of a sky that holds no promise of rain, a lot of dry barren land, and a weathered house that seems to be barely part of the setting. The film's opening seven shots are void of vibrant life and are melancholic and uninviting. *Ethan Coen; Universal DVD*

Almost 53¾ minutes into the film, viewers might see another flashing sign:

RETURN TO SEAT
GOBACKEN SIDONNA.

SUBJECTS

Like settings, subjects are crucial in understanding the expressiveness of mise en scène. In a fictional film, the subject is usually the film's characters. In a documentary film, real people are often a shot's main concern.

Action, Reaction, and Appearance

We learn about characters and people by observing their actions, such as dancing, marrying and divorcing, or writing a novel. Viewers may also learn volumes from facial reactions. As writer and director Jim Jarmusch said about the reactions of Forest Whitaker, the star of Jarmusch's *Ghost Dog: The Way of the Samurai* (1999), "Reacting . . . I think is the essence of acting. And just tiny things can fleet across his face and say a lot more than

FIGURE 1.13 Costume revealing character
Charlie Chaplin in his tramp outfit that he wore in many films, including here in *City Lights* (1931). At first glance, the character seems to be dressed as a gentleman: tie, hat, cane, jacket, vest, and carefully trimmed mustache. Closer inspection reveals, however, that the jacket is too tight, its sleeves too short, the trousers too loose. The cane is the flimsiest, cheapest one imaginable. His gloves are full of holes; his shoes are worn out and have holes. In some Chaplin films, including *City Lights*, the jacket elbows are patched or holey. He is not a wealthy gentleman, though he tries to look like one. His is a constant and often amusing battle to retain his sense of class and dignity. *Publicity still. Charles Chaplin; United Artists*

probably pages of dialogue." In movies, actions and reactions are the usual means of revealing characterization. Perhaps this is because films are superbly suited to single out actions and reactions, focus attention on them, and show them vividly and memorably. No one in the western *High Noon* (1952), for example, tells viewers that the town marshal lives by his principles and that his integrity and willpower are mightier than his fear. Those characteristics are shown by his resolute movements, proud carriage, and creased and worried face.

Often a character's possessions suggest something about the owner. Cars are a favorite means of characterization: station wagons for family members, sports cars for independent singles, VWs for the unassuming, and Volvos for the cautious and middle-aged. As in the choice of actors, the choice of vehicle may surprise and amuse audiences because characters may drive vehicles that audiences would not expect. An example is the Oldsmobile minivan that the John Travolta character, a Miami loan shark, drives and promotes in *Get Shorty* (1995).

We also learn about characters by their appearance, including physical characteristics, posture, gestures, clothing, makeup, and hairstyle. Charlie Chaplin's world-famous tramp outfit serves as an example (Figure 1.13). When a film has multiple main characters, appearance can be used to individualize them, as in *Mystery Men* (1999, Figure 1.14).

Clothing can be used to show or reinforce an aspect of a character, as in *The Graduate* (1967). For an early scene in which Mrs. Robinson is alone with Benjamin in her own home, the acclaimed production designer for the film, Richard Sylbert (*Rosemary's Baby*, *Chinatown*, *Reds*, and many others), wanted the Robinsons' backyard to have thick vegetation and look like a jungle. Such a setting is appropriate for an animal on the prowl, and against that background Mrs. Robinson wears revealing, enticing clothes (Figure 1.15a). The hotel bar where Benjamin waits for Mrs. Robinson

FIGURE 1.14 Appearance setting off characters from each other and from everyone else
In *Mystery Men* (1999), the story of superhero wannabes, six men and one woman with special but limited skills join forces to fight crime—with varying degrees of effectiveness. This image is from a little more than 92½ minutes into the film, when the wannabes have quit squabbling and are united in trying to thwart a catastrophic threat to their city, engineered by the gleefully evil Casanova Frankenstein. The fork-hurling character on the right (Jeff) insists on the moniker Blue Raja, and he dresses like a rajah, though, as his colleagues point out, he wears hardly any blue at all. The character in the middle, called Shoveler, often wears his son's baseball catcher's chest protector, a coal miner's light, and a large shovel on his back. Significant details are revealed in the characters' choices of adornments. For example, Bowler (on the left) always carries a clear plastic bowling ball containing the skull of her dominating father and wears a jacket embossed with a skull and crossed bowling pins. The varied costumes help viewers quickly identify characters, even in long and extreme long shots in action scenes. As befits their hardworking wearers (none of the characters seem to be wealthy), the costumes look like purchased party costumes or—in the case of the reluctant Mr. Furious— simple clothing with eccentric accessories, such as the metal Chevrolet insignia serving as a belt buckle (second from right). The costumes proclaim the characters' resourcefulness and individuality. *Lawrence Gordon Productions; Universal Studios Home Video DVD*

a)   b)

FIGURE 1.15 Costume (and setting) revealing an aspect of a character
(a) In an early scene in *The Graduate* (1967), Mrs. Robinson is alone with Benjamin in her own home, and she wears seductive clothing and appears against a jungle-like background. (b) Later, when she meets him in a hotel bar, she dresses in a leopard-skin coat, as if she is ready for the "kill." *Lawrence Turman and Embassy Pictures; MGM Home Entertainment DVD*

also has the same jungle look in one wall. Mrs. Robinson wears a leopard-skin coat when she shows up at the bar to meet young Ben Braddock before they go to a hotel room to initiate their affair (Figure 1.15b). Later in the film, the leopard-skin motif is picked up again both as Mrs. Robinson prepares to pack for the wedding a black jacket with leopard-skin lapels and cuffs and as she wears that jacket and a small leopard-skin hat at the wedding. The leopard is a large wild cat that is an agile stalker of its prey. Similarly, Mrs. Robinson pursues and captures her prey, then tries to maintain control over him: seducing Ben, continuing an affair with him, and later trying to thwart his relationship with her daughter.

Appearance may serve many other functions. It may be used to heighten the contrast between adversaries, as in the appearances of Obi-Wan Kenobi and Darth Vader (Figure 1.16). Appearance may conceal a character's identity, as in Darth Vader's costume (see Figure 5.19a on p. 242). Often a character's changing appearance reveals the character at different ages or under changed situations (Figure 1.17). As even the most casual viewer has noticed, costumes are often used to help show a place and time, and sometimes also to show the character's status and power (Figure 1.18). Appearance, including clothing, can be so expressive that a single image sometimes conveys the essence of a story. In the original *Star Wars* (1977), much of the story is conveyed by contending forces who dress differently and face each other from opposing sides of the frame against a backdrop of high-tech danger (see Figure 1.16).

FIGURE 1.16 Contending appearances, contending characters In *Star Wars* (1977)/*Star Wars IV: A New Hope* (1997), the softness of Obi-Wan Kenobi's robe and hood (left) contrasts with the heavier fabric and metallic helmet of Darth Vader. Obi-Wan Kenobi looks like a monk. Darth Vader looks militaristic, his helmet a blend of a helmet worn by German soldiers during World War II and one worn by warriors in the earlier Soviet film *Alexander Nevsky* (1938). Take away the light sabers and setting and one can almost imagine a monk confronting an armored knight. It looks as if Obi-Wan is poorly protected, but then the force is with him. *Lucasfilm Ltd., 20th Century Fox; Star Wars (1977) on Star Wars IV: A New Hope DVD*

Appearance reveals character. It can also create character. As film scholar James Naremore explains:

> Costumes serve as indicators of gender and social status, but they also shape bodies and behavior. "[We] may make them take the mould of arm or breast," Virginia Woolf wrote in *Orlando*, "but they mould our hearts, our brains, our tongues to their liking." . . . Who shall say how much the lumbering walk of Frankenstein's monster was created by [Boris] Karloff and how much by a pair of weighted boots? We even have Chaplin's word that the Tramp grew out of the costume, not vice versa: "I had no idea of the character. But the moment I was dressed, the clothes and make-up made me feel the person he was." (88–89)

Characters and Acting

Characters are imaginary personages in a fictional story. They are often based in part on real people—as the main character in *Ed Wood* (1994) is based on the real movie director Ed Wood—or on a combination of traits

FIGURE 1.17 Clothing used to reinforce changed situations
In *The Royal Tenenbaums* (2001), clothing is used to show how one of the major characters, Chas, the son played by Ben Stiller, was a formal, disciplined boy capitalist who wore a suit and tie as he conducted business (a). Years later, as a young man, Chas wears a red jogging suit on nearly all occasions (b). The suggestion is that no matter the occasion, clothing is unimportant. Wear what is familiar and comfortable. Here Chas appears with his two sons after a practice fire drill that he conducted.

Chas's renegade father, Royal, on the other hand, wears a greater variety of clothing and is represented as a more complex and variable character than Chas. He has been barred from practicing law, spent some time in prison, and lost his wealth when he finally attempts to rejoin his family. Like Charlie Chaplin in so many of his films (see Figure 1.13), Royal tries to appear wealthy—in his case, by wearing a suit, tie, and shirt with French cuff links and by carrying an umbrella (c). In spite of his fast talking, scheming, and charm, Royal is eventually reduced to working as an elevator operator in the hotel where viewers first saw him ensconced as a seemingly wealthy guest (d). *Wes Anderson, Barry Mendel, and Scott Rudin; Criterion DVD*

from several people. But some characters—such as the characters in most action movies—are entirely imaginary. In a fictional film, humans usually function as characters, but characters can be anything with some human features, such as talking animals or visitors from outer space. Characters' actions and language—and sometimes their thoughts, dreams, and fantasies—are the main ways we viewers come to understand them and to involve ourselves in the story. Depending on the needs of the story, characters may be round or flat. Round characters are complex, lifelike, multidimensional, sometimes surprising, and changeable. They tend to be

FIGURE 1.18 Costumes that reveal the wearers' status and power
In *The Nativity Story* (2006), the three Magi (in the film, Persian astronomers/astrologers/prophets) are seen in various scenes throughout the film. The costumes of the three quickly and clearly convey their status and wealth. Balthazar (center) in particular is always gussied up, whether traveling or working in the three's laboratory/observatory/library of scrolls. In fact, Balthazar seems to dress as regally as King Herod, though the two wear different headpieces. *Temple Hill Production and New Line Cinema; New Line Home Entertainment DVD*

the most important characters in a story. Flat characters are simple (stereotypical or minor), one-dimensional, and unchanging. They tend to play minor roles in a story, appearing in few scenes and rarely affecting the most significant actions. Narrative films tend to have only a few round characters because there is time to develop only a few characters in depth, and most viewers find it confusing to keep track of more than a few major characters.

TYPES OF ACTORS

> Far from the movies not being an actor's medium, there's probably been no other artistic medium in this [twentieth] century whose appeal rests so strongly on the human presence, and in which the human image has occupied a place of such primacy and centrality. (Pechter 69)

In the earliest years of cinema, film acting was considered so disreputable that in the United States and elsewhere, stage actors who appeared in movies would not let their names be publicized. How different is the situation today! Now American movie actors generally have more prestige, power, and wealth than anyone else involved in making a movie. The most popular actors can command many millions of dollars per movie. And by agreeing to do a particular film, a famous actor often ensures that it will be funded and made. Critics and film theorists have divided actors into various sometimes overlapping types, including stars, **Method actors**, **character actors**, and nonprofessional actors.

Some film industries—such as those of India, Brazil, France, and the United States—have film stars, famous performers who usually play a major if not the major role. Some American stars—such as Arnold Schwarzenegger and Sylvester Stallone—have played a narrow range of characters but often generated widespread interest, commanded enormous salaries, and often guaranteed a large box office, both in the United States and abroad. "Stardom seems more a state of being than a learned skill. . . . For

Method acting: The acting that results after the performer studies the background and personality of a character in depth and uses various techniques to immerse himself or herself in the role.

character actor: An actor who tends to specialize in well-defined secondary roles.

a performer like Stallone . . . the ability to convey subtle shades of emotion, to enter personalities foreign to him, is essentially irrelevant. His skill is that of existing intensely on screen, of communicating his uniqueness and inviting audiences to enjoy it and identify with it" (Kehr). With stardom come prestige and power. A star's power may extend to the choice of the director and even to the script. Sometimes stars and their previous roles are so well known that scripts are written with them in mind or are rewritten to suit them better once they are signed up for a movie. Sometimes the stars' contracts give them the right to insist on script changes. Writer John Gregory Dunne details how Michelle Pfeiffer and Robert Redford—who both had script approval before and during the filming of *Up Close and Personal* (1996)—suggested or insisted on many changes in the script (132–75).

Dustin Hoffman, Robert De Niro, Tom Hanks, Marlon Brando, Al Pacino, Jeff Bridges, Jack Nicholson, Peter Sellers, Alec Guinness, Daniel Day-Lewis, and others have been regarded as stars yet have played a wide range of roles, sometimes within the same film (Figure 1.19). In *Kind Hearts and Coronets* (1949), Alec Guinness plays eight brief roles, including a woman; and in *The Nutty Professor* (1996) and *Nutty Professor II: The Klumps* (2000), Eddie Murphy plays multiple roles, including all the members of the Klump family (Figure 1.20). Female stars—such as Vanessa Redgrave, Anjelica Huston, Jessica Lange, Meryl Streep, Maggie Smith, Faye Dunaway, Ellen Burstyn, and Glenn Close—have been no less versatile and accomplished though they rarely get to play multiple roles in the

a)    b)

FIGURE 1.19 Versatile acting
In *Tootsie* (1982), Dustin Hoffman plays a male actor (a) who sometimes plays a female actor (b). Here Hoffman is seen as (a) Michael Dorsey, an actor, and (b) Dorothy Michaels, who is in fact Michael Dorsey made up to look like a woman. With this film, Hoffman proved he was versatile enough to play two different yet related roles convincingly within the same film. *Sydney Pollack and Mirage; Columbia Pictures DVD*

FIGURE 1.20 One actor, one film, multiple roles
In *The Nutty Professor* (1996), Eddie Murphy plays (a) exercise guru Lance Perkins and all five members of the Klump family: Papa Klump, Ernie Klump, Mama Klump, (b) Grandma Klump, and (c) Professor Sherman Klump. On the right in (c) is Rick Baker, a special-effects makeup artist who won the first Academy Award for makeup for *An American Werewolf in London* (1981) and has also worked as makeup artist or special-effects artist in *King Kong* (1976), *Star Wars* (1977), *Gremlins 2: The New Batch* (1990), *Men in Black* (1997), *Mighty Joe Young* (1998), *Nutty Professor II: The Klumps* (2000), *How the Grinch Stole Christmas* (2000), *Planet of the Apes* (2001), *Men in Black II* (2002), *The Ring* (2002), *Hellboy* (2004), *Enchanted* (2007), and many others. *Publicity stills. Brian Grazer and Russell Simmons; Universal City Studios*

same film (Figure 1.21). Versatile foreign stars include the French actor Gérard Depardieu and Gong Li of China (Figure 1.22).

Some actors (for stage and screen), such as Marlon Brando, Al Pacino, and Joanne Woodward, are Method actors. These performers were trained at the Actors Studio in New York, which was founded by Elia Kazan and two others in 1947 and later brought to prominence by Lee Strasberg. Before filming begins, the Method actor tries to figure out the character's biography and psychology and immerses herself or himself in the role (for example, by not sleeping enough if the actor needs to create an exhausted or distraught character). During filming, Method actors try to become the

a)   b)

FIGURE 1.21 The versatile Vanessa Redgrave

Vanessa Redgrave (born in England in 1937) and her younger sister, Lynn, are the actor daughters of Michael Redgrave, who himself had a distinguished career on the stage and screen. Of Vanessa, David Thomson has written, "There is a case for her as the best actress alive, ready for further challenge" (719). Critic Stephen Holden has written, "Vanessa Redgrave fuses the passion of a true believer with a gift for empathy that allows her to get so thoroughly wired up to her characters' nervous systems that their minutest emotional responses detonate across her face like tiny time bombs. At the same time, this riveting actress conveys the unsettling radar-like intuition of someone who can see beyond the moment to a larger truth, and this gives her an aura of imperial power. Not only does she seem more sensitive than the rest of us, but she also appears stronger and more resolved." (a) In the biographical *Isadora* (1968), Redgrave plays the title role of Isadora Duncan, the unconventional 1920s dancer. (b) In *Orpheus Descending* (1990), which is based on a Tennessee Williams play and was made for TV, Redgrave plays a frustrated woman running her husband's mercantile store in a southern town as he is dying of cancer and often verbally abusing her. Other films from Redgrave's long and varied career include *Blow-Up* (1966), *Camelot* (1967), Ken Russell's *The Devils* (1971), *Julia* (1977), *Wetherby* (1985), *The Ballad of the Sad Cafe* (1991), *Howards End* (1992), the documentary *Looking for Richard* (1998), *Cradle Will Rock* (1999), *A Rumor of Angels* (2000), *Venus* (2006), and *Atonement* (2007). *Publicity stills. (a) Hakim, Universal. (b) Nederlander Film and Turner Pictures*

a)   b)

FIGURE 1.22 Chinese star Gong Li in two diverse roles
(a) *Ju Dou* (1990) is a Chinese film set somewhere in a small village in the 1920s. In it, Gong Li
is a bought wife of an abusive, stingy older man. She eventually takes a lover, has a son (perhaps
by the lover), and as the years go by suffers one misery after another. Here she is seen late in the
film, reduced to meeting her lover wherever she safely can, so the two can escape the censure
of family and village, not to mention the deadly hatred her son feels for her lover. (b) Gong Li
(on the right) as a dangerously unhappy aging top geisha in a geisha house in *Memoirs of a Geisha*
(2005). Here she is seen with her younger rival (played by Ziyi Zhang) well on her way to
replacing her in the geisha house pecking order. Ms. Gong has also played such diverse roles
as an innocent university-educated young woman trapped into becoming the fourth concubine
of a wealthy man in *Raise the Red Lantern* (1991), a golden-hearted prostitute in *Farewell My
Concubine* (1993), and, as Berenice Reynaud wrote, "an unglamorous, heavily pregnant, touch-
ingly obstinate heroine" in *The Story of Qui Ju* (1992). In the overheated *Curse of the Golden
Flower* (2006), Gong plays a powerful Chinese empress at war with her powerful emperor husband
and in love with her stepson from the emperor's first marriage. (a) *China Film Co-Production
Corp.; MagicPlay Entertainment DVD.* (b) *Columbia Pictures, DreamWorks Pictures, and Spyglass
Entertainment; Sony Pictures Home Entertainment DVD*

character and feel and act as the character would, in part by using people
they know as models and by remembering situations from their own lives
that evoke much the same emotion. Some Method actors, such as Robert
De Niro, may also change their bodies drastically to look and feel the part
(Figure 1.23).

Character actors specialize in more or less the same type of secondary
roles. Dennis Hopper, for example, has often played antisocial or deranged
characters (Figure 1.24). Actors such as Peter Lorre, Harrison Ford, Gene
Hackman, Morgan Freeman, and Kathy Bates began as character actors
then became stars; but most character actors do not.

And then there are nonprofessional actors, people with no training or
experience before the camera or theatrical audiences. Famed Soviet director Sergei Eisenstein preferred nonprofessional actors for ideological reasons: the Communist masses, not individuals, were the main subjects of his
films. Eisenstein also believed that nonprofessional actors could best rep-

a)

b)

FIGURE 1.23 Method acting
In *Raging Bull* (1980), Robert De Niro as Jake La Motta (a) in his early years when he was a successful boxer and (b) after his fighting days were over. To play the role of the aging prizefighter turned nightclub owner, dedicated Method actor De Niro put on more than 50 pounds during the three months the film's production was halted for just that purpose. *Robert Chartoff and Irwin Winkler; MGM/UA Home Video DVD*

resent the types of working-class men and women and their oppressors, such as capitalists, Russian Orthodox priests, and tsarist military forces. With nonprofessional actors, directors do not have to worry about audiences being distracted by the actors' previous roles or their activities in their private lives.

For reasons of novelty and greater authenticity, some filmmakers use at least some nonprofessional actors. Sometimes they have no choice. Films such as *Salt of the Earth* (1954; see Figure 7.28 on p. 336) and many films made in countries with widespread poverty may use few or no trained film actors because none are available locally and the production lacks the money to bring them in. Sometimes nonprofessional actors are so awkward and self-conscious, as in the low-budget *Night of the Living Dead*, that they are distracting, even unintentionally laughable, unless the film becomes a cult classic whose acting limitations have become part of the film's appeal. But some directors, such as Vittorio De Sica of Italy, are especially adroit at casting nonprofessional actors and eliciting effective performances from them.

A **cameo** is a small part usually limited to one scene and often unbilled. Though cameos are usually played by famous actors, they may also be played by famous people playing themselves or by insiders in the film community—a type of cinematic insider's joke. Often cameos are little unexpected treats for viewers, who enjoy spotting the cameo, as when attorney Johnnie Cochran and Reverend Al Sharpton appear briefly as protesters outside a building in *Bamboozled* (2000). The best-known cameos in cinema were done by film director Alfred Hitchcock, who put himself in *The Lodger* (1926) and every film he directed after it. Because he appears for only seconds and says nothing, Hitchcock contributes little as an actor to the movies he made. But his cameos are playful and enjoyable

a)

b)

FIGURE 1.24 A character actor
(a) Dennis Hopper as a drug-dealing and drug-consuming hippie cyclist in *Easy Rider* (1969).
(b) Hopper thirty years later in a cameo as a rehab patient who had been shot in the mouth by a former wife in *Jesus' Son* (1999). In addition to the roles illustrated here, Hopper plays a freelance photographer into drugs and his own mental world in *Apocalypse Now* (1979; see Figure 8.22a on p. 394). In *Blue Velvet* (1986), Hopper plays a sadistic, deranged, gas-inhaling, kidnapping lowlife whose mood ranges all the way from angry to furious! He plays a man trying to overcome his alcoholism and win respect from his son and his small-Indiana-town community in *Hoosiers* (1986), a drug-crazed recluse in *River's Edge* (1987), a Vietnam Marine veteran turned double-crossing hit man in *Red Rock West* (1994), a vengeful terrorist in *Speed* (1994), and in *Waterworld* (1995) a witty aquatic gang leader ironically called Deacon who has a shaved head, pirate-like eye patch, and codpiece. In all these and other roles, he is so compelling that many viewers automatically expect his characters to be unstable, unreliable, menacing, and perhaps into drugs or alcohol. *Publicity stills*. (a) *Peter Fonda and Raybert Productions; Columbia*. (b) *Jesus' Son Productions; Lions Gate*

tests of viewers' powers of observation and a challenge to Hitchcock's inventiveness because he did not want to make the same type of appearance twice (Figure 1.25).

CASTING

Once an actor becomes strongly associated with certain behavior outside the movies, for many viewers the actor in a film becomes more than the character. Sometimes those extra qualities supplement a role. Thus John

FIGURE 1.25 Hitchcock cameo
Hitchcock's *Lifeboat* (1944) takes place entirely on a lifeboat at sea. Should Hitchcock float in the water as a dead body, as was reputedly considered? Twenty-five minutes into the film, viewers can see his solution: in an ad for an "Obesity Slayer," a fictional weight-loss program in a newspaper plucked from the ocean some time after a ship had been torpedoed and sunk! As in all the films that he directed after 1926, Hitchcock makes a silent, fleeting appearance in *Lifeboat* that has no impact on the story but is fun to spot. *20th Century Fox; 20th Century Fox Home Entertainment DVD*

Wayne, who was well known for his conservative political beliefs, was cast in many conservative and patriotic roles. Conversely, Jane Fonda, who was well known for her liberal political views, has often played liberal characters. To make a character even more unappealing than the script does, filmmakers sometimes choose an actor who is well known for playing offensive roles. In the French film *Contempt* (*Le Mépris*, 1963), the part of the arrogant and pushy American film **producer** is played by Jack Palance, who was known for his portrayal of unsavory characters in such earlier films as the western *Shane* (1953).

Actors sometimes decide to be cast against type: to play a role unlike their usual previous roles. One of the most famous examples of casting against type occurs in Sergio Leone's western *Once upon a Time in the West* (1968). A widower homesteader and his three children are preparing for the arrival of the man's new bride from New Orleans. Nearly 20¾ minutes into the original and uncut version of the film, the man, his daughter, and his older son are outside near the house when some nearby birds take flight and a shot rings out loud and sharp. Soon there are more shots, and all three of the family members are killed by some unseen assailant(s). Then, the man's younger son runs out of the house and sees his dead father, sister, and brother. Five men emerge from behind desert plants and walk slowly toward the boy. Viewers cannot make out their faces. The men stop perhaps 15 feet from the boy, and the camera glides around from behind them to in front and to one side of the leader's head, and we see his face briefly. Is that the actor we think it is? We see the boy from the leader's point of view and then, a little more than 23 minutes into the film, we see the leader in an extreme close-up. By now, viewers can be certain which famous actor of the late 1960s they are seeing.

> The sense of violation is exacerbated by the familiar, reassuring smile on the face of the leader of these merciless specters. It's the smile of young Abe Lincoln, Tom Joad [Figure 1.26a], Wyatt Earp, and [U.S. Navy officer] Mister Roberts [in the 1955 film version of *Mr. Roberts*], a smile which for four decades in American movies has reflected the honesty, moral integrity, and egalitarian values synonymous with its owner—Henry Fonda [Figure 1.26b].
>
> By casting him as an almost abstract personification of evil . . . , Leone dramatically reversed the prevailing image of Fonda, at once complicating and commenting on our responses to that image. (Morris 220)

a)

b)

c)

d)

FIGURE 1.26 Casting against type

Throughout most of his career, Henry Fonda—the father of movie actors Jane Fonda and Peter Fonda and a grandfather to movie actor Bridget Fonda—played a succession of largely admirable characters. In 1939, he played Abraham Lincoln in *Young Mr. Lincoln*. (a) The next year, Fonda played the sympathetic Tom Joad in the film adaptation of the John Steinbeck Depression-era novel, *The Grapes of Wrath*. In the 1943 western *The Ox-Bow Incident*, he played a cowboy who questions a mob's highly charged, emotional thinking and intimidating behavior and resists those intent on hanging three men who might be innocent. He also played a low-key, trustworthy, and honorable Marshal Wyatt Earp in the western *My Darling Clementine* (1946). In *12 Angry Men* (1957), he played an intelligent, fair-minded juror whose questions and actions ensure that justice is served. (b) But in the spaghetti western *Once upon a Time in the West* (1968), in a striking example of casting against type, Fonda played a killer without a conscience.

Tom Hanks has played characters that are usually decent, likeable, sometimes romantic, sometimes funny. Generally, he has played characters viewers admire. (c) In *Saving Private Ryan* (1998), he plays an army officer who is under enormous pressure yet is dedicated to following commands, protecting the men under his command, and finally paying the ultimate price of duty to country. (d) In *Road to Perdition* (2002), however, Hanks is cast against type and plays a stoical, trustworthy, lethal enforcer for an early 1930s midwestern Irish mob boss. In *Perdition*, Hanks's performance was a bit of a stretch for him, but most viewers and critics found it credible. The role, however, did not call for Hanks to display a wide range of emotion or to play a character less admirable than the movie's other adult male characters. And occasional critics were unconvinced. John Powers, for example, said that Hanks "makes the hit man seem like a lumbering and doleful plumber rather than a killer burning with the need for revenge." (a) *Darryl F. Zanuck and 20th Century Fox; 20th Century Fox Home Entertainment DVD.* (b) *Fulvio Morsella and Paramount Pictures; Paramount DVD.* (c) *Steven Spielberg, DreamWorks, and Paramount; DreamWorks Home Entertainment DVD.* (d) *Sam Mendes and DreamWorks; DreamWorks Home Entertainment DVD*

33

There are also moral and economic implications in casting Henry Fonda as a killer working for a wealthy, powerful, immoral man. Unlike his earlier characters, the Fonda character of *Once upon a Time in the West* gives no hint of a conscience as he goes about doing his dirty work as a hired gun for the unbridled forces of wealth and power—an immoral, greedy railroad entrepreneur. Another example of casting against type can be seen by comparing and contrasting two films with Tom Hanks, who might be described as the Henry Fonda of his time, an actor who usually plays "good guys" convincingly and seems to be a genuine nice guy (Figure 1.26c–d).

Casting against type is chancy. Some viewers want a popular actor to play the same type of role repeatedly and may reject the actor in the new role. But as is illustrated by the casting of Henry Fonda in *Once upon a Time in the West*, casting against type can be effective. It can make viewers entertain new ideas: in this case, perhaps to be jolted into the realization that someone who looks virtuous and has a good reputation may in fact be evil. Casting against type may also intrigue viewers into seeing if the actors can succeed in the challenge they have undertaken (Figure 1.27).

In some animated films and some documentaries, the voices of famous actors are used. In those cases, actors may also be cast against type. Usually, though, actors' voices are used as one might expect. In *Toy Story* (1995) and *Toy Story 2* (1999), Don Rickles, who is known for his insulting grouchy humor, supplies the voice of the caustic, cynical Mr. Potato Head, and Wallace Shawn, who has played uncertain and insecure characters, supplies the voice of the unassertive (Tyrannosaurus) Rex. In *The Lion King* (1994), little Simba says to his malevolent uncle Scar, "You're so weird." In reply Scar, played by Jeremy Irons, says, "You have no idea." Scar's response echoes one of the most famous lines from one of Irons's earlier films, *Reversal of Fortune* (1990). In *The Lion King*, Irons's voice conjures forth the ironic, evil, duplicitous, weary characters he has played, whereas the deep, masculine, confident, commanding voice of James Earl Jones as the lion king evokes the mostly admirable characters from earlier in his career (Figure

FIGURE 1.27 Two stars cast against type
Before *Mad Dog and Glory* (1992), Robert De Niro (left) had been known for playing urban criminals—for example, in *The Godfather Part II* (1974) and in *Goodfellas* (1990). Bill Murray (right) had played various amusing laid-back characters—for example, in *Tootsie* (1982) and in *Ghost Busters* (1984). In *Mad Dog and Glory*, they switch roles. De Niro plays a sensitive, mild-mannered police photographer ironically called "Mad Dog" by his coworkers. Murray plays a Chicago hood who goes to a psychoanalyst and wants to be a stand-up comedian, but he also enslaves others and sanctions murders. The casting against type of the film's two central characters makes possible much of the film's comedy. *Barbara De Fina, Martin Scorsese, and Universal; Universal Studios DVD*

a)

b)

FIGURE 1.28 **Earlier roles, earlier characteristics**
(a) Jeremy Irons as complex twin gynecologists who come to a messy end in David Cronenberg's *Dead Ringers* (1988). Irons also played Dr. Claus von Bülow, a man charged with trying to murder his socialite wife in *Reversal of Fortune* (1990) and the snarling Uber-Morlock in the 2002 *Time Machine*. (b) James Earl Jones as an African American U.S. senator who becomes president of the United States in *The Man* (1972). In plays, on TV, and in films, Jones has brought a seriousness to the many admirable characters he has played, including a professional prize fighter in *The Great White Hope* (1970), actor Paul Robeson, writer Alex Haley, a writer in *Field of Dreams* (1989), and a South African backwoods minister in *Cry, the Beloved Country* (1995). (a) *David Cronenberg and Marc Boyman; 20th Century Fox.* (b) *Lee Rich, Lorimar Television; Paramount*

1.28). In Ken Burns's nine-part documentary film *Baseball* (1994), offscreen Gregory Peck—who has played a variety of well-known movie heroes—reads letters or statements by admirable men, such as the 1919 Chicago White Sox manager, who was unaware that eight of his players were involved in throwing the World Series. Elsewhere in the baseball documentary, Peck reads a passage from the Bible. In contrast, less recognizable actors were chosen to read the statements of "Shoeless" Joe Jackson, who was involved in the 1919 scandal, and the parts of other men the film represents partially negatively, such as Ty Cobb.

PROCESS AND PERFORMANCE

A good part for an actor begins with an effective script and shrewd casting. Without a well-written part, usually an actor can achieve little. Often a successful screen performance also owes much to the casting. Many film directors, including Martin Scorsese, say that if a movie is cast well, the acting will largely take care of itself. As Robert Altman has said, "Once I get a film cast, 85% of my creative work is finished, and the actors really kind of take over. . . . I have to be there because they would all be fighting with each other if I weren't" (quoted in Cheng).

Unlike stage actors, movie actors in big productions do their scenes one shot at a time, often doing multiple **takes** (versions) of each shot. Often

FIGURE 1.29 Understated comic acting
In *Mr. and Mrs. Bridge* (1990), the body language and facial expressions of Joanne Woodward and Paul Newman subtly and amusingly convey the doubts of their characters about the Parisian artist they are looking at. Immediately after this visual inspection of the artist, Mr. Bridge, who is a wealthy lawyer in 1930s–1940s Kansas City, says of artists, "Why don't they get jobs? Like everyone else. Then they can do their artwork on weekends. See, that's how I'd handle the situation." *Ismail Merchant and Miramax; Miramax Home Entertainment DVD*

actors have to do scenes out of order and with long waits between shots. Because filming is usually so time-consuming and costly, usually all the scenes at one setting are filmed together; then the crew moves to another setting and films all the scenes that take place there. Over many days, actors enact snippets here and snippets there. Unlike stage actors, film actors must be able to focus and deliver an appropriate performance after much waiting for the right weather, the right lighting, the right something or other.

Sometimes actors improvise during filming: they say spontaneously what they think their characters would say under the circumstances. Although many directors allow no improvisation, in some films directed by Robert Altman, Mike Leigh, Rainer Werner Fassbinder, and Martin Scorsese, improvisation plays a major role.[1] Those directors believe that what is improvised by an actor immersed in the character and the scene is likely to be truer to the character and situation than what has been imagined by the writer beforehand.

The actor's best allies are usually a skillful scriptwriter and a director who sets the contexts and establishes the moods for each shot. As is discussed in Chapter 3, the film actor can also be helped by an editor who selects the best take of each shot, shortens an ineffective shot, or **cuts** to a **reaction shot** during a lapse in the performance. Music can also cover weak moments in a performance. In films with many action scenes and frequent brief shots, the writer, director, and editor may strongly shape an actor's performance.

Usually an effective performance persuades viewers that the character is believable and helps keep viewers involved in the story. However, there is no

cut (verb): To change from one shot to the following shot seemingly instantaneously.

reaction shot: A shot, usually of a face, that shows someone or occasionally some other creature reacting to an event.

---

[1]Some critics would add John Cassavetes to this list of directors, but as Todd Berliner demonstrates, "John Cassavetes' dialogue comes so close to real speech that it often sounds peculiar, like ad-libbing. Many people think Cassavetes films are, in fact, ad-libbed, but they are not. . . . For all his later films, Cassavetes wrote complete scripts, and, although he and the actors changed the script in rehearsals, they rarely improvised on camera" (7).

one type of effective performance: what works depends on the film's **style** and to some extent on the viewers' culture. Droll, understated comedy—such as that found in *Mr. and Mrs. Bridge*—calls for restrained acting (1990, Figure 1.29). Many films, including many comic films, work best if the acting is exaggerated. Think Jack Black. Film acting should be judged not by one absolute standard but in light of the kind of film it is in.

Judging a performance of what is usually meant to be an invisible art is difficult after only one viewing. A second viewing, a comparison of a script and the performance, or a viewing of other films with the same actor can help viewers see the actor's successes and failures.

COMPOSITION: THE USES OF SPACE

Composition, the third and final major aspect of mise en scène, is the arrangement of lighting and subjects in relation to each other and to the sides of the frame. Before filming each shot, filmmakers may consider the following questions: What shape should the image be? When should empty space be used? Should the arrangement of subjects on the sides of the frame or in the foreground and background be used to convey or reinforce a meaning or mood? Should the width and depth of the image be used expressively within the same shot? Should the subjects of main interest within the frame balance each other or not? In this section, we examine some of the consequences of answers to those and related questions.

Shape of Projected Image

The **aspect ratio** indicates the *shape* of an image, specifically the relationship of the image's width to its height. Thus an aspect ratio of 4:3 means that the image is wider than it is tall by a factor of 4 to 3. Throughout film history the screen has nearly always been rectangular, but at different times the projected image has been relatively wider than at other times. From about 1910 to the early 1950s, most films were shown in the **standard aspect ratio**: approximately 4:3 or 1.33:1 (Figure 1.30a). Since the 1950s, wider formats have dominated in theatrical showings (Figure 1.30b–e). Figure 1.31 illustrates how

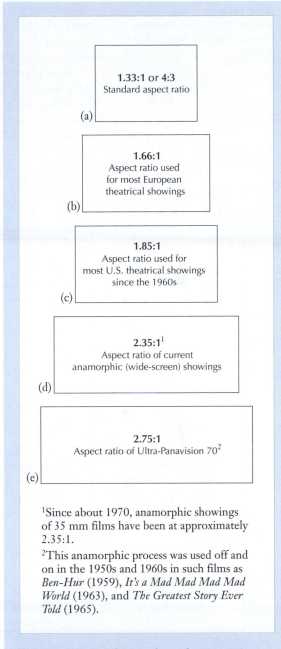

(a) **1.33:1 or 4:3** Standard aspect ratio

(b) **1.66:1** Aspect ratio used for most European theatrical showings

(c) **1.85:1** Aspect ratio used for most U.S. theatrical showings since the 1960s

(d) **2.35:1**[1] Aspect ratio of current anamorphic (wide-screen) showings

(e) **2.75:1** Aspect ratio of Ultra-Panavision 70[2]

[1]Since about 1970, anamorphic showings of 35 mm films have been at approximately 2.35:1.

[2]This anamorphic process was used off and on in the 1950s and 1960s in such films as *Ben-Hur* (1959), *It's a Mad Mad Mad Mad World* (1963), and *The Greatest Story Ever Told* (1965).

FIGURE 1.30 Five frequently used aspect ratios Movies have been shown in different rectangular shapes. Here are five of the most often used ones, drawn to scale.

wide-screen: A film format
with an aspect ratio or screen
shape noticeably greater than
1.33:1.

wide-screen films can be made and later projected by using an **anamorphic lens**, which makes possible the widest images by compressing the image onto the film during filming and expanding the image back to its original width during projection.

As wide-screen formats became commonplace in the 1950s to counter the growing popularity of TV and its screen in the standard aspect ratio, some skeptics claimed that the wider images would be suitable only for wide subjects, such as snakes and funeral processions! But filmmakers learned how to use the wide space effectively, as in *Once upon a Time in the West* (Figure 1.32).

Today, few filmmakers change the aspect ratio or shape of the image during filming. This was done more often in the silent era than since. A

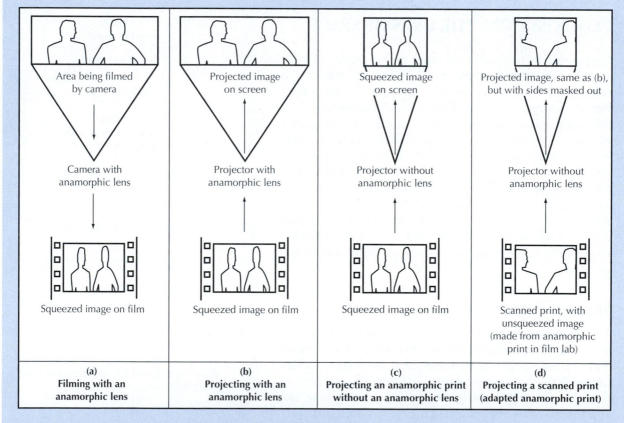

FIGURE 1.31 The anamorphic lens
An anamorphic lens can be used to compress a wide filmed image onto the film in the camera. Another anamorphic lens can be attached to a movie projector to unsqueeze the image during projection. These images are not drawn to scale.

FIGURE 1.32 Expressive use of wide-screen composition
Composition can suggest or reinforce a dramatic situation. Here, approximately 12 3/4 minutes into *Once upon a Time in the West* (1968), a man has arrived at a remote train station where he is greeted by three gunslingers. The "welcoming party" dominates the frame. They dominate it by being in the foreground and by being spread out and taking up most of the horizontal space in the frame. The wide-screen composition helps reinforce the idea that the newcomer—who is off to one side, distant from his antagonists, and very small in comparison to them—is in for a huge challenge. *Fulvio Morsella and Paramount Pictures; Paramount DVD*

1.33:1   1.85:1

FIGURE 1.33 Showing wide-screen films shot with spherical lenses
Many theatrical films since the 1960s have been shot with a spherical (nonanamorphic) lens with theaters *and* analog television in mind and can be shown in 1.85:1 in theaters (inner rectangle) or 1.33:1 elsewhere (outer rectangle). As illustrated by this frame from 5 minutes and 37 seconds into *Schindler's List* (1993), the visual information cropped from the top and bottom of the full image is of no importance. The wide-screen image is thus slightly more compact and ensures that when viewers look at the image they will see the most expressive parts. *Steven Spielberg, Gerald R. Molen, and Branko Lustig; Universal*

frame enlargement from *The Cabinet of Dr. Caligari* (see Figure 1.8) illustrates another way to change the shape of an image: parts of the image have been obscured by a process called **masking**. Other filmmakers change the shape of the image by simply illuminating only part of what is being filmed. As the frame from *Caligari* shows, obscuring part of the image directs viewers' attention to the visible subject.

For years, filmmakers have known that their nonanamorphic (spherical) films might be shown in theaters and on analog television sets and have filmed in the standard aspect ratio mindful that later some of the top and bottom of the image would be cropped for wide-screen theatrical showings (Figure 1.33).

masking: A technique used to block out part of an image (usually) temporarily.

CinemaScope: A wide-screen process introduced in 1953 and made possible by filming and projecting with anamorphic lenses.

Some videotapes and DVDs include a message that the image has been "formatted to fit your screen" or some similar message. But for a film originally shot with an anamorphic lens (for example, a film in **CinemaScope** or any other process with *scope* as part of its name), the full image will be visible only in a videotape, laser disc, or DVD in the **letterbox format** (Figure 1.34). Some videotapes and DVDs of foreign-language films in the letterbox format include subtitles in the darkened area under the images so that viewers can see the original images in their entirety and read distinct subtitles. Usually, the blacked-out bottom and top parts of the image are the same size, though occasionally only the bottom part of the screen is blacked out, which leaves more space for subtitles.

When considering the shape of an image on the screen, consider whether you are seeing the whole picture. If you are not, what you say about composition will probably not be true to the film as it was intended to be seen.

Empty Space

Empty space is often used to convey a sense of loss, as in the Japanese film *Ugetsu* (aka *Ugetsu monogatari*) (1953, Figure 1.35). Another film that uses empty space to suggest the feeling of loss is *Fargo* (1996), in which a husband arrives home and finds that his wife has been kidnapped, as he had

FIGURE 1.34 The Letterbox format
The letterbox format is used to retain a film's original aspect ratio (or a close approximation of it), as is seen here in a frame from almost 48 minutes into an early French New Wave film, *The Four Hundred Blows* (1959). Letterbox images have approximately the shape of a business envelope. *François Truffaut; Fox Lorber DVD*

a)

b)

FIGURE 1.35 Empty space to convey a sense of loss
(a) Almost 11 minutes into the Japanese film *Ugetsu* (1953), which was directed by Kenji Mizoguchi, the potter of the story is fashioning a pot as his wife powers the potter's wheel by turning the vertical pole round and round. By the time of the shot represented in (b), which appears about 94 1/2 minutes into the film, the wife has been killed during a civil war because of the husband's foolish choices. Frames (a) and (b) have the same composition, but the right side of (b) is void of pottery, of the wife, and of her movements. Notice how the filmmakers used light to highlight the emptiness on the right side of frame (b). The empty space (and the absence of the movements the wife made when powering the potter's wheel) help convey that the home has been drained of movement and companionship. So few pieces of pottery on the right side of frame (b) also suggest that the potter is not as productive as before the civil war. With different composition—one not emphasizing emptiness and loss—the shot would not have been so expressive and poignant. *Masaichi Nagata and Daiei Motion Pictures; Criterion DVD*

arranged. The reality of what the husband has set in motion, however, is quickly and visually conveyed largely by empty space (things being badly out of order also contributes to the effect) (Figure 1.36).

Like everything else in a film, empty space has no inherent meaning: its impact depends on context. Empty space is not always used in a negative context. It often reinforces a sense of power and freedom, as in countless scenes of flying airplanes, or a sense of energy and free-spiritedness, as in enormous vistas in many a western and scenes of the open road.

If we see largely empty space in a shot followed by something intruding abruptly, the results can be startling. A famous example occurs in *The Shining* (1980), where viewers see a locked bathroom door, then an ax cutting through it, followed by the face of the Jack Nicholson character—his face all exposed teeth, flared nostrils, staring eyes, scruffy beard, and straggly hair—eager to get to his wife to murder her. Suddenly, he has burst into his wife's space—and the viewer's. A more recent example of cinematic space being abruptly violated occurs in *The Bourne Identity* (2002, Figure 1.37).

a)   b)   c)

d)

FIGURE 1.36 Empty space suggesting disruption of order and loss
Seen here are four shots from three consecutive scenes beginning more than 23 minutes into *Fargo* (1996) in which the husband returns home and discovers that his wife has been kidnapped as he planned. (a) In the first scene, as in an earlier, happier scene, the husband enters through the front door carrying groceries. (b–c) In the second scene, from inside an upstairs bathroom in which one of the kidnappers had found the wife, we see no one, no life, no movement, just a mess, including an empty shower curtain rod seen from the husband's point of view. (d) In the third scene, downstairs again, viewers see the crumpled shower curtain on the floor and then broken glass and the TV that the wife had been watching when the two kidnappers broke into the house. Now the TV shows no picture—not because it would likely lack a signal at that time of day or because one of the kidnappers somehow disrupted the signal input but because the empty screen contributes to the sense of the disruption of order; it's a dramatically appropriate detail. *Ethan Coen and PolyGram Film Productions; PolyGram Video DVD*

a)   b)

FIGURE 1.37 Violating space
(a) A little more than 44 minutes into *The Bourne Identity* (2002), a shot shows Matt Damon's Jason Bourne standing before a pair of opaque glass doors. He seems to sense something is not right. (b) Just then a would-be assassin swinging on a rope comes bursting through one of the glass doors—toward Bourne and basically toward the viewers. This abrupt, in-your-face entry is about as rapid and startling a violation of someone's space as is cinematically possible without 3-D images. *Hypnotic; Kennedy/Marshall and Universal; Universal Studios Home Video DVD*

FIGURE 1.38 Framing to display contending forces
An often-used composition, illustrated by a shot from *The Grifters* (1990): two opposing forces appear on opposite sides of the frame, with the object of contention between them. Here, about 23½ minutes into the film, as elsewhere in *The Grifters*, a girlfriend and mother are competing for the young man's attention. *Robert A. Harris, Martin Scorsese, and Cineplex Odeon Films Production; HBO Home Video DVD*

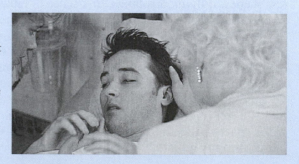

Taking Sides

The width of the film image may also be used expressively. Films often show two people on opposite sides of the frame to suggest their alienation from each other. Late in *Raging Bull* (1980), the Jake La Motta character spots his brother Joey, from whom he has been estranged for years. Joey glances at Jake and walks away without a word. As Jake follows Joey, the camera moves parallel to them, and all the while we see Joey near the left edge of the frame and Jake near the right edge. The composition—the two remaining on opposite sides of the frame, Joey keeping his back to his brother—conveys the physical and emotional distance Joey wants to maintain. As in many films and staged plays, *The Grifters* (1990) often shows two opposing forces on opposite sides of the frame, with the subject of their conflict between them (Figure 1.38).

a)

b)

FIGURE 1.39 Split screen serving different functions
Until near the end of *Napoléon* (1927), only the middle screen of three side-by-side screens is used. During the concluding approximately 18 minutes, three projectors and all three screens are used. (a) Viewers sometimes see one vast subject spilling over onto all three screens. Here Napoleon looks at his encamped troops. (b) More typically, late in *Napoléon*, three different images are projected at the same time, thus giving the audience the opportunity to absorb more information than is typical in a movie shown on a single screen. Often, though, the shots are so brief that viewers cannot absorb all of what is being shown. *Images Film Archive; The Museum of Modern Art/Film Stills Archive*

FIGURE 1.40 Split screen intensifying suspense
In *Run Lola Run* (1998), Lola is trying desperately to reach her
boyfriend, Manni, before he attempts to rob a grocery store when
the clock's minute hand reaches 12. The split screen intensifies
the tension of the situation as here, nearly 27 minutes into the
movie, where the two major characters briefly share the frame with
a clock whose second and minute hands are quickly approaching a
fateful moment. This example illustrates how split screen can be
used as an alternative to editing—here, for example, instead of
separate shots of Lola, Manni, and the clock. *Stefan Arndt; Columbia
TriStar Home Video DVD*

Occasionally filmmakers use split-screen
techniques to show two or more images simultaneously on the same screen. Abel Gance's
Napoléon (1927) occasionally divides a standard-
aspect-ratio screen image into three tall rectangles and early in the film divides the screen
space into nine equal small rectangles, each
one showing a different action. A split-screen
effect may also be achieved by using separate
films projected onto separate screens placed
side by side, as in the ending of *Napoléon*. Often
in *Napoléon*, multiple images allow the simultaneous viewing of events that are presumably happening at the same time (Figure 1.39
on p. 43).

A split screen may also contribute to a situation's suspense. In *Run Lola Run* (1998), the
split screen shows time running out as Lola
tries to reach her lover before he foolishly tries
to rob a grocery store in broad daylight (Figure
1.40). In one shot in the Venezuelan film *Secuestro [or Kidnap] Express* (2005), the split screen
is used to show two characters reacting to a crisis at the same moment in time (Figure 1.41).

There are alternatives to the use of the
split screen that can create similar results—for
example, filmmakers may use editing. Or they may use a transparent yet reflective surface (Figure 1.42). Or filmmakers may use a reflective surface but
not one that we viewers can also look through (Figure 1.43).

**FIGURE 1.41 Split screen used to show simultaneous
reactions**
Secuestro Express (2005) shows a late-night kidnapping of a
wealthy, engaged Caracas couple by three excited armed
men. Here, a little more than 20½ minutes into the film, a
split screen shows the simultaneous reactions of the couple. One shot could not show us how they are reacting to
their predicament at the same time because the kidnappers
have forced the young man to crouch on the car's floor and
have forced his lover to drive. Immediately after this split
screen, the screen is split into four equal rectangles to
show briefly two simultaneous telephone conversations.
*Sandra Condito, Salomón Jakubowicz, and Jonathan Jakubo-
wicz; Miramax Home Entertainment DVD*

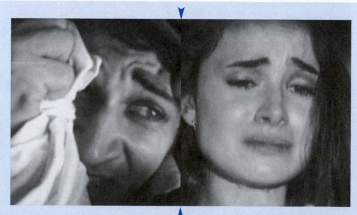

a)
b)
c)

FIGURE 1.42 Transparent, reflective surface and two subjects These images illustrate three of the ways filmmakers may use a transparent yet reflective barrier—in (a) and (b), a window; in (c), a mostly transparent plastic barrier—and additional lighting on one of the subjects to show in one frame both someone looking and what he or she is looking at. All such shots are alternatives to editing in which one shot shows a looker and the next shot shows what is looked at, or vice versa.

(a) A window and carefully chosen camera angle and lighting are used in this shot from *Schindler's List* (1993) to show simultaneously Schindler looking at his factory workers and the workers he sees. If the filmmakers had instead used two shots to convey much the same information—a shot of Schindler looking and a shot of what he sees (or vice versa)—they would have had to determine how much time to give to each shot, and the net effect would have been much different.

(b) In this frame almost 10½ minutes into *The Godfather Part II* (1974), viewers see the boy through a window and, elsewhere on the outside of the window, a reflection of what he sees. The filmmakers could have shown the boy followed by a point-of-view shot of what he sees, or vice versa. Instead they chose to present all the visual information in this one shot, which maintains continuity of action, space, and time. In this shot, the filmmakers also chose to keep the boy's face in much sharper focus than the Statue of Liberty.

(c) This image from a little more than 57¼ minutes into *The Silence of the Lambs* (1991) shows two subjects: he is in a prison cell, and she is on the other side of a mostly transparent plastic barrier. The camera is inside the cell and focused on the woman on the other side of the barrier. The face of the man inside the cell is partially reflected off the clear plastic. Like the image in (b), the image here shows a subject and simultaneously what the subject is looking at. But the image here also makes it look as if a ghostly image of this dangerous, threatening man is behind the woman and in her space when in fact they are face-to-face and separated by a barrier. (a) *Steven Spielberg, Gerald R. Molen, and Branko Lustig; Universal Studios Home Video DVD.* (b) *Francis Ford Coppola, The Coppola Company, and Paramount; Paramount Home Entertainment DVD.* (c) *Edward Saxon, Kenneth Utt, and Orion; Orion Home Video DVD*

Foreground and Background

How filmmakers position people and objects in the background and how they situate them in the foreground are options that influence what the

a)   b)

FIGURE 1.43 Reflective surface and two subjects
(a) This photo from the western *My Darling Clementine* (1946) shows the looker's face superimposed on what he sees. Doc Holliday, who is seriously ill and getting worse, drinks a shot of whiskey, looks at his medical certificate, says his own name scornfully ("Doctor John Holliday"), and throws the whiskey glass, which breaks the glass protecting the certificate. Here, the subject being looked at and the looker are both captured in the same frame. (b) In *Chinatown* (1974), a detective takes photographs of a man and a young woman. Here, the main subject being looked at is off-frame. Like the earlier examples of looker and a reflection of the object looked at within the same frame, this shot in *Chinatown* conveys much information quickly and economically and without editing. The filmmakers could have used a shot of the detective then a shot of the man and young woman, or vice versa. Instead, they chose to show the photographer and his subjects within the same frame. (a) *Samuel G. Engel; 20th Century Fox Home Entertainment DVD.* (b) *Robert Evans and Long Road Productions; Paramount Home Entertainment DVD*

images communicate. The background of an action may go unnoticed because it is obscurely lit or out of focus or because subjects in the foreground draw much of the viewers' attention. However, in some contexts, such as when a dangerous character may be lurking nearby, viewers may study the dark or out-of-focus background to see if they can discern a threat. Often the background is in focus, and details there affect how viewers respond to something in the foreground, or details in the foreground may influence how viewers react to something in the background.

A filmmaker may use **rack focus**: changing the focus *during* a shot (usually rapidly) from foreground to background, or vice versa. Rack focus directs viewers' attention to the relationship of foreground and background or to the action of a different subject. Often this shift in focus is done during a dramatic moment or while the primary subject of the shot is moving, or both, so that viewers do not notice the change in focus (Figure 1.44). In *Fatal Attraction*, the Michael Douglas character is being stalked by a former lover. As he reaches into his car for a rabbit cage and the cage momentarily crosses the screen, rack focus is used quickly and unobtrusively, and the previously out-of-focus background is replaced with a focused image of the stalker's black car. Like the use of reflective surfaces discussed in the

FIGURE 1.44 Rack focus
About 9 minutes into Jean Cocteau's *Beauty and the Beast* (1946), rack focus is used within a shot to shift the focus from the background subjects (a) to a foreground subject (b). As in many examples of rack focus, simultaneous movement (here the woman turning her head) helps disguise the changes in focus *during* the shot. (After this use of rack focus, the same shot continues with another use of rack focus.) *Jean Cocteau; Criterion DVD*

a)  b)

previous section, rack focus is an alternative to editing and maintains continuity of action, space, and time.

Foreground and background elements can be positioned to show how important something in the background is to the subject in the foreground, as in *The General* (1926, Figure 1.45). Another example of background subjects revealing the values of a subject in the foreground is seen in *Do the Right Thing* (1989, Figure 1.46).

FIGURE 1.45 Background conveying something about the subject in the foreground
In *The General* (1926), Johnnie, the Buster Keaton character seen here, wants to serve the Confederate cause in the U.S. Civil War and win the love of his sweetheart. This photograph is Johnnie's gift to her just a few minutes into the film. Overemphasizing the background at the expense of the earnest human subject in the foreground effectively—and amusingly—demonstrates the extreme importance of the train to Johnnie. *Joseph M. Schenck; Kino on Video DVD*

FIGURE 1.46 Expressiveness of background elements
In Spike Lee's *Do the Right Thing* (1989), the wall in the background reveals the values of the Italian American owner of the pizzeria seen here in the foreground. Although his clientele is mostly African American, he hangs only photos of famous Italian Americans on the "Wall of Fame," thus conveying a message of exclusiveness, not inclusiveness. *Spike Lee and Monty Ross; Universal DVD*

Sometimes viewers can see something significant in the background that a character in the foreground is unaware of. Such is the case in a scene in *Local Hero* (1983). The citizens of a small Scottish village have been meeting in a church but do not want the main character in the foreground to know about it. As the main character talks to his assistant in the foreground, viewers can see the villagers scampering out of the church in the distant background and be amused by the situation. In a scene in the German film *Good Bye Lenin!* (2003), viewers see what no one in a room initially notices, something outside in the background (Figure 1.47).

Conversely, the foreground may compete for the viewer's attention with action in the background (Figure 1.48). Sometimes filmmakers film *through* a foreground object, but viewers are so interested in the main subject in the background that they may not consider how the foreground object relates to the subject in the background. For example, when filmmakers impose something with bars (a door, a window, a headboard) in the foreground, often the suggestion is of entrapment or imprisonment for the subject in the background. An example occurs in *Wish You Were Here* (1987). Lynda—an insecure teenage woman involved with Eric, a much older man—goes to live with Eric after her father learns of the affair. Eric calls her to his bed, where he has stretched out. As she approaches the bed and sits on the edge of it, the camera moves so that it looks through the bars of the headboard at the two figures. The image suggests that being there with Eric is or will be a sort of imprisonment for Lynda. Another ex-

FIGURE 1.47 Background action seen by audience but initially not by the characters

Good Bye Lenin! (2003) is about a family of four—mother, absent father, adult daughter, and grown son—who lead eventful lives during a particularly eventful time in their nation's history. Most of the film's action takes place a short time before the 1990 upheaval in East Germany (Deutsche Demokratische Republik, or DDR) when the Berlin Wall was pushed and pulled down and some months after East Germany was reunited with West Germany and changed from communism and socialism to democracy and capitalism.

On her way to a celebration of the fortieth anniversary of the DDR, the mother crosses paths with street demonstrators, who are being attacked by the police, and sees her son beaten and arrested. The mother has a heart attack and lapses into a coma for eight months. After she comes out of the coma, a doctor tells her son (seen above) that any major shock will kill her, so the son attempts to deceive his mother into thinking that nothing major changed while she was in the hospital. In this part of a scene, which occurs approximately 62 minutes into the film, viewers see what no one in the scene has yet noticed, a huge red banner unfolding in the background. Soon, the mother notices it and sees that it reads "Trink [Drink] Coca-Cola." She is confused and concerned. Why is that Western company advertising in her beloved East Germany? *Stefan Arndt; Columbia TriStar Home Entertainment DVD*

a)

b)

FIGURE 1.48 Background action and foreground action
Frenchman Jacques Tati was a master of inconspicuous humorous details visible in the background. Tati's *Mr. Hulot's Holiday* (1953) mostly concerns Mr. Hulot's amusing disruptive experiences during a summer vacation at a beach resort. In the hotel lobby approximately 30½ minutes into the film, Hulot absentmindedly takes the bookmark out of a large book one of the other vacation guests had been reading. A few shots later, alert viewers can see the reader frantically flipping through the pages of his book, desperately trying to find his place. In (a), he is partly visible on the left of the frame and in the background. In the next shot (b), he can be seen far in the background, in the upper left-hand corner of the frame. Viewers may not notice the reader's desperation because his actions are seen far in the background and on the side of the frame. Then, too, these shots include prominent action in the foreground, and shot (b) is full of subjects that compete for the viewer's attention. Tati's films illustrate that viewers who remain attentive to all parts of the image will see the most and enjoy the most. *Fred Orain and Jacques Tati; Criterion DVD*

ample of filming through something in the foreground occurs early in *Easy Rider* (1969). After the two bikers have bought drugs, they stay outside overnight near what looks like an abandoned house. The next morning as they ride off on their motorcycles, somewhat ominously, they are seen from within the decaying abandoned house, whereas the two departing bikers could easily have been filmed without any intervening object. In addition, a shot may show the meaningful relationship of foreground, background, and intermediate subjects (Figure 1.49).

Occasionally, both width and depth are used expressively within the same shot. In *The Bicycle Thief* (1948; also known as *Bicycle Thieves*), when a boy is angry at his father, he is seen in the background and on the opposite side of the frame from the father (Figure 1.50).

Symmetrical and Asymmetrical Compositions

In symmetrical compositions with only one major subject, the subject is seen in the approximate center of the frame (Figure 1.51). In symmetrical

FIGURE 1.49 **Foreground, background, and in between**
Almost 9 minutes into the western *Unforgiven* (1992), as the Clint Eastwood character, William Munny, is trying to sort his sick pigs from the healthy ones, unexpectedly a stranger shows up. Before we viewers see him, we hear him addressing Munny ("You don't look like no rootin', tootin', son of a bitchin' cold-blooded assassin"); then we see a very long shot of the man on his horse, though we cannot see his face very well. Neither Munny nor the audience knows the stranger's mission. The composition of the following shot, seen here, and in a later shot helps sustain the possibility that the stranger is dangerous. In the foreground, the stranger is largely unseen off the left side of the frame with his rifle within easy reach and pretty much in a line with Munny's young daughter. In the background is Munny's daughter and in between the stranger and the girl in terms of depth and off to the right is the unarmed Munny. *Clint Eastwood; Warner Home Video DVD*

FIGURE 1.50 **Image's width and depth used expressively**
After the father slaps his son in the Italian neorealist film *The Bicycle Thief* (1948), the sulking boy keeps his physical and emotional distance, as seen here 55 minutes into the film. Their estrangement is reinforced by the framing: they are on opposite sides of the frame, and the boy is deep into the background. *Vittorio De Sica, PDS-ENIC; Criterion DVD*

FIGURE 1.51 **Symmetrical composition with one subject**
This symmetrical composition is from a film from India, Satyajit Ray's *The World of Apu* (1958). This image from almost 83 minutes into the film is the audience's first view of the boy who will play an important role in the rest of the film. Thus, it is not surprising the filmmakers single out his face by showing it in close-up and in the middle of a frame that has nothing else in focus. *Satyajit Ray Productions; Columbia TriStar Home Entertainment DVD*

compositions with two subjects, typically both are on the opposite sides of the frame, or both may be near the center (Figures 1.52–1.53). Even an image with many subjects can be symmetrical (Figure 1.54).

In asymmetrical compositions, major subjects are not offset or balanced by other subjects elsewhere in the frame. An expressive asymmetrical composition occurs at the end of the **French new wave** film *Shoot the Piano*

French new wave (cinema): A film movement consisting of a loose grouping of untraditional movies made in France in the late 1950s and early 1960s.

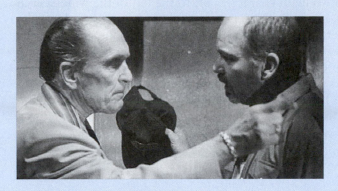

FIGURE 1.52 Symmetrical composition with two subjects on opposing sides of the frame
This composition from about 89½ minutes into Robert Duvall's *The Apostle* (1997) shows two subjects in a heated argument, one on each side of the frame. During confrontational situations, this composition seems so natural that it has been used frequently in paintings, photographs, plays, and films. *Butcher's Run Films; Universal DVD*

FIGURE 1.53 Symmetrical composition with two subjects near the center of the frame
A symmetrical composition from *Henry and June* (1990) shows two subjects near the center of the frame. Visually and emotionally, they are close and in harmony. *Peter Kaufman; Universal Home Video DVD*

FIGURE 1.54 Symmetrical composition with multiple subjects
In this publicity still for the musical *Cabaret* (1972), characters on the right balance characters on the left, and characters in the foreground are offset by characters in the background. Though filled with many subjects, the image could scarcely be more symmetrical. *Cy Feuer; Allied Artists–ABC Pictures*

Player (1960). By the penultimate scene, Charlie, the main character, has lost the woman he loves. In the last shot of the film, Charlie is on the extreme left side of the wide-screen frame; on the right side is a plain wall. Charlie appears alone and out of balance—and he is. (This effect is lost if the film is not seen in its original wide-screen aspect ratio.) A film may use asymmetrical compositions more than only occasionally. Michelangelo Antonioni's *L'avventura* (1960) uses them repeatedly, including in the film's last shot, an image of the two main characters off to the left of the wide-screen frame. In *L'avventura*, typically the setting or part of it on one side of the frame offsets character(s) on the opposite side; this composition suggests the importance of the film's settings—which have little movement, vegetation, or life—and reinforces the sense that some human element is missing in the characters' lives. A more recent example of asymmetrical compositions appears in a film from India, *The Terrorist* (2000, Figure 1.55).

For an examination of some of the choices filmmakers make about mise en scène, see the Close-Up on pp. 55–56.

FIGURE 1.55 Asymmetrical composition
In *The Terrorist* (2000), a boy has been abandoned by his family and lost his home. He serves as a guide for political rebels but is lonely, sensitive, and high-strung and is not well suited for the stresses of his duties. Here, nearly 33¼ minutes into the film, he watches the female would-be assassin whom he has been helping evade both authorities and booby traps as she leaves him. He is sad and thoughtful because she is moving on to the next stage of her assignment. It's appropriate that he is seen off to one side of the frame because he is losing a comfort and balance for his life (there are hints that the young female would-be assassin briefly functioned as both mother and sister to the boy). The space she occupied to the left of the boy is soon to be taken by the indistinct approaching murderous soldiers in the background. *Moderné Gallérie; Winstar TV and Video DVD*

MISE EN SCÈNE AND THE WORLD OUTSIDE THE FRAME

Sometimes filmmakers use settings, subjects, and composition to comment on the world outside the frame—for example, to express a political viewpoint or promote a product. Mise en scène can also be used amusingly to imitate human behavior outside the film, including in another film, or to pay tribute to another film.

Filmmakers may use an image to express political ideas that relate to the story yet promote the filmmakers' political views (Figure 1.56).

Mise en scène can also be used to promote businesses or corporations, products, or services. Moviemakers often make agreements with companies to display their products or services in exchange for money, promotion of the movie, or, much more often, goods and services (such as airline tickets or hotel accommodations). Sometimes the products and services shown are cited in the film's closing credits, as in "The Producers Wish to Thank Stanley Furniture, . . . Coca-Cola, . . . Black Death Vodka, Folgers

Coffee, . . . American Tobacco." (Businesses, products, and services acknowledged under "Special Thanks To" in the closing credits for *The Player* [1992] can be found on pp. 700–701.) So widespread has **product placement** become that some large companies pay specialists to arrange for placements in movies.

Movies may plug a related corporation. *Contact* (1997), which was released by Warner Bros., features Cable News Network (CNN) repeatedly. That's no accident. At the time *Contact* was being made, both Warner Bros. and CNN were owned by Time Warner (Figure 1.57). Sony used its Columbia Pictures branch to make *Panic Room* (2002), which conveniently and prominently features Sony video monitors. Increasingly in multicorporate businesses, one branch promotes another.

Product placement can be excessive and intrusive—sometimes for comic effect, sometimes not. A good example of egregious and amusing product placement is from a scene in *Wayne's World* (1992) that shows five name-brand products in a row, including Garth suddenly dressed in Reebok shoes, a Reebok jogging suit, and a hat with "Reebok" emblazoned under the brim and above it. So dressed, Wayne flaunts the Pizza Hut logo while declaring he would never do a product placement. More often, intrusive product placements are not amusing. During a three-minute stretch well into *EDtv* (1999), we hear that a major character prefers Pepsi over Coke, see a Pepsi machine, and see several characters with Pepsi cans.

FIGURE 1.56 Using mise en scène to promote a political viewpoint
In more than one shot of *Do the Right Thing* (1989), background graffiti include the slogan "Dump Koch." At the time of the film's making, Ed Koch was running for reelection as mayor of New York. The graffiti are credible in the film's story because many New York African Americans believed that Koch had failed to deal with racial strife effectively. The graffiti also allow director Spike Lee to express his own political views, at least indirectly. Before and during the making of *Do the Right Thing*, Lee openly opposed Koch's reelection. The publicity still seen here shows the "Dump Koch" graffiti more legibly than the film itself does. *Spike Lee and Monty Ross; Forty Acres and a Mule Filmworks; Universal*

FIGURE 1.57 Using mise en scène to promote a (related) corporation
During *Contact*, which shows humans establishing contact with extraterrestrial life, viewers often see TV coverage of spectacular unfolding (fictional movie) events, and that coverage is supposedly by CNN. Curious that CNN is so prominent, one might think. The reason: at the time *Contact* was released by Warner Bros. (1997), Time Warner controlled both Warner Bros. and CNN. The makers of *Contact* could either have made up a fictitious network or paid an existing network (say, NBC), or used CNN (for free or for lesser permissions fees). For the parent corporation Time Warner, the choice was obvious. *Steve Starkey and Robert Zemeckis; Warner Home Video DVD*

Product placements may be subtle and go unnoticed by many viewers. The documentary film *The Big One* (1998) focuses on a book tour and many side trips that satirist and filmmaker Michael Moore takes in hopes of questioning CEOs about corporate downsizing and sending jobs abroad even though the companies have been making huge profits. Moore gives considerable screen time to his visits to bookstores to give talks and to the long lines of people waiting for him to sign their copy of his book. There's also a shot of his book as number 1 on the *New York Times* list of best sellers. The message: his book is important (and so is Michael Moore). One could argue that promoting his book and the messages it contains indirectly supports the other main subject of the film: the pain suffered by workers who are victims of downsizing. But it could be argued that the emphasis on his book's popularity is also a self-promoting product placement. Regardless of Moore's motives, in *The Big One* Michael Moore's book functions as a pervasive product placement.

Some filmmakers sometimes conceal product identity to avoid possible lawsuits. If a movie shows someone committing a crime, filmmakers are usually careful not to associate the crime with a commercial product. That is why viewers will not see a character listen to a particular heavy metal number or drink a famous whiskey and then go out and murder someone.

Mise en scène can also be used to parody someone or something. A **parody** is an amusing imitation of human behavior or of a **text** (such as a book or film), part of a text, or texts. For example, the mise en scène of a shot inside Han Solo's spaceship in the original *Star Wars* movie is amusingly re-created in many later parodies, such as the 1987 movie *Spaceballs* (see Figure 5.15a and c on p. 237). Mise en scène can also be used to pay an **homage**, a tribute to an earlier text (such as a film) or part of one. For instance, some shots of the main character in the French new wave film *Breathless* (1959) re-create mannerisms that actor Humphrey Bogart used in his films (see Figure 7.30a–b on p. 339).

text: Something that people produce or modify to communicate meaning.

CLOSE-UP: MISE EN SCÈNE IN *CITIZEN KANE*

FIGURE 1.58 Expressive composition in *Citizen Kane* (1941)
In this frame from a scene that begins nearly 66 minutes into the film, a rival politician is trying to blackmail Kane (center) into quitting the governor's race or face public disclosure of Kane's affair with a single woman (left). Kane's wife, Emily, is seen on the right of the frame. *Orson Welles; Warner Home Video DVD*

For each scene, filmmakers decide how much to rely on mise en scène—settings, subjects, and composition.

In a scene in *Citizen Kane* that begins 65 3/4 minutes into the film, Charles Foster Kane, a wealthy newspaper publisher, and his wife, Emily, have gone to the residence of Kane's mistress, Susan, where they are met by Susan and a crooked politician (Gettys). During the scene Gettys tries to pressure Kane into withdrawing from the governor's race against him or face public exposure of Kane's affair with Susan. Early in the scene, one shot lasting 117 seconds contains the following compositions and major movements:

1. At the beginning of the shot, Kane is near the left of the frame facing Emily, who is on the right of the frame.

2. Susan joins Kane on the left (the camera pivots slightly to the left to accommodate her), and the three characters are positioned as they are in the frame shown in Figure 1.58.

3. Kane turns away from the two women and starts to walk toward the background. As he walks, the camera pivots slightly to the right to follow him, excluding Susan from the frame, and Emily pivots and looks toward the background, where Kane joins Gettys. Emily is in the left foreground; the two men are in the background.

4. Gettys walks forward while staying on the right of the frame. Kane remains in the background, in the center of the frame between Emily on the left and Gettys on the right. For the rest of the shot, Gettys and Emily remain in the foreground and on opposite sides of the frame.

5. Susan rushes into the frame from the left and joins Kane in the background, center.

6. Susan steps forward a few steps; Kane remains in the background.

7. Susan takes another step forward; Kane remains in the background.

8. Toward the end of the shot, Emily, Susan, and Gettys, all in the foreground, turn their heads and look toward Kane, who remains in the background (they await his response to Gettys's blackmail attempt).

Much is going on in this lengthy shot, both in groupings of characters (shifting alignments and confrontations) and in dramatic impact (who commands attention, who has power, who does not). For example, the shot begins with Kane between

55

his wife and mistress, though closer to the mistress than to his wife, and with the blackmailer out of the frame—in fact, waiting in a dark part of the room. The shot ends with Kane in the center of the frame facing his wife, mistress, and blackmailer in the foreground. By his own choice, he is physically and emotionally alone. In spite of his wife's practical advice and his mistress's emotional appeals, he is determined that only he will make the decision he is about to announce.

SUMMARY

In this and other publications, the term *mise en scène* signifies the major aspects filmmaking shares with staging a play. It refers to the selection of setting, subjects, and composition of each shot. Normally in complex film productions, the director makes final decisions about mise en scène.

Settings

- A setting is the place where filmed action occurs. It is either a set, which has been built for use in the film, or a location, which is any place other than a film studio that is used for filming.

- Depending on the needs of the scene, settings may be limbo (indistinct), realistic, or nonrealistic.

- A setting can be the main subject of a shot or scene but usually is not. Settings often reveal the time and place of a scene, create or intensify moods, and help reveal what people (in a documentary film) or characters (in a fictional film) are like. Throughout a film, changes in settings can also mirror changes in situations and moods.

Subjects

- In films, fictional characters or real people are the usual subjects, and their actions and appearances help reveal their nature.

- Performers may be stars, Method actors, character actors, or nonprofessional actors. There is some overlap among these categories: a star, for example, may also be a Method actor. Depending on the desired results, actors may be cast by type or against type.

- Usually film actors must perform their scenes out of order, in brief segments, and often after long waits.

- Effective performances may depend on the script, casting, direction, editing, and music. There is no one type of effective performance:

what is judged effective depends in part on the viewers' culture and the film's style or its manner of representing its subject.

Composition: The Uses of Space

- Filmmakers, especially cinematographers and directors, decide the shape of the overall image. They also decide how to use the space within an image. They decide when and how to use empty space and what will be conveyed by the arrangement of significant subjects on the sides of the frame, in the foreground, or in the background. Filmmakers also decide if compositions are to be symmetrical or asymmetrical.

- Composition influences what viewers see positioned in relationship to the subject and how the subject is situated within the frame; what information is revealed to viewers that the characters do not know; and what viewers learn about the characters' personalities or situations.

- Many films are seen in an aspect ratio (or shape of the image) other than the one the filmmakers intended, and the compositions, meanings, and moods conveyed are thus altered.

Mise en Scène and the World outside the Frame

- Mise en scène can be used to promote a political viewpoint or commercial product (the latter practice is called *product placement*).

- Mise en scène can be used to parody human behavior or a text (such as a film). It can also be used to pay homage or tribute to an earlier text or part of one.

Major Terms about Mise en Scène

Below, numbers in italics refer to the pages where the terms are explained. All terms are defined in more detail in the Illustrated Glossary beginning on p. 667.

anamorphic lens *38*
aspect ratio *37*
cameo *30*
character actor *29*
CinemaScope *40*
composition *37*
designer or production designer *11*
expressionism *16, 19*
frame *18*
letterbox format *40*
limbo *14*
location *13*

loose framing *17*
masking *39*
Method actor *27*
mise en scène *11*
product placement *52*
rack focus *46*
set *13*
setting *13*
standard aspect ratio *37*
tight framing *17*
wide-screen *38*

QUESTIONS ABOUT MISE EN SCÈNE

The following questions are intended to help viewers understand mise en scène and their responses to it. Not all the questions are appropriate for every film. In thinking out, discussing, and writing responses to the questions most appropriate for the film being examined, be careful to stick with the issues the questions raise, to answer all parts of the questions, to explain the reasons for your answers, and to give specific examples from the film.

Settings

1. Can you tell where sets are used and where the filmmakers filmed on location? If so, what does each type of setting contribute to the film?
2. Where and to what effect is each of the following type of setting used: limbo, realistic, or nonrealistic?
3. Where are settings used to reveal time and place?
4. Where and to what effect are settings used to create or intensify moods?
5. Where and to what effect are settings used to help reveal what people (in a documentary film) or characters (in a fictional film) are like?
6. Are settings used to mirror changes in situations and moods? If so, explain.

Subjects

7. What are the film's major subjects?
8. If the major subjects are people or characters, which actions are especially expressive?
9. If the film is fictional, who is the protagonist or main character? Why do you say so? Describe the character's appearance and personality.
10. Explain which performers are stars, Method actors, character actors, or nonprofessional actors.
11. Are any of the actors cast against type? If so, explain how so and what the effects are.
12. Are any of the actors cast to type? If so, cite some previous roles, and explain how they are consistent with the present role.

Composition: The Uses of Space

13. What is the film's intended aspect ratio? Are you seeing the film in its intended aspect ratio? If not, how does the changed aspect ratio alter the film's composition?

14. In significant excerpts from the film, how do background and fore-ground elements relate to each other?

15. In significant parts of the film, how do subjects on the sides of the image relate to each other?

16. Are significant subjects bunched up within the frame or spread apart? Are they in the center of the frame or off to a side?

17. In the fictional film, is composition ever used to reveal to viewers information that the characters could not know?

18. Are significant subjects arranged in such a way as to balance out the composition or to create an imbalance?

Mise en Scène and the World outside the Frame

19. Where is mise en scène used to promote a political viewpoint?

20. Where is mise en scène used to promote a business or corporation, a commercial product, or a service?

21. Where is mise en scène used to parody human behavior or a text (such as a film)?

22. Where is mise en scène used to pay homage to an earlier text or part of one?

WORKS CITED

Berliner, Todd. "Hollywood Movie Dialogue and the 'Real Realism' of John Cassavetes." *Film Quarterly* 52.3 (Spring 1999): 2–16.

Cheng, Scarlet. "It's All in the Acting." *Los Angeles Times* 8 Apr. 1999.

Dunne, John Gregory. *Monster: Living off the Big Screen*. New York: Random, 1997.

Erickson, Steve. "Taste of Cherry." *Film Quarterly* 52.3 (Spring 1999): 52–54.

Holden, Stephen. "A Rumor of Angels: A Friendship Based on Tough Love and Phony Tears." Review. *New York Times* 1 Feb. 2002, late ed.: E20.

Jarmusch, Jim. *Fresh Air*. Nat'l. Public Radio, 11 Apr. 2000.

Kehr, Dave. "Big Stars in Little Movies." *New York Times on the Web* 12 Sept. 1999.

Morris, George. "Henry Fonda." *The National Society of Film Critics on the Movie Star*. Ed. Elisabeth Weis. New York: Penguin, 1981.

Naremore, James. *Acting in the Cinema*. Berkeley: U of California P, 1988.

Pechter, William S. "Cagney vs. Allen vs. Brooks: On the Indispensability of the Performer." *The National Society of Film Critics on the Movie Star*. Ed. Elisabeth Weis. New York: Penguin, 1981.

Powers, John. Review of *Road to Perdition*. *Fresh Air*. Nat'l. Public Radio. 12 July 2002.

Reynaud, Berenice. "Gong Li and the Glamour of the Chinese Star." *Sight and Sound* Aug. 1993: 12–15.

Thomson, David. *The New Biographical Dictionary of Film*. New York: Knopf, 2002.

FOR FURTHER READING

Affron, Charles, and Mirella Jona Affron. *Sets in Motion: Art Direction and Film Narrative*. New Brunswick, NJ: Rutgers UP, 1995. On the status of art direction in cinema and how set design can function in narrative films, with interpretations of many specific sets and films.

Bruzzi, Stella. *Undressing Cinema: Clothing and Identity in the Movies*. London: Routledge, 1997. Citing detailed examples from a variety of mostly popular films, Bruzzi demonstrates how clothes are key elements in the construction of cinematic gender, identity, sexuality, and desire. The chapters are divided into three parts: "Dressing Up," "Gender," and "Beyond Gender."

Dyer, Richard. *Stars*. 2nd ed. London: British Film Institute, 1998. Discusses stars in terms of social phenomena, images, and signs and includes Dyer's detailed interpretations on such stars as Marlon Brando, Bette Davis, Jane Fonda, Marilyn Monroe, and John Wayne.

Fashioning Film Stars: Dress, Culture, Identity. Ed. Rachael Moseley. London: British Film Institute, 2005. A collection of essays examining the relationships between fashion, dress, and star image. The essays explore the significance of male and female star style in Hollywood, European, Asian, and Latin American contexts.

Heisner, Beverly. *Production Design in the Contemporary American Film: A Critical Study of Twenty-three Movies and Their Designers*. Jefferson, NC: McFarland, 1997. American films from the 1980s and 1990s are discussed under five headings: "Realistic Films Set in the Present Day," "Stylized Films Set in the Present Day," "Period Films," "Period Films That Move through Several Decades," and "Science Fiction and Fantasy Films."

Screen Acting. Ed. Alan Lovell and Peter Kramer. London: Routledge, 1999. Argues for the centrality of the actor's performance to a film's impact, offers directions for studying film performances, and discusses the acting styles of various movie actors.

Sennett, Robert S. *Setting the Scene: The Great Hollywood Art Directors*. New York: Abrams, 1994. Includes chapters on art direction in the silent film, the Hollywood musical, classic horror films, science fiction, and the western. Each chapter focuses on a few (usually famous) movies. Many photographs and sketches.

CHAPTER 2

Cinematography

W HAT MOVIES DO is make perception easier. The darkened theater cuts out the claims of peripheral vision. The large images on the screen open up the perceived world for analysis . . . and allow [viewers] to see details simply not available in ordinary experience. Because film makers can further assist perception by careful lighting, lens choice, and camera placement, and can guide expectations and discriminations in a thousand more subtle ways, they can radically enhance the efficiency of seeing. . . . And, in a sense, the film maker can make the viewer more intelligent perceptually, at least while the film is running. Movies use perception in ways that make being "perceptive" remarkably easy. That is one reason why they are so involving. (Eidsvik 21, 23)

> Terms in **boldface** are defined in the Illustrated Glossary beginning on page 667.

In the previous chapter we saw how **setting**, subjects, and **composition**—all essential components of staged plays—might function in a film. In this closely related chapter, we explore some of the cinematic aspects of filming, such as some of the many ways the **film stock**, lighting, camera lenses, camera distances and angles, and camera movement affect the finished images. We take up these topics in a temporal order: the film stock or videotape that is put into the camera; some of the ways the camera itself may be manipulated during filming; and after filming is completed, the ways the cinematography may be corrected or supplemented digitally. Whether through photochemical equipment or through the latest digital equipment, cinematography always strongly influences how viewers respond to the finished film: it helps convey the subject matter in expressive ways and powerfully shapes the viewers' emotional responses and the meanings viewers detect in films.

> **composition:** The arrangement of settings, lighting, and subjects within the frame.
>
> **film stock:** Unexposed and unprocessed motion-picture film.

FILM STOCK

Film stock is unexposed and unprocessed motion-picture film. It is made up of two basic components (Figure 2.1). The clear, flexible base resembles the **leader** on microfilm—the clear or opaque piece of film that is threaded into a microfilm reader. On top of the base is a thin gelatin coating called the **emulsion**, which contains millions of tiny light-sensitive **grains**. After the

> **leader:** The clear or opaque piece of film that begins and concludes a reel of film.

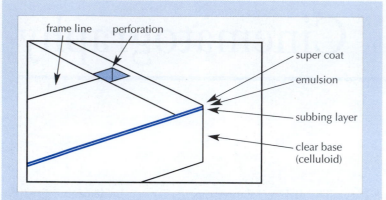

FIGURE 2.1 Film's components (not to scale)
A piece of film consists of a clear base, which constitutes most of the film's overall thickness, and the emulsion, which consists of a thin layer of gelatin in which are suspended the tiny light-sensitive crystals that make up the image after exposure to light. The emulsion is attached to the base by a clear adhesive called the *subbing layer*. A super coat on top of the emulsion protects it against scratching. Most film also has an antihalation backing (not shown) to prevent light reflection back through the base that would cause a blurred effect (halation) around the bright part of an image, as with bright oncoming headlights. (Adapted from Malkiewicz 50)

footage: A length of exposed motion-picture film.

emulsion is exposed to light, it can be chemically developed to hold an image. The emulsion is what has been scratched when you see continuous unwanted vertical lines in a projected movie.

The film or video stock influences the film's finished look, including its sharpness of detail, range of light and shadow, and quality of color. Cinematographers try to select film stocks that give the finished film an appropriate look. In preparing to film *Eve's Bayou* (1997), a family drama set in Louisiana in 1962, cinematographer Amy Vincent did extensive location scouting, shot hundreds of stills at various locations, and studied photographs of the period and place to be re-created in the movie. Later she chose different film stocks to achieve different effects. One stock was used for day interiors, one for day exteriors, one for night exteriors, and yet another for a character's "vision" **scenes** ("Collaboration"). Many **documentary films** combine older documentary **footage** with more recent footage shot on a different film stock. *Hearts of Darkness: A Filmmaker's Apocalypse* (1991), for example, combines footage shot during the making of *Apocalypse Now* (1979) with footage of interviews shot on a different film stock decades later. In that film, the different film stocks help viewers differentiate between the reactions of cast and crew then and their later recollections of the same events.

With the commercial viability of digital videotape in recent years, some cinematographers film parts of the movie on a particular film stock and shoot other parts using digital video, which is later transferred to film. Examples include Errol Morris's documentary *Fast, Cheap & Out of Control* (1997), the German fictional film *Run Lola Run* (1998), and Spike Lee's *Bamboozled* (2000). As we see in more detail in the next chapter, for various reasons, including costs and ease of use, more and more filmmakers film entirely on digital tape, edit the material with computers, and transfer the results to film for theatrical showings.

Gauge

Film stocks are available in various **gauges**, or widths (Figure 2.2). The most common width used for filming and projecting movies in commercial theaters is 35 millimeter (mm), though movies may be filmed in 16 mm,

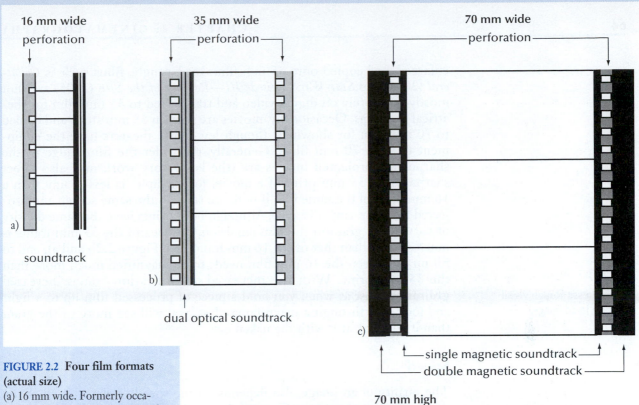

16 mm wide

perforation

a)

soundtrack

35 mm wide

perforation

b)

dual optical soundtrack

70 mm wide

perforation

c)

single magnetic soundtrack

double magnetic soundtrack

70 mm high

soundtracks

perforation

d)

FIGURE 2.2 Four film formats (actual size)

(a) 16 mm wide. Formerly occasionally used by small commercial theaters, TV stations, industry, military, and schools and universities. Usually, the aspect ratio of the projected image is 1.33:1. Other formats in 16 mm include anamorphic (squeezed) prints with an aspect ratio of approximately 2.4:1 when projected with an anamorphic lens. (b) 35 mm wide. Used in most commercial theaters, sometimes for major TV showings, and showings at some large universities. When projected, the screen image may have an aspect ratio of 1.33:1; 1.66:1 for many European theatrical showings; 1.85:1 for most U.S. spherical (nonanamorphic) theatrical showings; or 2.4:1 for anamorphic showings. (c) 70 mm wide, nonanamorphic (unsqueezed) image. Used only in selected large theaters. Aspect ratio: 2.2:1. In the United States and western Europe, films shown in 70 mm usually are shot on 35 mm and enlarged or are filmed in 65 mm and printed on 70 mm stock. (d) 15 perforation/70 mm format. Used by IMAX. Filmed and projected by running the film horizontally through the camera and projector. The space for each frame is about ten times larger than the area of the 35 mm frame. The projector aspect ratio is 1.43:1.

enlarged, and copied onto 35 mm film. Increasingly, films such as *Collateral* (2004) and *Star Wars: Episode III—Revenge of the Sith* (2005) are shot mostly or entirely on digital video and transferred to 35 mm film for theatrical showings. Occasionally, movies are shot on 65 mm stock and copied to 70 mm film for showings, though few movie theaters have the equipment to show 70 mm films. Generally, the wider the film gauge is, the sharper the projected images are (the laboratory work may also affect sharpness). A 35 mm print of a movie, for example, is less grainy than a 16 mm print of the same film if both are seen on the same screen and projected from the same distance. Although both prints have the same density of particles or grain in the film emulsion, the area of the 35 mm frame is much greater than that of the 16 mm frame (see Figure 2.2b and a), and to fill up the screen the 16 mm film needs to be magnified much more than the 35 mm print. With the increased magnification comes increased **graininess**, just as when you hold a piece of processed film up to a light and look at it through a magnifying glass, you will see more of the grain than if you look at it with the naked eye.

graininess: Rough visual texture in an image.

Speed

The quality of an image also depends on the speed of the film stock, its sensitivity to light. **Slow film stock**, which often requires considerably more light than **fast film stock**, can produce fine grain and a detailed, nuanced image. Filmmakers often use slow film stocks for musicals filmed on **sets** and for other films in which detailed images are important and the lighting can be carefully controlled during filming (Figure 2.3).

set: A constructed setting, indoors or outdoors, where action is filmed.

Fast film stock requires less light than a slow film stock. Often it is used in documentaries, especially when lighting options are limited, and in fictional films that capture a documentary look (Figure 2.4). Fast film stock is also used in fictional film scenes with little available lighting. In older films, fast film stock produces graininess. However, today's fast film stocks — and **fast lenses**, which transmit light efficiently — can produce remarkably

FIGURE 2.3 Fine-grain image
This fine-grain image of Salma Hayek appears in *After the Sunset* (2004). The choices made in film stock, lighting, and lab work ensured that this fine-grain image immediately reveals the details of the actor's appearance. Fine-grain images tend to be associated with controlled shooting conditions and professional quality and in some contexts can help nurture the impression that the shot was made on a set, not on location.
A Firm Films/Contrafilm Production and New Line Cinema; New Line Home Entertainment DVD

FIGURE 2.4 Rough-grain or grainy image
Grainy images may be achieved by using older fast film stock or by other means and tend to be associated with amateur filmmaking, newsreels, old footage, and old documentary films. Sometimes, as in parts of *Citizen Kane* and *Forrest Gump*, grainy images are deliberately created to support the illusion that old footage was used. In much of the Italian/Algerian film *The Battle of Algiers* (1966), film stock that produces high contrast and either washed-out, overly dark, or grainy images gives a documentary feeling to this film about the attempts by the French to eradicate an uprising in Algeria, one of its former colonies that gained independence in 1962. In this frame from a reaction shot, which appears approximately 96 1/2 minutes into the film, an Algerian woman reacts as she sees French soldiers torturing Algerian suspects. *Antonio Musu and Yacef Saadi; Criterion DVD*

detailed results even when shot with low levels of lighting, though current black-and-white stocks produce grainier results than current color stocks.

Film processing can also affect graininess. Some filmmakers ask the laboratory to make the processed film grainier to create or enhance certain effects. This may be done, for example, to represent harsh living conditions.

Color

> It's funny how the colours of the real world only seem really real when you viddy [see] them on a [movie] screen. — Narrator of *A Clockwork Orange* (1971 film)

As early as 1896, some films had some color. Some black-and-white films were hand-colored. Different colors were painted onto each frame with small, delicate brushes, sometimes in assembly-line fashion (Plate 1). (Color Plates 1–32 follow p. 70.) Other early black-and-white films, including many major **feature films** of the 1910s and 1920s, were **tinted** a uniform color (monochrome), or, more often, whole scenes or **sequences** were tinted a particular color. Either the black-and-white footage was dyed or the black-and-white **negative** was printed on a film stock of a particular, uniform color. The same color was used for similar scenes or sequences throughout the film (Plates 2–3). Different tints could also indicate **flashbacks** or fantasies, as in the famous French film *Napoléon* (1927).

By 1932, Technicolor combined three negatives, each sensitive to red, green, or blue, and in 1935, the first three-color Technicolor feature film was produced. Initially, color was used in ways that might surprise modern viewers: "In the 1930s and 1940s, . . . [Hollywood] decreed that colour

feature (film): A fictional film that is at least 60 minutes long.

sequence: A series of related consecutive scenes perceived as a major unit of a narrative film.

negative: Excluding reversal film, film that has been exposed and developed.

should be reserved for certain genres that in themselves were not particularly realistic—stylized and spectacle genres (musicals, fantasy, epics)" (Hayward 70). By the early 1950s, to counter the growing popularity of black-and-white television, more and more movies were made in color, and color was well on its way to becoming the usual way of showing **celluloid** lives.

celluloid: Movie, as in "celluloid heroes."

There are special considerations to be aware of when discussing the significance of color. Color may be used in so many ways that it is important not to overgeneralize. As with discussions of all **filmmaking techniques**, discussion of color is most useful when it is considered in context, including where the color is used in the film and how the color is used in conjunction with other filmmaking techniques. It is also important to remember that color associations vary from culture to culture. For example, in pre-Communist China, yellow was often associated with the emperor and saffron (orange-yellow) with Buddhist robes.

film(making) technique: Any aspect of filmmaking, such as the use of sets, lighting, sound effects, music, or editing.

Saturated color, which is intense and vivid, has been used in countless contexts, such as to render the heat and tension of a setting, to show powerful emotions, and to represent violent actions. Filmmakers may use mostly saturated color throughout an image as in the Japanese **anime** *Princess Mononoke* (1997). In the movie, people intent on industrializing the wilderness threaten nature, and at one point warriors of the iron foundry's boss fire guns that seem to shoot fire. Next, viewers see one of their targets, a boar running in a blazing forest (Plate 4). Saturated color may also be employed in only part of the image and perhaps draw attention to that part of it, as in Plate 5.

anime: Animated movie made in Japan.

Desaturated color is muted, dull, and pale. Filmmakers may use it to suggest a lack of energy or the draining of life, as throughout Werner Herzog's *Nosferatu, the Vampyre* (1979) and in the late scenes of *Terms of Endearment* (1983), where the Debra Winger character is losing her bout with cancer. The desaturated color in the Robert Altman western *McCabe and Mrs. Miller* (1971) has two purposes: Altman wanted the film to have the look of old, faded color photographs, and the desaturated color is appropriate to the story, which is set in a damp, cold environment and ends in death for one of the two main characters. Desaturated color may establish and reinforce certain moods throughout a film, as in the world created for Tim Burton's *Sleepy Hollow* (1999). It is a place where there are lots of clouds and fog, the sun never shines, nothing is in bloom, the trees are bare, it's cold, gloomy, and colorless, and the land is assaulted by a headless horseman intent on beheading those who still live (Plate 6). Other films use desaturated color only part of the time, as in *Gangs of New York* (2002, Plate 7).

To reinforce a basic contrast, parts of a film may be in desaturated color and other parts in saturated colors. The makers of *About Schmidt* (2002) did exactly that to reinforce the contrast between two of the film's most important characters. The Jack Nicholson character nearly always wears desaturated colors whereas his daughter's future mother-in-law, the Kathy Bates character, tends to wear saturated colors (Plates 8–9). Saturated and desaturated colors can also be used to contrast two time periods. In most of the many films that use flashbacks, the flashbacks are usually rendered in desaturated colors (or in black and white) and the story's more recent periods are seen in more saturated colors. However, in *Ray* (2004), which is about thirty or so years in the life of singer Ray Charles, the situation is the opposite (Plates 10–11).

A film may display only a limited color spectrum, as throughout *Road to Perdition* (2002, Plate 12). As that film's director said, the film's cinematographer deals in "muted shades of gray" (Zone 42). Conversely and more typically, color films show a wide range of color (Plate 13).

The German film *The Lives of Others* (2006) illustrates that for a drained-out look, a film may be permeated by both desaturated colors and a limited range of color (Plates 14–15). The film takes place in East Berlin beginning in 1984, five years before the wall separating communist GDR (German Democratic Republic) from West Germany came down, and the two countries were reunited. As the film shows in detail, during that time the East German government used an elaborate system of citizen surveillance, which was overseen by the Stasi, or secret police. In the director's commentary on the U.S. DVD, Florian Henckel von Donnersmarck says, "If you look at the color palette of this entire film, you have grays and greens and browns . . . beige, but you don't have any real blue, and you don't have any real red. And that wasn't a lab trick or anything. It was something that I devised very carefully with my production designer because we felt it would capture the essence of the GDR, and to all of the people in the GDR it did." And except for the deep greens of grass and shrubbery in some outdoor scenes, the film has no saturated colors until the story finally moves to the post-Stasi period.

Different colors may be used to offset different types of characters and different worlds. In *Tim Burton's Corpse Bride* (2005), the settings and characters of the repressed world of the living are rendered mostly in shades of grays, grayish blues, and browns. Ironically, the world of the dead is a livelier, more enjoyable place to reside and is represented in more vivid and more varied colors. When characters from the world of the living interact with characters from the world of the dead, the separate color schemes are retained (Plate 16). Contrasting colors are also used in *Amadeus* (1984), a fictional story about the composer Wolfgang Amadeus Mozart (Plate 17) and his nemesis, the pedestrian rival composer Antonio Salieri (Plate 18).

Colors are sometimes classified as "warm" or "cool." In most Western societies, warm colors (reds, oranges, and yellows) tend to be thought of as hot, dangerous, lively, and assertive and tend to stand forward in paintings and photographs. People trying to be sexy or feeling sexy may drive red sports cars, and women in Western cultures who want to emphasize their sex appeal (or sexual availability) have long been known to use red to draw attention to themselves. In Western cultures, the association of red with sexuality is at least as old as the "scarlet women" of the Bible. Warm colors may be used in countless other contexts—for example, to draw attention to nature's beauty. The contemporary western *The Three Burials of Melquiades Estrama* (2005), like so many other westerns and so many other films, includes brief shots that momentarily and wordlessly draw attention to the environment (Plate 19).

Colors on the other side of a color wheel (greens, blues, and violets) are often called "cool" or "cold." In Europe and the United States, these colors tend to be associated with safety, reason, control, relaxation, and sometimes sadness or melancholy. Green traffic lights and blue or green hospital interiors are supposed to calm and reassure. In *Reversal of Fortune* (1990), blue light is used in all the scenes with Sunny von Bülow in a coma. The room, her bedding, and her skin are all bluish. In those scenes, the blue suggests cold and lack of vitality, the opposite of a lively, passionate red. In the scenes in which windows are open and it's zero degrees Fahrenheit outside, and in a night scene in the von Bülows' bedroom after they have argued and turned out the light, blue adds to the sense of coldness. Blue is used in many other ways in our lives. In the United States, for example, dark blue has been worn with business suits, perhaps to downplay the clothing and body and to suggest restrained emotions. Cool colors can also emphasize the desolation and malevolence of a damaged environment, as in the brief views of the lifeless earth seen in *The Matrix* (1999)—the result of twenty-first-century warfare between humankind and a race of advanced machines spawned by artificial intelligence (Plate 20).

Pan's Labyrinth (2006) illustrates that warm colors may be used for certain parts of a film and cooler colors for other parts and other characters. The story takes place in 1944 Spain. The civil war has ended with General Franco's forces victorious, but armed men hidden in the mountains are still fighting the new Fascist regime, so military posts have been set up to fight the resistance. The leader of one such post, Captain Vidal, has married Carmen and impregnated her. Carmen's sensitive and imaginative 10-year-old daughter from a previous marriage, Ofelia, is the film's central character. She dislikes her mother's cruel new husband and escapes into her imaginative world populated with strange creatures. Those include a huge faun or satyr, who insists Ofelia is a princess but needs to pass three tests to prove she has not become a mortal, and a terrifying "pale man," who can see only when he places his eyeballs into the palms of his hands.

As John Calhoun wrote in *American Cinematographer*, "The initial color differentiation between the film's two worlds was simple: Ofelia's fantasy world would feature mainly warm colors, primarily 'deep crimsons and golden ambers, almost like amniotic fluids,' notes [the film's director] Del Toro [Plate 21]. . . . This warmth also infuses the worlds of the rebel fighters in the nearby hills and the friendly housekeeper, Mercedes . . . , who secretly aids the rebels and befriends Ofelia [Plate 22]. By contrast, the harsh reality represented by Vidal and his troops is coded in cold hues of blue and green [mainly blues] [Plate 23]" (36). But as Calhoun adds, "the filmmakers did not adhere to the color guidelines rigidly, even in the picture's early scenes," as is seen in Plate 24 where the Faun, like Captain Vidal, is rendered in a cold color (as he is throughout the film, except for the final scene).

Films may use mostly cool colors in the early scenes and increasingly use warm colors as the film progresses. Conversely, films may initially use mainly warm colors and as the film progresses use cool colors. At first, *The Iron Giant* (1999), which is initially set in autumnal rural Maine, uses warm colors (Plate 25). After the first snowfall and the action shifts to the American military attacking the extraterrestrial creature, the setting is awash in whites, grays, and black (Plate 26).

In Western cultures, white—which is not strictly speaking a color—has long been associated with innocence and purity, as in white wedding dresses. But white may also imply lack of emotion or subdued emotions, as in men's white dress shirts. Those deeply ingrained repressive associations are at work in George Lucas's first feature film, *THX 1138* (1971), which is set in a futuristic society that attempts to strictly control human behavior and to suppress emotion. People are dressed entirely in white, and all the interiors are white or off-white. People and their environments are not individualized by colors, and the feelings colors suggest are absent (Plate 27).

Black, which strictly speaking is also not a color, is often associated with death or evil, as in black hats on countless cowboy gunslingers; the black charioteer costume and black horses of the Roman tribune in *Ben-Hur* (1959, Figure 10.27c on p. 477); the black bra Janet Leigh has changed into when she decides to steal $40,000 in *Psycho* (1960); black capes on all those movie Draculas; and Darth Vader's helmet, face piece, and clothing. Darkness is also often used as in *The Blair Witch Project* (1999), where many scenes are set at night and the darkness and unidentifiable sounds may work on the viewer's imagination (Plate 28). Black is used in many situations, so it is important not to overgeneralize. For example, in Europe, the United States, Latin America, and Japan—though not in China—black is the preferred color for mourning. And in some formal contexts, black clothing can seem stately and elegant, at least to those raised in Western societies.

From the early days of cinema, filmmakers have occasionally combined color shots and black-and-white shots in the same film. The most famous example is *The Wizard of Oz* (1939; see Plates 29–30). *Schindler's List* (1993) reverses the situation: the opening and closing are in color and are set in the present, whereas, with the exception of a red coat on a little girl, the body of the film is in black and white and is set in the past. Alternating between color and black and white throughout a film may draw attention to the practice. Such alterations are used in the documentary *Madonna: Truth or Dare* (1991), where most of the concert footage is in color and the off-stage action in black and white; in *JFK* (1991), where most of the flashbacks are in black and white; and in *The Hurricane* (1999), where black-and-white shots are used for past boxing matches (see Figure 5.5 on p. 216) and for other background events, such as demonstrations on the boxer's behalf. Filmmakers can reverse the usual usage. In the Chinese film *The Road Home* (1999), the gloomy presence of death and grief is seen in black and white, whereas the glorious earlier times of youthful courtship and love are rendered in vivid colors.

As in other aspects of filmmaking, filmmakers may use color in countless creative ways, some of which have been illustrated in this section. They may also use colors intuitively, simply because they seem right. As cinematographer Allen Daviau has said of cinematographers in general, "We do some things that we don't even realize we're doing until we see the film put together. And we did them out of instinct." In addition, as in other aspects of moviemaking, colors in films are often more true-to-movies than true-to-life. Many viewers know, for example, that real blood in movies wouldn't look real enough (or exciting enough?), so various substitutes are used during filming.

For more on color in film, see the section "Digital Cinematography" on pp. 102–4.

LIGHTING

> Light [is] the paintbrush of the cinematographer. (Turner 96)

Filmmakers often spend an enormous amount of time and money lighting their subjects. They do so because lighting can convey meaning and mood in subtle yet significant ways. The importance of lighting is evident in our lives: on sunny days, people are more likely to be cheerful; on cloudy days, people tend to feel subdued. Studies show that some people in northern climates are subject to severe depression in winter if they receive too little light. The importance of lighting in filming is suggested by the word *photography*, which literally means "writing with light."

Two Types of Light

Hard light tends to show people in unflattering ways—for example, by creating shadows in the eye sockets—so it may reveal characters or people as plain or even unattractive (Figure 2.6). Two excellent sources of hard light are a focused spotlight and bright (midday) sunlight, when the sun functions as an intense spotlight.

Soft light, which can be bright or dim or something in between, reflects off at least one object before it illuminates the subject. An excellent (and free) source of soft lighting is available during the so-called magic hour of each

PLATE 1 Coloring parts of a black-and-white film
Like nearly all other early films, "The Great Train Robbery" (1903) was filmed in black and white. On some prints of that film, parts of some frames were hand-painted, a time-consuming and expensive process. In this frame and in the scene it is a part of, one woman's dress, the smoke from the fired pistol, and some of the overhead banners were hand-painted (so was the dress of another woman not much visible in this frame). *Edison; The Museum of Modern Art; Image Entertainment DVD*

Plate 2

Plate 3

PLATES 2–3 Tinting in early films
In the Kino on Video Restored Authorized Edition DVD of F. W. Murnau's classic *Nosferatu* (1922), exterior night scenes tend to be tinted blue, though sometimes they are in green (Plate 2). Interior scenes, whether day or night, tend to be tinted in the amber tint seen here (Plate 3). *Enrico Dieckmann and Albin Grau; Kino on Video DVD*

PLATE 4 Saturated color dominating a frame
In this image from the Japanese film *Princess Mononoke* (1997), saturated warm colors connoting the intensity of the fire and the ferocity of the situation permeate the image. *Studio Ghibli; Miramax Home Entertainment DVD*

Plates 1–4

PLATE 5 Saturated color in part of an image
In the popular Chinese film *House of Flying Daggers* (2004), the man seen here a little more than 33 minutes into the film is one of the film's three main characters. In most of the film, he wears this outfit of saturated purples and violets and therefore often stands out in the frame, as here against the desaturated background. *Zhang Yimou Studio; Columbia TriStar Home Entertainment DVD*

PLATE 6 Desaturated colors throughout a film
In *Sleepy Hollow* (1999), the colors are drained of intensity. Nearly all of the colors are desaturated: dull, drab, faint, grayish. Except for the face of the main female character, even the actors' faces are pallid. *Mandalay Pictures, Paramount; Paramount DVD*

PLATE 7 Desaturated colors, selective use
In *Gangs of New York* (2002), desaturated colors tend to be used in the scenes of poverty and working-class 1862 New York. *Initial Entertainment Group (IEG); Miramax Home Entertainment DVD*

PLATE 8 Characters contrasted by desaturated and saturated colors
In *About Schmidt* (2002), Warren Schmidt (Jack Nicholson) dresses in desaturated grays, blues, and greens as well as black and tans and is often seen in settings having desaturated colors. *New Line Cinema; New Line Home Entertainment DVD*

Plates 5–8

PLATE 9 **Characters contrasted by desaturated and saturated colors (continued)**
In contrast to the Jack Nicholson character in *About Schmidt* (2002), the Kathy Bates character tends to wear saturated colors (note that her home is full of color, too). *New Line Cinema; New Line Home Entertainment DVD*

Plate 10

PLATES 10–11 **Time periods contrasted by saturated and desaturated colors**
In *Ray* (2004), flashbacks to Charles's childhood are in saturated (and digitally enhanced) colors (Plate 10). In contrast, images from later periods of the story are usually desaturated (Plate 11). Note how the greenery in Plate 10 is much more saturated than the greenery in Plate 11. *Baldwin Entertainment, Anvil Films Production, Bristol Bay Productions; Universal Home Video DVD*

Plate 11

PLATE 12 **Limited spectrum of colors throughout a film**
Cinematographer Conrad Hall worked mightily to ensure that *Road to Perdition* (2001) is a color film that looks very close to black and white, as here in this period shot of Chicago. *DreamWorks; Dream-Works Home Entertainment DVD*

Plates 9–12

PLATE 13 Wide spectrum of colors
This frame from early in the Chinese martial arts/love story *House of Flying Daggers* (2004) illustrates the broad range of colors sometimes used in the film. Note, for example, the huge variety of colors in the background. No two hues are alike. *Zhang Yimou Studio; Columbia TriStar Home Entertainment DVD*

Plate 14

PLATES 14–15 Desaturated color and limited range of color
In *The Lives of Others* (2006), which is set at a time when the East German state police kept close tabs on the citizenry, everything and everyone in East Berlin seems drained of the vibrant colors of life. *Bayerischer Rundfunk (BR); Sony Pictures Home Entertainment DVD*

Plate 15

PLATE 16 Different colors to accentuate different characters and worlds
In *Tim Burton's Corpse Bride* (2005), the worlds of the dead and the living appear in contrasting colors. In this frame from almost 68 minutes into the film, the two characters from the world of the living (right) have less color than the corpse bride (on the left). *A Tim Burton Laika Entertainment Production, Warner Bros. Pictures; Warner Home Video DVD*

Plates 13–16

Plate 17

PLATES 17–18 Different colors to accentuate different characters and worlds
These two consecutive frames from *Amadeus* (1984) illustrate how usually the character of Mozart is associated with light and a wide range of colors (Plate 17), whereas Salieri is usually associated with darkness and a narrow range of dark colors (Plate 18). *The Saul Zaentz Company; Director's Cut (two-disc) Warner Home Video DVD*

Plate 18

PLATE 19 Warm colors and the beauty of a sunset
In this shot of a sunset in *The Three Burials of Melquiades Estrada* (2005), the subdued warm colors help convey some beauty. *Europacorp/Javelina Film Company; Sony Pictures Home Entertainment DVD*

PLATE 20 Cold colors, nature destroyed
In *The Matrix* (1999), what remains of earth are the types of ruins seen here a little more than 41 minutes into the film. The earth is rendered in shades of mostly desaturated greens and grays. *Warner Bros.; Warner Home Video DVD*

Plate 21

Plate 22

PLATES 21–24 **Warm colors and cold colors**
Plates 21–22: In *Pan's Labyrinth* (2006), the warm colors
of much of Ofelia's world are achieved by the choices of
color in setting and clothing (the earth tones in the clothing in Plate 22, for example) and the types of light used to
illuminate the subjects. Plate 23: Captain Vidal and his men
are nearly always seen in the cold color blue. Plate 24: The
imposing faun or satyr, who appears only to Ofelia, is nearly
always seen in cold colors: green or blues and greens. The
one exception is Ofelia's final, golden fantasy. *Bertha Navarro;
Alfonso Cuarón; Frida Torresblanco and Alvaro Augustin; Picture-
house; New Line Home Entertainment DVD*

Plate 23

Plate 24

Plates 21–24

Plate 25

PLATES 25–26 Warm colors, then cold colors in a film
Plate 25: In the first part of *The Iron Giant* (1999), warm, fall colors (shades of yellow, red, and orange) are used for the day scenes. (As usual, the night scenes are in blues.) Plate 26: Late in the film, winter weather has arrived. Initially many shots of the military are rendered in cold colors, especially blues and shades of gray. *Warner Bros.; Warner Home Video DVD*

Plate 26

PLATE 27 Extensive use of white
Here, a little more than 45 minutes into the George Lucas Director's Cut of *THX 1138* (1971), which is set in a repressive futuristic society, the natural skin tones of the two illicit lovers stand out against the white limbo setting and the lovers' white clothing in the background. *Warner Bros., American Zoetrope; Warner Home Video DVD*

PLATE 28 Extensive use of black
In *The Blair Witch Project* (1999), the leader of the student filmmakers is running in the dark, panting and screaming in confusion and fear. Blackness, and the possible dangers it might hide, engulf both setting and characters, so that neither participants nor viewers can know where they are and what (or who) is nearby. *Haxan Entertainment; Artisan Entertainment DVD*

Plate 29

Plate 30

PLATES 29–30 Black and white in parts of a film, color in others
The Wizard of Oz (1939) renders Dorothy's life in Kansas in black and white printed on a colored film stock and her adventures in Oz in early but very impressive Technicolor later restored for the DVD releases. These choices of monochrome and color seem natural and inevitable: her life in Kansas seems rather colorless in comparison to her "time in Oz," which is colorful. *MGM and Loew's; Warner Home Video DVD*

PLATE 31 Black and white and color within the same frame
In *Pleasantville* (1998), a couple who have been kissing are about to kiss some more. As the story progresses, the filmmakers used the digital intermediate process to show more and more people and more and more of the environment in color until by the end of the story everything is in color. *A Larger Than Life Production; New Line Cinema; New Line Home Video DVD*

PLATE 32 Digital intermediate to intensify color and contrast
The images in *Letters from Iwo Jima* (2006) are predominantly desaturated and monochromatic. At various places in the film, however, digital intermediate was used to highlight and enhance the amber-reds found in explosions, as here, nearly an hour into the film, where the intense colors of the fireball jump out of this otherwise single-color image. *Warner Bros. and DreamWorks SKG; Warner Home Video DVD*

Plates 29–32

day. According to cinematographer Nestor Almendros, the best of the magic hour light is available for only 20 to 25 minutes after sunset (in the middle latitudes, with fewer minutes near the equator and more minutes near the earth's poles). Sunlight before dawn is an equally useful source of soft light. Soft lighting tends to have the opposite effects of hard lighting. It softens the border between light and shadow, so, for example, it fills facial wrinkles and makes people look younger; it makes young people look even more attractive (Figure 2.7). Typically, cinematographers use soft light to present subjects in an appealing way, as in romantic films, or to make actors look their most youthful or most attractive, as in many Hollywood studio films of the 1930s and 1940s.

FIGURE 2.5 Three-point lighting
From the catchlight in Joel Grey's eyes in this publicity still for *Cabaret* (1972), we can see that the key light is to the right of the camera; a small fill light comes from slightly to the left and a little lower than the key light. Soft backlight is reflected off the back wall, but there is enough of it to highlight Grey's left shoulder a little and to set him off from the background. *Cy Feuer; Allied Artists–ABC Pictures*

Direction and Intensity of Light

The direction of light on a subject is another expressive option for filmmakers. Some ways to light a subject by using sources from different directions are illustrated in Figures 2.8 to 2.13. In all these examples, the model is the same and so is her makeup. The camera distance, lens, and angle are unchanged. But notice what different images a change in the direction of the lighting produces, what different moods and meanings. (You can usually detect the directions and intensities of most or all light sources by looking at the subject's eyes. **Catchlight**, a reflection of the light sources, is visible for all bright light that reaches the subject's eyes.)

For filming on a set, often at least three lights are used for each major subject: the **key light**, or main light; **fill light**; and a **backlight** (Figure 2.5). For filming, the key light is usually the first light set, or it may be handheld and moved around during a shot to keep the main subject illuminated appropriately. A key light and a fill light ensure adequate and fairly even illumination with few or no shadows on the subject. The backlight, often from above or below the subject, highlights at least some of the subject's edges, such as the hair or shoulders, and helps set the subject off from the

fill light: Soft light that usually comes from a source near the camera and is used to fill in unlit areas of the subject or to soften shadows or lines.

FIGURE 2.6 Hard lighting
The subject is illuminated by one direct, bright (spot) light. Hard light produces bright illumination; reveals many details, including imperfections in the subject; and creates shadows with sharp edges. *Model: Kimberlee Stewart; photographer: Jon Michael Terry*

FIGURE 2.7 Soft lighting
Soft light produces the appearance of smoother surfaces than hard light does by softening borders between light and shadow. If there are shadows, they will be faint. *Model: Kimberlee Stewart; photographer: Jon Michael Terry*

FIGURE 2.8 Backlighting
The model was illuminated by one light from behind. Often backlighting makes the subject seem threatening because viewers cannot interpret the subject's mood or perhaps discern the subject's identity. *Model: Kimberlee Stewart; photographer: Jon Michael Terry*

FIGURE 2.9 Top lighting
The model was illuminated by a single light from above. Top lighting used by itself is not flattering. Here the hair looks lighter than it is; a slight imperfection on the model's right cheek is visible; and she has shadows under her eyes. *Model: Kimberlee Stewart; photographer: Jon Michael Terry*

background to give a sense of depth. Lighting the main subjects and parts of a set is complicated and often requires more than three light sources.

One of the most fundamental decisions filmmakers make is how much light to shine on the objects within the frame. With **high-key lighting** the main subject is flooded with light, and all or nearly all parts of the frame are illuminated (see Figure 2.13). At the opposite extreme, **low-key lighting**, in which the subject is lit by very low levels of illumination and much of the image is bathed in darkness, may be the choice if the filmmakers want to create a dramatic or mysterious effect (Figure 2.14).

FIGURE 2.10 Bottom lighting
The model was illuminated by a single light from below. Like top lighting, bottom lighting is unflattering to the skin. Often bottom lighting also adds a touch of menace; it is often used to enhance a frightening mood, as in many horror films. *Model: Kimberlee Stewart; photographer: Jon Michael Terry*

FIGURE 2.11 Side lighting
Here the model is lit by one light from the side. Side lighting creates many shadows on the face, including prominent shadows under the eyes. It may be used to suggest someone with a divided personality or someone feeling contradictory emotions. *Model: Kimberlee Stewart; photographer: Jon Michael Terry*

◀ **FIGURE 2.12 Main, frontal lighting (also known as *key-light*)**
The model was lit by a single light in front of her and a little to the right of the camera. This lighting presents the subject in an attractive way, though not quite as much so as main or key and fill lighting together. *Model: Kimberlee Stewart; photographer: Jon Michael Terry*

FIGURE 2.13 Key light and fill light
Fill light is a soft light used to fill in unlit areas of the subject and reduce contrast. A combination of key light and fill light presents the subject's skin in the most appealing way. Here the slight imperfection on the model's cheek is less noticeable, and the right side of her face appears to be a little smoother than in the photo made with only main, frontal lighting (see Figure 2.12). *Model: Kimberlee Stewart; photographer: Jon Michael Terry* ▶

FIGURE 2.14 **Low-key lighting**
By using little or no frontal fill lighting, filmmakers can immerse parts of the image in shadows and other parts in deep dark tones. Such was the lighting used almost 8 minutes into *Touch of Evil* (1958, 1998) to show the complex main character played by Orson Welles. Low-key lighting often contributes to a dramatic or mysterious effect, as in many detective and crime films and in many horror films. *Universal International Pictures; Universal Studios Home Video DVD (restored 1998 version)*

It's not unusual to light different characters differently within the same scene, as German director Leni Riefenstahl did: "I always made sure the men, actors or not, were lit differently from the women. They were lit from the side so their features stood out. . . . With a young woman, who must look beautiful, you need a very soft light from the front. No side-lighting at all, so no facial lines or flaws are visible."

Lighting can support the type of character an actor plays. As film scholar Richard Dyer points out, in *Butch Cassidy and the Sundance Kid* (1969) the lighting tends to glamorize the tongue-in-cheek, romantic character played by Robert Redford (Figure 2.15a). Conversely, in *All the*

a)    b)

FIGURE 2.15 **A star lit two ways: soft lighting and hard lighting**
(a) In various scenes of *Butch Cassidy and the Sundance Kid* (1969), including here almost 101½ minutes into the film, soft lighting glamorizes Robert Redford. (b) By contrast, the harder lighting used on Redford in some scenes of *All the President's Men* (1976)—as here approximately 86½ minutes into the film—does not soften facial lines and enhance his appearance. In this movie, he plays an investigative reporter, and lighting that glamorizes him would not be appropriate. (a) *20th Century Fox Film; 20th Century Fox Home Entertainment DVD.* (b) *Wildwood Enterprises and Warner Bros.; Warner Home Video DVD*

President's Men (1976) Redford plays a no-nonsense investigative reporter and is sometimes lit by hard, bright lighting that does not conceal skin imperfections (Figure 2.15b).

Shadows

Light and shadows can emphasize and deemphasize parts of an image and thereby create moods and meanings (Figure 2.16). Light and shadows are also used to draw attention to part of an image in a scene late in *Schindler's List*. Oskar Schindler has arrived at the Auschwitz concentration camp to try to save a large group of Jewish women from extermination. For much of one scene in which he bribes a Nazi officer, the top half of the officer's face is in shadows. It's as if he wears a mask, which is appropriate because he is like an impersonal outlaw hiding in the dark. The shape of shadows can also be used expressively, as in the early Hitchcock film *Blackmail* (1929, Figure 2.17).

a)   b)

FIGURE 2.16 Expressive use of shadows
(a) In *Citizen Kane* (1941), Charles Foster Kane signs his "Declaration of Principles" for a newspaper he has recently taken over as his friend and employee Jed Leland (left) and Mr. Bernstein (right) look on. Kane's face is in shadows, which undercuts this supposedly noble moment (nearly 39 minutes into the film). Later in the film, we learn that Kane abandons these principles. The lighting on and the position of Bernstein remind us that Bernstein was a witness to this event, too. (This scene is part of Bernstein's version of events.) (b) A publicity still that approximates the same shot is less expressive than the image seen in (a) because Welles's face is not obscured by shadows. This posed still fails to capture the irony of the moment: Kane's face in the dark as he makes a show of presenting his declaration of principles and signing them. The publicity still also does not capture Leland's admiration as successfully as the frame from the film and directs too much attention to Bernstein, whereas, given the moment, most of the attention should be on Kane and his self-absorption. *RKO Radio Pictures, Mercury Productions; Warner Bros. DVD*

FIGURE 2.17 Shapes of shadows suggesting a possible future
In the British film *Blackmail* (1929), the woman seen here, who is the film's main character, has killed a man in self-defense. Late in the film, she feels guilty and decides to surrender to the police. In this shot, shadows from an offscreen window fall on and behind her and suggest her possible fate: prison and death by hanging. *British International Pictures; LaserLight DVD*

FIGURE 2.18 Shadows to hide the identity of a subject
The lighting in this scene approximately 47 1/4 minutes into *Psycho* (1960) helps hide the identity of the attacker and makes that person seem even more frightening. This effect is intensified by the low angle of the shot and a knife that seems as long as the attacker's forearm. *Universal City Studios; Universal Home Video DVD*

In the 1960 *Psycho* and many other films, shadows are used to heighten mystery and suspense (Figure 2.18). When used in combination with other lighting, however, shadows can have a different effect (Figure 2.19).

Depending on context, shadows on the side of someone's face can convey different meanings. In many films, including *Touch of Evil* (1958, 1998), a shadow cast on someone's face by a character standing over her or him can convey a threatening situation (Figure 2.20). In many films, too, shadows on the side of a character's face suggest an evil, perhaps split personality, as in the image of one of Shakespeare's major villains, Richard III, from the documentary film *Looking for Richard* (1996, Figure 2.21).

Shadows and other areas of darkness can be central to an entire film or even series of films. Cinematographer Gordon Willis lit the *Godfather* films as darkly as he dared—and darker than most other cinematographers would have dared. In the *Godfather* trilogy, many actors playing criminals are lit primarily from above, and frequently we can see their eyes only dimly, if at all (Figure 2.22). Given the dark and evil doings, the many dark scenes throughout the three *Godfather* films are appropriate. Then, too, darkness and shadows can be used in certain parts of a film, as in the criminal activities in *The Godfather*, and light used in contrasting parts of the film, as in most of the large family scenes (Figure 2.23).

Other Uses of Light

A film's contrasting settings may be lit differently. *All the President's Men* begins with scenes set at night, including the Watergate break-in. Many of the scenes showing the two reporters trying to get various possible sources to talk take place at night or in rather dark interiors. The parking garage where viewers glimpse the important unidentified in-

FIGURE 2.19 Shadows, unusual lighting, unusual situation
Near the end of the Senegalese film *Saaraba* (1988), the subject shown here believes that he has reached saaraba (a mythical place without life's misery and uncertainties). In the 11-second shot represented here, the subject is driving a motorcycle at night. This publicity still, however, was made indoors with the subject lit by three carefully positioned spotlights—one from each side and one from the back—and by one faint fill light. *Courtesy of California Newsreel, San Francisco, CA, or South Burlington, VT*

FIGURE 2.20 Shadows to suggest a threat
Approximately 70 minutes into *Touch of Evil* (1958, 1998), several menacing men enter a woman's motel room and approach her as she is on the bed. Twice, as here, a man's shadow passes across her face as she clutches a sheet to her chest. In this scene, as in Western cultures in general, extinguishing a light or plunging some place or someone into darkness is associated with danger and perhaps even death. *Universal International Pictures; Universal Studios Home Video DVD (restored 1998 version)*

FIGURE 2.21 Shadows on the side of a face to suggest two aspects of a character
This image from about 17½ minutes into the documentary *Looking for Richard* (1996) shows the title character of Shakespeare's play *Richard III* illuminated mainly from only one side. Given that Richard puts on one face for the public but shows a darker side when he is alone and plotting his ruthless ascension to power, the lighting seems entirely appropriate. That the lighting is also hard adds to the unglamorous results. Richard is not in any sense represented attractively. *20th Century Fox Film; 20th Century Fox Home Entertainment DVD*

FIGURE 2.22 Shadows to obscure eyes
In this frame from the first shot of the godfather's face almost 3¾ minutes into *The Godfather* (1972), overhead lighting creates shadows around the eyes, largely obscuring them. Here and elsewhere in the film, the shadows make the eyes hard to "read" or interpret, unnatural, and a little frightening. *Paramount; Paramount DVD*

a)

b)

FIGURE 2.23 General uses of darkness and light in *The Godfather*
Beginning with the opening sequence, *The Godfather* (1972) often
alternates between violent or dangerous actions in the dark and
(generally) safer events that take place in the light. (a) Here, as in
other films Gordon Willis has photographed, the lighting is minimal. In this shot, which occurs about 68½ minutes into the film, a
corrupt police captain arrives outside a hospital where the injured
godfather is recuperating. In many scenes in *The Godfather*, dangerous people, including the godfather himself, are often only partially
visible, and the characters' eyes are obscured by darkness or seem to
peer out of it (as here and as in Figure 2.22). For dangerous, powerful men—whose minds are difficult to read—the darkness seems
appropriate. (b) Many other scenes in *The Godfather*, as here nearly
26 minutes into the film, are filmed outdoors or in bright light, often
of happy family occasions, as in this photo of the Corleone family
after the daughter's wedding. *Paramount; Paramount DVD*

former (dubbed "Deep Throat") is always dark
and shadowy. It's as if the reporters are largely
working in the dark as they try to bring the truth
to light. In contrast, the newsrooms where the
journalists work to shed light on the perpetrators
of the Watergate break-in during Nixon's presidency are all lit with the same bright light that
largely precludes shadows. Those scenes are by far the most fully illuminated of all the scenes in the film.

Filmmakers may change the lighting during a film to modulate mood
and suggest meaning. Some films illuminate the main subject more and
more as they proceed. For example, as the main character of *American
Beauty* (1999) starts to loosen up and enjoy life, the illumination on and
around him gradually increases. Some films begin in the dark and end in
the dark (*Citizen Kane*, 1941). Other films begin in the light until the mood
and scenes tend to turn dark, and the films end in darkness (*I Am a Fugitive
from a Chain Gang*, 1932). *Batman Begins* (2005) also begins in light (and
innocence) but later has many dark scenes and ends in darkness (a kind of
rapid fade to darkness). And some films begin in the dark but end in the
light (*Jaws*, 1975).

THE CAMERA

To film, cinematographers need film stock, light, and a camera. What lens
or lenses are used on the camera and the location of the camera relative to
the subject also influence how the final images turn out and thus their impact on viewers.

Lenses and Focus

Images are filmed with three basic types of lenses: the **wide-angle lens**, the **normal lens**, and the **telephoto lens**. Each type of lens has different properties and creates different images. Often all three lenses are used at different times within the same film (Figures 2.24–2.26).

Three Types of Lenses

(Camera distance from the subjects is unchanged.)

FIGURE 2.24 **Wide-angle lens (here a 28 mm lens on a 35 mm camera)**

- The wide-angle lens may be used to emphasize distances between subjects or between subjects and setting because it causes all planes to appear farther away from the camera and from each other than is the case with a normal lens (see Figure 2.25).
- Deep focus: All planes are in sharp focus.
- More of the image's four sides is visible than is the case with a normal lens (see Figure 2.25).
- With extreme wide-angle lenses or with the subject close to the camera, there is much distortion or curvature of objects, especially near the edges of the image, as in Figure 2.27. This effect is sometimes called *wide-angle distortion*.
- Movements toward or away from the camera seem speeded up.

Models: Kimberlee Stewart and Carlos Espinola; photographer: Jon Michael Terry

FIGURE 2.25 **Normal lens (approximately 50 mm lens on a 35 mm camera)**

At most distances, this lens causes minimal distortion of image and movement. As its name implies, the normal lens creates images close to what the normal human eye would see in the same circumstances.

Models: Kimberlee Stewart and Carlos Espinola; photographer: Jon Michael Terry

FIGURE 2.26 **Telephoto lens (in this example, a 200 mm lens on a 35 mm camera)**

- All planes appear closer to the camera and to each other than is the case with a normal lens (see Figure 2.25).
- Shallow focus: only some of the planes very close to each other are in focus.
- Less of the image's sides is visible than is the case with a normal lens (see Figure 2.25).
- Movements toward or away from the camera seem slowed down.

Models: Kimberlee Stewart and Carlos Espinola; photographer: Jon Michael Terry

Sometimes the wide-angle lens has been used to show more of the two sides of a setting, sometimes to exaggerate the sense of depth between subjects in the image. Sometimes it is used to suggest that something is not right. Such a use was demonstrated memorably at the end of *Seconds* (1966, Figure 2.27). As we have seen before, a technique may be modified as the film's story progresses. For example, the lens used to film an important character may be changed as the story develops. In *Crossfire* (1947), an anti-Semitic character is seen early in the film through a normal 50 mm lens. As the story progressed, the director used shorter and shorter lenses. "Eventually in the last third of the picture . . . everything I shot with him was with a 25 [mm, a wide-angle lens]. . . . That slight subliminal distortion . . . made him a different kind of a character" (Dmytryk). The **fisheye lens** is the ultimate wide-angle lens. Filmmakers use it only rarely, in part because it causes so much distortion in the **representation** of the subject that the subject may be too difficult for the viewer to figure out. It was used for a publicity still for *Seconds* (p. 675) though it is not used in the finished film, and it was used in the hybrid film *David Holzman's Diary* (Figure 9.16a on p. 422).

representation: A likeness of a subject created in a text.

The normal lens is used most often in films because it most closely approximates what people see with their own eyes, and most films attempt to present the illusion of reality.

The telephoto lens has been used in many films to depict someone moving toward the camera laboriously slowly, as when the Dustin Hoffman character runs to prevent a wedding late in *The Graduate* (1967). The telephoto lens can also be used to help focus the viewer's attention on a particular subject, as in Figure 2.28. Or that lens can compress a long row

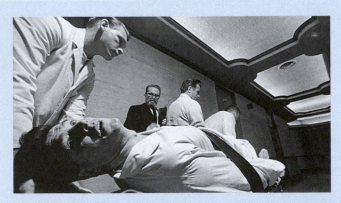

FIGURE 2.27 Wide-angle lens to intensify the sense that something is terribly wrong

Seconds (1966) shows the story of a dissatisfied middle-aged man who pays a secretive company to fake his death, do major cosmetic surgery on him, and set him up with a new identity and lifestyle (he is given the name Mr. Wilson). To convey some sense of the unusual situations that Wilson finds himself in, cinematographer James Wong Howe sometimes used wide-angle and extreme wide-angle lenses. Here, near the end of the film, Wilson has been strapped onto a gurney and is being wheeled to an operating room for "the next stage." Meanwhile, the man in the dark suit acts as a minister and hurriedly tries to comfort him. The extreme wide-angle lens used in this and related shots seems to elongate Wilson's body (note the seeming distance between the two most distant attendants). It also distorts the face and upper body of both Wilson and the attendant above him. Such distortions are in keeping with the shot's mood and subject: being terrified and helpless as Wilson is hurled toward his fate. *Joel Productions and Paramount; Paramount DVD*

a) b)

FIGURE 2.28 Telephoto lens and shallow focus to direct viewer attention
Maria Full of Grace (2004) is the story of Maria, a pregnant Colombian teenager who has agreed
to become a heroin carrier (called a *mule*) to earn money for her impoverished rural family. In
this scene, Maria's plane has landed in New York after a flight from Colombia. As seen here,
beginning a little more than 52½ minutes into the film, she and other passengers are walking
down a corridor. The first frame of the shot is seen in (a). Four seconds or approximately eight
or nine footsteps later, in (b), Maria is out of focus and a young woman on the right in the background is in focus. In frame (a) that same woman can be seen out of focus and in the background.
The effect of the shallow focus is to encourage viewer attention to only a few characters at any
time and for only briefly. *HBO Films and Fine Line Features; HBO Home Video DVD*

of signs, to seemingly crowd them together, as if to suggest the dense forest of signs in modern life. The telephoto lens is used similarly in a number of the opening shots in *Short Cuts* (1993, Figure 2.29).

Choice of lens, the lens **aperture**, or opening, and film stock largely
determines the **depth of field**, or the distance from foreground to background in which all objects are in focus. In **deep focus**, which is achieved
by using a wide-angle lens or small lens aperture or both, much or all of the
depth of the image is in sharp focus.[1] In low illumination, fast lenses and
fast film stock also help achieve deep focus. Film theorist André Bazin argued that deep-focus scenes consisting of **long takes** are more open to interpretation than heavily edited scenes. Certainly deep-focus shots of long
duration can let viewers experience clear images for lengthy segments of
uninterrupted time. Deep-focus scenes may be less manipulative than
edited footage. Viewers may be freer to look at the details in the frame and
select those that seem significant, though in deep-focus and other shots

deep focus: Photography in
which subjects near the camera,
those in the distant background,
and those in between are all in
sharp focus.

long take: A shot of long
duration.

---

[1]*Deep focus* is a term used by many film critics and scholars. For the same situation, filmmakers are more likely to use the phrase *great depth of field*. *Deep focus* can be confused with *depth
of focus*, which refers to the distance between the camera lens and the film in the camera in
which the image remains in acceptable focus.

FIGURE 2.29 **Telephoto lens compressing subjects in different planes**
Nearly 13 minutes into Robert Altman's *Short Cuts* (1993), five helicopters that have been spraying insecticide over Los Angeles are landing. Here—as earlier in the film—they are filmed with a telephoto lens; consequently, they look slowed down in their forward movement and bunched up. *Fine Line Features; Criterion DVD*

spherical lens: A lens that transmits the image to the film in the camera without squeezing or compressing the image.

filmmakers can guide viewers' attention through lighting, focus, camera placement, and composition (see the Close-Up on *Citizen Kane* on pp. 55–56). Unarguably, deep focus does give filmmakers more opportunities to use foreground-background interplay expressively (see Figure 1.45 on p. 47).

When filmmakers use **shallow focus**—for example, by using a telephoto lens or a large lens aperture in low light—usually either the foreground or the background will be in sharp focus, and viewers' attention is directed to the subject(s) in sharp focus (see Figures 2.26 and 2.28). Depending on the context, unfocused subjects may be ambiguous, disturbing, threatening (see Figure 1.42c on p. 45), or some other effect. Subjects may be out of focus because the director chose to focus on something else within the frame or because the lighting, film stock, and lenses available when the film was made precluded deeper focus.

Films are shot with a **spherical** (or flat) **lens**, which does not squeeze the sides of the image onto the film in the camera, or, less often, with an **anamorphic lens**, which squeezes the horizontal aspect of a wide image onto a normally shaped film frame (see Figure 1.31 on p. 38). On rare occasions, filmmakers use an anamorphic lens within a film otherwise shot with spherical lenses. Such shots make everything look tall and thin and easily suggest that something is not right or is out of balance. In *Summer of Sam* (1999), Spike Lee occasionally uses the anamorphic lens to increase the sense of the characters' and viewers' disorientation. In *Crooklyn* (1994), Lee had his cinematographer use the anamorphic lens throughout the two sequences of a Brooklyn girl's stay with her relatives in what to her is an alien Virginia. The first sequence of anamorphic footage begins approximately 68 minutes into the film and runs nearly 12 minutes; the second sequence begins at approximately 83 minutes into the film and runs for nearly 5 minutes. The anamorphic lens is also used in a scene well into the 1997 version of *Lolita* to show Humbert Humbert and what he sees during an attack of hysteria after he learns that Lolita is seeing another man.

An image's resolution and mood may also be changed by using a **diffuser**—material such as a nylon stocking, frosted glass, spun glass, wire mesh, gelatin, or silk—placed in front of the camera lens or a light source to soften the image's resolution. Figure 2.30 illustrates how diffusers soften facial lines.

a)

b)

FIGURE 2.30 Some functions of diffusers
A diffuser is a material placed over a light source or camera lens to soften the image.
(a) Depending on the context, a diffuser may glamorize, lend a more spiritual or ethereal look, obscure aging, or result in a combination of these consequences. (b) Heavy diffusion creates an even softer look. *Model: Eva L. Santos-Phillips; photographer: Jon Michael Terry*

Camera Distances

Camera distance from the subjects and setting helps determine what details will be noticeable in the frame, what details will be excluded, and how large the subjects and setting will appear.

Figures 2.31 to 2.36 illustrate six camera distances and the terms usually used to describe them. (In the last three photographs, a longer lens was used so that the photographer would not intrude into the model's space.)

When a film begins or when it shifts to a new setting, filmmakers often use an **extreme long shot** that reveals the setting (an **establishing shot**). Once viewers are oriented, the following shots are closer to the subject.

An extreme long shot or a **long shot** may create or enhance a humorous situation, sometimes because at that distance viewers cannot see the pain, discomfort, awkwardness, or embarrassment involved. The famous early film star and director Charlie Chaplin (Figure 1.13) reputedly said **close-up** for tragedy, long shot for comedy, and his own movies repeatedly illustrate that practice, as do many later movies (Figures 2.37–2.38).

establishing shot: A shot, usually a long shot or an extreme long shot, used at the beginning of a scene to show where the scene will take place.

Camera Distances

FIGURE 2.31 Extreme long shot
The entire subject will be visible (if not obstructed by some intervening object) but very small in the frame, and much of the surroundings will be visible. This camera distance is often used to show the layout and expanse of a setting. *Model: Carlos Espinola; photographer: Jon Michael Terry*

FIGURE 2.32 Long shot
Usually the subject is seen in its entirety, and much of its surroundings is visible. This camera distance has many possible uses—for example, to stress how small a human subject is in relationship to its environment. *Model: Carlos Espinola; photographer: Jon Michael Terry*

FIGURE 2.33 Medium shot
This camera distance tends to give equal importance to a subject and its surroundings. When the subject is a person, the medium shot usually shows the body from the knees or waist up. *Model: Carlos Espinola; photographer: Jon Michael Terry*

FIGURE 2.34 Medium close-up
The subject fills most of the height of the frame. When the subject is a person, the medium close-up usually reveals the head and shoulders. *Model: Kimberlee Stewart; photographer: Jon Michael Terry*

FIGURE 2.35 Close-up
The subject fills the height of the frame, and the shot reveals little or none of the surroundings. When the subject is a person, the close-up normally reveals all or nearly all of the head. *Model: Kimberlee Stewart; photographer: Jon Michael Terry*

FIGURE 2.36 Extreme close-up
The subject or, frequently, part of the subject completely fills up the frame and thus looks very large to the viewer. If the subject is someone's face, only part of it is visible. This camera distance shows the texture of a subject or part of it. With this camera distance, typically none of the background is visible. *Model: Kimberlee Stewart; photographer: Jon Michael Terry*

FIGURE 2.37 **Extreme long shot to deemphasize danger and instead to enhance humor**
The Motorcycle Diaries (2004) shows some of the South American adventures of two young Argentines, Ernesto Guevara, who was later to be known as Che, and his close friend. The men begin their travels on an old, unreliable motorcycle, on which they endure several accidents. The first such accident is represented here, about 8½ minutes into the film. Bags had fallen off the motorcycle onto the road, and the motorcycle had become unstable. The driver has lost control, and the men are about to crash into a ditch full of water. Since this shot showing the accident is an extreme long shot and viewers see none of the men's distress before or during the crash, for viewers the shot is amusing rather than alarming. (Moments before the accident, Ernesto, as the narrator, had commented, "I am glad we've left 'civilization' behind and are now a bit closer to the land." How close to the land they will soon become!). *FilmFour, South Fork Pictures; Universal Studios Home Entertainment DVD* ▼

▲ **FIGURE 2.38** **Extreme long shot contributing to the humor**
In *Smoke Signals* (1998), twice viewers see a van at an Idaho country crossroad as we hear the radio traffic report. During the opening credits, this is the July 4, 1976, traffic report by Lester Fallsapart from the broken down KREZ traffic van: "Big truck just went by. [pause] Now it's gone." A little later in the film, the story has jumped ahead to 1998, and the radio announcer informs listeners that the "KREZ traffic van [has been] broken down at the crossroads since 1972." The traffic reporter, Lester Fallsapart (note the name), then gives the traffic report for the reservation: "A couple of cars went by earlier. [pause] You know old Mrs. Joe? She was speeding. [pause] And, uh, Kimmy and James, they went by in a yellow car, and they were arguin.' [Lester looks to the right and left.] Ain't no traffic, really." These amusing imitations of big-city traffic reports coupled with the extreme long shots revealing nothing for vast distances contribute to the humor of the shots. *Sherman Alexie and ShadowCatcher Entertainment; Miramax Home Entertainment DVD*

Often a camera distance is chosen for surprising reasons. Ang Lee, the director of *Sense and Sensibility* (1995), used no close-ups during the movie's opening 14 minutes because the 35-year-old lead actor was older than the source novel indicated, and Lee wanted the audience to accept her in the part before he used close shots. At other times, an extreme long shot or a long shot distances viewers from a painful sight. In *Wish You Were Here* (1987), a teen, Lynda, feels unloved, so she seeks male attention in various ways, including displaying herself publicly and accepting as a sex partner her father's friend Eric, a man in his fifties who often belittles her. After her father discovers that Lynda has been having sex with Eric and evidently kicks her out of the house, she goes to Eric's. In a **medium shot** that begins about 63 1/2 minutes into the film, we see Eric start to unbutton her blouse; then she starts crying. He responds, "Come on. . . . What's all the fuss?" She says, "Hold me, please; just hold me," but he doesn't. He keeps undressing her during most of the rest of the shot and the following **medium close-up** shot. In a second medium close-up shot, he talks to her briefly. Then in a long shot, we see him over her and still undressing her. Here the long shot prevents the viewer from spying too long or too closely at Lynda's emotional pain. The long shot also discourages viewers who find her sexually attractive from enjoying seeing her being further exposed. In a sense, the camera distance protects her from further viewer intrusion.

The long shot or extreme long shot requires viewers to be especially attentive to what is happening. Such a shot may also have emotional rewards. For instance, a long shot or extreme long shot may suggest that viewers cannot get close to or entirely understand someone (Figure 2.39).

For close-ups, the camera can be positioned near a performer's face, or, much more often, a telephoto lens will be used so the camera does not have to get close to the subject, as in Figures 2.34–2.36. Close-ups and medium close-ups may show the many nuances and complexities of human feeling. Directors especially fascinated with the nuances of emotions, such as the famed Swedish director Ingmar Bergman, may often use lengthy close-ups and **extreme close-ups** of faces. One cannot overestimate the usefulness of close shots to reveal emotions and personality because of the incredible expressiveness of the human face. In his book *Kinesics and Context*, Ray Birdwhistell claims that the human face is capable of "some 250,000 different expressions" (8).

FIGURE 2.39 Extreme long shot to reveal character and environment
Seen here is a frame showing Kyuzo, the master swordsman in *The Seven Samurai* (1954), in an extreme long shot almost 96 minutes into the film. Kyuzo practices, in part for the art of it, alone in the woods, and even from this distance we can detect his focus, power, and gracefulness. The extreme long shot is also effective for showing the relationship of the subject to the environment. The camera is far enough back that viewers can see all of the swordsman's body yet see much of the surroundings—the trees, the rain, the stream that runs before his feet and basically toward the viewers. The extreme long shot here might also suggest that we viewers (and the film's characters) cannot get close to Kyuzo; he is a loner. *Toho Productions; Criterion DVD (207-minute version)*

Perspective

By changing the camera lens and the camera distance, filmmakers can change **perspective**: the relative size and apparent depth of objects in the image. Figures 2.40 to 2.42 illustrate three ways that filmmakers can use perspective.

Changing Perspective

In each of the following three figures, both the camera lens and the distance from the camera to the subjects are changed to create different perspectives.

FIGURE 2.40 Wide-angle lens (28 mm) at 8 feet 10 inches
This photograph was made by positioning the camera closer to the human subjects than in the comparable photograph made with a normal lens (see Figure 2.41). Here the camera angle seems to be a slight high angle, and the bench seat on the left seems elongated. This camera distance and lens could be used to stress the depth of the background, to show more of the sides, or to emphasize the distance of the subjects from the background. *Models: Kimberlee Stewart and Carlos Espinola; photographer: Jon Michael Terry*

FIGURE 2.41 Normal lens (50 mm) at 15 feet 6 inches
This photograph closely mirrors the distances and relationships the human eye sees. *Models: Kimberlee Stewart and Carlos Espinola; photographer: Jon Michael Terry*

FIGURE 2.42 Telephoto lens (200 mm) at 62 feet
This photograph was made by moving the camera back from its position for Figure 2.41 and using a telephoto lens. Here the background seems much closer and is more out of focus. The camera angle is not as high as in Figures 2.40 and 2.41, and the bench on the left now seems somewhat less long. (To see how the camera angle seems to change, look again at the three photographs, and note the angles from which the camera seems to view the cement area under the picnic table.) *Models: Kimberlee Stewart and Carlos Espinola; photographer: Jon Michael Terry*

In these three photographs, the main subjects are approximately the same size in the frame and appear in about the same position within the frame. By changing the lens and the distance together, cinematographers can emphasize or deemphasize certain areas of the image. They can change the relationships of people and settings in the frame to convey the information and the moods they intend. These two changes also affect how much of the setting can be seen and in how sharp a focus. In these three photos, notice how the lens and camera distance that are used determine how many trees are visible, how large the trees appear, and the sharpness of the focus. Often viewers cannot tell the distance of the camera from the subject or the type of lens used unless they know the subject and its setting well enough to detect distortion in their representation.

Filmmakers often change perspective from shot to shot, but occasionally they change perspective *within* a shot by **dollying** forward or backward as they simultaneously use a **zoom lens**—a lens that can be changed smoothly toward the wide-angle range or telephoto range while the camera is filming a shot. Depending on the movement of the camera and the simultaneous changes in the focal length of the camera lens, the background will seem to recede or to move forward as the main subject remains the same size and in approximately the same position within the frame. In several shots in *Vertigo* (1958, 1996), the camera dollies forward as the camera lens **zooms** out (changes from telephoto or normal to wide angle). The net effect of these two simultaneous changes is that the foreground of the image seems to change only slightly—note the handrail on the left of Figure 2.43a–b—but the background recedes and comes into sharper focus and more of the sides of the background come into view.

Another change in perspective during a shot occurs in *GoodFellas* (1990), but with the opposite camera movement and opposite simultaneous type of zooming (Figure 2.43c–d).

These rapid but fluid changes in perspective within shots from *Vertigo* and *GoodFellas* change the relation of the subjects to the setting in unsettling ways. They also briefly disorient viewers, in part because the changes are unnatural and unexpected. Although these changes in perspective last no more than a few seconds, they may momentarily draw viewers' attention to them.

Angles and Point-of-View Shots

Another important choice that cinematographers or directors make is the angle from which to film the subject. Figures 2.44 to 2.47 illustrate four basic camera positions: **bird's-eye view**, **high angle**, **eye-level angle**, and **low angle**. The camera may be placed at any angle above or below those indicated in the figures.

In a **Dutch angle** shot the subject appears to be on a slanted surface. It is often used to disorient viewers or make them somewhat ill at ease. As a **point-of-view shot**, the Dutch angle may suggest a character's confused

dolly (verb): To film while the camera is mounted on a moving wheeled platform, or a dolly.

point-of-view shot: Camera placement at the approximate position of a character or person (or occasionally some other creature) that gives a view similar to what that subject would see.

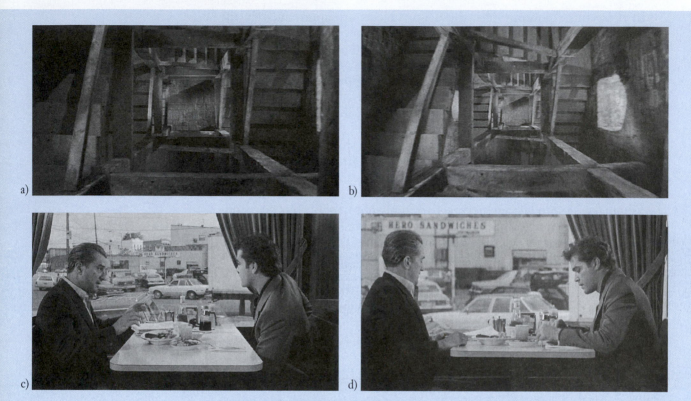

FIGURE 2.43 **Changing perspective during a shot: (a–b) background receding, (c–d) background coming forward**

(a–b) In several shots in *Vertigo* (1958, 1996), the main character, a detective, looks down a stairwell, and from his point of view, viewers see the background receding, with the background in the center of the frame receding much faster than parts of the building off to the sides and in the foreground. The shot illustrated here begins nearly 76 3/4 minutes into the restored version of the film and lasts about 2 seconds: (a) the first frame of the shot, the detective's view as he looks down the stairwell, (b) the last frame of the shot. In *Vertigo*, shots like this—achieved by zooming out (from telephoto to wide angle) while moving the camera forward—help viewers experience something like vertigo.

(c–d) These two frames illustrate the opposite effect: the background seems to come forward as the subjects in the foreground seem to remain much the same. Approximately 134 minutes into *GoodFellas* (1990), Jimmy (left) is meeting Henry in a restaurant. Jimmy is about to try to betray Henry and set him up so he will be killed. As they sit and talk, the camera tracks backward as it zooms in, going from normal to telephoto. The two men stay the same size and in the same positions within frames (c) and (d), but the background grows larger and its planes become more compressed. For example, the car parked across the street seems progressively closer to the large sign advertising hero sandwiches behind it. Perhaps the shot reinforces the sense that Jimmy's attempt to betray his friend is unnatural and unexpected. (a–b) *Alfred J. Hitchcock Productions, Paramount; Universal DVD (Newly Restored; Collector's Edition).* (c–d) *Warner Bros.; Warner Home Video DVD*

FIGURE 2.44 Bird's-eye view
This bird's-eye shot only 3¹/₃ minutes into the German film *Run Lola Run* (1998), which was made with the help of computer animation, shows a soccer ball that had been kicked high into the air returning toward the ground and the large group of people in formation spelling out the film's title in German, *Lola Rennt*.

For a bird's-eye view, the camera is often mounted on a crane. A moving bird's-eye view is used memorably late in *Taxi Driver* (1976) when viewers look down on the aftermath of a violent scene; the camera movement makes the shot even more disturbing than the usual bird's-eye view. In all instances, the effect is disorienting, perhaps even dizzying, since viewers look straight down on the subject. Most filmmakers avoid the bird's-eye view, probably because it can attract attention to itself and be distracting. *Westdeutscher Rundfunk (WDR); Columbia TriStar Home Video DVD*

FIGURE 2.45 High angle
In this shot from *Shakespeare in Love* (1998), Shakespeare himself is playing the part of Romeo as he appears below Juliet's balcony. From this angle (from Juliet's point of view) he seems somewhat small and a little helpless. High angles make the subject appear smaller and in some contexts shut off from the surroundings (sometimes all that is visible of the background is a part of a floor or the ground). In other contexts, the subject seen from a high angle appears vulnerable. *Bedford Falls Productions, Universal Pictures, and Miramax; Miramax Home Entertainment DVD*

a)

b)

FIGURE 2.46 Eye-level shots
(a) An eye-level angle—such as this one of the actor Chow Yun Fat in *Anna and the King* (1999)—creates the effect of the audience being on the same level as the subject. Viewers look neither up nor down at the subject.

(b) The height of the camera may depend on the filmmaker and the culture in which the film is made. In films directed by Japan's Yasujiro Ozu, such as *Tokyo Story* (1953), eye-level shots are often taken with the camera approximately 2 feet above the ground when the subjects are sitting on the ground or floor. In eye-level shots for films from Western societies, the camera is normally positioned 5 to 6 feet above the ground for standing subjects and 3 to 4 feet for sitting subjects. (a) *Fox 2000 Pictures, Lawrence Bender Productions; 20th Century Fox Home Entertainment DVD.* (b) *Shochiku; Criterion DVD*

FIGURE 2.47 Low angle
In this frame from nearly 81³/4 minutes into *Raging Bull* (1980), Jake La Motta is celebrating winning the world middleweight championship. At his moment of triumph, he is shown from a low angle that makes him seem prominent, dominating, and powerful. Filmmakers often use low angles in shots emphasizing a person's physique, sexual power, or powers of intimidation. As illustrated here, when the camera is positioned at a low angle, the surroundings are often minimized, perhaps with a lot of sky or ceiling visible in the background. *Robert Chartoff and Irwin Winkler; MGM/UA DVD*

state of mind. The Dutch angle is used in many scenes in *The Third Man* (1949), *Do the Right Thing*, and *Natural Born Killers* (1994). Documentarian Errol Morris often uses Dutch angles in his films, too (see Figure 8.8a on p. 381). Dutch angles are also used in the early scenes of *Bagdad Cafe* (1987) to suggest unhappy personal relationships (Figure 2.48).

In point-of-view shots (often called *p.o.v. shots*), the camera films a subject from the approximate position of a character, a real person (in a documentary), or occasionally an animal. Such camera placements contribute to the viewer's sense of identification with the subject who is looking and of participation in the action. In *Vampyr* (1932), the main character hallucinates that he is in a coffin with a small glass window. He thinks he looks up and sees (and viewers feel as if they are seeing) what it looks like from inside a coffin (Figure 2.49). In parts of more modern films, such as the two murders in the 1960 *Psycho*, periodically throughout *Halloween* (1978), and late in *The Silence of the Lambs* (1991), viewers are frequently put into the uncomfortable position of seeing horrendous events through the eyes of a killer. On a less threatening note, in *Toy Story*

FIGURE 2.48 Dutch angle
Early in *Bagdad Cafe* (1987), Dutch angles are used many times, particularly in shots of two quarreling couples. This image, from 16¹/2 minutes into the film, shows a crying woman who quarreled with her man, who then drove away in his car. Here the Dutch angle reinforces the sense that the woman's life is now out of alignment. *Bayerischer Rundfunk (BR); MGM Home Entertainment DVD*

FIGURE 2.49 Point-of-view shot
In *Vampyr* (1932), a coffin has a glass window where the head of the deceased would be. As the coffin is carried from inside a building to outside, the film cuts between shots of a man's head in the coffin and shots of what could be seen from the point of view of someone in the coffin. Here in a point-of-view shot about an hour into the film can be seen part of the coffin lid (the black frame) and through the coffin window the top of a building and in the upper right-hand corner some tree leaves. The sense of being confined in a coffin and of being carried along to the unknown combine to provoke an eerie and memorable response in viewers. *Filmproduktion Paris-Berlin; Image Entertainment DVD*

FIGURE 2.50 An experiment in sustained point of view
The original theatrical trailer for *Lady in the Lake* (1947) claimed the movie starred "Robert Montgomery and you!" While watching the film, viewers see nearly all the film's events from the main character's point of view. Exceptions are an occasional shot of a mirror showing the main character, detective Phillip Marlowe, and an occasional shot in which Marlowe talks directly to the camera. Here Marlowe is about to get slugged and knocked out by a man wearing brass knuckles. The image of the man in this shot is somewhat blurred because filming any extremely rapid movement at 24 frames per second results in some blurred individual frames. *MGM; Warner Home Video DVD*

(1995) and *Toy Story 2* (1999), viewers are often allowed to see impending dangers, such as a large menacing dog, from the same point of view as one of the toy characters. In 1946, a rare attempt was made to present an entire film from the point of view of a single character in *Lady in the Lake* (1947, Figure 2.50). Although *The Diving Bell and the Butterfly* (2007) does not show the main character's point of view as often as *Lady in the Lake* does, much of the movie is shot from the point of view of the paralyzed main character.

Much more often in films, the camera is placed outside the action, in an objective camera shot, and the audience is more spectator than participant.[2]

Moving Camera

A camera operator can tilt a camera up and down and pan from side to side. **Tilting** is a camera movement achieved during filming when a camera operator pivots the camera from down to up or from up to down while the camera is attached to a stationary base or is handheld. It is often used to reveal a subject gradually, frequently with a surprising or humorous conclusion. In **panning**, the camera is handheld or mounted on a tripod and pivoted sideways (right to left or left to right), as the two camera operators on the ground are doing in Figure 2.51. Panning is often used to show the vastness of a location, such as a sea, plain, mountain range, or outer space. As film scholar Ira Konigsberg points out, it may also "guide the audience's attention to a significant action or point of interest, . . . follow the movement across the landscape of a character or vehicle [as in Figure 2.51], and . . . convey a subjective view of what a character sees when turning his or her head to follow an action" (284). Rarely, as in Woody Allen's *Husbands and Wives* (1992), a 360-degree (circular) panning shot is

[2]For helpful explanations of lighting, color, camera angles, and camera lenses selected for the films he directed, see Sidney Lumet's discussion in Chapter 5, "The Camera: Your Best Friend," in his *Making Movies* (1995).

FIGURE 2.51 Panning and crane shots
For this shot for *Little Fauss and Big Halsy* (1970), two camera operators (left) pivot their cameras sideways on top of a tripod to follow the speeding motorcycles. At the same time, a camera operator on the crane films onrushing action. *Production still. Alfran Productions, Paramount*

used to show the surroundings on all sides of the camera, though that practice usually draws attention from the subjects to the technique itself.

Panning too quickly causes blurred footage; such a result is called a **swish pan** (Figure 2.52). It is seldom used in commercial films. An exception is found in *Schindler's List*, where swish pans done with an unsteady handheld camera intensify the chaos when Nazis roughly sort naked prisoners. Swish pans may also be point-of-view shots. Late in *The Wild Bunch* (1969), Angel, a member of the wild bunch, is upset when he realizes he is now under the control of a Mexican general. From Angel's point of view, we see some laughing Mexicans, then after a swish pan other people laughing at him. After a very brief shot of Angel, we see another point-of-view swish pan in the opposite direction and more laughter at his expense. The point-of-view swish pans help convey his extreme frustration and disorientation.

FIGURE 2.52 A swish pan
Nearly 22 minutes into *Touch of Evil* (1958, 1998), a female character is partially undressed in a darkened hotel room when a small bright light hits her (a). The shot continues with a swish pan from right to left (b–c) and concludes with a view of someone holding a turned-on flashlight in a room across the way (d). *Universal International Pictures; Universal Studios Home Video DVD (restored 1998 version)*

FIGURE 2.53 Early cinematography
The early American cinematographer Billy Bitzer hand-cranking a large and bulky Biograph camera as he films some of the U.S. Army Field Artillery in approximately 1905. Later, Bitzer worked closely with D. W. Griffith for sixteen years and filmed such classics as *The Birth of a Nation*, *Intolerance*, and *Broken Blossoms*. *The Museum of Modern Art/Film Stills Archive*

It is also possible to move the camera through space while filming. In the early years of cinema, however, filmmakers simply plopped down a camera before the subject, aimed it, and started turning the hand crank. The first films were extremely short, sometimes only a minute or so. Later, the camera was still so bulky it had to be mounted on a sturdy tripod and could be moved along with its subject only by placing the camera in some type of moving vehicle, such as the back of a flatbed (Figure 2.53). By the 1920s, however, various filmmakers had learned other ways to film while moving the camera. In a striking shot from *Napoléon*, the camera was mounted at the base of a huge swing device suspended from a very high ceiling, and as the camera swung back and forth over the room, it filmed the people below. Almost as notable are the concluding two shots of *The Crowd* (1928), which were taken from a camera above the film's central family and receding from it, showing the family more and more engulfed by a crowd at a theater. However, in the early years of synchronized sound on phonograph records or on the film itself (late 1920s), moving the camera during filming largely halted because the sound from the camera was being picked up by the sound recording equipment (see Figure 10.26 on p. 476). But gradually inventors developed camera shields (blimps and barneys) to muffle sound, and filmmakers learned how to record sound effectively while moving the camera. By the early 1930s, camera movement during shots had again become commonplace. For example, filmmakers could **track** or dolly. Such camera shots should not be confused with shots made with a stationary camera with a zoom lens. In zooming, the camera *appears* to move in or away from a flat surface, whereas in dollying or tracking, the camera is moved through space and viewers get some sense of contour and depth.

track (verb): To film while the camera is being moved around.

    With a **crane**, a camera may be positioned at a particular location in the air or moved smoothly through the air (see Figure 2.51). A crane makes possible otherwise impossible camera angles and distances. Crane shots may be unobtrusively slow, gracefully slow, or rapid and disorienting. Depending on the contexts, the effect can be soothing, exhilarating, or threatening. They may create or heighten many different effects (Figure 2.54).

a) b)

FIGURE 2.54 Filming from a crane
In *High Noon* (1952), the town marshal—who knows he is soon to confront four armed men intent on killing him—is seen in a close-up revealing his worry and fear. The next shot (a) begins as a medium shot. Then a little more than 74 minutes into the film the camera begins moving backward and continues moving backward and upward, stopping when it shows him in a high-angle extreme long shot (b). During this 18-second crane shot, viewers see the marshal turn away from the camera and eventually walk away alone toward a deadly showdown. Rather than show the action of this crane shot in two or more shots—for example, a medium shot followed by a high-angle extreme long shot—the director chose to preserve continuity of space, time, and action and also to emphasize increasingly how alone and how vulnerable the marshal is. *Stanley Kramer Productions; Artisan Home Entertainment DVD*

The **Steadicam**—a device consisting of a lightweight frame, torsion arm, movie or video camera, and small TV monitor—is another piece of equipment that allows the camera operator to move around smoothly while filming (Figure 2.55). Using a Steadicam has many advantages: "Visually, the Steadicam duplicates many benefits of handheld shooting without the lack of stability in the latter practice; indeed, to the crew, it can provide speed, flexibility, mobility, and responsiveness. And, of course, it can also energize the film with visual dynamism" (Geuens 12).

The Steadicam can be used in long, continuous shots, such as in a celebrated shot from *GoodFellas*. In this shot, which begins approximately 31 minutes into the film, Henry gives money to a car attendant across the street from the Copacabana nightclub; then Henry and Karen walk across the street, cut through a line of people waiting to get into the club, go in a side entrance and down some stairs, and walk through corridors and the kitchen to the nightclub itself. There a special table is set up for them, and Henry is greeted by men at nearby tables. Henry and Karen sit; they receive a complimentary bottle of wine from men at another table and talk

FIGURE 2.55 The Steadicam
This device for stabilizing moving handheld camera shots was first used in feature film production in the mid-1970s. Depicted here is a Steadicam Video SK with video monitor and Sony Hi-8 video camera below. A 35 mm movie camera is even larger and heavier than the video camera shown here. Operating a Steadicam expertly takes training and practice because it initially upsets the operator's sense of balance, especially when moving. It can also be tricky to maneuver in the wind, and achieving smooth starts and stops with one can be difficult. *"Steadicam" is a registered trademark of Cinema Products Corp., Los Angeles.*

a little; then Henry and Karen watch the beginning of a comedian's routine. For a little more than three uninterrupted minutes, the use of a Steadicam allows viewers to see and to some extent experience the deference, attention, and favors that Henry enjoys as a mobster.

A Steadicam is also used effectively near the end of *The Shining* (1980). As the ax-wielding main character chases his son through a large, snow-covered outdoor maze, hoping to catch him and murder him, the Steadicam follows the pursued then the pursuer without making viewers nauseous. With the increased capacity of digital video, it is now possible to use a Steadicam to shoot an entire feature film in one shot, as was done in the making of *Russian Ark* (2002), a dreamlike guided journey through the famed Hermitage Museum in St. Petersburg, Russia, during which the film's viewers glimpse artworks and meticulously costumed and choreographed reenactments of historical Russian events.

Camera movement may be used in countless ways. It is often used so viewers can follow along with a moving subject, as in the Steadicam shot from *GoodFellas* described above. Sometimes camera movement is used to show the subject from a very different angle, as when the camera moves to below Norman Bates's chin as the detective in the original *Psycho* questions him. Occasionally, camera movement is used to prevent the audience from learning information, as when a crane shot is used to position the camera overhead immediately before Norman carries his mother down the stairs in both the original version of *Psycho* and the 1998 remake.

Camera movement may allow viewers to see a subject more clearly. Moving the camera forward may create or intensify tension (what will we see next?) or slowly introduce viewers to the setting of the story, as in the beginnings of *West Side Story* (1961) and countless other films.

Conversely, camera movement away from the subject can reveal more and more of a setting. A good example is a tracking shot that begins approximately 47½ minutes into Gus Van Sant's *Last Days* (2005) and lasts nearly 5 minutes. As the shot begins, the camera is outside but close to a window, and viewers can easily see the musician inside. But as the camera very gradually tracks backward, viewers see less of him and more of the lush setting outside the window. Moving the camera backward during that shot may also encourage viewers to stay concentrated so they may see more or less what is going on in the background. During the 92-second opening shot of *A Clockwork Orange*, the camera reveals the main character in close-up, pulls back to show his collaborators in crime, then shows a major setting where the patrons are all drugged into immobility and where women are seen as sex objects to display and demean (Figure 2.56). Sometimes camera movement backward reveals more and more of a subject until viewers real-

FIGURE 2.56 Camera movement to reveal subjects and setting
Four frames representing the opening 92-second tracking shot of *A Clockwork Orange* (1971). (a) The film begins with a close-up of the main character, Alex. (b) After a few moments, the camera begins to dolly backward slowly, revealing Alex and the other three drugged gang members, with Alex's feet propped atop one of two interlocking tables in the form of two nude women. As the camera continues tracking backward, viewers can see an attendant in the background to the far right and in the background on the left the first of the nude female statues on pedestals. (A scene about 14 minutes into the film shows that these statues are also drug dispensers. The customer puts in a coin, gently pulls on the handle underneath the statue's genitals visible in [b] and [c], and some white liquid drug is dispensed from one of the statue's nipples.) (c) As the camera continues its slow backward movement, viewers see more and more of the setting, including other immobile (and drugged) patrons on both sides of this futuristic bar and the names of the liquid drugs available: Moloko (Milk) Plus and others. (d) As the camera continues to track backward, viewers can see more tables, more statues/dispensers on pedestals, and, toward the end of the shot, viewers can see two more immobile attendants (presumably present to prevent rowdiness). Finally the camera stops moving, and for a couple of seconds viewers get their most complete view of the setting's layout and size. *Stanley Kubrick Productions, Warner Bros.; Warner Home Video DVD*

Filmmakers Talk about Cinematography

The documentary film *Visions of Light* (1992) includes excerpts from interviews with many cinematographers and other filmmakers. All of the following quotations are from cinematographers, except for Robert Wise, who was an editor and later a film director.

> In the beginning all there was was a guy with a camera. There were no directors. . . . There was a guy and a camera, and he would shoot these subjects, and the subject may be twenty seconds long of a train coming at you, whatever it is. Then actors were brought in and because the cameramen were basically photographers and weren't that facile with performers, usually one of the performers directed the performers, so right in the very beginning you saw that there was the division of duties.
> —Stephen H. Burum

> A great DP [director of photography] adds to the material that already exists and really works to understand the subject matter and the language of the director they're working with. —Lisa Rinzler

> I think visually. I think of how if you turned off the soundtrack, anybody would stick around and figure out what was going on. —Conrad Hall

> Notice the beautiful jobs that were done on [actress] Marlene Dietrich where . . . if you light a set at 100 foot candles, she would be at 110, 15 foot candles. She would have just a little bit more light on her than anybody else so she would pop out amongst the crowd.
> —William A. Fraker

> By having the deep focus, he [cinematographer Gregg Toland] was able to give Orson [Welles] a lot more leeway on how he moved his actors and staged the scenes and freed him up. I think that was a tremendous contribution that Gregg gave to the film [*Citizen Kane*].
> —Robert Wise

> With [cinematographer John] Alton and the people in film noir they were not afraid of the dark, and in fact they were willing to sketch things just very very very slightly to see how you could use dark, not as negative space, but as the most important element in the scene.
> —Allen Daviau

> You see some of the scenes [from *Touch of Evil*, 1958, 1998], and you realize how much handholding [camera work] was done in the film, but it's extremely seamless. That film in particular was an inspiration to all of us because it was a textbook of what you could do. It was shot on a small budget in a short time, mostly on locations, and . . . you had almost simultaneously the breakout in France of the new wave. You had Orson Welles doing a new wave film in a Hollywood studio. And I think it has continued to be an inspiration to a lot of filmmakers. —Allen Daviau

> The films of the French new wave . . . captured a sense of life . . . by loosening up the camera and moving with it. . . . They would not think anything about picking up the camera and running with it. It had almost a documentary feel, and so that sort of quality about it would draw you into the film in the way that I think a more static camera would not.
> —Caleb Deschanel

> The director is going to be the author of the performances of the film, the story of the film. The cinematographer is the author of the use of light in the film and how that contributes to the story.
> —Ernest Dickerson

> Suddenly you're aware of the fact that things are not exactly as they seem. In other words, you create a representation of it, and lots of times that representation is more emotional than it is real.
> —Caleb Deschanel

ize that their initial impression was limited (Figure 2.57). Moving the camera back may give a sense of release or conclusion, as in the shots used for the endings of *The Shawshank Redemption* (1994) and many other movies.

Without a Steadicam, camera movement can disorient, confuse, or even sicken viewers, as in *Dr. Strangelove: Or, How I Learned to Stop Worrying and Love the Bomb* (1963). Immediately after a guided missile hits a bomber in *Dr. Strangelove*, the camera jars around vigorously and erratically and viewers feel momentarily at a loss. The erratic camera movement seen throughout *The Blair Witch Project*—which was intended to convince viewers that they were seeing amateur camera work—was so disorienting some viewers experienced "extreme nausea." Filming with a handheld camera while moving through a crowd usually results in footage that might make viewers feel something like the movement and excitement of crowd scenes.

Camera movement can also help control *when* during a shot viewers learn certain information. In *National Lampoon's Vacation* (1983), a shot begins with children asleep in the backseat of a moving car at night. The shot continues with the camera panning to the front seat, where the mother is

a) b)

FIGURE 2.57 Tracking to reveal surprising information
Sometimes a shot initially reveals part of its subject; then the camera keeps moving and moving away from the initial subject, and viewers see more and more of the surroundings, as was done memorably approximately 75 minutes into *Gone with the Wind* (1939). The shot that is represented here by its first frame and its last runs 55 seconds and shows Scarlett looking for a doctor to deliver a baby. As the camera moves back, upward, and sideways, viewers see more and more of the wounded, and Scarlett (and her mission) decrease in importance until viewers can no longer see her behind that tattered Confederate flag in (b). *Metro-Goldwyn-Mayer; Selznick International; Warner Home Video DVD*

also asleep; then the camera continues its movement, and we learn that the driver, the father, is also deep in sleep! Because of the context and camera movement, it's a hilarious moment.

For a sample of cinematographers' views on the roles and expressiveness of cinematography, see the feature on p. 100.

DIGITAL CINEMATOGRAPHY

Computers are increasingly being used to create or manipulate filmed images. Any image, just like any written language, can be scanned into a computer then changed in many ways. Computers can be used to composite (or combine) two or more images. They can also be used to **morph** images—to change the shape of the subjects—so that we can see a character's body change or even see a character morph into a different character (Figure 2.58).

a)

b)

c)

d)

FIGURE 2.58 Morphing
In morphing, at its simplest, filmed frames are scanned into a computer; then the parts of the image that are to change are marked manually and transformed in stages by a sophisticated computer program. The images are then transferred to film stock and incorporated into the finished film. Morphing was used in many shots during postproduction of *Terminator 2: Judgment Day* (1991). An example is the part of the shot represented here that shows the evil cyborg in its shiny protective coating transform into what seems to be an L.A. police officer. *James Cameron; Artisan Home Entertainment DVD*

Using a process eventually called **digital intermediate** (DI), filmmakers can transfer exposed film to digital, manipulate the colors and **contrast** with a computer program, then transfer the images back to film; or if the film was shot in digital to begin with, filmmakers can manipulate the colors and contrast before transferring the images to film for theatrical showing. One of the first uses of DI was in *Pleasantville* (1998), where the process rendered parts of an image in color and other parts of the same image in black and white. In the movie, two teens from the 1990s are trapped in a black-and-white 1950s television series. As the two introduce the complexities of the 1990s world into the **stereotypical**, idealized, black-and-white vision of small-town life, gradually the **mise en scène** gains in color. Plate 31 illustrates how initially colors begin to appear on or near those who experience strong emotion—at first in the film, romantic and sexual desires.

Using digital intermediate, filmmakers can alter color and contrast in part or all of a film. Digital intermediate is used in Clint Eastwood's *Letters from Iwo Jima* (2006). The story is set late in World War II before, during, and after massive U.S. forces invade the small, rocky, Japanese-held island of Iwo Jima. The Japanese defenders had prepared for the invasion by digging an extensive system of tunnels, and much of the film was filmed in caves. The film has a very narrow range of color; most of it is nearly monochromatic (single-color) and desaturated. The film also has lots and lots of black. In his article about the cinematography of the film, David E. Williams recounts how the film's **director of photography** (DP), Tom Stern, explained that he and the Technicolor DI colorist Jill Bogdanowicz "'added some color saturation and increased contrast here and there, just to have some visual relief.' . . . As they did on [the earlier companion film] *Flags* [*of our Fathers*], he and Bogdanowicz isolated and amplified reds, particularly blood and military insignia. 'In some of the early scenes we also highlighted and enhanced the amber-reds found in explosions and muzzle blasts,' he says. 'Set against the backdrop of this dry, dusty island [Iwo Jima], these colors of destruction really pop [out]'" (39) (Plate 32).

Computers can also be used to remove or cover up objects from images:

> They can eliminate scratches and remove objects which don't belong in period films. In one recent Western, bloodstains were removed from a character's shirt to make it acceptable for use in a trailer. In another PG-rated film, a brief bathing suit bottom was extended to cover some of an actress' exposed body . . . with the aid of "electronic paint." In *Wrestling with Ernest Hemingway* [1993], an actor was clearly breathing after he was supposed to be dead. The image was fixed by scanning the film into digital format, literally erasing parts of frames where the actor's shirt was moving or breathing, and replacing it with cloned images from frames where the shirt was still. (Fisher 101)

After Brandon Lee was killed in an accident with three days of filming left in making *The Crow* (1994), for a few scenes a computer was used to move

contrast: The difference between an image's lightest and darkest parts.

stereotype: A commonplace, simplified, and in some ways inaccurate likeness of a subject created in a text.

mise en scène: An image's setting, subjects, and composition (the arrangement of setting and subjects within the frame).

the image of his character to new settings. Now filmmakers with a large budget can use special effects during filming, as in *Wild Wild West* (1999), then clean up the images in the computer—for example, remove wires that supported actors as they were moved through the air.

Digital work allows filmmakers to correct mistakes that would be even more costly or impossible to correct (for example, perhaps the actor moved on to another project and cannot return to reshoot an indispensable shot or scene). Like animation, computer work makes possible extensive manipulation of the film's images and makes visible what was previously impossible to show. For example, for one scene in *In the Line of Fire* (1993), footage of the first President Bush and his wife getting out of the presidential airplane was scanned into a computer, and their faces were replaced with the faces of the movie's characters. Digital cinematography, however, is not without its limitations. Some people think it still too often looks a little fake; then, too, it remains enormously costly and time-consuming. Even films known for their digital creativity—such as *Jurassic Park* (1993), *The Lost World: Jurassic Park* (1997), and *Jurassic Park III* (2001)—continue to combine digital visual effects with shots made by filming models (life-size or miniature), robots, **animatronics**, and the like. It seems certain that transferring video footage and film to a computer, manipulating the digitized visuals, and transferring the visuals back to film will grow in importance in large commercial films.

Digital cinematography will probably eventually completely replace traditional cinematography, but the history of film technology shows that technological advances alone do not bring about radical changes in filmmaking and film exhibition. At least for big-budget movies, profits for those involved in production and distribution and the tastes of the paying public are also potent determinants. Now and in whatever future evolving technology and shifting economics bring us, cinematography will remain a powerful influence on films and in turn on viewer responses.

animatronic: A puppet likeness of a human or some other creature whose movements are directed by electronic, mechanical, or radio-controlled devices.

CLOSE-UP: CAMERA DISTANCES AND ANGLES IN A SCENE FROM *REVERSAL OF FORTUNE* (STUDENT ESSAY)

by Bret Lampman

In this flashback/vignette, which begins a little more than 80 minutes into the film (Table 2.1), the camera views a bedroom doorway (interior) in the first shot and shortly thereafter takes up the point-of-view shots of Claus and Sunny von Bülow: one representing Sunny's seated point of view from the settee (slightly low angle of Claus), the other Claus's standing point of view from near the window (slightly high angle of Sunny). The slightly high and low camera angles give the viewer a nearly point-of-view aspect at first, while about halfway through the scene we see Sunny and Claus closer to eye level. This technique seems appropriate for two reasons. First, the high and low angles at the beginning are conventional: since Claus is standing we get a high angle from his point of view, and likewise for Sunny. Also, as the confrontation heats up, seeing the characters more at eye level helps involve the viewer in the action.

This is an uncomfortable and emotional scene in which the two maintain a total physical separation. At no time in the scene do Sunny and Claus appear in the same frame. Two people casually chatting in a hotel lobby, keeping a respectful social distance, might have stood closer together than this man and his wife, who are in the privacy of their own bedroom. Even though Sunny eventually starts to fall apart emotionally, Claus does not approach to console or confront her. He does not even speak, despite her stinging barbs and her demand "Say something!" Their emotional distance is exquisitely portrayed as she remains on the settee, eventually beating her hands in her lap and sobbing, while he remains rooted in place. These two characters do not move; the camera moves instead, bringing viewers closer to each of them as the confrontation unfolds.

This is the closest we viewers come to either Claus or Sunny in the entire film spatially or emotionally. By this point, two-thirds of the way through the film, the background (their bedroom) is familiar to us, so the initial long shots do less to reveal mise en scène than to convey the characters' emotional distance. We find that Sunny is not so drugged up that she is beyond thinking or caring about her relationship with Claus; in fact, she is terribly upset that her marriage might be ending, that Claus might be leaving her or at least slipping from her control. Her plaintive emotional agony, honestly if angrily voiced, should have been enough to bring Claus to her side (there was plenty of room for two on the love seat), but he appears totally unprepared for her reaction; he does not move or even speak. His mostly passive face, even in medium close-up, is a stark contrast to Sunny's expressive face: she pleads, shouts, and sobs like a desperate child, for once holding nothing back.

As the emotional intensity builds, the camera brings us increasingly closer to Sunny and Claus (note particularly shots 8–14), while its eye-level angle involves us almost naturally in the confrontation. The predominant use of long shots earlier in this film leaves the viewer unprepared for the relative nearness of the camera here, making the viewer feel uncomfortably close. It is revealing that even a medium close-up should have the power to draw us into this exchange, presumably the last real communication Sunny and Claus ever had.

TABLE 2.1
Camera Distances and Angles in a Scene from *Reversal of Fortune*

SHOT	SHOT DESCRIPTION	DISTANCE*	ANGLE
1	Alexander and Claus enter through open bedroom door.	LS	eye level
2	Cosima on settee, looking toward Alexander and Claus (off-frame). Bathroom door in background opens, and Sunny emerges, leans on door frame. Cosima looks over her shoulder, gets up, and walks to her mother.	LS	sl.** high
3	As Sunny had requested, Alexander opens the window.	MS	sl. low
4	Sunny leans unsteadily on Cosima as they walk toward the settee. Sunny stands on her own, smiles kindly, and kisses her daughter, who leaves her side (walks off-frame). Sunny leans heavily on the settee.	MS	p.o.v.***
5	Claus kisses Cosima and walks her to the door. She and Alexander leave; Claus closes the door.	LS	eye level
6	Sunny sinks onto the settee, leaning her head back.	LS	sl. high
7	Claus adjusts fluttering drapes over the open window. He takes a few steps toward Sunny, then stops suddenly, looking toward her.	LS	sl. low
8	Sunny is speaking to Claus. With effort, she sits up.	LS	sl. high
9	Claus is listening, standing still. He is silent.	MS	sl. low
10	Sunny continues speaking but remains seated. She looks arrogant but frightened, then angry.	MCU	eye level
11	Claus reacts, looking injured, curious, or cautious (hard to read).	MCU	sl. low
12	Sunny shouts angrily.	MCU	eye level
13	Claus remains still and silent, quietly controlled, stunned or uncertain (still hard to read).	CU	sl. low
14	Sunny begins to sob and beat her hands in her lap, seemingly at her wit's end.	MCU	eye level

*LS = long shot; MS = medium shot; MCU = medium close-up; CU = close-up.
** = slight.
***All following shots are point of view (p.o.v.).

Of course, the flashback is Claus's, and we might believe that this is as near as Claus ever got to anyone, especially during an emotional display (except perhaps when making love). Were the memory related by Sunny, we may very well have found closer, higher, or lower camera distances and angles to reflect her feelings at the moment. But since this is Claus's narration, there is even here a feeling of distance that cannot quite bring us face-to-face with this sad couple.

They are separated by more than their physical distance. The emotional distance between them is equally noticeable. The camera brings us closer to Sunny, closer to Claus, than they are to each other. The scene is the film's most successful at helping us understand the relationship Claus and Sunny shared: even when they are together, they are somehow apart. Whether separated by a dinner table, a backgammon board, an affair, alcohol, night blinders and earplugs, or this emotional vacuum that not even Sunny's tearful collapse can bridge, the two are never close. We may believe that if only Claus had come as near to Sunny as this scene allows us viewers to, if only he had come down to her eye level as we do, rather than looking impassively down on her, she may have been reassured or encouraged. She may have lived.

But as we see in this scene, Claus keeps his social and emotional distance. In the end, so does Sunny.

SUMMARY

Cinematography involves the choice and manipulation of film stock or video, lighting, and cameras. Some of the main issues in cinematography are film grain, color, lenses, camera distance and angle from the subject, and camera movement. As with other aspects of filmmaking, the choices made in filming affect how viewers respond to the film.

Film Stock

- Film stock, which is unexposed and unprocessed motion-picture film, influences the film's finished look, including its sharpness of detail, range of light and shadow, and quality of color. Often professional cinematographers use different film stocks or videotape in different parts of the same film to support certain effects.

- Generally, the wider the film gauge is, the larger are the film frames and the sharper the projected images.

- Slow film stock, which requires more light during filming than fast film stock, can produce a detailed, nuanced image. In older films, fast film stock usually produces more graininess than slow film stock.

- Color associations vary from culture to culture, and a color's impact depends on context—where and how the color is used.

- In most Western societies, warm colors (reds, oranges, and yellows) tend to be thought of as hot, dangerous, lively, and assertive. Greens, blues, and violets are generally characterized as cool colors. In Europe and the Americas, cool colors tend to be associated with safety, reason, control, relaxation, and sometimes sadness or melancholy.

- Color may be saturated (intense, vivid) or desaturated (muted, dull, pale), and saturated and desaturated colors can be used to create or intensify countless possible effects.

Lighting

- Hard lighting comes directly from a light source, such as the sun or a clear incandescent electric bulb. Soft light comes from an indirect source. Hard lighting is bright and harsh and creates unflattering images. Soft lighting is flattering because it tends to fill in imperfections in the subject's surface and obliterate or lessen sharp lines and shadows.

- Low-key lighting involves little illumination on the subject and often reinforces a dramatic or mysterious effect. High-key lighting entails bright illumination of the subject and may create or enhance a cheerful mood.

- The direction of light reaching the subject—for example, from below or from only one side—can change an image's moods and meanings.

- Like light, shadows can be used expressively in countless ways—for example, to create a mysterious or threatening environment.

The Camera

- During filming, one of three types of lenses is used: wide-angle, normal, or telephoto. Often all three are used at different times within the same film. Each type of lens has different properties and creates different images.

- Choice of lens, aperture (or opening), and film stock largely determine the depth of field, or distance in front of the camera in which all objects are in focus.

- Diffusers may be placed in front of a light source or in front of a camera lens to soften lines in the subject, to glamorize, or to lend a more spiritual or ethereal look.

- Camera distance helps determine how large the subject will appear within the frame, what details will be noticeable, and what will be excluded from the frame.

- By changing the camera lens and the camera distance between shots or during a shot, filmmakers can change perspective: the relative size and apparent depth of subjects and setting in the photographic image.

- The angle from which the subject is filmed influences the expressiveness of the images. There are four basic camera angles—bird's-eye view, high angle, eye-level angle, and low angle—and countless other angles in between.

- In point-of-view (p.o.v.) shots, the camera films a subject from the approximate position of someone, or occasionally something, in the film. Such camera placements may contribute to the viewer's identification with one of the subjects and sense of participation in the action.

- A motion-picture camera may remain in one place during filming. While filming with a camera fixed in one place, the camera may be pivoted up or down (tilting) or rotated sideways (panning).

- Panning too quickly causes blurred footage. Such a result is called a *swish pan*.

- Ways to move the camera around during filming include dollying, tracking, using a crane, and employing a Steadicam. Like other aspects of cinematography, camera movement can be used in countless expressive ways.

Digital Cinematography

- Film and video images can be scanned or transferred into a computer, changed there, and transferred back to film. Computers can be used to modify colors and contrast (digital intermediate), correct errors, and change the images in ways impossible or more troublesome and costly to do with film alone.

- Mainly for reasons of economy and convenience, more and more movies are being filmed in high-definition video and transferred to film for theatrical showings, though the results do not yet match the detail and nuance of the best film stocks.

Major Terms about Cinematography

On p. 110, numbers in italics refer to the pages where the terms are explained. All terms are defined in more detail in the Illustrated Glossary beginning on p. 667.

QUESTIONS ABOUT CINEMATOGRAPHY

The following questions are intended to help viewers understand cinematography and analyze responses to it. Not all the questions are appropriate for every film. In thinking out, discussing, and writing responses to the questions most appropriate for the film being examined, be careful to stick with the issues the questions raise, to answer all parts of the questions, to explain the reasons for your answers, and to give specific examples from the film.

1. Are the images fine grain or rough grain? Are both looks used within the same film? What does the degree of graininess contribute to the film?

2. Does the film use cool or warm colors to achieve certain effects? Is color used in a symbolic way? Is color used to enhance mood? How lifelike is the color?

3. Does the film use saturated or desaturated colors to achieve certain effects? If so, explain.

4. For particularly expressive uses of light and shadows:

   a. Where is lighting used to support or create a particular mood? What mood?

b. Where is hard light used and with what consequences? Where is soft light used and with what consequences?

c. Where are shadows used to conceal information? To enhance mood? To reveal what a character is like or is feeling?

5. For an especially significant part of the film: What camera distances are used? To what effect? Are many close-ups used in the film? Generally, does the camera stay back from the subjects and show much of the setting? Or do the filmmakers favor closer shots? If so, explain where and with what consequences.

6. For some of the most significant shots in the film: What lens seems to be used: wide-angle, normal, telephoto? With what consequences?

7. In the film, does the subject tend to be filmed in high, eye-level, or low angles? Where are camera angles especially significant or effective? Why do you say so?

8. For especially expressive uses of camera placements:

a. Where are point-of-view shots used? How often are they used? What effects do they have on your viewing experience?

b. Where are camera placements used that make you feel like an outsider looking in on the action?

9. Characterize the camera movement.

a. If moving camera shots are used, does the camera dolly or track, or does it move up and down through the air? Are Steadicam shots used? If so, to what effect?

b. What is the effect of the camera movement or lack of movement?

10. Does the camera pan or tilt? Where and with what consequences?

WORKS CITED

Almendros, Nestor (cinematographer). Interview. *Visions of Light*. Documentary film. 1992.

Bazin, André. "The Evolution of the Language of Cinema." *What Is Cinema?* Ed. and trans. Hugh Gray. Vol. 1. Berkeley: U of California P, 1967.

Birdwhistell, Ray. *Kinesics and Context: Essays on Body Motion Communication*. Philadelphia: U of Pennsylvania P, 1970.

Calhoun, John. "Fear and Fantasy." *American Cinematographer* Jan. 2007: 34+.

"Collaboration Captures the South: Newcomers, Director Kasi Lemmons and Amy Vincent, Set *Eve's Bayou* in the Spiritual and Geographic Heart of Louisiana." *American Cinematographer* Nov. 1997.

Daviau, Allen (cinematographer). Interview. *Visions of Light*. Documentary film. 1992.

Dmytryk, Edward. Interview. *Hollywood: The Golden Years, Episode 5: Dark Victory*. BBC Television and RKO Pictures, 1987.

Dyer, Richard. *Stars*. 2nd ed. London: British Film Institute, 1998.

Eidsvik, Charles. *Cineliteracy: Film among the Arts*. New York: Random, 1978.

Fisher, Bob. "Looking Forward to the Future of Film." *American Cinematographer* Aug. 1994: 98–104.

Geuens, Jean-Pierre. "Visuality and Power: The Work of the Steadicam." *Film Quarterly* 47.2 (Winter 1993–94): 8–17.

Hayward, Susan. *Cinema Studies: The Key Concepts*. 2nd ed. London: Routledge, 2000.

Konigsberg, Ira. *The Complete Film Dictionary*. 2nd ed. New York: Penguin, 1997.

Lumet, Sidney. *Making Movies*. New York: Knopf, 1995.

Malkiewicz, Kris. *Cinematography: A Guide for Film Makers and Film Teachers*. 2nd ed. Englewood Cliffs, NJ: Prentice, 1989.

Riefenstahl, Leni (filmmaker). Interview. *The Wonderful, Horrible Life of Leni Riefenstahl*. Documentary film. 1993.

Turner, George. "A Tradition of Innovation." *American Cinematographer* Aug. 1994: 93–96.

Williams, David E. "A Line in the Sand." *American Cinematographer* Mar. 2007: 28+.

Zone, Ray. "Emotional Triggers." *American Cinematographer* Aug. 2002: 32+.

FOR FURTHER READING

Alton, John. *Painting with Light*. 1949. Berkeley: U of California P, 1995. Alton, an accomplished cinematographer, explains the duties of the cinematographer and how lighting, camera techniques, and choice of location determine the visual mood of films. This edition includes new introductory material and a filmography.

Coe, Brian. *The History of Movie Photography*. New York: Zoetrope; London: Ash and Grant, 1981. A short history of evolving filmmaking equipment and processes. Many photographs, some in color.

LoBrutto, Vincent. *Principal Photography: Interviews with Feature Film Cinematographers*. Westport, CT: Praeger, 1999. In-depth interviews with thirteen cinematographers; each interview is preceded by a short biography and a selected filmography. The book concludes with a glossary, bibliography, and index.

Lowell, Ross. *Matters of Light and Depth: Creating Memorable Images for Video, Film, and Stills through Lighting*. Philadelphia: Broad Street Books, 1992. The book's subtitle accurately describes its subject.

Rogers, Pauline. *Contemporary Cinematographers on Their Art*. Boston: Focal, 1998. Thirteen interviews cover such topics as preproduction, special effects, aerial photography, and second unit. Often the cinematographers tell how popular shots were lit and filmed.

CHAPTER 3

Editing

Stanley Kubrick's *The Shining* (1980) is in part about a writer who takes his wife and son to stay as lonely caretakers of a luxury hotel that shuts down during the worst months of the winter. It proves not to have been a good choice! He ends up attempting to kill his wife and son. The **trailer** "Shining" aka "The Shining Recut," which is available at various Web sites, takes **shots** from *The Shining* or parts of shots, reedits them, and adds upbeat music and narration to suggest that the film is about a writer looking for an inspiration, a boy looking for a dad, and the frustrated writer becoming the boy's foster father! This amusing and creative piece of editing or reediting suggests how powerful editing can be in formulating a story or redirecting it (the trailer's music and narration are crucial, too).

In general, how do film editors work? After the many labeled strips of film have been developed, the film editor or editors — often in the later stages of the work, in cooperation with the director — select the best version, or best **take**, of each shot for the finished film. Often the editor shortens the shot; sometimes the editor divides a shot and inserts another shot or part of it (a **cutaway shot**) into the middle of the split shot. Often the editor consults a **master shot**, which records an entire **scene**, usually in a **long shot**. Sometimes parts of the master shot are used in the **final cut** of the scene; occasionally the master shot is used in its entirety. All this work may be done on an editing table or editing machine (Figure 3.1). Increasingly, however, as we see near the end of this chapter, digitized shots are edited with a computer and sophisticated software and the results are transferred to videotape or, much more often, to DVD or film.

It's often said that an impressive performance is made in the cutting (or editing) room. The editor can make an actor look effective by selecting only the best takes and by cutting to a **reaction shot** if an actor even momentarily lapses out of character. The editor can also make writers look better, especially by dropping unnecessary words and by ensuring an appropriate **pace** to the dialogue and action. Editors can make everyone involved in the film look better by cutting the tedious and extraneous. In a movie, viewers never see, for example, all the reactions of someone in the film watching some important action. We should be grateful. As the film

Terms in **boldface** are defined in the Illustrated Glossary beginning on page 667.

shot (noun): An uninterrupted strip of exposed motion-picture film or videotape that represents a subject during an uninterrupted segment of time.

[handwritten: Continuity Editing / American Editing / D.W Griffin]

scene: A section of a narrative that gives the impression of continuous action taking place in continuous time and space.

final cut: The last version of an edited film.

pace: The rate of speed at which the film's subjects (such as events in a narrative film or information in a documentary film) are revealed.

FIGURE 3.1 An early flatbed editing table
Acclaimed Soviet filmmaker Sergei Eisenstein (1898–1948) works at an editing table with takes of 35 mm film. In the background, light behind frosted glass illuminates the film strips that hang before it. Note the scissors, which were used to cut the film that later would be discarded or spliced (connected) to another piece of film. *Courtesy Herbert Marshall Archives; Center for Soviet and East European Studies; Southern Illinois University*

feature (film): A fictional film that is at least 60 minutes long.

footage: A length of exposed motion-picture film.

shot (verb): Filmed.

director Alfred Hitchcock is reputed to have said, "Drama is life with the dull parts left out."

For a **feature film**, the editing process, which is often called "cutting the film," may require the efforts of two or more editors or an editor and assistants. Editing is so time-consuming that it's no wonder that for a feature film the job usually takes months and on rare occasions years. Although they faced extreme situations, the editors of *Crimson Tide* (1995) fashioned a 113-minute film out of 148 hours of **footage**. Documentary filmmakers often spend enormous amounts of time editing a film, too. Leni Riefenstahl had so much footage while making the **documentary film** *Olympia* (1936) that it took her ten weeks of ten-hour days just to view all the **dailies** (the prints made from one day's filming) and nearly two years to edit the film into its final version of more than three and a half hours (Riefenstahl). *Point of Order* (1963), a 97-minute documentary about the 1954 Army–McCarthy hearings, was constructed during a three-year period from 188 hours of footage. Frederick Wiseman's *Belfast, Maine* (1999), which documents everyday life in a small coastal town, is 245 minutes long and is the result of 110 hours of filming and fourteen months of long days of editing. Even if the film is edited on computers, the process is demanding and extremely time-consuming.

In large productions, editors typically work within the boundaries set by the script and the footage **shot**. Nonetheless, by selecting shots and arranging, doubling, and shortening them, editors can expand or compress an action, promote continuity or lack of it, affect the film's pace and moods, and intensify viewer reactions. Sometimes editing can even salvage an otherwise mediocre film.

In this chapter, we first review major developments in early film editing and the building blocks of editing: shots, scenes, **sequences**, and transitions between shots. After that, we focus on how viewer responses can be affected by how the pieces of film or digitized images are selected and combined. We consider how editing can be used (1) to promote continuity or disruption; (2) to superimpose and thus combine images; (3) to juxtapose images to make a point or to support a feeling or mood, intensify the viewer's reactions, or show parallel events; and (4) to affect the viewer's sense of pace, compress or expand time, and convey an enormous amount of information in a brief time. The chapter concludes with a discussion of how computers are increasingly used in editing.

sequence: A series of related consecutive scenes perceived as a major unit of a narrative film.

EARLY FILM EDITING

> In the first quarter of the twentieth century, the film editor's room was a quiet place, equipped only with a rewind bench, a pair of scissors, a magnifying glass, and the knowledge that the distance from the tip of one's nose to the fingers of the outstretched hand represented about three seconds. (Murch 75)

In the first motion pictures, from the 1890s, filmmakers positioned the camera and filmed until the short **reel** of film ran out. That was it: one shot (Figure 3.2). Later, editing was limited to deciding the shots to include in the finished film and their order. Georges Méliès's early films, such as "Cinderella" (1900) and "A Trip to the Moon" (1902), were longer than previous films and consisted of a succession of scenes, each made up of one shot and showing continuous limited action in one place (see the feature on pp. 116–17).

In "The Life of an American Fireman" (1902) and "The Great Train Robbery" (1903), Edwin S. Porter tried more daring editing strategies, such as suggesting actions occurring at two places at the same time and combining footage he filmed with others' footage. However, Porter's innovation was surpassed by the **filmmaking techniques** used by D. W. Griffith. In his short films from 1908 to 1913 and his first features, Griffith proved to be one of cinema's most innovative and adept editors. Griffith's controversial *The Birth of a Nation* (1915) has more than thirteen hundred shots of widely varying lengths, and parts

FIGURE 3.2 Early film without editing
The first films consisted of a single shot. This frame shows two actors engaging in the first known screen kiss in the very brief, one-shot film "The Kiss" (1896). *Edison Kinetoscope; The Museum of Modern Art; Image Entertainment DVD*

Editing of "A Trip to the Moon"

The most widely available version of Georges Méliès's 1902 silent film "A Trip to the Moon" runs about 14 minutes and consists of 15 scenes. Each scene in this French film is made up of only one shot. (The Roman numerals in the following outline indicate one way to divide the story into sequences.)

I. EARTH

1. Astronomers' Club: a gathering of men dressed as medieval wizards. Five female attendants bring in telescopes, which they give to men in the front row. Their leader arrives. The telescopes magically change into stools, and the men sit. The leader draws on a blackboard and leads an animated discussion. The leader and five others change clothes and leave.

2. Factory: workers constructing a rocket. The six men arrive, inspect the rocket, and leave.

3. Rooftop of the factory: the six explorers arrive and gesture toward the industrial scene with its smoking chimneys and a huge cannon barrel being cast.

4. Launch site on a rooftop: the six explorers arrive and get into the rocket; the hatch is closed; the female assistants push the rocket into the giant cannon and wave to the audience with their hats.

5. Launch site, another view of the cannon: a uniformed man with female attendants, brief ceremony with the French flag. The rocket is launched (Figure a), and the onlookers wave good-byes.

II. FLIGHT

6. Space: long shot of moon. The moon appears closer and closer until the "man in the moon" is hit in the eye by the rocket (Figure b).

III. MOON

7. Lunar surface: the rocket lands; the six explorers emerge from it; and the rocket disappears. The earth rises; the explorers bed down; their dreams: a comet, stars of a dipper, other astronomical sights. It snows, so the explorers get up and descend into the moon.

8. Interior of moon (Méliès's 1903 catalog calls it a giant mushroom grotto): the leader's umbrella is transformed into a mushroom then starts to grow rapidly. Moon creatures arrive. The earth leader hits them, and they vanish in puffs of smoke. More moon creatures arrive and overpower the explorers.

9. Throne room of the leader of the moon creatures: the earthlings are brought in. The earth leader tosses the moon leader to the floor, where he explodes and disappears in a puff of smoke. The earthlings rush off.

10. Elsewhere on the lunar landscape: the chase and further explosions, smoke puffs, and disappearing moon creatures.

11. Rocket perched over the edge of a precipice: all but the leader have gotten inside. Nearby, the leader hits a moon creature, who disappears in a puff of smoke, and closes the rocket hatch. The leader of the explorers climbs down the rope suspended from the front of rocket; soon a moon creature is clinging to the rocket's base (Figure c). As the rocket falls, the moon creature holds on to the base of the rocket. Other moon creatures arrive at the edge of precipice and gesture downward after the departing rocket.

a)

b)

c)

IV. RETURN TRIP

12. Space above ocean: the leader of the explorers, the rocket, and the moon creature are all falling.

V. HOME

13. Ocean: the rocket approaches the ocean (the leader still holding on to the rope; the moon creature still clinging to the rocket's base) and hits it.

14. Bottom of ocean: the rocket hits the bottom and floats upward.

15. Off a port: a ship tows the rocket toward land; the leader sitting on the rocket and moon creature being dragged along behind the rocket are barely discernible.

Early Editing
As in other early fictional films, throughout Georges Méliès's "A Trip to the Moon" (1902), the camera is stationary. The action plays itself out in front of the camera, and then a new scene consisting of one shot begins. (a) In one of the film's fifteen scenes, a huge cannon is fired, launching the rocket. (b) In the next scene, the rocket expedition from earth lands whimsically in the eye of the man in the moon. (c) After the explorers' adventures on the moon, a moon creature clings to the base of the rocket as it starts to fall. *Star Film; The Museum of Modern Art; Image Entertainment DVD*

117

of the film — such as the Civil War battles and the assassination of President Lincoln — are edited in a manner today's audiences still find engaging.

Some later Russian filmmakers—especially Lev Kuleshov, Dziga Vertov, Vsevolod I. Pudovkin, and Sergei Eisenstein—were much impressed with Griffith's editing (it is said that Pudovkin had planned to become a chemist until he saw Griffith's ambitious 1916 film *Intolerance*). These filmmakers studied some of Griffith's films closely and discussed or wrote about the art, craft, and theory of film editing. These four were part of a group of Soviet filmmakers who experimented with editing, and though they developed somewhat different editing styles, they promoted what came to be called **Soviet montage**, or simply **montage**. Such editing does not so much promote the invisible continuity of a story, strongly favored in **classical Hollywood cinema**; instead, it attempts to suggest **meanings** from the dynamic juxtaposition of many carefully selected details. As film theorist and scholar Dudley Andrew explains, Eisenstein

> was appalled at how inefficient and dull most cinema was, especially cinema which sought to give its audience the impression of reality. Reality, he felt, speaks very obscurely, if at all. It is up to the filmmaker to rip reality apart and rebuild it into a system capable of generating the greatest possible emotional effects. (69)

Soviet montage is illustrated in Eisenstein's films, such as *Strike* (1924). A memorable example occurs near the end of the film to suggest the plight of strikers in a capitalist society. Eisenstein cross-cuts shots of armed troops killing striking factory workers and their families with graphic shots of men slaughtering cattle. Another example of Soviet montage occurs in Eisenstein's (*Battleship*) *Potemkin* (1925) after the tsar's troops and mounted Cossacks have attacked unarmed civilians in 1905 Odessa, Russia. In retaliation, the guns on the *Potemkin* have fired at the headquarters of the generals, and shells are starting to land. Then a sleeping stone lion seems to spring to life (Figure 3.3). What the animation of the stone lion might signify is open to interpretation. Perhaps the scene suggests that the battleship and those in rebellion on it are so powerful that the ship's attack can bring stone to life. Maybe the three consecutive shots suggest that the Russian civilians (represented by the lion) are coming to life and will fight back. Or perhaps these three shots suggest some other meaning or some additional meaning. The shots do not help develop the story; they do not show any damage from the bombardment. Instead, they express an idea obliquely and somewhat obtrusively (probably many viewers will be impressed and distracted by the editing of the three shots). Ever since the films of Griffith and those of the later Soviet masters Pudovkin and Eisenstein, the expressiveness and power of editing have been beyond dispute.

classical Hollywood cinema: Films that show one or more characters facing a succession of problems while trying to reach their goals and that tend to use unobtrusive filmmaking techniques.

a)   b)   c)

FIGURE 3.3 Editing to animate the inanimate
In the classic Soviet film (*Battleship*) *Potemkin* (1925), the editing of three consecutive shots makes a stone lion seen in three different poses appear to sit up and take notice. In the context of the film, the editing suggests a reaction to the battleship firing shells. *Goskino; Image Entertainment DVD*

BUILDING BLOCKS

In constructing films that show stories, editors select shots to make scenes and sequences. They connect shots in various ways and usually try to maximize continuity. This unobtrusive style of editing helps viewers stay oriented as to time and location and follow the characters and action.

Shots, Scenes, Sequences

A shot is an uninterrupted strip of exposed motion-picture film or videotape made up of at least one **frame**, an individual image on the strip of film or videotape (Figure 3.4). A shot presents a subject, perhaps even a blank screen, during an uninterrupted segment of time. Typically, a feature film consists of hundreds of shots, sometimes more than a thousand. The original, uncensored version of (*Battleship*) *Potemkin* (1925), owned by the Museum of Modern Art in New York—which runs 72 minutes when projected at the silent speed of 18 frames per second—has 1,346 shots. *Toy Story* (1995), which is 77 1/2 minutes long, has 1,623 shots (Grignon). At the opposite extreme, some **experimental films** consist of a single, often very lengthy, shot. Andy Warhol's *Empire* (1964)—which is seemingly a single shot of a view of the Empire State Building and runs for hours—is an example of this sort of film.

A scene is a section of a **narrative** film that gives the impression of continuous action taking place during continuous time and in continuous space. A scene seems to have unity, but editors often delete tedious or unnecessary footage in such a way that viewers do not notice. For example,

experimental film: A film that rejects the conventions of mainstream movies and explores the possibilities of the film medium.

narrative: A representation of unified events (happenings and actions) situated in one or more settings.

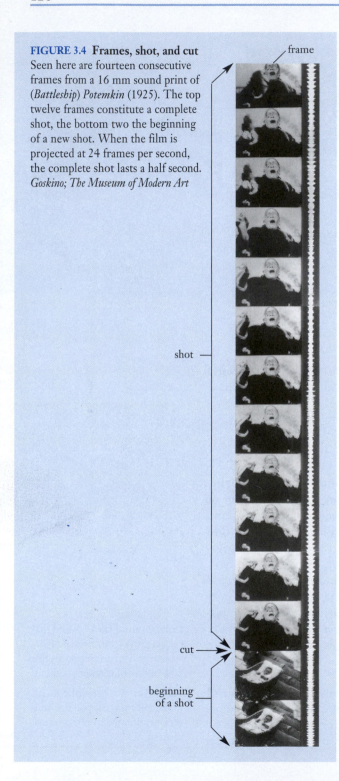

FIGURE 3.4 Frames, shot, and cut Seen here are fourteen consecutive frames from a 16 mm sound print of (*Battleship*) *Potemkin* (1925). The top twelve frames constitute a complete shot, the bottom two the beginning of a new shot. When the film is projected at 24 frames per second, the complete shot lasts a half second. *Goskino; The Museum of Modern Art*

frame

shot

cut

beginning of a shot

we may not see every step a character presumably takes in moving within a scene. A scene may consist of one shot and usually consists of two or more related shots, but on rare occasions a shot is used to convey multiple scenes, as in the more than 8-minute opening shot of *The Player* (1992). At various times during that shot, the camera moves closer to certain groups of characters so we viewers can see them interact and then moves to different characters elsewhere nearby (Table 13.1). In the opening of *The Player*, as in the famous opening shot of *Touch of Evil* (1958, 1998), there is not the usual scene consisting of a shot or shots but a shot consisting of scenes.

The word *sequence* is often defined differently by filmmakers, critics, and scholars. And comparison of several published outlines of sequences for the same film reveals different "sequences." It is most useful to think of a sequence as a group of related consecutive scenes in a narrative film, although what unifies the scenes is not universally agreed on.

To better understand sequence, scene, and shot, consider the opening of the restored 1989 version of *Lawrence of Arabia*:

Sequence 1 (in England)

Scene 1 (consisting of two shots):

Shot 1: On the left side of the **wide-screen** frame, Lawrence fusses with a motorcycle as the opening credits roll in the center and on the right side of the frame.

Shot 2: Lawrence starts the motorcycle, gets on it, and drives away until he is out of sight.

Scene 2 (consisting of twenty-three shots): As Lawrence rides quickly, even recklessly, up a hill, two bicyclists appear on his side of the road. He swerves and rides off the road.

Scene 3 (consisting of two shots): After Lawrence's funeral in St. Paul's Cathedral in London and before a bust of Lawrence,

Colonel Brighton and a cleric exchange brief and somewhat opposing views of Lawrence.

Scene 4 (consisting of four shots): Outside St. Paul's Cathedral, four people are questioned about who Lawrence was; they are evasive, claim to have not known him well, or point out contradictory qualities.

Sequence 2 (in Egypt) . . .

The film's first sequence, then, is made up of four scenes, and those four scenes consist of thirty-one shots. The next sequence begins at an earlier time in Egypt.

Narrative films stitch scenes together; if a film follows the traditions of classical Hollywood cinema, the scenes are usually combined in an unnoticeable manner. Feature films vary enormously in the number of scenes, but a hundred or more is common.

Transitions

Shots may be joined in many ways. The most common method is to **splice**, or connect, the end of one shot to the beginning of the next. This transition is called a **cut** (or *straight cut*) because pieces of film are cut and spliced together (see Figure 3.4). In narrative films, normally only cuts are used within a scene.

A **match cut** (sometimes called a *form cut*) maintains continuity between two shots by matching objects with similar or identical shapes or similar movements or both similar shapes and similar movements. An example of a match cut that matches similar shapes is from *2001: A Space Odyssey* (1968), in which a bone slowly tumbling end over end in the air is replaced by an orbiting spacecraft with a similar shape (Figure 3.5). A match cut in which the second shot continues a movement begun in the previous shot is found in *M* (1931, Figure 3.6).

A **jump cut** is a discontinuous transition between shots. For example, one shot shows a woman running on a beach toward the water, and the next shot shows her running away from the water. A jump cut is sometimes used to surprise or disorient viewers (see Figure 3.16b–c). It may also occur if the film print, video, or DVD has missing footage.

The **fade-out, fade-in** can provide a short but meaningful pause between scenes or sequences.

a)

b)

FIGURE 3.5 Match cut of similar forms
About 19 minutes into *2001: A Space Odyssey* (1968), one group of ape-men uses bones to kill a rival ape-man as the two groups confront each other at a water hole. Then in a moment of celebration, one of the victors tosses his bone into the air. The bone turns end over end in slow motion (a). The end of that shot is followed by a shot of an orbiting spacecraft (b). This match-cut transition suggests that both the bone and the orbiting spacecraft are weapons. (The movie gives the appearance of the bone becoming the orbiting spacecraft, and viewers do not notice that the angles of the two objects do not match.) *Metro-Goldwyn-Mayer; Warner Home Video DVD*

a)   b)

FIGURE 3.6 Match cut of form and movement
In the German film *M* (1931), (a) the head of Berlin's underworld begins a sweeping motion with his arm, and (b) the movement is picked up and completed by a match cut to the chief of police at a different meeting. The match cut provides continuity between scenes and suggests that the groups are similar. Both have the same goal: to catch a child murderer and restore order to their disrupted routines. *Nero Films; Criterion DVD*

Normally in a fade-out, fade-in, an image is gradually transformed into a darkened frame; then the next shot changes from the darkened frame into an illuminated one. However, many variations are possible. Early in *The Discreet Charm of the Bourgeoisie* (1972), a shot (and scene) ends with the camera **zooming** in as the image goes out of focus; the next shot (and scene) begins out of focus but quickly comes into focus. The transition functions much like the more traditional fade-out, fade-in. If a fade-out, fade-in is done slowly, it can serve as a leisurely transition; if done rapidly, it is less noticeable or not noticeable at all. Perhaps because of the current popularity of fast pacing in films, this transition is used far less often than it used to be.

In a **lap dissolve** (or *dissolve*), one shot fades from view as the next shot fades into view then replaces it. Lap dissolves may be rapid and nearly imperceptible or slow and quite noticeable, creating a momentary superimposition of two images, sometimes suggesting similarities or even meaning (Figure 3.7).

Throughout the history of film, lap dissolves have been used in many ways. They have been used *within* a scene—for example, to introduce and conclude a cutaway that shows what a character is thinking. In Buster Keaton's

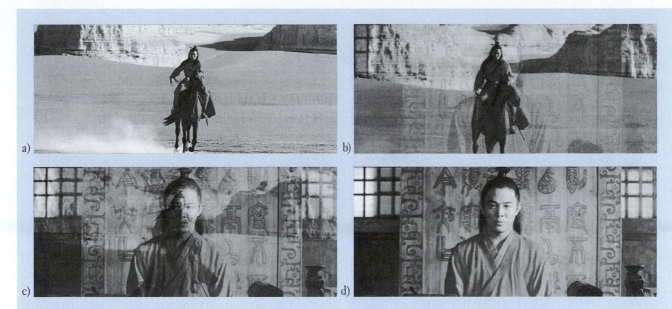

a)

b)

c)

d)

FIGURE 3.7 Lap dissolve between scenes
In a narrative film, filmmakers usually use lap dissolves to make a change from one setting to another, often at a later time in the story. Sometimes lap dissolves introduce what someone is thinking, remembering, or recounting. In this example, which begins a little more than 17 minutes into the 2002 Chinese film *Hero*, the lap dissolve serves both purposes. The character seen here is telling a powerful Chinese ruler how he traveled to a calligraphy school looking for two would-be assassins. (a) The beginning of the lap dissolve. (b–c) More and more, the image shows the traveler and his destination. (d) The transition is complete, and the story will now resume at this new location and later time. In almost 6 seconds, the lap dissolve allows the filmmakers to change locations and times. Sometimes lap dissolves involve a change of subjects, though not in this example. *Beijing New Picture Film Co.; Miramax Home Entertainment DVD*

Our Hospitality (1923), the Keaton character looks straight ahead, then a rapid lap dissolve introduces a brief shot showing what he is thinking about, and a second rapid lap dissolve returns to the shot of him looking straight ahead. Lap dissolves within a scene seem often to have been used simply to delete unnecessary time or action. Examples are seen in the scene in *Vertigo* (1958, 1996) where the James Stewart character carries the Kim Novak character from the edge of the San Francisco Bay to his nearby car and in the scene in *Election* (1999) when the Reese Witherspoon character rips down rival candidates' posters from a high school corridor's walls. Dissolves within a scene may serve more than one function (Figure 3.8). For many years now, though, lap dissolves have mainly been used *between* scenes to suggest a change of **setting**, the passage of time, or both, as in nearly all of the many lap dissolves used in *Citizen Kane* (1941).

setting: The place where the events of a narrative occur.

a)

b)

c)

FIGURE 3.8 Lap dissolve within a scene
Lap dissolves are now rarely used within scenes. Early films
occasionally used them—as in this fleeting example that
begins a little more than 17¾ minutes into *Citizen Kane* (1941)
and lasts slightly less than 2 seconds. The lap dissolve here
allows the editor to delete a little dead time in the long walk
from the Walter Parks Thatcher sign (and monument above
it) to the door to the library. The lap dissolve used here also
suggests how large (and pretentious) the library building is.
*RKO General Pictures, Mercury Productions; Warner Home Video
DVD*

serial: A low-budget action
film divided into installments,
one of which was shown each
week.

A **wipe** is a transition between shots in which the next shot seems to
push the current shot off the screen as it replaces it (Figure 3.9). The wipe,
which comes in many variations, has been popular in science fiction, **serials**,
and action movies, but it has also been used in such diverse films as the popular romantic comedy *It Happened One Night* (1934), *The Maltese Falcon*
(1941), *The Seven Samurai* (1954), and Tim Burton's *Ed Wood* (1994). Yet
other examples are found in the opening and closing credits of some Pink
Panther movies, where an animated pink panther seems to help push off one
shot as it is replaced with the next shot.

The six transitions discussed thus far are summarized in Table 3.1.

Many other transitions between shots are used less often than these
six. In many films from the silent era and some sound films that try to
evoke the silent era, an iris-in or iris-out may connect shots or bridge

a)

b)

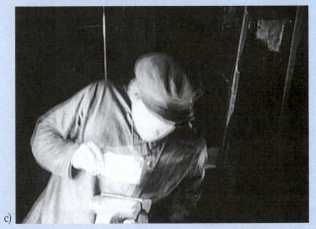

c)

FIGURE 3.9 A wipe
The Soviet film *Strike* (1924)—which is about the causes and consequences of a strike at a large factory in the U.S.S.R.—uses a variety of wipes. (a) At someone's workstation, a factory worker hurriedly leaves a Bolshevik flyer urging the factory workers to go on strike. (b) A wipe has begun from the frame's upper, left-hand corner. Part of the following shot can be seen in that corner, and some of the original shot remains visible in the lower right-hand corner. (c) The new shot is almost completely in view except for a little of the lower right-hand corner of the frame. In (c), we viewers can see the worker in another part of the factory placing another copy or copies of the flyer inside the top of a vise. Part of the image of the man is somewhat blurred here because the man is moving so rapidly. In this example, the wipe moves from the upper left-hand corner of the frame to the lower right-hand corner, but wipes may move across the frame from any direction—for example, on a diagonal from any of the four corners (as here), from above, from below, or from one of the sides (right to left or left to right). [U.S.S.R.] *First State Film Factory; Image Entertainment DVD*

darkness and a shot. In the **iris-in**, a widening opening reveals more and more of the next shot until it is more visible (Figure 3.10). In an **iris-out**, the image is closed out by a constricting shape, usually a circle.

Another unusual transition between shots and scenes is seen in *Easy Rider* (1969). Viewers see the last part of a scene's last shot, the beginning of the next scene, the last part of the previous shot again, the first part of the next scene again, and the same repetition two more times—all this consuming little more than a second before the second scene is finally allowed to play itself out. If 1 stands for several frames at the end of a scene and 2 for several frames at the beginning of the next scene, the transition

TABLE 3.1
Six Frequently Used Transitions between Shots

CUT	The end of the first shot is attached to the beginning of the second shot. The most often used of all transitions, the cut creates an instantaneous change in one or more of the following: angle, distance, subject. See Figure 3.4.
MATCH or FORM CUT	The shape or movement of a subject at the end of a shot matches or is very similar to a shape or movement in the beginning of the next shot. See Figures 3.5 and 3.6.
JUMP CUT	A transition in which the viewer perceives the second shot as abruptly discontinuous with the first shot. See Figure 3.16b and c.
FADE-OUT, FADE-IN	A shot fades to darkness (normally black); then the next shot fades in (by degrees goes from darkness to illuminated image).
LAP DISSOLVE or DISSOLVE	The first shot fades out as the second shot fades in, overlaps the first, then replaces it entirely. See Figures 3.7 and 3.8.
WIPE	The first shot seems to be pushed off the screen by the second shot. This is not a common transition but is not rare either. For a "wipe chart" illustrating 120 types of wipes, see Roy Huss and Norman Silverstein, *The Film Experience* (New York: Dell, 1968), 60. Examples they give include beginning with a small part of the second shot in one area of the frame and expanding the smaller area until it displaces the original, larger one. As Huss and Silverstein also explain, "a second image 'wipes' . . . a first from the screen . . . in several directional and formal ways: horizontally, vertically, diagonally, in the shape of a fan, like the movement of the hands of a clock, with a 'flip' (the frame revolves 360 degrees)" (59). See Figure 3.9.

between the two scenes in *Easy Rider* would be represented like this: 1 2 1 2 1 2 1 2.

Like other filmmaking practices, transitions between shots take on widely understood meanings or associations through repeated use. For instance, if enough filmmakers use lap dissolves to suggest that the action now shifts to a new setting, viewers come to associate lap dissolves with a shift to a new setting. (Similarly, people learn the meanings of most words by hearing or reading them in contexts, not by hearing, reading, or memorizing definitions.)

CONTINUITY EDITING

In narrative films and certainly in classical Hollywood cinema, **continuity editing** is normally used. Shots seem to follow one another unobtrusively,

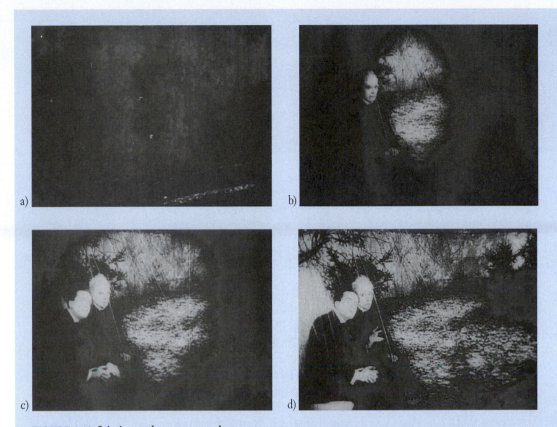

FIGURE 3.10 Iris-in used to connect shots
These four frames from the beginning of *The Cabinet of Dr. Caligari* (1919) illustrate an iris-in used to connect two shots. With an iris-in, the image is gradually exposed by a widening opening, usually a circle, though here an irregularly shaped opening. The first frame seen here (a) is from a very brief shot of a few black frames. The next three frames (b–d) reveal more and more of the next shot by means of a widening opening. As is common in *Caligari*, part of the image remains in the dark (is masked), as here in much of the right side of frame (d). Usually an iris-in begins in darkness but not always; occasionally it begins with a small opening exposing part of a shot, and then the opening is widened to include more and more of the shot. *Decla-Bioscop; Kino Video DVD Restored Authorized Edition DVD*

and viewers always know where the subjects of a shot are in relation to other subjects and in relation to the setting. Continuity editing allows the omission of minor details within scenes yet maintains the illusion of completeness and of the continuity of time, place, and action.

Continuity may be achieved in various ways. For example, **eyeline matches** may be used, in which a subject looks at something **offscreen**, and the next shot shows what was being looked at from approximately the point of view of the looking subject (Figure 3.11). Continuity is also maintained

a)

b)

FIGURE 3.11 Eyeline match
Almost 15¼ minutes into the Brazilian film *Central Station* (1998), the main character looks off-frame, in this case almost directly at the camera (a). Then from her point of view, the camera sees what she sees as the train doors are closing: a motherless boy she has reluctantly befriended (b). Such eyeline matches are one way filmmakers maintain continuity from shot to shot within a scene. *Canal + and others; Columbia TriStar Home Video DVD*

within scenes if all shots show the subjects from one side of an imaginary straight line drawn between them. This is sometimes referred to as the **180-degree system** (Figure 3.12).

A scene from *Life Is Beautiful* (1998) illustrates various ways continuity can be maintained within a scene (Figure 3.13). Eyeline matches are used in this scene, as when the man on the bicycle looks off-screen to the left (Figure 3.13c) and the next shot shows what he is looking at: the schoolchildren and the woman. Throughout the scene the viewer sees the man on his left side or from behind or in front but not on his right side (the 180-degree system). **Shot/reverse shot** is also used to promote continuity. A shot from over the first person's shoulder or to the side of it shows the face of a

a)

b)

FIGURE 3.12 180-degree system
These images from two consecutive shots of the Chinese film *King of Masks* (1996) illustrate the 180-degree system, sometimes called the *180-degree rule*. Envision an imaginary line drawn straight beneath the two subjects seen here. Notice how in both shots the camera is positioned on the same side of that imaginary line. In all shots in this scene, viewers would see the right side of the man and the left side of the little girl. No matter how many shots in a scene, filmmakers using the 180-degree system would always keep the camera positioned on one side of that imaginary line, and the background would remain essentially the same, though different shots often reveal different parts of that background. Here, for example, the shot of the girl reveals many bamboo canes behind her, whereas the shot of the man does not. *Wu Tianming; Columbia TriStar Home Video DVD*

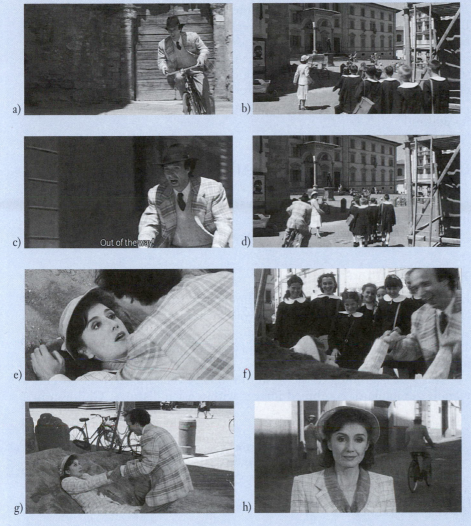

FIGURE 3.13 Continuity editing in a scene

The scene represented here, which begins almost 11 minutes into the Italian film *Life Is Beautiful* (1998), runs 29 seconds and consists of 8 shots:

(a) The man rounds a corner riding a bicycle in a hurry: an angry man, seen in the previous scene, is chasing him.

(b) A line of schoolchildren and a woman to the left of them are walking toward a nearby piazza.

(c) The man on the bike reacts with alarm because the children and the woman inadvertently block his path.

(d) The man runs into the woman and falls on top of her.

(e) Her reaction when she sees who it is (they had met briefly earlier when he broke her fall from a barn).

(f) His reaction to her.

(g) He helps her up, says good-bye, and runs off (he is still concerned that the man who was chasing him might catch up with him).

(h) Her reaction to his abrupt departure (the bicyclist behind her is a different man).

Cecchi Gori Group; Miramax Home Entertainment DVD

second person; in the next shot the camera is behind or to the side of the second person, and we now see the first person's face (Figure 3.13e–f). During both shots of a shot/reverse shot, the background remains the same or is consistent from shot to shot. (Shot/reverse shot is often used for scenes with dialogue.) Continuity editing is also achieved by cutting on action: one shot ends during a subject's movement, and the next shot, usually from a different distance or angle (or both), continues or concludes the action (Figure 3.13f–g). In such instances, often some of the middle part of the movement is omitted. Here, a little of the action is omitted between Figure 3.13f–g, yet continuity is maintained because the same subject moves in a consistent and seemingly uninterrupted way. For many movie scenes, editors delete fragments of time and action that will not be missed. Because of continuity editing, however, the action seems to flow from shot to shot smoothly and clearly yet concisely.

Although continuity editing is the usual way narrative films are edited, some filmmakers choose to ignore continuity from time to time, and other filmmakers—such as the French actor and director Jacques Tati and the Japanese director Yasujiro Ozu—often reject the conventions of continuity editing.

IMAGE ON IMAGE AND IMAGE AFTER IMAGE

Editors can combine two or more images into the same image—although it's usually hard for viewers to distinguish more than two images at the same time—or they can juxtapose images in expressive ways.

Superimpositions

superimposition: Two or more images photographed or printed on top of each other.

In creating a lap dissolve, editors momentarily **superimpose** images. The lap dissolve near the end of *Psycho* (1960) fleetingly juxtaposes three images (Figure 3.14). If a dissolve is slow enough—or even halts briefly midway, as is done on rare occasions—viewers are more likely to notice the superimposed images.

Near the beginning of the western film *The Wild Bunch* (1969) occurs a complex example of combined images within a lap dissolve. Children in a

FIGURE 3.14 Symbolic superimposition of three images
In a few frames near the conclusion of *Psycho* (1960), viewers may notice that three images are superimposed briefly: Norman from the shoulders up, a skull, and Marion's car being pulled from the swamp by a chain. In a 35 mm version of the film that is in good condition or a laser disc or DVD version viewed on a high-resolution monitor or projector-screen combination, viewers may notice the three superimposed images and consider their significance. (Viewers are unlikely to notice them on a videotape version.) There are various ways to interpret the significance of those three images. The brief triple superimposition suggests that underneath Norman is his dead mother and that Norman is, in at least one sense, already dead. The superimposed images also suggest that Norman, his mother, and death are a swamp and that Norman embodies death and destruction. A psychoanalytic critic might see the swamp as the vast, untamed id surrounding the human heart. *Universal City Studios; Universal Home Video DVD*

south Texas town are burning scorpions and ants. A slow lap dissolve combines images of the burning insects with images of many townspeople and railroad employees who had recently been shot in the crossfire between bounty hunters and the wild bunch. During the dissolve from the children to the scene of carnage, viewers hear the giggles of the children burning the insects mingled with some crying and the moans of the injured people. The combination of images and sounds suggests that people can be like helpless scorpions and ants, painfully destroyed by powerful forces indifferent to their well-being. The blending of images (and sounds) also undercuts any notion of youthful innocence: the children who enjoy destroying insect life may grow up and destroy human life, as did the bounty hunters and the wild bunch.

Juxtapositions   *Match on Action*

The **surrealist** film "Un chien andalou" (1928) begins with the following shots:

1. **Title card**: "Once Upon a Time."
2. A man's hands are sharpening a straight razor on a thick leather strap.
3. A man is smoking a cigarette and looking down.
4. The man's hands are sharpening the straight razor; he seems to test the sharpnesss of the razor against one of his thumbnails.
5. The man is smoking and looking down.
6. The man opens the nearby door and walks through the opening.
7. The man emerges on the other side of the door onto an exterior balcony and goes to the railing.
8. The man looks up.
9. Full moon in the dark sky.
10. The man is still looking up.
11. A woman looks straight ahead as a man stands next to her; the man holds open the eyelid of her left eye with his left hand and moves the razor blade toward the eye with his right hand.
12. A wisp of cloud seems to bisect the moon (Figure 3.15).
13. **Close-up** of an eye being sliced by a straight razor.
14. Title card: "Eight Years Later."

a)

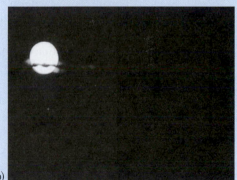

b)

FIGURE 3.15 Editing to mislead
In shot (a) from the experimental film "Un chien andalou" (1928), a man seems about to cut a woman's eye. In the next shot, a wisp of cloud crosses in front of the moon. The film is available online. These two consecutive shots occur near the beginning of the film. *Luis Buñuel; Les grands films classiques; Transflux Films DVD*

Since 1928, the film's opening has shocked and horrified audiences—pretty much as intended by the filmmaker Luis Buñuel, who himself plays the man in the opening shots. But it is not merely the subject matter that provokes such strong audience response. It is also a matter of the selection and arrangement of the shots. Buñuel, after all, could have presented the main action in two shots, shots 11 and 13. Instead, the film delays the shock by beginning with somewhat curious action: Why would a man be sharpening a straight razor when he does not seem to intend to shave, and why would he take that razor with him to the outside balcony? By near the end of shot 11, the action has become somewhat worrisome for viewers as the man moves the razor a little closer to the woman's eye. Shot 12, however, eases the tension for viewers, at least somewhat, only to be followed by the brief, explicit shot 13. A natural action (a wisp of cloud passing in front of the moon) is followed by a brutal human action. This, perhaps the most shocking match cut in the history of cinema, seems to end with a brutal act, but if viewers have the stomach and curiosity to study the film's opening section, they will notice that the sliced eye and eyebrow do not match the woman's eye and eyebrow. (In fact, a dead cow's eye was used.) So powerful can juxtaposed images be that viewers do not notice prominent inconsistencies. Then, too, there is that matter of the initial title card, "Once Upon a Time," which seems to promise a traditional narrative. Like "Un chien andalou" as a whole, this opening section proves to be neither traditional nor a narrative. The selection and juxtapositions of the film's opening thirteen shots illustrate how editing can help filmmakers guide and even mislead audiences and help intensify the audience's emotional responses.

Even in films that use continuity editing extensively (and as we saw illustrated above, "Un chien andalou" does not), filmmakers sometimes want to surprise, amuse, or confuse and may follow a shot with another shot that viewers don't expect. Occasionally the unexpected shot appears after a brief lap dissolve. In *Citizen Kane*, immediately after Kane marries Susan, his second wife, he decides she'll have a career as an opera singer. As the newlyweds are about to be driven off, Susan tells the reporters surrounding the car that if necessary Kane will build her an opera house. Kane shouts, "That won't be necessary." After a rapid lap dissolve, the next shot is the large newspaper headline "Kane Builds Opera House." The effect is surprising and amusing; the combination of shots also shows that Kane's judgment can be faulty. Sometimes filmmakers use jump cuts to confuse or disorient viewers, as in several scenes in the classic **French new wave** film *Breathless* (1959, Figure 3.16). Editing can also be used to show contradictory qualities of a place or situation (Figure 3.17).

Editors often join two shots to illustrate similarities. Near the end of *The Wild Bunch*, after the final shootout, appears a shot of gleeful bounty hunters swooping down on the dead to strip them of valuables, as birds (probably vultures) fly across the frame in the foreground and a vulture is visible briefly in the background. The next shot is of a vulture perched on

French new wave (cinema): A film movement consisting of a loose grouping of untraditional movies made in France in the late 1950s and early 1960s.

FIGURE 3.16 Jump cuts that create discontinuity
In Jean-Luc Godard's *Breathless* (1959), a man driving a car pulls off a country road to elude two pursuing motorcycle police officers. A few seconds later, nearly 5 minutes into the film, a motorcycle police officer pulls off the road, and the man shoots him and runs away. Sometimes, the scene is discontinuous, as if the camera were in the wrong position or shots or parts of them had been left out. The last seven shots of the excerpt illustrate three areas of confusion. Shot (b) shows the man facing left, but shots (c–e) show or imply that the man is now mysteriously facing right. The scene is not edited using the 180-degree system. The police officer's location when he gets shot (f) is also puzzling: he is not on or near the path shown in shot (a). Finally, the relation of shot (g) to the preceding shots is unclear: viewers cannot know where the man is and how far he is from the shot police officer. Perhaps (g) is a new scene consisting of one shot. Although the seven shots are elliptical and confusing in some details, the main action is clear, and one could argue that the discontinuous editing is appropriate for the subject: a sudden, unplanned murder. *SNC; Fox Lorber DVD*

a dead man. The juxtaposition of these two shots constitutes a none-too-subtle **filmic** metaphor suggesting that the bounty hunters are vultures.

Less obvious yet still damning by association is some of the editing in the films of satirical documentary filmmaker Michael Moore. About 25 3/4 minutes into *Roger & Me* (1989), we see a shot of a man scooping up horse dung from a parade route. The next shot is of Miss Michigan riding in a car with a sign for a Chevrolet dealer. Almost 28 minutes into the film, a

filmic: Characteristic of the film medium or appropriate to it, such as parallel editing.

a)

b)

FIGURE 3.17 **Consecutive shots revealing contradictory aspects of a setting** These two shots early in *The Third Man* (1949) suggest the contradictory aspects of Vienna shortly after World War II: (a) a statue of Beethoven and (b) two black marketeers. The consecutive, discontinuous images quickly convey that the story will be set in a city of both culture and crime. *London Film Productions; Criterion DVD*

man who had earlier spoken about labor unions getting weaker says, "Some people know what time it is; some people don't." The next shot is of Miss Michigan. Later still, we see brief footage of the 1988 Miss USA pageant and learn that Miss Michigan won the national title; the next shot (a little more than 29 3/4 minutes into the film) is a match cut to a man in Flint knocking on a door to evict people from their housing, presumably because they are out of work and behind in the rent. Because of Moore's selection and juxtaposition of shots, Miss Michigan is represented as someone who cares not about labor and living conditions but only about winning the national title. Moore also uses editing to undercut President George W. Bush and others in *Fahrenheit 9/11* (2004).

Moore is not the only filmmaker or even the first filmmaker to use editing that undercuts or contradicts someone. Not at all. This type of editing is used, for example, nearly 102 3/4 minutes into the 1975 anti–Vietnam War documentary, *Hearts and Minds*. A 21-second shot of a Vietnamese boy moaning and sobbing before a photograph on the coffin of his soldier father is followed by a shot of the U.S. general in charge of the Vietnam operations saying, "Well, the Oriental doesn't put the same high price on life as does a Westerner. Life is plentiful. Life is cheap in the Orient." The filmmakers do not use only that shot of the grieving boy to illustrate Vietnamese suffering. That shot is the culmination of 4 minutes of footage showing grief-stricken Vietnamese parents and children.

Consecutive shots may serve yet other purposes. For example, they may omit much of the action and subtly suggest what is happening (Figure 3.18). The filmmakers could have shown much more. Why were couples dancing on top of the houseboat? Were they dancing before the woman and Schultze arrived back at the boat? How and when was Schultze taken to the houseboat? How did he climb the interior ladder to the top of the houseboat? Did he do anything or say anything before he fell asleep? The filmmakers could have shown answers to any of these questions. They could also have shown explicitly that he died. Instead, they were highly selective in their selection of shots (and soundtrack). The results are subtle and perhaps touching because Schultze's last thoughts were of music and dancing.

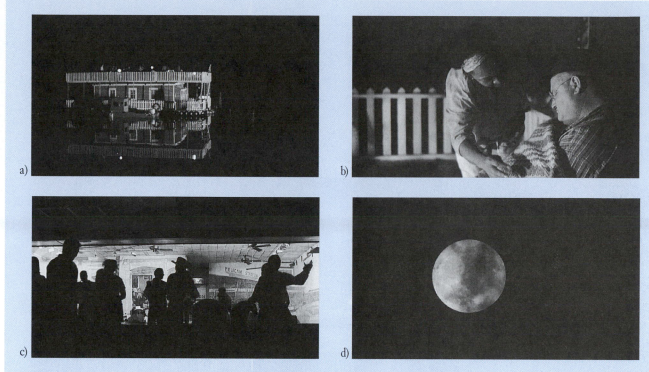

FIGURE 3.18 **Consecutive shots that omit much yet imply much**
In *Schultze Gets the Blues* (2003), Schultze, who has recently retired from his mining job in Germany, travels to Texas and then Louisiana, drawn initially by zydeco, but he stays on, looks around a bit, and seems to be intrigued by the music, lifestyles, and people. While dancing at a zydeco dance, he has to stop because he is in a lot of pain. Shortly after that, beginning a little more than 99 1/2 minutes into the film, occur four consecutive shots. (a) We see an extreme long shot of the house-boat where earlier Schultze had stopped to ask for a drink of water and been befriended there by a woman and her child. (Note the little blue boat that Schultze had rented is seen here beside the houseboat.) Couples seem to be dancing on top of the boat, but no music is heard. (b) On top of the houseboat, the dancing has stopped; it is later; and Schultze is asleep. The woman covers him with a blanket to keep him warm and leaves. (c) Couples dance (not where Schultze was dancing when he had his attack), but we cannot hear the music. Instead, we hear the ambient sounds from the previous shot and a long sigh or perhaps an expiration of breath. After that, the ambient sounds stop, and viewers may hear only very faintly some music or they may hear only silence. (d) As the extremely faint music of the end of the previous shot continues to play, the moon is seen partially covered by broken, dark, fast-moving clouds. Soon, the image fades to black, and while the screen is still black, the soundtrack fades to a brief silence. *Filmkombinat, Zweites Deutsches Fernsehen (ZDF); Paramount Classics DVD*

Fictional films are not the only type of film that can use expressive juxtaposition of shots. Nonnarrative films may also do so (Figures 3.19–3.20).

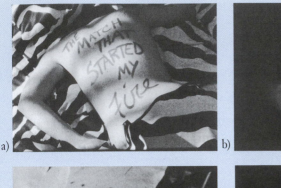

a)

b)

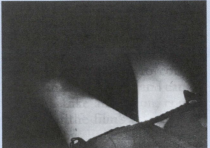

c)

d)

FIGURE 3.19 Consecutive shots creating meaning in a nonnarrative documentary
Three consecutive images from the non-narrative documentary film "The Match That Started My Fire" (1991) illustrate how the selection and arrangement of shots can create meaning beyond what the shots convey individually. In the film, various women describe their first aware-ness of their sexual feelings as viewers see a wide variety of images, some created for this film (b–c), some selected from exist-ing footage (d). The three consecutive images—a woman's bare legs illuminated in the dark (b), an open flower (c), and a mechanism pushing a load into a blazing furnace (d)—suggest various facets of a woman's sexuality. *Cathy C. Cook; Women Make Movies, New York*

FIGURE 3.20 Consecutive shots creating a brief visual poem in a nonnarrative experimental film
In (a), the first of four shots from the classic experimental film "Un chien andalou" (1928), a man begins to fall forward, presumably mortally wounded. In (b–c), as he continues to fall, his hands brush the bare back of a woman seated in the countryside as if he is try-ing to keep in touch with beauty and the living; then in (d) the woman's image fades away. The shots perhaps suggest that the dying man is unable to hold on to life and beauty and that nature endures though the man does not. The film is available on the Web. This example begins a little more than 12 minutes into the film. *Luis Buñuel; Les grands films classiques; Transflux Films DVD*

a)

b)

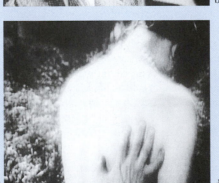

c)

d)

Action and Reaction

How viewers react to a movie is often intensified by how subjects in the film react. In nearly all narrative films (fictional and documentary), many scenes show actions and other people's reactions, and those reactions tend to intensify the viewer's responses. Humorous scenes are usually funnier because someone is shown to be bewildered, stunned, or in some other way uncomfortable. Horrifying scenes can be more frightening because of characters' reactions to scary sights or sounds. Suspenseful athletic contests, as in the **narrative documentary** *Hoop Dreams* (1994), are even more involving because of how individuals in the crowd are shown reacting to events. Sometimes actions and reactions are shown within the same shot (Figure 3.21).

narrative documentary: A film or video representation of an actual (not imaginary) narrative or story.

a)   b)   c)   d)

FIGURE 3.21 Action and reaction within the same shots
A single shot may be devoted entirely to an action or entirely to a reaction. Sometimes, however, a shot combines action and reaction in different proportions. Some shots are mostly of action. Others are mostly of reaction. About 113 minutes into *Pulp Fiction* (1994) occur two consecutive eventful shots. In the first shot—frames (a–b)—a young man rushes forward, repeatedly fires a gun at the film's two main characters, and misses in all six attempts even though his targets are close by. Toward the end of the shot—in (b)—after he realizes that he has fired his last bullet, for approximately 2 seconds he looks fearful and at a loss. In the second shot—frames (c–d)—the two characters who were shot at look straight ahead at their assailant, look down (as if to see whether they were somehow shot but have not yet realized it), look at each other, and again look straight ahead. The shot ends—in (d)—with the two men raising their guns and pointing them at their assailant. The first shot is devoted mostly to the young man's frantic actions and ends with a glimpse of his reaction to his predicament. The second shot draws out the suspense with which the previous shot ends; it concludes abruptly with the two men raising and pointing their guns. Shot 1: action, then reaction. Shot 2: more reactions, then action. *Miramax; Miramax Home Entertainment DVD*

a)

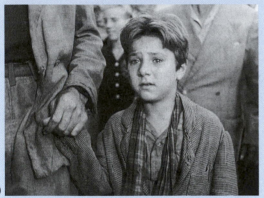

b)

FIGURE 3.22 Action, then reaction
In the last scene of the Italian neorealist film *The Bicycle Thief* (1948), many shots of action are followed by reaction shots. The boy has recently seen a crowd chasing, catching, and reviling his father, who in desperation had tried to steal a bicycle so he would not lose his recently acquired job. In (a), the third shot from the end of the film, the father is clearly distressed and probably embarrassed that his son, who has been shown to look up to him, has seen what he has done. The next shot shows the boy holding his father's hand and thrice looking up to check on how his dad is doing. The reaction shot of the boy represented here by (b) shows his anguish and empathy and intensifies viewers' response to his and his father's plight. *PDS-ENIC; Image Entertainment; Criterion DVD*

Often, shots of action are followed by reaction shots, which are (usually brief) shots showing someone's reactions to an event. Images of anguish can be more gripping if interspersed with reaction shots, as in the conclusion of *The Bicycle Thief* (1948, Figure 3.22). Action shots followed by reaction shots can be used in a limitless variety of situations.

But action followed by reaction is not the editor's only choice. Sometimes editors show first a reaction and then what caused it (Figure 3.23). Another example of reaction then action occurs at the end of a long scene in *Four Weddings and a Funeral* (1994). Approximately 7 minutes into the film, a wedding ceremony begins. Soon the best man realizes that in his rush that morning, he has forgotten to bring the rings. He pantomines to a friend in the congregation what the problem is, slips away from the couple and the minister, and meets with his friend in the back of the church. The two rings the friend gives the best man surprise him, but we do not get to see them yet. Later in the scene, we see the minister's startled reaction to the rings and the reactions of the bride and groom. Only then do viewers see the rings the friend has borrowed from those in attendance: hers is large, heart-shaped, and multicolored plastic; his looks like a pewter masked male's head with wings on both sides!

Filmmakers may even show a reaction shot but not the action that caused it and let viewers' imaginations supply the rest. An amusing example occurs in *There's Something about Mary* (1998, Figure 3.24). Then, too, it is possible to show a reaction then a second reaction within the same shot (Figure 3.25).

Parallel Editing

In **parallel editing**, or *cross-cutting*, the film shifts back and forth between two or more actions, often suggesting that the actions are occurring simultaneously and are related but sometimes depicting events from different times. Parallel editing that suggests simultaneous events in different locations is used in an early sequence in the classic German film *M* (Figure 3.26). A much more complicated example of parallel editing occurs in the musical *West Side Story* (1961). Approximately 93 minutes into the film, a sequence begins that uses competing, overlapping music ("Tonight") and rapid parallel editing to convey simultaneous actions by six subjects:

a)

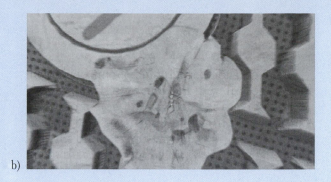

b)

FIGURE 3.23 Reaction, then action
(a) Nearly 51 3/4 minutes into *Antz* (1998), the main character, an ant named Z, looks at something off-frame. (b) The next shot shows viewers what Z is alarmed about: Princess Bala stuck in gum on the bottom of someone's shoe and, worse yet, the bottom of the shoe is heading straight toward Z. *DreamWorks SKG, PDI; DreamWorks Home Entertainment DVD*

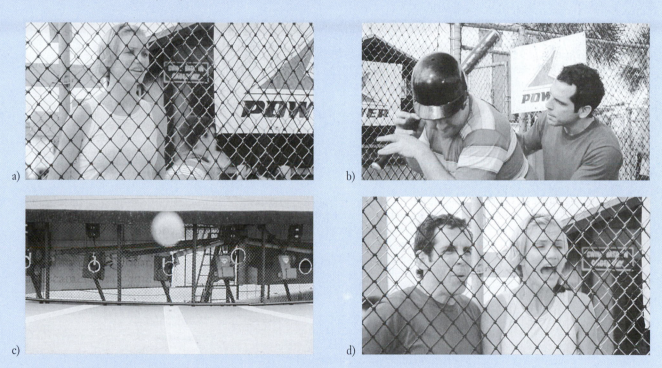

a)

b)

c)

d)

FIGURE 3.24 Reaction to implied action
These four frames represent four consecutive shots from nearly 94 1/2 minutes into *There's Something about Mary* (1998). (a) From outside a batting cage, Mary looks on at her brother. (b) The young man (Ted) helps Mary's brother get positioned in the batting cage. (c) A shot from the point of view of the boy shows a baseball whizzing toward him. (d) Mary and Ted react with pain and alarm. By implication, the ball has hit the boy and knocked him down. (In a later scene, viewers see that the boy got a big black eye from the experience.) In this scene, the editing shifts the emphasis from the boy getting hit (which could be alarming to viewers and not at all humorous) to the reaction of the two witnesses (which may amuse viewers since they do not see the boy's pain). For a situation to be humorous, it usually has to occur in a context involving little or no pain to someone whom viewers care about. *20th Century Fox; 20th Century Fox Home Entertainment DVD*

a)

b)

FIGURE 3.25 **Reaction followed by a different reaction in the same shot**
Some actors make a career mainly out of their reactions. An example is an amusing supporting actor popular in many 1930s and 1940s American comedies and musicals: Edward Everett Horton. In his films, often after someone says or does something, viewers see his reaction and then, after a beat, his second, very different reaction to the same stimulus. Sometimes he simply seems to have a second thought. At other times, he seems not too swift of thought. In the Fred Astaire and Ginger Rogers musical *Shall We Dance* (1937), Horton plays the director/owner of a ballet company. Approximately 5¼ minutes into the film, the Astaire character demonstrates a movement that combines ballet and tap. In the next shot (a–b), the initial reaction of the Horton character is surprise and pleasure, but he quickly catches himself and expresses his disapproval of the hybrid dancing. *RKO Radio Pictures; Warner Home Video DVD*

a)

b)

c)

d)

e)

FIGURE 3.26 **Parallel editing to convey mood and meaning**
Early in *M* (1931), a young girl, Elsie, leaves school and plays with a ball. Viewers learn that a child murderer is on the loose and see Elsie being greeted by a stranger who buys her a balloon. Elsie's mother waits for her daughter and frets that she is late arriving back at their apartment. As the mother calls out Elsie's name, viewers see (a) an empty stairwell in the building where Elsie and her mother live and (b) an empty attic, presumably in their building. In silence, viewers see (c) Elsie's empty chair and table setting. Somewhere outside the city, the ball Elsie played with earlier (d) rolls into view and stops, and the balloon the man had bought for her (e) floats up and briefly gets caught in wires before being carried away by the wind. These five shots suggest, at approximately the same moment in time, that Elsie is not in the stairwell, not in the attic, not at the table, and (somewhere outside the city) not in possession of her ball and the balloon. It is not only the parallel editing that contributes to the sequence's melancholic mood and ominous meaning: all five shots have no people, the last three shots of the sequence are without sound, and the last two shots end in disturbing stillness. *Nero Films; Criterion DVD*

1. the Jets, a New York gang on the way to a "rumble" or showdown with a rival gang, the Sharks

2. the Sharks, a Puerto Rican gang on the way to a showdown with the Jets

3. Anita, a Puerto Rican looking forward to an amorous evening with her boyfriend, Bernardo, the leader of the Sharks

4. Tony, the former leader of the Jets, who is looking forward to meeting with his beloved, Maria, that evening

5. Maria, a Puerto Rican who is looking forward to being with Tony

6. almost 95 minutes into the film, police officer Krupke checking his watch as he is being driven to the site of the gang fight

plotline: A series of related events, generally involving only a few characters or people, that can function as an independent story.

The parallel editing between the six subjects quickly shows almost simultaneously how all the subjects are anticipating the events of the evening.

Parallel editing is occasionally used throughout a movie to suggest two or more simultaneous **plotlines**, as in *Dr. Strangelove: Or, How I Learned to Stop Worrying and Love the Bomb* (1963). Except for that film's expository prologue, its doomsday device finale, and its third sequence, which is located in undisclosed residential quarters, all the film's sequences occur at one of three locations: a U.S. Air Force base where General Jack D. Ripper decides to order a group of U.S. bombers to attack Soviet targets; an American bomber containing a crew trying to reach a target in the Soviet Union; and the Pentagon War Room, where the U.S. president and his advisers, the Soviet ambassador, and via phone the Soviet premier all try to avert catastrophe. Although viewers get the sense of time moving forward as the film progresses, the parallel editing suggests that some of the events happen simultaneously.

Often parallel editing shows someone being menaced while someone else is on the way to help. Early in the twentieth century, D. W. Griffith perfected this technique and often used it in his films. It is still commonplace in movies, as in *Toy Story 2* (1999), which incorporates parallel editing of two plotlines during much of the film (Figure 3.27). Parallel editing may also be used to show one subject trying to achieve a goal as another subject tries to overcome various problems and prevent the first subject from achieving the goal. A memorable example occurs near the end of Hitchcock's *Strangers on a Train* (1951), where extensive and suspenseful parallel editing shows one character on his way to plant incriminating

FIGURE 3.27 Parallel editing of two plotlines Approximately half of *Toy Story 2* (1999) employs parallel editing of two plotlines. One plotline focuses on Woody, a toy cowboy who is stolen by a toy store owner. The other plotline involves Woody's friends, assorted toys, who mount a rescue mission. (a) Woody and his captor. (b) Four of Woody's friends in a toy car looking for Woody in the thief's toy store. *Pixar, Walt Disney Pictures; Buena Vista Home Entertainment DVD*

evidence at a murder site as another character tries to overcome various obstacles and arrive there before him.

Parallel editing can show a contrast. In *A Fish Called Wanda* (1988), it is used amusingly to contrast a bored married couple getting ready for bed with a young unmarried couple fully attending to each other as they undress and have sex. In the documentary film "The Heck with Hollywood!" (1991), which is about the difficulties of marketing one's own low-budget film, parallel editing is briefly used to contrast the views of an independent filmmaker with those of her distributor.

Parallel editing can also highlight a similarity. Throughout *M*, parallel editing shows that the police, organized beggars, and organized crime in a German city of the early 1930s are all trying to capture a child murderer. Griffith also used parallel editing throughout the monumental silent film *Intolerance* to present four stories illustrating intolerance in four places and eras.

As we see so many times in this book, a technique is not restricted to a certain type of film. Parallel editing can also be used in films that tell no story, as in the **nonnarrative documentary** *Titicut Follies* (1967), where it is used to compare and contrast the same subject at different times. Shots of an inmate being force-fed by a psychologist in a mental hospital are alternated with shots of the corpse of the same man being prepared for display before his burial.

nonnarrative documentary: A film or video that uses no narrative or story in its representation of mainly actual (not imaginary) subjects.

PACE AND TIME

A film's pace is the rate that a film's subjects (such as events in a narrative film or information in a documentary film) are revealed or presented—such as rapidly or slowly or somewhere in between. Although the viewer's sense of pace is subjective and is influenced by many aspects of the film, a film's pace can help keep viewers involved or alienate them.

Fast and Slow Cutting

A shot may be as brief as one frame, but when it is, few viewers see its content. At the opposite extreme, as Hitchcock demonstrated in *Rope* (1948), a shot may run for as long as the reel of film in the camera, whereas a single shot in video may run more than two hours. Shots in feature films typically range from several seconds to about 20 seconds. **Fast cutting** refers to consecutive shots of brief duration (say, a few seconds or less) or to editing dominated by brief shots. **Slow cutting** refers to consecutive shots of long duration or to editing dominated by long-lasting shots. Because, again, so much depends on context, it's difficult to set a number here, but an average shot length (ASL) of 15 or more seconds will seem slow to many viewers in Western cultures.

Fast cutting may impart energy to its subjects. It is also an effective way to convey a lot of information in a brief time, as in many trailers. Makers of music videos and other filmmakers often use fast cutting to intensify a sense of confusion or loss of control or to add urgency or energy. It's no accident, for example, that the opera montage in *Citizen Kane* uses fast cutting throughout. During that section of the story, Susan is under unbearable pressure, and the fast cutting reflects the fact that events seem to gallop out of her control.

For some descriptions of the opera montage in *Citizen Kane*, see the Web site for this book: <bedfordstmartins.com/phillips-film>.

Fast cutting is sometimes used to show images flashing through someone's mind during a crisis, as when late in *Spanking the Monkey* (1994) the main character has jumped from a high cliff and is plunging toward water. Fast cutting is also used for countless movie fights, climaxes to races, and montages summarizing past events. Editing may not only be fast but also have a regular rhythm (Figure 3.28).

Slow cutting may be used in scenes of calm or reflection. It can be used to establish a subdued mood before fast cutting injects energy. And filmmakers can use slow cutting to slow down the pace, just as the second movement of a symphony or concerto typically does and just as a slow number on a CD full of energetic numbers does.

Too much of any technique—fast cutting or slow—causes viewers to lose interest, so editing is used to vary a film's pace. Like poets writing in meter, filmmakers can establish a more or less regular rhythm, maintain it,

FIGURE 3.28 Fast cutting and a regular rhythm
Fifteen or so minutes into the Soviet film *October* (1928), which was codirected and edited by Sergei Eisenstein, two frames of a soldier firing a machine gun are alternated with two frames of the gun being fired. This extremely rapid alternation between soldier and gun, soldier and gun, soldier and gun, sets up a regular rhythm, as if the man is relentless, as if he is a machine or part of one, or as if the weapon

a)

b)

consists of man plus gun. Through editing, the man and the gun become one. To recapture some of the experience of seeing these two alternating images in the film, look at (a) only long enough to see its subject (much less than a second); then do the same with (b); then allotting the same fraction of a second to each image, look back and forth, back and forth, and so on. *Sovkino; Image Entertainment DVD*

or work expressive variations on it. In the last sequence of the classic Soviet film (*Battleship*) *Potemkin*, for example, the battleship is steaming along. The cutting is brisk but by no means hurried or frantic. After possible rival ships are spotted and the men called to their battle stations, the cutting becomes faster and faster until it is clear there will be no battle after all; then the pace of the editing slows. Pace mirrors mood.[1]

Studies of editing show that since the mid-1970s, movies have had a much shorter average shot length than in earlier decades. Film scholar Barry Salt reports that from 1976 to 1987, the ASL of a large sample of movies was about 8.4 seconds (296). Of course, some shots are 25 or even many more seconds, but there are also many stretches of fast cutting. Why there is so much fast cutting in recent movies, TV, and music videos in Western cultures is not easy to determine. It is widely believed that modern viewers absorb the meaning of a shot more quickly. Perhaps we are visually jaded and need more of a kick. If a narrative is poor, editors may dazzle or distract viewers with exciting editing techniques, according to Michael Hoggan, a past president of American Cinema Editors. Or perhaps the fast cutting reflects the fast pace most people feel is an inescapable part of their lives. Maybe it's a combination of these or other causes. Music videos with their fast cutting and jump cuts bombard viewers with such an overload of information that it is often impossible to discern in them any coherence or meaning, and for many viewers this lack of coherence and meaning is characteristic of contemporary life.

The pace of individual scenes can make or break them. In comedy, for example, pacing is crucial. Pause too long and the moment is lost. Rush forward too soon and the moment is also lost. Consider a sight gag in *Airplane!* (1980), which lasts from 73:47 to 73:51 in the film; in other words, approximately a mere 4 seconds. An Air Israel plane is glimpsed taxiing with a huge prayer shawl draped over the front of the plane. If the shot were shorter, hardly anyone would get the joke. If it were longer, viewers would quickly lose interest, or at least the gag would not carry as much punch.

Condensing Time and Stretching It: Montage and Other Editing Techniques

The Japanese director Yasujiro Ozu and the Danish director Carl Theodor Dreyer, some experimental filmmakers, occasional documentary filmmakers, and a relatively few other filmmakers deliberately include shots

---

[1]David Mayer's detailed cutting continuity script for (*Battleship*) *Potemkin* includes the number of frames for each shot in one version of the film. The descriptions reveal that as the men on the *Potemkin* prepare for possible battle, many shots are only a second or two long or even less than a second (calculated at 16 frames per second, which many experts believe is the speed that best approximates the original showings). After it is clear that no confrontation will occur after all, the average shot length tends to increase (208–52).

that most directors and editors would consider unnecessary. For the vast majority of filmmakers, however, one of the main goals of editing is to eliminate dead time—any footage that does not contribute to the immediate desired effects. The sense of dead time, however, depends on who is doing the viewing, and shots that were engaging in former eras often seem uneventful to viewers of a later generation. For example, the many shots in classic western films of cowboys riding and riding on and on are dead time to many of today's young viewers. One of the most effective means of cutting dead time and showing viewers much information quickly is a montage, or a "quick impressionistic sequence of . . . images, usually linked by dissolves, superimpositions or wipes, and used to convey passages of time, changes of place, or any other scenes of transition" (Reisz and Millar 112). One of the most famous montages in cinema is from *Citizen Kane*, the montage of breakfasts experienced by Kane and his first wife as the years pass. In twenty-seven brief shots (plus brief blurry transitions that look like swish pans) lasting altogether only 133 seconds, the filmmakers show the couple's deteriorating marriage (Figure 3.29).[2]

Another montage—this one without lap dissolves—occurs in *Raging Bull* (1980). One scene ends with the boxer Jake La Motta soaking his fist

---

[2]For a detailed description of the breakfasts montage in *Citizen Kane*, including ten frame enlargements and an analysis of the sequence, see Reisz and Millar (115–21).

a)   b)

FIGURE 3.29 **The breakfasts montage in *Citizen Kane* (1941)**
(a) At the beginning of a sequence that begins almost 52 minutes into *Citizen Kane*, Charles Foster Kane and his new first wife are close to and attentive to each other, but by stages they become alienated. (b) At the end of the sequence they are far apart, sitting at opposite ends of a long table and reading rival newspapers. In slightly more than 2 minutes, this montage shows their growing alienation and failing marriage. *RKO General Pictures, Mercury Productions; Warner Home Video DVD*

in a bucket of ice water. Then we see a title card announcing a La Motta fight, a few still photographs from the fight, and snippets from home movies. The same pattern is repeated, during which six fights are accounted for; Jake and Vicki date, marry, indulge in horseplay beside and in a swimming pool, and begin a family; and Jake's brother Joey marries and begins a family. In 2 minutes and 35 seconds, the story jumps ahead more than three years, from January 14, 1944, to sometime after a March 14, 1947, fight. This montage shows Jake's work and personal life and Joey's personal life all going well, but the filmmakers chose to skim through those events. Perhaps the montage that condenses the most amount of time of any montage in the history of film, and does so in only about a minute, occurs early in *Adaptation* (2002, Figure 3.30).

Montages usually consist of many brief shots, often connected by lap dissolves, but a montage can be as simple as a few shots without lap dissolves. In *Hook* (1991), we see three consecutive shots from behind a seated Wendy. Each shot ends with Wendy turning around and revealing that she is older; this simple montage represents an expanse of forty or so years in a matter of seconds.

a)

b)

FIGURE 3.30 **Beginning and ending of a montage condensing an eon—in less than a minute** The main character in *Adaptation* (2002), screenwriter Charlie Kaufman, is plagued by self-consciousness, self-doubts, and crippling shyness. Sometimes the film visualizes what is going on in his mind. The first time it does so is only a few minutes into the film after he thinks, "I've been on this planet for forty years, and I'm no closer to understanding a single thing. Why am I here? How did I get here?" What follows is a montage that seems to answer his questions by giving a speedy recap of developments on earth. The first shot of the montage, in (a), reveals a hot bubbly mass—earth presumably, Hollywood in particular, at near its beginning. A quick succession of shots reveals later and later stages of the earth, including the emergence of life from the sea, the growth of vegetation, the destruction of dinosaurs, the coming and going of an ice age, other massive changes in geology, the emergence of *Homo erectus* or *Homo sapiens*, the founding and development of the L.A. area, and finally, in (b), the birth of a baby, presumably Charlie Kaufman. The montage represents "Four billion and forty years" in a mere 56 seconds! *Good Machine, Intermedia, and others; Columbia Pictures DVD*

Montages are not the only method editors have of condensing time. Sometimes editors provide much information by a succession of relatively brief shots, as in the ending of *Breaking Away* (1979). The film presents the story of four unemployed young men living in a university town; they have graduated from high school but have not yet found their places in life. The most important of the four is Dave Stoller, whose father runs a used car lot and disapproves of Dave's zealous imitation of professional Italian bicycle racers and his attempts to emulate everything Italian. The four young men are harassed by university students and decide to prove themselves by entering the annual university team bicycle race, which they win in a close race against thirty-three fraternity teams.

After the race, the film has three more scenes, which presumably take place at the beginning of the following fall semester:

Scene (2 shots, 12 seconds)

Shot 1. Used car lot: Mr. Stoller is leaving on a bike; his pregnant wife is talking about a car to an interested couple, though we do not hear her.

Shot 2. On a bike, Mr. Stoller leaves the Cutter Cars lot and rides into the street.

Scene (3 shots, 19 seconds)

Shot 3. On campus: a young woman with a French accent asks Dave where the "office of the bursar" is.

Shot 4. After hesitating, he replies, "You must mean the Bursar's Office."

Shot 5. She agrees and smiles.

Scene, the film's last (3 shots, 22 seconds)

Shot 6. Dave and the French woman are biking; Dave tells her he was thinking about studying French and talks to her about the major French bicycle race.

Shot 7. Dave continues to talk to the French woman. Mr. Stoller is riding a bike from the opposite direction, passes Dave and the woman, and calls out to Dave. Dave replies hello in French.

Shot 8. Mr. Stoller's startled reaction and a **freeze frame** of it.

freeze frame: An unmoving motion-picture or video image that looks like a still photograph.

Without these last three scenes, the film would end after the bicycle race as a working-class success story, with four sons of limestone cutters as victors, working-class brothers united (one of the four young men and his police officer brother), and Dave and his parents reconciled. But the last three scenes, as in so many American movies, quickly shift emphasis from social class to individual psychology.

The last scene suggests that Dave may be about to take on a new role—that of would-be cosmopolitan student studying French rather than Italian. He's still an adolescent trying out roles. The Stollers also assume new roles, probably too many in too short a time to be believable if we think about the situation. Mr. Stoller has changed the name of the car lot from Campus Cars to Cutter Cars, suggesting that he will henceforth seek the town market and that the victory by the four young men has renewed his social class pride. The father has also imitated the son and taken up bicycle riding. For the first time in the film, he allows his wife to help with the work at the car lot. Finally, the Stollers are going to start a new family. Mr. Stoller is more relaxed, more accepting of his son, more willing to accept his own limitations (his wife helping at the car lot). His calling out to Dave in the last scene reminds viewers of an earlier scene in which he snubbed Dave in public—when Dave was deep into his Italian period. The last two shots are of Dave (and the French woman) and Mr. Stoller, as it should be: throughout the film, Dave acts, and Mr. Stoller reacts. In these last eight shots, viewers are swept along on a rapid river of images until the final one, without noticing that all these changes in the lives of the Stollers are depicted in a very brief time. All this and more is conveyed by only eight shots, in 53 seconds of carefully edited film.

Editors nearly always try to condense time. But a few films—nearly all of them outside the classical Hollywood cinema—occasionally and briefly expand time, allowing more time to show an action than the action itself would take. Eisenstein used this technique in several of his films. In *October* (1928), he often stretches out an action slightly by including shots that repeat part of a movement, as in the toppling of a statue of a former tsar: one shot ends with the statue well on its way to the ground; the next shot begins with the statue not as far from the ground; the shot after that does the same thing. Three somewhat overlapping shots are used to show one brief action. Later, we see parts of the raising of a drawbridge more than once. Two other famous examples of expanded time are from Eisenstein's (*Battleship*) *Potemkin*. In one scene, an angry sailor breaks a plate, but the scene has been edited so that viewers see parts of the sailor's arm movement twice, from above first his left shoulder and then his right.[3] Later in the film, parts of the famous massacre of civilians on the Odessa steps are edited so that the running time is longer than the **story time**. Because of the surprising **structure** of "An Occurrence at Owl Creek Bridge" (1962), the film's running time (28 minutes) is longer than its story time (slightly more than 10 minutes). Another example of expanding time slightly by repeating part of an action is found in *Bamboozled* (2000, Figure 3.31).

story time: The amount of time represented in a film's story.

structure: The arrangement of all the parts of a text.

---

[3]For frame enlargements for each of the sixty-one frames making up the eight key shots in this scene, see Mayer, 23–30. For Mayer's analysis of these shots, see 13–14, 15.

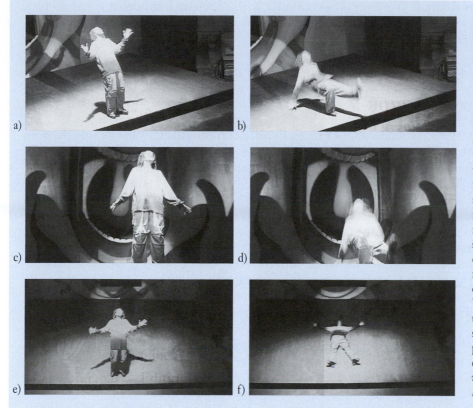

a)
b)
c)
d)
e)
f)

FIGURE 3.31 Expanding film time by repeating parts of an action
A little more than 112 minutes into Spike Lee's *Bamboozled* (2000), one of the two main performers in the TV minstrel show, who has become disillusioned with the show and is going to quit, comes onto the stage in his street clothes and tells the audience that he wants them to go to their windows and yell out about their frustrations. He then falls backward, an action seen in three consecutive, repetitive, brief shots. The beginning and ending of the first shot are seen in (a–b). The beginning and ending of the second shot are seen in (c–d). The beginning and ending of the third shot are seen in (e–f). Using editing to expand the time used to represent an action prolongs slightly the already tense and suspenseful moment and gives it greater emphasis. *Forty Acres and a Mule Filmworks; New Line Home Entertainment DVD*

(Although it is not a matter of editing, time can also be expanded when the camera films at a faster rate than the film is projected, as when an explosion is filmed at 300 frames per second but is projected at 24: an explosion that would normally last approximately a quarter of a second will last about 3 seconds.)

For a sample description and an analysis that illustrates the expressiveness and impact of editing, see the Close-Up on pp. 151–52.

DIGITAL EDITING

As in other aspects of filmmaking, increasingly computers are being used in editing. Editing can be done by transferring videotaped or filmed images (and sometimes sounds) to a computer and using sophisticated software. With the power, speed, and flexibility of the computer, editors can do **nonlinear editing**—that is, access and edit shots in whatever order is desired. Working on a computer with adequate hard drive space, editors can quickly access any of the digitized shots and select and combine them (Figure 3.32).

Since the beginning of editing history, editors have been able to shorten any shot by deleting its beginning or ending or any fragment or fragments within the shot. With nonlinear editing, they can still do all that, but they can also lengthen or shorten the duration of a shot and thus change the speed of subjects within the shot, as is often done by editors working on trailers. Digital editors can also create certain effects, such as split screens and superimposed titles, and use various transitions between shots, such as lap dissolves and wipes. With some software and some films, editors can also select and synchronize sound to image. At any stage, editors can play back any part of the results and see if they are satisfied. Digital versions may even be sent long distances electronically. If **film stock** was used during filming and the results will eventually be shown on film, the editor can transfer the shots to a computer, edit them, and use the computer to print out an *edit decision list* to use while cutting and splicing the final version of the film. If digital video was used for filming and the results were edited on a computer, the final edited results can be transferred from the computer to a videotape, DVD, or film for showings.

Some films—such as *Buena Vista Social Club* (1999), *The Original Kings of Comedy* (2000), and *Star Wars: Episode III—Revenge of the Sith* (2005)—have been shot on digital video cameras, edited digitally, and transferred to 35 mm film for showings in theaters. Filming with digital video cameras has several major advantages, including the ease with which the content of digital videotape can be copied to a computer and edited there. As digital filming supersedes the older technology, digital editing is sure to grow even more widespread. Regardless of these and other technological editing advances, however, what will count for viewers are the skill with which the final creation is edited and the effect of the way the shots are chosen and arranged.

film stock: Unexposed and unprocessed motion-picture film.

FIGURE 3.32 Advanced digital editing set-up
Seen here about 70 1/2 minutes into the TV documentary *The Cutting Edge: The Magic of Movie Editing* (2004) is master editor Walter Murch with his digital editing equipment (left to right: monitor showing one of the shots he selected from the setup on the right wall, computer workstation, and on the right wall images from shots to choose from). Most editors do not stand during the long and arduous job of editing a feature film, but Murch prefers to do so. *A.C.E., BBC, TCEP Inc.; Warner Home Video DVD*

CLOSE-UP: THE EXPRESSIVENESS OF EDITING (AND OTHER TECHNIQUES): AN EXCERPT FROM *HIGH NOON*

In the 1952 western *High Noon*, Will Kane, the town marshal of Hadleyville, has learned that Frank Miller, a man Kane helped convict years ago, is on the noon train to Hadleyville. There he will be joined by three men; then the four men plan to kill Kane. For various reasons, the townspeople do not rally behind Marshal Kane. During the 11:55 a.m. to noon section, which begins almost 67½ minutes into the film, viewers see the following sixteen scenes (each scene is divided into its shots):

Scene 1: Kane's Office

1. Kane looks at the boy as the boy (who had volunteered to help Kane in the coming showdown) leaves. Kane turns and glances at the clock on the wall (it reads 11:55); then he starts to sit down.

2. Kane sits at desk, takes a pistol from the drawer, checks the hammer of its firing mechanism, tucks the gun between his belt and his abdomen, opens a box of bullets, and dumps them into his hand.

Scene 2: Train Station

3. Near the train tracks, all three members of the Miller gang check to make certain their gun cylinders move freely and are full of bullets.

Scene 3: Kane's Office

4. Kane takes out a sheet of paper and begins to write.

5. He writes at the top of the sheet: "Last Will and Testament."

6. He looks up from his writing.

7. As the music begins, the camera tilts up from a swinging clock pendulum to reveal it's 11:58.

8. Kane looks down from the clock and resumes writing his will.

Scene 4: Train Station

9. The three members of the Miller gang are by the railroad tracks.

10. The empty railroad tracks.*

Scene 5: Inside a Church

11. Congregation at prayer.

12. In a pew, Joe Henderson, a town leader, looks straight ahead.

13. Ezra, a man who urged the townspeople to stand by Kane during a debate that took place in the church, looks down.

Scene 6: Ramirez Saloon

14. At the bar, men smoke, wait, and look at each other.

15. A man with a dark eye patch gazes at his drink as he sits alone at a corner table.

16. The bartender, who is behind the bar, looks tense.

Scene 7: Kane's Office

17. The swinging clock pendulum.

18. Kane writing.

Scene 8: Town Street

19. View of a deserted town street.

_____

*According to Leonard J. Leff, shots 10 to 31 last 3.2 seconds each (159).

151

20. Another section of a deserted town street.

Scene 9: Outside Train Station

21. View of empty train tracks (nearly the same shot as shot 10).

22. The three Miller men (presumably looking down the train tracks).

Scene 10: Above a Town Street

23. On a second-floor verandah, two old townsmen watch and wait.

Scene 11: Fuller House

24. Sam Fuller and his wife look at one another briefly, then look down (and the wife also turns away slightly).

Scene 12: Martin's Place

25. Martin, the former sheriff, looks offscreen.

Scene 13: Mrs. Ramirez's Residence

26. Mrs. Ramirez, Kane's former lover, waiting.

27. Mrs. Kane waiting.

Scene 14: Kane's Office

28. The clock reads 11:59.

29. The swinging pendulum.

Scene 15: Train Station

30. The three Miller men looking straight ahead.

Scene 16: Kane's Office

31. Kane writing.

32. The camera tilts up from the swinging pendulum and reveals that it is 12:00.

This excerpt uses parallel editing to show three major kinds of information:

- How Kane prepares for the coming showdown: he gets out his pistol and bullets and writes his will.
- What Miller's men do: they check their guns and wait for the arrival of the noon train.
- What the townspeople do: they do nothing to help Kane as they wait for the arrival of Frank Miller.

The editing here illustrates the enormous amount of simultaneous information edited film can convey. In little more than 2 minutes, we viewers see what characters are doing or not doing in nine settings. And the film shows what is occurring at different places at about the same time by rapidly cutting between Kane in his office, Miller's three men at the train station, and residents of Hadleyville in different parts of town. As the shots of the empty streets reveal, Kane's potential allies do nothing but wait indoors in safety.

Shots of brief duration are used within and between the scenes, but there is little movement within each shot. Indeed, many shots look like still photographs. It's as though the townspeople are frozen in inaction. People do little but wait, think, and feel (or try not to feel). And they do so alone. Many shots show only one individual. In shots of groups, there is little interaction, little community. Together the brief shots, regular rhythm of the editing, and inaction within the shots reinforce the sense that the people of Hadleyville are frozen in nervous, isolated paralysis as a momentous showdown moves steadily and inevitably toward them. All this—and more—the editing and other filmmaking techniques help us experience and understand.

SUMMARY

Editing involves decisions about which shots to include, the most effective take (version) of each shot, the duration of shots, the arrangement of shots, and the transitions between them. Regardless of the equipment used for filming and editing, editing can strongly affect viewer responses. It can be used, for example, (1) to promote continuity or disruptions; (2) to superimpose images; (3) to juxtapose shots to make a point, support a feeling or mood, intensify the viewer's reactions, or show parallel subjects or events; and (4) to affect the viewer's sense of pace, compress or expand time, and convey an enormous amount of information in a brief time.

Early Film Editing

- The first films of the 1890s consisted of one shot or a series of one-shot scenes.

- By the time of *The Birth of a Nation* (1915), editing was used to maintain continuity while telling complex stories.

- In the 1920s, the editing of some Soviet filmmakers conveyed a story and promoted ideas by the juxtaposition of shots.

Building Blocks

- The shot is the most basic unit of editing. It is a piece of continuous film or videotape depicting an uninterrupted action or an immobile subject during an uninterrupted passage of time.

- A scene is a section of a narrative film that gives the impression of continuous action taking place during continuous time and in continuous space. A scene consists of one or more shots although on rare occasions, a shot will convey multiple scenes.

- A sequence is a series of related consecutive scenes that are perceived as a major part of a narrative film.

- Editors can use one or more of many possible transitions between shots, such as a cut, lap dissolve, or wipe. Depending on conventions and context, editing transitions can be used to convey or reinforce information or moods. For example, often a lap dissolve suggests that the next shot takes place at a later time or different location—or both.

Continuity Editing

- Continuity editing, which is used in most narrative films, maintains a sense of clear and continuous action and continuous setting within each scene.

■ Continuity editing is achieved in filming and editing by using eyeline matches, the 180-degree system, and other strategies. The aim of continuity editing is to make sure viewers will instantly understand the relationship of subjects to other subjects, subjects to settings, and each shot to the following shot.

Image on Image and Image after Image

■ A momentary superimposition of two or more images is possible in a lap dissolve, as in the ending of the 1960 *Psycho*.

■ Consecutive shots can stress differences or similarities. They may also be used to surprise, amuse, confuse, or disorient viewers.

■ Reaction shots often intensify viewers' responses. Usually a reaction shot follows an action shot, but it may precede one, or it may occur alone with the action not shown but only implied.

■ Parallel editing can be used to achieve various ends, including to give a sense of simultaneous events, contrast two or more actions or viewpoints, or create suspense about whether one subject will achieve a goal before another subject does.

Pace and Time

■ Usually fast cutting is used to impart energy and excitement. Slow cutting may be used to slow the pace or help calm the mood.

■ Depending on the context, a succession of shots of equal length may suggest inevitability, relentlessness, boredom, or some other condition.

■ Shifting the pace of the editing can change viewers' emotional responses, as in the excerpt analyzed from near the end of (*Battleship*) *Potemkin*.

■ Montage compresses an enormous amount of information into a brief time, as in the montage of Susan's opera career in *Citizen Kane*.

■ Editing usually condenses time (for example, by cutting dead time), but it can expand time—for instance, by showing certain fragments of an action more than once.

Digital Editing

■ Increasingly, computers are being used for editing. Images shot on film are scanned into computers; images shot on videotape are simply transferred to computers.

■ Once in the computer, the shots can be edited there and later transferred to DVD or film for showings.

Major Terms about Editing

Below, numbers in italics refer to the pages where the terms are explained. All terms are defined in more detail in the Illustrated Glossary beginning on p. 667.

180-degree system *128*
continuity editing *126*
cut *121*
cutaway shot *113*
dailies *114*
eyeline match *127*
fade-out, fade-in *121*
fast cutting *142*
final cut *113*
footage *114*
iris-in *125*

iris-out *125*
jump cut *121*
lap dissolve *122*
master shot *113*
match cut *121*
montage *118, 145*
nonlinear editing *149*
pace *142*
parallel editing *138*
reaction shot *138*
scene *119*

sequence *120*
shot *114, 119*
shot/reverse shot *128*
slow cutting *142*
Soviet montage *118*
splice *121*
superimpose *130*
take *113*
wipe *124*

QUESTIONS ABOUT EDITING

The following questions are intended to help viewers understand the use of editing in a film and analyze their responses to it. Not all the questions are appropriate for every film. In thinking out, discussing, and writing responses to the questions most appropriate for the film being examined, be careful to stick with the issues the questions raise, to answer all parts of the questions, to explain the reasons for your answers, and to give specific examples from the film.

1. Generally, is the film's editing characterized by fast cutting or slow cutting? To what effect?

2. Is continuity editing used? If so, give examples and explain in at least one of the examples what strategies the filmmakers use to create continuity editing.

3. What transitions other than cuts does the film employ? What do those transitions contribute to the film's impact?

4. Where are shots joined for a particular effect, such as to stress similarities or differences or to create or enhance a mood? What do those special juxtapositions contribute to the film?

5. Does the film use parallel editing? If so, where and to what effect?

6. Where is editing used to delete time within a scene or section? Where is editing used to make viewers use their imaginations (for example, by use of a cutaway shot)?

7. Is editing ever used to expand time? If so, explain how that is achieved and what the expanded time contributes to the film.

8. How would you characterize the film's overall pace? Did you notice changes in pace in particular parts of the film? If so, explain.

9. Does the film include any montages? If so, explain their components and functions within the film.

WORKS CITED

Andrew, J. Dudley. *The Major Film Theories: An Introduction*. New York: Oxford UP, 1976.

Grignon, Rex. Address. "The Making of *Toy Story*." Monterey, CA, Conf. Center. 10 Apr. 1996.

Hoggan, Michael (former president, American Cinema Editors). Telephone interview. July 1994.

Huss, Roy, and Norman Silverstein. *The Film Experience: Elements of Motion Picture Art*. New York: Dell, 1968.

Leff, Leonard J. *Film Plots: Scene-by-Scene Narrative Outlines for Feature Film Study*. Vol. 1. Ann Arbor: Pierian, 1983.

Mayer, David. *Sergei M. Eisenstein's* Potemkin: *A Shot-by-Shot Presentation*. New York: Grossman, 1972.

Murch, Walter. *In the Blink of an Eye: A Perspective on Film Editing*. 2nd ed. Los Angeles: Silman-James, 2001.

Reisz, Karel, and Gavin Millar. *The Technique of Film Editing*. Enlarged ed. New York: Hastings, 1968.

Riefenstahl, Leni (filmmaker). Interview. *The Wonderful, Horrible Life of Leni Riefenstahl*. Documentary film. 1993.

Salt, Barry. *Film Style and Technology: History and Analysis*. 2nd ed. London: Starword, 1992.

FOR FURTHER READING

Balmuth, Bernard. *Introduction to Film Editing*. Boston: Focal, 1989. An introduction for someone who wants to edit film.

Fairservice, Don. *Film Editing: History, Theory, and Practice: Looking at the Invisible*. Manchester, Eng.: Manchester UP, 2001. A comprehensive examination of the film editor's craft from the beginning of cinema to the present day.

Oldham, Gabriella. *First Cut: Conversations with Film Editors*. Berkeley: U of California P, 1992. Interviews with twenty-three award-winning editors, including editors of documentary films.

Selected Takes: Film Editors on Editing. Ed. Vincent LoBrutto. Westport, CT: Praeger, 1991. Interviews with twenty-one film editors plus a glossary and bibliography.

The student essay "Stretching Time to Create Tension in (*Battleship*) *Potemkin*" can be found on the Web site for this book at <bedfordstmartins.com/phillips-film>.

CHAPTER 4
Sound

W<small>E TAKE SO MUCH FOR GRANTED</small>, in life and in the movies. Perhaps more than any other component of a film, viewers tend not to notice and not to appreciate the soundtrack—what it can consist of and what it can contribute to the viewer's responses. So by way of introduction and illustration, let's begin by considering an example: the soundtrack in the opening of a film. Not just any opening. Not just any film. But one with an especially expressive soundtrack. *Contact* (1997) is a fictional film about listening for life elsewhere in the universe and some of the consequences (scientific, political, and personal) after extraterrestrial life makes contact with earth. At the beginning of *Contact*, the camera seems to be positioned in space and looking down on a part of the earth. Then the camera seems to travel farther and farther away from earth, then from the planets and galaxies. All the while, viewers hear snippets of sound, mainly overlapping music and speech from earlier and earlier TV and radio broadcasts (see the feature on p. 158). This simultaneous visual and aural information suggests—as the author of the film's source novel, astronomer and writer Carl Sagan, stated—that ever since the first radio transmissions near the beginning of the twentieth century, earthlings have in effect proclaimed to the universe that there is life on earth. In the previous chapter, we were reminded of how much information can be conveyed by skillfully edited film—such as the montage early in *Adaptation* (2002, Figure 3.30, p. 146). Similarly, the initial audio sequence of *Contact* demonstrates that a wealth of history can be evoked in a very short time if filmmakers choose the details carefully.

What are a few of the many ways that other typically unobtrusive film sounds are created, how might film sounds be used, and, most important, how do they affect viewers? This chapter gives some answers to those questions by examining some specific uses of a soundtrack's four major components, possible sound transitions, and general uses of sound in **narrative** films.

Terms in **boldface** are defined in the Illustrated Glossary beginning on page 667.

narrative: A representation of unified events (happenings and actions) situated in one or more settings.

Opening Soundtrack for *Contact* (1997)

As images of the receding earth, solar system, and galaxies are seen, the following sounds can be heard:

Loud, indistinct, overlapping music
SONG: "Be There" by All for One
SONG: "Doot, doot, doot . . ."
Song by Hootie and the Blowfish
1997 SONG: "I wanna be there when you're (gonna be there)" from "Wanna Be" by the Spice Girls
SONG: "God Shuffled His Feet" by Crash Test Dummies
SONG: "You wanna get with me, you gotta . . ."
SONG: "Clearly, I've never been there, but it feels like . . ."
SONG: "Broken Wings" by Mr. Mister
1986, announcer at launch of *Challenger* space shuttle: "situation obviously a major malfunction"
Music for *Dallas* TV show

. . .

1979 (music): "Funkytown" by Lipps, Inc.

. . .

MUSIC: "Boogie Oogy"
MUSIC: "Sometimes you feel like a nut" commercial theme for Almond Joy candy bars
Song by The Trammps
Sounds of asteroids in space [these are the only sounds not originating from earth]
1973, President Nixon: ". . . your president's a crook. Well, I'm not a crook."
SONG: "Got to Give It Up" by Marvin Gaye
1969, Neil Armstrong on the moon: ". . . for man. One giant leap for man . . ."
SONG: commercial theme for Coca-Cola
1968, announcer: "Robert Kennedy was shot in that ballroom."
SONG: ". . . golden hair"
SONG: whistled theme for *The Andy Griffith Show* TV show
1963, Martin Luther King, Jr.: ". . . God almighty, we are free at last."

Music theme from *The Twilight Zone* TV show
1963, announcer: "A sniper has fired at President Kennedy."
SONG: "Teeny Yellow Polka Dot Bikini"
SONG: "Mr. Postman"
1961, President Kennedy's inauguration: "Ask not what you . . ."
1958: Dean Martin singing "Volare"
1954 (?) Army–McCarthy hearings: "Communist Party or have you ever been a member of the Communist Party?"
1951, General Douglas MacArthur (addressing U.S. Congress): "Old soldiers never die . . ."
SONG: ". . . my lucky . . ."
Lone Ranger shouting "Hi ho Silver" on radio show. Gunshots.
Dance music played by a big band
1942 (?) Edward R. Murrow broadcasting from England (?): "something before never experienced"
December 7, 1941, President Franklin D. Roosevelt: "1941, a date which will live in infamy"
1940 (?): Hitler speech and crowd response
1939 song: "Somewhere over the Rainbow"
1939, radio announcer: "and we continue this evening's final edition of our *Maxwell House Good News of 1939*."
Walter Winchell radio broadcast: "Good evening, Mr. and Mrs. North America and all our ships at sea. Let's go to press."
SONG: "We're in the Money"
ANNOUNCER: "lurks in the hearts of men" from *The Shadow* radio program
Man singing "happy times are here again"
1933, President Roosevelt's inauguration: "The only thing we have to fear is fear itself."
Early instrumental jazz music heard on radio
1920 (?), announcer of an early radio broadcast: "Let us know if this broadcast is reaching you. Please drop us a card."
1900 (?): Morse code (ends at 2 minutes and 7 seconds from beginning of film)
Static (which is a sound effect)
Silence

FILM SOUND: EARLY AND RECENT

Sound has always been a part of film viewing. Even during showings of the first projected short films in the 1890s, music was usually played to cover the sounds of the audiences and projectors and to reinforce mood and support continuity. Later in film history, the theater management also supplied **sound effects**. As is demonstrated repeatedly in *Monty Python and the Holy Grail* (1975), to make sounds like horses' hooves people could beat half co-conut shells against a hard surface or against each other. Large pieces of sandpaper might be rubbed together to sound like a running river; a flexible strip could be stuck into spinning bicycle spokes to simulate the sound of an early airplane engine. Some theaters even had a sound effects machine that included a whistle, bell, horn, chains, drum, and sheet metal. "Silent" films were rarely silent (Figure 4.1).

sound effect: In film, a sound other than spoken words or music.

By the late 1920s, some sound films were shown using the **Vitaphone** system, a large phonograph disc played on a record player that was syn-

FIGURE 4.1 Allefex sound effects machine
This sound effects machine was first marketed in Britain in 1909. Film historian David Robinson writes that the Allefex "was capable of producing upwards of fifty sound effects from storm noises, bird-song, and barking dogs to gun-fire, escaping steam and the rattle of pots and pans" (159). Historian Brian Coe includes a quotation that explains how some of the sounds were made: "The shot of a gun is imitated by striking a drum on the top of the machine, on which a chain mat has been placed. . . . Running water, rain, hail and the sound of rolling waves are obtained by turning a handle, which rotates a ribbed wooden cylinder against a board set at an angle from the top of which hang a number of chains. . . . The puffing of an engine is made by revolving a cylinder with projections against a steel brush. . . . Pendant tubes serve to produce the effects of church bells, fire alarm, ship's bell, and similar noises; the sound of trotting horses is caused by revolving a shaft carrying three tappets which lift up inverted cups . . . ; the cry of the baby is emitted by the dexterous manipulation of plug-hole and bellows" (91–92). *British Film Institute Stills, Posters and Designs*

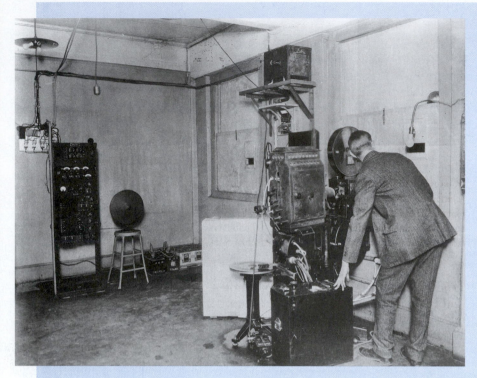

FIGURE 4.2 Vitaphone projection system
In the late 1920s, the Vitaphone system was used in the United States during filming and projecting.

During filming or often after filming, early film sound specialists recorded all the spoken words, sound effects, and music on a large phonographic disc, but they could not later remix. As Walter Murch has explained, "There was no possibility of cutting out the bad bits, because there *was* no way to cut what was being chiseled into the whirling acetate of the Vitaphone discs. It had to be right the first time, or you called 'Cut!' and began again" ("Sound Design" 240).

During projection of a Vitaphone movie, as seen here, the 35 mm projector was synchronized to the attached record player and disc. *The Museum of Modern Art/Film Stills Archive*

chronized with the projector (Figure 4.2). Warner Bros. created a sensation with the Vitaphone system in *The Jazz Singer* (1927), which was basically a silent film with synchronized musical numbers and a little ad-libbed dialogue. In 1928, Warner Bros. used the system in *The Lights of New York*, the first all-dialogue motion picture. There were drawbacks to the Vitaphone system: the records could be played only twenty or so times before they became worn, and it was hard to keep the record always synchronized with the images being projected.

In the same year as *The Lights of New York*, two rival and not entirely compatible sound-on-film systems were used on **feature films**, and the days of Vitaphone were numbered. With a sound-on-film system, the projector displays the image on the screen as it simultaneously converts the optical information in the soundtrack into electrical information. That electrical information is amplified and sent to the theater speakers. (Figure 2.2 on p. 63 illustrates where optical and the later magnetic soundtracks may be located on film.) Since 1928, if theaters have adequate sound equipment, audiences have been able to hear the spoken words, sound effects, music, and silence more or less the way the filmmakers intended. In the late 1920s and early 1930s, such directors as René Clair, Ernst Lubitsch, Rouben Mamoulian, Alfred Hitchcock, and Walt Disney experimented with film sound and dis-

feature (film): A fictional film that is at least 60 minutes long.

covered new uses for it, and in the 1940s and 1950s, Orson Welles, who did some innovative work in radio before turning to filmmaking, did highly original and influential work in film sound, beginning with his first film, *Citizen Kane* (1941).

In recent years, Robert Altman, George Lucas, Walter Murch, and other filmmakers have experimented with film sound and made major advances in its uses. Today film sound specialists can record sound on Digital Audio Tape (DAT) and can also create, store, manipulate, and mix sounds on computers. Many theaters have installed **THX sound**. All have multispeaker sound systems that are vastly superior to the sound systems that were available in the early years of sound cinema. And digital film sound systems—such as Digital Theater Sound (DTS) and Sony Dynamic Digital Sound (SDDS)—bring new levels of clarity, range, and fidelity that are now the standard in movie projection (Figure 4.3). Because of technology

THX sound: A multispeaker sound system developed by Lucasfilm and used in selected movie theaters to improve sound quality.

(b) Sony Dynamic Digital Sound (SDDS)

(a) Digital Theater Sound (DTS)

(d) Dolby Stereo (dual analog tracks)

(c) Dolby Digital Sound (DDS)

FIGURE 4.3 **Digital and analog sound on 35mm films** (larger than actual size)

There are three competing digital sound systems and one analog system.

(a) The Digital Theater Sound (**DTS**) system consists of a timing code that runs the length of the film print, a special optical reader, and a computer that controls one or more compact disc players and discs. The discs, which are the size of a standard CD but are incompatible with CD and DVD players, contain the film's digital soundtrack. Like the 1920s Vitaphone system (see Figure 4.2), DTS uses a separate disc for the soundtrack synchronized with the projector.

(b) The Sony Dynamic Digital Sound (**SDDS**) system includes an identical digital soundtrack on the two edges of the film. (If one strip of digital coding is damaged, the other acts as a backup.) On the projector, the digital sound is decoded with a reader. Unlike the other two digital sound systems, which create six channels of sound, SDDS creates eight.

(c) The Dolby Digital Sound (**DDS**) system consists of digital coding in the spaces between the sprocket holes on one side of the film print, a Dolby Digital reader in or on the projector, and a Dolby Digital Processor. DDS produces six channels of sound: five plus one for low rumbling sounds (often referred to as 5.1).

(d) Also still widely included on film prints is Dolby Stereo, an analog system consisting of two optical audio tracks that create four distinct channels of sound in theaters. Most current movie prints include more than one sound format—for example, one or two of the digital formats plus Dolby Stereo (with Dolby Stereo sometimes functioning as a backup). Because each of the available sound formats—three digital and one analog—uses a different area of the film print, movie prints such as the one seen here from *Saving Private Ryan* (1998) may include all three digital formats and Dolby Stereo. *Amblin Entertainment; DreamWorks SKG; Mark Gordon Productions; Mutual Film; Paramount*

and human creativity, today film sound is more faithful, creative, dynamic, varied, and expressive than ever before.

COMPONENTS OF THE SOUNDTRACK AND THEIR USES

Filmmakers can include spoken words, sound effects, music, and silence in the soundtrack (Table 4.1). Each may be used in the usual manner, but each also may be used in surprising ways. "Dialogue is usually dominant and intellectual, music is usually supportive and emotional, sound effects

TABLE 4.1
Possible Soundtrack Components

SPOKEN WORDS	SOUND EFFECTS	MUSIC	SILENCE
■ **Dialogues and monologues,** including vocals that convey meaning. Example: "Hmmm" = "I don't know," "Let me think about that," or some other meaning depending on context. ■ **Narration** = spoken comments about subjects on screen or off	■ **Sounds made by objects.** Example: a falling tree crashing onto an asphalt pavement ■ **Sounds made by people (other than spoken words).** Example: a person walking on gravel ■ **Ambient sound** = typical, usually unnoticed sounds of a place. Examples: the wind blowing through backyard bushes and indistinct conversations at a party	■ **Instrumental sounds** • Electronic. Examples: Moog synthesizer, computer-generated music • Nonelectronic materials. Examples: wood, plastic, glass, a combination of materials • Electronic and nonelectronic combinations. Example: selective use of the Theremin and elsewhere orchestral music in *The Day the Earth Stood Still* (1951) ■ **Vocals.** Examples: singing, chanting, humming, rhythmic grunting, rhythmic forced laughing, whistling, yodeling, and the throat singing heard in the documentary *Genghis Blues* (1999) ■ **Instrumental sounds and vocal combinations**	Examples: an astronaut tumbling lifelessly through space in *2001: A Space Odyssey* (1968) and a dream in Ingmar Bergman's *Wild Strawberries* (1957) 

are usually information. Their uses, however, are not inflexible. Sometimes dialogue is nonintellectual and aesthetic, sometimes music is **symbolic**, and on occasion sound effects may serve any of those functions. Any of these elements may be dominant or recessive according to the sharpness or softness of the sound and the relationship of the sound to the image" (Murch, "Sound Designer" 298).

In this section of the chapter, we consider some of the choices filmmakers make and the consequences of those choices.

Spoken Words

Most sound films since 1930 include dialogue, monologues, or **narration**. Movies such as *When Harry Met Sally* (1989) have a dense mix of words, and dialogues and monologues cascade and swirl throughout them. These and other films may use overlapping dialogue. Viewers cannot make out all the words, but they hear most of them and sense the busy, chaotic atmosphere that overlapping dialogue can help create. In films using overlapping dialogue, characters speak without being entirely heard by those they speak at, and flash floods of words may suggest the characters' nervousness, isolation, or unconscious attempts to mask their painful situations. Many films directed by Howard Hawks—such as *Bringing Up Baby* (1938) and *His Girl Friday* (1940)—and several films directed by Orson Welles—perhaps most notably *Citizen Kane*, *The Magnificent Ambersons* (1942), and *Touch of Evil* (1958, 1998)—use extensive overlapping dialogue. Films directed by Robert Altman—such as *MASH* (1970), *McCabe and Mrs. Miller* (1971), *California Split* (1974), *Nashville* (1975), *The Player* (1992), *Gosford Park* (2001), and *A Prairie Home Companion* (2006)—also use extensive overlapping dialogue.

Overlapping dialogue may also be used in a brief section of a film, as in *Saving Private Ryan* (1998). At the beginning of one **scene**, many typists are busy typing letters. Soon we viewers begin to hear fragments of letters read by different male voices (presumably the commanding officers). The first voice begins, "Dear Mr. Brian Boyd: No doubt by now you have received full information about the untimely death of your son; however, there are some personal details . . . ," and is overwhelmed and replaced by another male voice reading another fragment of a letter. The voices are always cut off in midsentence. The images of many typists busily typing and the continuous typing sounds and overlapping and interrupted dialogue suggest how many letters had to be sent, how many men were lost in the battles of World War II, and how enormous was the number of families devastated by the loss of their sons, brothers, and husbands.

Often in a theater or in our home viewing environment, we hear film dialogue more distinctly than we could in a similar situation in real life (another movie **convention**). Usually dialogue in movies is louder and more distinct than it would be in actuality. At the beginning of a shot 6½ minutes into Woody Allen's *Manhattan* (1979), two male characters are

symbol: Anything perceptible that has meaning beyond its usual meaning or function.

scene: A section of a narrative that gives the impression of continuous action taking place in continuous time and space.

convention: A subject or technique that makers of texts and audiences accept as natural or typical in certain contexts.

seen perhaps 50 feet in the background ambling toward the camera as they talk. For more than 30 seconds, as they approach the camera, the volume of their dialogue remains essentially the same. In a comparable situation outside the movies, someone watching them at that distance could not initially hear them so clearly (and without at least occasional extraneous distracting city noises), nor would the volume of their talk remain largely unchanged as they approach so closely.

Spoken words may also be deliberately distorted in movies to portray a character's confusion. In several scenes in *Nick of Time* (1995), what is being said to the main character is distorted. The effect is analogous to a visual **point-of-view shot**: viewers hear the same speech and other sounds as the distracted character presumably does.

point-of-view shot: Camera placement at the approximate position of a character or person (or occasionally some other creature) that gives a view similar to what that subject would see.

Dialogue is invaluable for revealing a character's ideas, goals, and dreams, though often it does so more concisely, obliquely, and revealingly than conversation in life. Consider the following dialogue from *Betrayal* (1983). Robert and his wife, Emma, are on holiday. Robert has discovered a letter at the American Express office addressed to Emma, and he recognizes the handwriting as that of his friend, Jerry. The next day Robert tells Emma there was a letter for her at American Express. After a while, she says that she got it and it was from Jerry. Shortly after that, their dialogue in the film runs as follows:

> ROBERT: What do you think of Jerry as a letter writer? [pause] You're trembling. Are you cold?
>
> EMMA: No.
>
> ROBERT: He used to write to me at one time. Long letters about Ford Madox Ford. I used to write to him, too, come to think of it. Long letters about, ooh, W. B. Yeats, I suppose. That was the time when we were both editors of poetry magazines. Him at Cambridge, me at Oxford. Did you know that? We were bright young men and close friends. Well, we still are close friends. All that was long before I met you. Long before he met you. I've been trying to remember when I introduced him to you. I simply can't remember. I take it I did introduce him to you. Yes. But when? Can you remember?
>
> EMMA: No.
>
> ROBERT: You can't?
>
> EMMA: No.
>
> ROBERT: How odd. [pause] He wasn't best man at our wedding, was he?
>
> EMMA: You know he was.
>
> ROBERT: Aah, yes. Well, that's probably when I introduced him to you. [pause] Was there any message for me in his letter? [pause] I mean in the line of business. To do with the world of publishing. Has he discovered any new and original talent? He's quite talented at uncovering talent, ole Jerry.
>
> EMMA: [pause] No message.
>
> ROBERT: No message? [pause] Not even his love?
>
> EMMA: [pause] We're lovers.
>
> ROBERT: Ah, yes. I thought it might be something like that, something along those lines. . . .

This passage reveals writer Harold Pinter's skill in creating characters that say one thing when they feel and think something else. In this passage, Robert also does not say directly what is important to him. Evidently he suspects his wife has been unfaithful, but he does not come right out and say so. Part of the time, he feigns forgetfulness: "He wasn't best man at our wedding, was he?" Part of the time, Robert muses about the past and brings up the points that Jerry is an old and dear friend, that he has known Jerry in fact longer than he has known Emma, that he introduced Jerry and Emma, and that Jerry was best man in their wedding.

By not coming right out and saying what he fears, Robert is able to hold Emma in painful suspense about whether he suspects her affair. Like many other Pinter characters, Robert knows when to pause for effect. Often he asks a difficult question and pauses; Emma doesn't reply, so Robert continues. Emma is soon put on the defensive. She gives short answers (less chance of a slipup there). Reread all of Emma's responses. None is longer than four words! Toward the end of this exchange, she pauses before she replies, admitting, "We're lovers." Perhaps she thinks that Robert will now at least stop his cat and mouse game.

After Robert hears Emma's admission, he again does not say what is bothering him, how painful for him Emma's words are: "Ah, yes. I thought it might be something like that, something along those lines." Elsewhere in the film, we see how painful his wife's affair is for Robert, but he never comes out and says so directly. Like most believable characters (and most people, for that matter), Robert often says one thing when he means another. And he never comes right out and says what is most important to him. We viewers must watch, listen, and figure that out for ourselves—and by doing so, we stay involved with the characters.

Sometimes word choices and accents provide clues about a character's background: country or region of origin, ethnic group, social class, occupation. Tone, volume, speed, and rhythm of speech also reveal what a character is like. So infinitely expressive is the human voice that the words "You had better go" can be threatening, pleading, sad, indifferent, questioning, **ironic**, amusing, matter-of-fact, or something else. Perhaps second only to an expressive face, a flexible voice can convey countless meanings and unlimited shades of emotion.

Many movies, however, use limited or no spoken words because given the **settings** or goals of the film, few or none are needed. In *Quest for Fire* (1981), which is set eighty thousand years ago, the hominids use an assortment of grunts, pants, screams, and so forth, but the film has no intelligible dialogue, only imaginary prehistoric languages that are not translated and are only vaguely understandable. The first and fourth parts of *2001: A Space Odyssey* (1968) are without intelligible dialogue, and only 43 of the film's 141 minutes contain dialogue. Other feature films employing little dialogue are *Blood Wedding* (1981)—which consists of backstage preparations, a brief warm-up session, and a flamenco version of most of Federico

setting: The place where the events of a narrative occur.

Garcia Lorca's famous play of the same title—and *Sidewalk Stories* (1989), which has no dialogue during its 97 minutes except for a few lines near the end that are not integral to the story. Some short films use little dialogue; other short films that could use dialogue use none. The films' images, music, and perhaps sound effects convey story, meanings, and moods. The short French film "The String Bean" (1962) uses no spoken words, and they are used only occasionally and briefly in another classic French film, "The Red Balloon" (1955).

Often films begin with music and no words: the opening scenes reveal the setting, major character(s), and mood without the help of the human voice. Many movie scenes with sound forgo the use of the human voice, and many movies use dialogue less than half the time. As scriptwriting books and scriptwriting teachers typically advocate, many filmmakers use dialogue only to reveal important information that cannot be conveyed visually.

Sound Effects

> Almost all the really great sounds that you hear in movies are recordings of real things made with microphones in the real world, and we're constantly looking for new things to record. (Thom)

Sound effects specialists tend to use sound effects highly selectively. In life we hear but usually ignore insignificant and potentially distracting sounds, such as an airplane overhead, a beeping watch, or a ringing cell phone. In cinema, such sounds are usually omitted from a soundtrack, and the sound effects that are included tend to be inconspicuous because they are usually played at low volume and often along with music or dialogue or both.

location: Any place other than a film studio that is used for filming.

Sound effects are often used to help create a sense of a **location**, and they can make a place seem more lifelike than it is (Figure 4.4). Sound effects can also make viewers feel more involved. In the popular German film *Das Boot*, or *The Boat* (1981; expanded and reissued with eight-channel digital sound in 1997), when the German submarine is trying to evade detection deep below the surface, viewers hear sheet metal groaning and bolts popping from pressure they were not designed to withstand.

Effects are often used to intensify a mood. Sometimes a sound effect, such as a beating heart, intensifies the mood of the moment even though we wouldn't hear such a sound outside the movies—yet another movie convention. Throughout most of *The Blair Witch Project* (1999), strange, unidentifiable sounds emanating from the dark woods contribute to the tension in the characters lost in the woods and in the viewers ensconced in the dark theater. In the theater or out, a sound from an unknown source—in the basement, in the attic, outside the window, under the bed—may frighten us. We are rattled by the unknown, so films often use sound from

FIGURE 4.4 Sound used to fill out a set
In *Citizen Kane* (1941), sound sometimes adds to the verisimilitude of a set. The budget for the film was limited, and the set shown here was flimsy and incomplete. The elaborate windows above Kane are painted, and the back wall on the left is largely in the dark. The set alone could not have nurtured the right sounds for the scene, but the reverberations in the soundtrack help mightily to convey the size, emptiness, and sterility of Kane's and Susan's lives in their huge Florida retreat. *RKO General Pictures, Mercury Productions; Warner Home Video DVD*

beyond the lighted **frame**, in the darkness. Even if we know the source of the sound, such as a tree limb brushing against a window, hearing a sound and not seeing its source leaves much to the imagination. We have paid to be emotionally involved, and filmmakers try to oblige us.

Another example of sound effects used to support a mood comes from *The Godfather* (1972). After Michael prevents an attack on his hospitalized father, a corrupt police captain and his men arrive at the hospital entrance. During the men's arrival and their confrontation with Michael, we viewers hear thunder three times: first as Michael pushes another man away and as police officers grab Michael, second as the police captain gets out of his car and approaches Michael, and third as we see the police captain's reaction after slugging Michael. We hear this thunder, though we may not much notice it, as we see the police in action. The thunder underscores the power of the police, especially the captain. In many other films, thunder often accompanies danger and violence and can be almost a cliché.

Sound effects are often used to enhance humorous or light moments. Early in Jacques Tati's *Mr. Hulot's Holiday* (1953), the sputtering and backfiring as Hulot drives his shaky, 30-year-old car, which is not much bigger than an elongated bathtub, are amusing in themselves, and the scenes in which they appear are funnier because of them. Sound effects from an unexpected source can create a humorous effect. In *Bowfinger* (1999), as the Eddie Murphy character is walking in a darkened parking garage, he hears the sounds of a woman's high heel shoes. Because he cannot see the source for the sound, he is puzzled and concerned. Soon viewers see the source: high heels on a dog's front paws.

Sound effects can be used just as effectively to intensify a sad or melancholy occasion. In the last shot of a **documentary film** about a much-admired Italian actor, *Marcello Mastroianni . . . I Remember* (1999), Mastroianni, who died before the film was released, is off to one side of the frame, concluding his comments about the brevity of life while looking off-frame; then the sound of wind is heard before the final fade-out and continues into the end credits. The suggestion is of desolation, loneliness, and perhaps cold and death.

Sound effects can, in fact, be used to create or enhance any situation, including suspense and surprise. A famous example occurs about 44 minutes into the 1942 *Cat People*. Alice is walking home at night in a deserted part of town and fears that she is being stalked by a woman who the film has hinted transforms into an aggressive panther when she experiences strong emotions. Initially, we see and hear both Alice and the woman who might be following her; then we see and hear only Alice, who grows apprehensive, stops, and looks back. For a split second, the beginning of a large cat's low growl is heard and is immediately followed by the loud, startling sound of air brakes as a city bus abruptly pulls to a stop between Alice and the camera. But perhaps some viewers hear the beginning of a large cat's low growl because previous scenes have hinted that panthers have some special powers.

Another use of sound effects is to conceal an action. About 68 minutes into *Chinatown* (1974), Jake, the detective, goes to the hall of records to investigate recent land sales. After he finds the page he wants, he lines up a ruler against the page and coughs loudly as he rips out part of the page. When Jake coughs, the clerk looks up but does not hear the ripping sound and resumes his work. A character also uses sound to conceal his action nearly two hours into *The Shawshank Redemption* (1994). As the main character attempts to break out of prison during a storm, he uses a large stone or piece of concrete to hit a sewer pipe, hoping to rupture it. To mask the noise he makes and thus his action, he hits the pipe only during the thunder.

Another example of filmmakers using one sound to mask another occurs in *On the Waterfront* (1954). The Marlon Brando character (Terry) unwittingly contributed to the murder of the brother of the woman Terry later becomes attracted to. Some 63 minutes into the film, in front of an industrialized riverfront, Terry finally tries to explain to her that he did not realize what the murderers had intended to do, but most of his anguished explanation is drowned out by a loud steam whistle. Viewers already know about his situation anyway and need not hear what he says here; instead, they can more readily concentrate on the two characters' extremely expressive faces.

Like light and shadow, sound effects often add to a film in significant yet inconspicuous ways. In many of the examples discussed above—such as the timely confluence of thunder and police in *The Godfather* and the amusing sound of the sputtering old car in *Mr. Hulot's Holiday*—the effects are not true to life. Only occasionally, however, are the effects so untrue to life as to draw attention to themselves, especially during a first or even second listening.

Sound effects specialists use sound sources that viewers are only very rarely aware of. Frank Serafine has said that in the 1983 TV movie *The Day After* he created the sound of a nuclear explosion by blending animal screams that had been processed so that viewers could not recognize the sources. In a June 27, 2005, interview on NPR, sound specialist Randy Thom said that for the walking sounds of the four-legged robotic Imperial walkers in *Star Wars: Episode V—The Empire Strikes Back* (1980), he used the sounds of a special blade cutting giant thick rolls of sheet metal. Ironically, sounds that are faithful to their sources sometimes do not seem "real," so moviemakers substitute or add sounds, sometimes provided by a **Foley artist**, a person who creates and records sound effects as he or she watches the action in the film projected on a screen (Figure 4.5). The sounds of footsteps on snow that were recorded during filming may not sound right, so a Foley artist may use instead the sound of walking on cornstarch. To simulate the sounds of walking in grass, a Foley artist may take audiotape from a cassette, crumple it, then walk on it in synchronization with the film's action. For the sounds of insects in the animated film *A Bug's Life*

a) b)

FIGURE 4.5 A Foley studio and a Foley artist at work
(a) Part of a Foley studio with some of the objects used for making various sounds. (b) Foley artist about to break a bottle in synchronization with the image being projected from the glassed-in projection room behind him onto the screen before him. During the process someone else records the sound for later inclusion in the film's soundtrack. *Brian Vancho, Foley artist; Sound One Corp., New York*

FIGURE 4.6 Recording sounds in nature
In *Blow Out* (1981), the John Travolta character is a sound specialist who records and mixes sounds for the soundtracks of low-budget movies. This publicity still shows him using headphones, a microphone wand, and (offscreen) a reel-to-reel magnetic tape recorder to record sounds of the night. *Filmways Pictures, Cinema 77, and Viscount Associates*

(1998), the sound engineer mixed such sounds as the cracking open of uncooked crabs and various World War II bombers in flight (Rydstrom).

A sound specialist may speed up or slow down the original recorded sound in digital format. At least as early as 1938, sounds were played backward to create new sounds. In that year Loren L. Ryder—the eventual winner of six Academy Awards in sound—recorded a pig's squeal and played it backward as the sound of an ice avalanche. Similarly, a suction sound may be made by running the sound of an explosion backward.

Sound effects may be recorded during filming, added later from a library of sound clips, or recorded separately on location for later use (Figure 4.6). Often sound effects are composite effects, made by combining simpler sounds (many of which might already have been modified themselves). For the sounds of the giant creature's "voice" in *Godzilla* (1998), six sound specialists worked on blending sounds from a rare two-CD set of Godzilla sound effects plus metal grinding and metal stressing sounds and modified animal cries (of bears, walruses, sea elephants, and a hawk) ("Making Godzilla Roar").

Sometimes synthetic sounds are created and blended. Other times, especially in action movies, animal sounds—such as a monkey screaming, a pig squealing, a lion roaring, or an elephant trumpeting—are distorted or used as is and blended with other sounds because many sound experts believe that animal sounds or variations of them can affect listeners more powerfully than human-made sounds. *Top Gun* (1986) includes many sounds of jet airplanes, but the recording of their sounds could not capture the excitement of the original noise, so animal sounds and human screams were blended in (Hall). In this and other uses of sound, the effect is usually subliminal: viewers are unaware of why they respond as they do.

Music

Just how crucial music can be to a movie's dramatic texture was illustrated by an exercise [the lyricist] Mrs. [Marilyn] Bergman devised in which [the film composers] Mr. [Henry] Mancini, Mr. [Mark] Isham and Mr. [Dick] Hyman each provided music for the same 19-second film clip. The seemingly innocuous little scene shows a woman walking into a darkened house at the end of the day, turning on a light, mounting the stairs, entering a bathroom and starting to brush her teeth.

Mrs. Bergman gave each of the composers a different scenario to musicalize. Mr. Hyman was told that the woman comes home to a house that is blissfully empty and quiet now that her husband and his two children from a previous marriage have finally left. Mr. Mancini was told that she is coming home to the house that she shared with a husband who had walked out on her. Mr. Isham's instructions explained that the woman is unaware of something the audience knows—that there is probably an intruder waiting for her.

While the scene was replayed, Mr. Hyman and Mr. Mancini each conducted a small orchestra on the stage. Mr. Isham played an electronic fragment written at home. In all cases, the clip came alive. Mr. Hyman's jaunty tongue-in-cheek music expressed quiet comic relief, Mr. Mancini's was wistfully romantic, Mr. Isham's tinglingly suspenseful.   — Stephen Holden

As is suggested above, music can serve countless functions and strongly affect a scene's moods and meanings. Music may, for example, mirror a film's central conflict while intensifying it, as in *The Omen* (1976). The movie shows what happens as Robert and Kathy come to realize that their son, Damien, is the son of the devil. For the movie, Jerry Goldsmith created two types of music, which I call *demonic music* and *Kathy and Robert's music*. The demonic music is sometimes dissonant and electronic but more often is conveyed by many low male voices accompanied by relentless and pronounced rhythms. In contrast, Kathy and Robert's music is much more melodic and more varied to fit different moods. It is usually played on a piano or stringed instruments. Unlike the demonic music, Kathy and Robert's music is never loud and threatening, never persistently rhythmical, and never electronic. As Kathy and Robert's prospects grow more gloomy, though, their motif is played briefly and in minor keys: it's still beautiful but sadder and less prominent. Throughout the film, the two kinds of music war with each other, mirroring the film's evil versus good conflict. Sometimes they battle within the same scene. By the end of the film, the demonic music triumphs over Kathy and Robert's music—within the scene and in the film as a whole—just as Damien and evil triumph over Kathy and Robert and those who have tried to help them.[1]

An example of two basic types of music being used to highlight the differences but not conflict between two aspects of a film can be seen in *Tim Burton's Corpse Bride* (2005). It is difficult to generalize about all the varied music of the two different worlds of the film. By turns, the music of the world of the living may be subdued, threatening, or amusing. And that music suggests or reinforces yet other moods, but never pleasure or happiness. In Burton's film, the world of the living is a pretty dreary place. The music in the land of the dead is also varied but never dreary, and it is

---

[1]The Special Edition of the DVD for *The Omen* includes a bonus feature in which composer Jerry Goldsmith discusses four parts of his film score and corresponding excerpts from the finished film are shown. Another example of the use of two competing types of music to reinforce the film's central conflict is Quincy Jones's score for *The Pawnbroker* (1965), the making of which is described by the film's director, Sidney Lumet, in his book *Making Movies* (175–77).

sometimes happy, playful, and lively, as in the scenes accompanied by jazzy 1930s music.

As in *The Omen*, a musical motif may be played in different ways at different times to help convey something about a character. In *Citizen Kane*, Bernard Herrmann's music suggests how Kane feels at the six times his own song is heard. The first time it is played, Kane is near the height of his power and happiness. He has recently bought the staff of a rival newspaper, and a party has been arranged to celebrate the occasion. During the party, a band plays Kane's song loudly, briskly, and in a major key. After his affair with a young woman becomes known and he loses the election for governor, his song is played softly, slowly, and in a minor key. It is so subdued that many viewers do not notice it, though it adds to the melancholy of the scene. (The visuals of these two scenes also reinforce this contrast. At the party, the screen is alive with movement. The scene after the election defeat contains only two people: Leland and a man who is sweeping the sidewalk outside Kane's election headquarters, and their movements are lethargic, as if Leland and the worker were sapped of energy and hope.) Herrmann uses a similar strategy for his music for the breakfasts montage from *Citizen Kane* (approximately 52 minutes into the film). He begins with a romantic waltz that was heard about 4 minutes earlier in the film and follows it with increasingly unromantic variations for each of the montage's scenes.

Film music can help establish the place or time period of a story. In *Tom Jones* (1963), the lively harpsichord music helps establish the time of the narrative because the harpsichord was popular in the eighteenth century. In many movies, such as *American Graffiti* (1973), *Stand by Me* (1986), and *The Ice Storm* (1997), popular music helps establish when the story takes place.

Often music suggests what a character feels. In *My Life as a Dog* (1985), as a girl plays a recorder with other students in front of a class, she sees another girl pass a note to the boy they both like and unintentionally starts playing badly. In the first scene of *The Purple Rose of Cairo* (1984), a young woman looks at a poster for a romantic adventure movie as viewers hear the famous movie dancer Fred Astaire singing. The woman's expression and the music show that she is lost in romantic thoughts, until her daydreaming and the music are abruptly cut off by the sound of a letter from the marquee crashing onto the sidewalk behind her. As in many films, music and an expressive face convey emotional nuances that words cannot.

Changing musical motifs can reinforce the changing moods of a situation. In a confrontation that begins approximately 132 minutes into *West Side Story* (1961), the mood changes from unfriendliness and taunting, to emotional and physical harassment, and then to the threat of a rape. After the Puerto Rican Anita enters Doc's store and Jets gang members confront her, one of the young men whistles part of "La Cucaracha," which means "the cockroach." Soon the same mambo played earlier at the dance is heard playing on the jukebox, and the Jets begin to taunt Anita and call her names. As the situation turns even uglier, "America," a song-and-dance number heard earlier in the film, begins. (In the earlier version of the song, which begins a little more than 49 minutes into the film, Anita and five other Puerto Rican women sing about the merits of life in America and the limitations of life in Puerto Rico, and six Puerto Rican men sing about the limitations of life in America and the merits of life in Puerto Rico.) As the ethnically hateful treatment of Anita continues, off and on, one can hear the "America" music in the background, an ironic reminder of Anita's advocacy of American life (Figure 4.7). As two Jets pick up a third Jet and move to place him on top of Anita, who has been pushed to the floor, the same three chords are played repeatedly, as if to suggest the rape that presumably is about to occur. When Doc shouts "stop," the action and music cease simultaneously.

Another example of music played different ways at different times to reveal a character or situation occurs in *The War of the Roses* (1989). The song "Only You" is heard three times. The first time we hear it, Barbara Rose is watching and listening to the song on TV. The song is undistorted, but it is accompanied by her husband's snoring. Love has flown. Later in the scene, Barbara tells Oliver, her husband, she wants a divorce. The second playing occurs after Barbara has led Oliver to believe that she has killed his beloved dog and used it to make the pâté that Oliver has been savoring. In a fury, Oliver spits out the remaining pâté, overturns the table, and chases Barbara up the stairs. As he grabs at her and she kicks him down the stairs, "Only You" is played briefly, faintly, and in a minor key, accompanied by a sustained bass note (pedal point). The song is distorted and used ironically: it accompanies Oliver's attempts to hurt Barbara and her forceful rejection of him. The song is an appropriate choice because Oliver is obsessed with Barbara and wants only her, although she has declared she wants out of the marriage. The third time we hear the song, a drunken Oliver sings the first three notes as he tries to accompany himself with the musical notes he

FIGURE 4.7 Musical motifs reinforcing the changing moods of a situation
In a scene late in *West Side Story* (1961), various musical motifs, some of them used earlier in the film, are used to support the changing moods of the scene. As the disrespectful treatment of the Puerto Rican Anita grows more threatening, a gang member holds her sash before her as if she were a bull and he a matador. As a running comment on much of this scene, off and on in the background can be heard the song "America." *Mirisch Corp., Beta Productions, Seven Arts Productions; Special Edition MGM DVD*

FIGURE 4.8 Music to express a changed situation
The Michael Douglas character uses a collection of partially full wineglasses to "play" part of "Only You" to his estranged wife in *The War of the Roses* (1989). "Only You" is heard three times in the film, each time more discordant than the last. *Publicity still. Gracie Films, 20th Century Fox*

makes by dipping a finger in wine and running it along the rims of partially full wineglasses (Figure 4.8). Again, how the music is played is appropriate. Oliver's mood is no longer loving, and he's no longer entirely in control of himself, so the song is crudely rendered: he sings somewhat drunkenly and off-key, and the wineglass notes are only crude approximations.

Sometimes a musical motif is associated with a character or group of characters, and the music is played the same way every time it accompanies the character or group. In *The Seven Samurai* (1954), the samurai who is an outsider has his own (jazzy) melody, and the other six samurai have their own group melody.

Music is often used to intensify an emotional effect. In *Jaws* (1975), a relentless, strongly rhythmical, and accelerating bass melody accompanies the shark attack on a boy. As the shark approaches its victim, the music is played more loudly and more quickly, suggesting the shark's power and acceleration. Once viewers have heard the shark theme and associated it with the shark, the mere melody sets their nerves on edge because music and viewers' imaginations can be a powerful combination.

Filmmakers sometimes use music—knowingly or not—to distract viewers from a weak part of the script or to enhance a performance. *The Omen* illustrates both uses. Certain details about the film's **plot** may trouble viewers, but the music is so effective it helps involve viewers and keep them from dwelling on narrative weaknesses. Though the acting in *The Omen* is generally convincing, as in many films the music enhances the performances. Billie Whitelaw is entirely credible as the frightening, evil governess, but she is often accompanied by a fiendishly able assistant: the demonic music. Gregory Peck is also well cast and is convincing, but in the scene where he learns of his wife's death, he is convincing only up to a point. As Peck buries his head in his hands in grief, the slow, melancholy strings and woodwinds increase in volume and build on the emotion he began.

In other films, the music is not as integral as in *The Omen*. Inappropriate or intrusive music can distract viewers—and insult them and the actors. As film composer Thomas Newman said, "I just don't want the actors to be angry with me. They've put all this work into the scene, come up with all these subtle moves and gestures to communicate what they're trying to get across, so the last thing they want is that the music just explodes all over the place. How insulting is that to the actors? It's like you're saying to the audience, 'You're not sure what they're doing? Okay, let me tell you what they're doing!'" (Edwards). Films may also use music to disguise shortcomings.

Film music may reference earlier film music. Like visuals, music may be used **intertextually**—for example, to repeat earlier music or to make a joke. Sometimes, the music is the same as in an earlier film. Beginning approximately 74 minutes into the documentary *Wild Man Blues* (1997), viewers hear music before and after a Woody Allen press conference in Italy that was originally used in the press conference scene 122 minutes into Italian director Federico Fellini's *8½* (1963). Sixty-nine minutes into *Zoolander* (2001), the music of Richard Strauss helps create a brief parody of part of *2001: A Space Odyssey*. Elsewhere, the music being referenced is not from the original film but approximates it closely enough that viewers can recognize the reference. Seventy-two minutes into *Zoolander*, the music evokes Nino Rota's music in the corresponding part of *The Godfather Part II* (1974). Here, as in other movies, for copyright, budgetary, or artistic reasons, the original music was not used but is strongly suggested. Similarly, in the animated film *Jonah: A Veggie Tales Movie* (2002), after Jonah has been forced to walk the plank and is floating some distance from the ship, we hear music reminiscent of the famous prowling shark motif in *Jaws*. The music suggests that Jonah will soon be attacked from below. He is. By the whale.

> **intertextuality**: The relation of one text (such as a film) to another text or texts (such as a play or another film).

More than ever, movies help sell recorded music. *Evita* (1996), *Buena Vista Social Club* (1999), and *O Brother, Where Art Thou?* (2000) are examples of movies that helped make their music into huge successes. In turn, the music sales and music videos—sometimes with clips from the films—created more interest in the movies. As never before, movies have a symbiotic relationship with CDs and MP3 downloads. The fame of the composer or performer may also be a factor in selecting music for a movie. Names such as Elton John, Whitney Houston, and Jennifer Lopez generate interest not only in the movie but also in future music sales. In some movies, the music may be emphasized so that another division of the corporate conglomerate that made the film can sell CDs based on it.

At its most effective, music—which draws from the same creative well as poetry—helps elicit feelings and moods that are difficult or impossible to explain in words. As Irwin Edman has written:

> But just because music cannot be specific it can render with voluminousness and depths the general atmosphere or aura of emotion. It can suggest love, though no love in particular; worship or despair, though it does not say who is worshiped or what is the cause of the despair. Into the same music, therefore, a hundred different listeners will pour their own specific histories and desires. . . .

Words are too brittle and chiseled, life too rigid and conventional to exhaust all the infinity of human emotional response. The infinite sinuousness, nuance, and complexity of music enable it to speak in a thousand different accents to a thousand different listeners, and to say with noncommittal and moving intimacy what no language would acknowledge or express and what no situations in life could completely exhaust or make possible. (116–17)[2]

Silence

Although they rarely do, filmmakers may use silence realistically. In *2001*, some scenes in outer space are aptly silent because space lacks air to carry sound waves. In the opening battle scenes of *Saving Private Ryan*, silence can plausibly indicate the loss of hearing due to injury and perhaps the nightmarish quality of intense, deadly warfare. Then, too, soldiers hitting the beaches of Normandy might not notice or hear the sounds if they are so intent on *seeing* the deadly dangers in front of them. Silence may also be used more symbolically.

From time to time, silence has been employed during unpleasant dream scenes in sound films, as in Bergman's *Wild Strawberries* (1957) and Hallström's *My Life as a Dog*. The effect is unsettling and, if prolonged, can be distancing.

Filmmakers have often used silence to suggest dying or death. In *2001*, as astronaut Frank Poole goes outside the spaceship, we hear Poole's breathing and the hiss of pressurized air. After the space pod has presumably cut Poole's air tube, all sounds stop as Poole struggles with his air tube and tumbles lifelessly through space. These deadly silent scenes outside the spacecraft are alternated with scenes containing **ambient sound** as the other astronaut, Dave Bowman, tries to help. Later when Bowman explodes the pod door of the spacecraft and is catapulted into the vacuum of the emergency air lock, at first we hear nothing. Then he pulls a switch that starts to close the spaceship's outer door and send air surging into the entry chamber, returning him and us listeners to the normal world of glorious and in this case life-affirming sound. Silence can also be used to underscore the profound difference between life and death. One section of the documentary film *Titicut Follies* (1967) cuts back and forth between an asylum inmate being force-fed and shots of his body being prepared for display before burial.

ambient sound: Unobtrusive background sound that people tend not to notice.

---

[2]Some listening exercises can help the viewer gain a greater appreciation of the powers of effective film music. Here are two exercises I have used in class: Watch a powerful scene, such as the last scene of *Citizen Kane*, with the soundtrack turned down so low that you cannot hear any of it. Watch the scene again with the soundtrack set at its normal level. You may want to then close your eyes and just listen to the soundtrack for the scene. Here's another way to study the contributions of film music: Choose a DVD that includes a music-only option—such as *North by Northwest* (1959), *Amadeus* (1984), or *Tim Burton's Corpse Bride*. Next, watch the movie or a large part of it with the music-only option, and notice what the music adds to the scenes in which it is used.

The shots of his being force-fed include the usual sounds; the shots of his corpse are silent. A similar use of silence occurs in *The Body Snatcher* (1945). A singing woman walks into the darkness in the background of the frame and is followed by a slow-moving horse-drawn carriage. For 8 to 10 seconds after the woman and carriage disappear into the darkness, her voice remains strong and clear; then her singing stops abruptly in midsong. The rest is silence. The suggestion created by the interruption of the sound—and the engulfing darkness of much of the frame—is that she has been murdered.

As with any other technique, silence can be used in countless creative ways in countless contexts. Sometimes silence can be effective when words would be inadequate. A long silence occurs near the end of the Japanese film *Shall We Dance?* (1996) as the dance instructor slowly approaches her former student to ask him to dance before a large group. At that moment, emotion is best served by silence.

More generally, silence can function as a pause might in music or poetry: as a break in the natural rhythm of life, a change that can be unsettling and make us eager, even nervous, to return to the sounds of life.

For an illustration of how the different components of a soundtrack can function within a movie, see the two Close-Up sections on pp. 184–88.

ADDITIONAL USES OF SOUND

As this chapter has suggested, spoken words, sound effects, music, and silence may be used in countless creative ways within a film. Sound may also be used as a transition to foster continuity or promote discontinuity. In narrative films, sound may be used from an on-screen source or offscreen, as part of the story or not.

Transitions

One way sound designers direct viewer attention and promote continuity or discontinuity is by the type of sound transition they use between shots. Sound may be used to connect shots in many ways.

Often the sound ends with the visuals of one shot and is replaced by new sound at the beginning of the next shot. The sound ending one shot may be similar to the sound beginning the next shot (if so, this transition is comparable to a visual **match cut**). Sometimes the sound of the first shot is quite unlike the sound beginning the next shot (something like a **jump cut**) (Figure 4.9).

A **sound dissolve** is the sound equivalent of a visual lap dissolve (see Figure 3.7 on p. 123). In a sound dissolve the first sound begins to fade out as the next sound fades in and overlaps the first sound before replacing it (Figure 4.10). Sound dissolves may be used to shift sound and mood gradually from one shot to the next and to promote continuity. Continuity may

jump cut: A transition between shots that causes a jarring shift in space, time, or action.

also be promoted when the same sound is used in two consecutive shots (Figure 4.11). Sometimes the same sound is used to connect three or more shots (Figure 4.12). If only music is used as a transition between scenes, the transition is often called a **bridge**. On rare occasions, continuity is supported when the sound from the following shot occurs at the ending of the preceding shot (Figure 4.13).

Depending on their similarity or difference, the sounds between shots contribute to continuity or disruption. Usually, in **classical Hollywood cinema** the new sound with the new shot is different but not noticeably so, and continuity is supported. Nonetheless, as with the editing of images, occasionally a discontinuous transition is used to surprise, amuse, or confuse viewers, as in the cockatoo example from *Citizen Kane* (see caption for Figure 4.9).

classical Hollywood cinema: Films that show one or more characters facing a succession of problems while trying to reach their goals and that tend to use unobtrusive filmmaking techniques.

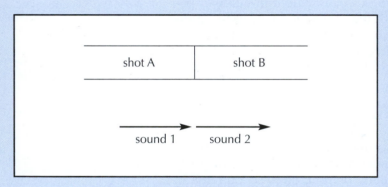

FIGURE 4.9 Sound ends with a shot; then a new shot and new sound begin

A frequent sound transition between shots is for the first shot and its accompanying sound to end and a new shot and its new sound to begin. This transition can promote continuity between shots or discontinuity.

If the sound of the first shot is even vaguely like the sound in the following shot, the transition seems continuous. An example of a similar, linking sound occurs in *Local Hero* (1983). A shot at an office ends with a woman office worker responding to the main character's request for a date: she simply says, "No." The next shot, in the main character's apartment, begins with him on the phone saying, "No, it's not. It's Mac." Although the speaker and tone of voice are different, the linking word *no* is the same.

If the sound of the earlier shot does not match the sound of the next shot, the transition is discontinuous, even startling. One shot late in *Citizen Kane* ends with the butler saying that he knew how to handle Kane, "like that time his wife left him." The next shot begins with a cockatoo shrieking and flying away. The result of this sound transition: surprise and discontinuity.

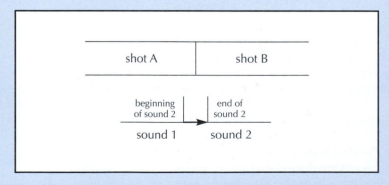

FIGURE 4.10 A sound dissolve

At the end of *Betrayal* (1983), a man and woman are about to begin an affair. As the man takes the woman's hand, the party music begins to fade out as melancholy music gets louder, momentarily coexists with the party music, replaces it, and finally becomes louder still. In this example, the sound dissolves gradually shift the mood from festive to subdued.

FIGURE 4.11 The sound from one shot continues into the next shot
Fairly often, the sound from the ending of one shot carries over, perhaps diminished in volume, into the following shot. In *Schindler's List* (1993), an outdoor shot shows a girl shouting "Goodbye Jews!" In the next shot, which takes place inside a well-furnished residence that Schindler is taking over from a Jewish family, the girl's same taunts can be heard three times at lower volume.

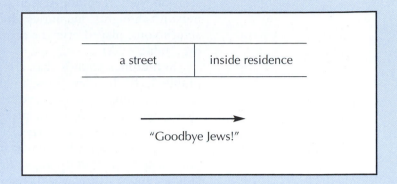

FIGURE 4.12 A sound used to connect multiple shots
Often a sound continues from one shot into the following shots. Approximately 69 minutes into the classic western *High Noon* (1952), the town marshal is in his office writing his will because he has learned that the noon train is bringing a man planning to join three others to kill him. Immediately after the clock shows that it is noon, we see a shot of a chair, and near the end of that shot a train whistles abruptly and loudly with only two slight interruptions until the beginning of the seventh shot/scene (of the marshal's face); then the sound fades out quickly.

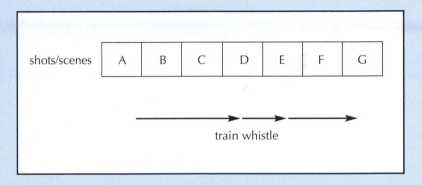

FIGURE 4.13 The sound for the second shot begins before the shot does
As a shot nears its conclusion, viewers may hear the sound from the following shot before they see its visuals. Early in *The War of the Roses* (1989), the sounds of rain, thunder, and wind can be heard. The wind sounds continue loudly during a brief visual fade-out, fade-in. In the next shot, which takes place in a different setting, it is a stormy day, and the sounds of rain and thunder can still be heard.

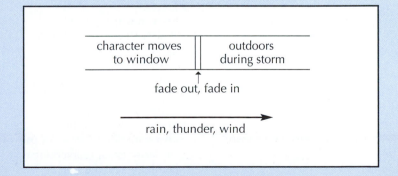

General Uses of Sound in Narrative Films

Table 4.2 illustrates sources and some possible functions of sound for narrative films. In most films, spoken words, occasional sound effects, and music that someone hums, whistles, sings, or plays all come from sources seen on the screen. On-screen sound in narrative films can also include a person's thoughts, memories, dreams, or fantasies, conveyed by the character's voice played over the action while the person is not directly speaking (Table 4.2A).

Sometimes sounds that are part of the story come from **offscreen** (Table 4.2B). In a few films, a **narrator** who is also a character in the film says something about a scene he or she is not in, as in *Double Indemnity* (1944) and *Citizen Kane*, or makes a few introductory comments in some scenes, as in *Menace II Society* (1993) and *The Virgin Suicides* (1999). A particularly imaginative use of narration occurs in the soundtrack for the biographical documentary *Tupac Resurrection* (2003), which came out after famed rapper Tupac Shakur had been murdered. The narration for the documentary is by none other than Tupac himself, obviously excerpts from recorded comments by Tupac during his lifetime. Only 2 minutes into the film, the screen goes black as the film's first song is interrupted by loud

TABLE 4.2
General Uses of Sound in Narrative Films

	ON-SCREEN SOUND **A**	**OFFSCREEN SOUND** **B**
■ PART OF THE STORY Sound derives from someone or something that is part of the story	■ INTERNAL Spoken words to convey thoughts, memories, dreams, or fantasies ■ EXTERNAL Spoken words Sound effects Music	Spoken words Sound effects Music
	C	**D**
■ NOT PART OF THE STORY Sound derives from a source outside the story	EXAMPLES ■ Someone looks at the camera and says something that is not part of the story or says something that comments on the story ■ The source of background music is visible, as in a scene in *Blazing Saddles* (Figure 4.14)	EXAMPLES ■ Music that is not heard by those *in* the film but serves a function—for example, to create or intensify a mood ■ Spoken words, often narration, by someone who is not in the story

gunshots, and then while the screen is still dark Tupac's voice says, "I got shot" (his murder was the second time in his life he had been shot). Then the film's visuals return, and the narration resumes and runs off and on throughout the rest of the film.

Often, offscreen sound effects, such as ambient sound, are part of the story's environment. They may function as more than mere background noise. In *American Graffiti*, Curt and John are talking when a car revving its engine is heard offscreen. Curt says, "Hey, John. Someone new in town." We viewers need not see the car; hearing it is enough. Occasionally, we hear spoken words and music that are part of the narrative though we do not see their sources. It's even possible to hear the sounds of one scene as we see a later scene. Late in the French film *Nelly and Monsieur Arnaud* (1995), we hear Arnaud's voice on a telephone imploring Nelly to come to him as we see her hurrying along a sidewalk in response to his call.

Sometimes—as in *Ferris Bueller's Day Off* (1986), *Just Another Girl on the I.R.T.* (1992), *Double Happiness* (1995), *High Fidelity* (2000), and *24 Hour Party People* (2002)—a character looks at the camera and says something that is not part of the story (Table 4.2C). Another example of a sound that is not integral to the story yet whose source is visible on-screen occurs in *Blazing Saddles* (1974, Figure 4.14). In classical Hollywood cinema, however, viewers rarely hear a sound that is not part of the story as they see its source.

Sounds that are not part of the narrative are more typically used offscreen (Table 4.2D). An example of this film convention is music that creates or reinforces a mood. For example, the screeching violins in both the 1960 and the 1998 versions of *Psycho* tend to frighten viewers. Of course, the string section of an orchestra is not part of the story: viewers have no sense of a string orchestra holding a timely rehearsal in the Bates Motel. Another example of offscreen sound that is not part of the story is narration by someone outside the story, as in *Tom Jones*, *The Age of Innocence*

FIGURE 4.14 Visible source of background music
As in many movies directed by Mel Brooks, *Blazing Saddles* (1974) sometimes makes viewers aware of movie conventions by presenting something unconventionally. Immediately before this point of *Blazing Saddles*, the main character is riding along on a horse as high-society big-band swing music plays in the background. Then the man rides up to the music's source: Count Basie and his band! *Crossbow Productions, Warner Bros.; Warner Home Video DVD*

(1993), and the opening of *Dr. Strangelove: Or, How I Learned to Stop Worrying and Love the Bomb* (1963).

Most often sounds are synchronized with their sources, as when spoken words match lip movements. But filmmakers may use **asynchronous sound**—a sound from a source on-screen that precedes or follows its source. And movie sounds usually sound like what we expect from their sources: a scream, for example, usually emanates from a frightened or upset person. In Hitchcock's *The 39 Steps* (1935), however, the sound of a loud, onrushing train briefly seems to emanate from a woman's mouth (Figure 4.15). Other disjunctions between image and sound are possible. As Walter Murch has shown in his own work on film sound and has explained in his writings, "By choosing carefully what to eliminate, and then adding sounds that at first hearing seem to be somewhat at odds with the accompanying image, the film-maker can open up a perceptual vacuum into which the mind of the audience must inevitably rush" ("Sound Design" 247). A famous instance of sound briefly but not exactly corresponding with the image (created by Murch himself and later explained by him) occurs in a scene about 88½ minutes into *The Godfather:*

> The rumbling and piercing metallic scream just before Michael Corleone kills Solozzo in *The Godfather* is not linked directly to anything seen on screen and so the audience is made to wonder at least momentarily, if perhaps only sub-

a)   b)

FIGURE 4.15 A sound from an unexpected source
Almost 20¾ minutes into *The 39 Steps* (1935), directed by Alfred Hitchcock, (a) a cleaning woman has discovered a body with a knife sticking out its back and opens her mouth and seems to scream. (b) In the next shot, viewers see a loud onrushing train and realize that its sound is the sound that seemed to come from the cleaning lady. *Gaumont British Picture Corp.; Criterion DVD*

consciously, "What is this?" The screech is from an elevated train rounding a sharp corner, so it is presumably coming from somewhere in the neighbourhood (the scene takes place in the Bronx). But precisely *because* it is so detached from the image, the metallic scream works as a clue to the state of Michael's mind at the moment—the critical moment before he commits his first murder and his life turns an irrevocable corner. It is all the more effective because Michael's face appears so calm and the sound is played so abnormally loud. This broadening tension between what we see and what we hear is brought to an abrupt end with the pistol shot that kills Solozzo: the distance between what we see and what we hear is suddenly collapsed at the moment that Michael's destiny is fixed. ("Sound Design" 249)

Today surround sound (360-degree sound) is available in theaters equipped with projectors capable of reading multiple soundtracks on the film and speakers in front of, on the sides of, and behind the audience. For such showings, sound can be used in new, more flexible ways. For example, viewers can hear the corresponding sounds as something seemingly approaches the audience and goes over or beside it. An airplane can be shown firing a machine gun as it approaches viewers in the audience and flies over them, and a split second after it is beyond the viewers' peripheral vision a booming explosion can be heard behind them. Nobody is going to remain uninvolved through that.

No aspect of film is so taken for granted as the soundtrack. Perhaps part of the reason we disregard sound is that even if we want to discuss it, we who use a variation of one or more of the languages of Europe have a paltry vocabulary to do so. English and many other languages have many more words for visuals than for sounds, so to describe a sound we must often compare it to other, well-known sounds.

Viewers are seldom meant to notice the shadings of a trained voice, sound effects, music, and silence, but an effective soundtrack helps involve us in the film and amplifies our responses to it. Like **designers**, directors, cinematographers, and editors, sound designers can direct viewers' attention and powerfully influence how audiences respond. In movies the results usually seem true to life—and they are, in spirit—but they are also true to cinema, its illusions and its artistry.

designer: The person responsible for the appearance of much of what is photographed in a movie, including locations, costumes, and hairstyles.

CLOSE-UP: SOUND IN ONE MINUTE OF *FATAL ATTRACTION* (STUDENT ESSAY)

by Christy Casmer

Beginning at 1:51:47 into *Fatal Attraction* (1987), sound is used effectively in the scenes in which Alex (Dan's unstable short-term former lover) attacks Dan's wife Beth in the upstairs bathroom while downstairs Dan puts the teakettle to boil (see Table 4.3).

In this 60-second excerpt, there is not much dialogue at all. The vocals consist mostly of screaming, crying, and heavy breathing. The screaming and crying add to the already intense action and put the viewers even more on edge. Both Alex and Beth are highly emotional. Beth fears for her life and is so terrified that she cannot even speak. When Alex talks, she does so in intense, angry tones as her body trembles with emotion. Alex's vocals show her feelings and mood clearly. Without these vocals, the excerpt would not seem as real or exciting.

Another expressive component of sound in this excerpt is the sound effects. The most effective sound effect used is the whistling teakettle. This sound is heard several times during this excerpt and is used mainly to delay the resolution of a suspenseful situation. The whistling teakettle drowns out the screams and noise coming from the upstairs bathroom so that Dan does not hear them. The viewers know that there is a life-and-death struggle going on between Alex and Beth, but downstairs Dan does not. Viewers have no idea how long the struggle will go on before Dan hears the screaming or if he will hear it in time. If the teakettle were not whistling, Dan would have heard the screaming immediately and there would be no suspense. The other sound effects also contribute to this part of the film. While the loud struggle is going on upstairs, it is peaceful and quiet downstairs. We hear Dan unwrap a fruit roll-up and hear the relaxing crackling in the fireplace. The differences in the sound volume and intensity from upstairs and downstairs show the drastic differences in the characters' emotions and the situations.

The last component of sound in this excerpt is the music. If the viewer did not listen to the vocals or sound effects during this scene, the music alone would still be highly expressive. At first, the music is slow and eerie, which indicates that something exciting may be about to happen. As the struggle between Alex and Beth begins, the music speeds up and becomes louder. For the most part, the faster and the more intense the struggle becomes, the faster and louder the music is played. Each time a shot of Dan is shown, the music quiets and becomes less intense, which again helps contrast the emotions and situation upstairs with the mood and situation downstairs. The music is also subordinated to the sound of the whistling teakettle when we see Dan downstairs. I think this helps to show the importance and expressiveness of the whistling teakettle once again. Viewer attention is directed away from the music and the intense struggle to scenes in which Dan is close by but simply cannot hear the screaming. Once again, sound intensifies the mood and situation of the scene.

This one-minute excerpt illustrates how vocals can intensify actions shown and make them seem more real. Sound effects, such as the whistling teakettle, can be used to delay a resolution, to make actions more intense and suspenseful, and to support the differences between characters' emotions and situations. Music can mirror the intensity of actions and be used to contrast mood and situation in different locations. Without the expert use of vocals, sound effects, and music, this part of *Fatal Attraction* would not be nearly as vivid and expressive as it is.

TABLE 4.3

Sound in One Minute of *Fatal Attraction*

VISUALS	VOCALS	SOUND EFFECTS	MUSIC
The dog looks up at water dripping from the ceiling.		Water dripping.	Slow, eerie music continues from earlier shots.
Dan opens and starts to eat a fruit roll-up in the living room.		Fruit roll-up wrapper being unwrapped. Crackling fire.	Music continues at low volume.
Alex yells at Beth in the bathroom and then raises knife to frighten her.	"If you weren't so stupid you'd know that, but you're just so stupid. You're a stupid selfish bitch. You're a stupid selfish bitch!" Beth: Screaming.	Dripping and running water.	Music becomes more intense and louder.
Dog licks water off the floor.		Sound of dog lapping up water. Water dripping.	
Dan stands in living room looking around.		Teakettle starts to whistle.	Music is overwhelmed by the sound of the teakettle.
Alex out of breath in bathroom raises knife to attack Beth.	Alex: Heavy breathing. Beth: Screaming.	Dripping and running water. Knife hitting wall.	Music gradually gets louder.
Steam starts to emerge from the teakettle in the kitchen.		Teakettle whistles full blast.	Music is not as loud as the teakettle.
Dan walks toward the kitchen eating.		Teakettle whistling.	
Alex and Beth struggle in bathroom. Beth is pinned against wall, and Alex tries to stab her with the knife. Beth hits Alex, who falls to the ground. Alex gets partially up and goes after Beth again.	Alex: Screaming. Beth: Screaming. "Dan . . . Dan . . . Dan!"	Hitting sound. Sounds of person falling to the ground and hitting it hard, and of knife sliding across the floor.	Music louder and very fast.
Dan removes teakettle from stove in kitchen. He jumps and sets it down after he hears the upstairs racket.		Teakettle whistling. Teakettle being set down on stove.	Music not as loud as the teakettle.
Alex and Beth struggle and fight on the bathroom floor.	Alex and Beth: Crying and screaming.		Music played rapidly, louder, in faster rhythm.
Dan runs from the kitchen.		Dan's footsteps.	
Alex and Beth struggle on the bathroom floor.	Alex and Beth: Screaming and shrieking.	Knife being stabbed into floor.	

CLOSE-UP: VOCALS, SOUND EFFECTS, AND MUSIC IN AN EXCERPT FROM *PSYCHO* (1960)

An excerpt from *Psycho* illustrates some major ways filmmakers can use the soundtrack.

In a motel where she is staying, Marion Crane steps into a shower bath. Viewers hear the shower curtain being pulled, Marion sighing, a bar of soap being unwrapped, and water running. At first, there is no music (see Figure 4.16). The sound of the water continues as we see through the shower curtain the indistinct image of someone coming toward Marion (and seemingly toward the audience). As that person pulls the shower curtain aside and begins to attack Marion with a large knife, the sound of water disappears from the soundtrack. At the beginning of the attack, we hear Marion's screams and, more loudly, a slashing sound and Bernard Herrmann's pulsating music. During the attack, the loudest sounds are the pulsating extreme high notes played by an orchestra of string instruments. After the attack is well under way, the sound of the running water gradually reemerges, and briefly and simultaneously we hear screams, slashing sounds, music, and running water. (When the film was first released in 1960, some viewers also heard the audience's screams.)

After the attacker leaves and Marion is losing consciousness, the screams stop, and bass strings play loudly and slowly but still rhythmically. As she reaches for the shower curtain and holds on to it momentarily, the music slows and decreases in volume, while the sound of the water gets louder. The music stops, and, while popping the shower curtain hooks in succession, Marion falls forward in death.

As is usually the case in films, in this scene from *Psycho* sound effects, only six in all, are used selectively. The first sounds are neither unusual nor particularly expressive. The soft tone and regular rhythm of the running water, for example, seem uneventful: all sounds normal. Once the attack begins, however, the sound of splashing water is not dramatic enough; instead we hear the sounds of Marion screaming and panting, music, and a knife supposedly slashing flesh. After the attacker leaves and Marion falls, the sounds of the shower curtain being pulled free and of her falling forcefully to the floor suggest life rushing from her body.

If we listen to this part of the film several times, we begin to notice that some of the sound effects don't sound as they would in life. When Marion unwraps the new bar of soap, for example, the paper sounds more crinkly and louder than any actual soap wrapper. And the running water in the shower doesn't sound like water running in a shower. It sounds nearly the same as the heavy rain Marion drove in while arriving at the motel. But the sound of the water in the shower also includes a sound like that of a liquid being sloshed around in a large container. The sound of the knife stabbing Marion is probably different from and more noticeable than that sound in life. One of my students said it sounded as if someone were slicing cabbage with a knife. Another said it sounded as if someone were chipping away on a block of ice with an ice pick.

The sound effects in this 106-second excerpt illustrate a commonplace in movies: what we see and hear normally seems true to life—which can be a source of cinema's enormous power—but under close examination is revealed to be artificial or modified. In most popular movies, such deceptions are to be expected. Normally, audiences are meant to believe in what they see and hear and to stay caught up in what happens before them, but the techniques used are often truer of movies than of life.

Notice two sound effects *not* supplied in this section of *Psycho*: When the attacker pulls the shower curtain aside, we do not hear it slide on the rod, though we did earlier when Marion got into the tub. What is more effective is the loud, pulsating music that accompanies the shower curtain being pulled aside. The other significant sound not supplied is noise coming from the attacker, but the

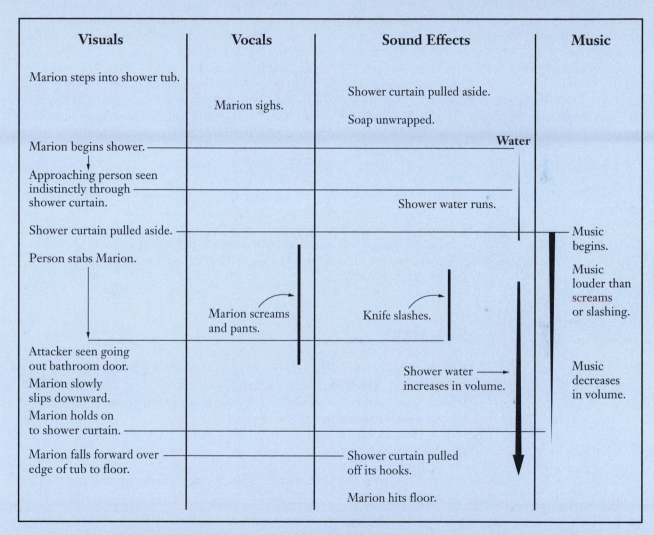

FIGURE 4.16 Sound in *Psycho* (1960), before, during, and after Marion's shower
From the time Marion steps into the shower until she half falls out of it, about 106 seconds elapse. During this time, what happens is so riveting and upsetting that few viewers notice the soundtrack. However, this figure shows that it is not only the visuals and editing that make this part of *Psycho* effective and memorable.

high-pitched music during the attack suggests both the attacker's violent and sexual frenzy and Marion's (and the viewers') panic.

Music is not used before the attack. Unlike countless film scenes, this excerpt lacks music to establish a mood or create suspense. But as the attack begins, Bernard Herrmann's music intensifies the audience's shock. During the attack, the music is louder than any other sound. The people mixing the sounds could have relied more on the screams or the slashing sounds, or both, but they chose to emphasize the music. During the attack, the loud, piercing string music sounds like bird cries (perhaps many viewers hear bird cries in the music because images of birds and references to them appear earlier in the film). The music also suggests Marion's heartbeat. When the attack begins, the music is rapid and frantic, as Marion's heartbeat would be. As the attacker leaves and Marion slips toward death, the music slows but retains a regular rhythm. And as Marion loses her grip on life, the music loses its jagged up and down melody, and its volume or force then comes to a halt. The melodies and rhythms of life fade out. What remain are only a silent body and the sound of water streaming on indifferently.

 A similar figure and analysis for a sound excerpt from *The Conversation* (1974) can be found on the Web site for this book at <bedfordstmartins .com/phillips-film>.

SUMMARY

The chapter briefly explains a few of the many ways that film sounds have been created. More important, it explores some specific uses of a soundtrack's four major components, possible sound transitions, and general uses of sound in narrative films.

Spoken Words

- In films, spoken words may take the form of dialogue, monologues, or narration.

- Overlapping dialogue can create or reinforce a sense of nervousness, stress, and isolation.

- Spoken words, such as those by Darth Vader, may be distorted for effect.

- Dialogue is invaluable for revealing a character's ideas, goals, and dreams, though usually it does so more concisely, obliquely, and revealingly than conversation in life does.

- Although spoken words can be extremely expressive, many films and many film scenes rely heavily on visuals and use only limited spoken words.

Sound Effects

- Sound effects consist of sounds that objects make, sounds that people make other than spoken words, and ambient sound.

- Some of the many possible uses of sound effects are to help create a sense of a location, intensify a mood, enhance a humorous situation, or conceal an action.

- Sound effects specialists have many options in manipulating sounds, such as playing them backward, playing them faster or slower than they were recorded, constructing them, and blending them in different proportions.

Music

- Film music may serve countless functions, such as to mirror a film's central conflict, direct viewers' attention, establish place and time, suggest what a character feels or an animal is like, and cover weak acting.

- Film music may reference earlier film music. Sometimes the same music is used; other times an approximation is composed and used.

- In large-budget movies, sometimes the film music is selected with an eye to future recorded music sales.

Silence

- Possible uses of silence in films include during dreams, to suggest dying or death, or to interrupt the regular rhythm of life's sounds.

Transitions

- There are many possible ways to use sound between shots, such as to have the sound of the first shot end as the shot does.

- Sound transitions between shots are used to reinforce continuity or contribute to discontinuity.

General Uses of Sound in Narrative Films

- Sound in narrative films may come from on-screen or offscreen and may derive from a source in the story or outside the story.

Major Terms about Film Sound

Below, numbers in italics refer to the pages where the terms are explained. All terms are defined in more detail in the Illustrated Glossary beginning on p. 667.

ambient sound *176*	narration *163*	sound effect *166*
asynchronous sound *182*	narrator *180*	THX sound *161*
bridge *178*	offscreen *180*	Vitaphone *159*
Foley artist *169*	sound dissolve *177*	

QUESTIONS ABOUT FILM SOUND

The following questions are intended to help viewers understand the use of sound in a film and analyze their responses to it. Not all the questions are appropriate for every film. In thinking out, discussing, and writing responses to the questions most appropriate for the film being examined, be careful to stick with the issues the questions raise, to answer all parts of the questions, to explain the reasons for your answers, and to give specific examples from the film.

1. Where is sound used to suggest the size of a location or the texture of the surfaces?
2. How frequently is dialogue used? Is the dialogue always distinct? Does it sometimes overlap? If it does, with what consequences?
3. Where is the volume of the dialogue raised or lowered for effect?
4. Does the film use narration? If so, what functions does the narration serve?
5. Were any of the sound effects particularly important? If so, explain.
6. Consider the film's music.
   a. Where is music used? For what purposes? Is the music always subordinated to the rest of the film, or is it sometimes dominant? If the music is ever intrusive, explain where and with what consequences.
   b. What are the major melodies or tunes? Are they repeated? With or without variation?
   c. Is the music a part of the story itself, or is it played as complementary to the story (viewers hear the music, but the characters cannot)?
   d. Where does the music suggest a particular place or time or both?
   e. Where is music used to suggest what a character is feeling?
7. Is silence ever used in the film? If so, where and with what consequences?
8. Where is sound used between scenes to create a certain effect? What effect is created or supported?
9. Where is sound distorted? What does the distortion contribute?

10. Is sound ever used from a source offscreen? If so, explain its use.

11. Is any component of the sound ever at odds with the accompanying image, as in the example of the screeching elevated train in *The Godfather*? If so, explain.

WORKS CITED

Coe, Brian. *The History of Movie Photography*. New York: Zoetrope, 1981.

Edman, Irwin. *Arts and the Man: A Short Introduction to Aesthetics*. New York: Norton, 1939.

Edwards, Mark. "Moving Sounds for Moving Pictures." *The Times* (U.K.) 23 Apr. 2000.

Hall, Cecelia (executive sound director, Paramount Pictures). Telephone interview. 5 Aug. 1994.

Holden, Stephen. "Composers Show How to Make a Movie Sing." *New York Times* 9 July 1988: 12.

Lumet, Sidney. *Making Movies*. New York: Knopf, 1995.

"Making Godzilla Roar." *Morning Edition*. Nat'l. Public Radio. 20 May 1998.

Murch, Walter. "Sound Design: The Dancing Shadow." *Projections 4: Film-makers on Film-making*. Ed. John Boorman, Tom Luddy, David Thomson, and Walter Donohue. London: Faber, 1995. 237–51.

———. "The Sound Designer." *Working Cinema: Learning from the Masters*. Ed. Roy Paul Madsen. Belmont, CA: Wadsworth, 1990.

Robinson, David. *The History of World Cinema*. New York: Stein, 1973.

Rydstrom, Gary. Audio Commentary. *A Bug's Life: Deluxe Edition* (DVD) 1999.

Serafine, Frank. "Audio Cinemagic." Lecture. Art Institute of Chicago. 27 Apr. 1985.

Thom, Randy. Interview. *All Things Considered*. Nat'l. Public Radio. 27 June 2005.

FOR FURTHER READING

Brown, Royal S. *Overtones and Undertones: Reading Film Music*. Berkeley: U of California P, 1994. The book focuses "on how the interaction between a film and its score influences our response to cinematic situations." Includes interviews with eight major film composers, including Miklós Rózsa, Bernard Herrmann, and Maurice Jarre. An appendix contains an outline of what to listen for and consider in a film score.

Schelle, Michael. *The Score: Interviews with Film Composers*. Los Angeles: Silman-James, 1999. Conversations with contemporary film composers of various styles, backgrounds, and positions in Hollywood.

Sound-on-Film: Interviews with Creators of Film Sound. Ed. Vincent LoBrutto. Westport, CT: Praeger, 1994. Includes glossary, filmographies, and bibliography.

The Sounds of Early Cinema. Ed. Richard Abel and Rick Altman. Bloomington: Indiana UP, 2001. The first book to examine the sounds that accompanied "silent" movies.

Thomas, Tony. *Music for the Movies.* 2nd ed. Los Angeles: Silman-James, 1997. A history of Hollywood film music with discussion of the lives, works, and influences of such film composers as Alfred Newman, Miklós Rózsa, Max Steiner, Bernard Herrmann, Aaron Copland, Elmer Bernstein, Jerry Goldsmith, and Lalo Schifrin.

A lengthy analysis of the expressiveness of the mise en scène, cinematography, editing, and sound in *The Third Man* (1949) can be found on the Web site for this book at <bedfordstmartins.com/phillips-film>.

Obvious vs. Subtle Film Techniques

T HE INTRODUCTION TO PART ONE (pp. 9–10) explains three major points about **film techniques**: the use of a particular technique, such as the use of a **wide-angle lens**, may be changed as the film progresses; the technique's contribution to a particular **shot** depends on the context in which it is used; and an effect is achieved by several different techniques used at the same time. There is another point to be made about techniques. It is a point better understood after you have read all or most of the first four chapters, hence its placement here: techniques may be used obviously or subtly.

First, an example of some of the choices one group of filmmakers made: during the opening credits of *Walk the Line* (2005), viewers learn that the initial **setting** is Folsom Prison (California) in 1968. At the end of the opening credits, 2 minutes and 29 seconds into the film, viewers see these shots:

1. Part of the top of a table saw that is not running is shown as the director's name is briefly **superimposed** then **fades out.** A hand reaches toward the saw's teeth and lightly rotates the round blade a little.

2. The face of Joaquin Phoenix (who plays Johnny Cash) is shown looking down (presumably at the saw), and **offscreen** a man's voice speaks three times, "Mr. Cash," but the Johnny Cash character does not respond.

3. The film **cuts** to Dyess, Arkansas, in 1944 (so identified in subtitle).

The story progresses from 1944 back to 1968; then at 115:48 into the film, viewers see the last part of the shot labeled #1 above: the top of a table saw and a hand reaching out, touching it, and starting to rotate its blades. The next shot begins the same way as shot #2 above, but after the second time the man's voice says "Mr. Cash," we see its source; we soon learn the speaker is the prison warden.

shot (noun): An uninterrupted strip of exposed motion-picture film or videotape that represents a subject during an uninterrupted segment of time.

superimposition: Two or more images photographed or printed on top of each other.

cut (verb): To change from one shot to the following shot seemingly instantaneously.

193

representation: A likeness of a subject created in a text.

The first use of shots 1 and 2 discussed above comes at a dramatic time, right before Johnny Cash goes onstage at Folsom Prison to entertain the enthusiastic inmates and get his career back on track. By the second time the two shots are used, we viewers have seen that Johnny's young brother had been killed working on the same type of saw, and we understand why Cash reaches out to the saw and what he must be thinking and feeling some twenty-plus years after his brother's death. It's a poignant moment, rich in understatement and resonant in feeling. And it is achieved because of the filmmakers' subtle **representation** that doesn't explain but rather encourages viewers to make connections. How different the effect if the filmmakers had chosen to show the same two shots but then flashbacked briefly to the accident itself and then quickly resumed the story begun by the earlier two shots.

zoom: To use a zoom lens on a movie or video camera to cause the image of the subject to either increase in size as the area being filmed seems to decrease (zoom in) or to decrease in size as the area being filmed seems to increase (zoom out).

Cinematic techniques may be used in an obvious manner—for example, the filmmakers may unnecessarily **zoom** in on a subject when the viewers have already noticed it. Or filmmaking techniques may be used subtly—for example, filmmakers might include a significant detail in the background of the frame and expect viewers to notice it and consider its significance. The subtle use of cinematic techniques may have more impact on viewers than an obvious one because they are forced to stay involved, make connections, imagine what happens, or help create meaning (Figure 1).

scene: A section of a narrative that gives the impression of continuous action taking place in continuous time and space.

Some viewers believe that erotic situations are sexier if restraint is used in their representation. Sometimes a look can carry more erotic charge than kissing or more obvious representations of attraction. And often the images that viewers *imagine* are more erotic than images on a screen. Novelist Leslie Epstein recounts that for her, "Perhaps the most erotic **scene** in all the sixties occurs in *Persona*. . . . Bibi Andersson tells the half-catatonic Liv Ullmann about the time she and a friend had been lying on a beach [sunbathing nude]. . . . Nothing [much] moves but the one actress's lips and the other's eyes" (289). About 28 2/3 minutes into the film, the Bibi Andersson character's account begins as follows:

> Suddenly I saw two figures leaping about on the rocks above us who kept hiding and peeking. "There are two boys looking at us," I said to the girl. Her name was Katarina. "Let them look," she said, turning over on her back. It was such a strange feeling. I just lay there with my bottom in the air not a bit embarrassed. I felt very calm. Wasn't it funny? And Katarina was beside me with her big breasts and thighs. She just lay there giggling to herself. Then I saw that the boys had come closer and were staring at us. They were awfully young. Then the bolder of the two came over and squatted down beside Katarina and pretended to be busy with his foot and started to poke between his toes. I . . . I felt all funny. Suddenly I heard Katarina say: "Come here a minute." Then she helped him off with his jeans and shirt. Then he was on top of her. She showed him how and held him by his fanny. The other boy sat on the rock watching. I heard Katarina whisper and laugh. The boy's face was close to mine. It was all flushed and puffy. I turned over and said: "Won't you come to me too?" And

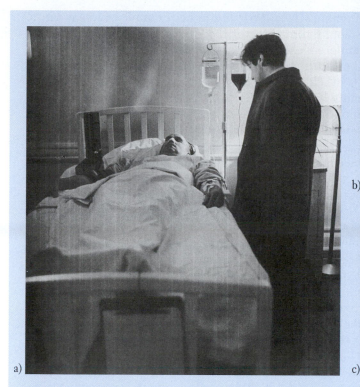

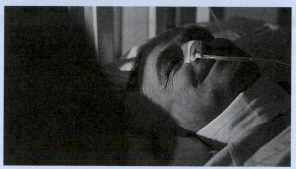

FIGURE 1 Obvious vs. subtle use of film techniques
(a) This publicity still for *The Godfather* (1972) shows an image that was posed for the benefit of a still photographer and was used in publicizing the film but does not appear in it. Frames (b–c) are from the last two shots of the same scene, which begins approximately 65 3/4 minutes into the film. They reveal some of the scene's subdued lighting, two expressive faces, restrained acting, and in the scene's last shot the complex feelings conjured up by actor Marlon Brando's slight smile and a tear near his right eye. The film's mise en scène subtly suggests a love, respect, and affection not captured by the publicity still's greater camera distance from the subjects, brighter lighting, and greater emphasis on the setting than on the faces of the two human subjects. (a) *Paramount.* (b–c) *Paramount; Paramount DVD*

> Katarina said: "Yes, go to her now." So he left her and fell roughly on top of me and grabbed one of my breasts. It was over for me almost at once.

If the film instead showed a **flashback** of what happened, that part of the film would be less erotic for some viewers because instead of hearing once and briefly that the two boys were "awfully young," viewers would continuously see how young they were, and that would be troubling for some viewers who would interpret the scene as being about adults seducing children. For many viewers, the restrained representation in *Persona* is more erotic than a more obvious rendition.

medium shot: A shot in which the subject and surroundings are given nearly equal prominence.

extreme long shot: A shot in which the subject appears to be far from the camera.

montage: A series of brief shots used to represent a condensation of subjects and time.

Near the end of Fellini's *8½* (1963) is another example of less is more. After Guido, a distraught film director, has hidden under a table at his nightmarish press conference and pulled a pistol from his pocket (almost 127 minutes into the film), we see a scene consisting of only one shot: Guido's mother on a beach turning and calling offscreen "Guido. Guido. Where are you running, you low-life?" We first see her in **medium shot**, but as she stops running and begins to call out, the camera seems to race away from her, and we end up seeing her in **extreme long shot**, her face no longer discernible. In the next shot, we see Guido under the table again, hear a gunshot, and see his head drop. In the 6 or so seconds before Guido's fantasized death, we experience not the expected rush of images and sounds from Guido's life but one brief, spare, evocative scene. We do not even see Guido. We see only his mother being annoyed with him because he is evidently running away. By the end of the scene, Guido is presumably gone (in more than one sense), and she has shrunk in size and importance. The scene displays great restraint. Much more time, many more images, a much richer soundtrack could have been used, but the muse whispered into director Federico Fellini's ear, "Federico, less is more." For many viewers, it is off-putting for movies to explain their ideas, so scriptwriting teachers and scriptwriting books implore future scriptwriters to "show, don't tell": don't tell viewers anything that can be shown instead or has already been shown.

Subtle technique is not without risks. If the image or sound is too indistinct or too fleeting or both, or if viewers are otherwise engaged, they may miss a significant detail, even on many later re-viewings. An example of excessive subtlety is from *Citizen Kane*. After Susan's disastrous opera career, Kane insists she persevere. Then come the famous opera **montage** (described on the Web site for this book) and the aftermath of Susan's suicide attempt. If viewers listen especially carefully just before Susan revives, they can hear an instrumental version of a fragment of an aria that Susan had struggled with during a singing lesson earlier in the film (at 86 minutes and 28 seconds into the film). After Susan's revival, the music plays faintly for about 50 seconds while she tells Kane she couldn't make him understand how she felt and how the audience simply didn't want her. As Kane says, "That's when you've got to fight 'em," the music stops.

The music is in a minor key and sounds as if it's coming from a faraway calliope, the kind of instrument you may have heard played on merry-go-rounds. The music is a subtle reminder of Susan's disastrous singing career: she was as ill-suited for singing opera as that calliope was to render an aria. However, the music after Susan's suicide attempt is so faint that many viewers never hear it. It is so faint that I heard it only after many viewings of the film over the years and then only on a laser videodisc version (no movie projector noise to contend with). Even after I told a class about the music and played the excerpt from the laser disc version for them, some did not hear it. Like so much of *Citizen Kane*, it's a brilliant touch, but in this instance it is too subtle.[1]

Another example of filmmakers being too subtle occurs 20 minutes and 43 seconds into another widely admired film, *The Searchers* (1956). Ethan Edwards hates Comanches because early in the film they kill his brother Aaron, two of Aaron's three children, and, most important, Aaron's wife, for whom Ethan has special feelings (the film is restrained in suggesting why and how deeply). Understandably, many critics seem not to have noticed that Comanches had also killed Ethan's mother. When Comanches are about to attack Aaron Edwards and his family, Aaron and his wife send their little daughter Debbie to hide by her grandmother's grave. Before Debbie sits in front of the tombstone, at about 20 2/3 minutes into the film, for 6 video frames (out of 30 per second) the following is legible:

HERE LIES
MARY JANE EDWARDS
KILLED BY
COMANCHES
MAY 12, 1852
A GOOD WIFE AND MOTHER
IN HER 41ST YEAR

If viewers noticed this detail, they could better understand Ethan's feelings about Comanches and his obsession to retrieve from them what is evidently his sole surviving relative, his niece Debbie (who is the third female relative of Ethan killed or abducted by Comanches). But how many viewers read the tombstone, since they have only a fifth of a second to do so?

Like all who hope to communicate effectively regardless of the medium, filmmakers are challenged to have a clear sense of their audiences and not to insult them by being too obvious or lose them by being so subtle that audiences have no chance of getting the point, even during later re-viewings. For those who make texts, it is a judgment call, sometimes wisely made, sometimes not.

In these examples and elsewhere, the filmmakers may have known how demanding they were being when they used these subtle techniques. Perhaps sometimes filmmakers include them for those in the audience who are especially observant. Maybe they include such subtleties for those who see the film more than once, as rewards for the faithful. Perhaps they include such touches for their own pleasure in being creative and sly. Then,

---

[1]On the Criterion CAV laser disc version of *Citizen Kane*, the music can be heard on side 4, **frames** 20,200 and following. If the volume is turned way up, the music is also audible about 96 minutes and 57 seconds into the Criterion DVD version.

too, possibly the filmmakers were unaware of how demanding they were being and simply goofed, which is possible even in otherwise brilliantly made films.

Sometimes viewers miss the significance of a technique because they watch a videotape version. Films shown in commercial theaters and on some DVD systems usually have detailed images. But when films are shown on an analog television set (a pre-high-definition set), the results are somewhat blurred and grainy (since video images have less definition than film images). The lighting is without subtle shades (**high contrast**), and in shadowed areas details tend to get lost because analog TV has far less range of tones than film; thus, many details in dark scenes are especially difficult to see. That is why films with many dark scenes—such as *The Third Man* (1949), the *Godfather* films, some of the *Batman* films since the late 1980s, and most **films noirs**—are frustrating to watch on analog television or

film noir: A type of film first made in the United States during and after World War II, characterized by dangerous characters and frequent scenes with dark, shadowy (low-key) lighting.

a)   b)

FIGURE 2 **Subtle visual clues**

(a) In *Citizen Kane* (1941), a doll belonging to Susan, Kane's second wife, is seen on the bed in Susan's room 104 1/3 minutes into the film, on the day Susan walks out of her marriage (the doll is also visible 108 1/2 minutes into the film). Even though the doll is large and prominent in the frame shown here, many viewers do not notice it, let alone consider its possible significance. (Like the doll, Susan has been mainly a pretty plaything; the doll being on Susan's bed could also be symbolic.) (b) Even more subtle is the last appearance of Susan's doll, visible only for a few seconds 115 2/3 minutes into the film, amid the vast collection of objects from Kane's life. Its presence there reveals that even though Susan left Kane and he then tore up her room in anger, he kept her doll (he also kept her glass paperweight, which he holds at the moment of his death). When one is watching a videotape or a broadcast of the film on an analog TV, it is extremely difficult to see the doll among all that other stuff, destined for a fiery furnace. *RKO General Pictures, Mercury Productions; Warner Home Video DVD* videotape. Even in well-lit scenes, viewers watching on analog TV are likely to miss such significant details as the fleeting triple superimposition of the last shot of *Psycho* (see Figure 3.14 on p. 130). On analog TV it is also difficult to spot significant details in *Citizen Kane*, including the whiskey bottle Kane finds in the bookcase of Susan's room (109 $\frac{1}{2}$ minutes) and her doll (Figure 2).

WORK CITED

Epstein, Leslie. "The Movie on the Whorehouse Wall/*The Devil in Miss Jones*." *The Movie That Changed My Life*. Ed. David Rosenberg. New York: Viking, 1991.

Part Two
FICTIONAL FILMS

NEARLY SINCE THE BEGINNING of projected films in the 1890s, fictional films have proven the most popular with audiences all over the world. By far. They also have garnered the most attention from critics. And many more studies and publications are devoted to them than to films of any other type. Fictional films have attracted so much attention that we examine them in some depth before turning our attention (in Part Three) to the major alternatives to them. The three major subjects of Part Two are sources for fictional films (such as history, fiction, and TV), components of fictional films (structure, treatment of time, and styles), and some of the major types of fictional films.

Links to a variety of sources, including supplementary readings and short films, are available for each chapter on the Web site for this book at <bedfordstmartins.com/phillips-film>.

◄ Typically, fictional films have multiple sources, as is illustrated here by frames from Oliver Stone's movie *JFK* (1991). The film includes actual historical footage of President and Mrs. Kennedy as they are being driven in a convertible that fateful 1963 day, re-created footage of the events of that same day in Dallas, and fictional characters partially based on actual people. *Warner Bros.*

CHAPTER 5

Sources for Fictional Films

A FILM IS ONE OF MANY kinds of **texts**, things that people produce or modify to communicate **meaning**, such as photographs, paintings, newspaper articles, and T-shirt messages and images. Some theorists refer to the relationship of one text to another as **intertextual**, a term that means "between texts." Films are intertextual in an immense variety of creative ways: other texts that they use as sources include scripts, **storyboards**, written history, fiction, plays, TV and video games, and other films. Intertextuality in films may take many forms, including adaptation, remake, **allusion**, **parody**, **homage**, **sequel**, and **prequel** (Figure 5.1).

Usually, a fictional film is based on a script. The script may be a more or less original story, but often it is based mainly on historical events, a fictional work (usually a novel), a play, a TV show or series, or other films. In this chapter, we focus on some of the most frequent major sources for

Terms in **boldface** are defined in the Illustrated Glossary beginning on page 667.

storyboards: A series of drawings (or occasionally photographs) of each shot of a planned film or video story.

homage: A tribute in a text to a person, to another text (such as a film), or to part of a text.

Of all the people Skywalker could have been stranded with ...

FIGURE 5.1 Intertextuality
This cartoon is an example of intertextuality. It makes an allusion, or reference, to earlier texts—to the *Star Wars* movies and specifically two of the most prominent characters, Luke Skywalker and Darth Vader. In general, people who know the earlier text(s) can understand whatever forms of intertextuality are in play. Since the *Star Wars* movies are so popular throughout much of the world, people in many different cultures can "get" the joke seen here. Other examples of intertextuality—such as a political cartoon in the local newspaper about a local politician—are more culturally specific and thus less accessible to large audiences. *Dave Blazek, "Loose Parts," 18 May 2005. Used with permission of The Permissions Group, on behalf of TMS Reprints.*

fictional films and on the processes of transforming sources into films. In doing so, we will come to understand the film medium more completely — to understand, for example, some characteristics of fictional films and their sources, the extensive connections that films have with other films and other types of texts, and the influences of various cultures on the creation of a film.

SCREENPLAYS, SHOOTING SCRIPTS, AND STORYBOARDS

Written and graphic sources for a fictional film may take the form of a screenplay, shooting script, or storyboard.

Screenplays and Shooting Scripts

scene: A section of a narrative that gives the impression of continuous action taking place in continuous time and space.

shot (noun): An uninterrupted strip of exposed motion-picture film or videotape that represents a subject during an uninterrupted segment of time.

The **screenplay** is the earliest version of a script. It is written before filming begins and describes or supplies the **settings**, action, vocals including dialogue, and **structure**. A **shooting script** is the version of the script used during filming. It includes changes made in the screenplay, usually breaks **scenes** into **shots**, and normally includes instructions on camera placement and use.

In creating a screenplay, writers select from experiences (their own, others they know about, and experiences they imagine), transform them, and arrange them in an involving and meaningful order (Figure 5.2).

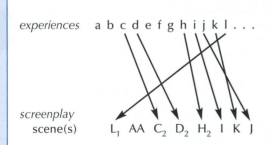

experiences   a b c d e f g h i j k l . . .   Continuous and chronological; full of both significant and seemingly trivial details.

screenplay
scene(s) L_1 AA C_2 D_2 H_2 I K J   Not necessarily chronological; usually discontinuous; many insignificant details omitted so that significant details and patterns are more evident.

FIGURE 5.2 The making of a sample screenplay
When experiences are transformed into scenes in a screenplay, here are some of the possible outcomes:

- Certain experiences may not be included in the script (a, b, e, f, and g).
- Experiences may be altered (c, d, and h become C_2, D_2, and H_2).
- Events may be rearranged (j and k become K and J).
- Experiences may be altered and transposed (l becomes L_1).
- New scenes without corresponding experiences in life may be made up (as in the case of AA).

Adapted from Phillips (Analyzing Films 58).

TABLE 5.1
Creative Territories for Making Fictional Films

THE WRITER'S TERRITORY

- SETTINGS: where and when the action takes place and in general terms what the settings look like

- SUBJECTS: the characters' actions and vocals (if any)

- STRUCTURE: the selection and arrangement of vocals and narration (if any) and actions

- MEANINGS: what the film explains about its subjects in general terms or, more often, what it implies by showing subjects in particular situations

THE TERRITORY OF PRODUCTION PERSONNEL

- CASTING AND PERFORMANCE: people, animals, or creatures selected to play the roles; behavior, gestures, tone of voice

- CINEMATOGRAPHY AND MISE EN SCÈNE: camera distances, camera angles, lenses, lighting, composition, and so forth

- EDITING: length and arrangement of shots; transitions between shots*

- MUSIC AND SOUND EFFECTS*

*Occasionally, the writer supplies directions for editing transitions, music, and sound effects, and the production personnel may follow them.

Source: Adapted from Phillips (*Writing Short Scripts* 170).

Table 5.1 distinguishes between the elements of a film that are usually the responsibility of the screenplay writer and those that are the contributions of others. In large productions, arrangements with the **producer**, director, and perhaps actors determine how closely the screenplay writer's wishes are followed. Usually all other aspects of a film—such as camera angles and transitions between shots—are the domain of the other filmmakers, such as the **cinematographer** and editor, usually under the guidance of the director.

The screenplay writer's territory, and the territory of those shooting and editing the film, can be further explored by examining the last scene of *The Royal Tenenbaums* (2001). The left column in Table 5.2 reprints the scene from the screenplay. The right column provides a description of the last scene in the finished film. Note in the left column that the two screenplay writers for *The Royal Tenenbaums* indicate the setting (a cemetery and day) and something about what the setting looks like: snowy and darkening. They describe all the characters' actions, lowering the casket, firing the BB guns, and so forth, but they exclude dialogue from the scene. By indicating what happens and in what order, the screenplay writers determine

producer: A person in charge of the business and administrative aspects of making a film.

cinematographer: The person responsible for motion-picture photography during the making of a film.

TABLE 5.2
Last Scene of *The Royal Tenenbaums* (script and film)

SCRIPT

EXT. CEMETERY. DAY

Snow falls lightly, and the sky is getting dark. Everyone in the family is gathered around as Chas, Richie, Henry, Raleigh, Eli, Dusty, and Pagoda lower the casket. They are all bundled up in coats and scarves. They step away from the grave.

Henry stands next to Etheline. She takes his arm. Pagoda wears Royal's sunglasses. Tears stream down his face. Dusty stands beside him. Margot has her arm around Richie's shoulder. She smokes a cigarette. Raleigh stands next to Dudley. Eli stands next to Walter. The priest is on crutches.

Chas looks to [his young sons] Ari and Uzi standing a few yards away. He nods. Ari and Uzi fire several shots into the air with Chas' and Royal's old B.B. guns.

Royal's gravestone sits in a wheelbarrow next to a pile of dirt. It reads Royal O'Reilly Tenenbaum (1932–2001). Epitaph: Died tragically rescuing his family from the wreckage of a destroyed sinking battleship. The priest sees this and hesitates. He looks puzzled. He smiles slightly.

Richie throws a white flower into the grave. They all stand in silence for a minute before they turn away and walk to their waiting cars.

Source: Anderson and Wilson (149–50).

FILM

Shot number:

1. It is a damp, gray day, and the trees are without leaves. Chas, Dusty, Eli, Henry, Raleigh, and Richie finish lowering the casket into the ground. Pagoda tosses white flowers onto the lowered casket. The men turn away from the grave. Henry moves toward Etheline.

2. Medium close-up as Henry finishes joining Etheline and they stand under an umbrella she holds. The camera pans to the left and briefly pauses to show Dusty in his elevator operator clothes and somewhat in front of him and to his left Pagoda wearing sunglasses. The camera resumes panning to the left and stops briefly to show Richie holding an umbrella and Margot behind him with her chin on his right shoulder; she puts her other hand on his left shoulder and viewers see she is holding a cigarette. The camera resumes panning to the left and pauses briefly before Raleigh and Dudley, who share an umbrella. The camera pans further to the left and pauses before the priest, Eli, and Walter; the priest steps forward and out of the frame to the right. The camera resumes its motion to the left and pauses before Chas, who is looking down toward the grave; he turns his head to his right and nods.

3. Chas's two young sons, Uzi and Ari, each raise a BB gun rifle, as their spotted dog sits nearby; one of the boys says "Fire," and both of them shoot. The camera resumes its leftward panning as we hear the boy shout "Fire" again and hear the guns shooting a second time. The camera stops some distance from the engraved headstone, and the priest (on crutches) reenters the frame on the right and facing toward the headstone.

4. A medium close-up shot of the priest as he looks toward the headstone. He furrows his eyebrows slightly.

5. Cutaway shot revealing the headstone inscription:
   ROYAL O'REILLY TENENBAUM
   1932–2001
   DIED TRAGICALLY RESCUING HIS
   FAMILY FROM THE WRECKAGE OF A
   DESTROYED SINKING BATTLESHIP

6. Long shot showing everyone in the small, enclosed area surrounding the gravesite except for the priest, the two boys, and the boys' dog. The rest of the funeral party slowly walks out of the enclosed area and out of the frame (during the last part of the shot, it appears that all movement is in a slight slow-motion). Richie and Pagoda are the last two to leave the enclosed area. Richie looks down into the grave and tosses in one white flower as Pagoda pauses and looks on. Richie turns and leaves the fenced-in area. Pagoda comes through the opening, closes the waist-high gate, and walks off-frame to the left. The camera lingers on the gate's inscription; it reads "TENENBAUM."

The film then cuts to the beginning of the end credits, beginning with the director's credit.

the scene's structure. And by selecting setting and actions, they make it possible for readers to formulate a range of possible meanings the scene suggests.

The scene in the finished film, which consists of six shots and runs for 125 seconds, generally honors the scriptwriters' wishes but makes many changes as well. The day is not snowy and darkening. During the time that the filmmakers had for filming the scene, the **location** probably was gray and drizzling. The actions in the film follow the script generally, but the film makes many changes. For example, the film shows six men lowering the casket, not seven, and it shows the seventh man (Pagoda) on the far end watching and then tossing in the flowers. The film also omits some details included in the script. For example, the film does not show Pagoda crying.

Sometimes the filmmakers added details. For example, the film includes the boys' spotted dog. He is a reminder of Royal's finest hour, when he saved the boys from an out-of-control car that killed the boys' first dog. Royal quickly bought a new one and gave it to the boys to help ease their anguish.

Nowhere in the script do the two screenplay writers stipulate which actors should be cast and how they should perform (one of the writers directed the film, and the other acted in it). Also, in this last scene and elsewhere in the script, the writers never indicate camera placement, camera movement, and composition. Nor do the scriptwriters indicate how many shots the scene should have and where to begin and end each shot. It was left to the production personnel to decide whether to include any **narration** in the last scene (they did), whether to include any music (they included two discontinuous excerpts), and whether to include **sound effects** (they did — for example, the firing BB guns).

Unless we have access to a version of the script that was written by the screenplay writers, we cannot know the writers' contributions to a film. In a large production company, many people — especially the producer, director, actors, and editors — may rewrite or edit parts of the script or insist on changes in it. In large, complicated productions, one or more "script doctors" may be hired to rewrite the script, sometimes again and again, and they often are uncredited. Comparing a screenplay or shooting script with the finished film sometimes reveals the different contributions of the writer(s) and others, especially the director. We can see these relative contributions by comparing a scene from the shooting script for *The Third Man* (1949) with the comparable section of the finished film. In the film, Holly Martins has come to Vienna to work for an old friend, Harry Lime. Martins learns that Lime has been involved in stealing penicillin, diluting it, and selling it at an enormous profit. Late in the film Calloway, a British officer trying to enlist Martins's aid in trapping Lime, has brought Martins to a children's hospital. Two scenes from the shooting script are reprinted in the left column of Table 5.3.

location: Any place other than a film studio that is used for filming.

narration: Commentary in a film about a subject in the film or about some other subject, usually by someone offscreen.

sound effect: In film, a sound other than spoken words or music.

TABLE 5.3
The Third Man:
Two Scenes from the Shooting Script and the Film's Comparable Section

SHOOTING SCRIPT (two scenes)

123. *CHILDREN'S HOSPITAL (NIGHT):*

> *As they* [Calloway and Martins] *come through the doors, a nurse passes and Martins realizes he has been shanghai-ed, but it is too late to do anything.*

CALLOWAY: I want to take a look in No. 3 Ward.

NURSE: That's all right, Colonel Calloway.

CALLOWAY (*to Martins*): You've been in on this story so much, you ought to see the end of it.

124. *CHILDREN'S WARD (NIGHT):*

> *He pushes open a door and, with a friendly hand, propels Martins down the ward, talking as he goes in a cheerful, professional, apparently heartless way. We take a rapid view of the six small beds, but we do not see the occupants, only the effect of horror on Martins's face.*

CALLOWAY: This is the biggest children's hospital in Vienna— very efficient place. In this ward we have six examples— you can't really call them children now, can you?—of the use of the Lime penicillin in meningitis. . . . Here in this bed is a particularly fascinating—example, if you are interested in the medical history of morons . . . now here . . .

> *Martins has seen as much as he can stand.*

MARTINS: For pete's [sic] sake, stop talking. Will you do me a favour and turn it off?

> *As they continue their walk past the small beds, dissolve.* (*The Third Man* 123–24)

FILM (one scene, 88½ minutes into the film)

Martins and Calloway enter a large ward of a hospital. As they walk past beds and Martins looks into them, Calloway tells Martins, "This is the biggest children's hospital in Vienna. All the kids in here are the result of Lime's penicillin racket." Calloway moves away from Martins and talks to a nurse (unheard) as Martins walks on slowly, still looking into each bed. Martins stops at the foot of one bed and looks into it. Calloway joins him (see photo) and says, "It had meningitis. They gave it some of Lime's penicillin. Terrible pity, isn't it?" Calloway then walks away from Martins, and Martins turns away and walks a few steps. (We do not see Calloway and Martins together again during the scene.) Nurses tend the offscreen children: taking temperatures, giving oxygen, marking a chart, tossing aside a teddy bear (presumably the child who had it won't need it anymore).

London Film Productions; Criterion DVD

Like the excerpt from the script for *The Royal Tenenbaums* reprinted in the left column of Table 5.2, this version of the *Third Man* script is written in the **master-scene format,** which often indicates the scene number, the setting, and the segment of the 24-hour day (such as day, night, dawn, noon, late afternoon). The scriptwriter describes the action briefly and supplies all the dialogue but does not indicate how the dialogue is to be spoken. The writer knew that well-written dialogue usually suggests its delivery and that the director and actors would probably have ignored overly specific directives.

In the right column of Table 5.3, a description of the actual scene in the finished film indicates that the film is true to the script in showing only Martins's reactions to the children and not the patients themselves. But the film differs in several ways from the script. The hallway and ward scenes in the shooting script have become one ward scene in the film—a wise decision because the script's hallway scene adds little to the story. The film also has far less dialogue (34 words versus 103) and relies more on visuals, especially the expressions on Martins's face, which we see in six of the scene's fifteen shots. In the film, Martins says nothing and Calloway is subtler. He talks less and does not push Martins along. Instead, he brings Martins into the ward and lets the sights of the place work on Martins, while the director lets the images of Martins's face work on the film's viewers, who can infer the extent of the suffering that Lime's actions have spawned. The film also portrays a large ward full of Lime's victims; the script indicates victims in only six beds. The film shows many nurses busy tending the children; the script says nothing about the nurses' work. When we compare screenplays or shooting scripts with the corresponding films, we find that, as in the case of *The Third Man*, the film is usually more concise, less reliant on dialogue, and more visual.

Although we cannot say with certainty who is responsible for all the changes in this part of *The Third Man*, we can see roughly what the scriptwriter, Graham Greene, wrote and the final filmed and edited product. Director Carol Reed probably deserves much credit for the changes from the script, which compress the action and present the information and moods more visually and more subtly.

Storyboards

Storyboards are a series of drawings (or occasionally photographs) of each shot (or sometimes part of a shot) of a planned film or video story, often accompanied by brief descriptions or notes (Figure 5.3). Storyboards are the visual equivalent of a rough draft of a written story. They allow filmmakers to see how the finished film might look before the laborious and costly processes of filming and editing begin. Storyboards are useful for deciding how to divide the script into shots, determining how to arrange the shots (a sort of preediting), and deciding camera placement.

In **animation**, storyboarding is crucial because creating each **frame** of an animated film is usually extremely time-consuming and expensive. Typically, once the storyboards for an animated film have been worked out in detail and the voices cast and all the vocals recorded, the creation of individual frames begins.

frame (noun): A separate, individual image on a strip of motion-picture film.

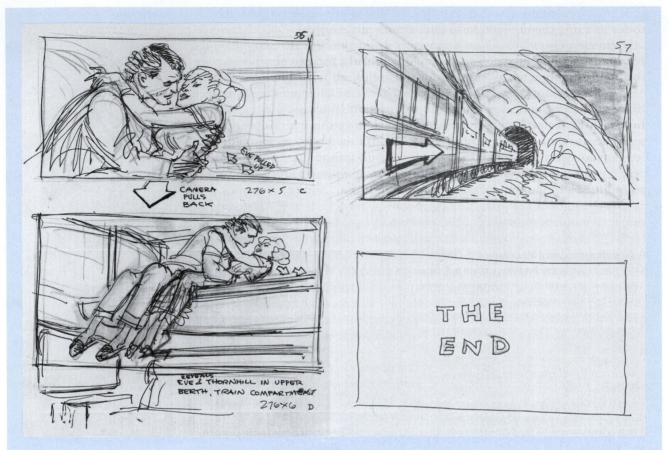

FIGURE 5.3 Sample storyboard
A storyboard is the visual equivalent of an outline for a story. Each panel represents an intended shot or part of a shot. Here are the final panels for Hitchcock's *North by Northwest* (1959). The first two represent the film's penultimate shot: the camera begins close to the two subjects and pulls back to reveal the surprising setting, the upper berth of a train compartment. The final shot is of the train speeding into a darkened tunnel. No part of a storyboard is binding on filmmakers; the panels are simply explorations of a film's possible shots. Hitchcock, however, worked out all of a movie's shots before filming began and rarely deviated from his plans once shooting was under way. *MGM; The Museum of Modern Art/Film Stills Archive*

INDIVIDUAL SOURCES

The history of cinema shows that just about any human subject can become the source of a fictional film. Possible, but infrequent, sources include nonfiction magazine articles (*Pushing Tin*, 1999, and *Isn't She Great*,

2000), video games (*Tomb Raider* films, 2001 and 2003; *Resident Evil* films, 2002, 2004, and 2007; and *Doom*, 2005), comic books (*X-Men*, 2000, and *X2: X-Men United*, 2003), comic strips (the Peanuts films), musical albums (*Pink Floyd the Wall*, 1982), operas (*Carmen*, many times), and even (loosely) amusement park rides (*Pirates of the Caribbean: The Curse of the Black Pearl*, 2003). Although fictional films can have other sources, five of the most frequent ones are history, fiction, plays, TV, and other films. As is illustrated in this chapter's last section, a film is often based on a series of sources, and even films based on one major source inevitably have been influenced by additional sources.

An adaptation of a primary source may be one of three basic types: (1) *loose* (it retains only a few major aspects of the original—for example, only the title and one or two of its subjects); (2) *faithful* (it imitates the subject and perhaps style of the original and captures its mood or spirit but with some changes); (3) *literal* (in nearly all aspects, it re-creates the source). Literal adaptations are rare but most likely to be attempted when plays are adapted into films. Which type of adaptation is "best" is subject to debate. Some critics advocate literal adaptations, assuming that re-creating the original as closely as possible is most important. At the opposite extreme, those who support loose adaptations believe that how closely a text adapts earlier texts is unimportant and that what matters is the quality of the adaptation.

History

Many fictional films—such as *Stand and Deliver* (1987), *The Hurricane* (1999), *Hotel Rwanda* (2004), *Munich* (2005), *Flags of Our Fathers* (2006), and *Letters from Iwo Jima* (2006)—are based on historical events. Often a single historical event is the source for multiple, very different film interpretations, as in the case of the sinking of the Titanic—*Saved from the Titanic* (1912), *Titanic* (1943), *Titanic* (1953), *A Night to Remember* (1958), and *Titanic* (1997). Usually movies based on historical events must attract large audiences to recoup the fortunes needed to make and market them. Consequently, filmmakers do not typically aim to teach audiences the accounts that are found in written histories because movies that include those tend to be unengaging, unpopular, and unprofitable. When a film deals with news or history, filmmakers usually omit, add, or change details to make the film more entertaining or to imply different meanings, or both. For centuries, novelists and playwrights, including Shakespeare, have done the same. (For a sample of the debate about the issues involved in one movie's interpretation of history, see pp. 212–14.)

Typically, fictional films based on history blend fiction and fact throughout. One example is *Stand and Deliver*, the story of a real Latino high school math teacher, Jaime Escalante, and one of his largely Latino

JFK: **Fact and Fiction**

Someone assassinated President John F. Kennedy in Dallas, Texas, on 22 November 1963, and shortly afterward the accused murderer himself was murdered while in custody. Soon a flood of theories about who was behind the two murders surged forth. The Warren Commission, appointed by President Lyndon B. Johnson, investigated the matter at length and issued a report that failed to gain widespread acceptance. To this day, many people remain uncertain about the causes of Kennedy's death. Oliver Stone's *JFK* (1991) combines actual documentary footage, reconstructed documentary-like footage, and fictionalized versions of people involved to present one theory about the Kennedy assassination. However, it is very much a minority interpretation, one to which few or no published historians subscribe. Even before Stone's film came out in December 1991, a controversy about its merits broke out around the United States. Following are excerpts from the wide-ranging debate.

Below are excerpts from a seven-page statement by Jack Valenti, the president and chief executive of the Motion Picture Association of America and a former top aide to President Johnson, as reported in the national edition of the *New York Times*, 2 April 1992:

> Does any sane human being truly believe that President Johnson, the Warren Commission members, law-enforcement officers, C.I.A., F.B.I., assorted thugs, weirdos, Frisbee throwers, all conspired together as plotters in Garrison's [the prosecutor's] wacky sighting? And then for almost 29 years nothing leaked? But you have to believe it if you think well of any part of this accusatory lunacy.
>
> In scene after scene Mr. Stone plasters together the half true and the totally false and from that he

manufactures the plausible. No wonder that many young people, gripped by the movie, leave the theater convinced they have been witness to the truth.

> In much the same way, young German boys and girls in 1941 were mesmerized by Leni Riefenstahl's *Triumph of the Will*, in which Adolf Hitler was depicted as a newborn God. Both *J.F.K.* and *Triumph of the Will* are equally a propaganda masterpiece and equally a hoax. Mr. Stone and Leni Riefenstahl have another genetic linkage: neither of them carried a disclaimer on their film that its contents were mostly pure fiction.

This op-ed piece in the 7 March 1992 national edition of the *New York Times* was written by David W. Belin, a former counsel to the Warren Commission:

> What far right-wing extremists tried to persuade a majority of Americans to believe in the 1960's with their "Impeach Earl Warren" billboards, Hollywood has been able to achieve in the 1990's in its impeachment of the integrity of a great Chief Justice.
>
> Earl Warren is not the only victim. The Kennedy assassination is called a "coup d'etat," a "public execution" by elements of the C.I.A. and the Department of Defense, while President Lyndon B. Johnson is called an accessory after the fact—in other words, a murderer.
>
> When the film not only alleges conspiracy but names the guilty parties, it goes beyond just artistic license and entertainment. It crosses the threshold of slander and character assassination—a 1990's version of McCarthyism.

A letter from John Roberts in the 18 August 2000 issue of the *Chronicle of Higher Education* included the following:

> In his [Stone's] preposterous film *JFK*, the only unassailable fact presented in the movie is that Kennedy is dead. The numerous threads of Mr. Stone's paranoid

Poster for *JFK* (1991)
From this poster, potential viewers learn that the film will focus on one man's difficult and dangerous task in pursuing a noble goal, a frequent subject in popular American movies. Because of the placement and size of the lettering, certain groups of words receive more prominence than others. The largest lettering and the boldface is for *JFK* (the movie's name); the next largest lettering is for *Kevin Costner* (the name of the popular actor playing the main role). Also prominent is lettering for *The Story that Won't Go Away* (a reminder that the causes of the Kennedy assassination are still in dispute).

As the movie *JFK* does, the visuals on the right side of the poster combine fiction and fact—an image of the actor playing the main role combined with fragments of three historical images: a photograph of part of the motorcade shortly after President Kennedy was shot, a newspaper headline announcing Kennedy's assassination, and a photo of the accused assassin, Lee Harvey Oswald, holding a rifle. *Warner Bros.*

conspiracy theories can be held together only by his creating out of whole cloth a person who did not exist (Donald Sutherland's character) who breathlessly tells the hero (Kevin Costner) that "Yes, this assassination was a coup!" All of it was done to keep Kennedy from doing something he never intended to do in the first place—namely, get out of Vietnam. . . . Kennedy understood the logic of the cold war, the danger of authoritarianism, and the threat of passivity in the face of real oppression. Keep in mind, this is the man who wrote *Why England Slept*. He was not into appeasement.

Mr. Stone seems to think this is a minor triviality. But it cuts to the core of his and others' conspiracy theories about the case. And without evidence to support the assertion that Kennedy was killed because he wanted to pull out of Vietnam, the conspiracy evaporates into thin air, whence Mr. Stone seems to have pulled it in the first place.

As film critic Roger Ebert, writing in the 20 December 1991 *Chicago Sun-Times*, saw it,

Stone's film is hypnotically watchable. Leaving aside all of its drama and emotion, it is a masterpiece of film assembly. The writing, the editing, the music, the photography, are all used here in a film of enormous complexity, to weave a persuasive tapestry out of an overwhelming mountain of evidence and testimony. Film students will examine this film in wonder in the years to come, astonished at how much information it contains, how many characters, how many interlocking flashbacks, what skillful interweaving of documentary and fictional footage. The film hurtles for 188 minutes through a sea of information and conjecture, and never falters and never confuses us. . . .

The achievement of the film is not that it answers the mystery of the Kennedy assassination, because it does not, or even that it vindicates Garrison, who is seen here as a man often whistling in the dark. Its achievement is that it tries to marshal the anger which ever since 1963 has been gnawing away on some dark shelf of the national psyche. John F. Kennedy was murdered. Lee Harvey Oswald could not have acted alone. Who acted with him? Who knew?

David Ansen, one of the film critics for *Newsweek*, wrote in the 23 December 1991 issue:

By turning Jim Garrison—a troubling, shoot-from-the-hip prosecutor whose credibility has been seriously questioned—into a mild-mannered, four-square Mr. Clean, Stone is asking for trouble. *JFK*'s Garrison is perhaps best viewed more as a movie convention than as a real man. Stone has always required a hero to worship, and he turns the D.A. into his own alter ego, a true believer tenaciously seeking higher truth. He equally idealizes Kennedy, seen as a shining symbol of hope and change, dedicated to pulling out of Vietnam and to ending the cold war.

But it is possible to remain skeptical of *JFK*'s Edenic notions of its heroes and still find this movie a remarkable, necessary provocation. Real political discourse has all but vanished from Hollywood filmmaking; above and beyond whether Stone's take on the assassination is right his film is a powerful, radical vision of America's drift toward covert government. What other filmmaker is even thinking about the uses and abuses of power?

Finally, historian Robert A. Rosenstone wrote in his 1995 book *Visions of the Past: The Challenge of Film to Our Idea of History* (123–24):

JFK, despite the many documentary-type elements that it contains, belongs to what is certainly the most popular type of film, the Hollywood—or mainstream—drama. This sort of film is marked, as cinema scholars have shown, by a number of characteristics, the chief being its desire to make us believe in [sic] that what we see in the theater is true. To this end, the mainstream film utilizes a specific sort of film language, a self-effacing, seamless language of shot, editing, and sound designed to make the screen seem no more than a window onto unmediated "reality."

Along with "realism," four other elements are crucial to an understanding [of] the mainstream historical film:

- Hollywood history is delivered in a story with beginning, middle, and end—a story that has a moral message, and one that is usually embodied in a progressive view of history.
- The story is closed, completed, and ultimately, simple. Alternative versions of the past are not shown; the *Rashomon* approach is never used in such works.
- History is a story of individuals—usually heroic individuals who do unusual things for the good of others, if not all humankind (ultimately, the audience).
- Historical issues are personalized, emotionalized, and dramatized—for film appeals to our feelings as a way of adding to our knowledge or affecting our beliefs.

Such elements go a long way toward explaining the shape of *JFK*. The story is not that of President Kennedy but of Jim Garrison, the heroic, embattled, uncorruptible investigator who wishes to make sense of JFK's assassination and its apparent coverup, not just for himself but for his country and its traditions—that is, for the audience, for us.

classes. The film shows various barriers the students face, the methods the teacher uses, and the students' hard work. The film presents all this in such a way that viewers are led to believe that the account is factual. In spirit, yes; in some details, no. For example, in the film the entire class seems to have to retake a national test because authorities at the testing service suspected cheating, but in fact only fourteen of the eighteen students had to take the test again. The film shows the students having only one day to review for the second test. The actual second test was administered several months later. Yet another example of a change made for the movie: as in nearly all fictional films, the movie character is livelier and more engaging than the real person (Figure 5.4).

FIGURE 5.4 Actor and subject
Actor Edward James Olmos (left) as Jaime Escalante in *Stand and Deliver* (1987), with the real high school math teacher Jaime Escalante. Comparison of clips of the celluloid Escalante teaching with documentary footage of the real Escalante teaching illustrates that, as in most movies based on real people, the movie character seems more lively and engaging than the actual person. *Publicity still. American Playhouse; Warner Bros.*

The makers of *The Hurricane*—which shows the story of Rubin (Hurricane) Carter, a successful boxer imprisoned for a triple murder but eventually freed—take great pains to make the film look historically accurate (Figure 5.5). The story is based on historical events about which there is disagreement. Before and after the film's opening in December 1999, reporters and attorneys involved in the original case painted a very different picture of the Carter case than the movie does.[1] The changes made seem to be the usual ones for movies based on history. Thus, for example, nine Canadians living on a commune become three Canadians doing some sort of work to end injustices in society. The detectives, prosecutors, witnesses, judges, and juries whose work led to two convictions of Carter become one racist police officer and two suspect witnesses. A trial, a conviction, nine months of liberty for Carter and John Artis (the other man arrested for the triple murder), a second trial, and a second conviction in the movie become one brief courtroom sentencing. In the film, Artis becomes a minor character while the young Lesra Martin, who worked with the Canadians on Carter's behalf, plays a major role.

Some actual events after Carter's second release from prison are at odds with the movie's concluding explanations about the main characters' fates. After his release from prison, Carter married one of the Canadians but eventually became disillusioned with her and the others of the commune

---

[1]For example, a former newspaper reporter who covered the case and is highly critical of the movie's accuracy has maintained a Web site with a video and links to many newspaper articles about the case.

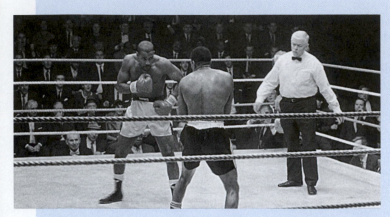

FIGURE 5.5   Re-creating the look of an earlier time and place
Like other commercial films based on historical events, the images in *The Hurricane* (1999) look authentic. Here about 4 1/2 minutes into the film, actor Denzel Washington (in white trunks) and others reenact part of a 1963 title fight. The scene was filmed in black and white, as photographs of the time would have been. Everything else about the scene—including the men's short haircuts and an audience made up mostly of white men in suits and narrow ties—looks true to the story's time and place. *Beacon, Universal; Universal DVD*

and evidently remains alienated from them all. The film informs viewers before the movie's closing credits only that "Terry, Sam, and Lisa returned to Canada. Rubin Carter joined them there and makes his home in Toronto. He is the Executive Director of the Association in Defence of the Wrongly Convicted."

Like so many other movies based on historical events, *The Hurricane* illustrates all of the following points made by historian Robert Brent Toplin:

> Filmmakers must attend to the demands of drama and the challenges of working with incomplete evidence. In creating historical dramas they almost always need to collapse several historical figures into a few central characters to make a story understandable. Often they are pressed to simplify complex causes so that audiences will comprehend their movies' principal messages and not lose interest, and the dramatic medium often leads them to attribute changes in history to the actions of dynamic individuals rather than to impersonal forces. Cinematic historians often lack detailed evidence about situations in the past, so they invent dialogue and suggest impressions about the emotions and motivations of historic figures. Also, they suggest **closure** on a story, revealing few doubts, questions, or considerations of alternative possibilities. (10)

closure: A sense of coherence and completion at the end of a narrative.

A fictional film based on historical events always fictionalizes the material to a greater or lesser extent.

Some filmmakers and film distributors downplay the fictional elements of movies based on history—for example, by burying the disclaimer (if there is one) at the end of the film when only a few viewers remain in the theater. In theatrical showings, *Gladiator* (2000), *The Hurricane*, and other movies end with disclaimers that are on screen only a few seconds. Here is the disclaimer for *The Hurricane*: "While this picture is based upon a true story, some characters have been composited or invented, and a number of incidents fictionalized." "Some" and "a number of" conceal the extensiveness and nature of the changes made. After the prolonged controversy about the historical accuracy of *The Hurricane* when it was released in theaters, the video and DVD releases carried the disclaimer at the beginning and ending. Filmmakers may even hide their fiction by claiming factuality. *Fargo* (1996) begins as follows:

> THIS IS A TRUE STORY.
> The events depicted in this film took place in Minnesota in 1987.
> At the request of the survivors, the names have been changed.
> Out of respect for the dead, the rest has been told exactly as it occurred.

Some reviewers of *Fargo* were skeptical of that claim, and an investigation by the *Minneapolis Star Tribune* failed to unearth any case like the one the movie represents. A fictional film may even falsely imply at its conclusion that it has been factual. The 1994 Russian-French film *Burnt by the Sun* has an epilogue explaining the fates of the main characters, but the film's director and cowriter, Nikita Mikhalkov, has said that "he added the epilogue for dramatic effect and invented the characters himself" (Stanley B1).

Other fictional filmmakers enhance their films' semblance of actuality by including **documentary**-like material. *Schindler's List* (1993) includes **title cards** about actual events, and the main body of the movie concludes with documentary footage of survivors and their relatives honoring Schindler by placing stones on his grave. *JFK* (1991) begins with documentary footage of President Dwight D. Eisenhower warning of the powers of the military-industrial complex and includes frequent excerpts from historical films and TV newscasts. *Apollo 13* (1995) uses old TV clips, interviews, subtitles conveying factual information, and (concluding) narration to enhance the appearance of factuality.

With a fictional film based on historical events, let the buyer beware: such a movie should be regarded primarily as a fictionalized entertainment that nearly always focuses more on satisfying storytelling than on written accounts regarded as historical. In both *Stand and Deliver* and *The Hurricane*, for example, as in so many American movies, the two major goals of the films are to entertain and to give hope that individuals or small groups that work hard and persistently can eventually triumph over society's flaws.

title card: A card or thin sheet of clear plastic on which is written or printed information included in a film.

The student essay "Understanding the History of the 1870s West with *The Ballad of Little Jo*" can be found at <bedfordstmartins.com/phillips-film>.

Many historical sources for films are cited in the first column of the chronology for 1895 to 2008 (see pp. 607–66).

Fiction

film theorist: A person who formulates a general explanation of the film medium or part of the medium.

According to critic and **film theorist** Dudley Andrew, "Well over half of all commercial films have come from literary originals" (98). To see what changes may be made when fiction is adapted into a film and what each medium is capable of, let's consider a passage of fiction and the corresponding section of a film based on the fiction. The fictional passage is from the end of Chapter 12 of *The Woman in the Dunes* (1964), Kobo Abé's Japanese novel about a man trapped in a large sand pit with a woman who lives there in a shack (left column, Table 5.4). The comparable section of the film version consists of the conclusion of one shot and three additional shots, begins nearly 35 minutes into the film, and runs about 45 seconds. A description appears in the right column of Table 5.4 (the dialogue is from the film's subtitles in the Criterion DVD).

There are many differences between the experience of reading the passage and seeing and hearing the corresponding section of the film. Some of the differences result from choices made by the filmmakers. For example, the filmmakers chose to have the man laugh, catch himself, and become brusque, whereas in the book the man shrieks and the woman laughs. Although filmmakers typically prune the dialogue they adapt from fiction, in this scene the filmmakers of *Woman in the Dunes* chose to supply slightly more dialogue than is in the novel.[2]

Many differences between the passage in Abé's novel and the corresponding section of the film, however, result from the limitations of film in comparison with fiction. The novel gives many of the man's thoughts, including a memory of how on the first night "she had laughed in that strange voice . . .," but to render these mental states in a film might confuse viewers. Look again at the last two paragraphs reprinted from the book. How can film accurately convey what those words do? Without words, how can a filmmaker convey the simile and the two implied metaphors in the sentences "Her charms were like some meat-eating plant, purposely equipped with the smell of sweet honey. First she would sow the seeds of scandal by bringing him to an act of passion, and then the chains of blackmail would bind him hand and foot"? The figurative language cannot be entirely converted into visual images and sounds, including music. Similarly, neither images nor sounds can convey well the experiences of smell, taste, and feeling. Thus, "A stagnant smell of sun-heated water, coming from her mouth, nose, ears, armpits, her whole body, began to pervade the room around him" cannot be captured by film.

Other differences between the passage and the film result from the limitations of fiction in comparison with film. In 45 seconds, the film gives viewers an excellent sense of place, shape, volume, textures, and sounds.

---

[2]The title of the English translation of the novel is *The Woman in the Dunes*. The title of the English translation of the film is *Woman in the Dunes*.

TABLE 5.4
The Woman in the Dunes (novel) and *Woman in the Dunes* (film)

NOVEL EXCERPT

The woman sidled up to him. Her knees pressed against his hips. A stagnant smell of sun-heated water, coming from her mouth, nose, ears, armpits, her whole body, began to pervade the room around him. Slowly, hesitantly, she began to run her searing fingers up and down his spine. His body stiffened.

Suddenly the fingers circled around to his side. The man let out a shriek.

"You're tickling!"

The woman laughed. She seemed to be teasing him, or else she was shy. It was too sudden; he could not pass judgment on the spur of the moment. What, really, was her intention? Had she done it on purpose or had her fingers slipped unintentionally? Until just a few minutes ago she had been blinking her eyes with all her might, trying to wake up. On the first night, too, he recalled, she had laughed in that strange voice when she had jabbed him in the side as she passed by. He wondered whether she meant anything in particular by such conduct.

Perhaps she did not really believe in his pretended illness and was testing her suspicions. That was a possibility. He couldn't relax his guard. Her charms were like some meat-eating plant, purposely equipped with the smell of sweet honey. First she would sow the seeds of scandal by bringing him to an act of passion, and then the chains of blackmail would bind him hand and foot. (Abé 90–91)

FILM EXCERPT

Shot 1. . . . *At the end of this lengthy shot, the woman, carrying a pan of water and a rag, approaches the man—who is lying on his back, naked from the waist up—and kneels beside him.*

WOMAN: How do you feel?

Shot 2. *The man turns his head slightly away from her and groans.*

MAN: Not too bad.

WOMAN: I'll wipe you down.

> *As she helps turn him on his side, he lets out more groans. The camera moves slightly to the left, and we see and hear her rinse and wring the rag in the metal pan; the camera moves right and we see her begin to wipe the man's back with the damp rag* (see photo). *She turns the rag over.*

Shot 3. *Part of the man's back and side is visible. The camera follows the woman's hand as she slowly wipes near his side. Offscreen, she transfers the rag to her left hand. With a finger of her right hand, she thumps or tickles his side.*

Shot 4. *As we see the man's face and shoulders, he giggles then quickly turns his head back toward the woman.*

MAN (*angry and loud*): Stop it!

> *With a serious look on his face, he lowers his head and faces forward again.*

WOMAN (*unseen*): It hurts?

MAN (*still serious*): Yes!

Source: Teshigahara Productions and Toho; Pathe Contemporary Films; Criterion DVD

For example, we can see the forms and sizes of the man and woman; we can see the texture of the man's skin; we hear his groans and the tone of voice of the man and woman. Most of these details are not rendered in the comparable passage of fiction. To do so would require enormous space and slow the story to a crawl, and even then the images in the reader's mind would be less precise than the images and sounds of the film. The movie camera can select actions and render them with clarity and force (as in the second shot where the camera moves left, then right); it can capture movements and gestures and their significance (such as the man's spontaneous laugh, followed by a quick suppression of it). Film can convincingly show places, real and imaginary. It can juxtapose images more quickly than the blink of an eye.

Film can present visual details such as faces, the viewing of which, as scientist and educator David Attenborough has said, is itself extraordinarily expressive:

> Letting others know how you feel is a basic part of communication. No creature in the world does so more eloquently than man, and no organ is more visually expressive than his face. Even in repose, the human face sends a message and one that we tend to take for granted. Each face proclaims individual identity. In teams, recognition of other members is of great importance. A hunting dog in a pack proclaims its identity by its own personal smell. Primates, with their reduced sense of smell but their very acute vision, do it by the infinite variety of their faces. We have more separate muscles in our faces than any other animal. So we can move it in a variety of ways that no other animal can equal and not only convey mood but send precise signals. By the expression on our face, we can call people and send them away, ask questions and return answers without a word being spoken.

Adept actors can express mood and meaning with facial expressions and can contribute much more. Michael Cunningham, author of *The Hours* (1998), has written with admiration about what the main female actors contributed to the 2002 film adaptation of his novel: "Actors . . . this good can introduce details you can't convey on paper. If only because by writing them down, you'd render them too obvious. Actors have the incidental at their disposal. Ms. [Meryl] Streep's Clarissa is stunningly complex, in part because she creates a whole person out of movements, expressions, and inflections. . . . And when she finally begins to lose her desperate composure, there's a moment, you miss it if you blink—when she literally loses her balance, tips over to the left, and immediately rights herself. If there's a way to do things like that on paper, I haven't found it" (1).

Film can also capture well the nuances of sound and music. Prose is hard-pressed to compete with cinema in presenting what can be seen and heard and in making us feel that we are at a particular place.

As we see illustrated by the Robert Altman film *The Player* (1992; see Chapter 13), fictional films that are based on novels or short stories rarely re-create the source fiction in its entirety. In film stories, passages of characters' thoughts, descriptions of characters' backgrounds, analysis by the author, and a more or less consistent point of view or means of perception are uncommon. The order of scenes may also be changed. Especially in popular movies, the ending of the source novel is often changed to a happier, more crowd-pleasing conclusion (Figure 5.6). Nor does the fictional film usually re-create all the characters and action of a novel. *Greed*—the 1925 American film classic, which is a literal adaptation of the novel *McTeague*—attempted to do so, but the initial version reportedly ran 9 1/2 hours. Such a length was quickly judged too long to be marketable because it could be screened only in two or three lengthy installments, whereas a two-hour film can be shown several times a day and thus can generate more revenue. Soon *Greed* was edited down to about two hours. Even *Tom Jones* (1963), which critics have praised for capturing the structure, **events**, and moods of the long, complicated British source novel, omits characters and events.

FIGURE 5.6
Jonik. Cartoon Arts International/CWS. Reprinted with permission.

Reading fiction and seeing a film are different experiences because each medium has its own techniques, strengths, and limitations. Perhaps the basic difference between fiction and film is that fiction requires its audience to visualize and subvocalize from printed words, whereas film presents images and sounds directly. People who enjoyed a novel are rarely satisfied with a film made from it because, in part, they visualize the characters and events as they read, and the film presents different visuals and sounds. Then, too, sometimes readers are disappointed that film adaptations do not include all of the novel's characters or **plot**.

Fiction and film are distinct media, with their own strengths and weaknesses. It is misleading to judge a film by how closely it re-creates the story one visualizes while reading. Instead, the film is something related yet new and separate, a creative expression in a different medium with its own resources and techniques. Likewise, whenever a novel or play is based on a film, it is unfair and misleading to evaluate the later work in another medium by how well it re-creates the source film. If one takes the view that a derivative creative fictional work should be judged by its fidelity to its

event: In a narrative or story, either an action by a character or person or a happening (a change brought about by a force other than a person or character, such as a lightning strike).

plot: The structure or arrangement of a narrative's events.

source(s), then, for example, many of Shakespeare's plays, such as *Macbeth* and *Richard III*, would be judged deficient: they are not reliable history but make for effective theater.

Instead of evaluating a film by comparing it to its fictional source, it is more helpful to compare the film version to other, similar films (and to compare the fiction with other, similar fiction). However, a close comparison of a film and its fictional source can be instructive, revealing what creative decisions were made during the transformation, what the two forms share, and what is distinct to each.[3]

For a sample student essay about a fictional work adapted into a film, see the Close-Up section of this chapter on pp. 247–48, and for a detailed comparison of a source novel and the film made from it (*The Player*), see the section "Novel and Film" in Chapter 13, pp. 590–92.

Plays

In the early years of cinema, many fictional films closely imitated plays. After all, plays had existed in the Western world for more than two thousand years, and in the 1890s people on both sides of the footlights had a good sense of what a play was. For this reason, many early films look like awkwardly filmed theater (Figure 5.7). Gradually, though, film developed its own identity. Today, the two forms are still cousins but are not as close as they were in film's first few decades.

Basically, plays are the more verbal medium. If you listen to a recording of a play, you will notice that the lines of dialogue and their delivery communicate much of the play's moods and meanings. So expressive is the human voice that a trained actor can convey a world of information and feeling by pauses, volume, timbre, timing, and pronunciation.

Films, in contrast, tend to be much more visual. Several times I have begun a film course by giving students a list of questions to answer about a film, such as "Who is the main character? What does he or she seem to want? What does that character's personality seem to be like? Where and when does the story take place?" Then I turn off the volume and show students the beginning of a British film few of them have seen. I show the film

---

[3]Some authors, such as Gabriel García Márquez and E. L. Doctorow, and some film scholars have written about the many general ways movies have influenced the ways fiction is now often written—for example, with little initial description of setting, sparse initial exposition, shorter scenes, and a faster **pace**. Movies have also been responsible for a type of fiction, *novelizations*—paperback novels that re-create and expand the plots of recent movies. By initially appearing usually a few weeks before the movie first comes out, these books help publicize the movie, but they are written and published rapidly and are usually judged as inferior fiction when compared with other published fiction.

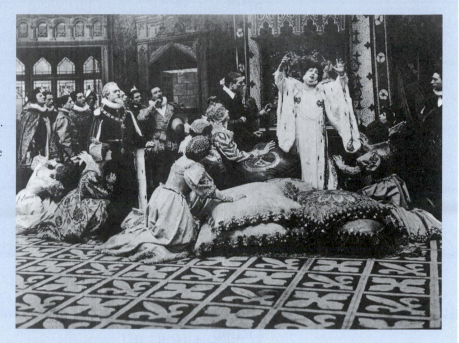

FIGURE 5.7 Early film actors with theatrical backgrounds
In the 1912 "Queen Elizabeth," Sarah Bernhardt, one of the most famous actors of her era, played her part with the broad stylized gestures that actors of the day used so that they could be seen from distant seats in large theaters. Actors with theater experience had not yet learned to restrain their acting style for the movies. *The Museum of Modern Art/Film Stills Archive*

clip twice. After each showing, I ask students to jot notes in answer to my questions and about anything else they noticed in the silent clip. Then I collect and read the responses aloud. The results: students generally come close to what the film is showing—with only its moving pictures. Films can convey so much information visually that the acclaimed 1924 silent German film *The Last Laugh* includes readable words only four times. Many movies—for example, *2001: A Space Odyssey* (1968) and Jane Campion's *The Piano* (1993)—have scenes with little or no dialogue or with sign language. If you watch a foreign-language film with inadequate subtitles—and do not allow yourself to be distracted with thoughts about how annoying it is not to know all that is being said—you will understand a great deal from only the film's visuals.

Some would argue that the essence of a play is at least one actor acting and reacting. Actors also interact with the audience. Experienced theater actors attest to how much an alert, responsive, and supportive audience contributes to an effective performance. Live acting differs markedly from the rehearsed, edited, larger-than-life performances shown from different distances and angles on the movie screen. The live actor is more nearly what we see in our lives outside the theater, someone who might even occasionally seem to look us in the eye, someone who makes imperfect delivery or has all-too-human movements. In small theaters where the audience is close to the stage, live acting may also be more intimate.

Because of these basic differences between plays and films, certain changes tend to be made when a play is transformed into a film. Most filmmakers want to make a film, not simply record a performance of a play. A film version of a play tends to locate some of the scenes outdoors. This process is called "opening up" the play. With more scenes, it's not unusual for a film to have more characters than its source. The film derived from a play often prunes the play's dialogue and relies more on the visuals, music, and sound effects. And as we watch a film, we seem to get to sit in many seats and view the action from different distances and angles.

In staging a play, directors, actors, costumers, set designers, and others decide what words and actions to include, how to show the action and deliver the dialogue, how to costume the characters, and what the lighting and settings will be like. In the stage directions printed with their plays, some playwrights include details about how the plays should be staged. Other writers, such as Shakespeare, supply few such directions (perhaps in Shakespeare's case in part because he himself did not prepare his own plays for publication).

mise en scène: An image's setting, subjects, and composition (the arrangement of setting and subjects within the frame).

As we saw in the chapter on **mise en scène**, when a play is filmed, filmmakers make many of the same decisions that are made by people staging a play—about the selection of dialogue and actions, lighting, costuming, settings, and the like. However, filmmakers have many additional concerns, such as camera distances and angles, editing, and nearly always a more complex mixture of spoken words, sound effects, and music than is found in a staged play.

To see some of the differences between a play and one of its film adaptations, consider Shakespeare's *Richard III*, which was a play (probably first published in 1597) before it was a film (the version discussed here is the 1995 production with Ian McKellen; Figure 5.8). Table 5.5 illustrates some of the similarities and differences between the play and the 1995 film version. In its fundamentals, the film adaptation remains faithful to the original play. The film's opening, for example, retains most of the play's dialogue, the personalities of the major characters are unchanged, and the

FIGURE 5.8 Main determinant of actions, consequences, and meanings
As in most Shakespearean film adaptations, in the 1995 version of *Richard III*, many changes were made between the play and film. The focus of the film, however, remains on Richard—his charm and political skills but also his utter ruthlessness (even to those who support him), his overreaching, and his fall from power—and finally, as in other Shakespearean tragedies, the restoration of political order. *Bayly/Paré Productions, United Artists, and others; MGM Home Entertainment DVD*

focus stays on a disgruntled Richard setting in motion schemes to hurt others while advancing himself into a position of power.

Nevertheless, as in most plays transformed into films, there are many differences. The film shows actions only mentioned in the play—the murders of the Prince of Wales and his father, the king. As is usually the case when a play is compared with its corresponding film, the film version also has many more scenes and settings. In Shakespeare's play, the entire first scene takes place on a London street. The opening of the McKellen *Richard III*, however, takes place in King Henry VI's field headquarters, on a London street, in the palace, at an airport, back at the palace, and near a docked boat. The film changes the setting of the play's opening soliloquy (which takes place on a London street) to two settings: before a large party and in a men's restroom. In the film, objects (car, airplane, palace, clothes) show the York family's wealth and power. Viewers may also notice that the uniforms and banners resemble those used by the Nazi regime in Germany, suggesting that York-ruled England is a fascist state. Unlike the play, the film uses five brief title cards to supply basic information about settings and situations. The film also has less dialogue than the play. During the film's first 8 minutes and 47 seconds, only nine spoken words are heard (not counting the lyrics that a woman sings at the party). Of the play's first soliloquy, which is forty-one lines long, only thirty lines are used in the film plus three lines inserted from Act 3, Scene 2, of Shakespeare's *Henry VI, Part 3* (see the three consecutive lines in boldface in Table 5.5). Like nearly all films based on plays, the film relies more heavily on visuals than does the play.

Shakespeare's plays have been a deep and enduring well of inspiration for films. Most of the stories have remained of interest to viewers, and Shakespeare's insights into human behavior are matched by perhaps only a few other writers in the history of Western literature. His language—though often difficult for modern audiences and in places obscure even to scholars who have dedicated their lives to its study—is often striking, apt, and memorable.

In transferring a play to the screen—especially Shakespeare's plays—filmmakers often take major liberties. Period, settings, costumes, and props may all be added or altered. Lines are nearly always pruned. The actors' gestures may suggest possible new interpretations. Consider the 2000 film *Hamlet*, with Ethan Hawke playing Hamlet. The setting is shifted from Denmark in approximately the year 1600 to New York City in 2000. Instead of scenes taking place in a castle at Elsinore, they are set in the Hotel Elsinore, a high-rise luxury hotel presumably near Times Square; a laundromat; a diner; and the Guggenheim Museum. In the action videos section in the neighborhood Blockbuster, Hamlet delivers part of his "To be, or not to be" soliloquy. Instead of traveling to England in a boat, Hamlet is transported in a jet. Costumes are not period clothing but what early-twenty-first-century New Yorkers might wear. Props include the

TABLE 5.5
Richard III: Scene 1 of the Play and the First 14 Scenes of the 1995 Film

[ ] = Dialogue deleted for the film. **Boldface** = Dialogue added in the film. {   } = Additional information.

THE PLAY (first scene)

Act 1, Scene 1
London. A street.

Enter Richard, Duke of Gloucester, solus.

GLO. Now is the winter of our discontent
Made glorious summer by this sun of York,
And all the clouds that lowered upon our house
In the deep bosom of the ocean buried.
Now are our brows bound with victorious wreaths,
Our bruisèd arms hung up for monuments,
Our stern alarums changed to merry meetings,
Our dreadful marches to delightful measures.
Grim-visaged war hath smoothed his wrinkled front,
And now, instead of mounting barbèd steeds
To fright the souls of fearful adversaries,
He capers nimbly in a lady's chamber
To the lascivious pleasing of a lute.
But I, that am not shaped for sportive tricks,
Nor made to court an amorous looking-glass;
I, that am rudely stamped, [and want love's majesty
To strut before a wanton ambling nymph;
I, that am curtailed of this fair proportion,
Cheated of feature by dissembling nature,]
Deformed, unfinished, sent before my time
Into this breathing world, scarce half made up,
And that so lamely and unfashionable
That dogs bark at me as I halt by them—
Why, I, in this weak piping time of peace,
Have no delight to pass away the time,
Unless to spy my shadow in the sun
And descant on mine own deformity.
And therefore since I cannot prove a lover,
[To entertain these fair well-spoken days,]
I am determinèd to prove a villain
And hate the idle pleasures of these days.
Plots have I laid, [inductions dangerous,
By drunken prophecies, libels, and dreams,]
To set my brother Clarence and the King
In deadly hate the one against the other,

THE FILM
(first 14 scenes, 11 minutes, 34 seconds)

1. Field headquarters of King Henry VI's army at Tewkesbury. Richard kills the Prince of Wales and the prince's father, King Henry VI. Only dialogue in the scene: Son: "**Goodnight, your Majesty.**" King: "**Goodnight, son.**" Son: "**Father.**"

2. Richard is driven in an escorted car in London.

3. At the palace, young prince Edward playfully tries to avoid being dried after his bath.

4. Nurse to King Edward IV: "**Your Majesty.**" She gives him his medicine.

5. Clarence finishes developing some photos, grabs his coat and camera, and rushes off.

6. At the airport, Rivers gets off a plane and gives a stewardess his card.

7. Richard's motorcade arrives at the palace, and Richard gets out.

8. Richard addresses the Duchess of York as "**Mother,**" but she and her granddaughter, the young Elizabeth, pass by Richard without a word.

9. Clarence sets the camera timer and takes the York family photo.

   {Up to this point, the film has supplied information on three title cards and two superimposed title cards.}

10. At a party the Yorks throw to celebrate their victory over King Henry VI and the House of Lancaster, King Edward IV dances with his queen, Elizabeth. Richmond asks the young Elizabeth to dance. Buckingham and Richard greet each other warmly.

11. Outside, Rivers, the queen's brother, arrives by car; he gets out of the car and walks up the steps toward the party.

12. The queen dances with young Edward, her son and the heir to the throne. Rivers greets various people and dances with the queen and his young nephew Edward. Clarence is led away by several men. Richard steps up to the microphone and begins to speak {8 minutes, 47 seconds into the film}:

THE PLAY (continued)

[And if King Edward be as true and just
As I am subtle, false, and treacherous,
This day should Clarence closely be mewed up,
About a prophecy, which says that G
Of Edward's heirs the murderer shall be.
Dive, thoughts, down to my soul—here
     Clarence comes.]

*Clarence enters, under guard. He is being taken
as a prisoner to the Tower. Richard acts surprised
and vows to help him.*

*After Clarence is led away, Richard, alone,
reveals he plans to have Clarence killed.*

*Lord Hastings, who has recently been released
from imprisonment in the Tower himself, tells
Richard that King Edward IV is very ill.*

*Alone again, Richard reveals more about his
plans for Clarence and how Richard for tactical
reasons plans to marry Lady Anne, whose husband and father-in-law (King Henry VI) Richard
himself had killed.*

THE FILM (continued)

Now is the winter of our discontent
Made glorious summer by this sun of York,
And all the clouds that lowered upon our house
In the deep bosom of the ocean buried.
Now are our brows bound with victorious wreaths,
Our bruisèd arms hung up for monuments,
Our stern alarums changed to merry meetings,
Our dreadful marches to delightful measures.
Grim-visaged war hath smoothed his wrinkled front,
And now, instead of mounting barbèd steeds
To fright the souls of fearful adversaries,
He

13. {Richard enters men's room} capers nimbly in a lady's
     chamber
To the lascivious pleasing of a lute.
But I, that am not shaped for sportive tricks,
Nor made to court an amorous looking-glass;
I, that am rudely stamped,
Deformed, {flushes urinal} unfinished, sent before my time
Into this breathing world, scarce half made up,
And that so lamely and unfashionable
That dogs bark at me as I halt by them—
Why, I, in this weak piping time of peace,
Have no delight to pass away the time,
Unless to espy my shadow in the sun
And descant on mine own deformity.
Why I can smile and murder while I smile
And wet my cheeks with artificial tears
And frame my face to all occasions.
And therefore since I cannot prove a lover,
I am determinèd to prove a villain
And hate the idle pleasures of these days.
Plots have I laid {Richard leaves men's room}

14. {above a pier leading to a boat and some distance from it}
To set my brothers Clarence and King **Edward**
In deadly hate the one against the other.

latest electronic gadgets, a pistol to supplement fencing foils, and a briefly
glimpsed little rubber duck that Ophelia nearly returns to Hamlet along
with his love letters. King Claudius is now a dapper new CEO of the
Denmark Corp., although he is as smooth and treacherous as ever. Hamlet
is an aspiring film/videomaker whose mousetrap to test the conscience of
the king is not a play within the play but a film within the film. In this as in
other *Hamlet*s, lines are pruned, characters are dropped, and whole scenes

filmic: Characteristic of the film medium or appropriate to it, such as parallel editing.

are eliminated. The performances also add new or at least unusual interpretive possibilities. The Laertes of this first **filmic** *Hamlet* of the new century, for example, seems to have a stronger than brotherly attachment to his sister Ophelia. She seems here more emotionally pained and more prone to serious instability than she does in many earlier productions. Gertrude seems to sense that the cup of wine Claudius offers Hamlet is poisoned but drinks from it anyway. The results are another *Hamlet*: same basic plot, same language—in what remains of Shakespeare's lines—but a *Hamlet* that the makers of the film doubtless hoped would attract and engage a new generation.

There are exceptions to the foregoing generalizations about films and plays. Some films—*My Dinner with André* (1981), for example—have much in common with traditional plays: few scenes, much dialogue, and limited visuals. And some recent plays have much in common with films—scores of short scenes, many settings, and sparse dialogue.[4]

Television

Television has long been a source for movies, especially since the box office success of *The Addams Family* (1991). Since then, U.S. studios have made a slew of TV shows into movies, including *The Fugitive* (1993), *The Beverly Hillbillies* (1993), *The Flintstones* (1994), *Mission Impossible* (1996), *The Rugrats Movie* (1998), *The X-Files* (1998), *South Park: Bigger, Longer, and Uncut* (1999), *Mission: Impossible 2* (2000), *Charlie's Angels* (2000), *Traffic* (2000), *I Spy* (2002), *Charlie's Angels: Full Throttle* (2003), *The Simpsons Movie* (2007), and many others. TV has been a frequent source for the characters and plots of movies and the writers, actors, and directors who bring them to

---

[4]In recent decades, films increasingly influence plays, in both the writing and the staging. Sometimes plays discuss or allude to films. This happens in *The Baltimore Waltz* (1990), a play that refers to the films *The Third Man* (1949), *Dr. Strangelove: Or, How I Learned to Stop Worrying and Love the Bomb* (1963), and *Wuthering Heights* (1939). Plays may also be structured as a film typically is. In general, recent plays consist of many more brief scenes than plays had before the arrival of cinema. *The Baltimore Waltz*, for example, has thirty scenes during its approximately 80 minutes of playing time. Often, staging is influenced by films. A 1996 production of *Four Dogs and a Bone* added video versions of imaginary film footage made during a day's work.

For many decades, Broadway was a source for many of Hollywood's most successful musical films: *Oklahoma!*, *South Pacific*, *West Side Story*, *My Fair Lady*, *Chicago*, and many others. Now that trend has somewhat reversed, as films become the sources of musical plays. Examples are *Sunset Boulevard*; *Victor/Victoria*; the MGM musicals *Singin' in the Rain*, *Meet Me in St. Louis*, and *Seven Brides for Seven Brothers*; the Disney hits *The Little Mermaid*, *Beauty and the Beast*, and *The Lion King*; *The Full Monty* (with an American setting); *The Producers*; *Hairspray*; and *Gray Gardens*, which was originally a documentary film. From time to time, films are still the basis of nonmusical plays, as with *The Graduate*, which has played in both New York and London. Plays may also be based on a movie topic or type. An example is *Action Movie: The Play—The Director's Cut*, a 1998 parody of action movies.

life on the big screen. Perhaps almost as often, TV borrows from films. It is a two-way street with heavy traffic. The mutual dependence of one medium on the other has become so commonplace that knowledge of the relationship of the two media deepens one's understanding of both.

The TV medium itself has also been a subject for films. Commercial television's proclivity to present a sanitized and artificial world was a subject of several late-1990s films. In *Pleasantville* (1998), David wishes that his life were more like the TV series *Pleasantville*, a re-creation of 1950s sitcoms such as (*The Adventures of*) *Ozzie and Harriet* (1952–1966) and *Leave It to Beaver* (1957–1963). Because David's family life and social life are frustrating, he is attracted to the stable and comforting lives he sees on the show. In this fictional world, it's always 72 degrees and sunny, divorce is nonexistent, there is no conflict, Mom is always home to make dinner and cookies, and one of the prettiest girls in school is eager to date David. Nevertheless, when he and his sister become trapped in the TV show as two black-and-white characters, David slowly realizes that the sanitized world of Pleasantville is artificial and constricting. While this fifties TV world is safe, it also precludes opportunity for individualism, creativity, and deeply felt emotions (orgasms, too). Like the widely held view of the 1950s as a decade, Pleasantville is initially colorless and is characterized by a restricted range of options. *The Truman Show* (1998) provides much the same image of TV shows. The movie focuses on a character who eventually realizes that his life in an idealized small town is controlled by a television producer and that his entire life is being broadcast for the benefit of a huge television audience. Like Disneyland, which itself is a creation of the 1950s, *Pleasantville* and *The Truman Show* present a world that is safe, sanitized, and reassuring—at least initially.

Movies often **satirize** television. Oliver Stone's *Natural Born Killers* (1994) shows the story of two murderous lovers and their victims. The film has many satiric targets: law enforcement officers, prison guards, the police officer/author who murders a prostitute, the warden who is twisted by hatred of the murdering couple, and the TV tabloid host of *American Maniacs*, who will do anything to get a story and high ratings (see Plate 33 in Chapter 13). The film especially goes after the TV journalist for his self-absorption and self-promotion, thin veneer of self-control, pride, and pandering to the worst in human nature. The film also satirizes the American public's love affair with violence—especially when it is largely used against authorities—by showing how ratings-hungry journalists turn two killers into international celebrities. One of the most prominent satiric targets in Spike Lee's *Bamboozled* (2000) is the programming of commercial TV run by European Americans who do not understand African American culture(s) yet are eager to present tired, offensive racial **stereotypes** in the name of entertainment. The film also satirizes TV audiences who eagerly lap up the rancid old wine poured from new bottles (see Figure 6.24 on p. 291).

satire: A representation of individual or group thinking or behavior that indirectly exposes the subject as flawed.

stereotype: A commonplace, simplified, and in some ways inaccurate likeness of a subject created in a text.

Two other sources for films, though rarely the main sources, are TV commercials and music videos. Commentator Maria Demopoulos points out that directors of music videos seek "to translate into film the ethos characteristic of the young demographic of the music: rebellion, defiance, individuality, teen angst. Music videos, by design, reflect a youth-driven agenda, distinguished by impermanence and disposability" (36). Often, these are the same subjects and outlook of teen movies. Demopoulos also points out that the techniques and ideas of TV commercials and music videos have influenced filmmakers and vice versa:

feature (film): A fictional film that is at least 60 minutes long.

> The techniques and ideas behind these short formats have crossed over to **feature films**. Commercials and music videos have long served as a testing ground for visual styles migrating upward, and at the same time have spawned a new generation of directors. . . . Still, the influence flows both ways. Much of the raw material mined for music videos and commercials derives from films in the first place. The video-as-movie-adventure-epic, for instance, dates back to MTV's infancy with Duran Duran's video "Hungry Like the Wolf" ([directed by] Russell Mulcahy, [19]82). (35)

Commentators concur that the two short TV formats have influenced moviemaking most notably in editing. It seems likely that viewing both TV commercials, including movie **trailers**, and music videos has conditioned a new generation of viewers to process a succession of images more quickly than earlier generations. Because so many viewers have seen so many TV commercials and music videos, filmmakers have the option of doing less **continuity editing** and more editing by association, intuition, or accident, as in sections of *Natural Born Killers*.

trailer: A brief compilation film to advertise a movie or video release.

TV has also borrowed from film. Television parodies of movies or parts of movies have a long history in the United States, going all the way back to TV's birth and providing subjects for performers like Milton Berle, Sid Caesar, Imogene Coca, and Carol Burnett and later *Saturday Night Live*. A Thanksgiving episode of *South Park* (Episode 109, "Starvin' Marvin," 1997) provides another instance of TV borrowing from film. In that episode, an attack by vengeful turkeys is made even more amusing because it parodies the epic battle scenes in *Braveheart* (1995). Over the years, various popular movies, such as *MASH* (1970) and *Buffy the Vampire Slayer* (1992), have also led to TV series. And we should not overlook the repeated influences of the *Godfather* movies on *The Sopranos*.

The relationship between the two media is sometimes complex. The successful transformation of the 1966–1969 *Star Trek* TV series into six films is an example of this mutual dependence. The first *Star Trek* movie, *Star Trek: The Motion Picture* (1979), reunited the television cast from the U.S.S. *Enterprise*; it was followed by five sequels and inspired a new television series. In the second TV series, crew members can walk onto the "holograph deck" of the *Enterprise* and enter simulated environments that are often inspired by films or are informed by film aesthetics.

Although television and film now provide innumerable sources for each other, they have not always coexisted amicably. When television appeared on the American national scene in force during the 1950s, Hollywood was floundering. During the war years of 1941 to 1945 and the postwar years from 1946 to 1948, Hollywood experienced its most profitable period. During the war, weekly attendance was estimated at ninety million people, a number that was five times the weekly attendance number in the mid-1990s (Cook 442). This wartime boom for the movie industry, however, slowed in the late forties and early fifties as television viewing grew. By 1949, movie attendance had dropped from ninety million to seventy million. In the same year, there were one million television sets in the United States. By 1951, the number of sets had climbed to ten million, and by 1959, it had reached fifty million (Cook 459). For some years, television and film competed intensely for the same audience. Hollywood's initial reaction was to refuse to interact with television or even acknowledge its existence. Members of the Motion Picture Association of America would not lease or sell their films for broadcast until 1956, and many film studios refused to allow their stars to appear on television (Cook 459). Gradually and haltingly, movie studios got into TV production, and media conglomerates included movie and TV production components under one corporate umbrella. Today, TV and film have grown more comfortable with—or at least more resigned to—their marriage, though from time to time flashes of envy and condescension appear.

For more information on the development of TV and other mass media, see the third column of the chronology for 1895 to 2008 (pp. 607–66).

Other Films

> I'm often asked by younger filmmakers why do I need to look at old movies. . . . I'm always looking for something or someone that I can learn from. I tell the younger filmmakers and young students: do it like painters used to do, what painters do. Study the old masters. Enrich your palette. Expand the canvas. There is always so much more to learn.   —Martin Scorsese

IMITATIONS

Filmmakers may imitate an earlier film, either part of it or (less commonly) all of it. Like an adaptation of any text, an imitation may be one of three basic types. The imitation may be loose (it retains only a few major aspects of the original, such as only the title and one or two of its subjects); faithful (it imitates the subject and perhaps style of the original and captures its mood or spirit but with some changes); or literal (as nearly as possible it re-creates the sources). These three types of imitation are of only limited help. With some texts, it is difficult to be certain whether to label them as one type of imitation or another, or as sharing characteristics of two of the types. Some thoughtful viewers might label a film that imitates an earlier film "loose," others might label it "faithful," and still others might judge it loose in some respects but faithful in others. At any rate, imitations of texts or, more often, parts of texts may take the form of a remake, an allusion, a parody, or an homage.

In a remake, the original film or part of a film is re-created but usually updated: changes are made in the hope that the remake will seem more appealing to current audiences. Remakes are attractive to producers because the original film usually made a lot of money and some of the public will remember it favorably and be curious to see a modern version of it. For economic reasons, then, remakes have been plentiful in Hollywood.

A good example of a remake of an entire film is Gus Van Sant's remake of Alfred Hitchcock's *Psycho*. Although many critics have labeled the 1998 *Psycho* as an exact re-creation of the 1960 film, it is not. Yes, many scenes are extremely close. The dialogue is close, often exact. Many of the camera setups and the editing are largely the same. But.

The remake omits at least one scene and changes other scenes. The scene in the original where Lila and Sam meet Sheriff Chambers and his wife outside a church after the Sunday service is nowhere to be found in the remake. Scenes are changed by the addition of new shots. A striking example: as Detective Arbogast is being murdered and falling down the stairs, the remake includes two new shots, supposedly samples of what he visualizes during his last moments alive: a shot of darkened, roiled, fast-moving clouds and a circumspect shot of a naked woman. Language that is dated—such as Arbogast's observation that "if it doesn't jell, it isn't aspic"—has been changed or deleted. The scene that is most changed, however, is the first one: Sam and Marion in a hotel room (Figure 5.9).

Two of the most fundamental changes: the remake film is in color—so, for example, blood is red, not a shade of gray—and the film uses saturated colors as it proceeds. And then the remake has recent, mostly recognizable actors, who along with their director were interested in developing their characters and in figuring out the characters' motivations and ways to play a scene. Sam, for instance, is now a man on the make who would hop in bed with Marion's sister Lila if given the chance. But Lila, in turn, is played (subtly) as a lesbian and uninterested. In the remake, Norman is more obviously sexually aroused by Marion than could be shown in 1960: as he watches her through a peephole, he masturbates to completion.

Probably most young people, who generally do not watch black-and-white films, have not seen the Hitchcock original, and director Gus Van Sant hoped to entice them into seeing his version of the story. Some people were predisposed against the remake even before seeing it. Some asked, for example, why remake a masterpiece? But remakes are a matter

a)

b)

FIGURE 5.9 A scene from a film and a remake of it
Gus Van Sant directed the 1998 remake of Alfred Hitchcock's 1960 *Psycho*. By Van Sant's own account in the DVD commentary, the scene changed most drastically between the original *Psycho* (a) and his own *Psycho* (b) is the first. In a hotel room, Sam and Marion are more intimate than in the original. To underscore the nature of the hotel in the remake, briefly and subtly, another couple can be heard having sex in the next room. The scene also includes glimpses of below-the-waist (male) nudity from behind, something strictly forbidden in the days of the original. (a) *Universal City Studios; Universal Home Video DVD.* (b) *Universal Pictures, Imagine Entertainment; Universal DVD Video*

of degree: later imitators inevitably make changes. The key question is how significant are they? A film that imitates an earlier film is always an approximation, not a replication. When viewers and critics judge an imitation to be "close" to the original, they think of it as a remake. In other words, a film remake can be defined as an imitation of an earlier film that is judged basically faithful to the original.

Loose remakes are plentiful. Examples are the remakes of the classic American comedy *It Happened One Night* (1934), which has twice been remade in India as *Chori Chori* (1956) and *Dil Hai Ke Manta Nahin* (1991) but with major changes:

> Whenever a Hollywood film is remade in India it has to be recast in the Indian mould, that is, emotions have to be overstated, song, dances, and spectacle have to be added, family relationships have to be introduced if they do not exist in the original, traditional moral values such as dharma (duty) must be reiterated, and female chastity must be eulogised. Only then will the film find success at the box office. (Kasbekar 412)

In their fast pace, frequent cliff-hanging action, and exotic costumes and locations, the *Star Wars* movies, Indiana Jones movies, and many other action movies can be seen as loose but high-budget remakes of **serials**, including the Buck Rogers serials and the Flash Gordon serials (Figure 5.10).

FIGURE 5.10 A serial
From the 1910s to the early 1950s, serials were shown in short weekly installments in neighborhood and downtown movie theaters. They featured extensive, fast-paced action; danger for the heroes; occasional episodes of tepid romance; and exotic villains, costumes, and settings. Seen here is a lobby card for Chapter 6 of the twelve-chapter popular serial *Flash Gordon Conquers the Universe* (1940). Flash Gordon, played by Larry (Buster) Crabbe, is the second character from the left. *Universal*

A remake may be of the soundtrack only. In *What's Up, Tiger Lily?* (1966) Woody Allen remade only the soundtrack of a Japanese movie by deleting the original soundtrack and adding new dialogue, music, and sound effects to tell a very different, often amusing story about the complicated adventures of a Japanese James Bond–like secret agent, Phil Moscowitz. In various ways, the soundtrack reuses parts of many earlier texts. Two examples: viewers briefly hear voice imitations of such famous earlier movie stars as James Cagney and Peter Lorre, and occasionally the film includes clips of The Lovin' Spoonful performing songs that have nothing to do with the story.

If you examine one of the reference books, CD-ROMs, or Web sites that describe and evaluate thousands of films, you may be surprised by how many hundreds and hundreds of them are remakes. A later film with the same title, however, is not necessarily a remake because many titles are reused for a different story (both film stories and titles get recycled, but not necessarily together).

An allusion is a reference to an earlier text or part of one. Filmmakers may allude to a text for various reasons—for example, "to acknowledge their own debt to other directors, to enrich their work with the themes and emotions associated with the earlier work, or simply as an ironic contrast to their own characters and situations" (Konigsberg 9). Allusions are also a way to share aspects of a culture. Occasionally, filmmakers make allusions to their own earlier films. In two scenes in *The Sure Thing* (1985), directed by Rob Reiner, a poster for *This Is Spinal Tap* (1984), also directed by Reiner, is visible briefly in the background. In a scene in Mel Brooks's *Spaceballs* (1987), a shelf on a spaceship contains videotapes of films directed by Brooks, including the videotape for *Spaceballs* (a little more than 36 minutes into the film)! In *American Graffiti* (1973), director George Lucas makes a sly allusion to an earlier film directed by the film's co-producer (Figure 5.11). A filmmaker may even make an allusion to a work that initially seems to have been made by someone else but was in fact also made by the person making the allusion. Pedro Almodóvar's *Talk to Her* (2002) includes excerpts from an unusual black-and-white silent film called "The Shrinking Lover," which was in fact the creation of Almodóvar. One could label such usages *mock allusions* (Figure 5.12).

FIGURE 5.11 An allusion to a friend's earlier work
George Lucas directed *American Graffiti* (1973); his friend Francis Coppola co-produced it. A little more than 79¾ minutes into the film and on a background movie marquee, the attentive viewer can briefly spot *Dementia 13*, the title of an early Coppola film. (If *American Graffiti* is not seen in letterbox format, the title on the marquee may be only partially visible.) *Universal Pictures, Coppola Company, and Lucasfilm; Universal DVD*

Allusions are not usually to one's own work (or to the work of friends). More often, allusions are made to others' earlier texts. *Babe: Pig in the City* (1998) includes frequent references to other texts as amusing, enjoyable rewards for informed adult viewers (Figure 5.13). Approximately 49¾ minutes into the film, the bull terrier tells Babe, "I have a professional obligation to be malicious. . . . It's in the bloodline you see. We were once warriors. Now there's just the urge. A murderous shadow lies hard across my soul." And in both her personality and her manner of speaking, the pink poodle in *Babe: Pig in the City* is reminiscent of a major character in *A Streetcar Named Desire*, both the play and the first film adaptation of it. A scene about 85 minutes into *American Pie* (1999) alludes to the popular 1967 film *The Graduate*. The scene shows a situation similar to one in the earlier film and includes an excerpt from "Mrs. Robinson," one of *The Graduate*'s best-known songs. In the scene, a virginal high school male is alone with the earthy mom of one of his classmates, and we sense that they are becoming attracted to each other as a few bars of the popular song are heard.

A parody is an amusing imitation of human behavior or of a more serious text, part of a text, or groups of texts. A good example occurs in *Analyze This* (1999, Figure 5.14). As in *Babe: Pig in the City*, the parody in *Analyze This* rewards those who know the earlier texts and watch and listen attentively.

In a parody, viewers who know the subject that is being parodied recognize similarities yet see amusing differences. Parody may result from re-creating highly selected excerpts from the original story, as in "The Fifteen Minute Hamlet" (1996), which reenacts snippets

FIGURE 5.12 A mock allusion
Beginning a little more than 61 minutes into Pedro Almodóvar's *Talk to Her* (2002), the film includes excerpts from a black-and-white silent film that Almodóvar himself created. In the film within the film, the man had consumed an untested drug and shrunk to the size seen here, but he and his lover remain devoted to each other. *El Deseo S.A., Good Machine, and others; Sony Pictures Classics DVD*

FIGURE 5.13 Allusion as a bonus
In *Babe: Pig in the City* (1998), the bull terrier's manner of speaking and low, gravelly voice make him sound like a movie gangster. In a speech recalling the making-an-offer-that-he-couldn't-refuse story in *The Godfather*, after Babe (on the right) saves the bull terrier's life, the dog steps forward and (nearly 48½ minutes into the film) addresses the other animals: "I'd like to offer up a solution that I feel confident you'll all respond to. Whatever the pig says goes. Anyone hostile to the notion?" Such allusions to gangster films and sophisticated, formal language are a source of amusement and pleasure for viewers with a broad knowledge of American culture and language but will pass unnoticed by those unfamiliar with the earlier texts. *A Kennedy Miller Film; Universal DVD Video*

a)

b)

FIGURE 5.14 A parodied scene
One scene in *The Godfather* (1972) is amusingly imitated in a scene in *Analyze This* (1999). (a) In a scene beginning a little bit more than 44 minutes into *The Godfather*, two men attempt to assassinate the godfather as he is buying oranges from a street vendor, and the godfather's youngest son fumbles his gun and fails to protect his father. (b) Approximately 54½ minutes into *Analyze This*, the Billy Crystal character dreams that he is the godfather, and his patient, the gangster played by Robert De Niro, is the fumbling youngest son who fails to protect his father from the gunmen. The scene in *Analyze This* also includes auditory allusions to *The Godfather* soundtrack: a trumpet seemingly being played far offscreen and, after the shots are fired, a distant barking dog and a crying baby. The scene in *Analyze This* concludes with a much louder sound, an audio allusion to a different section of *The Godfather*: the screeching elevated train heard 88½ minutes into that film, shortly before Michael kills the corrupt police captain and his gangster companion (see pp. 182–83). (a) *Paramount; Paramount DVD.* (b) *Tribeca Productions, Village Roadshow Pictures, and others; Warner Home Video DVD*

of the original play (and delivers the lines at maximum speed). For example, as Laertes is dying, he is cut off in midsentence, and instead of the original "Exchange forgiveness with me noble Hamlet," we hear "Exchange forgiveness with me noble Ham." A feature film may be a pastiche of allusions and parodies. *Scary Movie* (2000) parodies the various *Scream* and *What You*

Did Last Summer movies and parts of *The Exorcist* (1973), *The Blair Witch Project* (1999), *The Sixth Sense* (1999), *The Matrix* (1999), *The Usual Suspects* (1995), and others. *Not Another Teen Movie* (2001) parodies subjects and scenes from numerous (mostly) teen movies, including *The Breakfast Club* (1985) and other John Hughes movies, *Cruel Intentions* (1999), *American Pie, Bring It On* (2000), *Never Been Kissed* (1999), and *American Beauty* (1999). A single movie is rarely the main subject of an entire movie parody, although the original *Star Wars* (1977) is an exception (Figure 5.15).

Films that parody a specific category, or **genre**, of movies include *The Rocky Horror Picture Show* (1975), mainly a musical parody of classic horror movies like the 1931 *Frankenstein* (Figure 5.16). Other films that poke fun

genre: A group of fictional films that share enough similarities that both filmmakers and audiences recognize the films as members of the same group.

a)

b)

c)

FIGURE 5.15 Parodies of a film or films

Star Wars (1977) is parodied by "Hardware Wars" (1978). The original *Star Wars* movie and other science fiction movies are parodied by Mel Brooks's *Spaceballs* (1987). (a) A well-known image from the original *Star Wars* film shows (left to right) Chewbacca, Luke Skywalker, Obi-Wan Kenobi, and Han Solo in Solo's Millennium Falcon. (b) This image is from a little more than 5 minutes into "Hardware Wars," which is a 13-minute trailer for a film that does not exist. The scene takes place inside a "space vehicle" (actually a very large appliance, an iron, that sports dangling oversized dice in the back window). The characters in the scene are (from left to right), Chewchilla, Fluke Starbucker, Augie "Ben" Doggie, and Ham Salad.

(c) Almost 66 minutes into *Spaceballs*, this scene takes place inside a spacecraft shaped like a recreational vehicle and includes Barf (who's half man, half dog, and his own best friend), Dot Matrix (a robot chaperone with the voice of comedian Joan Rivers), Princess Vespa (the endangered damsel), and Lone Starr (the heroic pilot).

How marvelous the powers of the human mind: while watching both "Hardware Wars" and *Spaceballs*, many viewers immediately recognize similarities to *Star Wars* and laugh at the differences. The settings are roughly the same, the compositions are much the same, but the characters and their names are amusingly different.

Parodies of the various *Star Wars* films and *Star Wars* characters—such as "Star Wars Gangsta Rap," "Who Wants to Marry Darth Maul?," "Trooper Clerks," and "Pink Five"—and parodies of trailers for *Star Wars* films have been extremely popular on the Web. (a) *Lucasfilm Ltd., 20th Century Fox; Star Wars (1977) on Star Wars IV: A New Hope DVD.* (b) *Pyramid Films, 20th Century Foss* [sic]; *The Original Hardware Wars Collector's Edition DVD.* (c) *Brooksfilms, MGM; MGM DVD*

a)

b)

FIGURE 5.16 A parody of a film genre
The Rocky Horror Picture Show (1975) is a parody mostly of horror films, especially various Frankenstein movies. (a) The Dr. Frankenstein–type character is the "scientist" Dr. Frank-N-Furter, a bisexual, "sweet transvestite from [the distant planet of] Transexual, Transylvania." (b) His assistant, Riff Raff, at first looks and sometimes acts like Dr. Frankenstein's hunchback assistant of the 1931 *Frankenstein* movie. But in (b), Riff Raff dresses (at least from the hips up) and acts as if he stepped out of a 1930s sci-fi serial or movie. His sister, Magenta, is dressed as if she comes from the same serial or movie, but her hairstyle and that flash of gray hair are right out of the 1935 horror movie *Bride of Frankenstein*. (a) *20th Century Fox; 20th Century Fox Home Entertainment DVD.* (b) *Publicity still. 20th Century Fox*

convention: A subject or technique that makers of texts and audiences accept as natural or typical in certain contexts.

cinéma vérité: A type and style of documentary filmmaking developed in France during the early 1960s whose aim was to capture events as they happened.

at a genre, or type, of fictional films include *Blazing Saddles* (1974), a parody of westerns (see Figures 4.14 and 7.22) and the Austin Powers movies, which parody James Bond films.

Other films are parodies of documentaries. At first, these **mock documentary** films (sometimes called *mock docs* or *mockumentaries*) may seem to be factual and to follow the **conventions** of documentary filmmaking, such as the use of interviews, subtitles, and handheld camera shots. Mock documentaries do not *mock* documentaries; they *imitate* them and do so in playful, humorous ways. They are amusing fictional imitations using documentary filmmaking techniques. *This Is Spinal Tap* purports to be a documentary about an inept, aging heavy-metal band (Figure 5.17). *Fear of a Black Hat* (1994) poses as a documentary about the endless problems confronted by a hip-hop group (a lot like N.W.A.), including troubles with various recording companies, rivalries with other hip-hop groups, and loss of the group's managers to gunfire—six of them in a row! The film uses (and sometimes exaggerates) the techniques of **cinéma vérité**, such as handheld

FIGURE 5.17 The mock documentary: a fictional film that parodies documentary films
Two minutes into *This Is Spinal Tap* (1984), we viewers see its title and below that this explanation: *A rockumentary by Martin Di Bergi*™. The film, which imitates rock documentaries in amusing ways, has two main subjects. One is an imaginary earnest documentary filmmaker (Martin Di Bergi) who interviews and supposedly films the heavy-metal band, Spinal Tap. The other main subject is the aging and largely forgotten band itself, which "earned a distinguished place in rock history as one of England's loudest bands," and various people connected to the band, including its hapless manager and the manipulative girlfriend of one of the band members. *This Is Spinal Tap* uses the techniques of many documentaries—such as handheld camera work, clips from TV shows, subtitles, and interviews—to record the group members as they suffer one amusing setback after another. Once viewers figure out that *This Is Spinal Tap* is a parody of earnest rock documentary films, they can enjoy its creativity, playfulness, and good-natured humor. *Publicity still. Embassy Pictures*

camera work, interviews, and surprising, even embarrassing developments for the film's subjects. *A Mighty Wind* (2003) uses interviews, subtitles, excerpts from TV news programs, and clips from home movies to impart a documentary feel. But it's a completely fictional and wryly satirical film about a reunion concert featuring three 1960s folk music groups, each of which takes itself very seriously. Some viewers will recognize professional movie actors in the cast, such as Bob Balaban and Paul Dooley, and infer that the film is not a documentary.

Occasionally, however, it is difficult to be certain if a film is a documentary or a mock documentary (Figure 5.18). Many reviewers interpreted *20 Dates* (1998) as a documentary with perhaps a few staged scenes. Other viewers see the film as a mock documentary. By the end of the film, no viewer can say with certainty which parts are factual and which are fictional. So many things go wrong for Myles, and the film has such a tidy happy ending (Myles succeeds in both his work and his love life) that the whole film or most of it may be a mock documentary or an amusing fictional film disguised as a documentary. In general, reviewers who

FIGURE 5.18 Documentary or mock documentary?
In *20 Dates* (1998), the main subject, Myles, is on a date with Christian, who called herself a feminist ballerina. After he points out to her that a hidden movie camera has been photographing their date, Myles says "her reaction was disappointing—and surprisingly violent." In the next scene, viewers learn she had attacked him, necessitating twenty stitches in his hand, and was suing him for invasion of her civil rights (the second of his dates to file a lawsuit). Is *20 Dates* a documentary or an amusing mock documentary where a lot goes wrong for the main subject? *Phoenician Films*

interpreted the film as a documentary judged it negatively, and those who saw the film as a "mock doc" and were amused by it valued it more highly.

Unlike a parody, an homage (in French and in film studies, pronounced "oh MAZH") is a tribute to a person or to a text or part of one. It may be a respectful reference to or an affectionate re-creation of parts of an earlier film. An example occurs near the end of *Play It Again, Sam* (1972), which echoes part of the ending of *Casablanca* (1942), but the laughter is not at *Casablanca*'s expense but at Woody Allen's movie (Table 5.6). Homages may be verbal or visual or—as the example from *Play It Again, Sam* illustrates—both. Perhaps the films of Alfred Hitchcock have elicited the most homages. A British Film Institute booklet lists twenty selected homages to Hitchcock in such films as *High Anxiety* (1977), *Basic Instinct* (1992), and *Twelve Monkeys* (1995) (*Hitchcock* 14).

Often a part in a film (or the entire film) is clearly an allusion, a parody, or an homage. However, as with so many related terms, it is sometimes difficult to decide which of several labels to apply. Sometimes, it is debatable if a part of a particular film or the complete film is an allusion, parody, or homage. Does the film simply re-create from the earlier source? Does the later film amusingly imitate the earlier source? Or does the later work pay tribute to the earlier one? Sometimes the answers are not simple and clear-cut.

SEQUELS AND PREQUELS

Another source for a movie is a sequel, a narrative film that further develops at least some of the story from an earlier narrative film. If a film is popular and later filmmakers see ways to continue the story and develop it, they may make a sequel. Because Hollywood sequels have proven generally profitable in recent years, more and more of them have been made. If the ending of a popular fictional film seems too final (the main character dies, for example), a sequel based on one of the main characters' offspring may be made, as in the sequel to *King Kong* (1933), *Son of Kong* (1933). Since 1997, the death of a protagonist no longer precludes a sequel. Thanks to cloning, the main character of the *Alien* movies was reconstructed from leftovers before the plot of *Alien Resurrection* (1997) begins.

Although sequels are often profitable, they usually disappoint viewers. Todd Berliner has studied sequels and concluded, "The almost inescapable failure of sequels results from the fact that, at the same time a sequel calls to mind the charismatic original, it also recalls its absence, fostering a futile, nostalgic desire to reexperience the original aesthetic moment as though it had never happened. . . . Sequels . . . can only *remind* us of the original film, and continually and conspicuously fail to reinvoke that initial pleasure" (109). He goes on to point out that the makers of a sequel usually try to compensate for the sequel's "sense of absence and loss" by supplying excessive

TABLE 5.6
Part of an Homage

. . .

RICK: I'm staying here with him [Renault] till the plane gets safely away.

ILSA: No, Richard, no! What happened to you? Last night we said —

RICK: Last night we said a great many things. You said I was to do the thinking for both of us. Well, I've done a lot of it since then and it all adds up to one thing. You're getting on that plane with Victor where you belong.

ILSA: But Richard, no, I—

RICK: Now you've got to listen to me. Do you have any idea what you'd have to look forward to if you stayed here? Nine chances out of ten we'd both wind up in a concentration camp. (looking offscreen) Isn't that true, Louis?

RENAULT: I'm afraid Major Strasser would insist.

ILSA: You're saying this only to make me go.

RICK: I'm saying it because it's true. Inside of us we both know you belong with Victor. You're part of his work. The thing that keeps him going. If that plane leaves the ground and you're not with him, you'll regret it.

ILSA: No.

RICK: Maybe not today, maybe not tomorrow, but soon, and for the rest of your life. . . .

. . .

ALLAN [the character played by Woody Allen]: Linda, we have to call it quits.

LINDA: Yes, I know.

ALLAN: (shocked) Pardon me?

LINDA: Suddenly everything became very clear. And when I asked myself, do I really wanta break off my marriage? The answer is no. I love Dick. And although somebody as wonderful as you is very tempting, I can't imagine my life without'm.

ALLAN: You can't?

LINDA: He needs me, Allan. In some unexplainable way, I need him.

ALLAN: I know he needs you.

LINDA: This is the first time I've ever been affected by anyone besides Dick. I'm already in love with you. And unless I stop it now, I'll become too deeply involved to be able to go back to him. Oh, I don't regret a moment of what's happened because—what it's done for me is to reaffirm—my feelings for Dick.

ALLAN: Linda, I understand, really.

LINDA: Are you sure? You're not just saying that to make things easy?

ALLAN: No, I'm saying it because it's true. Inside of us, we both know you belong to Dick. You're part of his work. The thing that keeps him going. If that plane leaves the ground and you're not on it with him, you'll regret it. Maybe not today, maybe not tomorrow, but soon, and for the rest of your life.

LINDA: That's beautiful.

ALLAN: It's from *Casablanca*. I waited my whole life to say it. . . .

Sources: Casablanca: *Warner Bros.* Play It Again, Sam: *Paramount*

amounts of whatever audiences seem to have enjoyed in the original, such as fast-paced action and violence (109).

Occasionally, a movie is the inspiration for a prequel: a movie that depicts some of the characters from a previous film at earlier stages of their lives. *Butch and Sundance: The Early Days* (1979) is a prequel to *Butch Cassidy and the Sundance Kid* (1969). More widely known examples of prequels are the three prequels *Star Wars: Episode I—The Phantom Menace* (1999), *Star Wars: Episode II—The Attack of the Clones* (2002), and *Star Wars: Episode III—Revenge of the Sith* (2005, Figure 5.19). It's also possible but rare for a film to be both a prequel and a sequel, as in the case of *The Godfather Part II* (1974), which has related events involving the same characters that precede and follow the story of *The Godfather* (1972). Many other family trees are possible: *Nutty Professor II: The Klumps* (2000), for example, is a sequel to a remake.[5]

---

[5]Sometimes art is an important source for films. At various times in film history, painters and other visual artists have been especially prominent in making films. Two such periods were the 1920s in Europe and the 1950s and 1960s in the United States (pop art). Filmmakers have also long learned from painters, especially in the use of lighting, composition, color, and grain. Such filmmakers as Martin Scorsese in *The Last Temptation of Christ* (1988), Stanley Kubrick in *Barry Lyndon* (1975), Tony Richardson in *Tom Jones* (1963), Derek Jarman in *Caravaggio* (1986), Peter Greenaway in *The Cook, the Thief, His Wife and Her Lover* (1989), and Carlos Saura in *Goya in Bordeaux* (1999) have all imitated particular painters and sometimes specific paintings. In recent years, some filmmakers have made artworks, including temporary museum exhibitions involving two or more arts (**installation art**), and increasingly museums of modern or contemporary art include film or video art combined with other media (see pp. 414 and 416).

a)   b)

FIGURE 5.19 A film and its prequels The second three *Star Wars* movies made are prequels to the first three that were made, and viewers are introduced to the adult Darth Vader (a) in the first three films before meeting his younger self (b) as here in the first of the three prequels. *Publicity stills. Lucasfilm Ltd., 20th Century Fox*

MULTIPLE SOURCES

Although most fictional films derive mainly from history, fiction, a play, a TV show or series, or previous films, they inevitably have more complicated ancestries. Such is the case with the movie *Cabaret* (1972). A story—"Sally Bowles" in the 1939 book *Goodbye to Berlin* by Christopher Isherwood—was the basis for the play *I Am a Camera*, which was filmed in 1955 and made into the Broadway musical *Cabaret* in 1966. The film version of *Cabaret*, with Liza Minnelli and Joel Grey, appeared in 1972.

Even when a film seems to have one main source, lesser influences are involved. The film *Dangerous Liaisons* (1988), with a screenplay by Christopher Hampton, is based on Hampton's 1985 British play *Les liaisons dangereuses*, but that play is based on the 1782 French novel of the same title, which has many other sources itself, including two epistolary novels (Table 5.7). Another influence on the 1782 French novel is the story of Don Juan in its many variations, including the popular 1665 Molière play, *Dom Juan ou le festin de Pierre*. The 1988 film, then, is the product of three countries: French and English sources influenced the 1782 French novel, which in turn influenced the 1985 English play, which in turn helped shape the 1988 French-English-U.S. film, which to date is the best-known film version of the story.

Many factors complicate discussions of sources. In interviews, filmmakers often tell of being impressed by a technique or detail in one film and later using it while making an unrelated movie. Even a film that is based primarily on one source is also the product of the scriptwriters', directors', and actors' experiences. Influences on creative work are varied and not always easily identifiable by audience or artist. After all, successful creative people spend most of their time and energy creating (and revising)—not reflecting on their sources. Then, too, few people are aware of the full range and interdependence of their sources, their intertextuality.

Human creativity being limitless, the combination of sources may be even more original and complex than the examples examined so far (Figure 5.20). *Adaptation* (2002) is primarily about three characters whose names are identical to those of three real people, and

a)

b)

c)

FIGURE 5.20 Multiple sources, creatively combined
The playful, satirical, and knowing *Adaptation* (2002) cuts back and forth in place and time between multiple fictional subjects. (a) Uptight nonfiction writer Susan Orlean forms a relationship with eccentric, self-taught exotic wildlife specialist John Laroche, whose life and ideas she recounts in her book, *The Orchid Thief.* Here Susan and John have caught Charlie Kaufman snooping around John's place in Florida. (b) Screenwriter Charlie Kaufman encounters persistent difficulties in adapting Orlean's book into a viable movie script. (c) Charlie's temperamentally opposite twin brother Donald (center of frame) decides to try scriptwriting himself and by following commercial formulas enjoys rapid success. Here Charlie is shocked at his brother's declaration about and playful demonstration of how he plans "a little push, push in the bush" of his girlfriend (on the left). *Good Machine, Intermedia, and others; Columbia Pictures DVD*

TABLE 5.7
A Highly Selective Chronology of a Story's Versions

Clarissa (The History of Clarissa Harlowe) **(1747)** English novel of letters by Samuel Richardson.

Julie (Julie, ou la nouvelle Héloïse) **(1761)** French novel of letters by Jean-Jacques Rousseau.

Les liaisons dangereuses **(1782)** French novel by Choderlos de Laclos consisting of 175 letters by about a dozen characters.

According to Milos Forman, director of the movie *Valmont* (1989), there were several stage adaptations of *Les liaisons dangereuses* in the nineteenth century and at least three stage adaptations in the twentieth century.

Les liaisons dangereuses **(1959)** French black-and-white, modern-dress film adaptation set in Paris and a Swiss ski resort, with Jeanne Moreau and Gerard Philipe as the two main characters who are married to each other and aware of each other's seductions. Directed by Roger Vadim. (106 minutes)

Les liaisons dangereuses **(1985)** British period play by Christopher Hampton, based fairly closely on the source novel with two former lovers still warily attracted to each other and scheming with and against each other as he seduces a very young woman and a pious married woman. The play enjoyed critical and commercial success in London and then New York.

Dangerous Liaisons **(1988)** American and British period film in color with Glenn Close and John Malkovich as former lovers. Direction by Stephen Frears and screenplay by Christopher Hampton, based closely on Hampton's own play, which in turn was "adapted from the novel" by Choderlos de Laclos. Compared with the play *Les liaisons dangereuses*, this film version captures more of the epistolary quality of the original novel by dramatizing some brief scenes that are only recounted in the play. (120 minutes)

Valmont **(1989)** French/U.S. period film with updated language, filmed in color on location in France with extensive attention to visual details. Stars: Annette Bening and Colin Firth; screenplay: Jean-Claude Carrière and Milos Forman; direction: Forman. The film is based loosely on the French novel: the endings of the novel and film, for example, differ widely. Compared with other adaptations, *Valmont* also devotes much more time to 15-year-old Cecile, her innocence and social education. (137 minutes)

Cruel Intentions **(1999)** American film in color with Sarah Michelle Gellar and Ryan Phillippe as stepbrother and stepsister. The stepbrother seduces a willing young virgin and eventually an unwilling young virgin with whom he soon falls in love. Directed and scripted by Roger Kumble. Modern-dress version with young cast and characters set in New York City. The film's credits include the following: "Script suggested by the novel *Les liaisons dangereuses*." (97 minutes)

Les liaisons dangereuses **(2003)** Miniseries filmed in Scotland and Canada and set largely in the wealthy society of 1960s France. Directed by Josée Dayan, who had seen and admired the 1959 and 1988 film versions, and featuring an international cast, including Catherine Deneuve and Rupert Everett. (According to IMDb.com, there are three DVD versions available in one place or another: in French with English subtitles [two parts totaling 200 minutes], in English, and in a 252-minute, three-disk set in French with English subtitles.)

Note: Unavoidably, this table simplifies. For example, a later creative work is not shaped equally by all previous influences, and later works are typically also influenced by sources outside the lineage represented here.

the actions of the three movie characters are based closely on the lives of the three real people. The sources for the movie might be listed as follows:

Before the movie was made:

Susan Orlean (person) and John Laroche (person) meet and interact.

Susan Orlean (person) writes a magazine article ("Orchid Fever") and a book (*The Orchid Thief*, 1999) about John Laroche (person).

Charlie Kaufman (person) writes the script for the movie *Adaptation* (2002).

In the movie (which is nonchronological):

Susan Orlean (character) has already published her nonfiction book.

Susan Orlean (character) and John Laroche (character) meet and interact.

Charlie Kaufman (character) struggles to adapt the book into a movie script.

Charlie's twin brother, Donald Kaufman (character), takes up commercial scriptwriting and quickly achieves success.

The sources of *Adaptation*, then, are multiple, complex, and creative: real people and real experiences are adapted into versions of the real people and their experiences.

FIGURE 5.21 Multiple cultural sources

This publicity still illustrates the opening shot of the Senegalese *Karmen Geï* (2001), a loose adaptation of Prosper Merimée's *Carmen*, a French novella that also served as the main source for Bizet's 1875 opera *Carmen*. The statuesque woman with the broad smile seen here soon dances with so much vitality and self-possession that it helps her bewitch the beautiful female prison warden (after they go to bed together, Karmen is allowed to slip out of the prison later that night). Before this film, there had already been Bizet's opera and more than fifty film versions of *Carmen*, but probably no bisexual Carmen and perhaps no Carmen who so defiantly rebels against police authority and so decisively wields power over various men. The languages used in the film are French and Wolof (a language widely used in Senegal). Unlike in the source novella and the Bizet opera, the setting is contemporary Senegal, and the dancing and most of the music are indigenous (there are also frequent jazz passages composed by the American David Murray). The script—by the film's Senegalese director Joseph Gaï Ramaka—has more differences than similarities to the original source novella. France, the United States (Murray's jazz), and Senegal are sources for the film. *Publicity still. Courtesy of California Newsreel, San Francisco, CA, or South Burlington, VT*

Discussions of sources also get complicated when the sources come from different times and different cultures. The Japanese film *Shall We Dance?* (1996), for example, is mostly Japanese in its sources, but U.S. and British cultures are also influences (see pp. 531–32). The 2001 Senegalese film *Karmen Geï* (pronouned "gay") provides another example of multicultural sources (see Figure 5.21 on p. 245).

Texts do not emerge *ex nihilo*, out of nothing. Neither do they emerge from a single human imagination or from a team of people working on the same creative project. Texts are always intertextual, always related to the chaos of other texts. And they are always influenced by the cultures that nurture them.

CLOSE-UP: "THE DEAD": NOVELLA TO FILM (STUDENT ESSAY)

by William Meyer

Contemporary film critics praise Tony Huston's adaptation of "The Dead" for its faithfulness to James Joyce's original text. Tim Pulleine calls the film "a close literary adaptation" (67). Richard Blake asserts that the adaptation is "extremely faithful to the text" (194–95). And Vincent Canby simply calls the film a "magnificent adaptation." However, despite its reputation for faithfulness, a careful analysis reveals that the film is unlike Joyce's novella in three major ways. First, the adaptation expands the scope of the original narrative by adding new scenes. Second, the adaptation deletes important contextual elements from its literary source. Finally, the adaptation modifies significant dramatic elements in the literary source.

Perhaps the most apparent difference between the film and its source is the addition of new scenes not found in the novella. For example, the opening scene of the film is shot from the **exterior** of the Morkans' home. It includes images of snow falling, carriages stopping, guests arriving, and people dancing. The scene effectively establishes the social context and physical setting of the film, but it does not appear in Joyce's novella. A second example is a scene in which Freddy Malins walks into a bathroom, washes his face, combs his hair, and relieves himself. The elements of this scene clearly reinforce Joyce's depiction of Malins as a disheveled drunkard, but the scene itself fails to appear in the literary source. Although Huston's new scenes extend elements of the narrative introduced by Joyce, they are still invented. It seems clear that Tony Huston's addition of scenes to the screenplay supports Michael Klein's observation that the brevity of short stories provides scriptwriters with room for "imaginative expansion" (10).

A second major difference between the film and its literary source is the deletion of important contextual elements from the novella. For example, in the original text, we learn the context of Molly Ivors's relationship with Gabriel: "They were friends of many years' standing and their careers had been parallel, first at the University and then as teachers" (Joyce 204). This background information is deleted from the screenplay. Consequently, the audience never fully understands the professional and academic nature of their relationship. Another contextual element that is deleted from the film is a scene in which Gabriel becomes discontent with the party and wishes to leave the Morkans' home. In the novella, we learn that he walks to a window, taps his fingers on a windowpane, and stares outside (Joyce 208). Moreover, we learn that he wonders "how much more pleasant it would be there than at the supper-table" (Joyce 208). Because this scene is cut from the screenplay, viewers of the film cannot accurately gauge the depth of Gabriel's discontent. Therefore, they can never fully appreciate the emotional context in which his words and actions are expressed.

A third major difference between the film and the novella is the modification of significant dramatic elements in the original novella. For example, Molly Ivors's exit from the party is modified to clarify her political significance for contemporary audiences. In the novella, "Joyce allows his patriot to depart quietly, offering only that she does not choose to join the party for dinner" (Blake 194). However, in the film, Molly's exit is modified to include the lines "I'm off to a union meeting at Liberty Hall. A Republican meeting." Film critic Richard Blake argues that in the novella, "Her farewell is shot through with irony: 'Beannacht libh' (a blessing upon you all). The point would not be lost on the original readers, but for film audiences Huston must underline Molly's political function in the story" (194). In this case, Huston's modification of the literary source effectively clarifies the political significance of an important dramatic element in the film.

By addition, deletion, and modification, Tony Huston created a screenplay adaptation that is different from its literary source. However, commentary by professional film critics seems to indicate that *different* does not necessarily mean unfaithful (Blake 194–95; Canby; Pulleine 67). Perhaps this is why Huston's adaptation of "The Dead" received so much critical praise. Such praise clearly underscores Huston's skill at weaving his way through what film critic Gabriel Miller calls the filmmaker's "dilemma of remaining faithful to the novel's spirit while realizing the necessity of altering its design" (xi).

Works Cited

Blake, Richard A. "The Living and the Dead." *America* 20 Feb. 1988: 194–95.

Canby, Vincent. "The Party's Over." *New York Times* 17 Dec. 1987, nat'l. ed.: C19.

Joyce, James. "The Dead." *The Portable James Joyce*. Ed. Harry Levin. New York: Viking, 1966. 190–242.

Klein, Michael. "Introduction: Film and Literature." *The English Novel and the Movies*. Ed. Michael Klein and Gillian Parker. New York: Ungar, 1981. 1–13.

Miller, Gabriel. *Screening the Novel*. New York: Ungar, 1980.

Pulleine, Tim. "A Memory of Galway." *Sight & Sound* (Winter 1987–88): 67–68.

SUMMARY

A text is something that people produce or modify to communicate meaning. Fictional films are based on one or usually more texts. A fictional film may be based on a screenplay, which may be an original story but often is not. Frequently, a screenplay is based on historical events, a fictional work (usually a novel), a play, a TV show or TV series, or other films. Texts, including fictional films, are always intertextual, always influenced by earlier texts and by the culture(s) that helped bring them to light.

Screenplays, Shooting Scripts, and Storyboards

- Typically the screenplay writer determines the settings, subjects (action and vocals), and structure of a fictional film and directly or indirectly many of its meanings.

- The shooting script is the version of the script used during filming. It includes changes made in the screenplay, usually breaks scenes into shots, and normally includes instructions on camera placement and use.

- Comparing a screenplay or shooting script with the finished film seldom reveals who contributed exactly what, but typically the film is more concise, less reliant on dialogue, and more visual than the script.

- Storyboards are a series of drawings or photographs of each shot or part of a shot for a planned film or video story. They help filmmakers visualize how the story might look and function before filming and editing begin.

Individual Sources

Nearly any subject can become the source of a fictional film, but five of the most frequently used sources are history, fiction, plays, television, and other films.

HISTORY

- Fictional movies based on history inevitably omit, change, or fabricate some of the events.

- In spite of the advertising claims and the documentary qualities of a historical movie, commercial fictional films based on history, such as *The Hurricane*, tend to give priority to drama and entertainment, not to the accepted written historical accounts.

FICTION

- Short stories, novellas, and novels are well suited to render a character's mental activity. Other strengths of fiction include descriptions of characters' backgrounds, analysis by the author, figurative language, and a more or less consistent point of view or means of perception.

- Film is adept at presenting sights and sounds. It can also show the nuances of faces and the infinite flexibility and expressiveness of movement. It can render the human voice and music in much of their fullness. And through editing, it can condense the time needed to present significant events and transport viewers through time and space instantaneously.

- People who admire a novel are usually disappointed with a film adaptation of it because as they read the novel, they visualized it and later usually find the filmmakers' visualization inadequate or misleading. Then, too, a novel is usually too long and involved for a complete rendition on the screen, so parts of it are omitted.

- A film based on a fictional source should be understood and assessed as a film, not as adapted fiction.

PLAYS

- Plays, in general, are a verbal medium; films, a visual one. Plays filmed with minimal variations in the camera work and editing tend to be disappointing as films because they do not take advantage of film's capabilities.

- Fundamentally, plays rely on the give-and-take of audience and live performer, whereas films rely on the audience's responses to controlled moving images and usually a soundtrack.

TELEVISION

- Although initially American TV and film were in fierce competition and their makers refused to cooperate with each other, now the two media are intertwined and often borrow actors, writers, directors, characters, stories, and techniques from each other.

- Often film and TV represent each other critically, even satirically. Sometimes each medium uses the other medium as a source for parody.

OTHER FILMS

- Films are often based, at least in part, on earlier films or parts of them.

- A film may imitate earlier films in various ways. It may be a remake. A movie or part of one may include allusions (references) to earlier films, an amusing imitation of a more serious film (parody), or a respectful imitation of parts of an earlier film (homage).

- A movie may also be a sequel or, far less commonly, a prequel. It is even possible, though rare, for a film to be both.

Multiple Sources

- Texts are always intertextual, always related to earlier texts.

- Even when a film seems to have one main source, other influences, including the filmmakers' culture and other cultures, are at work.

Major Terms about Sources for Fictional Films

Below, numbers in italics refer to the pages where the terms are explained. All terms are defined in more detail in the Illustrated Glossary beginning on p. 667.

allusion *234*	parody *235*	serial *233*
homage *240*	prequel *242*	shooting script *204*
intertextuality *203*	remake *232*	storyboard *209*
master-scene format *208*	screenplay *204*	text *203*
mock documentary *238*	sequel *240*	

QUESTIONS ABOUT SOURCES FOR FICTIONAL FILMS

The following questions are intended to help viewers understand sources for fictional films. Not all the questions are appropriate for every film. In thinking out, discussing, and writing responses to the questions most appropriate for the film being examined, be careful to stick with the issues the questions raise, to answer all parts of the questions, to explain the reasons for your answers, and to give specific examples from the film.

1. Is the film based on an original screenplay, or is it an adaptation? If the film is based on a screenplay that is accessible to you, describe the major differences between the screenplay and the finished film. What are the major similarities between the screenplay and the finished film?

2. Is the film based on written historical accounts? If it is, how closely does the film follow the earlier accounts? Where does the film make changes for dramatic effect? Where does it make changes unnecessarily?

3. Is the film based on fiction? If it is, how closely does the film follow the source fiction? Where does the film make changes for dramatic effect? Where does it make changes unnecessarily?

4. Is the film based on a play? If it is, how closely does the film follow the source play? Where does the film make changes for dramatic effect? Where does it make changes unnecessarily?

5. Is the film based on a TV show or series? If it is, how closely does the film follow the source? Where does the film make changes for dramatic effect? Where does it make changes unnecessarily?

6. Is the film based on other films? Does the film allude to, parody, or pay an homage to earlier film(s)? Is the film a sequel or prequel?

7. Is the film based on multiple sources? If it is, what are the main ones? Is the film the product of more than one culture? If so, explain.

WORKS CITED

Abé, Kobo. *The Woman in the Dunes*. Trans. E. Dale Saunders. New York: Knopf, 1964.

Anderson, Wes, and Owen Wilson. *The Royal Tenenbaums*. London: Faber, 2001.

Andrew, Dudley. *Concepts in Film Theory*. New York: Oxford UP, 1984.

Attenborough, David. "The Compulsive Communicators." *Life on Earth*. Program 13. BBC Bristol. 1979. (The wording is from the television program, not the book based on the series.)

Berliner, Todd. "The Pleasures of Disappointment: Sequels and *The Godfather, Part II.*" *Journal of Film and Video* 53.2–3 (Summer/Fall 2001): 107–23.

Cook, David A. *A History of Narrative Film.* 3rd ed. New York: Norton, 1996.

Cunningham, Michael. "My Novel, the Movie: My Baby Reborn; *The Hours* Brought Elation, but Also Doubt." *New York Times* 19 Jan. 2003, late ed.: sec. 2: 1.

Demopoulos, Maria. "Blink of an Eye: Filmmaking in the Age of Bullet Time." *Film Comment* 36.3 (May/June 2000): 34–39.

Hitchcock. Ed. Nick James. London: British Film Institute, 1999.

Kasbekar, Asha. "An Introduction to Indian Cinema." In *An Introduction to Film Studies.* 2nd ed. Ed. Jill Nelmes. London: Routledge, 1999. 381–415.

Konigsberg, Ira. *The Complete Film Dictionary.* 2nd ed. New York: Penguin, 1997.

Phillips, William H. *Analyzing Films: A Practical Guide.* New York: Holt, Rinehart and Winston, 1985.

———. *Writing Short Scripts.* 2nd ed. Syracuse: Syracuse UP, 1999.

Scorsese, Martin (filmmaker). Commentary. "The Director as Smuggler." *A Personal Journey with Martin Scorsese through American Movies.* Documentary film. 1995.

Stanley, Alessandra. "Surviving and Disturbing in Moscow." *New York Times* 21 Mar. 1995, nat'l. ed.: B1+.

The Third Man: A Film by Graham Greene and Carol Reed. New York: Simon, 1968.

Toplin, Robert Brent. *History by Hollywood: The Use and Abuse of the American Past.* Urbana: U of Illinois P, 1996.

FOR FURTHER READING

Armes, Roy. *Action and Image: Dramatic Structure in Cinema.* Manchester, Eng.: Manchester UP, 1994. The first of the book's three parts, "Film as Drama," consists of four chapters: "Readings and Viewings," "Showing and Telling," "Text and Performance," and "Stage and Screen."

Based on a True Story: Latin American History at the Movies. Ed. Donald F. Stevens. Wilmington, DE: SR Books, 1997. Various essays on how films have represented Latin America from the late fifteenth century to the present.

Custen, George F. *Bio/Pics: How Hollywood Constructed Public History.* New Brunswick, NJ: Rutgers UP, 1992. Using a sample of over a hundred biographical films from 1927 to 1960, Custen argues that Hollywood created a nearly monochromatic view of history that was systematically distorted in regard to race, gender, nationality, and profession.

Film Adaptation. Ed. James Naremore. New Brunswick, NJ: Rutgers UP, 2000. An investigation of how cinema transforms stories from other sources, such as literature and history, into films. Contributors examine the process of adaptation in both theory and practice, discussing a wide variety of films.

Revisioning History: Film and the Construction of a New Past. Ed. Robert A. Rosenstone. Princeton: Princeton UP, 1995. Theoretical issues about films based on history.

Rosenstone, Robert A. *Visions of the Past: The Challenge of Film to Our Idea of History*. Cambridge: Harvard UP, 1995. Argues that history is a mode of thinking that can use "elements other than the written word" and that history can be done through films.

Tibbetts, John C., and James M. Welsh. *The Encyclopedia of Stage Plays into Film*. New York: Facts on Film, 2001. Three hundred entries classified in one of three sections: "Dramatic Adaptations," "Shakespearean Adaptations," and "Musical Adaptations."

———. *Novels into Film: The Encyclopedia of Movies Adapted from Books*. New York: Checkmark Books, 1999. More than 120 entries, each describing a novel and one or more of its film adaptations. Each entry concludes with a brief references section.

Toplin, Robert Brent. *Reel History: In Defense of Hollywood*. Lawrence: UP of Kansas, 2002. Using examples mainly from contemporary movies, Toplin argues that critics often do not recognize how fictional movies often convey important ideas and information about the past.

CHAPTER 6

Components of Fictional Films

Terms in **boldface** are defined in the Illustrated Glossary beginning on page 667.

meaning: An observation or a general statement about a subject, such as a film.

U NLIKE ORDINARY EXPERIENCE, which mixes the meaningful with the amorphous and random, a story's ingredients are selected for appropriateness to the story's intended effects, **meanings**, and **structures**. A story can therefore be almost free from redundancy, meaninglessness, and, especially, inexpressiveness. . . . Thus a story promises comprehensibility in a way that ordinary experience does not. (Eidsvik 61)

By definition, **narrative** [or story] always recounts one or more **events**. . . . It does not simply mirror what happens; it explores and devises what can happen. . . . Narrative can thus shed light on individual fate or group destiny, the unity of a self or the nature of a collectivity. . . . [B]y marking off distinct moments in time and setting up relations among them, by discovering meaningful designs in temporal series, by establishing an end already partly contained in the beginning and a beginning already partly containing the end, by exhibiting the meaning of time and/or providing it with meaning, narrative deciphers time and indicates how to decipher it. In sum, narrative illuminates temporality and humans as temporal beings. (Prince 60)

A few years after the first motion pictures were created in the 1890s, the new medium was used to present short, entertaining fictional stories. Fictional films became so popular that during the late 1910s, **feature films** became commonplace, drew large audiences, served as an evening's or afternoon's major pastime, and supported a large and growing industry. Since then, people have remained captivated by fictional films, in no small part because most people are endlessly fascinated by the causes and consequences of human behavior.

In this chapter, we briefly consider narrative (factual and fictional) and then examine the short fictional film and some of the ways the feature-length fictional narrative film can handle the basic components of structure, time, and **style**.

style: The way that subjects are represented in a text, such as a film.

254

NARRATIVES: FACTUAL AND FICTIONAL

> I believe the life of every person is worthy of scrutiny, containing its own secrets and dramas. People don't talk about them because they are embarrassed, because they do not like to scratch old wounds, or are afraid of being judged unfashionably sentimental. (Kieslowski)

As part of the opening **narration** of *Blood Simple* (1984, 2000) indicates, "Nothing comes with a guarantee. I don't care if you're the Pope of Rome, the President of the United States, or Man of the Year. Something can all go wrong." Often narrative films show how neither the audience nor characters (or people in a documentary film) can anticipate how things "can all go wrong." Some stories show that developments can be profound and far-reaching. In *A Simple Plan* (1998), credible events early in the story set in motion a chain of events that eventually result in unexpected complications and grief. A fox runs across the path of a pickup truck with three men inside. The driver swerves to miss the fox; his truck hits a tree; his dog chases after the fox in the deep snow. The driver goes trudging off after his dog and the other two men go along, but they do not find it. After a brief, somewhat heated exchange between two of the characters, the annoyed one throws a snowball at nothing in particular. When it lands, snow falls away revealing a small downed plane. Inside is a dead pilot and a duffel bag containing lots and lots of money. The decisions of the three very different men about what to do with the money lead to all sorts of complications that are unexpected by both the characters and the film's viewers (Figure 6.1).

Another narrative that illustrates that unexpected events can have important unforeseen consequences is the **animated** film "T.R.A.N.S.I.T." (1997), in which a suitcase falling off the back of a sports car makes all the difference in the worlds of several characters (for a description of the film, see p. 427). Had it not fallen, the man would not have seen and become infatuated with the attractive woman, and none of the ensuing tragedies would have transpired.

narration: Commentary in a film about a subject in the film or about some other subject, usually by someone offscreen.

FIGURE 6.1 Decisions and actions leading to unexpected complications
Early in *A Simple Plan* (1998), three men find a small crashed airplane in the woods. Inside are a dead pilot and a duffel bag full of hundred-dollar bills. After some deliberation, the three decide what to do with the money, and that decision leads to complications and more complications—and eventually the death of six characters. The consequences of "a simple plan" turn out to be anything but simple. *Mutual Film Company, BBC, Toho, Paramount, and others; Paramount Pictures DVD*

text: Something that people produce or modify to communicate meaning.

Most people are so drawn to narratives or stories that when they are confronted by any type of **text** with no obvious story, they still try to find one. As film archivist and critic Robert Rosen writes,

> Film and painting . . . display intriguing points of convergence, among them the inescapability of narrativizing spectators. Even in the face of totally nonrepresentational works, viewers have a powerful urge to uncover or invent narrative—a basic need to normalize the challenge of the unfamiliar by situating it in a comfortably recognizable sequence of events. (252)

representation: A likeness of a subject created in a text.

Factual or fictional "narratives" or stories are commonplace in every society. We all produce them, and almost everyone can enjoy them and sometimes learn from them. Most of us experience narratives by listening to others tell stories, by going to movies and plays, or by reading factual or fictional stories. Yet explanation of what precisely constitutes a narrative is a complex, frequently debated issue in critical theory. *Narrative* can be defined as a **representation** of unified events (**happenings** and actions) situated in one or more **settings**. The representations of the events may be arranged chronologically or nonchronologically, and the events themselves may be factual, fictional, or a blend of the two (Figure 6.2).

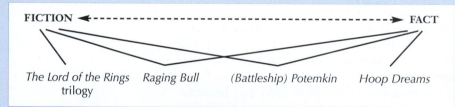

FICTION ◄- -► FACT

The Lord of the Rings trilogy   *Raging Bull*   *(Battleship) Potemkin*   *Hoop Dreams*

FIGURE 6.2 The narrative films continuum
Many narrative films are completely fictional. Many blend fiction and fact. And some narrative films are predominantly factual.
The Lord of the Rings: The Fellowship of the Ring (2001) and its two sequels are completely fictional: as we watch them, we recognize no character as being based on an actual person and no actions as re-creating real events.
Raging Bull (1980) is a fictional film that is also partially factual: certain aspects of the movie Jake are the same as those of the famous boxer Jake La Motta. Some narratives are more difficult to categorize. The Soviet classic *(Battleship) Potemkin* (1925) is a blend of fiction and fact, and though scholars usually categorize it as a fictional film, some consider it a narrative documentary. (Narrative films that blend fiction and fact and have as their subjects recent news or history are sometimes called *docudramas*, especially if they were originally made for TV.)
Finally, some narratives are documentary films (see pp. 382–85 in Chapter 8). They show or tell a factual story. A good example is *Hoop Dreams* (p. 385), which is mainly the true story of two inner-city young men who hoped to eventually play in the National Basketball Association. However, narrative documentary films that seem to be completely factual usually are not. For example, a significant detail might be omitted, or the order of some events might be changed during editing.

As an example of narrative, consider the main events of the 17-minute wordless French fictional film "The String Bean" (1962):

1. An old woman finds a discarded potted plant near her apartment building.
2. In her apartment, she replaces the dead plant with a seed that she took from a package.
3. In her apartment, the plant grows to only a certain size.
4. The woman transplants the plant to a park, where it thrives.
5. One day, she sees park caretakers uproot the thriving plant and discard it. The woman takes pods from the discarded plant.
6. In her apartment, she removes seeds from a pod, plants them, places the pot outside on the sill, and looks on as rain begins to fall on the pot.

This narrative consists of selected, chronologically arranged events in the life of one character. Most viewers can figure out the relationship of later events to earlier ones. For example, between the major units of the narrative (or **sequences**) numbered 3 and 4, viewers can infer that the woman transplants the plant to the park because she hopes it will grow even larger and healthier outdoors. If the film showed only sequences 1 through 5, there would still be a narrative, though one with an unhappy ending, both for the woman and for people in the audience who identify with her. If the film showed only sequences 1 through 3, there also would still be a narrative, though most viewers would find it unsatisfactory because it lacks complications and resolution of them.

> **sequence:** A series of related consecutive scenes perceived as a major unit of a narrative film.

A narrative's events must be unified—related—in some manner. Consider the following actions, which are not clearly related:

5. An old woman in a park sees park caretakers uproot a healthy plant and discard it. The woman takes pods from the discarded plant.
3. In the woman's apartment, a plant grows to only a certain size.
1. The old woman finds a discarded potted plant near her apartment building.

If a film showed only these actions and in this order, viewers could make no sense of them. The film would not convey a narrative.

Some films—such as many films directed by the French directors Jean-Luc Godard and Alain Resnais—make it difficult or impossible for viewers to perceive the unity of events. Other films—such as *Mr. Hulot's Holiday* (1953), *Nashville* (1975), *Short Cuts* (1993), *Clerks* (1994), and *Gosford Park* (2001)—are only loosely unified overall. Although individual **scenes** are unified and easy to follow, some scenes could be moved to a different place

> **scene:** A section of a narrative that gives the impression of continuous action taking place in continuous time and space.

in the story with little consequence. Such films are said to have an **episodic plot**.[1]

The settings of narratives may be fictional, as in most science fiction stories, or they may be essentially factual, as in the many movies that were filmed on largely unaltered **locations**. As we saw in Chapter 1, on **mise en scène**, settings can help reveal what characters are like in a fictional film or what people are like in a factual narrative.

A fictional film is a narrative that shows mostly or entirely imaginary events. On rare occasions, filmmakers combine fictional events with **footage** of actual events, as in the scenes beginning 91¾ minutes into *Medium Cool* (1969) in which one character attends the actual 1968 Chicago Democratic National Convention as a reporter while on the streets outside the convention another character gets caught up in an actual demonstration and is threatened by tear gas and police violence.

SHORT FICTIONAL FILMS

From 1895 to about 1906, all fictional films ran for less than 60 minutes, a frequent definition of **short film**. During movie showings until the 1960s, short fictional films were often part of the program. Today, short films are seldom shown in theaters and are rarely available in video stores. They *are* shown at film festivals; by film societies, museums, and libraries; on some cable channels, including the Sundance Channel, the Independent Film Channel, and Turner Classic Movies; in various school and college courses; and on many Web sites. In addition, collections of short films— such as the series of collections beginning with *Short 1* and continuing through *Short 11* (2001)—have been available on DVD. Helping to make a short film is usually required of filmmaking students. Occasionally, short films attract attention at film festivals or on the Web and lead to funding for feature productions.

At its best, a short fictional film is not a shortened and compressed feature but a flexible and expressive form in its own right. Its brevity, like that of a short story, can be an advantage. Compared with a feature film, a short film may be more compressed, demanding, and subtle. And since its budget is relatively small, its makers are under far fewer financial pressures to

---

mise en scène: An image's setting, subjects, and composition (the arrangement of setting and subjects within the frame).

footage: A length of exposed motion-picture film.

---

[1]Digital technology has made it possible to rearrange a film's parts. For example, "digital technology [was used] to shuffle audio and visual tracks, reassembling a different story on each viewing" of "City Hall 2.0" on the Web site *The Bit Screen: Films Made for the Internet* (Stables 5). *The Onyx Project* (2006)—which comes on a CD designed to be played on any late-model Windows XP PC with DVD drive and QuickTime—tells (rather than enacts) a story if viewers stay involved with it long enough. As viewers watch one excerpt, links to other excerpts pop up on the bottom of the screen, so viewers choose which excerpts to watch and in what order.

conform to the usual Hollywood movie format and are freer to be true to their vision. To get some sense of the range of possibilities in the short film, let's examine briefly two very different short fictional films: "Leon's Case" and "The Other Side."

"Leon's Case" (1982), which is 25 minutes long, shows the often amusing story of the idealistic Leon Bernstein, who resides in 1980s Los Angeles but still thinks of himself as a Vietnam War protester and a fugitive from the military draft. Accordingly, he still thinks and acts as he did two decades earlier. In trying to publicize his opposition to the U.S. military-industrial complex, Leon goes through the following steps:

1. In his basement apartment, Leon is dressed as a priest. He puts on a false mustache and leaves.

2. At the house of his friends Keith and Karen, Leon discusses his plans and hides his manuscript about his life resisting the war and the draft. His two friends offer him no direct support and sometimes ignore him.

3. At a duplicating shop, Leon has copies made of a press release and a flyer announcing a demonstration he plans to stage. The worker in the store, a former hippie, does not give Leon a "discount for the movement."

4. At the *Los Angeles Times* building, Leon is unable to see his friend Keith, who writes a real estate column, to give him a copy of the press release.

5. At a university, wary students accept Leon's flyers and quickly discard them. Leon finds the discarded flyers in a nearby trash can.

6. Leon has trouble gaining access to a lawyer he knows, and when he does, he learns the lawyer doesn't do resistance work anymore "'cause there's no resistance."

7. At a telephone booth, Leon calls the FBI to announce that his demonstration is being held the next day, but he learns that President Carter pardoned war resisters long ago.

8. Back at his apartment, Leon's friends give him a surprise party. He is uncomfortable and uncharacteristically speechless; his friends do not entirely support him in his cause.

9. The next day, Leon cuts his hair short, puts on conventional clothing, goes to the Los Angeles airport, presumably chains himself to a military airplane on display there, gets arrested, and is glimpsed smiling happily on a local television news show.

Like "Leon's Case," most short fictional films exhibit the major characterstics of **classical Hollywood cinema** (pp. 308–10) but have fewer major characters and fewer events. Most short fictional films have

1. One or two major characters, who usually do not change goals or personality during the story

classical Hollywood cinema: Films that show one or more characters facing a succession of problems while trying to reach their goals and that tend to use unobtrusive filmmaking techniques.

story time: The amount of time represented in a film's story.

2. A brief **story time**, usually a few days or less

3. One goal, which the main character usually does not state explicitly but which viewers can figure out early in the film

4. One or more obstacles or conflicts, none of them very time-consuming, thwarting achievement of the goal

5. Success or failure in reaching the goal

A minority of short fictional films rejects the conventions of classical Hollywood cinema. A good example is "The Other Side," an $8^1/_2$-minute 1966 black-and-white film from Flemish Belgium. The film is a **symbolic** story about masses of people in an unidentified town who are forced to keep their hands against the walls of buildings as they move slowly sideways. Eventually, some try to rebel but are gunned down by an unseen machine gun. The film has no dialogue, no narration, and no music except during the opening credits and the final moments. The only **sound effect** is occasional machine-gun fire. "The Other Side" is a brief, complex, and somewhat **ambiguous** film that calls for multiple viewings, which are easier to manage with short films than with features.

sound effect: In film, a sound other than spoken words or music.

In classical Hollywood cinema, conflict between characters is used to show what individual characters are like and to initiate and develop the **plot**. But in "The Other Side," we viewers see only one side of the conflict. We never learn about the persons who are shooting the people in the street, nor do we know why they do so. The oppressors kill individuals one at a time and evidently kill no more than necessary to keep the rest in line (literally and figuratively). The film shows that they shoot rebels. Also, in contrast with classical Hollywood cinema, "The Other Side" reveals little about individual characters. The film has no spoken words and no written language except the final "1966." There are no revealing **close-ups** of faces, so we viewers cannot infer what the characters are feeling. No one looks happy, yet no one looks angry either. In nearly all of the film, people move lethargically, like drugged inmates in an institution or animals in a zoo. The lack of emotion and of interaction among characters are two of the film's most prominent features. The film focuses not on individual psychology but on the political issues of force and conformity.

plot: The structure or arrangement of a narrative's events.

As in most short films of classical Hollywood cinema, the main characters in "The Other Side" have a single goal: freedom from oppression and conformity. Failing at that, they want to survive, even if survival requires conformity, lack of interaction, and the absence of vitality. Unlike the main characters in most films of classical Hollywood cinema, the characters in this short film fail to achieve their goal, and the film ends as it began—except with more bodies filling the street.[2]

---

[2]Descriptions and analyses of "Leon's Case" and "The Other Side" are adapted from Phillips.

FEATURE FILMS

The events of a fictional film are selected and arranged in a meaningful order (structure). They are represented over time (chronologically or not). In addition, the events are represented in one or more styles. In the remainder of this chapter, we explore how feature films handle the basic components of structure, time, and style.

Structure

Structure, which some scholars and theorists call *form*, refers to the arrangement of the parts of a text. This section focuses on (1) the basics of fictional structure (characters, goals, conflicts, and resolution); (2) some functions of beginnings, middles, and endings; and (3) the combining of different brief stories—**plotlines**—into a larger, more complex story.

CHARACTERS, GOALS, CONFLICTS, AND RESOLUTION

Fictional films always include at least one character, and that character is usually based on characteristics of one or more actual people. Nonhuman characters featured in fictional films—such as extraterrestrials, robots, zombies, ghosts, animals, and even abstract shapes—are portrayed as having human qualities (Figure 6.3). A fictional narrative nearly always includes at least one character that wants something but has problems obtaining it (Figure 6.4). People are fascinated with characters that have trouble reaching their goals, in part because in such circumstances viewers learn about human nature or think they learn about how they themselves might handle a similar situation. Perhaps viewers also sometimes enjoy seeing others struggling with problems. Whatever their motivations, viewers tend to be fascinated by how others behave in adverse situations and how their decisions and actions could affect them and others around them.

Typically, a main character's goals in a fictional film are not immediately apparent, though one major goal usually becomes clear early in the film so that viewers do not lose interest. As a story

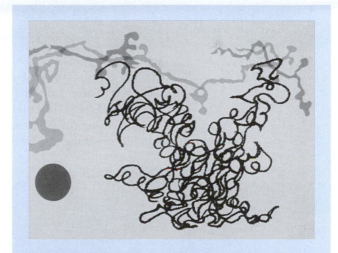

FIGURE 6.3 Abstract shapes functioning as characters
Most fictional films include characters that are enacted by humans, but occasionally characters are imaginary beings with human qualities. "The Dot and the Line: A Romance in Lower Mathematics" (1965), which was co-directed by Chuck Jones and Les Goldman, presents the story of a female dot and two contending males: a straight line and an ever-changing squiggle (the squiggle is represented here by the darker squiggly lines). In this image, a tad more than 9 minutes into this 10-minute film, the narrator has said, "Dot wondered why she'd never noticed how hairy and coarse he [the squiggle] was, how untidy and graceless, and how he mispronounced his L's and picked his ear." She has decided to choose the line as her mate. *MGM; Warner Home Video DVD [Special Feature on the 2005 DVD for* The Glass Bottom Boat*]*

FIGURE 6.4 The basics of a fictional narrative: character, goal(s), setbacks, and resolution
This graph for "The String Bean" (1962) illustrates how a central character seeks a goal (described at the top of the vertical axis), makes progress or encounters setbacks in reaching the goal, and then either succeeds or not. Similar graphs can help scriptwriters as they work on their scripts and film students as they study a plotline's structure. *Source: Phillips, 101*

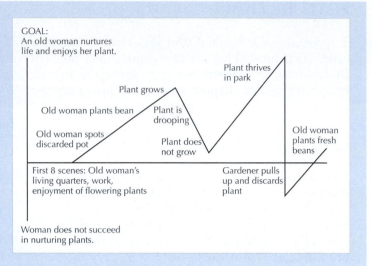

GOAL:
An old woman nurtures life and enjoys her plant.

Plant thrives in park

Plant grows

Old woman plants bean   Plant is drooping

Old woman spots discarded pot

Plant does not grow

Old woman plants fresh beans

First 8 scenes: Old woman's living quarters, work, enjoyment of flowering plants

Gardener pulls up and discards plant

Woman does not succeed in nurturing plants.

progresses, sometimes a second goal emerges. In the French film *Ridicule* (1996), the main character pursues a goal and then a second goal emerges (Figure 6.5). Initially, another character, the worldly woman of the court, helps the main character make progress toward his first goal, but she hinders his reaching the second goal (winning the love of Mathilde, a younger

a)

b)

FIGURE 6.5 Character with one initial goal and later a second goal
Nearly all of *Ridicule* (1996) takes place in 1783 France (six years before the beginning of the French Revolution), a time when wit was king and ridicule could kill. The main character is Gregoire Ponceludon, seen on the left in (b), an engineer who seeks royal support to clear a swamp and thus eradicate a fatal disease. While staying in Versailles, he is soon pursuing a second goal: Mathilde, a young, intelligent, individualistic woman who is not of the king's court, seen in (a). As Gregoire pursues his two goals, he becomes entangled with a calculating, worldly woman of the court, seen in (b). She helps him gain the king's ear but later, in anger at his choice of Mathilde over her, assures his downfall. As a postscript, the film informs viewers that in 1794, French aristocrats fled the French Revolution, and "In 1795, Citizens Gregoire and Mathilde Ponceludon proceeded with the draining of the Dombes. Their lives were rid of pestilence, royal caprice, and the savage sting of aristocratic ridicule." (Note that the construction of the last sentence gives *equal* weight to *pestilence*, *royal caprice*, and *aristocratic ridicule*.) *Canal+, France 3 Cinéma, and others; Miramax Home Entertainment DVD*

woman). The main character then fails in his first goal but succeeds in his second, though, as the film's final **title card** informs us, he (and Mathilde) eventually succeed in reaching his initial goal. Sometimes the main character fails to achieve either of two major goals. In *Citizen Kane* (1941), Charles Foster Kane has two major goals in his life: to win a woman's lasting love and to win the love of the populace, most notably by being elected governor. He fails to achieve either goal: his first wife leaves him after his affair with another woman becomes public, his second wife leaves him because of his self-centeredness and her isolation and boredom, and voters decline to send him to the governor's office.

In films with two or more major characters, the characters usually have different goals or they seek the same goal, at least initially. The result is conflict, with or without humor. Conflict largely without humor is prominent in many movies, including most war movies and westerns. Conflict with humor abounds in most romantic comedies, such as *It Happened One Night* (1934), *Bringing Up Baby* (1938), *My Best Friend's Wedding* (1997), *Bridget Jones's Diary* (2001), *Down with Love* (2003), *Mr. and Mrs. Smith* (2005), and *Waitress* (2007).

Although action movies tend to show a lot of action involving many characters fighting or chasing one another, a film story may concentrate on a conflict within a single character. It may show the character torn between two difficult choices. An example is *The Terrorist*, which is set in the south Indian jungle and is about Malli, a young woman who has volunteered to assassinate an important opposition leader by blowing herself up in his presence (2000, Figure 6.6).

title card: A card or thin sheet of clear plastic on which is written or printed information included in a film.

FIGURE 6.6 Conflict within a character
In *The Terrorist* (2000), Malli, a 19-year-old, is trained to be an assassin. Before she arrives at the fateful time and place, however, she has many conflicting thoughts and feelings. In various parts of the story, Malli savors the beauties and wonder of life with new awareness. However, she also experiences strong competing thoughts and feelings. For example, here, approximately 82 1/4 minutes into the film, she has failed her final assassination rehearsal, and her contact reminds her of a number of points, including how many others are counting on her to assassinate an opposition leader. The contact concludes, "Lastly, don't betray yourself. Your great sacrifice, your valiant death will stir the hearts of our people. Our future generations will pay homage to you. Your death will herald a new era for our people. Think only about that." Most of what viewers learn about Malli's conflicting thoughts and feelings is conveyed by the film's visuals and sound effects (her heavy breathing during times of stress, for example). Although she is the main character and is on the screen during nearly the entire film, she says little. It is largely up to her expressive face, as seen here, to suggest her conflicted thoughts and feelings. *Moderné Gallérie, Wonderfilms; Winstar TV and Video DVD*

In pursuing goals, people inevitably encounter conflict or problems, in fiction as in life. In *Jaws* (1975), a huge killer shark is menacing swimmers who venture into the waters off a New England island that caters to summer tourists. The film exemplifies the three traditional types of conflict (Figure 6.7). At the film's end, however, the conflicts are resolved: the veteran fisherman Quint is destroyed by his shark adversary, and soon afterward the shark is destroyed; Hooper and Brody resolve their differences and later paddle back to the beach; and Brody no longer feels divided in his allegiances because the townspeople and tourists are no longer in danger. Often fictional stories take the form of two opposing characters or of two opposing groups of characters (see Plates 34–37 in Chapter 13).

In classical Hollywood cinema, the main characters typically achieve all their major goals. If a feature film has only one major character, that character normally has more than one major goal. For example, in countless movies—such as *Rocky* (1976), *Top Gun* (1986), *The Mask* (1994), *Mission: Impossible 2* (2000), and almost any James Bond movie—the central male character tries to succeed in both love and work or in some other major goal and does so. In many musicals, the main male character eventually wins the woman of his dreams and is instrumental in the successful staging of a show or making of a movie.

In most movies, especially the popular ones, the major characters don't just succeed; they succeed against enormous odds. In *Stand and Deliver* (1987), an overworked high school math teacher in a Los Angeles barrio wins the respect of his students, who overcome their various problems at home, work diligently to pass the math Advanced Placement test, and pass the test a second time after being allowed only one day to review. *Music of the Heart* (1999) is yet another movie in which the main character—a violin teacher in an East Harlem elementary school—endures setback after setback but eventually succeeds spectacularly. Her long list of problems includes a husband who abandons her and their two sons; loss of income and resultant housing problems; resentment from fellow teachers and resistance from some parents; difficulties in handling her two sons, especially the older one, who misses his father; a boyfriend who is not interested in a long-term relationship; unending parking tickets because she never gets a parking space at work; and loss of her position and funds for her violin program, even after it becomes so successful that students have to enter a lottery for a chance at admittance. Early in the story,

FIGURE 6.7 The three types of conflict
The three main human subjects of *Jaws* (1975) are (left to right) the chief of police (Brody), a veteran fisherman (Quint), and a marine-life specialist (Hooper). During the film, each comes into conflict with each of the others. All three come into conflict with a great white shark. And Brody has conflicting desires to accommodate the political leaders and businesspeople yet protect townspeople and tourists against shark attacks. In short, the film illustrates the three basic types of conflict possible in stories: people versus people, people versus nature, and a character conflicted in his or her thinking. *Publicity still. Zanuck/Brown Productions; Universal*

she decides to do without a social life and instead to focus on her two sons and her work. Like the stories of so many popular movies, hers shows that despite seemingly unending hurdles, one person who works hard can achieve a dream.

Nevertheless, an occasional popular movie has a resolution in which the main (usually male) character does not achieve all his major goals (Figure 6.8).

BEGINNINGS, MIDDLES, AND ENDINGS

The beginning of a fictional film tends to involve viewers and to establish where and when the story starts. Many fictional films start with one or more **shots** of the setting before introducing the subjects. Soon after that, the story begins to unfold and draw viewers into anticipating and readjusting to developments that take place before their eyes.

shot (noun): An uninterrupted strip of exposed motion-picture film or videotape that represents a subject during an uninterrupted segment of time.

Typically, a fictional film's beginning provides minimal **exposition** (information about events that supposedly transpired before the beginning of the plot). Too much exposition, especially early in a narrative, tends to keep audiences uninvolved. Tellers of tales—whether in print, online, on the stage, or on the screen—usually feed their audiences tidbits of background information when needed as the story progresses.

Beginnings usually introduce the major characters and encourage viewers to infer their goals. The events of fictional films are so intertwined that often a character's need or desire at the story's beginning largely determines the story's ending. Early in *Finzan: A Dance for the Heroes* (Mali, 1990), a man's desire to force his late brother's widow to marry him sets off a chain of actions and consequences (Figure 6.9). *The Maltese Falcon* (1941) also begins with characters seeking something, which leads to lots of complications and eventually a resolution (Figure 6.10).

Mind you, a beginning may withhold a lot of important information and challenge viewers to try to figure out what is going on and how it all ties together. A good example is the first three minutes of Ernst Lubitsch's 83-minute film *Trouble in Paradise* (1932; Table 6.1). Less imaginative filmmakers might have begun *Trouble in Paradise* with the usual **establishing shot(s)** so that viewers

FIGURE 6.8 Main character, his goals, his partial achievements
Here on the right with his four best friends is the main character in *8 Mile* (2002), Jimmy Smith, Jr. (Rabbit), who is a budding hip-hop artist partially based on and played by Eminem. By the end of the film, Rabbit has won an important freestyle battle and is on his way to success, and his mother, to whom Rabbit is close, is rid of a bad boyfriend and has won a lot of money at bingo and thus has temporarily solved her money problems. But Rabbit has not fared well with the two major young women in his life, both seen only briefly in the film but both proving untrustworthy. The film ends with Rabbit alone, heading down an alley to go back to work (to finish an extra shift he had promised to do) and choosing to go his own way in his future hip-hop career. *Imagine Entertainment; Universal DVD*

FIGURE 6.9 A character's initial need or desire causing consequences
Seen here is Nanyuma, the main character in *Finzan: A Dance for the Heroes* (1990). Early in the film, Nanyuma's husband dies, and soon her husband's brother, the village idiot, wants to marry her. In pursuing that goal, he sets in motion most of the film's complications. The story ends with the man not getting what he wants: the widow evades the consummation of her forced marriage but only by exiling herself and her young son from her village and chancing an uncertain future. *Courtesy of California Newsreel, San Francisco, CA, or South Burlington, VT*

FIGURE 6.10 Something sought at the beginning shaping the fictional film's middle and ending
Early in *The Maltese Falcon* (1941), viewers learn that several characters seek the Maltese Falcon, which is a statuette thought to be valuable. The large middle section of the story shows the consequences of their trying to acquire it and the extremes to which people will go to acquire "the stuff that dreams are made of." This frame, from nearly 88 minutes into the film, shows three seekers finally in possession of what they think is the long-sought fabled object. *Warner Bros.–First National; Warner Home Video DVD*

instantly identify the setting. In this film, however, initially the setting could be any city at night. First, Lubitsch shows us darkness and garbage. Later, we see that the setting is Venice. From the beginning, the film implies that it will not show more of the same old same old. At first, it is difficult to figure out the function of the two Italian women ringing the doorbell. Much later in the film the unconscious man on the floor calls them "business associates," but those attuned to Lubitsch's subtlety will figure out that they are prostitutes. The film also does not start developing one story line. Instead, it introduces viewers to two of the film's major characters: the man unconscious on the floor and the man who, we learn later, is responsible for putting him there. By this point, the film is into its third minute and the situations have not yet come into clear focus.

The middle section of fictional feature films typically includes a series of obstacles that prevent or delay the main characters from achieving their goals. In the long central section of *Schindler's List* (1993), for example, Schindler tries to thwart the Nazis and help save as many Jews as possible, but in pursuing his goals, he faces setbacks, dangers, and delays. In dealing with the impediments to reaching their goals, the central characters in films reveal their natures and the consequences of their decisions and actions for themselves and others. Consider the structure of the western *Unforgiven* (1992). The film begins with acts of injustice both by a cowboy who slashes a woman's face and by the sheriff who cavalierly acts as law officer, jury, and judge. The large middle section of the film shows those who will avenge the injustice against the woman, how they will do so, and what consequences their actions cause. The middle section of a fictional film tests the filmmakers' inventiveness and skill in

TABLE 6.1
The Opening Eight Shots of *Trouble in Paradise* (1932)

1. In the partial darkness, a man picks up a loaded garbage can and carries it to a nearby small boat. In the background, viewers can see water and other small boats and soon can infer that the setting is Venice.

2. The man dumps the load of garbage into the boat, sets down the empty can, turns, starts walking, and starts singing *O sole mio*.

3. The man gets in the boat and starts to move the oar to propel the boat forward.

4. Inside a dark room, a man in a suit is running away with his back to the camera; he goes out an open window and begins to climb down a tree.

5. Seen as shadows only, on the ground the man looks to the right and left and then takes off a false beard and mustache.

6. Back in the same room that is seen in shot 4, the moving camera reveals the legs and feet of an unmoving man on the floor.

7. Outside the same room, two women speaking in untranslated Italian are frustrated that no one has answered their repeated ringing of the doorbell.

8. With the camera outside a window to that same room and looking in, viewers can see the man get up part way but then fall unconscious again. Outside the building, the camera moves through space from left to right, seemingly continuing the shot, but in fact the long middle section where the camera is moving is of a miniature. The camera stops outside a lighted room. In the background is a small table set for two. In the foreground and on the right stands a man dressed in a suit and deep in thought. A waiter walks toward the man, stops, gives him a large piece of printed paper, and asks him with what to begin the upcoming meal. The man asks for the waiter's suggestion; he gives it; and the man accepts it.

creating satisfying surprise and suspense and in using other ways to keep the audience involved with the story.

An ending may serve many functions—for example, to reverse the mood and meanings of what has gone before. Thus, a film suffused with pain, suffering, and blood might end not in darkness and silence, not in defeat and despair, but in light, music, and triumph (Figure 6.11a–b). An earlier representation of much the same story ends very differently (Figure 6.11c–d).

Narrative endings show the consequences of the major previous events. Filmmakers, however, sometimes include an ending that isn't well integrated with the rest of the story. Consider *Schindler's List*. Early in the film, Schindler is portrayed as a complex, multidimensional man—exploitative, philandering, and callous, yet shrewd, self-confident, powerful, and somewhat inexplicable. Later in the film, after he retrieves the Jewish women from the Auschwitz concentration camp, he seeks out his wife to be reconciled with her and presumably strays no more. Viewers learn that his factory workers build deliberately flawed armaments to sabotage the

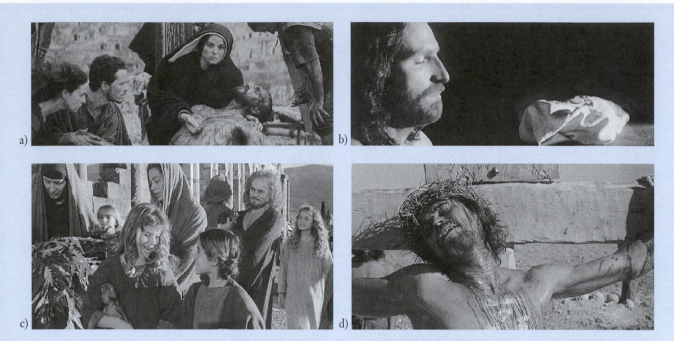

FIGURE 6.11 Different endings to the same basic story

(a) The penultimate scene of Mel Gibson's *The Passion of the Christ* (2004) concludes with a carefully composed bloody pietà. Jesus has died after extensive beatings, crucifixion, and a spear stab in the ribs. This image fades to darkness and silence. What follows is anything but dark and silent. (b) In the film's last scene, the image fades in, but at first we viewers can see very little and what we see are only fragments of the whole. As a massive, flattish rock blocking the entrance of Jesus' tomb is moved by some unseen force, the darkness is replaced by changing patterns of darkness and light and finally by a gently collapsing empty shroud (on the right) and by a seated, resurrected, and restored Jesus. He seems to pray briefly, then gets up and starts to walk, and we viewers can glimpse that he is naked and that his right hand retains a large hole from the crucifixion. As he moves forward (screen right) to off-screen, the image fades to black.

(c–d) Martin Scorsese's *The Last Temptation of Christ* (1988)—which is based not on the Gospels but on an imaginative novel—also shows the story of Jesus' last days but has a very different ending. As in Mel Gibson's later film, the crucifixion is bloody and graphic. But Scorsese's film ends not with the resurrection but with the crucifixion, then a long sequence illustrating the stages of the normal family life Jesus did not get to lead (c), and then back to the crucifixion (d), where Jesus finally accepts his fate as he looks upward and shouts and then repeats more softly, "It is accomplished."

Both films have as their central subject the human and divine aspects of Jesus. And both dwell on his pains, Gibson's mostly on physical pain, Scorsese's mostly on the psychological. The two films present two different endings to the same well-known story. (a–b) *Icon Productions; 20th Century Fox Home Entertainment DVD.* (c–d) *Universal, Cineplex-Odeon Films; Criterion DVD*

German war effort. Schindler urges the rabbi who works for him to pre-pare for the Sabbath and spends a lot of money sustaining his workers and bribing Reich officials. At the war's end, he credits his Jewish workers with saving themselves and persuades the armed camp guards to leave without harming the workers. Later, as the music swells, he breaks down and says that he squandered money and should have saved even more Jews; then he is quietly and lovingly enfolded by many of those he did save. By the end of the movie, the Schindler character has been reduced to one dimension as the filmmakers try hard to make sure no one misses his admirable qualities. The movie ends not with modulated chords but with a single repeated note. The ending may be emotionally satisfying for many viewers—and understandable, given the filmmakers' desire to honor Schindler—but it does not mesh with the film's earlier restraint and complexity.

Sometimes a film has an improbable ending because the filmmakers respond to political or societal pressures. The Chinese film *Not One Less* (1999) shows both the inadequate conditions of a rural Chinese primary school and later the brusque or uncaring attitudes of the people whom the main character meets in a Chinese city (Figure 6.12). But as the film nears its end, it changes into a fairy tale. The thirteen-year-old girl who takes over the teaching while the adult teacher is away is suddenly rewarded in highly unlikely ways. A TV broadcast helps her locate the boy she went to the city to retrieve; a TV crew drives the boy and girl back to their home-town while recording the happy developments; and the village receives gifts and money to rebuild the school and refurnish it. A final title card informs viewers that a million Chinese children drop school for work each year. The happy ending and inaccurate final title cards (the number of Chinese school dropouts is much higher) were included because the direc-tor (Zhang Yimou) had trouble with Chinese censorship in the past and feared that the authorities would object to too unfavorable a representa-tion of life in contemporary China. Perhaps other endings are wrong for

FIGURE 6.12 Ending shaped by the context of the production
Not One Less (1999) is the story of a resolute girl who is put in charge of a small rural Chinese primary school while the teacher is away for a month. The film shows the difficult conditions in which the children are taught—for example, a run-down schoolroom with only one piece of chalk per day, a badly pitted chalkboard, a leaky roof, no books, and an unqualified substitute teacher. Most of the story shows the conditions at the school and in a city in a credible way. *Columbia Pictures, Film Production Asia, and others; Columbia TriStar Home Video DVD*

their stories because filmmakers know how unpopular unhappy endings can be. Director Stanley Kubrick observed, "'Maybe the reason why people seem to find it harder to take unhappy endings in movies than in plays or novels is that a good movie engages you so heavily that you find an unhappy ending almost unbearable'" (quoted in Hohenadel).

Films with **closure** end by showing the consequences of events that viewers have become curious about. Closure supplies viewers with the answers and a sense of completion that real life so often withholds. Films, however, may lack closure—that is, be open-ended, leaving the fate of a significant character or person uncertain or the causes or consequences of a significant event unknown or unknowable. Generally, films of classical Hollywood cinema provide a sense of completion because mainstream audiences tend to dislike inconclusive or puzzling endings. The endings of **independent films**, in contrast, are more likely to be open. Examples are *The Crying Game* (1992) and *L.A. Confidential* (1997). At the end of *The Crying Game*, viewers cannot know what Fergus and Dil's relationship will be. They can only review relevant events from the film and make informed guesses. In *L.A. Confidential*, the ending for one of the two main characters is open. Viewers cannot know Ed Exley's fate. He has survived an attempt on his life and been awarded honors again. For now, Exley is aware that the police chief and the district attorney are using him to repair damage done to the image of the Los Angeles Police Department. But in the long run, can he trust the police chief and the DA, especially now that his colleague, a powerful ally, is leaving the police force?

THE END OF ENDINGS: LAST SHOTS

Usually the ending of a film is more important than almost any other part. And the end of the ending, the film's last shot, can serve any number of important functions, including contributing to the film's closure and extracting the viewer from the film's world. Some of the possible **filmmaking techniques** used to support these results include the following: the final image increasingly going out of focus, a **cut** to black, or a **fade-out** to a color or to black. Like many TV shows, a film may end with a **freeze frame**, which distances the viewer from the film's movements. A film may end with a freeze-frame **reaction shot**, as in the classic **French new wave** film *The 400 Blows* (1959), where the main character, a male teen escaping from a juvenile detention facility, runs up to the edge of a body of water, stops, and turns and looks directly at the camera. The filmmakers also use a concluding reaction shot in *Le petit lieutenant* (2005), where the main character looks at the camera and through subtle facial expressions reveals the deep anguish she is feeling. **Slow motion** is another option that can support results similar to those of a freeze frame. A film's human subject may move away from the camera, or the camera may move away from the

independent film: Film made mainly or entirely without support or input from the dominant, established film industry.

cut (noun): A transition between shots that is made by splicing or joining the end of one shot to the beginning of the next.

reaction shot: A shot, usually of a face, that shows someone or occasionally some other creature reacting to an event.

French new wave (cinema): A film movement consisting of a loose grouping of untraditional movies made in France in the late 1950s and early 1960s.

subject. The camera may pull back or up into the air, or both, perhaps while mounted on a crane (see Figures 2.51 and 2.54) or while located in a helicopter. Similarly, filmmakers may use a **zoom lens** to distance viewers from the film's subject and setting. Filmmakers often use several of these or other techniques in combination, as in the last shot of the 2004 Chilean film *Machuca* (Figure 6.13).

The House of Mirth (2000) also uses more than one technique in its last shot, which shows a man kneeling by a bed, grieving, and holding the hand of a woman he had loved. Soon a freeze frame is used, and shortly after that, we viewers see the title card "New York 1907," which soon fades out. Very gradually, the still image of the man and woman begins to fade and go out of focus, starting at about the time the final credits are superimposed on the final image and begin to roll. Soon, the image of the man and especially of the woman has become indistinct, and the main areas of color—the woman's red hair and a small red piece of clothing she wears on her chest— gradually transform to shades of light brownish gray. The final image may signify the woman's fading of life and consciousness, the finality of her death, the man's immobility caused by grief, and the conclusion of the film's movements and clarity.

FIGURE 6.13 **Multiple techniques used in a film's concluding shot**
Here in the first frame of the last shot of the 2004 Chilean film *Machuca*, the film's main subject is seen badly out of focus in the foreground, and the background is even more out of focus. During this shot, the boy slowly walks away from the camera, and his indistinct form soon disappears into the darkness in the bottom part of the frame. After a pause, the image fades to black. Setting, focus, and movement are all used to increasingly distance the viewer from the film's main subject and his world. *Wood Producciones, Toanasol Films*

Sometimes a film's conclusion is so appropriate and effective that it is one of the most memorable parts, sometimes even the most memorable part, of the film. Two examples are from the American movies *The Searchers* (1956) and *The Godfather* (1972) (Figure 6.14).

The departure from the film's world can be gradual or abrupt, coming as a surprise or as what viewers largely anticipated. Often music is used to help convey or reinforce the final transition as well (Figure 6.15). Like images, music can fade out or end abruptly. Then, too, like the freeze frame, silence may conclude a film. As in any part of a film, creative filmmakers may use countless combinations of techniques to end a film. How well they succeed depends in part on the techniques chosen for the film's context.

PLOTLINES

A plotline is a brief narrative—a series of related events situated in one or more settings—that usually involves only a few characters or (in documentary films) a few people. A plotline can function as a complete short narrative, as it typically does in a short film. A feature film, however, often has

a)

b)

FIGURE 6.14 Appropriate, resonant, and memorable concluding shots
(a) The main character in *The Searchers* (1956) has devoted years of his life to retrieving his young niece from American Indians sometime after the conclusion of the American Civil War. By the end of the film, he has finally succeeded and brought her home to surviving family only to be forgotten and ignored by both her and her family. After the moment seen here, he turns and slowly walks away, the door closes on his image in the windy wilderness, and darkness fills the screen. In *The Searchers* the main agent of European American civilization is complex, admirable, yet deeply flawed and finally without a home in the wild.

(b) At the end of *The Godfather* (1972), Michael is in his home office surrounded by three of his men. Both Michael's wife Kay and we viewers see one of the men kiss Michael's hand and hear him say, "Don Corleone"—acknowledging Michael as the new head of the Corleone family and its criminal business. The second man kisses Michael's hand, and, at nearly the same time, the third man goes to the door and closes it. In the last shot, seen here, taken from inside Michael's office, the closing door serves as a kind of concluding wipe to darkness (from left to right on the screen). The final shot shows that Kay is to be shut out of knowledge of her husband's criminal life.

The concluding shots of *The Searchers* and *The Godfather* not only end the stories in ways that are completely credible given the characters and the stories up to this point but also serve to emphasize that characters are excluded and to distance viewers from the film's main subjects. Beyond that, for many viewers the two shots and the music that accompanies them also evoke emotions difficult to express in words, though two words useful here are *loss* and *melancholy*. (For discussion of the symbolic use of doors in all three *Godfather* films, see p. 526.) (a) *C. V. Whitney Pictures, Warner Bros.; Warner Home Video DVD 50th Anniversary Two-Disc Special Edition.* (b) *Paramount; Paramount DVD*

two or more plotlines. Plotlines may be combined in countless creative ways and serve many different functions.

To compress a wide-ranging story into a movie, plotlines can be consecutive yet have large gaps of story time between them. *2001: A Space Odyssey* (1968) contains the consecutive plotlines of four groups: man-apes, scientists, a computer and two astronauts, and the star-child. *Being Human* (1994), with Robin Williams, has five plotlines (set, for example, in cave times, ancient Rome, and the modern era) with vast gaps of time between them.

Multiple alternating plotlines can be used to show relationships between different time periods. *The Godfather Part II* (1974) and *Heat and Dust* (1983) alternate between a narrative primarily about one character and a story set years earlier about a relative. *Intolerance* (1916), directed by

FIGURE 6.15 Music to help conclude a fictional film
Fat City (1972) is about two young men—Tully on the left and Ernie on the right—who try to achieve some success through boxing but whose dreams come to little. In the film's last scene, the two have gone out for coffee. They sit and chat briefly; then Ernie says he needs to get going. Tully asks him to "stick around" and at the beginning of the film's last shot adds, "talk a while." Ernie agrees and they sit and sip coffee but say not a word. During the last part of the shot, the end credits begin (right) while part of the song "Help Me Make It through the Night" is heard once again. As the singing and instrumentals conclude, so do the shot and the film. The music helps reinforce the film's overall melancholy mood. It also supports some of the film's meanings—the uncertainty of the future, the undesirability of being alone, and the desirability of companionship. Then the music fades out as the image does. The film's concluding seconds consist of darkness and a momentary silence as we viewers sit before a screen in the dark and silence. *Rastar Pictures, Columbia Pictures; Sony Pictures Home Entertainment DVD*

D. W. Griffith, alternates four plotlines, each set in a different place and historical period: Babylon in 539 B.C., Judaea toward the end of Christ's life, France in 1572, and the United States early in the twentieth century. As might be expected from a film with so complicated a structure, many viewers detect little unity in the film and are confused about its purpose.

A film can alternate between simultaneous plotlines to heighten suspense. *Dr. Strangelove: Or, How I Learned to Stop Worrying and Love the Bomb* (1963) has three major simultaneous plotlines: at a U.S. Air Force base where the paranoid General Jack D. Ripper has ordered U.S. military planes to attack the Soviet Union; on a U.S. plane on its way to bomb a Soviet target; and in the Pentagon war room, where the U.S. president, military commanders, and Dr. Strangelove, the leading scientist, try to call back the plane and prevent the catastrophe.

The Mexican film *Amores Perros* (2000), which is set in contemporary Mexico City, also has three major plotlines. Each is announced by a title card: "Octavio and Susana," "Daniel and Valeria," and "El Chivo and Maru." In the first plotline, Octavio (played by the Mexican star Gael García Bernal) is a young man obsessed with Susana, the wife of his hot-headed older brother Ramiro. In the second plotline, Valeria is a successful young model having an affair with Daniel, a married father who leaves his family and sets up a luxury apartment for her and himself. And in the third plotline, El Chivo ("The Goat"), a bearded former revolutionary who years earlier had abandoned his family, is an occasional hit man who lives alone with his dogs and yearns for a relationship with his grown daughter Maru. As Table 6.2 illustrates, it's possible to interpret the film as having

TABLE 6.2
Selected Excerpts from the Three Parts of the Plot for *Amores Perros* (2000)*

PART 1

during a car chase (1:03)
car accident (3:05)
Octavio and Susana title card (3:20)
Jarocho arrives at dog-fighting site
　　with his dog . . .
(P3) El Chivo collecting junk and
　　putting it into his cart
dogfight continues
Octavio with Susana and her baby,
　　then Ramiro arrives . . .
(P3) El Chivo murders a man
(P2) Daniel in car with wife and two
　　young daughters . . .
Ramiro and a friend begin holdup of a
　　pharmacy . . .
(P3) El Chivo watches funeral of his
　　daughter's mother . . .
Octavio and Susana become lovers . . .
　　Octavio has Ramiro beaten . . .
　　Ramiro, Susana, and their baby
　　leave for locations unknown
(P1 & P2) TV show with Valeria
　　cross-cut with Octavio and his
　　friend watching the show . . .
Octavio stabs Jarocho
car chase again (56:50 = 1:03)
car accident (57:31)

Octavio with Susana and her baby before
Ramiro comes into the scene.

PART 2

Daniel trying to comfort Valeria after her
return from the hospital.

end of TV show with Valeria as guest
　　(57:30) . . .
(P3) El Chivo observing Solares
(P2 & P3) Valeria drives past El Chivo
car accident (62:51)
Daniel and Valeria title card (63:02)
Daniel at hospital after Valeria's car
　　accident . . .
(P3) El Chivo breaks into Maru's place
　　and looks around
Valeria's dog lost under the apartment
　　floor . . .
Valeria and Daniel have heated argu-
　　ments . . .
Daniel rings his wife but cannot bring
　　himself to talk to her . . .
Valeria gets advanced case of gangrene
　　and loses her leg . . .
Daniel with Valeria as she looks out
　　window at spot where she had been
　　featured in an ad (94:00)

PART 3

El Chivo after he has shaved off his
beard and is in his daughter's place where
he is leaving a message on her answering
machine.

El Chivo and Maru title card (94:00)
To El Chivo's, Leonardo brings
　　Gustavo, who asks El Chivo to kill
　　his business partner, Luis Miranda
　　Solares
(P1 & P3) El Chivo sees Susana,
　　Ramiro, and their baby (101:00) . . .
(P2 & P3) As Valeria drives by El
　　Chivo, she calls to her dog, Richi.
　　As El Chivo observes Solares, two
　　cars crash behind him
car accident (105:41)
El Chivo takes Octavio's money and
　　his injured dog . . .
(P1) Ramiro and his friend rob a bank.
　　Ramiro shot . . . (P1) Funeral home,
　　Ramiro dead. Octavio there on a
　　crutch and asks Susana to go away
　　with him
El Chivo kidnaps Solares and later
　　arranges to leave him face-to-face
　　with Gustavo
(P1) Octavio at bus station waiting in
　　vain for Susana . . .
(P2) "Enchant" advertising sign with
　　Valeria on it being lowered
El Chivo at Maru's place leaving
　　money and messages
El Chivo sells Gustavo's SUV and
　　walks away

*(P1) = plotline 1. (P2) = plotline 2. (P3) = plotline 3.
. . . = Omission of scene(s) from table. Number in parentheses = the time into the film.
Source: Altavista Films, Zeta Film; Lions Gate Home Entertainment DVD

three major parts, each part mainly about one plotline but containing scenes from one or both of the other two plotlines.

Part 1, which is mostly about the "Octavio and Susana" plotline, begins well into the first plotline: a car chase and car accident. The film then flashes back to the earliest point of the first plotline and proceeds chronologically, though with frequent brief interruptions for scenes from the film's other two plotlines (see Table 6.2). The main body of Part 2, which is mainly about the "Daniel and Valeria" plotline, begins with Valeria as a guest on a TV talk show and proceeds chronologically but with brief interruptions for scenes from the third plotline. Part 3, which has many scenes from the "El Chivo and Maru" plotline, begins with two men in an SUV on the way to a meeting with El Chivo. Part 3 shows events before the accident, the accident yet again, and developments after the accident; and it ends at 149 minutes into the film. Part 3 also includes a brief scene where viewers see characters from the first plotline in the background, more scenes that finish up the first plotline, a shot in which viewers can hear Valeria call out to her dog shortly before the accident, and a glimpse of an advertising sign featuring Valeria. (The third part also includes two scenes seemingly out of chronological order: Leonardo is seen in a bank and later in a scene saying he is going to the bank.)

The film's unusual structure demands that audiences be unusually attentive and thoughtful. The cutting between events from the different plotlines gives viewers a sense of what different characters are doing before or after the accident or in some cases at about the same time that it occurs. Since all three plotlines converge in the auto accident, the film's structure also suggests that entirely dissimilar characters may converge in unexpected ways and then experience unanticipated consequences.

The structure of *Babel* (2006), which is a later film by the writer and director team of *Amores Perros*, also shows how life's occurrences may have unexpected connections and unanticipated consequences. The film has four nonchronological plotlines that initially seem unrelated. The plotlines are introduced in the following order:

1. Plotline about a rural Moroccan family, mainly a father, his two young sons, and his daughter
2. Plotline about a U.S. couple's two children whose Mexican nanny takes them on a trip to Mexico and back
3. Plotline about the two children's parents (plotline 2), who have recently lost their third child and are on a tense vacation tour in Morocco when the wife gets shot while riding in a tour bus
4. Plotline about a frustrated, troubled Japanese deaf-mute girl and her widower father.

Here's the **fabula** in brief: A Japanese man had given a hunting rifle to a guide in Morocco, and it is eventually used to seriously injure an American

fabula: The reconstruction of the events of a nonchronological narrative into chronological order.

wife, which in turn disrupts the vacation of her fellow travelers. The incident causes the eventual sending of a Red Cross helicopter, an international incident, and international news coverage. The husband is so upset about possibly losing his wife that he telephones the nanny and orders her not to let their two children out of her sight. She cannot find a caretaker she trusts, so she ends up taking them to her son's wedding in Mexico. On the return trip, the nanny and the two children nearly perish in the desert (and thus the father nearly loses his two children and his wife in a few days' time). The nanny gets arrested and is summarily deported. At various times during all these and other complications, two Japanese police officers try to locate the Japanese father to question him about his hunting rifle, which he used to own, because it was later used in the incident in Morocco, and the man's virginal teenage daughter becomes infatuated with one of the officers and tries to seduce him. By the end of the film, someone has been killed, a second person has been shot during a shoot-out, and someone has been badly beaten. On a larger scale, the U.S. government's response to the incident in Morocco is based on a false assumption that it was a terrorist act. That interpretation in turn delays Moroccan authorities from sending an ambulance to aid the American couple.

Other than the film's scriptwriter, who would imagine that the gift of a gun could begin such a chain of events? So much happens at such distant places, yet much of it is related in unexpected ways. The film's multiple plotlines show how connected human endeavors can end up being. The multiple plotlines also show that actions can have unexpected and far-reaching consequences. Finally, the multiple plotlines show some of the possible varieties and complexities of parent-children relationships, so it is not surprising that the film concludes with this dedication:

> To my children,
> Maria Eladia and Eliseo
> . . . the brightest lights in the darkest night.

To show various aspects of a large group, plotlines may be numerous, chronological, simultaneous, and sometimes intersecting. *Short Cuts* includes nine pairs of major characters plus six other important characters, but the film has so many groupings of characters that one cannot say with certainty how many plotlines the film has. Different critics have detected "nine interlocking narratives," "approximately ten stories," or "a dozen stories." There are at least ten (Figure 6.16). The film's multiple plotlines are arranged chronologically or simultaneously—the viewer cannot tell which—and each couple interacts with at least one other major character. With so many characters and intersecting plotlines in something as fleeting and onrushing as a film, however, a viewer may sometimes lose track of who is who. There is also the danger that, with so many events, some may be implausible (one murder seems insufficiently motivated and its cover-up

FIGURE 6.16 Multiple, simultaneous, and intersecting plotlines
Short Cuts (1993) has twenty-four major characters and many different groupings of them. For example, (a) Howard Finnigan (a TV news commentator) and his wife, Ann, have a son Casey, who is hit by a car, walks home, falls asleep, lapses into a coma, and is treated in a hospital. Two other characters are seen in the film only in relation to the Finnigans: (b) Mr. Bitkower, a baker who as requested has made a special birthday cake for Casey, and (c) Howard's father, Paul, who unexpectedly appears at the hospital after years of alienation from his son. Other characters have lives in the film beyond their interactions with the Finnigans: (d) Doreen, a waitress, drives the car that Casey darted in front of; (e) Ralph Wyman is the physician in charge of Casey's care; and (f) Zoe is a disturbed cellist who lives next door to the Finnigans with her mother and is extremely upset by news of the boy's fate. *Fine Line Features; Criterion DVD*

highly unlikely). Nonetheless, a story consisting of many intersecting plot-lines can effectively present a panoramic view of a society or group. In *Short Cuts* as in *Nashville* (1975), *A Wedding* (1978), *The Player* (1992), *Gosford*

Park, and *Prairie Home Companion* (2006), director Robert Altman and his collaborators explore how inclusive a narrative can be—in terms of both the number of characters and the various combinations of plotlines—yet remain unified enough and comprehensible enough to be a satisfying narrative. Like many Altman films, the Iranian film *The Circle* (2000) uses many plotlines to focus on a group, rather than the backgrounds, situations, and personalities of individual characters (Figure 6.17).

In *Time Code* (2000), director Mike Figgis also has experimented with how inclusive a narrative can be. The film consists of multiple, chronological, simultaneous, and intersecting plotlines that present a panoramic view of a group, in this case an assortment of small-time independent Hollywood moviemakers and others with ties to them. But the film uses no editing. Instead, it shows simultaneous, often converging, uninterrupted plotlines on different quadrants of the screen (Figure 6.18). While viewing *Time Code*, the viewer probably most often watches the quadrant with the loudest or most distinct soundtrack. At other times, the viewer is less guided about which quadrants to observe and for how long. (Each viewer

FIGURE 6.17 Chronological plotlines that emphasize a situation The Iranian film *The Circle* (2000) has nine plotlines that are arranged chronologically. During the film's opening credits, noises of a woman's suffering are heard, then the sounds of a crying baby. Immediately after the conclusion of the credits, a woman's voice is heard, and in the English-language version of the film, "It's a girl!" appears as a subtitle against a black background. The film's first image of something other than words appears, and the first plotline begins: a woman learns that her daughter had given birth to the baby girl. The following, brief events reveal that the baby's father and his family will be bitterly disappointed that the baby was not a male. In the next plotline (represented by the image on the left), viewers see these three women trying to reach someone by telephone and failing. Later, viewers learn that the women had been released from jail early that morning. The woman on the right is quickly rearrested, and for a while the camera shows the experiences of the other two women (and subtly implies that the woman on the left prostitutes herself to raise some money quickly); then the camera follows only the woman in the center of the image above (she has an unexplained bruise on her right cheek). Sometime later, she too disappears from the film as the film begins a fifth plotline about another woman and her difficult situation, then another female character and plotline, and another, and another. The film ends in a large dim jail cell, where viewers again see the initial trio of women and learn that the unseen woman who gave birth to a daughter at the beginning of the film had also recently been a prisoner in that same cell. The film's nine plotlines, all devoted to various women and their problems, leave a lot of details unexplained, reveal no character in depth, and are little developed as stories. Instead, the plotlines illustrate the limitations placed on women in contemporary Iran. The concluding setting being a jail is significant. *Jafar Panahi Film Productions and others; Winstar TV and Video DVD*

in effect edits the film and constructs a somewhat different story.) With more than twenty characters to keep track of, many visuals bombarding the viewer from four sources simultaneously, and sometimes more than one soundtrack competing for the viewer's attention, no viewer can completely reconstruct the plot after only one viewing. *Time Code* invites multiple viewings. However, like viewers struggling with the four alternating plotlines of *Intolerance*, many viewers may find trying to figure out the story of *Time Code* too demanding and frustrating to give the film a second chance.

Plotlines may be viewed consecutively even though they occur simultaneously. Jim Jarmusch's *Night on Earth* (1992) has five consecutive brief plotlines. Each is set in one of four different time zones but begins at the same moment in time: 7:07 p.m. in Los Angeles, 10:07 p.m. in New York, 4:07 a.m. in Paris and Rome, and 5:07 a.m. in Helsinki. Viewers are offered the rare opportunity to see what happens simultaneously at various places around the world. In its use of simultaneous nonintersecting plotlines that are presented successively, the film's structure is rare, perhaps even one of a kind.

FIGURE 6.18 Four interconnected plotlines shown simultaneously
In *Time Code* (2000), action in one plotline occasionally intersects with action from another plotline, but viewers usually see four unedited plotlines simultaneously. *Publicity still. A Red Mullet Production*

Plotlines may be nonchronological and from many time periods, yet all of them or nearly all of them may intersect at one time and place, as in *The Joy Luck Club* (1993), which has eight major plotlines: for four middle-aged women born in China and for each woman's American-born grown daughter (Figure 6.19).

Plots may be extremely complicated yet entertaining and easy to follow, as in *Run Lola Run* (see the feature on pp. 282–83). The film begins and proceeds chronologically except for some brief **flashbacks**. From the time Lola begins to run, the story progresses chronologically (with three scattered brief **flash-forwards**) toward an ending. But the story begins again as Lola begins to run again; this time with a different three brief flash-forwards and a very different ending. The film is still not over. The story begins a third time as Lola begins to run yet again and includes a brief flash-forward as the story races to its conclusion.

As in all aspects of human creativity, the ways to structure a fictional film seem limitless.

flash-forward: A shot, scene, or sequence—though usually only a shot or two—that interrupts a narrative to show events that happen in the future.

FIGURE 6.19 Multiple interwoven plotlines
Wayne Wang's film adaptation of Amy Tan's novel *The Joy Luck Club* (1993) tells the stories of four Chinese mothers and each mother's Chinese American daughter. The film illustrates how complex the combinations of multiple plotlines may be. In the months before the plot of *The Joy Luck Club* begins, Suyuan (on the left) has died, and Suyuan's middle-aged women friends (seen here) have written to friends and relatives in China to locate Suyuan's abandoned daughters, left behind as babies decades earlier during a war in China. The movie begins with a going-away party for Suyuan's daughter June (the second woman from the left), who plans to leave for China the next day to meet her two half-sisters. Most of the movie consists of flashbacks from the going-away party to each middle-aged woman's painful childhood or early adulthood in China, present-tense scenes from the party, and flashbacks to selected events from the lives of the four adult American daughters. The film concludes with June's arrival in China and her meeting with her two half-sisters. Except for Suyuan, all the other seven major characters meet at one place and time, the going-away party. *Publicity still. Hollywood Pictures*

Time

Fictional films have three main tenses: present, future, and past. Also considered in this section are the amount of time it takes to show a film and the time span represented by a film's story.

PRESENT TIME, FLASH-FORWARDS, AND FLASHBACKS

> In an exchange with [the film director] Georges Franju in the 1960s, after granting that a film should have a beginning, a middle, and an end, [Jean-Luc] Godard [also a director] famously added: "but not necessarily in that order." (Perez)

Most makers of narrative films agree with Franju and arrange scenes chronologically. But the earliest scenes of a film's story may occur late in the film or even at its ending, and the latest scenes of some other story may occur early in the narrative. These and countless other temporal arrangements of scenes are possible because of flashbacks and flash-forwards.

Only a few movies use chronological order with an occasional flash-forward. *Easy Rider* (1969) is one of them. About 77¼ minutes into the film, the Captain America character is in a brothel; he looks up past a small statue toward a plaque that reads "Death only closes a man's reputation and determines it as good or bad." Next we see from a helicopter a one-second shot of something burning off to the side of a country road. In the brothel, Captain America looks down, and the action resumes. Does the **cutaway shot** suggest he vaguely glimpses the future, or are viewers meant to see the shot as a glimpse of the future, or is the cutaway shot meant to puzzle viewers because it doesn't fit in and make sense at the moment? Or does the shot function in two or more ways? Viewers cannot even recognize it as a flash-forward unless they remember that one-second shot approximately 16 minutes later as they see the end of the film, when Captain America is shot by a passing motorist and, in the film's last shot, his motorcycle is seen in flames off to the side of that country road. Occasionally during the opening credits, a flash-forward shows events that are repeated well into a film, as in *My Life as a Dog* (1985), *GoodFellas* (1990), *Go* (1999), *American Beauty* (1999), and *L.I.E.* (2001).

> **cutaway (shot):** A shot that briefly interrupts the representation of a subject to show something else.

Although flash-forwards are usually mainly visual, they may be auditory. At the end of *Medium Cool*, $108^{1}/4$ minutes into the film, the car radio announces a serious car accident that we witness nearly 50 seconds later. According to the French scholar Marc Vernet, this filmmaking technique was used years earlier in Alain Robbe-Grillet's *L'immortelle* (1962): "We hear the sound of an accident at the beginning of the film even though that crash will occur later in the film" (92).

Flash-forwards "can only be recognized retrospectively" (Chatman 64) and are demanding of viewers. They can be confusing and frustrating if the events shown are too far into the future or if the flash-forwards are frequent or lengthy. Perhaps because flash-forwards let viewers glimpse consequences they do not yet anticipate or are not yet interested in, they are rarely used.

Flashbacks are much more common than flash-forwards. Often a flashback briefly interrupts a chronological progression of events to show what influenced a character earlier. Flashbacks also may be used at the end of a film to reveal causes of previously puzzling events, as in the Canadian film *Exotica* (1994). Near the end of that film, a flashback reveals how the discovery of a murdered girl affected an enigmatic young woman, and in the film's last two scenes a flashback to an even earlier time reveals more information about the enigmatic young woman's relationship to the troubled main male character. By withholding these revelations until the last scenes, which is what some theorists refer to as a "privileged" placement, the final scenes help clarify the whole. A flashback also may be used within a flashback, as in the 2002 film *City of God* (Figure 6.20).

In some films—such as the Italian classic *8 1/2* (1963) and the Japanese classic *Rashomon* (1950)—it is sometimes difficult, sometimes impossible, to know if certain scenes are flashbacks to events that happened or are dreams, fantasies, or lies. In *8 1/2*, a director tries to regain his creativity and

Structure of *Run Lola Run*

EXPOSITION [author's term] (11 min., 51 sec.)

Crowd seen in fast motion. Actors are highlighted briefly. Bank guard kicks soccer ball high up in air. Film's title formed by masses of people. Opening credits over animation of Lola running. Photo IDs of characters and cast. Establishing shots. Inside Lola's apartment, she answers phone call from a desperate Manni. In black-and-white flashbacks, we see how Lola's moped was stolen and learn she could not pick up Manni after his criminal transaction. We also learn Manni had to get on a subway train, on which he left a bag with the money he was to deliver to his criminal boss, Ronnie. Lola has 20 minutes to reach Manni with DM 100,000 (at that time, nearly $60,000). She runs by a room in which her mother is on the phone. On the nearby TV, we see a cartoon Lola running toward stairs and down them.

I (22 min., 26 sec.)	II (20 min., 15 sec.)	III (20 min., 57 sec.)
■ Cartoon Lola runs by cartoon dog on the stairs.	■ Cartoon boy on stairs trips cartoon Lola, and she tumbles down stairs.	■ Cartoon Lola jumps over cartoon dog on stairs.
■ On sidewalk, Lola brushes against a woman pushing a baby stroller.	■ Running outside, Lola limps for a while.	■ Lola does not brush against the woman with a baby stroller.
■ Flash-forward photos: authorities take the woman's baby; the woman steals a baby.	■ She bumps against the woman with the baby stroller.	■ Flash-forward photos: the woman becomes a Jehovah's Witness.
■ Lola's father with his disgruntled mistress.	■ Flash-forward photos: the woman wins a lottery.	■ On sidewalk, nuns do not part, so Lola runs into street and nearly hits cyclist.
■ On sidewalk, nuns part and allow Lola to run through their group.	■ On sidewalk, nuns part and allow Lola to run through their group.	■ Cyclist rides off and stops at a snack place; he offers to sell his cycle to the homeless man.
■ Nearby cyclist offers to sell Lola his bicycle.	■ Nearby cyclist offers to sell Lola his bicycle.	■ Lola runs into Meyer's car and ends up on its hood; the white car passes by. Lola runs off.
■ Flash-forward photos: cyclist beaten up; courtship; marriage.	■ Flash-forward photos: cyclist's unhappy fate.	■ Lola rounds a corner where we previously saw the homeless man with the bag of money.
■ Lola runs in front of Mr. Meyer's car (Figure a).	■ Lola runs over hood of Mr. Meyer's car (Figure b).	■ Homeless man cycling.
■ Meyer's car hits side of white car driving by.	■ Meyer's car hits side of white car driving by.	■ Lola's father learns that his mistress is pregnant and assumes the child is his. He hurriedly leaves his office as Lola runs toward his office.
■ Lola runs by the homeless man carrying Manni's bag of money.	■ Lola bumps into the homeless man carrying Manni's bag of money.	■ Lola's father gets in Meyer's car, and they drive off as Lola vainly shouts after them.
■ Mistress tells Lola's father that she is pregnant.	■ Lola runs by woman in bank hallway.	■ A blind woman by a phone booth helps Manni spot the homeless man who is cycling by. Manni chases him.
■ Lola runs by woman in bank hallway.	■ In Lola's father's office, mistress has already told Lola's father that she is pregnant but not by him. . . . Lola calls the mistress a stupid cow. Lola's dad slaps Lola; she wrecks part of his office as the frightened mistress looks on.	
■ Flash-forward photos of that woman's tragic fate.		

a)

b)

Run Lola Run (1998) consists of initial filmic exposition (author's term, not the film's) followed by three variations of the rest of the story. In the film, some actions are repeated with variation, such as Lola and Mr. Meyer's car. (a) In the first version, Lola runs in front of it without being hit.

(b) In the second version, Lola runs over the hood of Mr. Meyer's car. In the third version (not shown here but occurring a little more than 58 minutes into the film), Lola runs into Mr. Meyer's car and briefly ends up on its hood. *Westdeutscher Rundfunk (WDR) and others; Columbia TriStar Home Video DVD*

I (continued)

- Lola's dad escorts Lola out of his office and tells her he is not her birth father.
- Outside bank, Lola asks old woman the time of day.
- Red ambulance stops short of hitting large plate glass being carried across the street.
- Lola is a second too late, and Manni enters market and begins robbing it. Lola hits armed guard on back of head with a plastic bag of groceries and helps Manni with the robbery.
- Outside, they run as the song "What a Difference a Day Makes" is heard on soundtrack.
- Police stop Lola and Manni and accidentally shoot Lola.
- Her dying thoughts: she asks Manni many questions related to his feelings for her.

II (continued)

- In bank hallway, Lola shouts at woman.
- Lola takes bank guard's pistol and takes her father hostage.
- Flash-forward photos for woman in bank hallway: romantic happiness with male bank colleague.
- Bank guard places his hand near his heart as if the stress were causing him pain as Lola robs the bank.
- Lola tosses the gun aside then leaves the bank. Outside, police push Lola aside, assuming that someone else is trying to rob the bank. She runs away.
- Red ambulance runs through large plate glass being carried across the street.
- Lola arrives in time to stop Manni from robbing market, but looking straight ahead at Lola, he walks in front of ambulance.
- Manni's dying thoughts: Lola will soon forget him and find another lover.

III (continued)

- The homeless man and Manni indirectly cause the car with Meyer and Lola's father to run into the white car after all. The man who stole Lola's moped runs into the back of the white car.
- Lola runs in front of a large truck and is nearly hit by it.
- She goes into a nearby casino and wins a lot of money.
- Manni pulls his gun on the homeless man on the cycle, gets back the bag of money, but gives homeless man the gun.
- After the red ambulance stops to avoid hitting the plate glass, Lola gets into the back of the ambulance. It contains the bank guard, who has a life-threatening heart problem. After Lola holds his hand, his heart recovers.
- At the intersection where she is supposed to meet Manni, Lola gets out of the ambulance.
- Down the block, Manni arrives in black car with Ronnie. All is OK between them.
- Manni kisses Lola briefly; then they walk away. Lola is carrying the sack of money. Freeze frame. (75:48 total)

a)

b)

FIGURE 6.20 Flashbacks within a flashback
Early in the Brazilian film *City of God* (2002), the central character, a young man called Rocket, finds himself in the middle of a standoff between a gang of armed youths and police officers. Before viewers can see the outcome of the standoff, a match cut introduces action at an earlier period, when Rocket is a boy, and soon a title card reads "THE SIXTIES." Many scenes from the sixties show major characters, including the boy Li'L Dice. A later title card reads "THE SEVENTIES." In the seventies section, viewers learn that the grown Li'L Dice is now called Li'L Zé. Also, in the seventies section, about 40½ minutes into the movie, occurs the superimposed title seen in frame (a), which is followed by flashbacks featuring Li'L Dice, seen in frame (b), as a boy in the sixties. In the first flashback, Li'L Dice is murdering people indiscriminately at a motel/brothel that three young men from the sixties section of the film had robbed as Li'L Dice was supposed to be on watch outside. In the second, Li'L Dice and his friend Benny are hitting a man and robbing him. In the third, Li'L Dice is murdering Rocket's brother Goose, one of the main characters from the sixties part of the film. The fourth flashback is a montage of Li'L Dice and then Li'L Zé at different times and in different places presumably shooting still others. The filmmakers could have supplied all the sixties information in the sixties section of the film, but they chose to withhold certain information until the seventies section (Li'L Dice murdering people at the motel/brothel and later murdering Goose). In the sixties flashbacks within the seventies flashback, viewers also learn that ever since his childhood Li'L Dice/Li'L Zé has been a psychopath who laughs gleefully as he murders people. *O2 Filmes, VideoFilmes; Miramax Home Entertainment DVD*

confidence and finish a costly and complicated film while trying to cope with his wife, lover, producer, actors, and the press. That much of the narrative proceeds chronologically but is intercut with frequent scenes of the director's dreams, fantasies, or memories, although sometimes viewers cannot know which is which. In *Rashomon*, viewers cannot know which of four quite different accounts of a man's death and the events leading up to it is the most reliable and which are self-serving lies. Both *8½* and *Rashomon* are not based on "the assumptions on which all conventional (Hollywood-style) film narrative is based, namely that the world is wholly decipherable, that people's motivations can be understood, that all events have clear causes and that the end of a fiction will offer us the chance to fuse all elements of the plot into a single coherent dramatic action" (Armes 103–4).

On rare occasions, a film is basically chronological but includes flashbacks and flash-forwards, as in *Run Lola Run* (see the feature on pp. 282–83). *Don't Look Now* (1973) is also mostly chronological but sometimes uses flashbacks and occasional flash-forwards. One memorable flash-forward occurs when the main male character glimpses his wife on a passing boat with two other women and all three are dressed in black. Near the film's ending, viewers see some shots related to that earlier scene, but they are from the man's funeral procession in Venice. The flash-forward earlier in the film reveals that the man is so psychic he can briefly see beyond his own life although at the time he does not realize what he is seeing. One movie narrative that jumps around in time extensively is *Slaughterhouse-Five* (1972). Like its source novel, it uses many flash-forwards and flashbacks, some of which are difficult to place in a chronological ordering of the events but seem appropriate because the central character has become "unstuck in time."

CHRONOLOGICAL TIME AND NONCHRONOLOGICAL TIME

Plot is the selection and arrangement of a story's events. Fabula is the chronological reconstruction of all the events of a nonchronological plot. Both a plot and its corresponding fabula contain the same events, but the nonchronological arrangement of events changes focus, mood, and viewer interest—sometimes considerably.

Storytellers have used flashback at least since the time of Homer and his *Odyssey* (perhaps the eighth century B.C.), which begins in the middle of the story, flashes back to the beginning, then returns to where the first section left off and concludes the story. *Out of the Past* (1947) has the same basic structure (Figure 6.21). The plot begins not with the earliest event, when Jeff, the main character, is given the job of retrieving Kathie and thus is about to be sucked into a dangerous, uncertain life. Instead, it begins at a later stage, when he is seemingly free of his past and in love with a woman he can trust, so by the end of the film his loss of security and happiness is all the more pronounced and poignant.

For another example of a nonchronological film's plot and fabula, see the Close-Up section about *Pulp Fiction* on pp. 299–301.

The human inclination to try to sort through events and make sense of them is deep-seated. That's one reason most people are endlessly fascinated by narratives. It's also a reason most viewers attempt to construct fabulas out of nonchronological plots. But as demonstrated by *Slaughterhouse-Five*, *Jacob's Ladder* (1990), *Lost Highway* (1997), *Mulholland Drive* (2001), *Inland Empire* (2006), and occasional other movies, constructing the fabula may be problematic because different attentive and thoughtful viewers will disagree about whether certain events are present, past, or future events or are only imagined (fantasized or dreamed). Then, too, some films, such as *Amores Perros*, are constructed so that making a complete fabula is impossible.

FIGURE 6.21 Plot and fabula of *Out of the Past* (1947)

PLOT = Parts 3, 1, 4, 2, 5

1 minute into the film

Part 3: Joe, Whit's assistant, arrives at Jeff's gas station and tells Jeff that Whit, a big-time gambler, wants to see him. . . . As Jeff and Ann, his girlfriend, drive to Whit's Lake Tahoe residence, Jeff begins to tell Ann about his past in New York, where he and his partner Jack Fisher worked as "detectives."

12 minutes into the film

Part 1: Whit gives Jeff the job of finding Kathie, who shot him and ran off with $40,000 of his money. . . . In Acapulco, Jeff locates Kathie—and promptly falls for her. . . . During Whit and Joe's surprise visit to Jeff in Acapulco, they learn nothing about Kathie's whereabouts and leave. Soon thereafter, so do Jeff and Kathie.

33 1/2 minutes into the film

Part 4: We are very briefly reminded that Jeff is still telling Ann about his past as they drive toward Lake Tahoe.

34 minutes into the film

Part 2: Jeff and Kathie hide out in San Francisco, but Fisher spots them and Jeff and Kathie split up. . . . When the couple is finally reunited, Fisher shows up and tries to blackmail them, but Kathie kills Fisher and drives off.

39 1/2 minutes into the film

Part 5: After Jeff finishes telling Ann about his past, they arrive at Whit's residence, and Ann drives off. Inside, Jeff sees that Kathie has returned to Whit. To repay Whit for his betrayal with Kathie, Jeff agrees to steal some papers from an attorney in San Francisco but is framed for the man's murder, which viewers learn later Joe committed. . . . Joe intends to shoot Jeff, but Jeff's helper hooks Joe with a fishing hook and pulls him down to his death. . . . Jeff discovers that Kathie killed Whit. She threatens to tell authorities that Jeff committed three murders and makes it clear she intends to be in charge henceforth. Jeff acts as if he will go along with her but makes a telephone call. At a police roadblock, Kathie quickly realizes Jeff called the police and shoots him, but she is shot and their car crashes. . . . Later Jeff's helper lies to Ann so she can more readily get on with her life with a man who has long loved her.

96 minutes into the film

The End

FABULA = 1, 2, 3, 4, 5

The Past	Part 1	Part 2
The Present	Part 3 Part 4	Part 5

A description and a brief analysis of the plot and fabula of *Citizen Kane* can be found on the Web site for this book at <bedfordstmartins.com/phillips -film>.

RUNNING TIME AND STORY TIME

Running time is the amount of time it takes to view a film, including the opening and closing credits. Sometimes the credits accompany images of the film's subjects; sometimes they do not. Running times of features originally intended for theaters vary from one hour (the cutoff length in many definitions of *feature film*) to maybe 7 1/2 hours for the 1994 Hungarian film *Sátántangó* (1993).[3] (See bottom of p. 287.)

Story time is the amount of time covered in a film's narrative or story. For example, if a film's earliest scene occurs on a Sunday and its latest scene takes place on the following Friday, the story time is six days. Beginning with some of the early short silent films, story time has nearly always been much longer than running time. At least as early as Georges Méliès's "A Trip to the Moon" (1902), story time stretched out over days but running time was only minutes (pp. 116–17). The story time of the Chinese film *To Live* (1994) is approximately twenty-five years (from "the 1940s" to "the 1960s" plus five or six more years); the running time is 129 minutes. The plot of *Women on the Verge of a Nervous Breakdown* (1988) begins one morning and ends approximately 36 hours later, on the evening of the following day; the film's running time is 88 minutes.

A film's story time may be approximately the same as the running time. For example, the story time of the western *High Noon* (1952) is about 102 minutes (from about 10:30 a.m. to 12:12 p.m.), and the film's running time is 81½ minutes. *United 93* (2006) is mainly about the last flight of the hijacked United Airlines plane on the fateful day of September 11, 2001. In actuality, the flight lasted around 81 minutes. In the film, the plane finally takes off almost 31 minutes into the movie and crashes about 70 minutes later. Because the actual flight time and the film flight time are nearly the same, viewers see and hear and partially experience the whirlwind of emotion during roughly the same amount of time the film passengers do and real passengers did.

Only very rarely does a movie's running time seem to equal its story time. A good example is a **film noir** called *The Set-Up* (1949), which is about a man called Stoker, who is an aging, small-time boxer still dreaming about a successful career and refusing to cooperate with his manager and throw a fight. As in the relatively few other films in which the story time seems to equal the running time, the minute-by-minute equivalence is only a matter of appearance. The film's major fight begins nearly 39 minutes into the movie and consists of four rounds. Each round, which includes many reaction shots of people watching the fight, exceeds the usual three minutes of a round in a professional boxing match. The time between rounds, which is supposed to be one minute, is not strictly adhered to by the film either (Table 6.3). Overall, though, the film's running time and story time are nearly the same

film noir: A type of film first made in the United States during and after World War II, characterized by dangerous characters and frequent scenes with dark, shadowy (low-key) lighting.

---

[3]The longest film for theatrical release cannot be identified because many early films have not survived. There are no known copies of more than 70 percent of all feature films made before the 1920s or of about 50 percent of all American films made before 1950. Moreover, many films that have survived may be incomplete. In addition, before the late 1920s, not all projectors ran at the same speed. The French film *Travail* (1919) may have run 8 hours. The 1925 *Les misérables* reputedly consisted of thirty-two 35 mm reels (each reel could be from 13 to 16 minutes long), so that movie might have run anywhere from 7 to 8½ hours.

The running times for multipart films originally shown on TV and later in theaters (however briefly) is another matter. *Heimat II* (1992), a German TV series later shown in theaters, runs about 23½ hours. Polish director Krzysztof Kieslowski's ten-part TV series later called *Decalogue* (1989) was shown at film festivals and occasionally in theaters and now on DVD runs about 9½ hours. Rainer Werner Fassbinder's 1980 *Berlin Alexanderplatz* was shot on 16 mm film for German TV, was later restored and screened, and since 2007 has been available on a seven-disc DVD set from Criterion running more than 15½ hours.

TABLE 6.3
Running Times and Story Times in *The Set-Up* (1949)

	RUNNING TIME	STORY TIME
Round 1	3 minutes, 17 seconds	3 minutes
Time between rounds	nearly 1 minute	1 minute
Round 2	3 minutes, 37 seconds	3 minutes
Time between rounds	1 minute, a few seconds	1 minute
Round 3	3 minutes, 51 seconds	3 minutes
Time between rounds	nearly 1½ minutes	1 minute
Round 4	3 minutes, 54 seconds	3 minutes
Totals	**18 minutes, 10 seconds**	**15 minutes**

(about 71 minutes), and viewers may get the impression that throughout the film the running time matches the story time. Overall, yes. Minute by minute, no.

Examples of films in which running time and story time are exactly identical are extremely rare, although, excluding its opening credits, *Time Code* (see Figure 6.18) is such a film.

On extremely rare occasions, a film's story time is less than its running time. *Night on Earth* consists of five plotlines, each beginning at the same moment in time and each having a story time of 35 minutes. Although the film's story time is 35 minutes, its running time is 125 minutes. Another film with a story time less than its running time is the short French film "An Occurrence at Owl Creek Bridge" (1962), a story of a civilian facing being hanged from a railroad bridge during the American Civil War. The film's story time is slightly more than 10 minutes; its running time is almost 28 minutes.

Nearly all fictional films are imprecise about how much time supposedly elapses between scenes. "The String Bean" (described on pp. 257 and 262) shows an old woman finding a discarded plant, planting seeds, nurturing the new plant, finding it uprooted, then planting seeds from it, presumably to begin the cycle again. How much time passes between the time the woman first plants the seeds and one seed sprouts? How much time passes altogether in the film? What is the story time: one month, two months, three? This imprecision is not a weakness of the film but a characteristic of fictional films, which are generally less specific about their story time than are fiction or published plays.

Filmmakers can present many events selected from a brief story time, as in *High Noon*, or relatively few events taken from a long story time, as in *2001*, which represents highly selective events from 4 million B.C. to an unknowable future time. Storytellers may even repeat the same block of story time and segments within it—for example, a 24-hour period and various minutes within it—over and over, though with many variations in the events during each repetition of the time. That was done for parts of a day in *Groundhog Day* (1993). Repetition of the same part of a story is also used in the three versions of the sequence that shows Lola running to save her boyfriend in *Run Lola Run* (pp. 282–83).

Style

Style is one of those terms that has different meanings for different critics and theorists. In this book, *style* refers to the way a text, such as a film, represents its subjects. Possible styles include farce, **black comedy**, **fantasy**, **realism**, **magic realism**, **socialist realism**, and **parody**. A style may be used in any kind of film. For example, a parody (an amusing imitation of human behavior or of a text) may be used in any **genre** (type of fictional film). A western or horror film may include a parody of an earlier well-known character or situation, or an entire film may be a parody. For reasons of space and focus, this section cannot present a comprehensive discussion of film styles. Parody and socialist realism are discussed elsewhere in the book (see p. 235 and following, as well as p. 460). In the remainder of this section, we focus on three styles that beginning film students are likely to find especially challenging: satire, black comedy, and magic realism.

SATIRE

Satire is a representation that indirectly exposes and perhaps ridicules individuals or groups for their shortcomings. Makers of satire often use **irony**, exaggeration, parody, black comedy, and other means to amuse but more often to chide, inform, or perhaps reform. The mood of a satire may range from scathing and bitter to genial and good-natured or lie somewhere in between (Figure 6.22). The meanings conveyed by satire are normally **implicit meanings**, and it is up to readers or viewers to figure out what behavior is satirized and what in general is implied about the behavior. Let's consider some of the uses of satire in film.

Life of Brian (1979) is Monty Python's take on the times of Jesus' last days on earth and on the hapless Brian, who was born in a neighboring manger on the same night as Jesus. As envisioned by the film, the time was one of competing would-be prophets. For example, about 45^2/$_3$ minutes into the film, one man prophesies, "And the young shall not know where lieth the things possessed by their fathers that their fathers put there only just the night before—about eight o'clock," which can be understood as

black comedy: A narrative style that shows the humorous possibilities of warfare, death, illness, and other subjects often considered off-limits to comedy.

magic realism: A style in which occasional wildly improbable or impossible events occur in an otherwise realistic story.

socialist realism: A Soviet doctrine and style in force from the mid-1930s to the 1980s that decreed that Soviet texts must promote communism and the working class.

implicit meaning: A generalization that a viewer or reader makes about a text (such as a film) or a subject in a text.

FIGURE 6.22 Mood of a satire
Kitchen Stories (2003) is a Norwegian/Swedish film about a man hired by the Swedish government to observe without interference the kitchen routines of a cantankerous single Norwegian and later to submit his scientific observations. As this image from a little more than 16 1/2 minutes into the film might suggest, the film is satirical. Doesn't that man in the corner remind you of an earnest overgrown child in a huge high chair? While watching the film, the viewer does not sense that its makers were angry or bitter about the subject. Instead, the mood or tone of the satire is gentle and good-natured: the main characters are represented as flawed but not seriously so (the one exception: the cantankerous old man's best friend uses his tractor to put the observer in serious harm's way). The film pokes fun at the idea that people can observe individuals long-term without interfering or interacting with them. It also shows that people want interaction with other people, and that prolonged scientific observation of human behavior has its challenges. But throughout this satirical film, the mood is good-natured. *Svenska Filminstitutet (SFI) and others; MGM Home Entertainment DVD*

satirizing or making fun of the trivial and unnecessary specificity of some prophesies. The film satirizes various aspects of human behavior, perhaps none more prominently than desperation to find a savior (Figure 6.23).

In Spike Lee's *Bamboozled* (2000), Pierre Delacroix, an African American TV writer, proposes a TV minstrel show made up of offensive African American **stereotypes**, which he believes will be a disastrous failure and get him fired from a job he loathes (if he quit, he would be hit with a lawsuit and lose a lot of money). The show, however, quickly becomes a hit. Part of the film's satire is conveyed by parody, as in the imitations of minstrel shows, and, about 68 1/2 minutes into the film, by two TV advertisements. The spots for "Da Bomb 1/2 gal. malt liquor," which is "125% pure," and for "Timmi Hill-

stereotype: A commonplace, simplified, and in some ways inaccurate likeness of a subject created in a text.

FIGURE 6.23 Satire of group behavior
In *Life of Brian* (1979), a crowd has quickly convinced itself that the unlucky Brian is the messiah and has gathered outside his window. Here, nearly 67 minutes into the film, Brian tells them, however, "You don't need to follow anybody. You've got to think for yourself. You're all individuals." In unison they respond: "Yes, we're all individuals." This part of the film satirizes both the tendency of crowd members to think alike and the human desperation to fashion a messiah from the flimsiest of evidence. *HandMade Films, Python Pictures; Anchor Bay Entertainment DVD*

nigger 125% authentic ghetto [pronounced "GEE toe"] active wear," which comes complete with the bullet holes, are satirical imitations of TV ads and inner-city African American stereotypes.

Bamboozled has multiple targets of satire. The black TV writer and his boss, the white TV executive, Dunwitty, are most often caught in the satirist's crosshairs (Figure 6.24). The film also satirizes African American TV shows with large writing staffs but no blacks; Dunwitty's superiors, unseen TV executives who quickly greenlight the minstrel show; American TV audiences composed of various ethnicities, races, and ages who quickly ape the new minstrel show; and TV critics who hail the show with such superlatives as "earthshaking." Additional satiric targets include a misguided gangster-rap group called the Mau Maus and some New York City police officers, who seem to be exclusively white, shoot first and ask later, and kill all the dark-skinned people but spare the one person who looks white.

Life of Brian and *Bamboozled* are primarily satires. But satire may be a secondary concern of any text that has human behavior as its subject. The

FIGURE 6.24 The two major characters satirized
In Spike Lee's highly satirical *Bamboozled* (2000), the two characters most often satirized are (a) Pierre Delacroix and (b) Thomas Dunwitty. Delacroix is a college-educated African American TV writer who overestimates the tastes of American TV audiences and suffers the consequences after his deliberately racist minstrel (variety) show becomes an unexpected hit. Thomas Dunwitty, a white man, is Delacroix's boss. Dunwitty's wife is African American, and his office is full of African figurines and photographs of African American sports stars. Dunwitty thinks he has so fully appropriated a black identity that he tells Delacroix, "Brother, man. I'm blacker than you." Soon, however, Dunwitty shows his true color (and it is not black). He quickly embraces Delacroix's proposed show, replete with many of the oldest, most offensive stereotypes of African Americans: a plantation setting; two "ignorant, dull-witted, lazy, and unlucky" headliners; a tall, deep-voiced emcee who looks like a black Abraham Lincoln dressed in the parts of an American flag; a troupe of dancing stereotypes, including Jungle Bunny and Aunt Jemima; and a small group of musicians called the Alabama Porch Monkeys, who are dressed in prison outfits, wear shackles, and carry a ball and chain. All the black minstrel performers wear blackface.

a)

The most important character that the film does not satirize is Delacroix's assistant, Sloan, who asks her boss probing questions, warns of consequences, and occasionally objects to the goings-on. As in (a), Sloan is often seen concerned and skeptical about Delacroix's plans and behavior. *A Forty Acres and a Mule Filmworks, New Line Cinema; New Line Home Entertainment DVD*

b)

musical *Chicago* (2002) can serve as an example. Like *Bamboozled*, it has multiple objects of satire, including the public, journalists, and the Chicago justice system. The populace is satirized for getting caught up in the latest murder case and then quickly forgetting about it when the next public drama unfolds. People are shown to get excessively caught up in the latest fad, whether it is wearing a hairstyle like that of a notorious murder suspect, buying dolls in her image, or purchasing her underwear at inflated prices. Journalists are shown to stampede to get the latest coverage of each case in which a woman murders a man. They are also repeatedly manipulated by the defense lawyer, Billy Flynn, perhaps most memorably in "The Press Conference Rag" ("We Both Reached for the Gun") (46 minutes into the film), where the reporters are seen in the background as puppets and toward the end of the number Flynn pulls their strings as they dance to his tune. The justice system comes in for other criticisms. Life in jail is oiled by bribes. The most successful attorney is entirely motivated by greed and pride (for winning every case) and is not above using distracting courtroom antics and tampering with evidence. The film shows that you can murder someone, bribe jail officials, hire an expensive lawyer, tell lies (about a pregnancy), and walk away free. But those who lack money, such as the Hungarian woman who seems to be innocent, can end up on the wrong end of a hanging rope. That description may make *Chicago* sound grim, but the characters and their actions are exaggerated perhaps to the point of caricature, and the film's satire is mostly genial (least so in the fate of the Hungarian woman), so that it does not upset or outrage viewers but amuses them.

Normally satire is used in fictional films. It also can readily be used in **experimental films** or **hybrid films**, such as "Neighbours" (1952; see Figure 9.18 on p. 425), which satirizes men's tendency to become possessive and then violent over a trivial matter. Satire, however, is rarely used in documentary films. Exceptions are the films of Michael Moore—such as *Roger & Me* (1989), *The Big One* (1998), *Bowling for Columbine* (2002), *Fahrenheit 9/11* (2004), and *Sicko* (2007)—and Morgan Spurlock's *Super Size Me* (2004).

Like all documentaries, Moore's films represent actual, not imaginary, subjects. Like many documentaries, they imply criticism of their subjects. But unlike most other documentaries, Moore's films often imply criticism by using satire. Consider shots 2 through 15 of the opening of *Bowling for Columbine* (Table 6.4). The combination of the images and narration suggests a number of satiric points—for example, that it is as typical for the American president to order the bombing of obscure countries as it is for a farmer and a milkman to do their routine work, for a man to take a morning walk, and for a teacher to tend her flock of students. The next shots imply that it also is typical for two boys to go bowling at six o'clock in the morning. But we viewers may wonder about this example, especially since these events are occurring on a school day (we learn later that the two boys

experimental film: A film that rejects the conventions of mainstream movies and explores the possibilities of the film medium.

hybrid film: A film that has characteristics of two or all three film categories: fictional, documentary, or experimental.

TABLE 6.4
Shots 2–15 of *Bowling for Columbine* (2002)

The visuals are accompanied by an instrumental version of "Battle Hymn of the Republic" and the calm narration of Michael Moore.

VISUALS (the shots)	NARRATION
A shot made using **time-lapse cinematography** of the sun rising behind the Washington Monument; an aerial shot of a town full of trees; a helicopter shot of a wheat field; shots of a farmer and milkman doing their morning work; a shot of bombed-out buildings; shots of a man leaving for a morning walk and an elementary school teacher shepherding her students in a hallway; a **zoom**-in shot of a building with mountains in the background; a bowling ball missing the remaining nine pins; a scantily dressed muscular young woman posing with a large automatic rifle; and an encircling aerial shot of the Statue of Liberty's head and shoulders.	"It was the morning of April 20th, 1999. And it was pretty much like any other morning in America. The farmer did his chores. The milkman made his deliveries. The President bombed another country whose name we couldn't pronounce. Out in Fargo, North Dakota, Carey McWilliams went on his morning walk. Back in Michigan, Mrs. Hughes welcomed her students for another day of school. And out in a little town in Colorado, two boys went bowling at six in the morning. Yes, it was a typical day in the United States of America."

referred to were the ones who committed the Columbine High School massacre). The juxtaposition of the bowling (supposedly by the two unseen boys) with the following shot of the scantily dressed woman with the large assault rifle might be ominous. And the juxtaposition of that armed woman with the Statue of Liberty links two divergent representations of America: armed (and represented as sexy) and pacific (and platonic). As the film unfolds and viewers come to understand the film's subjects even more clearly, they can better understand the satiric implication of the concluding shots of this early part of the film: America encompasses the possibility of both gun violence (even by a woman) and the promise of refuge from the problems of the world. Here and throughout the film, Michael Moore does not often come out directly and voice his criticisms; instead, he uses satire to imply them.

Life of Brian, Bamboozled, Chicago, Bowling for Columbine, and many other texts exaggerate and in other ways distort the representations of their subjects. Satires are less concerned with attempting to show true-to-life representations of subjects than with indirectly revealing the shortcomings of various human behaviors. Consequently, satiric works should be judged not by the standards of realism but by their effectiveness in exposing human folly.

BLACK COMEDY

Some writers, filmmakers, and other weavers of tales have by implication asked viewers to consider the possible humor in subjects often considered inappropriate for comedy, such as warfare, cannibalism, murder, death, and illness. Such a narrative style is usually called black humor or black comedy. Often black comedy is used in satires. After its first 15 minutes or so, *Citizen Ruth* (1996) satirizes the extreme behavior of both anti-abortion groups and abortion rights groups, daring choices for the main subjects of a comedy.

In plot summaries, black comedies rarely sound amusing because they often involve violence, death, or at least emotional or physical pain. To make them work, their makers must have an acute sense of their audience and handle **pace** and mood masterfully. Typically, black comedies amuse some viewers and shock or offend others. Because John Waters's *Female Trouble* (1974, 2004) represents serious subjects, such as violent crime, in unconventional ways, some viewers are offended, some are amused, and still others are by turns offended and amused (Figure 6.25).

Comedy involves pain—such as embarrassment, confusion, or a fall— for someone else. Successful makers of comedies know where and how to distance the pain or exaggerate something about the situation so it no longer seems realistic—or to do both. Because the sounds of someone being hit could be alarming to audiences of the new sound films in the late 1920s and early 1930s, the comedy team of Laurel and Hardy exaggerated

pace: The rate of speed at which the film's subjects (such as events in a narrative film or information in a documentary film) are revealed.

FIGURE 6.25 A black comedy that may offend or amuse
Like other black comedies, John Waters's *Female Trouble* (1974, 2004) represents serious subjects—such as parenthood and violent crime—in amusing or at least unconventional ways. The film shows the story of Dawn Davenport (played by the drag queen Divine). Dawn's problems start in her unhappy high school days, which culminate when she throws a tantrum, overturns the Christmas tree onto her mother, and runs away from home. Nearly everything that could go wrong in a woman's life goes wrong in Dawn's. For example, she is raped and ends up with an uncontrollable child, who years later is nearly raped by the same man. Dawn's face is scarred when her former husband's aunt throws acid at her. Later, she becomes more and more obsessed with fame and increasingly violent. Seen here with her attorney, she is tried for kidnapping and multiple murders and is sentenced to die in the electric chair—a fate she welcomes because she believes it will be "the most theatrical moment" of her life and her best chance for lasting fame. When the film was restored and re-released on DVD in 2004, it was rated NC-17 for its sexuality and nudity. For some viewers, *Female Trouble* is mostly offensive; for others, it is mostly an amusing right-on satirical black comedy. *Dreamland; New Line Home Entertainment DVD*

those sounds to achieve comic results. *Eating Raoul* (1982) also distances the pain or exaggerates some aspect of the moments of black comedy. The film is about a married couple who hit upon the scheme to murder men seeking nontraditional sex so that the couple may get money to start their own restaurant. The film downplays the reality of multiple murders in a number of ways. For one thing, the soundtrack contributes to the film's amusing results. The weapon of choice is usually a large cast-iron frying pan, and the sound effect of it hitting a head (which viewers hear often) is never realistically squishy, squirting, bone crushing, or snapping. For another thing, the killings are never messy or seen close-up. We never see blood and only in one instance (a knife-like comb plunged somewhere into the front of a man) sense that the victims suffer: one minute they are alive; seconds later they are still and breathless (Figure 6.26). Makers of black comedies dare to represent subjects such as murder that viewers are not usually used to seeing in comedies. Depending on

FIGURE 6.26 A black comedy deemphasizing pain and emphasizing humor
Paul Bartel's *Eating Raoul* (1982)—a U.S. black comedy classic that a narrator informs viewers is "the story of Hollywood today"—includes many murders, but viewers never see any clearly. One way of hiding the deed is by interposing something or someone between the victim and the camera. Here, almost 36 1/2 minutes into the film, the man wielding the large iron skillet bonks a victim who is sitting on the floor. Another way of hiding the deed: three times the victim is offscreen, and viewers hear only the familiar bonking sound made by the skillet presumably hitting yet another head. *Bartel, Quartet, Films Incorporated; Columbia TriStar Home Entertainment DVD*

the filmmakers' skill in anticipating viewers' responses and on the viewers' backgrounds and tastes, black comedies may amuse, offend, or both.

MAGIC REALISM

Another style, which has been used mainly in fiction, is magic realism—wildly improbable or impossible events in an otherwise realistic narrative. Most of *Erendira* (1982)—based on a script by a master of literary magic realism, the Colombian writer Gabriel García Márquez—is rendered in a realistic style. But the film also has many scenes incorporating magic realism. In one series of scenes that begins 87 1/2 minutes into the film, the cruel grandmother consumes an enormous amount of rat poison mixed into a birthday cake and collapses onto her bed. After she starts to revive, the young man who has poisoned her observes, "Incredible! She's tougher than an elephant! There was enough poison to kill a million rats!" The next morning, the grandmother wakes up, smiles, then says to her granddaughter Erendira, "God bless you, child. I hadn't slept that well since I was 15! I had a beautiful dream of love." The only ill effect from the previous night's dessert is that her hair is falling out, which amuses her. The episode is unreal or magical (and symbolic to some viewers): no one could survive so huge a dosage of poison or would react with amusement as her hair falls out.

In the 1992 Mexican film *Like Water for Chocolate*, the scrumptious food that Tita prepares causes those who eat it to feel as she felt when she prepared it—for example, sad or lustful. Some of the film's magic realism is unrelated to food (Figure 6.27). Examples of magic realism also appear in the French film *Amélie* (*Le fabuleux destin d'Amélie Poulain*, 2001, Figure 6.28). A film may use magic realism only occasionally. In *Trainspotting* (1996), a film that is overwhelmingly gritty and realistic, one of the most memorable scenes is rendered as magic realism (Figure 6.29).

A film may use more than one style or may switch styles as it progresses. *Fargo* (1996) uses mainly realism. Sometimes, however—as about 44 minutes into the film when the kidnapped wife who has a hood over her head attempts to run away from her two kidnappers but merely makes odd noises as she zigzags here and there—some viewers chuckle (as does one of the kidnappers), and some cringe. Likewise, about 88 minutes into the film when one of the kidnappers uses a wood chopper in a novel way, the moment can be seen as black comedy or grim or gross realism—or some of both. At first, the Italian film *Life Is Beautiful* (1998), like so many crowd-pleasing movies, blends fantasy and realism as a man courts a woman in an amusing and romantic manner. Later, though, disquieting signs of fascism and anti-Semitism begin to emerge, and the film turns darker, literally and figuratively. In the last part of the film, which is set in a Nazi concentration camp, the style is grittier and somewhat more realistic than it was at the film's beginning.

Styles can strongly influence how viewers react to a film. If viewers refuse to go along with the magic realism of *Erendira* or *Like Water for Chocolate*, they will miss much of the pleasure of interacting with the film on its own terms. Likewise, if viewers beginning to watch the famous experimental film "Un chien andalou" (1928) expect the usual mixture of realism and fantasy so prevalent in popular Hollywood movies, they will

FIGURE 6.27 Magic realism as symbol
Most of the story of *Like Water for Chocolate*—the Mexican novel and the faithful 1992 film adaptation of it—is plausible or realistic. At times, however, the novel and film include symbolic magical events. Here, approximately 47 3/4 minutes into the film, Tita (background, right) is being driven off in a horse-drawn carriage. Why does her shawl trail on the ground all the way back to near the woman on the left of the frame? Not because Mexican women prefer absurdly long shawls. Instead, the situation symbolizes how cold Tita is feeling. *Arau Films International, Secretaria de Turismo, and others; Miramax Home Entertainment DVD*

a)

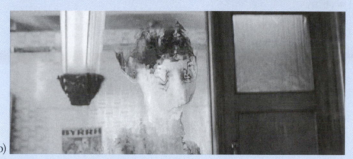

b)

FIGURE 6.28 Magic realism in *Amélie*
From time to time, magic realism is used in *Amélie* (2001). Photographs talk. A statue winks. And as seen here in two frames from a 6-second shot approximately 106 1/2 minutes into the film, Amélie's disappointed face and her body morph into water that splashes onto the floor after the man she is attracted to does not see the note she has written for him. *Claudie Ossard Productions and others; Miramax Home Entertainment DVD*

FIGURE 6.29 Magic realism as central symbol
In *Trainspotting* (1996), a young man addicted to drugs has inserted two suppositories of illegal drugs. Soon thereafter, he goes to a filthy public toilet. After relieving himself, he realizes the suppositories have fallen into the toilet. Then, approximately 10 minutes into the film, the magic realism begins. (a) The man plunges into the toilet, swims down through clear water past a large spiked mine to the bottom, snatches up the two suppositories, turns to swim back up, and while still submerged says something unintelligible. (b) He tosses out the two suppositories of drugs, starts to emerge from the toilet, and spits out some water. These actions, impossible in reality, symbolically and memorably show to what depths a person hooked on drugs might descend. In addition the extreme filth and the spiked mine suggest the degradation and dangers in the man's drug addiction. *Channel Four Films, A Figment Film, and others; Miramax Home Entertainment DVD*

a)

b)

remain uninvolved and perhaps bitterly disappointed. Viewers who quickly recognize that "Un chien andalou" consists of a series of discontinuous dreamlike scenes are much more likely to become intrigued by the film and even want to see it a second time. If audiences are watching a film that uses a style that they have not previously seen, such as magic realism, they need to figure out the film's style quickly and give the film a chance to do what it can within the parameters it has set for itself. If viewers know nothing about the film's style and cannot figure it out quickly or if they refuse to play along with a style they do know (for example, if they decline to be amused by a parody), they will sit glumly and hope for a different style and a different film—in vain.

CLOSE-UP: THE PLOT AND FABULA OF *PULP FICTION* (1994)

THE PLOT OF *PULP FICTION*

B.2. In a grill, Ringo and Honey Bunny talk about robbery; Ringo calls out "Garçon" to the waiter. Ringo and Honey Bunny talk some more; then they decide to rob the grill and its customers, pull out their guns, and shout that it's a holdup.

[Opening Credits]

A.1. Vincent (John Travolta) and Jules (Samuel L. Jackson) in a car. The two arrive at a building. When they are about to go inside an apartment, it's 7:22 a.m. Inside one of the apartments, they confront two men who had been trying to get away with an attaché case containing something valuable and belonging to the two men's "business partner," Marsellus (Ving Rhames). Jules and Vincent locate the attaché case and kill the two men.

Title card: "Vincent Vega & Marsellus Wallace's Wife"

C. At Marsellus's business, Marsellus tells Butch (Bruce Willis), a prizefighter, that Butch's best times are past and offers him an envelope full of money. After Butch accepts it, Marsellus tells him he's to take a dive in his upcoming boxing match. Vincent and Jules arrive with the attaché case. Marsellus calls to Vincent and embraces him.

D. Vincent buys powerful heroin, shoots up, and (now night) goes to take out Marsellus's wife, Mia (Uma Thurman), as Marsellus had asked him to do while he is away. Vincent and Mia go out (Figure 6.30) then return to her and Marsellus's place, where she overdoses on drugs and almost dies. . . .

E. Before his fight, Butch dreams about receiving a watch originally acquired by his great-grandfather.

FIGURE 6.30 **Vincent and Mia's night out**
Here, almost 48 1/2 minutes into *Pulp Fiction* (1994), at Mia's insistence Vincent and Mia take part in a dance competition. They win. *Miramax Films; Miramax Home Entertainment Collector's Edition DVD*

Title card: "The Gold Watch"

Butch wins the fight and escapes. Vincent and Marsellus's bartender (Paul) report about the search for Butch to Marsellus, who is furious. Butch joins his lover, Fabienne, then the next morning returns to his apartment, fetches his watch, and kills Vincent. At a nearby stoplight, Butch "runs into Marsellus" and tries to kill him; Marsellus then tries to kill Butch (Figure 6.31). Both enter a pawnshop and are captured and tied up. Marsellus is sexually assaulted; Butch saves him, takes the motorcycle of one of their captors, and picks up Fabienne, and they drive off (111 1/2 minutes into the film).

Title card: "The Bonnie Situation"

A.1. (parallel to part of A.1 at beginning of film). A man in the next room hears Jules speaking immediately before the second of the two murders seen near the film's beginning. Repeating the end of A.1 at the beginning of the film, Jules and Vincent shoot the second man.

299

A.2. The man from the next room bursts into the room that Jules and Vincent enter at the beginning of the film, shoots at them, but misses; they kill him (see Figure 3.21 on p. 137). Jules thinks it's a miracle he wasn't killed. In a car, Jules says he is going to retire. Vincent accidentally shoots and kills their own accomplice (Marvin), thereby splattering blood all over the car and the two men. At Jimmie's house, Jules and Vincent seek help (it's 8:00 a.m.). Calls are made, and at 8:50 Mr. Wolf (Harvey Keitel) arrives to supervise the cleanup before Jimmie's wife, Bonnie, will arrive home from work at about 9:30. At Monster Joe's Used Auto Parts, Mr. Wolf has presumably arranged for the elimination of the car with the accomplice's body in the trunk. Vincent and Jules decide to go for breakfast.

B.1. At a grill, Jules again tells Vincent that he plans to quit the business and "walk the earth."

B.2. (repeat of a line from near the beginning of the film). Ringo calls out "Garçon."

B.2. (parallel to the time at the beginning of the film between the time Ringo calls "Garçon" and Ringo and Honey Bunny begin the robbery). Jules and Vincent talk some more; then Vincent leaves to go to the restroom.

B.2. (repeat of the end of B.2 at film's beginning). Ringo and Honey Bunny pull their guns and begin the holdup.

B.3. After many complications, Ringo and Honey Bunny complete the robbery and leave; soon afterward Vincent and Jules leave (Jules still has the attaché case he plans to deliver to Marsellus).

THE FABULA OF *PULP FICTION*

A. Vincent and Jules in a car. The two arrive at an apartment building. When they are about to enter an apartment, it's 7:22 a.m. Inside one of the apartments, they confront two men who had been trying to get away with something valuable belonging to Marsellus. Jules and Vincent retrieve an attaché case full of Marsellus's valuables and kill the two men. The man from the next room bursts into the room and shoots at Vincent and Jules but misses; they kill him (see Figure 3.21). Jules thinks it's a miracle he wasn't killed. In a car, Jules says he is going to retire. Vincent accidentally shoots and kills their own accomplice (Marvin), thereby splattering blood all over the car and the two men. At Jimmie's house, Jules and Vincent seek help (it's 8:00 a.m.). Calls are made, and at 8:50 Mr. Wolf arrives to supervise the cleanup before Jimmie's wife, Bonnie, will arrive home from work at about 9:30. At Monster Joe's auto wreckers, the clean car with the assistant's body in the trunk is left. Vincent and Jules decide to go for breakfast.

B. At a grill, Jules again tells Vincent that he plans to quit the business and "walk the earth." Ringo and Honey Bunny talk about robbery; Ringo calls out "Garçon" to the waiter. Ringo and Honey Bunny talk some more as Vincent and Jules talk, and Vincent leaves to go to the restroom. Ringo and Honey Bunny decide to rob the grill and its customers, pull out their guns, and shout that it's a holdup. After many complications, Ringo and Honey Bunny complete the robbery and leave; soon afterward Vincent and Jules leave (Jules still has Marsellus's valuables in the attaché case).

C. At Marsellus's business, Marsellus is telling Butch, a prizefighter, that Butch's best times are past and gives him an envelope full of money. After Butch accepts it, Marsellus tells him he's to take a dive in his upcoming boxing match. Vincent and Jules arrive with the attaché case. Marsellus calls to Vincent and embraces him.

D. Vincent buys powerful heroin, shoots up, and (now night) goes to pick up Marsellus's wife, Mia, as Marsellus had asked him to do while he is away. Vincent and Mia go out (see Figure 6.30), then return to her and Marsellus's place, where she overdoses on drugs and almost dies. . . .

E. Before his fight, Butch dreams about a watch originally acquired by his great-grandfather. Butch wins the fight and escapes. Vincent and Marsellus's bartender (Paul) report about the search for Butch to Marsellus, who is furious. Butch joins his lover, Fabienne, then the next morning returns to his apartment, fetches his watch, and kills Vincent. At a nearby stoplight, Butch "runs into Marsellus" and tries to kill him; then Marsellus tries to kill Butch (see Figure 6.31). Both enter a pawnshop and are captured and tied up. Marsellus is sexually assaulted; Butch saves

him, takes the motorcycle of one of their captors, and picks up Fabienne, and they drive off (111 1/2 minutes into the film).

The plot for *Pulp Fiction* includes many deviations from a straight chronology. For one thing, unlike most other fictional films, the film's plot includes repeated actions and parallel actions. In the plot, Jules is prominent at both the beginning and the ending. In the fabula, he does not appear in the last two major sections, though for many viewers he is probably the film's most complex and intriguing character. The nonchronological plot of *Pulp Fiction* makes possible a more exciting and engaging beginning (the beginning of a robbery) than a chronological arrangement of all the film's events (two guys talking in a car). The plot also results in a less upbeat ending: at the end of the film's plot, we know that death lurks around the corner for Vincent; at the end of the fabula, Butch picks up his girlfriend, and they drive off. The plot's last scene also allows viewers to experience the unusual situation of learning what happens before and after the film's first scene. Because the plot shows two versions of the action in the grill and revisits the apartment where men get killed, we can better understand the context of actions we saw earlier and the perspectives of different characters at the same event. For example, the film first focuses entirely on Ringo and Honey Bunny at the grill and the second time at the robbery in the grill focuses on the couple, Vincent, and especially Jules. The plot for *Pulp Fiction* is so intricate that few viewers can completely reconstruct the fabula after only one showing. The plot is much more demanding of the audience than its fabula, and for some viewers the film's complex structure is both a challenge and a pleasure.

SUMMARY

This chapter discusses what a narrative is, what is possible in a short fictional film, and then the major components of the feature-length fictional film: structure, time, and style.

Narratives

- A narrative—in film and in other texts—may be defined as a representation of a series of unified events (represented actions and happenings) that are situated in one or more settings.

- A narrative may be factual or fictional or a blend of the two. Its parts may be arranged chronologically or nonchronologically.

- A fictional film is a narrative film including at least one character (imaginary person) and largely or entirely imaginary events; its settings may be real or imaginary.

Short Fictional Films

- Short fictional films typically have only one or two major characters, and they do not change much during the film's brief story time. The major characters of a short fictional film usually have a goal, have obstacles to overcome, and succeed or fail in reaching the goal.

Feature Films

STRUCTURE

- In feature films, the major characters usually have one or more goals but face problems in trying to reach them.

- Typically, the beginning of a feature film does not supply much exposition, although it usually establishes where and when the story begins. It also attempts to involve audiences in the story.

- Among other functions, the middle section of a feature film shows how the central characters deal with problems that impede progress toward their goals and reveals how happenings and the characters' decisions and actions affect them and others.

- The ending of a feature film usually shows the consequences of major previous events. In stories with closure, the consequences of previous major events are obvious or clearly implied by the end of the narrative. Most films of classical Hollywood cinema have closure, but many other narrative films do not.

- A plotline is a brief narrative that is focused on a few characters or (in a documentary) on people and could function on its own as a separate story. Typically, short films have only one plotline, and feature films have more than one plotline.

- In feature films, many combinations of plotlines are possible. For example, plotlines can be consecutive but with large gaps of story time between them, can alternate between different time periods, or can be chronological and simultaneous and occasionally intersect.

TIME

- Flash-forwards are used only occasionally in feature films, usually to suggest a premonition or inevitability. Flashbacks are often used and can serve many different purposes, such as showing how a character's past has influenced the character or continues to trouble the character. On very rare occasions, feature films combine present-tense action with flash-forwards and flashbacks.

- A fabula is the mental reconstruction in chronological order of all the events in a nonchronological plot. Although a nonchronological plot contains the same events as its corresponding fabula, the plot (as in *Pulp Fiction*) creates different emphases and therefore causes different responses in viewers.

- How much time is represented in a feature film (story time) is usually unspecified and difficult to determine, but story time nearly always far exceeds the film's running time.

STYLE

- A style is the way subjects are represented in a text, such as a film. A film may use a style—such as satire, black comedy, or magic realism—only occasionally or may use it throughout the film.

- Satire, which is one of the most often used styles, is a representation of an individual or group that indirectly exposes and perhaps ridicules the human subjects for being foolish, evil, or stupid or for having some other shortcoming. Satire suggests meaning indirectly, so it is up to readers or viewers to figure out what is being implied about the subject. Satires are not realistic but distorted representations of human folly.

- Black comedy, another style used in films, depicts subjects often considered inappropriate for comedy, such as warfare, cannibalism, murder, death, and illness.

- Magic realism, a third style occasionally used, includes wildly improbable or impossible events in an otherwise realistic narrative.

▪ If viewers know nothing about a film's style, such as black comedy, and cannot figure it out quickly, the film probably will not engage them. If viewers know about a film's style yet refuse to accept it, they also are not likely to become engaged by the film.

Major Terms about Components of Fictional Films

Below, numbers in italics refer to the pages where the terms are explained. All terms are defined in more detail in the Illustrated Glossary beginning on p. 667.

black comedy *294*	flashback *281*	satire *289*
closure *270*	flash-forward *280*	short film *258*
episodic plot *258*	magic realism *295*	story time *286*
event *256*	narrative *256*	structure *261*
exposition *265*	plot *285*	style *289*
fabula *285*	plotline *271*	
feature film *261*	running time *286*	

QUESTIONS ABOUT COMPONENTS OF FICTIONAL FILMS

The following questions are intended to help viewers understand the components of fictional films. Not all the questions are appropriate for every film. In thinking out, discussing, and writing responses to the questions most appropriate for the film being examined, be careful to stick with the issues the questions raise, to answer all parts of the questions, to explain the reasons for your answers, and to give specific examples from the film.

Narratives

1. Is the film narrative fictional, factual, or a blend of the two? How do you know?

Short Fictional Films

2. If the film is less than 60 minutes long, how is it fundamentally similar to a feature film? How is it different?

Feature Films

3. Structure:
   a. What are the goals of the main characters?
   b. What are the major conflicts? How are they resolved?

c. Do any of the characters have internal conflicts (such as uncertainty, conflicting values or conflicting duties, or guilt)?

d. Does the film have a chronological or nonchronological structure? What are the advantages of the choice?

e. Does the film have more than one plotline? If it does, how are the different plotlines related?

f. How appropriate is the film's ending? Why do you say so?

g. Does the film have closure? If not, what is left unresolved? What are the consequences of that lack of closure for the viewer?

4. Time:

a. How long is the film's running time? How long is its story time?

b. If the film has a nonchronological plot, what is its fabula?

c. In what sequences is the story time longer than the running time? Conversely, and much less commonly, in what excerpt is the running time longer than the story time?

5. Style:

a. What styles are used? How do they affect your responses to the film?

b. Which, if any, behavior or attitudes are satirized or made fun of? How strongly implied is the disapproval? Is the satire obvious or subtle? Why do you say so?

c. Is black comedy used in the film? If so, where and with what consequences for you as a viewer?

d. Is magic realism used in the film? If so, where and with what consequences for you as a viewer?

WORKS CITED

Armes, Roy. *Action and Image: Dramatic Structure in Cinema*. Manchester, Eng.: Manchester UP, 1994.

Chatman, Seymour. *Story and Discourse: Narrative Structure in Fiction and Film*. Ithaca: Cornell UP, 1978.

Eidsvik, Charles. *Cineliteracy: Film among the Arts*. New York: Random, 1978.

Hohenadel, Kristin. "'Happily Ever After' Fading Fast from Film." *New York Times* 13 Jan. 2002, late ed.: sec. 2: 13.

Kieslowski, Krzysztof. "An Introduction to the Decalogue." 1991. In pamphlet with Facets Video Special DVD Edition of *The Decalogue*.

Perez, Gilberto. "Self-Illuminated." Rev. of *Godard: A Portrait of the Artist at 70*, by Colin MacCabe. *London Review of Books* 26.7 (1 Apr. 2004).

Phillips, William H. *Writing Short Scripts*. Syracuse: Syracuse UP, 1991.

Prince, Gerald. *Dictionary of Narratology*. Lincoln: U of Nebraska P, 1987.

Rosen, Robert. "Notes on Painting and Film." *Art and Film since 1945: Hall of Mirrors*. Ed. Kerry Brougher. Los Angeles: Museum of Contemporary Art, 1996.

Stables, Kate. "Zap the Gerbil, Blend the Frog." *Sight and Sound* ns 10.1 (Jan. 2000): 5.

Vernet, Marc. "Cinema and Narration." *Aesthetics of Film*. Trans. and rev. Richard Neupert. Austin: U of Texas P, 1992.

FOR FURTHER READING

Hayward, Susan. *Cinema Studies: The Key Concepts*. 3rd ed. London: Routledge, 2006. Especially pertinent to the study of the fictional film are the entries *flashback*, *form/content*, *narrative*, *sequencing/sequence*, *setting*, and *space and time/spatial and temporal continuity*.

Mamber, Stephen. "Simultaneity and Overlap in Stanley Kubrick's *The Killing*." *Postmodern Culture* 8:2 (Jan. 1998). One of several essays in this special issue on film, Mamber's essay incorporates various graphics to illustrate the complexity and achievements of the film's structure.

Phillips, William H. *Writing Short Scripts*. 2nd ed. Syracuse: Syracuse UP, 1999. Includes three unproduced scripts for short films, detailed descriptions of two award-winning short films, discussions of the general characteristics of the short script and short film, and partial credits and brief descriptions for many short fictional films.

Raskin, Richard. *The Art of the Short Fiction Film: A Shot by Shot Study of Nine Modern Classics*. Jefferson, NC: McFarland, 2002. Each film has a chapter of its own, including a shot-by-shot reproduction of the film with a frame enlargement for every shot. In most cases, an interview with the director and an original screenplay and storyboard are also included. Films covered include Roman Polanski's "Two Men and a Wardrobe," Jim Jarmusch's "Coffee and Cigarettes," and Marianne Olsen Ulrichsen's "Come."

Stam, Robert, Robert Burgoyne, and Sandy Flitterman-Lewis. "Film-Narratology." *New Vocabularies in Film Semiotics: Structuralism, Post-structuralism, and Beyond*. London: Routledge, 1992. Part 3, 69–122. Theoretical issues about narrative for the advanced student.

CHAPTER 7

Types of
Fictional Films

FICTIONAL FILMS ARE NUMEROUS, popular, and enduring. Perhaps that is one reason critics, scholars, and others often try to classify them (Figure 7.1). Seeing similarities and patterns in films helps viewers place a film in a context and understand it more completely. Considering some of the types of fictional films also helps viewers understand the properties and potentials of the film medium.

In this chapter, we examine a few of the most frequently used ways to group fictional films: **classical Hollywood cinema** (throughout the world the most popular and influential type of fictional film) and a few alternatives to it: **Italian neorealist cinema**, **French new wave cinema**, **independent films**, **Bollywood**, and **Hong Kong cinema**. Although various groupings of films are discussed in this chapter and in Chapter 8, it is important to remember that filmmakers are not ruled by formulas or books. Instead, they may be influenced by earlier films, cinema traditions, intuition, creativity, demographic patterns (such as the percentage of teens who attend movies), box office potential, and other factors. As a consequence and increasingly so in recent years, some films are not exclusively one type.

Terms in **boldface** are defined in the Illustrated Glossary beginning on page 667.

French new wave (cinema): A film movement consisting of a loose grouping of untraditional movies made in France in the late 1950s and early 1960s.

Bollywood: Extremely popular Hindi-language movies made in India.

FIGURE 7.1

CLASSICAL HOLLYWOOD CINEMA

> The film experience resembles a fun house attraction, a wild ride, the itinerary of which has been calculated in advance but is unknown to the spectator. By spurts and stops, twists and roller coaster plunges, we are taken through a dark passage, alert and anxious, yet confident we shall return satisfied and unharmed. (Andrew 144)

convention: A subject or technique that makers of texts and audiences accept as natural or typical in certain contexts.

Film scholars have explored many ways of grouping fictional films. David Bordwell, Janet Staiger, and Kristin Thompson studied representative American films across the years to see if they could discover recurrent **conventions**. In their book *The Classical Hollywood Cinema: Film Style and Mode of Production to 1960* and in other publications, they argue that most American **feature films**—and indeed most movies worldwide—share certain qualities, which are explained below.

Characteristics of Classical Hollywood Cinema

According to Bordwell, Staiger, and Thompson (1–84), classical Hollywood cinema tends to have the following characteristics:

point-of-view shot: Camera placement at the approximate position of a character or person (or occasionally some other creature) that gives a view similar to what that subject would see.

1. The story is set mainly in a present, external world (not necessarily in the current era) and is seen largely from outside the action, although **point-of-view shots**, memories, fantasies, dreams, or other mental states are sometimes included.
2. The film focuses on one character or a few distinct individuals.
3. The main characters have a goal or a few goals.
4. In trying to attain their goals, the main characters confront antagonists or a series of problems.
5. The emphasis is on clear causes and effects of actions. What **events** happen and why they happen are clear and unambiguous.
6. The film has **closure**—a sense of resolution or completion at the end of a **narrative**—and often the main characters succeed in reaching their goals (happy endings).
7. The film uses unobtrusive **filmmaking techniques**.

narrative: A representation of unified events (happenings and actions) situated in one or more settings.

film(making) technique: Any aspect of filmmaking, such as the use of sets, lighting, sound effects, music, or editing.

Bordwell, Staiger, and Thompson argue that in American films of recent decades, "the classical paradigm continues to flourish, partly by absorbing current topics of interest and partly by perpetuating seventy-year-old assumptions about what a film is and does" (372). They also point out that many foreign films exemplify the traits of classical Hollywood cinema. Recent examples are *Shall We Dance?* (1996) from Japan (see Figure 11.18 on p. 532) and *Not One Less* (1999) from China (Figure 7.2a).

So pervasive are the basic story components of classical Hollywood cinema that they also shape animated narratives. *Antz* (1998) is the story of a male ant seeking to win a society's most highly prized female while in the end attempting to save his society from a deadly outside threat. Throughout the story, the protagonist confronts a series of problems, but the story ends with closure and a happy ending as the main character, who was initially full of self-doubts, achieves his goals and gains his society's adulation (Figure 7.2b).

a)    b)

FIGURE 7.2 Classical Hollywood cinema: two examples
So widespread is classical Hollywood cinema that most fictional films, including foreign films and animated stories, exhibit its characteristics. The Chinese film *Not One Less* (1999) and the animated feature *Antz* (1998) are examples.

(a) *Not One Less* is set in the present world and is largely seen from outside the action. It shows only a few distinct characters and focuses on one character: the girl substitute teacher seen here. The young girl has been hired to keep order in a small, rural school and to deter students from dropping out. In pursuing her goals, she faces a series of problems, including the disobedient boy seen above. The film leaves the viewer with no major unanswered questions and no uncertainty as to what happened and why. It has closure, or a sense of completeness and completion. As in most movies of the classical Hollywood cinema, the ending is happy for the main character and for those in the audience the film intends to please. *Not One Less* uses only unobtrusive filmmaking techniques: viewers are never distracted from the story by some unusual or obtrusive technique.

(b) *Antz* also is set in the present world and is largely seen from outside the action. It features only a few distinct characters and focuses on one character: Zee, who is voiced by Woody Allen, as seen above at a therapy session. Zee has two goals: to win the princess and later to thwart the mass extermination of the ant colony. In pursuing his goals, Zee confronts a succession of problems. The film leaves no major unanswered questions and no uncertainty as to what happened and why. It has closure, or a sense of completeness and completion. As in most movies of the classical Hollywood cinema, the ending is happy for the film's main character and for those in the audience the film intends to please. *Antz* has no distracting filmmaking techniques.
(a) *Columbia Pictures Film Production Asia and others; Columbia TriStar Home Video DVD.* (b) *PDI, DreamWorks SKG; DreamWorks Home Entertainment DVD*

So widely seen is classical Hollywood cinema that it has influenced almost all narrative films: filmmakers either imitate characteristics of classical Hollywood cinema or ignore or reject its conventions.

Film Genres: Related Fictional Films

> What genre does is recognize that the audience [watches] any one film within a context of other films, both those they have personally seen and those they have heard about or seen represented in other media outlets. . . . In general, the function of genre is to make films comprehensible and more or less familiar. (Turner 97)

Action, war, western, comedy, science fiction, horror, mystery/suspense, drama, family, and children. Sound familiar? These and other major categories are commonly used for ease of marketing in video stores. Many other films are seen as part of a group, including adaptations of literature (for example, movies based on the novels of Jane Austen or the plays of Shakespeare), road movies, urban comedies, and ethnic films. Filmmakers, film critics, film scholars, and film viewers all think of films in terms of categories, although for different reasons.

Most films of the classical Hollywood cinema are **genre** films—members of widely recognized groups of fictional films, such as westerns, musicals, romantic comedies, detective films, gangster films, science fiction movies, horror, and war movies. Each genre has characteristics accepted by both filmmakers and audiences. For example, westerns, at least the traditional ones, tend to share the same basic conflict (civilization versus the wilderness) and usually the same type of **setting** (sparsely settled region—often frontiers—west of the Mississippi River, in northern Mexico, or in the Canadian Rockies). All detective films share the same basic story: the uncovering of causes (who did what when and why). Musicals share nothing more than frequent prominent interludes of music and perhaps dancing during a story.

It is difficult to be precise about the characteristics of particular genres because critics and scholars define genres in somewhat different ways. Genres that do not die out evolve as social attitudes change. Many westerns before World War II represented Native Americans in **stereotypical** negative ways that encouraged European Americans to continue to think of themselves as superior. For example, the comedy western *My Little Chickadee* with W. C. Fields and Mae West (1940) consistently depicts American Indians in stereotypical ways and as the butt of tired jokes that many viewers today do not find amusing. Of that film, an anonymous customer reviewer at Amazon.com wrote, "as a Native American, this film is really offensive. . . . W. C. Fields treats this supposedly Native American companion [whom he calls "Milton"] like a dog he can kick around who still comes and licks him on the face at night. Fields literally abuses the com-

setting: The place where the events of a narrative occur.

stereotype: A commonplace, simplified, and in some ways inaccurate likeness of a subject created in a text.

panion physically and verbally and that's supposed to be funny. Furthermore, the supposed Indian [played by a non-Indian] says crap like 'Ugh' and 'Big Chief gottem new squaw?' It's sickening." But times and attitudes changed, and later westerns such as *Little Big Man* (1970) and *Dances with Wolves* (1990) show Native Americans in a sympathetic light, sometimes more favorably than they portray the European American settlers. Even more recently, the first feature movie made by and about Native Americans, *Smoke Signals* (1998), and *The Business of Fancy-dancing* (2002), do much to dispel stereotypes about American Indians—for example, that they are stoic and humorless (Figures 2.38 and 7.3).

Makers of genre films are inevitably influenced by previous films of the same genre. They either imitate earlier films, reject the genre's fundamentals, or follow the genre in some ways but not in others. Let's consider three of the most enduring genres: the western, **film noir**, and the musical.

THE WESTERN

According to scholar Charles Musser, "The Great Train Robbery" (1903) was "the most commercially successful film of the pre-**nickelodeon** era, perhaps of any film prior to *The Birth of a Nation* (1915)" (18). "The Great Train Robbery" includes what was to become the basic story of many western films: a threat to civilization (outlaws committing a crime by robbing the passengers on a train) and the eventual reestablishment of order (a posse giving chase, catching the four outlaws, killing them, and recovering the stolen goods) (see Plate 38 in Chapter 13). Ever since that film, viewers have enjoyed westerns.

Westerns have proven so popular that they have been made in many countries, including Mexico, Spain, Italy, and East Germany. The **documentary film** "The Spaghetti West" (2005) claims that "between 1964 and 1973, over five hundred westerns were produced or co-produced by Italians." "Between 1965 and 1983, the East German studio . . . produced fourteen westerns. **Shot** on **location** in Yugoslavia, Czechoslovakia, Romania, Bulgaria, the Soviet Union, and Cuba, and usually starring a hulking former

FIGURE 7.3 Dispelling stereotypes
Although traditional westerns helped perpetuate demeaning stereotypes about American Indians, later westerns and nonwesterns such as *Smoke Signals* (1998) present a different picture. *Smoke Signals* repeatedly undercuts the stereotype that Native Americans lack humor. Here Thomas, on the left, and Victor are talking to two Indian women who gave them a ride:

FIRST WOMAN: Ain't you guys got your passports?

THOMAS: Passports?

FIRST WOMAN (with mock seriousness): Yah. You're leaving the rez and going to a whole different country, cousin.

THOMAS (seriously): But it's the United States.

SECOND WOMAN: Damn right it is. That's as foreign as it gets. Hope you two got your vaccinations.
(The women laugh.)

ShadowCatcher Entertainment, Welb Film Pursuits; Miramax Home Entertainment DVD

nickelodeon: A small storefront theater where a brief program of short films could be seen for a nickel in the United States from approximately 1905 to 1915.

location: Any place other than a film studio that is used for filming.

physical-education instructor . . . , these so-called *Indianerfilme* are as clumsy and predictable as many of Hollywood's cowboy films. There is one notable distinction: in East German westerns, the American Indians are always the good guys" (Shulman), fighting "wars of liberation against the capitalists" (Barton Byg, quoted in Ingalls).

Typically the setting of a western film is the United States plains, the Rockies, the Northwest, the Southwest, northern Mexico, or perhaps the Canadian Rockies, and some **shots** usually linger on the vastness, openness, beauty, or menace of the terrain (see Plate 19 in Chapter 2). The focus of traditional film westerns is people who stand for law and order, for settling and taming the West (often territories before they were states), and for bringing the refinement and civility of the eastern United States or Europe to the rough-and-tumble West (often women perform this last function). The transformations so often celebrated in westerns can be seen in an excerpt from *Bend of the River* (1952), where a settler says, "We'll use the trees that nature has given us. Cut a clearing in the wilderness. We'll put in roads. . . . Then we'll build our homes. . . . There'll be a meeting house, a church. We'll have a school. Then we'll put down seedlings." To achieve the traditional western's goals, those who represent civilization usually have showdowns and shoot-outs with one or more of the following: Native Americans, Mexicans, and men wearing black hats.

Most westerns directed by John Ford are generic but not without complexities, subtleties, and surprises. They may also include music, dancing, and humor. In many respects Ford's *My Darling Clementine* (1946) reenacts the generic western story. The film's basic conflict involves the attempt of Wyatt Earp and his brothers to establish order in a town (which includes reining in the ill, troubled, and dangerous Doc Holliday) and to bring the murderers of their 18-year-old brother to justice. Another important conflict is between Chihuahua—the sensual, emotional Mexican saloon singer—and Clementine, the less sensual, more emotionally restrained Boston nurse. By the end of the film, the following events have taken place: A drunken, unruly Native American has been silenced and disappears from the movie; a crooked professional gambler has been run out of town; and a traveling actor has recited Shakespeare, the quintessence of British culture. The town's first church has been dedicated, and an outdoor dance has been held as American flags blow in the breeze. Chihuahua, the dishonest and unfaithful Mexican beauty, has died; and Clementine—the restrained, churchgoing easterner—plans to stay and teach school. Most significantly, two of the four Earp brothers survive. They are leaving, although Wyatt may return to Clementine. He has achieved what he set out to do: see that the evil ones are brought to justice (though at the cost of brothers and sons killed) and that order is established in the town. Civilization as many European Americans might think of it is coming to the dusty desert community of 1882 Tombstone, Arizona (Figure 7.4).

shot (noun): An uninterrupted strip of exposed motion-picture film or videotape that represents a subject during an uninterrupted segment of time.

FIGURE 7.4 Generic western
Although *My Darling Clementine* (1946) surprises viewers with its low-key Marshal Earp, a complex Doc Holliday, and the lack of closure to the budding Wyatt Earp–Clementine Carter romance, the film is a generic western. In this frame from the film's last scene, Earp is seen riding away from Clementine and toward the wilderness, Monument Valley. Most of the basics of westerns such as *Shane* and *The Searchers* are contained within this image: the wilderness, the promise of domesticity, and a man's tug of allegiance between those two forces. *20th Century Fox; 20th Century Fox Home Entertainment DVD*

Since about 1950, most westerns have been **revisionist**: they ignore or challenge the fundamental traditions of the western film. Fifties revisionist westerns include *Broken Arrow* (1950), which depicts Native Americans at least as sympathetically as the European American settlers; *High Noon* (1952), which attacks the cowardly behavior of townspeople afraid of or sympathetic to those in black hats; and *The Searchers* (1956), which shows the human cost of pursuing vengeance so passionately and for so long (Figure 7.5).

revisionist: A novel or revised interpretation or representation of a subject.

FIGURE 7.5 A 1950s revisionist western
The Searchers (1956), directed by John Ford from a script by Frank Nugent, begins in 1868 with Ethan Edwards (on the right) arriving unexpectedly at his brother's ranch in Texas. Here we see Ethan shortly after the reunion with his brother, nephew, two nieces, and sister-in-law, Martha. (The way Ethan here picks up his younger niece Debbie has emotional resonance near the end of the film.) Ethan proves to be a complex hero, more complex and flawed and even mysterious than any seen in westerns before and few if any since. He has many of the typical western hero's qualities—including knowledge of a Native Indian culture, skill with guns and horses, bravery, self-sacrifice, and perseverance. Details such as the tender way Martha hangs up Ethan's coat hint that the two share deep though unrevealed feelings. Sometimes he seems worthy of an admirable woman's love. Ethan, however, becomes consumed by vengeance and murderous suppressed rage and is doomed to remain an outsider to family and home. *C. V. Whitney; Warner Bros.; Warner Home Video DVD*

The sixties also saw various revisionist westerns. John Ford's *The Man Who Shot Liberty Valance* (1962) exhibits major creative variations of the western. In that film, the agent of civilization is a man of the law, a lawyer who doubles as a teacher of English and civics. But the film shows that without skill in using a gun, the agent of law and order is helpless in the face of a bullying murderer. *The Man Who Shot Liberty Valance* also shows that legend masks the truth, in this case the bravery and integrity of the real hero. As indicated in the first column of the book's chronology (pp. 607–66), the United States experienced massive domestic upheaval from late in 1963 to the end of the sixties: political and racial assassinations; an increasingly unpopular war in Vietnam and growing demonstrations against the war; and civil rights unrest, violence, and demonstrations. During the late 1960s, many viewers who had become disillusioned with the U.S. federal government and with others in power identified with the outlaws of *The Wild Bunch* (1969) and *Butch Cassidy and the Sundance Kid* (1969), all of whom defy authorities and try to cope during changing times (Figure 7.6).

Robert Altman's *McCabe and Mrs. Miller* (1971) is also about trying to defy an outside force during changing times. The two central characters are not settlers bringing the usual socially acceptable goods or services to the untamed West. Mrs. Miller is a practical, intelligent, opium-smoking prostitute and madam who has financial goals and a clear sense of how to achieve them. McCabe is a card shark–businessman–pimp who ignores Mrs. Miller's sound advice, lacks the confidence and power he initially seems to have, and is too naive to see when to cut a deal with those with power. Near the end of the film, the townspeople are more concerned with saving the burning church, which they had ignored and will likely continue to ignore, than with helping McCabe in his deadly confrontation with three murderous thugs sent by an acquisitive corporation. As scholar John H. Lenihan points out, the film implies that "the future of America lay not with the individual but with the corrupt and indomitable corporation" (164).

In *McCabe and Mrs. Miller*, Altman also deliberately rejected the major conventions of the western genre:

> Mr. Altman's interest in film genres was candidly subversive. He wanted to explode them to expose what he saw as their phoniness. He decided to make "McCabe & Mrs. Miller" for just that reason. "I got interested in the project because I don't like westerns," Mr. Altman said. "So I pictured a story with every western cliché in it."
>
> His intention, he said, was to drain the glamour from the West and show it as it really was—filthy, vermin-infested, whisky-soaked, and ruled by thugs with guns [Figure 7.7]. His hero, McCabe (Mr. [Warren] Beatty), was a dimwitted dreamer who let his cockiness and his love for a drug-addicted prostitute (Ms. [Julie] Christie) undo him.

FIGURE 7.6 A double bill: revisionist westerns with outlaw protagonists

The Wild Bunch and *Butch Cassidy and the Sundance Kid* were first shown within three months of each other in 1969. Both are revisionist westerns featuring not lawmen taming the western frontier but sympathetic outlaws who rob banks and trains but whose criminal options are fast disappearing in the changing American West. Both movies quickly proved popular with American audiences. (a) *The Wild Bunch*, which is set in 1913, begins and ends with prolonged and elevated levels of violence never before seen in a western. The image here represents action near the end of the film when four of the wild bunch are on their way to try to free a Mexican colleague regardless of the considerable danger to themselves. (b) *Butch Cassidy and the Sundance Kid* focuses on a bickering, often witty criminal odd couple, Sundance (left) and Butch Cassidy (right), along with Sundance's game girlfriend.

a)

b)

Unlike traditional westerns, both movies are set in an era that is coming to an end as railroad owners spend a lot of money to hire others to track down the outlaws and kill them. Both films end in countries south of the U.S. border, supposedly where new opportunities await the outlaws. In keeping with the growing disillusionment in late-1960s America, both films show the central characters scornful of business and government. As the leader of the wild bunch says with amusing understatement almost 58½ minutes into the original director's cut of the film, "We share very few sentiments with our government." However, unlike *The Wild Bunch*, *Butch Cassidy and the Sundance Kid* is playful and humorous throughout. For example, in a scene shortly after 18½ minutes into the film, a sheriff implores a group of the town's men to join a posse and go in pursuit of Butch and Sundance: "How many of ya can bring your own guns?" No response. ". . . well, how many of ya are going to want me to supply you with guns?" Again, no takers. The scene illustrates widespread defiance of authority and an amusing refutation of those countless earlier western scenes where sheriffs quickly raise a posse of eager townsmen. Here and throughout, *Butch Cassidy and the Sundance Kid* has a subversive humor that vast American audiences of the time found pertinent and satisfying. (a) *Warner Bros./Seven Arts; Warner Home Video Original Director's Cut DVD.* (b) *Campanile Productions; 20th Century Fox Home Entertainment DVD*

"These events took place," Mr. Altman said, of westerns in general, "but not in the way you've been told. I wanted to look at it through a different window, you might say, but I still wanted to keep the poetry in the ballad." (Lyman)

In Italy from 1964 to the mid-1970s, the many Italian or **"spaghetti" westerns** also reflected the unsettled political and social environment of the time. An Italian film director of the era explains that in Italy the period was one of "political and social unrest. . . . The good guy who wins in the name of the law and restores the law was no longer valid. So a new, ambiguous

spaghetti westerns: A film movement consisting of hundreds of westerns filmed from 1964 to the mid-1970s mostly in Italian studios and often on barren locations.

FIGURE 7.7 Revisionist representation of a western
Unlike nearly all earlier westerns, Robert Altman's *McCabe and Mrs. Miller* (1971) was filmed on location (in British Columbia, Canada) and teems with the messiness of life. One way Altman and the film's designer drained "the glamour from the West" was in their choices of settings: the buildings in the remote young village are incomplete, and the area is a mess. Here viewers see McCabe (on a horse) near the beginning of the film arriving in the rainy, remote, rain-soaked town. Even the film's weather is untraditional for westerns: except for a few shots, it is persistently gloomy. The film shows lots of mud, rain, gray skies, fallen snow, light snowing, and near the end heavy snowing. Throughout most of the exterior scenes, there is also a howling wind. It is the first sound viewers hear in the film (occurring along with the Warner Bros. logo even before the story begins) and continues throughout most of the opening credits. The sound of the howling wind also returns during the film's ending, including all the closing credits, and thus is the last sound viewers hear in the film. *David Foster Productions, Warner Bros.; Warner Home Video DVD*

character was born, a character that played both sides, a person who didn't want to have anything to do with anyone" (Baldi). The best-known practitioner of Italian westerns was Sergio Leone, who in *A Fistful of Dollars* (1964), *The Good, the Bad, and the Ugly* (1966; see Figure 1.1 on p. 12), *Once upon a Time in the West* (1968; see Figures 1.26b and 1.32), and other **widescreen** color films favored slow **pacing**, dramatic music, expressive **mise en scène**, and extended preliminaries to intense acts of violence, often including **extreme close-ups** of faces. But spaghetti westerns include many other filmmakers and many other subjects and **styles**, perhaps most notably Sergio Corbucci, who made such influential films as the enormously popular *Django* (1966), which is often imaginatively staged and includes more cruelty and slaughter by guns than any American western up to that time and few since. Probably Corbucci's most-admired

pace: The rate of speed at which the film's subjects (such as events in a narrative film or information in a documentary film) are revealed.

mise en scène: An image's setting, subjects, and composition (the arrangement of setting and subjects within the frame).

style: The way that subjects are represented in a text, such as a film.

film is *The Great Silence* (1968), which is set in snowy, mountainous Utah but filmed in Italy (Figure 7.8).

In the 1980s and into the 1990s, some critics were writing about the death of the western. Then came *Unforgiven* (1992), which set off another wave of revisionist westerns. The setting and subject of *Unforgiven* make it instantly recognizable as a western, but for those who have seen many westerns, the film has many surprises. The major antagonist is not a Native American, a Mexican, or an evil cowboy but the sheriff himself; he's so brutal that the townspeople are both embarrassed and afraid when he starts (literally) kicking someone around. The film's killings, which are committed in the name of justice, are based on rumor and dubious moral grounds and are messy, excruciating, and in one instance protracted. Perhaps most surprisingly, the hero is not a macho cowboy. He is an aging pig farmer aching to forget his past and to be left alone and longing for his deceased wife, who helped him give up alcohol and helped civilize him. Furthermore, the hero has a nagging conscience: he regrets murders he committed years before.

Other nineties westerns explored the possibilities of subjects usually pushed to the sides or backgrounds of movie screens, such as single women, African American males, and female prostitutes. *The Ballad of Little Jo* (1993) shows the trials, triumphs, and civilizing effects (such as compassion) of a woman in the man's world of 1870s Montana territory (Figure 7.9). Another western that focuses on a group usually on the periphery of westerns, if included at all, is *Posse* (1993). Most of its main characters are

FIGURE 7.8 An esteemed Italian or "spaghetti" western
Seen here—almost 60¼ minutes into Sergio Corbucci's *The Great Silence* (1968)—are the film's two major antagonists. Silence (on the left, played by the French actor Jean-Louis Trintignant) is a hired gun who was made mute as a boy when his throat was cut by bounty hunters after they had killed his father and mother. On the right is Loco (Spanish for *crazy*), a bounty hunter, played by German actor Klaus Kinski, who leads a group of bounty hunters intent on making lots of money, not in helping promote the law. Another important character is the sheriff, who is played by an American, Frank Wolff, and who is often unintentionally comic in the film and finally ineffective. Like many other westerns, *The Great Silence* deals with the issues of law and order and with attempts to tame and civilize the wild, in this film and many other westerns, the wild in human nature. *Adelphia Compagnia Cinematografica, Les Films Corona; Fantoma DVD*

FIGURE 7.9 A feminist revisionist western
In *The Ballad of Little Jo* (1993), (a) Josephine Monaghan is first seen dressed much as she is here, but carrying a suitcase and protecting her head from the sun with a parasol. Viewers eventually learn that she has had a baby out of wedlock and been exiled by her family. (b) In the West, men menace her—she is nearly raped—so to avoid further danger and abuse, Josephine becomes Jo by inflicting a scar on her cheek, dressing as a man, and gradually learning how to act as one. Unlike most westerns, *The Ballad of Little Jo* shows both the limited options available to nineteenth-century American women and the civilizing influences that a woman doing men's work could bring to the wild West. *Publicity stills. PolyGram Filmed Entertainment, Joco*

 a)

 b)

African American (Figure 7.10). *Bad Girls* (1994) also focuses on characters normally peripheral in the conventional western (Figure 7.11).

In recent years, commentators yet again revived talk about the death of the western. Though not numerous, westerns still get made. Some of them can help viewers reconsider what a western is. Many reviewers referred to *The Three Burials of Melquiades Estrada* (2005) as a western even though the film is set in the present time; includes illegal Mexican immigrants and members of the U.S. Border Patrol; contains flashes of **black comedy**; and represents the plights of two female characters in some depth. But otherwise, the film's settings (Texas and Mexico), major characters (ranch foreman, cowboy, and law enforcement officer), and subjects (law and order,

black comedy: A narrative style that shows the humorous possibilities of warfare, death, illness, and other subjects often considered off-limits to comedy.

FIGURE 7.10 An African American revisionist western
Posse (1993)—which focuses on five African Americans and one European American—gives a contemporary African American perspective on a group rarely seen in mainstream westerns, even in recent years. In *Posse*, blacks do not face opposition from the usual western antagonists, such as Native Americans, Mexicans, or an assortment of obvious outlaws. Instead, they have to contend with the white power structure. The posse's major antagonists are two European Americans. One is a cruel, corrupt army officer and his motley band of Spanish-American War veterans eager to steal war booty from the "posse" while exacting revenge. The posse's other major antagonist is a racist, greedy, power-hungry sheriff and his followers who years earlier had killed blacks with impunity. It is not clear if the white sheriff and his followers constitute the local version of the Ku Klux Klan or if that is a separate group, but the KKK is also a threat. Another problem for the African American community in the film is that the black marshal of an all-black town has naively struck an illegal business deal with the racist white sheriff and fails to oppose him when the sheriff treats blacks unjustly. *PolyGram Filmed Entertainment, Working Title Films; MGM DVD*

FIGURE 7.11 Taming the wild West
Throughout *Bad Girls* (1994), the four major female characters fight back against injustice. Initially, they are prostitutes wronged by men's laws, but when provoked, they outsmart, outride, and outshoot the men. Early in the film one of them catches up with a runaway horse-drawn carriage, jumps into it, and reins it to a halt. Among their many accomplishments as a group are rescuing one of their own from being hanged, killing four armed outlaws, and evading two detectives on their trail. While they are at it, two of them also win the love of two attractive young men. In their own fashion, they help tame the West. *Publicity still. Ruddy Morgan Productions, 20th Century Fox Film Corp.*

loyalty, retribution, and redemption) all fit within the western domain. *The Proposition* (2005) has an 1880s frontier setting beset by violent lawlessness. It features a "captain" in charge of trying to "civilize" the area, and he and his wife have brought with them as much of their faraway culture as they can. The film also includes a minority that is treated at best as second-class citizens, in part because of their skin color. To the minds of many critics, the film is unquestionably a western. The catch? The story is set in Australia. The captain and his wife are British. The minority is dark-skinned aborigines. But the basic frontier setting, the characters (lawful and lawless), the conflicts between the forces of law and order and the forces of lawlessness or self-appointed law enforcement, and subjects such as attempting to civilize a wild area and to bring in a culture and lifestyle of a more established civilization—all are present in the film (Figure 7.12). *The Three Burials of Melquiades Estrada* and *The Proposition* help us viewers understand what a revisionist "western" might be. Certainly, as *The Proposition* illustrates, it need not be set somewhere in North America.

Only time will tell whether the western is now largely corralled, but given its long history and filmmakers' record of adapting it to different times, places, and circumstances, I think it unlikely.

FILM NOIR

> This large body of films, flourishing in America in the period 1941–58 [from *The Maltese Falcon* to *Touch of Evil*], generally focuses on urban crime and corruption, and on sudden upwellings of violence in a culture whose fabric seems to be unraveling. Because of these typical concerns, the film noir seems fundamentally about violations: vice, corruption, unrestrained desire, and, most fundamental of all, abrogation of the American dream's most basic promises—of hope, prosperity, and safety from persecution. (Telotte 2)

Film noir (pronounced "nwahr") is a partial translation of *cinéma noir* (meaning "black or dark cinema"), the term first used by some French critics to describe a group of American films made during and after World War II. Various critics and scholars have defined *film noir* as a genre, a "sub-genre of the crime thriller or gangster movie," a **film movement**, a "quasi-generic category," a "fluid concept," a mode, a mood, a style, a visual style, and a "stylistic and narrative tendency." I consider film noir a genre of films that tend to have many **scenes** with dark, shadowy, **low-key lighting** and many night scenes (Figure 7.13). Other characteristics of film noir

FIGURE 7.12 A western's two worlds
The Australian western *The Proposition* (2005), which is set in an 1880s frontier area of Australia, includes many shots of the dry, largely barren wild. It also includes many shots of the home of the captain and his wife and what the wife facetiously refers to as their "lawn" (foreground above). This image from a little more than 18 3/4 minutes into the film shows both worlds. *UK Film Council, Surefire Film Productions, and others; First Look Home Entertainment DVD*

FIGURE 7.13 Film noir lighting and darkness
Seen here is a frame from the last shot of *The Big Combo* (1955). The film's cinematographer was John Alton, who later wrote a book on cinematography, *Painting with Light*. In his introduction to a reprinting of that book, Todd McCarthy writes, "In fashioning the nocturnal world inhabited by noir's desperate characters, Alton was ever consistent and imaginative in forging his signature, illuminating scenes with single lamps, slanted and fragmented beams and pools of light, all separated by intense darkness in which the source of all fear could fester and finally thrive. . . . Often, the light would just manage to catch the rim of a hat, the edge of a gun, the smoke from a cigarette. Actors' faces, normally the object of any cameraman's most ardent attention, were often invisible or obscured, with characters from *T-Men* to, perhaps most memorably, *The Big Combo* playing out their fates in silhouette against a witheringly blank, impassive background. . . . [In *The Big Combo*] Alton pushed his impulse toward severe black-and-white contrasts and silhouetting of characters to the limit. . . . And the final shot, with the figures of a man and woman outlined . . . against a foggy nightscape and illuminated by a single beacon, makes one of the quintessentially anti-sentimental noir statements about the place of humanity in the existential void" (x, xxix). *Security Pictures, Theodora Productions; Image Entertainment DVD*

are urban settings and characters who are motivated by selfishness, greed, cruelty, and ambition and are willing to lie, frame, double-cross, and kill (Figure 7.14).

Often noir films are fatalistic, and the main characters seem doomed. *Detour* (1945), for example, includes such lines as "Until then, I'd done things my way, but from then on something else stepped in and shunted me off to a different destination than the one I had picked for myself" and "That's life. Whichever way you turn, Fate sticks out a foot to trip you." Also, noir films tend to exhibit embittered or cynical moods and to have compressed and convoluted stories. *Double Indemnity* (1944) begins and ends in the present and has five **flashbacks.** Robert Siodmak's *The Killers* (1946) has eleven flashbacks that are arranged mostly chronologically. Early in the film, a man knows that two men are looking for him and plan to kill him. But he does not attempt to run away and is murdered. As the film's insurance detective tries to discover the sources of the murder, he talks with various people who begin to tell him what they know related to the case (in one instance, a newspaper article being read aloud provides the introduction to the flashback and the substance of it), and soon viewers are seeing and hearing earlier scenes. *Out of the Past* (1947) also includes flashbacks (see Figure 6.21 on p. 286).

Because these films were made when the American production code was strongly enforced (see pp. 462–64), characters who commit crimes are eventually punished. By the end of *Murder, My Sweet* (1944), for example,

flashback: A shot or a few shots, a brief scene, or a sequence that interrupts a narrative to show earlier events.

a)

b)

FIGURE 7.14 Film noir classic
Some film noir specialists regard *Touch of Evil* (1958, 1998) as the last of the classic films noirs. It has all the characteristics of film noir, including (a) many scenes with dark, shadowy, low-key lighting (here a man and his shadow follow another man and his shadow) and (b) as the central character a man (on the left) who is shrewd, driven, complex, and flawed. *Universal International Pictures; Universal Studios Home Video DVD (restored 1998 version)*

the three who commit murder have murdered each other; by the end of *The Lady from Shanghai* (1948), the three lethal characters have also killed each other. Near the end of *Force of Evil* (1948), the three major criminal characters confront one another in a dark room; two are shot; then the third calls the police and says he'll be turning himself in.

Often films noirs feature a femme fatale, invariably an attractive, young, worldly woman who thinks and acts quickly and is verbally adroit. She is also manipulative, evasive, sexy, dangerous, perhaps even lethal, especially to men who succumb to her wiles and charms—and do they ever. In *The Lady from Shanghai*, the femme fatale is a Circe who figuratively enchains her husband's business partner and nearly lures the film's central character to his doom (Figure 7.15). The original title of another film noir, *Deadly Is the Female* (1950), states what many other films noirs show (later the film was renamed *Gun Crazy*, and that is how it is usually referred to today). The film's femme fatale, Laurie, is first seen as a sharpshooter in a traveling carnival. Later, viewers learn that Laurie is involved with her sleazy boss because he knows that she murdered a man and is blackmailing her. Laurie is attractive, seductive, manipulative, assertive, and sexual. Unlike Bart, her new lover and later husband and partner in crime, she is anything but naive and is quite willing to murder (Figure 7.16). *Out of the Past* also contrasts a more traditional woman (Ann) with a femme fatale (Kathie). In Nicholas Christopher's **reading**, Ann is "antiseptic, static, sexually repressed, socially rather dull, she lives with her parents and works as a schoolteacher; she wants to marry and have kids and never leave her hometown. Should we be surprised that when [Jeff, the main male character,

reading: An interpretation of a text or part of one.

a)

b)

FIGURE 7.15 Two faces of a femme fatale
Initially, Rita Hayworth plays the innocent victim in need of male protection, but she proves to be a femme fatale in the film noir *The Lady from Shanghai* (1948). (a) She is on a boat deck singing, and her song lures the main male character up to the deck; she's a Circe (which is also the name of the boat). (b) Near the end of the film, viewers learn she has killed a man who she had hoped would kill her husband, and here in a fun house full of mirrors she will soon pull a gun on her husband and he then on her. Soon, they are blazing away at the reflections of each other. She kills him, but the film was released in 1948 and was subject to the production code, so she does not go unpunished. *Columbia Pictures and Mercury Productions; Columbia TriStar Home Video DVD*

FIGURE 7.16 Film noir good woman–bad woman dichotomy
Often in films noirs the femme fatale contrasts with a more conventional woman. In *Gun Crazy* (1950), the femme fatale is Laurie (dressed in black), who like most femmes fatales is young, worldly, attractive, calculating, and resourceful. The film's other main female character is the sister of Laurie's lover, the antithesis to Laurie in her choices of motherhood, domesticity, lawfulness, and even clothing. Significantly, when the two females meet late in the film, as here a little more than 71 minutes into this 87-minute film, they do not hit it off. *King Bros.; Warner Home Video DVD*

is] reunited with Kathie, who is freewheeling, worldly, intellectually (if criminally) active, dangerous, and highly sexed, Jeff finds it so easy to fall back under her spell?" (198–99). Kathie is so dangerous that when Ann says of her, "She can't be all bad. No one is," Jeff, who is no innocent yet succumbs to Kathie more than once, replies, "Well, she comes the closest."

The changing role of women in 1940s U.S. society influenced film noir. During World War II, women were urged to take over factory jobs traditionally held by men, and millions did. After the war, the men returned and displaced the women workers, often unceremoniously. The self-sufficiency many women showed during the war doubtless threatened many men, perhaps including those involved in making films noirs.

"A large number of the postwar noir thrillers are concerned to some degree with the problems represented by women who seek satisfaction and self-definition outside the traditional contexts of marriage and family" (Krutnik 61).

Film noir can be understood as in part a reaction against the brightly lit **studio** entertainment films of the 1930s. The look of noir films was also influenced by German and Austrian immigrant filmmakers attuned to **expressionistic** lighting and mise en scène. Then, too, it is likely that the urban painting of such American artists as Edward Hopper influenced the look of film noir: "When Abraham Polonsky, the director of *Force of Evil*, was dissatisfied with the look his cinematographer . . . was getting, he took him to an exhibition of Hopper's paintings at a Greenwich Village gallery and said, 'This is how I want the picture to look.' And it did: full of black windows, looming shadows, and rich pools of light pouring from recessed doorways and steep stairwells" (Christopher 15).

The detective fiction of such writers as Raymond Chandler, Dashiell Hammett, and James M. Cain was a major influence and provided sources for some of the major scripts. Films noirs reject the nationalistic films of World War II. They also reflect the disorientation and lack of clear identity many experienced after surviving the severe economic depression of the 1930s; the massive casualties, genocide, torture, and atomic clouds of World War II; and the difficult readjustment to civilian life by returning soldiers.

Many film scholars see the 1941 version of *The Maltese Falcon* as the first film noir. That film does have most of the characteristics outlined here, but it is not nearly as dark and shadowed as many later films noirs. In addition, as critic and scholar Foster Hirsch points out, various earlier films have elements of the genre (12–13). Undisputed major films noirs include *Double Indemnity*; *Murder, My Sweet*; *Detour*; *The Big Sleep* (1946); the 1946 version of *The Killers*; *Out of the Past*; *The Lady from Shanghai*; *Force of Evil*; *Criss Cross* (1949); *Gun Crazy*; *The Asphalt Jungle* (1950); *The Big Combo* (1955); and *Touch of Evil*.

Many later American color films also are films noirs or were influenced by that genre (Figure 7.17). Others are *The Long Goodbye* (1973); *Chinatown* (1974); *Body Heat* (1981); *Pulp Fiction* (1994); *Devil in a Blue Dress* (1995); *Fargo* (1996); and *L.A. Confidential* (1997). *The Man Who Wasn't There* (2001) is in black and white and is set within the period of classic films noirs: 1949. It is immersed in darkness and shadows and features an unassuming, ambitious main character who

studio (era): The period of U.S. film history from the 1920s to the 1950s during which large studios used a factory-style system to make movies.

expressionism: A style of art, literature, drama, and film used to represent not external reality in a believable way but emotions in striking, stylized ways.

FIGURE 7.17 A night scene in a modern film noir in color
Approximately 42 1/2 minutes into *Chinatown* (1974), Detective Jake Gittes (left) is about to get his nose cut by two thugs hired to guard secrets in the night. In its night scenes filled with mystery, danger, and violence and in its lying, duplicitous, and murderous antagonists, *Chinatown* is a film noir in color. *Long Road Productions, Paramount; Paramount Pictures DVD*

seems anything but in charge of his own fate. *Sin City* (2005), which is mostly in black and white though with occasional areas of color, often *looks* like film noir (Figure 7.18). One of its three main stories is about a good cop with a weak ticker and nearing 60 who rescues a pretty 11-year-old girl from the clutches of the pedophile son of a corrupt senator. The cop is framed for crimes he didn't commit, serves eight years in prison, and is released. He locates the young woman only to discover she is in love with him and he with her. Realizing that they are trapped by circumstances threatening her life, once again he sacrifices himself for her.

Some French films—such as *Breathless* (1959), *Shoot the Piano Player* (1960), and *Alphaville* (1965)—also have been labeled films noirs or were influenced by this genre. Another important noir film, *Night and the City* (1950), might be labeled Brit-Yank noir. The story is set in England. Some of the actors and characters are unmistakably English. The film seems British, but it also seems American. The leading actor, Richard Widmark, is an American who had already appeared in many American films as an American and in *Night and the City* somehow seems American in his schemes to become rich and powerful, his determination, and his energy (the film begins and ends with him running away from trouble). The film also seems American because of the character played by a glamorous well-known American female actor, Gene Tierney. Critics speak of certain British crime films as Brit noir. An example is a British-Irish-German-French co-production, *Croupier* (1998)—a twisted tale set in a nocturnal city. The story includes crime, intrigue, lies, betrayal, and a beautiful, worldly, mysterious, duplicitous, and potentially dangerous woman.

Writing in 1998, Hirsch summarizes noir's subjects, evolution, and enduring appeal:

> The private-investigation quest; crimes of passion and profit; stories involving masquerade, amnesia, split identity, and double and triple crosses continue to be the genre's abiding concerns. . . . Noir endures, but, inevitably, not in the

FIGURE 7.18 Continuing presence of film noir look
In this scene, a little more than 6 minutes into *Sin City* (2005), a police officer's partner (on the left) tries to convince the cop played by Bruce Willis to call for backup instead of rushing in to try to save an 11-year-old girl from rape and possible murder. As illustrated here, many of the film's scenes are set at night in a dangerous big city. *Sin City* is film noir in its pervasive darkness and shadows around, on, and within the characters. *Dimension Films, Troublemaker Studios; Dimension Home Video DVD*

same way as forty and fifty years ago. Like any genre that survives, it has had to adapt; and as a set of narrative patterns, a repertoire of images, a nucleus of character types, it has proven remarkably elastic. Against the odds, and after several premature obituaries, noir is a mainstay of commercial narrative film-making. (14, 320)

Film noir is not restricted to one period (1941–1958) or to one country (the United States). It is not a movement restricted to a place and time period but a large, diverse genre that has been adapted to different times and places and has had enduring appeal.

THE MUSICAL

Musicals come in an enormous variety, but essentially, a musical features some combination of intermittent but prominent instrumental music, singing, and dancing in combination with a narrative or story. The musical genre has existed since the introduction of movie sound technology in the late 1920s. The term *musical* came into use in the early 1930s to describe such films (Altman 32), which constituted one of Hollywood's most presti-gious genres throughout the era of the studio sys-tem, commanding impressive resources and attracting large audiences. To date, nine of the Academy Awards for Best Picture have gone to musicals, including *Broadway Melody* (1929), *An American in Paris* (1951), *West Side Story* (1962), *My Fair Lady* (1964), *The Sound of Music* (1965), and *Chicago* (2002). *The Wizard of Oz* has been a staple of American culture since it first lit up screens in 1939. Two of the most endearing and enduring cult movies are musicals, *The Rocky Hor-ror Picture Show* (1975) and the *Sing-a-Long Sound of Music* (see p. 509). For many years, the musical held the place in American cinema now occupied by action films: many were big-budget extrava-ganzas aimed at a mass audience, appealing on the level of visual spectacle, and emphasizing the strength, speed, flexibility, grace, and expressive-ness of the human body (Figure 7.19). In addition to visual spectacle, musicals showcase the expres-siveness of instrumental music, the human body moving in sync with music, and the range and nu-ance of emotion possible with the singing voice.

Hollywood is the best-known source for mu-sicals but hardly the world's only one. Film indus-tries in the Middle East, Latin America, Europe, and especially South Asia have made musicals part

FIGURE 7.19 Musicals celebrating the human body
Like sporting events, gymnastics, and yoga, musicals cele-brate the human body by showing its flexibility, balance, strength, and grace. Here, a dancer seen for less than a second 4 3/4 minutes into *Chicago* (2002) whirls her legs around with superior flexibility, range, and ease. The shot also celebrates human sexual appeal, a frequent aspect of musicals. The dancer's well-proportioned body is neither cloaked nor hidden in the shadows, nor is she wearing pantyhose and clogs! From her high heels and up, she is adorned in ways many societies consider both enhancing and celebratory of female sexual allure. *Miramax Films and others; Miramax Home Entertainment DVD*

of their output. India is the most prolific producer of musicals, which are made in many different languages. Most Indian films have many musical numbers, and the "playback singers," who are major Indian pop stars and attract audiences in their own right, sing the songs as the actors lip-sync along (a section on Bollywood begins on p. 344).

The origins of the American musical genre are diverse. European influences include opera and operetta. American sources include **vaudeville**, minstrel shows, burlesque, and especially the Broadway stage.

Most musicals are **live action**, but many are **animation** or a blend of live action and animation. As it has evolved, the musical has not been limited by setting, subject, or style. Some musicals are set in the past, others in the present; some aim for **realism**, others for fantasy or a blend of realism and fantasy. A musical may be a tragic romance set in an urban world of ethnic mistrust (*West Side Story*) or a fairy tale with a happy ending (*Snow White and the Seven Dwarfs*, 1937). A musical might be set during the era of rising Nazi power (*Cabaret*, 1972). It might very well include a story of courtship: the man pursuing the initially reluctant female (Figure 7.20a). A musical could be a genial gangster **parody** and **homage** with a cast with the average age of 12: *Bugsy Malone* (1976) is a British gangster musical, small time. Everything is scaled down, from the **sets** to the pedal-powered cars to the characters themselves in a film that parodies prohibition-era gangster movies. A musical may be a remake of both an opera and a later staged musical based on the opera, and the same musical may replace characters from Spain with an all African American cast and have different settings (the American South and Chicago), plentiful selections from the original operatic score, and new lyrics replete with stereotypical dialect such as *dese* and *dem* (*Carmen Jones*, 1954, Figure 7.20b). A musical may be an animated **satire** of recent events and trends (*South Park: Bigger, Longer and Uncut*, 1999) or a parody of a movie genre (*The Rocky Horror Picture Show*; see Figure 5.16 on p. 238). Alternatively, it may be an animated film such as *The Lion King* (1994) that entertains both children and adults. A musical may set some of the numbers within the mind of a character and **cross-cut** between what is happening in the story and what the character is fantasizing about (*Chicago*). It may even be about an East German youth who suffers a botched sex change operation and thereafter dresses and functions as a female (Figure 7.20c). A musical, like so many 1930s U.S. musicals, may tell a "backstage" story of a popular entertainment (Figure 7.20d). As this sampling suggests, the possible settings and subjects for the musical are limitless.

Musicals also may use a huge range of filmmaking techniques. Some musicals use a **long-shot/long-take** camera style that emphasizes the uninterrupted performances of the leads. The athletic Gene Kelly, for example, could dance seemingly effortlessly for long fragments of time (see Figure 1.5 on p. 15). So could Fred Astaire, who insisted on minimal editing. In *Swing*

vaudeville: A type of live U.S. theatrical show that consisted of various short acts and was the most popular form of entertainment in the United States early in the twentieth century.

homage: A tribute in a text to a person, to another text (such as a film), or to part of a text.

satire: A representation of individual or group thinking or behavior that indirectly exposes the subject as flawed.

cross-cut: In editing, to alternate between events occurring at different settings and often presumably at the same time.

long shot: A shot in which the subject may be seen in its entirety and much of its surroundings is visible.

long take: A shot of long duration.

a)

b)

d)

c)

FIGURE 7.20 **The scope of the musical**

Musicals may be set anywhere and show any story. They may use any type of music and any type of dance style. These four films suggest some of the vast range of the musical. (a) Almost 68 minutes into *Top Hat* (1935), the Fred Astaire and Ginger Rogers characters dance to the music "Cheek to Cheek." The story of *Top Hat* is about courtship and prolonged comic misunderstandings that can alienate a couple. (b) *Carmen Jones* (1954) is an American musical based on *Carmen*, Bizet's tragic opera, but the film is set in the United States and acted entirely by American blacks, not Europeans or European Americans. Here, in the final minutes of the film, Joe (Harry Belafonte) and Carmen (Dorothy Dandridge) sing their final duet, in which he desperately tries to convince her to come back to him and she resolutely refuses. (c) *Hedwig and the Angry Inch* (2001) combines live action and animation and has wry standup comedy, music, and a story told in action and songs. The film shows the story of Hedwig, a put-upon transsexual seeking musical success, respect, recompense, and love. Here Hedwig (center) performs before an initially unsuspecting and then largely unappreciative audience: customers at one of a chain of "Bilge-water's" seafood restaurants (think of a Red Lobster restaurant with a maritime disasters motif and note the glimpse of a photo of a sinking ship on the back wall). (d) Robert Altman's final film, *A Prairie Home Companion* (2006), is a backstage musical that shows what happens immediately before, during, and sometime after a special show. Unlike a number of 1930s musicals, in the movie *A Prairie Home Companion* the special show is not a play but a radio show. The movie takes place mostly within St. Paul's Fitzgerald Theater, home to Garrison Keillor's long-running radio program *A Prairie Home Companion*. The film has an abundance of genial humor and music aplenty, some of it related to the film's uncomplicated story. The movie also has an angel of death, who moves quietly around the backstage and touches lives; other reminders of the passing of time and of mortality; and ongoing examples of the disposition to celebrate the past and to try to cling to it through memories, stories, humor, music, and reenactments of traditional communal events. (a) *RKO Radio Pictures; Warner Home Video DVD.* (b) *Carlyle Productions; 20th Century Fox Home Entertainment DVD.* (c) *Killer Films, New Line Cinema; New Line Home Entertainment DVD.* (d) *Sandcastle 5 Productions, Prairie Home Productions, and others; New Line Home Entertainment DVD*

Time (1936), the Astaire and Rogers numbers consist of mostly extremely long-lasting shots that necessitated lengthy rehearsals to get the right **take**. For example, the penultimate shot of *Swing Time*, "Never Gonna Dance," runs 150 seconds and reportedly required 48 takes to get the details just right. In contrast, other musicals inject energy by using frenetic choreography (as frequently in Bob Fosse musicals), abrupt camera movements, and fast-paced editing, a style familiar from TV commercials and music videos. The most extreme cases are *Moulin Rouge* (2001) and *Chicago*, in which some scenes have such **fast cutting** that sometimes viewers' eyes can scarcely take in the mise en scène.

fast cutting: Editing characterized by frequent brief shots.

In the first few decades of the American film musical, the dominant style of music was popular standards, with melody and harmony deriving from European traditions. The most respected talents in American popular music in those years were as much the songwriters as the performers. Irving Berlin, George and Ira Gershwin, Jerome Kern, Cole Porter, and Richard Rodgers wrote scores of songs that are still often heard today. Many of these were written for Hollywood musicals, including Gershwin's "They Can't Take That Away from Me" (*Shall We Dance*, 1937), Kern's "The Way You Look Tonight" (*Swing Time*), Porter's "I've Got You under My Skin" (*Born to Dance*, 1936), and Berlin's "Cheek to Cheek" (*Top Hat*, 1935) and "White Christmas" (*Holiday Inn*, 1942).

Although musicals in the traditional popular music style of earlier decades were still made into the 1960s, beginning in the 1950s, American film musicals adopted other musical styles. During this time, popular music changed drastically. Musical influences were less European and more American: folk, western swing, jazz, and especially rock and roll and the blues. Films starring Elvis Presley, such as *Love Me Tender* (1956) and *Jailhouse Rock* (1957), draw on these new musical sources. These films started appearing in the mid-1950s and continued at a pace of more than one a year through the end of the 1960s. In the 1970s, *The Wiz* (1978), *Nashville* (1975), and both *Saturday Night Fever* (1977) and *Grease* (1978) incorporated African American pop, country, and disco (respectively) into the genre.

In more recent examples of the genre, no single musical style dominates. Films are made in various different musical idioms and sometimes even an eclectic mix of styles within a single film. *Hedwig and the Angry Inch* features original punk rock. *Dancer in the Dark* (2000) uses Björk's original songs, in her inimitable alternative techno-rock sound, whereas *Chicago*, based on a 1975 stage musical, has John Kander and Fred Ebb's retro, Jazz Age tunes. *Moulin Rouge*, which uses mostly existing compositions for its score, contains a grab bag of hit pop songs of the past few decades but only one number, "Diamonds Are a Girl's Best Friend," from the popular standards era.

Musical numbers may be clearly motivated and serve many possible functions, such as to support characterizations, express **meanings**, or advance actions. In Bob Fosse's *All That Jazz* (1979), for example, the songs and dances help reveal the personality and situation of the driven, creative, yet self-destructive central character. A dance number in *Seven Brides for Seven Brothers* (1954) illustrates how a number can serve more than one function (see Plate 39 in Chapter 13). The opening number of Disney's *The Lion King*, "The Circle of Life," is another example of a number serving more than one function (Figure 7.21). Musical numbers are also integral to *Chicago*. Beginning about 69½ minutes into that film, "Mr. Cellophane" highlights the nonassertive personality of the John C. Reilly character, whereas 10 minutes later in the film, "Razzle Dazzle" shows Billy Flynn's circus/flimflam/magical courtroom strategies perhaps more completely than any other part of the film.

   In most musicals, the motivations for most numbers seem conventional, not realistic. Viewers are asked in effect to accept the convention that most or all of the singing or dancing, or of both, can occur in the movie even though they would not occur in a comparable real-life situation. *Meet Me in St. Louis* (1944)—which is set in 1903–1904 St. Louis, a time when horse-drawn carriages share the streets with "horseless carriages"—works its music into the film through such situations as characters traipsing through the house, saying goodnight, riding on a trolley, and singing at the piano. The first three examples seem contrived. After all, do families sing as they traipse through their house? Not many sane ones do. But the husband and wife at the piano seems much more natural and is an example of the integration of narrative events and music (as well as an example of the power of music to bring people together). The number is "You and I," and it takes place approximately 77 minutes into the film. Minutes before, the father had announced to the assembled family that they would all be moving from St. Louis to New York. The reactions are shock, hurt, and resentment. Everyone leaves the room except the mother and father. Soon the mood shifts a bit, and she sits down and starts playing the piano. As he joins in singing and the mother joins him during a repetition of the chorus, all the

FIGURE 7.21 Possible varied functions of a musical number During the opening of Disney's animated feature *The Lion King* (1994), animals from far and wide make their way to at first we know not where. Soon we learn their destination: a presentation ceremony for Simba, the lion toddler who will one day be the lion king. This opening action is accompanied by the song "Circle of Life," which immediately suggests the African setting and also conveys various meanings—that life is abundant and varied, that different creatures react to life differently and fare differently, and that life is ongoing. The songs of *The Lion King* reinforce setting, characterizations, plot development, meaning, or mood. *Walt Disney Pictures, Walt Disney Feature Animation; Walt Disney Home Entertainment DVD*

other family members, drawn by the music, return and resume where they had left off before the disruptive paternal announcement.

One rare musical in which all the musical numbers arise spontaneously and credibly from the story is a 2006 film from Ireland called *Once*. The film shows the story of a male musician and a female musician who have much in common: both sing, play an instrument, and either compose music or write lyrics. Both are deeply involved in a disrupted relationship. Unlike nearly all other musicals, all the songs in *Once* arise naturally from the story (he is a street musician and she plays the piano and sings).

A number of times, though, the music that arises so naturally in a scene serves as background music for the following scene(s) or part of a scene. One example begins about 8 1/4 minutes into the film. It is evening and the male musician is in his room. He is playing his guitar and singing a song about his ex-girlfriend. Sometime after that, he tries to reach her by telephone. Although he is clearly not then singing and playing, he can still be heard singing that same song; then we see him on his bed again continuing seamlessly to sing and play the same song. That music continues nearly 2 minutes beyond when we viewers last see him singing and playing his song about his ex and serves as background music for the next few brief scenes the following morning, fading out only when he is at the spot where he sings to passers-by and the female musician approaches him.

In recent years, the U.S. movie musical has retained some popularity because of the continued success of animated musicals (such as *Happy Feet*, 2006), the cult favorites *The Rocky Horror Picture Show* and *Sing-a-Long Sound of Music*, and the popularity of musicals such as *Hedwig and the Angry Inch*, the Academy Award–winning *Chicago*, and on a lesser scale *Dreamgirls* (2006) and *Once*. The coming years may see a surge of musicals—or they may not. Like all genres, the musical is subject to changing times and interests, evolution, and cycles of prominence and eclipse.

Times change and many filmmakers seek fresh takes on stories that have had widespread and enduring appeal. Like all genres that last, the western evolved to the point that sometimes critics and viewers are not certain if a particular film can be squeezed under its umbrella. An example of this phenomenon is *Brokeback Mountain* (2005), which some critics labeled a "gay western." That designation is short and memorable but inaccurate. For one thing, the two main male characters are bisexual though more passionate about gay sex than straight. Is the story a western? Only very loosely.

It begins in 1963 rural Wyoming and consists of **sequences** set in Wyoming and Texas in the 1960s, 1970s, and 1980s. The two men look like cowboys and wear cowboy hats, jeans, and boots, and they ride horses, carry rifles, and camp out in beautiful, unsettled areas—all of which results in familiar western iconography. But the two men are hired to protect a large herd of sheep against attacks by wild animals, and eventually one drunken night they share a tent and a rough sexual union, and they begin an affair that lasts as opportunity permits over the years. By 1963, when the story begins, Wyoming and Texas had long become states, and the movie shows no threats from the usual western suspects: American Indians, Mexicans, or evil men with six-shooters and black hats. Instead, the main impediments to the happiness of the two men come from a society strongly partial to heterosexual unions and—as implied by some of the film's dialogue and seen in two brief flashbacks—the biggest danger to gay behavior comes from intolerant, violent straight men. If one applies a short label to *Brokeback Mountain*, it's more accurate though admittedly less striking to label it a forbidden love story. Particularly after a genre has evolved into different permutations, labeling a film as a member of the genre can be problematic.

Occasionally a film is a parody of a genre: an amusing imitation of traditional films in the genre. Examples of parodies of westerns are Paul Bartel's *Lust in the Dust* (1985) and Mel Brooks's *Blazing Saddles* (1974, Figure 7.22). In another western parody, a supremely poised ("cool") fighter for hire arrives in a town torn by two greedy, violent, warring factions. Amused by the shortcomings of both groups, he plays one against the other and partially orchestrates their eventual mutual destruction. Though greatly outnumbered, he also kills some of each group and then strides away. The story re-creates many elements of the western, such as *High Noon* and *Shane* (1953), but much of its characterization and action is rendered humorously, even satirically. The country and film: Japan and *Yojimbo* (*The Bodyguard*) (1961).[1]

---

[1]For a comparison and contrast of *Yojimbo* and *High Noon*, see Alan P. Barr, "Exquisite Comedy and the Dimensions of Heroism, Akira Kurosawa's *Yojimbo*," *Massachusetts Review* 16 (1975): 158–68. *Yojimbo* was remade fairly loosely, mostly in Spain, as the first of the spaghetti westerns, Sergio Leone's *A Fistful of Dollars* (1964), and later remade in the United States as a story of an outsider and two rival groups of gangsters in a prohibition-era Texas town in *Last Man Standing* (1996).

FIGURE 7.22 A parody of westerns
The bad (and dense) guys rein up to pay the toll for the Governor William J. Le Petomane Thruway 79 1/2 minutes into *Blazing Saddles* (1974). Here, as elsewhere in the film, the subjects (cowboys) and settings (the nineteenth-century American West) are those of the traditional western, but such actions as building a railroad, saving a town from corruption, and brawling in a saloon are exaggerated and mocked. As illustrated here, often *Blazing Saddles* also includes details from twentieth-century life. *Crossbow, Warner Bros.; Warner Home Video DVD*

Many filmmakers combine elements of two or more genres. Occasionally, they do so in only part of a film (see Plate 40 in Chapter 13). *Curse of the Undead* (1959) and *Billy the Kid vs. Dracula* (1965) combine elements of horror films and westerns (Figure 7.23). Some films written and directed by David Cronenberg, including *Scanners* (1981) and *eXistenZ* (1999), combine science fiction and horror. So do *Alien* (1979) and its **sequels** (Figure 7.24). *Blade Runner* (1982, revised and rereleased in 1992, and revised and rereleased again in 2007) combines visual and story elements of film noir, characters typical of a horror film (a Dr. Frankenstein type and his dangerous yet finally pitiable creation), and a decayed futuristic science fiction setting. All three *Matrix* movies can also be seen as a combination of elements from three genres (Figure 7.25).

Although a blending of genres can be inventive, refreshing, and fun, sometimes combined-genre films yield curious narrative results, as in *Plan 9 from Outer Space* (1959; see Figure 10.25 on p. 475). That film mixes science fiction and horror by showing a story of aliens who travel to earth in wobbly flying saucers to try to reason with humans to end scientific exper-

sequel: A narrative that continues the story begun in an earlier narrative.

FIGURE 7.23 A vampire western
In this publicity still for *Billy the Kid vs. Dracula* (1965), a vampire in western clothes and in a western setting menaces a beautiful woman. "The text [is] endowed with a strong degree of logical coherence, largely through a kind of process of condensation, whereby elements common to both genres [horror and western] . . . receive heavy emphasis. A key site of such condensation is the film's lead player, [John] Carradine [seen here], being an iconographic figure for both the horror and western genres, having played both numerous poverty-row vampires and numerous western character roles. . . . His nineteenth-century costume, the horse-drawn carriages he often travels in, and the cave–turned–silver mine he sleeps in all seem appropriate to both the western and the horror film" (Knee 145). *Circle Productions*

FIGURE 7.24 Science fiction settings, horror stories
As so often happens in the *Alien* movies, in *Alien³* (1992) people in futuristic settings are cut off from others and are destroyed by a swift, voracious, evasive, and unrelenting monster. Here, a little more than 56½ minutes into the film, the Sigourney Weaver character is once again in mortal danger from an alien with two mouths, but she survives this encounter because of a surprising condition viewers learn about later. Like the other *Alien* movies, *Alien³* combines a science fiction setting and the horror film components of

shadows, disturbing sounds, unsettling music, and a lurking monster. *Brandywine Productions Ltd.; 20th Century Fox; 20th Century Fox Home Entertainment DVD*

a)

b)

c)

FIGURE 7.25 Kung-fu, sci-fi, action movie
The Matrix (1999) blends elements of kung-fu movies, science fiction, and action. (a) The Carrie-Anne Moss character does a somewhat slow-motion cartwheel off a wall as bullets and stone chips fly all around her. Many acrobatic movements here and elsewhere are reminiscent of kung-fu movies. The filmmakers had seen many Hong Kong action movies, and the major cast members were trained for months with a system of wires used to support them. (b) Neo, the Keanu Reeves character, tries to dodge bullets that he and we viewers can more or less see, an image one might expect in a science fiction movie. (c) The Laurence Fishburne character leaps out of a building on the right as Neo, who is tethered to a helicopter, jumps toward him. Such exciting actions are not of this world but of the world of action movies. *Silver Pictures, Warner Bros., and others; Warner Home Video DVD*

iments that would result in the destruction of the "universe." Earthling governments will have none of it and even refuse to acknowledge that flying saucers exist. The male aliens, who are at least as patriarchal as their earthly counterparts, eventually begin "Plan 9," which entails resurrecting recently killed earthlings—including a woman with an hour-glass figure much on display—and turning them against the living. Much goes wrong for both sides of the conflict. And for the audience.

OTHER CINEMAS

There are many influential groups of fictional films other than classical Hollywood cinema, but the limited space here and limited accessibility to certain groups of films allow us to consider only a few of them: Italian neorealist cinema, French new wave cinema, European and American independent cinemas, Bollywood, and Hong Kong cinema. We consider them in the order in which they first elicited attention in film studies.

Critics and scholars sometimes group films into movements—groups of films sharing innovative styles or subjects (or both) that emerge from the same country or region over a period of a few years and that are in opposition to the dominant cinema(s) of the time. Two widely studied film movements are Italian neorealist cinema and French new wave cinema.

Italian Neorealist Cinema

> Along with [Luchino] Visconti, such other directors as Roberto Rossellini and Vittorio De Sica strove to create a film art of authenticity. . . . Feeling that reality could better be conveyed through created situations than through the direct recording of actual events, they employed a synthesis of documentary and studio techniques, merging actual situations with a scripted story line. The essentials of neorealist films were the use of nonprofessional actors, authentic settings, naturalistic lighting, simple direction, and natural dialogue. (Phillips 686)

In *The Bicycle Thief* (aka *Bicycle Thieves*, 1948), a long-term unemployed family man finally gets a job pasting up movie posters, but soon he loses his bicycle to a thief and his accomplices and faces losing his job if he cannot retrieve the bicycle by Monday morning. Most of the film is devoted to showing the man and his young son searching for the bicycle in various parts of Rome and the mostly difficult conditions under which different people live. *The Bicycle Thief* exhibits the characteristics of Italian neorealism: heavy but not exclusive use of nonprofessional actors (in the three major roles), mostly unaltered location settings, and a chronological story. Generally, the film uses unobtrusive filmmaking techniques: few **close-ups**, **wipes** that are about as inconspicuous as an editor could make them, and little or no supplemental lighting (Figure 7.26). The film's dialogue is natural, not rhetorical, and includes a range of dialects.

wipe: A transition between shots in which one shot appears to be pushed off the screen by the next shot.

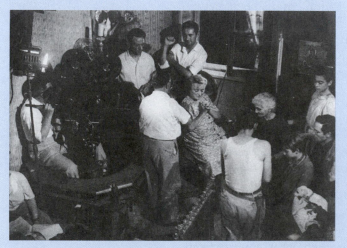

FIGURE 7.26 The Italian neorealist film *The Bicycle Thief* (1948)
This photograph illustrates how Italian neorealistic filmmakers use real people, actual locations, and little or no supplemental lighting. The seated woman is an untrained actor playing the part of a fortune-teller. Like other neorealist films, *The Bicycle Thief* deals with ordinary, believable characters—often played by nonactors—caught up in difficult social and economic conditions. The main character and his son (the actors playing those two central characters are seen on the right side of the photograph) have come to see the fortune-teller in hopes she can give the man information that will help him regain the stolen bicycle he needs to retain his desperately needed, recently acquired job.
Production still. PDS-ENIC; The Museum of Modern Art/Film Stills Archive

For an outline of the scenes of *The Bicycle Thief*, see the Web site for this book at <bedfordstmartins.com/phillips-film>.

In addition to *The Bicycle Thief*, other important neorealist films include *Open City* (1945), *Shoeshine* (1946), and *Umberto D.* (1952). *Open City*, which is set near the end of World War II in Europe, shows Catholics (especially a humane and compassionate priest), Communists, and others working together to resist the brutal Nazi occupation of Rome and exposes the myth of German superiority. A year later, *Shoeshine* showed two boys, who are best friends, trying to survive in the streets of Nazi-occupied Rome but getting into trouble and suffering arrest, prison, reform school, and mutual betrayal. *Umberto D.* is the story of an old pensioner increasingly distraught because he is behind in his payments to his wealthy, uncaring landlady. He is comforted only by his dog and to a lesser extent by his landlady's young, pregnant, unmarried servant (Figure 7.27).

The characters in neorealist films are ordinary and believable, but they are not probed for their psychological complexities. Instead, the focus is on characters caught up in the difficult conditions of Italy during and after World War II, such as poverty and unemployment. Generally, these films

FIGURE 7.27 *Umberto D.* (1952) as an Italian neorealist film

In *Umberto D.*, a childless retired civil servant named Umberto Domenico Ferrari is struggling to live in Rome on his limited pension. Added to his problems is a callous landlady intent on getting him out of his room after she has had it torn up as part of a major renovation during the man's absence. Also seen here, approximately 67 1/2 minutes into the film, are the man's only two reliable friends: a kind young woman who works for the landlady and the man's dog, which plays a major role in the story. Like *The Bicycle Thief*, *Umberto D.* exhibits the characteristics of Italian neorealist films: mostly nonprofessional actors (the man playing Umberto was a university professor without previous acting experience), location filming, and a chronological story. Generally, the film uses unobtrusive filmmaking techniques (although its music is sometimes prominent, especially near the ending). The everyday people in the story are in no way glamorized or idealized. Like *The Bicycle Thief*, *Umberto D.* shows believable characters trying to cope with difficult social and economic circumstances. But the film shows even more. As scholar and author Roy Armes concludes, the film operates "as social study and meditation on solitude, as a critique of bourgeois rapacity [the landlady] and a defence of bourgeois dignity [the old pensioner], as stark tragedy and warmly human story" (*Patterns* 163). *Rizzoli–De Sica–Amato; Criterion DVD*

failed to make money in Italy because audiences found them depressing and not diverting enough and an affront to national pride. They fared better at foreign box offices, especially in the United States.

The movement began in Italy during World War II and largely died out there by the early 1950s. In part, it was a product of the economic and social conditions of the times. In part, neorealism was also a reaction to prewar and wartime Italian cinema that often presented idealized images of fascist Italy, studio-made comedies, and costume histories.

Neorealism did not set out mainly to be an alternative to classical Hollywood cinema; indeed, in its clear linear **plots** and unobtrusive filmmaking techniques, neorealism is similar to it. However, in its frequent use of nonprofessional actors, unadorned location settings, simplified lighting, natural dialogue, concern for the social and economic problems of everyday people, and credible unhappy endings, neorealism was an alternative to the studio-made classical Hollywood cinema of its time.

Neorealist films influenced some later films—such as the early films directed by acclaimed Italian directors Federico Fellini and Michelangelo Antonioni, French new wave directors (see p. 337), the Bengali filmmaker Satyajit Ray, and some American directors working after World War II, such as Nicholas Ray, Elia Kazan, Jules Dassin, Joseph Losey, Robert Rossen, and Edward Dmytryk (Cook 438). Other films—such as *Salt of the Earth* (1954)—have strong resemblances to Italian neorealist films (Figure 7.28). In recent years, many of the most cineliterate film critics have

plot: The structure or arrangement of a narrative's events.

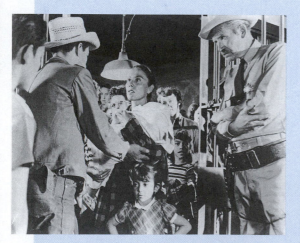

FIGURE 7.28 American neorealist-like film
Salt of the Earth (1954) shows zinc miners in New Mexico striking to gain a safe and fair deal from the callous mine owners, who control the district attorney, the sheriff, and the sheriff's deputies. The workers, mostly Mexican Americans, go on strike. When their efforts seem to be at a dead end, gradually the women become involved in the protests. Eventually, some of them are arrested illegally and jailed, including the film's narrator and main character, seen here in jail giving up her baby to its father so he can see that it gets its formula.

Like Italian neorealist films, *Salt of the Earth* was shot on location on a low budget, and except for the woman shown and four other professional actors playing minor roles, the large cast is nonprofessional. Like Italian neorealist films, *Salt of the Earth* uses mostly unobtrusive filmmaking techniques, blends fact and fiction, and focuses on the difficult social and economic conditions under which poor workers try to survive with some dignity. However, the film is unlike neorealism in its overt messages, its use of a narrator who explains many of the story's important points, and its hopeful ending. It is no accident that the film's central character is named *Esperanza*, which means "hope." *Publicity still. Independent Productions Corp., The International Union of Mine, Mill and Smelter Workers; The Museum of Modern Art/Film Stills Archive*

pointed out the neorealistic qualities of some recent Iranian films and how other films are at least partially neorealistic. An example is David Riker's *The City* (*La ciudad*, 1999), which was filmed in black and white and consists of four vignettes showing the difficult economic conditions of Latin American immigrants in New York. The film is neorealistic in its subject, location shooting, nonprofessional actors, documentary quality, and unresolved endings.

Since the 1950s, students of Italian neorealist films have come to see their artifice more clearly. Nonetheless, the stories and contexts of neorealist films continue to fascinate and engage film students and film scholars.

French New Wave Cinema

French new wave films were a diverse group of fictional films made in France in the late 1950s and early 1960s as a reaction to the carefully scripted products of the French film industry and as explorations of more current subjects, which were sometimes rendered with untraditional techniques.

> The New Wave—however we define it—captures the surface texture of French life in a fresh way, if only because the low budgets with which most young directors work initially necessitate a certain contemporary flavour lacking in the 1951–57 period, when the characteristic works were . . . period reconstructions. The newcomers had no money to build elaborate sets, pay for costumes, or employ star names: they shot on location, with reduced crews and fresh young performers. But this contemporary flavour was not accompanied by any real social or political concern. . . . The post-1958 feature film industry . . . remains essentially a Parisian cinema, dealing with middle-class problems in middle-class terms, and above all concerned with the "eternal" issues of human emotions and relationships. (Armes, *French* 169, 170)

The films of the French new wave were made by such directors as François Truffaut, Jean-Luc Godard, Claude Chabrol, and, to a lesser extent, Eric Rohmer and Jacques Rivette.[2] Most new wave directors had watched many films at the Cinémathèque Française (French national film archive) and various film clubs and had written about films and the film medium in the journal *Cahiers du cinéma*. In their writings they advocated that directors should have control over all creative stages of production, and they criticized traditional French films, especially those of the preceding decade. Before the new wave, French movies—as typified by the 1945 film *Children of Paradise*—tended to be period pieces and more literary than **filmic** (Figure 7.29).

filmic: Characteristic of the film medium or appropriate to it, such as parallel editing.

---

[2]Susan Hayward points out that Agnès Varda's 1954 film *La Pointe Courte* is a forerunner of French new wave cinema (146).

FIGURE 7.29　French film before the new wave
In the theatrical and literate *Children of Paradise* (*Les enfants du paradis*) (1945), one of the main characters is a mime (left) and the object of his affections on-stage and off is the woman posing as a statue. As a costume film and period piece that was shaped more by the script than by the direction, *Children of Paradise* was the type of film the French new wave directors rebelled against in their publications and their filmmaking. *S. N. Pathé Cinéma; Criterion DVD*

fast film (stock): Film stock that requires relatively little light for capturing images.

cutaway (shot): A shot that briefly interrupts the representation of a subject to show something else.

jump cut: A transition between shots that causes a jarring shift in space, time, or action.

New wave films are often imbued with an awareness of earlier films, especially American genre films, and are marked by unpredictable plot developments and the independent spirit of their directors. Jeanne Moreau, whose independent and openly sexual characters embody quintessential qualities of new wave films, said that the new wave way of making films freed up actors:

> In other films I made . . . the lighting was so complicated. There were shadows on one side and another light on the other side, so, really, when you are in close-ups you are in a corset. It was impossible to move. That's what the new wave was about, that absolute freedom. The light was made in such a way that you could move and do whatever you wanted, like in real life.

New wave films were set in the present or recent past. Like a type of documentary filmmaking evolving in France at about the same time (**cinéma vérité**), they were often shot on location with portable handheld cameras and sound equipment, **faster film stock**, and new, more portable lighting equipment. Sometimes they included surprising or whimsical moments, perhaps the product of improvisation while filming.

New wave cinema may also include homages or tributes to earlier films or parts of them (Figure 7.30). An homage results when visual details from the two main characters in Charlie Chaplin's *The Kid* (1921) are re-created in *Jules and Jim* (1961, Figure 7.31).

New wave films abound in editing rarely used in classical Hollywood cinema. Sometimes the results are surprising and whimsical. In *Shoot the Piano Player*, a gangster says to a boy he is kidnapping, "I swear it on my old lady's head. May she die if I lie." In a **cutaway shot**, a woman old enough to be the gangster's mother moves her hand toward her chest, falls down backward, and briefly kicks her legs straight up in the air. In the next scene, the boy says, "Then I believe you," and the gangster replies, "Didn't I tell you so?" And the film resumes its story. *Breathless* sometimes uses **jump cuts**, as in the scene where Michel shoots the motorcycle police officer; as edited, the scene is a little disorienting and confusing (see Figure 3.16 on p. 133). Jump cuts are also used in a later scene in which a couple is talking in a moving car and between shots the background changes in inexplicable ways. There is continuity in the conversation in the foreground (continuity of action and time) but discontinuity of settings in the back-

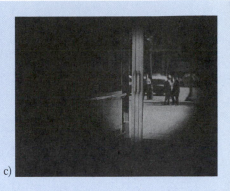

a)   b)   c)

FIGURE 7.30 Homages to another actor and to an earlier transition in film
In the French new wave film *Breathless* (1959), the main character, Michel, sometimes pays homage to American actor Humphrey Bogart. For example, in various scenes Michel runs his thumb across his lips and back as Bogart did in many films. In the last three shots of the scene represented here (beginning almost 18 1/4 minutes into the film) viewers see (a) a lobby card (photograph advertising a movie) of Bogart and (b) a shot of Michel rubbing his thumb across his lips as he looks at the lobby card. (c) The next shot ends with another homage: an iris-out, a popular optical effect used in silent films. *SNC; Fox Lorber DVD*

a)   b)

FIGURE 7.31 A source and a French new wave homage
(a) The source: the two main characters in *The Kid* (1921): Charlie Chaplin as the tramp and Jackie Coogan as the abandoned boy the tramp is raising. (b) An homage from one filmmaker (François Truffaut) to another (Chaplin): Jeanne Moreau as she appears in a brief section of Truffaut's *Jules and Jim* (1961): her shoes and mustache are reminiscent of Charlie Chaplin's in *The Kid*; her cap and sweater are like the boy's. *Publicity stills.* (a) *Charles Chaplin Productions.* (b) *Sédif Productions, Les Films du Carrosse*

ground. In *The 400 Blows* (1959), two boys emerge from a movie theater and start running; then their movement blends into a blurred horizontal image (**swish pan**) that ends by blending with the boys arriving at another movie theater. In one brief scene of *Shoot the Piano Player*, a couple is in bed; as she talks to him, five times the scene alternates with even briefer shots of them together in bed at some other time. Quite unconventionally, each of these five cutaway shots is preceded and followed by a rapid **lap**

swish pan: The shot that results when a movie camera is pivoted too rapidly during filming and blurred footage results.

dissolve: as the first shot fades out, the next shot fades in, momentarily overlapping it before replacing it.

For a student essay on the French new wave film *Jules and Jim*, see pp. 571–73.

European Independent Films

Neorealism and new wave cinema are not the only European alternatives to classical Hollywood cinema. Various films since the 1960s directed by European directors working outside the commercial mainstream—such as Jean-Luc Godard and François Truffaut (throughout their careers, not merely during their earlier new wave years), Ingmar Bergman, Federico Fellini, Michelangelo Antonioni, and Luis Buñuel—are also alternatives to classical Hollywood cinema. Sometimes these films are called art cinema, but it is more descriptive to refer to them as European independent films. Perhaps the easiest way to begin considering these films is to compare and contrast their features with the features of classical Hollywood cinema (see the list on p. 308):

1. The characters' memories, fantasies, dreams, and other mental states are rendered more often than in classical Hollywood cinema. Such films are more likely to be fragmented and are more likely to shift quickly and without explanation between different states of consciousness.

2. As in classical Hollywood cinema, the films focus on only one character or a few distinct characters.

3. Often the main characters' goals are unclear or shifting. Often the characters are ambivalent and hard to figure out (as in most films directed by Antonioni).

4. The main characters confront various antagonists or a series of problems, but the antagonists and problems are not always as evident (for example, as obviously evil) or as simple as in classical Hollywood cinema.

plotline: A series of related events, generally involving only a few characters or people, that can function as an independent story.

5. Often the films lack closure and have unresolved **plotlines**, and the protagonists do not succeed in reaching a goal (the endings are more likely to be true to life than the endings of most commercial American movies of the time).

6. The emphasis is not as emphatically on clear causes and effects of actions; ambiguity may be pervasive; and sometimes the plots are **episodic**: scenes could be shifted without changing the film substantially, as in films directed and cowritten by Jacques Tati.

narration: Commentary in a film about a subject in the film or about some other subject, usually by someone offscreen.

7. As in classical Hollywood cinema, filmmaking techniques tend to be unobtrusive, but European independent films are more likely to have authorial **narration**.

8. European independent films are more likely than classical Hollywood cinema to be **self-reflexive**, to be in part about the film medium or filmmaking or to interrupt the viewers' involvement to draw attention to themselves as films (Figure 7.32). Ingmar Bergman's *Persona* (1966) is also highly self-reflexive: on one level, it is about the nature of film and film presentation. At one point, for example, the story is interrupted with a **title card** reading "One moment please while we change **reels**," and after a **fade-out**, we see briefly only blackness and hear silence before a rapid **fade-in** introduces the next scene.

title card: A card or thin sheet of clear plastic on which is written or printed information included in a film.

reel: A metal or plastic spool to hold motion-picture film.

European independent films are also likely to stress relationships between people and to have a pace and intensity that approximate those of normal human experience, whereas the films of classical Hollywood cinema are more likely to emphasize physical action and to have a pace and intensity exceeding normal experience. The European independent cinema is also more likely to be explicit about sexuality, whereas classical Hollywood cinema is more likely to be explicit about violence.

Finally, films directed by independent European directors are much less likely to be genre films than are the films of classical Hollywood cinema. *Run Lola Run* (1998), *Amélie* (2001), *Good Bye Lenin!* (2003), and *The Lives of Others* (2006), for example, are not recognizable as any genre.

Although few films have all the characteristics described above, all European independent films have many of them. The Italian film *8 1/2* (1963)—which was directed by Federico Fellini and is partly autobiographical (Fellini himself had completed eight films before directing *8 1/2*)—exemplifies all the major features of European independent cinema. It focuses on Guido, an exhausted movie director besieged with doubts and fears about the film he is trying to complete and beset with problems with his wife and his mistress, his producer and actors, and the press (Figure 7.33).

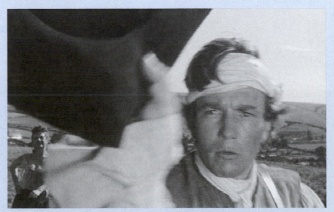

FIGURE 7.32 Self-reflexiveness
From time to time, Tony Richardson's *Tom Jones* (1963) playfully interrupts the usual, nonobtrusive representations that viewers expect in commercial movies and instead uses various untraditional techniques such as fast motion or a freeze frame. Quite a number of times, the usual agreement between filmmakers and viewers is also breached when a character briefly interrupts what she or he is doing at the moment and looks directly at the audience, sometimes saying something to the viewers, sometimes only making a gesture. Here, nearly 76 minutes into this British film adaptation of Henry Fielding's novel, Tom sees that the audience has been peeking at the partially disrobed Mrs. Waters in the background and takes it upon himself to protect her modesty by covering the camera lens with his hat and thus end that scene. *Woodfall Film Productions; MGM Home Entertainment DVD*

FIGURE 7.33 European independent film
Guido, the main character of *8 1/2* (1963), is a film director who often evades the many problems in his personal and professional lives by escaping into fantasies and memories. After his wife berates him as a liar, he retreats into two fantasies: a fantasy of his wife and mistress getting along fabulously and then a fantasy of a harem full of the important women in his present and past life. After the women in his harem temporarily rebel, he takes up a whip and quickly restores order—but then it is *Guido's* fantasy. Seen here, almost 104 1/2 minutes into the film, Guido has reestablished order (the woman sitting on his right is his wife, here consigned to be a servant). The frequent transitions from present-tense reality to fantasy or dream or memory are a feature more common in European independent films of the 1960s than in films of the classical Hollywood cinema.
Cineriz, Francinex; Criterion DVD

For an outline of the sequences of *8 1/2*, see the Web site for this book at <bedfordstmartins.com/phillips-film>.

For a discussion of a later European film movement, Dogme 95, see the Web site for this book at <bedfordstmartins.com/phillips-film>.

American Independent Cinema

American independent films since the 1960s, which tend to be relatively low budget and focus on personal relationships, originate outside the Hollywood studios and are made all over the United States, not only in southern California. Because of their low budgets, American independent films are usually made without costly directors, writers, and stars (or with personnel willing to work for a relatively small salary, a percentage of any profits, or both). An early example of American independent cinema is *Carnival of Souls* (1962, 1989), which was filmed in Lawrence, Kansas, and to a lesser extent Salt Lake City, Utah, on a very tight budget. The director had a crew of only five and only a few weeks of long, busy days to do the filming. The movie also had unknown (and sometimes limited) actors and some stilted dialogue, but it is strong on spooky organ music and occasional striking visuals, such as pairs of ghosts formally attired dancing in a huge, dark, abandoned, remote, weathered pavilion. As an early American independent film, *Carnival of Souls* exemplifies what is possible outside the Hollywood studio system of the time if the filmmakers have imagination and work hard. Another, much later example of American independent cinema is *Just Another Girl on the I.R.T.* (1992), which is a candid film about a bright 17-year-old African American living in Brooklyn who plans to go to college but gets pregnant. The movie concludes with a title card reading "A Film Hollywood Dared Not Do."

Until recent years, when corporate Hollywood saw possible new sources for profits and began to invest in or buy out small independent cinema groups, funding for an American independent film came from one of a variety of sources or, more often, a combination of sources, such as a series of maxed-out credit cards, relatives, friends, investor groups, grants, semi-independent film companies such as Fine Line, Canadian-based companies, and European TV firms. In recent years, cable TV networks such as HBO, Showtime, TNT, A&E, Lifetime, USA Networks, and Independent Film Channel have helped to finance and then show independent films. Later some of those films are shown in theaters. However, many independent films are never accepted at film festivals, and most of them that get shown never get distribution. In fact, such is the competition and the marketplace that most independent films are never shown in theaters.

So varied are American independent films that it is difficult to generalize about their subjects and techniques, as we can about neorealist films, new wave cinema, and European independent films. With lower budgets, American independent films need not draw huge crowds to turn a profit, and the filmmakers are freer to take on a controversial subject or a subject of limited interest, so independent films tend to be more varied, less formulaic, and more individualistic than films of the classical Hollywood cinema. They are more likely, for instance, to deal with a controversial subject without showing audiences what they *want* to see and to include an unhappy ending if the story has been building toward it.

Independent films such as *Night of the Living Dead* (1968), *Blood Simple* (1984, revised and rereleased in 2000), *Daughters of the Dust* (1991), *El Mariachi* (1993), and *Memento* (2000) have won awards or been nominated for awards and often secured a distributor at a major film festival such as Cannes, New York, or Sundance. Many independent films that find distribution garner excellent reviews, and some win critics' awards, like those given by the National Society of Film Critics, a group of writers for major U.S. newspapers and magazines.

Independent filmmakers have two major cooperating organizations: the Association of Independent Video and Filmmakers (AIVF) and Independent Feature Project (IFP). Both groups foster independent filmmakers and promote the independent film. Each organization also publishes a magazine: AIVF publishes *The Independent Film & Video Monthly* and IFP publishes *Filmmaker*. Each year since 1986, members of Independent Feature Project/West, one of four branches of IFP, have gained publicity for independent films by giving Independent Spirit Awards. Best feature awards for 1990 to

2007 films have gone (in order) to *The Grifters*; *Rambling Rose*; *The Player*; *Short Cuts*; *Pulp Fiction*; *Leaving Las Vegas*; *Fargo*; *The Apostle*; *Gods and Monsters*; *Election*; *Crouching Tiger, Hidden Dragon*; *Memento*; *Far from Heaven*; *Lost in Translation*; *Sideways*; *Brokeback Mountain*; *Little Miss Sunshine*; and *Juno*. Beginning with films from 2007, the Independent Spirit Awards include the Robert Altman Award for a filmmaker, casting director, and acting ensemble cast. The first winner: *I'm Not There*. With the increase of investments in independent films in recent years, budgets have grown, and the definition of an "independent film" has become less clear, so a $20 million budget cap was set for all films submitted for the 2007 Independent Spirit Awards nomination.

Two cable channels devoted solely to the independent film—the Independent Film Channel (since 1995) and the Sundance Channel (since 1996)—have also been important in promoting independent films, including fictional shorts and documentaries, from countries throughout the world.

Chapter 13 is devoted to a detailed description and analysis of an American independent film that was a winner of the Independent Spirit Award, Robert Altman's *The Player*.

Bollywood[3]

In 2001, the Hindi-language film *Lagaan* (*Tax*, sometimes called *Land Tax*) depicted the mythic formation of the first all-Indian cricket team under British colonial rule and a momentous match between Indian and British teams (Figure 7.34). After playing to packed theaters around the world, the film was nominated for an Academy Award. *Lagaan* was some viewers' first exposure to a popular Hindi film, a form that has nonetheless entertained one of the world's largest film audiences and been one of Hollywood's rivals for decades. (Previously, if Western viewers saw Indian films, they were likely directed by the Bengali master Satyajit Ray, whose realist narratives were widely viewed only by an intellectual elite within India [see Figures 1.51 and 10.1].) Also in 2001, the star-filled family melodrama *Kabhi Khushi Kabhie Gham* (*Sometimes Happiness, Sometimes Sadness*) ranked in the American top-ten box office charts, though few non–South Asians were aware of the film's sell-out run in North American theaters.

For South Asian audiences, *Lagaan* dealt with a fresh topic through a familiar formula established by the Hindi-language popular cinema produced in Bombay (now officially called Mumbai) or *Bollywood*, a term that

---

[3]Thanks to Professor Corey Creekmur of the University of Iowa for helping me write the following two sections.

FIGURE 7.34 International Bollywood hit

Lagaan: Once upon a Time in India (2001) is set in "a small [agricultural] village in the heart of India" in 1893, a time when Victoria was queen of England and the English had permanent military installations in colonial India and imposed an unpopular land tax. The film exemplifies the "masala" (spicy mix) typically found in Bollywood films. *Lagaan* devotes a lot of its nearly 4 hours running time to an underdog sports story that includes making the cricket equipment needed, recruiting a team that ends up consisting of representatives of different castes and different religions, training long and hard, and playing a three-day match in which the stakes are huge and it all comes down to the last play.

It is only you that I love

Also prominent in the film are two relationships. One involves the film's two main characters: Bhuvan on the left above and Gauri on the right. (He is about to flick her earring mischievously.) In the scene represented here, which appears nearly 2 hours into the film, Bhuvan and Gauri sing about their love for each other in a scene in which Indian audiences would recognize the pair to embody archetypes of the Hindu god Krishna and his divine consort. The film's other relationship involves an English woman who in the spirit of fair play helps the village men learn how to play cricket and ends up falling deeply in love with Bhuvan. The film also includes narration of historical background; the exposure of the arrogance, prejudice, and capriciousness of the younger British military men, particularly Captain Russell; and a story of one man's betrayal of his team and thus his village and district. *Lagaan* also gives viewers some insight into the role of religion in the village and the issues of disability and caste (the team includes an "untouchable" and a Brahmin). On a lighter note, *Lagaan* has scenes of comedy and bantering and plentiful music and dancing. But perhaps above all, the film focuses on the peerless Bhuvan, a playful, sometimes teasing Krishnaesque character with so many positive traits it would be difficult to list them all. Finally, the film includes rousing speeches but also some fresh dialogue, such as the comment the jealous Gauri makes to Bhuvan that the moment her English rival comes around, "you flutter around like a silly pigeon." *Aamir Khan Productions, Ashutosh Gowariker Productions; Columbia TriStar Home Entertainment DVD*

some use affectionately and others reject as belittling and condescending. While India actually produces popular films in many languages, including the major south Indian languages of Tamil and Telegu, and at times has supported a vibrant art or "parallel" cinema, popular Hindi cinema plays a dominant role in South Asia, similar to Hollywood's impact throughout much of the world. Hindi cinema has also consistently allowed Indian audiences to resist American cinema; in most other countries, Hollywood overwhelms local productions. Hindi cinema also has a long history of exhibition outside of India, especially in China, the Soviet Union, Africa, and the Middle East. It is the world's largest popular cinema, producing hundreds of films annually, though it remains largely unknown among mainstream North American and European audiences.

The term *Bollywood* is usually applied to recent films, but Hindi cinema extends back into the silent period. The father of Indian cinema, D. G. Phalke, began making films based on Hindu myths in 1913, and by the 1930s a vibrant film industry built around a Hollywood-style studio system was active. World War II, India's independence movement, and the 1947

Partition of India (creating the Muslim nation of Pakistan) somewhat derailed the film industry, but by the 1950s, Bombay was producing films that invoked India's ancient culture and mythology while exploring the nation's contemporary identity: Hindu epics were dramatized in "mythologicals," while contemporary issues were treated in films termed "socials."

Popular Hindi cinema resembles classical Hollywood in its reliance on melodramatic narratives and a prominent star system, but it is distinctive for its reliance on "picturized" film songs, which are a prominent element of nearly all Indian films (contributing to their often approximately 3-hour **running time**). Moreover, the songs, often with poetic lyrics, are performed not by the stars on screen but by prominent "playback singers" whose voices are often more famous than the actors they dub. Among these legendary singers, Lata Mangeshkar has provided the musical voice of Indian actresses for almost fifty years and is one of the world's most prolific recording artists. Hindi film songs are a common feature of everyday life throughout South Asia: they are heard constantly on radio and television and sung at parties, festivals, and weddings. Often seen as unnecessary intrusions by Western viewers, film songs are central to the appeal of Hindi films to their audiences: a film without hit songs is rarely successful at the box office, and film songs are fondly recalled long after many movies are forgotten.

Bollywood is also a star-driven cinema, and film heroes and heroines (as they are called) are the objects of adoration as well as endless gossip in India's many glossy movie magazines and on Web sites. Films are often tailored to the images and talents of their stars, who remain consistent in their character types.

Since a half dozen songs are a common feature of films that also include action, romance, drama, and comedy, critics have identified contemporary Hindi cinema as a "masala," or spicy mix of ingredients. More so than Hollywood movies, Bollywood films typically combine and juxtapose diverse elements for audiences seeking a feast rather than a single flavor or two or three. Subplots and digressions are common since Hindi films rarely strive for the seamless story of Hollywood films.

Bollywood films are commonly dismissed as superficial entertainment. But controversial films such as *Bombay* (1995) and *Gadar* (*Mayhem*, 2001) have explored "communal" (Hindu-Muslim) violence in India's recent history, and blockbuster family films like *Dilwale Dulhania Le Jayenge* (*The Lover Wins the Bride*, 1996) and *Hum Aapke Hain Koun … !* (*Who Am I to You?*, 1994) consider the dynamics of romance in a culture that both celebrates and increasingly questions arranged marriages. At the same time, violent gangster films such as *Satya* (*Truth*, 1998) and *Company* (2002) compete for audiences with slapstick comedies like *Hero No. 1* (1997).

Recently, independent films produced by South Asian filmmakers in North America and Britain have examined the Indian diaspora, the global movement of people who leave India and develop hybrid cultures abroad.

running time: The time that elapses when a complete film is projected.

Directors such as Mira Nair, in *Mississippi Masala* (1992) and *Monsoon Wedding* (2002), and Gurinder Chadha, in *Bhaji on the Beach* (1993) and *Bend It like Beckham* (2002), rely on popular Hindi films for **allusions** and affectionate parody, even though the international audience for these films may not recognize those sources. Even more so than *Bend It like Beckham*, Chadha's *Bride and Prejudice* (2004) seems aimed at a broad audience, not just Indians in India, not just Indians living in the U.K. and elsewhere, but also general audiences in the U.K. and the United States (Figure 7.35). At the same time, hints of Bollywood have shown up in innovative films such as *Moulin Rouge* and *Ghost World* (both 2001). On the whole, however, Western viewers, especially in the United States, are just beginning to acquaint themselves with a cinema enjoyed by close to a billion people around the globe.

allusion: A reference in a text to a person, an event, or another text.

In summary, as a popular cinema influenced by Western models, Bollywood relies on many of the same elements as classical Hollywood cinema, including goal-driven protagonists and a star system that places popular actors in familiar roles. But Bollywood films also draw on classical Indian forms to mix moods and narrative forms that Hollywood isolates. Bollywood films often combine action, romance, and comedy and most

FIGURE 7.35 **An attempt to broaden Bollywood's appeal**
Some of the promotional material for Gurinder Chadha's *Bride and Prejudice* (2004) proclaims that the film is "a classic romance . . . reinvented in a new globally connected world." The film draws on varied sources. The story and title are more or less from Jane Austen's 1813 British novel, *Pride and Prejudice*. Like the novel but with an Indian family instead, the film focuses on a family with multiple unmarried daughters and a mother eager to see them spoken for. The second oldest daughter (right, played by former Miss World and Bollywood superstar Aishwarya Rai) is not only a stunning beauty but also educated, rational, and feminist though sometimes gullible and not without pride herself. The film has four major male characters. One is an honorable London barrister of

Indian origin. A second is an Indian who had moved to California and succeeded as a materialist. The British male character is handsome but deceptive and a cad (like the corresponding character in Austen's novel, his last name, Wickham, sounds something like *wicked*). The American male character (above) initially appears as an opinionated, condescending capitalist obsessed with his financial work, but in the course of the film he broadens his outlook and eventually succeeds romantically.

In keeping with the varied cast of characters and intended audiences, the film's major locations are India, the United States, and the U.K. The music is by an Indian composer and an American composer who lives in England. Not insignificantly, the film also has plenty of aural and visual Bollywood appeal: joyful songs and lively dancing; lavish colorful costumes; and lots of big production numbers with numerous seemingly enthusiastic extras. *Publicity still. Bride Productions, Kintop Pictures, Pathé Pictures International, and UK Film Council*

notably feature elaborate song sequences using the voices of famous off-screen (or "playback") singers. Though made for popular audiences, Bollywood films are also highly self-referential and stylistically playful, breaking the rules of cinematic realism even as they involve audiences in highly emotional family melodramas.

Hong Kong Cinema

Ang Lee's *Crouching Tiger, Hidden Dragon* (2000) introduced millions of viewers to a new kind of action film and to actors Chow Yun Fat and Michelle Yeoh. The hit film was a big-budget homage to the immensely popular 1980s and 1990s movies produced in Hong Kong and starred two of that cinema's superstars. By the time *Crouching Tiger* was released, films produced in the former British colony had redefined action films worldwide. In fact, the increased demand for spectacular action in Hollywood films in recent decades suggests a belated response to Hong Kong's challenge.

Hong Kong cinema refers to the commercial film industry produced (by the 1980s) in the local Cantonese dialect, as distinguished from the *Taiwanese New Cinema* and from films produced in official Mandarin Chinese in the People's Republic of China. Popular Chinese films were produced in Shanghai before the Communist takeover in 1949, when commercial filmmaking shifted to Hong Kong. But the first Chinese movies to reach an international audience were the kung-fu or martial arts (*wuxia pian*) films produced in Hong Kong, especially those featuring the charismatic Bruce Lee, including *The Big Boss* (1971) and the international co-production *Enter the Dragon* (1973). After Lee's untimely death in 1973, the vogue for such films dwindled, but a decade later a new, reinvigorated cinema emerged from a generation of filmmakers informed by the cosmopolitan values of the highly industrialized British colony as well as Chinese tradition. After attracting local viewers and a cult audience in the West, this cinema would influence filmmakers around the world.

Although Hong Kong continued to produce films in a range of genres, including comedies and romances, its most popular and influential films emphasize dynamic action, either in martial arts competition or urban gun battles. In groundbreaking films such as *Peking Opera Blues* (1985) and *Once upon a Time in China* (1990), director Tsui Hark staged wildly inventive fight scenes, often relying on the "wire work" that allowed his warriors to defy gravity. (Hong Kong's stunts do not adhere to the realism Western viewers often expect.) John Woo's "heroic bloodshed" films, beginning with *A Better Tomorrow* (1985) and including *The Killer* (1989) and *Hard-Boiled* (1991), all starred the suave Chow Yun Fat and stunned audiences with their highly stylized violence and operatic emotions (Figure 7.36). During the same era, the actor-director Jackie Chan became a superstar by combining his kinetic martial arts skills with ingenious comic stunts (sometimes reminiscent of the stunts of the silent-era superstars Charlie

Chaplin and Buster Keaton) in films like *Project A* (1982) and *Police Story* (1985, Figure 7.37).

Hong Kong action films are characterized not just by the action on screen but by their relentless stylistic energy. Quickly paced, the films can leave audiences breathless. The films often switch moods suddenly, from high tragedy to low comedy, and display a playful visual style through an accumulation of bizarre angles, distorted close-ups, and jarring perspectives,

FIGURE 7.36 Hong Kong action cinema

The Killer (1989), which was written and directed by John Woo several years before he made his first U.S. movie, was filmed in Hong Kong. It stars Chow Yun Fat as Jeff (his name in the English language version), an ace hitman with a conscience, sense of style, and strong convictions about friendship and honor. Although *The Killer* includes numerous chases on foot, in boats, and in a variety of motorized vehicles and more than a few loud, fast-paced, stylized killings (one observer counted 120!), it also has three male characters developed in some depth, especially Jeff. As Inspector Li, one of the other three main male leads, says of him, "He looks determined without being ruthless. . . . He doesn't look like a killer. He comes across so calm, acts like he has a dream, eyes filled with passion." As seen here, 44 minutes into the film, Jeff looks to be in a bad way, but he's actually testing the honor and friendship of the man holding that humongous gun. *Tsui Hark; Film Workshop Co., Ltd.; Fox Lobner DVD*

FIGURE 7.37 Jackie Chan's Hong Kong cinema

In *Police Story* (aka *Jackie Chan's Police Force*, 1985), Chan directs the film, functions as the stunt coordinator and fight choreographer, and plays the main role of Ka Kui ("Kevin" in at least one other version of the film), an honorable Hong Kong police officer beset with problems. In pursuit of a drug baron, Ka Kui had snatched a woman's umbrella, chased a speeding bus, hooked onto the back of it, is briefly dragged along, and here, about 13 1/2 minutes into the film, starts to pull himself up and soon gets into the bus, fights off the drug baron's henchmen, and arrests the man. The action is typical of Jackie Chan's inventiveness and athleticism. *Police Story* also includes an abundance of cartoonish violence, situations where damage and danger multiply, people fight fiercely, yet no one seems to suffer any pain that the audience would take seriously. The film's frequent verbal and physical humor, often at Ka Kui's expense, illustrates the dictum that comedy is a man in trouble. Ka Kui has girlfriend problems (she wrongly assumes that he is unfaithful) and work difficulties (at one point, he even kidnaps the police superintendent at gunpoint). And although Ka Kui is shown to be capable of extraordinary agility, strength, and gracefulness (as in the image seen above), he is often amusingly awkward with people and objects. *Paragon Films, Golden Way Films; Weinstein Company Home Entertainment DVD*

such as the point of view of a bullet leaving a gun and passing through a body in Ringo Lam's *Full Contact* (1992). Hong Kong films are also full of allusions to and parodies of previous films, rewarding loyal fans with the sort of self-reflexivity often associated with art cinema rather than popular entertainment. The lush sounds of local Canto-pop music also link the films to Hong Kong's youth culture, and many of the stars of Hong Kong films also have careers as popular singers.

Contemporary Hong Kong cinema clearly shows Hollywood's influence, especially in its reliance on streamlined plots and conventional genres such as comedies and gangster films. But in drawing on more traditional Chinese elements, such as martial arts and Chinese opera, Hong Kong action films often feature highly stylized action, achieved through rapid editing, surprising camera positions, and the dynamic choreography of actors and camera movement. Hong Kong films thus seek to startle, amuse, and jolt audiences, often at the expense of believability.

Along with outrageous comedies and blood-drenched gangster sagas, Hong Kong has allowed for the production of more subtle films, such as Clara Law's *Song of the Exile* (1990) and Stanley Kwan's *Center Stage* (aka *Actress*, 1989), starring Maggie Cheung as the actual 1930s Shanghai star Ruan Lingyu. Hong Kong's most distinctive filmmaker is perhaps Wong Kar-Wai, whose portraits of urban ennui in *Chungking Express* (1994) and *In the Mood for Love* (2000) reduce narrative to a minimum while featuring restrained performances (achieved through improvisation with actors), lush images, and inventive soundtracks. His distinctive technique of blurring images (developed with cinematographer Christopher Doyle) makes his films resemble modern paintings as much as photographic images.

Since the expiration of Great Britain's 99-year lease on Hong Kong in 1997, the return of sovereignty to China, and a severe economic recession in 1999, Hong Kong cinema has scaled back. Many of its most prominent figures—including stars Jackie Chan, Jet Li, and Chow Yun Fat and director John Woo—have established careers in the United States, though many of their fans think their Hollywood films haven't matched the quality of their earlier work. Meanwhile, the influence of Hong Kong cinema is evident in such films as the French art film *Irma Vep* (1996), starring Maggie Cheung as herself; the Hollywood sci-fi action kung-fu film *The Matrix* (1999; see Figure 7.25); *X-Men* (2000); and *Kill Bill, Volume 2* (2004). More recently, Martin Scorsese's *The Departed* (2006) is a reworking of a popular 2002 Hong Kong movie, *Infernal Affairs*. Retaining some independence as a commercial cinema, recent Hong Kong films are again exploring their simultaneously Chinese and international identities in stories that allude to recent history and politics. Despite fears that Hong Kong's popular cinema would disappear under China's administration of the island, creative work continues to appear.

● ● ●

Classical Hollywood cinema is so much a part of the world that most of us were born into and grew up in that many viewers do not easily adapt to other cinemas. Initially other films seem odd and perhaps too demanding. But in seeing more of these films, studying them, and learning about the contexts in which they are created, many viewers come to enjoy and appreciate them and to broaden their understanding of the possibilities and achievements of the fictional film.

CLOSE-UP: *OUT OF THE PAST* AS FILM NOIR (STUDENT ESSAY)

by Zach Finch

[*Out of the Past* (1947) has a complicated plot. If you have not seen the film recently, please study Figure 6.21 on p. 286 before you read this essay.]

Out of the Past exhibits many characteristics of film noir, such as dark, shadowy cinematography; urban settings; complex and flawed main male characters; a complex, flawed femme fatale; and a protagonist who is a loner and emotionally restrained.

Dark lighting and prominent shadows permeate many films noirs. *Out of the Past* is no exception. Films noirs focus on the darker side of human nature, and the cinematography is appropriately dark. In *Out of the Past*, the darkness of the San Francisco scenes contrasts with the bright lighting of the exterior scenes in Mexico and the exteriors of the small California town where Jeff lives. In Mexico, Jeff says of Kathie, the film's femme fatale, "I never saw her in the daytime. She seemed to live by night." The dark lighting is appropriate for dark dealings such as double-crossing, revenge, and murder.

In *Somewhere in the Night: Film Noir and the American City*, Nicholas Christopher points out similarities between the city setting of a film noir and Greek mythology's labyrinth. In Greek mythology, Theseus enters the labyrinth, attempts to reach the center, but finds that the way is impossibly hard with many traps, twists, turns, and confusing passageways. Similarly, the protagonist of a film noir tries to find his way through the city's figurative twists and turns, and the barriers of deception and double-crossing that he encounters are reminiscent of a labyrinth. Often the protago-

nist is caught in this labyrinth only to discover that it has no center and that he is playing a small role in a game he understands only slightly (7–8). In *Out of the Past*, San Francisco serves as the labyrinth that Jeff returns to after leaving his previous life in the dark of San Francisco for a quiet, brightly illuminated, small-town existence where he could easily find his way around. Early in the film, a former colleague recognizes Jeff pumping gas, and Jeff is soon forced to reenter a dark world. When Ann, Jeff's small-town girlfriend, accompanies him to Whit's home and drives away, Jeff must confront the consequences of his past by himself: find his way through a dark, treacherous big-city labyrinth and then cope with Whit and Kathie.

In film noir, the main male players are complex and flawed. Their motivations tend to be greed, self-interest, and ambition. These motivations fuel threats of blackmail, double-crossing, and convoluted plots. In *Out of the Past*, Whit hires Jeff to find Kathie and bring her back; however, when Jeff finds her in Acapulco, he decides to keep her for himself. When Jeff and Kathie return from Mexico and go to California, Jeff's old partner tries to blackmail the couple. Whit is obviously flawed too: he is a tax cheat who employs dense, thuggish hit men like Joe and plans to frame Jeff for a murder.

The noir femme fatale is also complex and flawed. Her power lies in her cold, calculating intellect and her sexual appeal to men. Even if the protagonist knows that she is bad news, her sexual allure and guile are usually too much for him. When Jeff finds Kathie in Mexico, he is instantly enchanted by her even though he knows that she has recently tried to kill Whit. The femme fatale sees the protagonist as a means to achieve her goals. Early in the film, Kathie uses Jeff to distance herself from Whit. Throughout the film, she deceives both Jeff and Whit. She lies to cover up her own crimes and switches sides without blinking. During a moment of clarity, Jeff says she's like a leaf that is blown by the wind from one gutter to another. Should the femme fatale's powers of persuasion fail her, she may resort to violence. Before she is finished, Kathie, who has outbursts of temper, shoots and kills three men.

The loner and "tough guy" protagonist of a film noir is also characteristic of the genre. These characters are generally men in their thirties or forties. Like Jeff, they are almost always unmarried. Jeff has a male working partner but seems to not particularly like or respect him, and Jeff is seen always working alone and spending a lot of time alone. There is no indication he has family or friends other than Ann and perhaps the mute young man who works for him. The typical film noir protagonist also reins in his emotions and exudes a "tough guy" image. Jeff rarely shows anything more than a poker face and rarely confides his private thoughts or feelings to anyone, so his personal thoughts and emotions remain shrouded in mystery.

In these and other ways, *Out of the Past* remains an illuminating example of film noir.

Works Consulted

Christopher, Nicholas. *Somewhere in the Night: Film Noir and the American City*. New York: Holt, 1998.

Phillips, William H. *Film: An Introduction*. 3rd ed. New York: Bedford/St. Martin's, 2005.

SUMMARY

Most fictional films, including foreign films and animated stories, exhibit the major characteristics of classical Hollywood cinema. Alternatives to classical Hollywood cinema include Italian neorealist cinema, French new wave cinema, European and American independent films from the 1960s to the present, Bollywood, and Hong Kong cinema.

Classical Hollywood Cinema

- Throughout the world, classical Hollywood cinema has been the most influential group of fictional films.

- Such films show one or more characters who face a series of problems in reaching a goal or goals. These films stress continuity and the clear causes and effects of actions, and they tend to use unobtrusive filmmaking techniques.

- A film genre is a commonly recognized group of fictional films that share characteristics that both filmmakers and audiences recognize as making the films members of the group.

- Three widely studied film genres are the western, film noir, and the musical. Traditionally the western features civilization versus the wilderness and is set west of the Mississippi River, in northern Mexico, or in the Canadian Rockies.

- Film noir features scenes with low illumination, convoluted plots, and complex, flawed characters caught up in crime.

- Musicals always give prominence to intermittent music and often also dance, but there are no restrictions on the types of music used or on the settings and the subjects of their stories.

- A genre film may be traditional or revisionist. Most westerns made since about 1950, for example, are revisionist and vary widely from the traditional western.

- Occasionally, a film parodies a genre. Or a film may combine elements of two or more genres, such as horror and science fiction, or western and musical.

Other Cinemas

- Italian neorealist films, French new wave cinema, the European independent cinema since the 1960s, many American independent films since the 1960s, Bollywood, and Hong Kong cinema offer alternatives to classical Hollywood cinema.

- Neorealism was a film movement in Italy during and after World War II. Neorealist films, which are a mixture of scripted and actual situations, are located for the most part in real settings and show ordinary and believable characters caught up in difficult social and economic conditions, such as poverty and unemployment.

- French new wave films were a diverse group of fictional films made in the late 1950s and early 1960s in reaction to the carefully scripted products of the French film industry of the time and as explorations of more current subjects sometimes rendered with untraditional filmmaking techniques.

- Since the 1960s, films directed by such Europeans as Ingmar Bergman, Federico Fellini, Michelangelo Antonioni, and Luis Buñuel also have been alternatives to classical Hollywood cinema. These films are likely to have a pace and intensity that approximate those of normal human experience. Compared to classical Hollywood cinema, they are more likely to be explicit about sexuality, less likely to be explicit about violence, less likely to belong to a genre, and more likely to be self-reflexive.

- Since the late 1960s, American independent fictional films have been made all over the United States, not just in southern California. They have smaller budgets than their Hollywood counterparts, are free or freer of Hollywood studio creative control, and tend to be more varied and less formulaic than classical Hollywood cinema.

- Bollywood (India's Hindi-language popular cinema) is the most prominent component of the world's largest film industry. Bollywood films typically offer a full mix of drama, action, comedy, and romance, with prominent songs an especially vital element. Often rooted in Indian mythology while exploiting current trends, Bollywood films display India's balance of tradition and modern life, often through highly melodramatic plots involving multigenerational families. Like Hollywood in its heyday, Bollywood films rely on a star system that features favorite actors in familiar roles.

- As a popular cinema, Hong Kong action films resemble Hollywood movies in their reliance on character-driven and goal-oriented plots, as well as familiar genres and stars. But Hong Kong films also draw on traditional Chinese elements, such as martial arts, and often rely on a highly kinetic style that breaks the bounds of realism. Hong Kong cinema's over-the-top action scenes and sudden shifts into low comedy seek to startle and jolt viewers rather than represent a convincing reality.

Major Terms about Types of Fictional Films

Below, numbers in italics refer to the pages where the terms are explained. All terms are defined in more detail in the Illustrated Glossary beginning on p. 667.

Bollywood *344*
classical Hollywood cinema *308*
film movement *333*
film noir *319*
French new wave cinema *337*

genre *310*
Hong Kong cinema *348*
independent film *340, 342*
Italian neorealism *334*
revisionist *313*

QUESTIONS ABOUT TYPES OF FICTIONAL FILMS

The following questions are intended to help viewers understand some of the many types of fictional films. Not all the questions are appropriate for every film. In thinking out, discussing, and writing responses to the questions most appropriate for the film being examined, be careful to stick with the issues the questions raise, to answer all parts of the questions, to explain the reasons for your answers, and to give specific examples from the film.

1. If the film is fictional, how may it be further classified—as classical Hollywood cinema or in some ways an alternative to it? Why do you say so?

2. If the film is a genre film—such as a western, musical, or horror film—consider the following questions:

    a. What major similarities and differences does the film have with earlier films of the same genre?

    b. Is the film revisionist? If so, explain in what ways.

    c. Is the film typical of its genre in some ways but atypical in others? If so, explain.

    d. Is the film a parody of earlier films of the same genre? In what ways does it imitate earlier films of the same genre? In what ways does it treat the subject(s) humorously? What conventions of the genre does the parody make fun of?

    e. Is the film a combination of genres? If so, explain which genres and which features of them the film incorporates.

3. If the film is an alternative to classical Hollywood cinema—for example, Italian neorealism, Bollywood, or a Hong Kong action film—consider the following questions:

    a. In what major ways is the film like classical Hollywood cinema, and in what major ways is it unlike classical Hollywood cinema?

    b. In what major ways is the film like and unlike earlier examples of the same type of alternative to classical Hollywood cinema?

WORKS CITED

Altman, Rick. *Film/Genre*. London: British Film Institute, 1999.

Andrew, Dudley. *Concepts in Film Theory*. New York: Oxford UP, 1984.

Armes, Roy. *French Cinema*. New York: Oxford UP, 1985.

———. *Patterns of Realism: A Study of Italian Neo-Realist Cinema*. Cranbury, NJ: Barnes, 1971.

Baldi, Ferdinando. Interview in the 2005 Independent Film Channel documentary *The Spaghetti West* (quotation begins 15 minutes and 40 seconds into the film).

Bordwell, David, Janet Staiger, and Kristin Thompson. *The Classical Hollywood Cinema: Film Style and Mode of Production to 1960*. New York: Columbia UP, 1985.

Christopher, Nicholas. *Somewhere in the Night: Film Noir and the American City*. New York: Holt, 1998.

Cook, David A. *A History of Narrative Film*. 4th ed. New York: Norton, 2004.

Hayward, Susan. *Cinema Studies: The Key Concepts*. 2nd ed. London: Routledge, 2000.

Hirsch, Foster. *Detours and Lost Highways: A Map of Neo-Noir*. New York: Limelight, 1999.

Ingalls, Zoë. "Notes from Academe." *Chronicle of Higher Education* 12 Nov. 1999: B2.

Knee, Adam. "The Compound Genre Film: *Billy the Kid versus Dracula* Meets *The Harvey Girls*." *Intertextuality in Literature and Film: Selected Papers from the Thirteenth Florida State University Conference on Literature and Film*. Ed. Elaine D. Cancalon and Antoine Spacagna. Gainesville: UP of Florida, 1994. 141–56.

Krutnik, Frank. *In a Lonely Street: Film Noir, Genre, Masculinity*. New York: Routledge, 1991.

Lenihan, John H. *Showdown: Confronting Modern America in the Western Film*. Urbana: U of Illinois P, 1980.

Lyman, Rick. "Robert Altman, Director with Daring, Dies at 81." *New York Times on the Web* 22 Nov. 2006.

McCarthy, Todd. "Introduction." In John Alton, *Painting with Light*. Berkeley: U of California P, 1995.

Moreau, Jeanne. Interview. *Morning Edition*. Nat'l. Public Radio. 11 Mar. 1994.

Musser, Charles. "The Innovators 1900–1910." *Sight and Sound* ns 9.3 (Mar. 1999): 16–18.

Phillips, William H. "Neorealist Cinema." *Benét's Reader's Encyclopedia*. 3rd ed. Ed. Katherine Baker Siepmann. New York: Harper, 1987.

Shulman, Ken. "From a Vanished Country, a Viewable Cold-War Archive." *New York Times on the Web* 26 Oct. 1997: Arts and Leisure sec.

Telotte, J. P. *Voices in the Dark: The Narrative Patterns of Film Noir*. Urbana: U of Illinois P, 1989.

Turner, Graeme. *Film as Social Practice*. 4th ed. London: Routledge, 2006.

FOR FURTHER READING

Altman, Rick. *The American Film Musical*. Bloomington: Indiana UP, 1999. Nine chapters on theory of genre analysis, dual-focus narrative, structure, style, genre history, fairy-tale musicals, show musicals, folk musicals, and genre and culture.

Bordwell, David. *Planet Hong Kong: Popular Culture and the Art of Entertainment*. Cambridge: Harvard UP, 2000. An appreciative and detailed analysis of the form and style of Hong Kong cinema.

Film Genre Reader III. Ed. Barry Keith Grant. Austin: U of Texas P, 2003. A wide variety of essays by a variety of film scholars, stills, and bibliography.

Gopalan, Lalitha. *Cinema of Interruptions: Action Genres in Contemporary Indian Cinema*. London: British Film Institute, 2002. Close readings of specific films and filmmakers, emphasizing interactions between Indian narrative forms and international genres such as the gangster film.

Hollywood Musicals, The Film Reader. Ed. Steven Cohan. New York: Routledge, 2002. Each of the book's sections explores a central issue of the musical, including the musical's significance as a genre, the musical's own particular representation of sexual difference, and the displacement of race in Hollywood's representations of entertainment.

Kabir, Nasreen Munni. *Bollywood: The Indian Cinema Story*. London: Channel 4 Books, 2001. An introductory overview based on interviews with industry insiders.

Larkin, Colin. *The Virgin Encyclopedia of Stage and Film Musicals*. London: Virgin, 1999. A 680-page one-volume encyclopedia covering both American and British musicals that traces the history of the genre from Busby Berkeley to Andrew Lloyd Webber.

Levy, Emanuel. *Cinema of Outsiders: The Rise of American Independent Film*. New York: New York UP, 1999. Surveys the major cycles in the indie film movement from the late 1970s to 1999, including regional cinema, the New York school of film, African American, Asian American, gay and lesbian, and movies made by women.

Neupert, Richard. *A History of the French New Wave Cinema*. Madison: U of Wisconsin P, 2003. Captures the dramatic impact these films made on their release, closely examining such movies as *The 400 Blows* and *Breathless* as well as many less studied films.

Pierson, John. *Spike, Mike, Slackers and Dykes: A Guided Tour across a Decade of American Independent Cinema*. New York: Miramax/Hyperion, 1995. An introduction to American independent films from 1984 to 1994 by someone involved in their making and marketing. Appendix I lists all American independent features from late 1984 to 1993.

Prats, Armando José. *Invisible Natives: Myth and Identity in the American Western*. Ithaca, NY: Cornell UP, 2002. A study of the representation of Native Americans in the western film since the genre's beginnings. Certain films—such as *Stagecoach*, *The Searchers*, and *Dances with Wolves*—are discussed at length.

Stokes, Lisa Odham, and Michael Hoover. *City on Fire: Hong Kong Cinema*. New York: Verso, 1999. A study of Hong Kong cinema emphasizing social and political contexts.

Teo, Stephen. *Hong Kong Cinema: The Extra Dimensions*. London: British Film Institute, 1997. A history of Hong Kong cinema up to 1997, with full filmographies for major figures.

Thompson, Kristin. *Storytelling in the New Hollywood: Understanding Classical Narrative Technique*. Cambridge: Harvard UP, 1999. Argues that Hollywood's storytelling techniques are still used to make complex, clear, entertaining movies that are based on the narrative system used by earlier generations of Hollywood filmmakers.

Virdi, Jyotika. *The Cinematic ImagiNation: Indian Popular Films as Social History*. New Brunswick, NJ: Rutgers UP, 2003. A study of postindependence cinema in terms of nationality with particular attention to representations of gender and sexuality.

Westerns: Films through History. Ed. Janet Walker. New York: Routledge, 2001. Leading scholars unpack the ways in which westerns have embellished, mythologized, and erased past events. Essays also explore how the genre addresses key issues of biography, authenticity, race, and representation.

Part Three
ALTERNATIVES TO LIVE-ACTION FICTIONAL FILMS

S O FAR, WE HAVE STUDIED the expressiveness of film techniques and the sources, components, and types of fictional films. Part Three discusses some alternatives to live-action fictional films. Chapter 8 introduces the documentary film, and Chapter 9 explores experimental, hybrid, and animated films.

Examining a variety of films helps us understand the film medium more fully: the properties, techniques, forms, and possible effects of different films. The film medium is far more inclusive and diverse than what is found on the screens of the nearest multiplex, in the neighboring video store, on movie channels, and in music videos. Viewers who have studied alternatives to mainstream movies are more likely to avoid overgeneralizing about the film medium. A film, for example, does not always

◄ *Witchcraft through the Ages* (*Häxan*), which was directed by the Dane Benjamin Christensen and made in Sweden in 1922, illustrates how varied a film can be and how problematic it can be to classify one. *Witchcraft through the Ages* combines elements of narrative and nonnarrative, of documentary film and experimental film, and of realism with surrealism as it re-creates and illustrates a variety of historical and contemporary manifestations of witchcraft and witch-hunting. The film abounds with information for students of witchcraft and memorable expressive images for students of film. Seen here is one of the film's most famous and most striking images: a re-creation of part of a witches' Sabbath as the lascivious bearded Satan leans over a woman to embrace her as she reaches up to embrace him and presumably surrender herself to him. This scene like various others before and after it is a dramatization of an old woman's "confession" that she is a witch, a "confession" that medieval Catholic monks extract from her with torture and the threat of even more torture. *Svensk Filmindustri; The Museum of Modern Art/Film Stills Archive*

361

last 80 to 180 minutes and convey a fictional story. Indeed, a film does not even necessarily aspire to coherence, completeness, and popularity. As the next two chapters demonstrate, film has been and is much more.

 Links to a variety of sources, including supplementary readings and short films, are available for each chapter on the Web site for this book at <bedfordstmartins.com/phillips-film>.

CHAPTER 8

Documentary Films

D OCUMENTARIES, which are more or less films about reality, are actually not considered by most people to be real films, but Hollywood films, which usually have an extremely high fantasy quotient, are considered to be real.
— Ross McElwee's **narration** in his documentary *Six O'Clock News* (1997)

Terms in **boldface** are defined in the Illustrated Glossary beginning on page 667.

narration: Commentary in a film about a subject in the film or about some other subject, usually by someone offscreen.

Every summer since 1988, the U.S. Public Television's series *Point of View* (aka *P.O.V.*) has shown a series of documentary films. Since early in 2006, the Documentary Channel has been broadcasting documentaries 24/7. Cable television networks — such as HBO, the History Channel, Discovery Channel, and Bravo — have financed and shown many documentaries. Bell Auditorium at the University of Minnesota became the first U.S. theater to show only documentary films. Film festivals such as Sundance are swamped with submissions of documentary films, many of them later praised as among the festival's highlights. The Full Frame Documentary Film Festival, the Hot Springs Documentary Film Festival, the Yamagata (Japan) Documentary Film Festival, and other film festivals are all devoted exclusively to the documentary. Magazines such as *Dox* focus on the documentary film. The magazine *Documentary* is published by the International Documentary Association, which also champions the documentary film on its Web site. Numerous academic conferences and articles in scholarly journals are devoted to studying documentaries. Many books are being written about the subject. College and university courses are devoted to it. Some U.S. graduate programs in "documentary media studies" and "documentary production studies" have begun in recent years. Students in introduction to film courses are increasingly shown documentary films. In my courses, they rate such documentary films as *The Thin Blue Line* (1988), *Hearts of Darkness: A Filmmaker's Apocalypse* (1991), *Hoop Dreams* (1994), *The Celluloid Closet* (1996), *Fast, Cheap & Out of Control* (1997), and *The Fog of War: Eleven Lessons from the Life of Robert S. McNamara* (2003) among their course favorites. More than ever, documentary films are being made, seen, promoted, studied, and enjoyed. They are a major alternative to the fictional films discussed in the previous chapters, and they deserve their own chapter.

This chapter explores four questions: What are documentary films? What might documentaries do? What steps might be taken to construct them? How does filmmaking technology affect the documentary films made?

WHAT ARE DOCUMENTARY FILMS?

Definition

representation: A likeness of a subject created in a text.

footage: A length of exposed motion-picture film.

Anyone who has seen a wide variety of documentaries has a good sense of what a documentary film is, yet because of their immense variety, coming up with a precise definition is difficult. In this book, the term **documentary film** refers to a film or video **representation** of actual (not imaginary) subjects. Documentary filmmakers select what subjects to film and in what ways (or they select from existing **footage**, or they combine footage that they **shot** with footage shot by others). Sometimes documentary filmmakers stage or re-create situations; and they nearly always **edit** the resultant footage. As this chapter illustrates, "Documentaries adopt no fixed inventory of [**filmmaking**] **techniques**, address no one set of issues [or subjects], display no single set of forms or **styles**" (Nichols 21).

style: The way that subjects are represented in a text, such as a film.

Documentary films are sometimes referred to as *nonfiction films*. I prefer the older and more widely understood term *documentary films* because *nonfiction films* identifies this group of films not by what they are but by what they are *not* (they are *not* fiction). Also, *nonfiction film* suggests that this type of film is the opposite of fictional films, whereas, as we will see, a documentary may have much in common with fictional films.

Mediated Reality

> In every documentary, every edit you make, every choice you make is yours, the filmmaker's judgment call.
> —Michael Apted, director of the *Up* series of documentaries (2007)

According to many critics, documentary films are mediated reality. *Mediate* can mean to work as an intermediary between two sides or to function as a go-between. The following diagram visualizes how the documentary film mediates between reality and the viewer:

$$\text{reality} \rightarrow \text{documentary film} \rightarrow \text{viewer}$$

The documentary is not reality. It is an intermediary between reality and the viewer.

running time: The time that elapses when a complete film is projected.

A documentary film may *seem* to represent reality objectively, but it does not. Consider Frederick Wiseman's documentary *Belfast, Maine* (1999), which has a **running time** of slightly over 4 hours and shows different aspects of life in and near the seacoast town of Belfast, Maine (such as a social worker picking lice out of a woman's hair and a high school English teacher lecturing on *Moby Dick*). The film has no narration, no interviews, no **title cards**, and no music that does not derive from a source shown in the film. The opening title card does not cue viewers about the film to come. In plain lettering, it simply announces the film title.

At first glance, the filmmakers seem only to have selected the subjects, filmed them, and selected the footage to include. However, in constructing the film, the filmmakers made many significant decisions that influenced the outcome and viewers' responses to the film. For example, the film-makers selected which subjects to film and which to ignore. They selected the time of year in which to film (autumn) and often the time of day (many **shots** were filmed in the morning hours or in the late afternoon, when objects outdoors are bathed in flattering **soft light**). They decided how many shots would be of **locations** without people, which shots would be of run-down or even polluted areas, and which would not. For each shot, they decided camera location, distance from subject, and lens. They decided how long to hold a shot, when to use a **zoom lens** (rarely in this film), and when to move the camera during a shot (also rarely).

Later, the filmmakers decided which shots to include and their dura-tion, the order of shots, and the transitions between them (one black screen of a few seconds, otherwise only **cuts**). During 14 months of editing, 110 hours of footage was fashioned into the 4-hour film. During editing, prob-ably whole sections that had been filmed were dropped. Often a section begins with one or two **establishing shots**, frequently including a build-ing's identifying sign; sometimes an identifying sign is seen in a section's concluding shot. During the editing, decisions also were made about where to include **reaction shots** and how often, as during a lawyer's presentation to the Belfast city council. The filmmakers decided the order and duration of each major section and the **pacing** of the parts and of the whole film. In addition, they decided what sounds would be prominent (the many sounds of motorized vehicles, for example, remind viewers that even in this small town and surrounding area, motorized vehicles are an integral part of life). The filmmakers also decided to occasionally use sound from a source before we viewers see the source, and to carry over a sound from one location into the following one.

Documentary films like *Belfast, Maine* might seem to be simple, straight-forward representations of reality, but they are actually complex mediations of reality. A documentary film is never an objective, indisputable truth. Rather, it is the product of the selections, recordings, and manipulations of one group of filmmakers.

Another documentary in which the mediation of reality is not readily apparent is the French documentary *To Be and To Have* (2002). Viewers might assume that all the filmmakers had to do was select the human subjects and the **exterior** and **interior** locations, film them, include one or more interviews, and then decide what footage to include in the final

---

title card: A card or thin sheet of clear plastic on which is written or printed information included in a film.

shot (noun): An uninterrupted strip of exposed motion-picture film or videotape that represents a subject during an uninter-rupted segment of time.

zoom lens: A camera lens with variable focal lengths that can be adjusted by degrees dur-ing a shot so that the size of the subject and the size of the area being filmed both change.

cut (noun): A transition between shots that is made by splicing or joining the end of one shot to the beginning of the next.

pace: The rate of speed at which the film's subjects (such as events in a narrative film or information in a documentary film) are revealed.

version. The whole process might seem straightforward. But it was not (Figure 8.1).

Marcello Mastroianni . . . I Remember (1999) provides another example of mediated reality. The film focuses on the Italian actor's stage and film acting, his films, his travels and thoughts about various cities, and his work with different directors. Mastroianni himself supplies all the narration. The film includes no interviews with family, friends, or filmmaking colleagues and little information about his adult personality. Unaddressed are many questions: Was Mastroianni easy to work with? Was he aloof in his personal life? Was he as modest and charming **offscreen** as in interviews and in his narration of the documentary? What was he like when he was not making a movie? Was he ever married? Who was the mother of his daughter? Was he close to his daughter? The director and editor of the film, Mastroianni's companion of more than two decades, decided to focus on his films and filmmaking and largely avoid his personal life and any perspective other than his and hers. Is the film the objective truth about Marcello Mastroianni? Not at all. Rather, it is largely or perhaps entirely the perspective of one person — and a biased person at that, his companion of more than two decades.

Other documentarians make changes in a film's subject before filming it (Figure 8.2). The director of *Crumb* (1994), which is a documentary about cartoonist Robert Crumb, also fudged some of the details. An interviewer on the Sundance Channel observed that a large wall cabinet full of 78-rpm records in Terry Zwigoff's house looked a lot like Crumb's record cabinet. Zwigoff responded, "We actually shot fake scenes in this room where he's [Crumb's] sitting here with, like, a drawing board and we moved this lamp

offscreen: The area beyond the frame line.

FIGURE 8.1 More mediation of reality than viewers can know
To Be and To Have (2002) is a French documentary about a grade school teacher (seen here trying to help a student) and the teacher's small class in a rural school. As in the making of perhaps all documentary films, the making of *To Be and To Have* involved more manipulation of the materials than viewers can realize. Beginning 8 3/4 minutes into an interview included with the U.S. DVD release of the film, the film's director, Nicolas Philibert, confides, "Certain sequences occurred spontaneously. Others were more constructed. It depended on the situation. . . . People often say of documentaries that what makes them exciting is that reality does not repeat itself. That it has to be recorded in a single take. Whereas with fiction, you can do it over a hundred times. That's not entirely true. . . . If I wasn't satisfied with a scene, I could usually do it over. . . . There are also a few scenes I suggested. . . . For instance, when the teacher talks about his retirement. But it only works . . . if it also could have occurred without my input." *Maïa Films, Arte France Cinéma, Les Films d'Ici, Centre National de Documentation Pédagogique, and others; New Yorker Video DVD*

that used to be in his house over here, and this [indicating Zwigoff's record cabinet] is the background. We faked it for his house because we didn't want to drive back up there." Near the beginning of cinema, in Edison's "The Execution of Mary, Queen of Scots" (1895), the filmmakers wisely substituted a dummy for the person enacting Queen Mary immediately before the beheading. Since then, countless documentary filmmakers have staged actions or re-created them or in other ways changed details about the way things were.

Some filmmakers change the order of presentation through editing. A title card at the beginning of *Dead Birds* (1963), a film about the lifestyles of similar warring New Guinea tribes, states that the film "is a true story composed from footage of actual **events** photographed. . . . No scene was directed and no role was created. The people in the film merely did what they had done before we came and, for those who are not dead, as they do now that we have left." Yet the director Robert Gardner later wrote that the film has "compressions of time which exclude vast portions of actuality. There are events made parallel in time which occurred sequentially" (346–47).

Like fictional filmmakers, for various reasons—including the need to save time and money or to show something judged important in an engaging way—documentary makers sometimes fudge the details. Sometimes a lot of them.

WHAT MIGHT DOCUMENTARIES DO?

Documentaries tend to inform, entertain, criticize (and sometimes try to motivate viewers to take certain actions), and celebrate.

Inform

All documentaries inform. Viewers watching Errol Morris's *The Thin Blue Line* learn about the circumstances of a man wrongly imprisoned for

a)

b)

FIGURE 8.2 More mediation of reality in the making of a documentary
While making *Nanook of the North* (1922, restored 1976), director Robert Flaherty took many liberties with his subjects, a small group of Canadian Inuits, including asking them to restage or modify their behavior or the world they live in. For example, Flaherty found that the igloos were too small to accommodate his bulky 35 mm camera and tripod and too dim to provide enough light for filming, so for certain shots he had the Inuits build a larger igloo without a top. (a) *Frame enlargement. Revillon Frères; The Museum of Modern Art/Circulating Film Library.* (b) *Production still. The Museum of Modern Art/Film Stills Archive*

murdering a Dallas police officer and about the man who probably committed the crime. Viewers watching *Standing in the Shadows of Motown* (2002) can learn about the role that an unheralded group of backup musicians played in many popular recordings from an earlier era. And viewers watching the short documentary "A Girl like Me" (2005) learn that high school filmmaker Kiri Davis's interviews with Harlem 4- or 5-year-olds reveal that some racial attitudes may be much the same as those that were expressed when a similar test was conducted in 1954 (see Plate 41 in Chapter 13).

Entertain

Documentaries are nearly always meant to entertain. Most filmmakers know that they must entertain and hold viewer interest if they are to achieve any other goals. Thus, for *The Thin Blue Line*, director Errol Morris made sure that the images, music, editing, interviews, and investigative story that unfolds all work together to rivet audience attention. Conversely, Michael Moore's films entertain largely by his wry, **satirical** takes on his subjects (see Table 6.4 on p. 293).

satire: A representation of individual or group thinking or behavior that indirectly exposes the subject as flawed.

Criticize

Films such as Morris's *A Thin Blue Line*, *Mr. Death: The Rise and Fall of Fred A. Leuchter, Jr.* (1999), and *The Fog of War* report on various aspects of a subject and more or less let viewers make up their own minds about the issues raised. Many documentary films, however, more obviously directly or indirectly criticize at least one subject. A sizable number of documentaries are made primarily to criticize. These films are made out of the filmmakers' conviction that something is wrong. A film may function as an editorial or op-ed piece and mainly try to convince viewers of the validity of certain viewpoints. In all his films—including *Roger & Me* (1989), *The Big One* (1998), *Bowling for Columbine* (2002), *Fahrenheit 9/11* (2004), and *Sicko* (2007)—Michael Moore takes a satirical, entertaining stand on the films' issues. Then, too, his films include few credible, unmocked sources arguing an opposing view. Like Moore's films, Robert Greenwald's films inform and promote strongly held views. In *Outfoxed: Rupert Murdoch's War on Journalism* (2004) and *Wal*Mart: The High Cost of Low Price* (2005), Greenwald sometimes shows a clip of someone talking followed by footage that contradicts or mocks what was just said. Even the subtitles of Greenwald's films reveal the importance of their viewpoints. Like Michael Moore, in his recent films Greenwald also argues a particular position without allowing another side much voice. The end credits of his *Wal*Mart: The High Cost of Low Price* include this statement: "[no company reps agreed to be interviewed]." The film includes no explanation of why authorities on the subject—such as authors, professors, or governmental officials who championed tax breaks to get Wal*Mart to build in a particular location—were not given a chance to air their views.

Documentary filmmakers who inform and criticize sometimes hope to motivate viewers to take action. Michael Moore declared repeatedly in the media that in large part he made *Fahrenheit 9/11* to motivate U.S. voters to deny the second President Bush a second term. Patricia Foulkrod's *The Ground Truth* (2006) makes a number of points about the problems endured by American military personnel in the second Iraq war, including the claim that the U.S. military cares little for the psychological problems of returning vets. The film's last shot, a title card, includes a call to action:

www.thegroundtruth.net
Meet the veterans. Get involved. Go to:
www.aimpages.com/thegroundtruth

An Inconvenient Truth (2006)—a documentary on the campaign of former U.S. Vice President Al Gore to convince people to understand global warming as a seriously dangerous threat and a worldwide problem—supplies lots and lots of information in hopes of swaying uninformed viewers and skeptics into believing that global warming is real and perilous. The film concludes with a Web site address, followed by the end credit for the film's director and then specific suggestions on how viewers can reduce their carbon emissions "to zero." These fleeting suggestions appear amid the other end credits, traditionally a time in theatrical showings when most people get up and block the view of those of us who usually try to read them.

Celebrate

By way of contrast, some documentary films celebrate a subject, presenting it in a way that viewers can appreciate or admire. Examples of laudatory documentaries include *Marcello Mastroianni . . . I Remember*, about the famed Italian film actor; "A Great Day in Harlem" (1994), which pays tribute to many great American jazz musicians; and *The Life and Times of Hank Greenberg* (2000), which extols the personality and achievements of the first American Jew to become a major league baseball star. Another celebratory documentary is *Calle 54* (2000), which includes brief comments by some of the musicians featured and occasional brief narration, but viewers do not *learn* very much about the music and the musicians from Cuba, Puerto Rico, Spain, Argentina, Brazil, the Dominican Republic, and the United States. The film also supplies little information about the various influences on the musicians, including one another's music, U.S. jazz, and above all else music from Africa. Instead, the film's emphasis is on presenting the music. And what glorious, life-affirming music it is, a dozen complete numbers, recorded and filmed in the Sony Music Studios on Manhattan's 54th Street.

Another example of a celebratory documentary is *Winged Migration* (2001), a French film about migratory birds. The film illustrates how a documentary may be educational but even more so celebratory. The visuals convey much of the film's information. For example, the film shows without comment that being a migratory bird is dangerous. Birds may become mired in industrial waste; birds nesting in a field may be run over by a combine; migratory birds may be shot out of the sky by hunters; birds in the Amazonian jungle may be captured and hauled away in wooden cages affixed atop boats. Avalanches and storms may threaten their lives; migrating birds may be so exhausted and in danger of perishing that they may stop en route (even alighting onto a ship) and quickly fall asleep; baby birds may be consumed by larger birds of a different species; and injured birds are easy prey for other animals, such as crabs.

Winged Migration has few subtitles; mainly they identify the birds being seen on the screen and inform viewers how far they fly each year to their migratory destination. The narration is infrequent, brief, and not terribly informative. Viewers are not told, for example, how far a group of migrating birds may fly in a day, how many days are needed to reach their destination, and why so many different types of birds choose the same destination. By the end of the movie, some viewers and reviewers believe they have not learned very much (Roger Ebert, Stephen Holden, and others). Critic James Berardinelli wrote that "numerous questions are left unanswered and many **sequences** could have benefited from some **exposition**." But by dwelling on so many birds in many different locations and by showing them from different distances and angles for an hour and a half, the film also celebrates their grace, beauty, and endurance. In addition, sometimes the film also celebrates the variety and expanse of the amazing planet we live on. And the film indirectly celebrates technology (such as ultralight aircraft) and modern **cinematography** (perhaps especially the **telephoto lens**) and its ability to show subjects in ways otherwise impossible to show and to represent nuances of color, variations of light, and a range of animal movement otherwise fleeting and usually taken for granted by human observers.

Celebratory can also be wed to promotional. *That's Entertainment* (1974) is an MGM film about MGM films, specifically MGM musicals. The film includes not only many clips from MGM musicals but also testimonials and narration by former movie stars—Elizabeth Taylor, Debbie Reynolds, Gene Kelly, Fred Astaire, and others. Their testimonials and narration mostly pay tribute to MGM musicals and their stars. For example, beginning approximately 54 minutes into the film and running for nearly 12 minutes, Gene Kelly speaks of his admiration for Fred Astaire's work as we viewers see clips from Astaire movies. About 88 3/4 minutes into the film and running approximately 10 1/2 minutes, Astaire introduces clips from some Gene Kelly musicals and praises Kelly's work. All four of the musicals that Astaire identifies in his narration were by MGM. You scratch my back, I'll scratch yours? *That's Entertainment* is celebratory but promo-

exposition: Information supplied in a narrative about characters (or people in a narrative documentary) and about events that supposedly transpired before the earliest event in the plot.

telephoto lens: A lens that makes all subjects in an image appear closer to the camera than does a normal lens.

tional, too. It has testimonials and narration, which are largely of the same cloth, covering over nuance and variety of viewpoints and making no pretense to be objective, balanced, or fair. Then, too, the film excludes interviews with any authority on the American musical.

All documentaries inform. All either entertain or fail to hold the audience's attention. Many documentaries criticize or celebrate their subjects. Most documentaries achieve more than one goal.

A documentary that achieves more than one goal is *Justifiable Homicide* (2001), which informs viewers about the killings of two Puerto Rican youths by two New York City police detectives. The film explains why the two young men and the police were where they were at the time of the shootings, the 12-to-8 vote by a Bronx grand jury that the killings were "justifiable homicide," and the subsequent investigation by the city Civilian Complaint Review Board. The film also includes a report and demonstration by a representative for an independent pathologist, justifications for the police action by a police official and Mayor Rudolph Giuliani, the finding of the Civilian Complaint Review Board that the police detectives had used unnecessary and unjustified force in the shooting deaths, and the police commissioner's prompt dismissal of that report. The film also shows the parents' responses to the death of one of the young men; other people's frustration and anger over police killings of loved ones; the grief, abiding love, and dedication of the mother of one of the slain youths; and her role in the establishment of the group Parents Against Police Brutality. *Justifiable Homicide* primarily criticizes the actions and reactions of some NYPD officers and city officials. The film has additional less prominent goals. It also informs about the context of a police shooting, entertains with its investigative organization (what led to the two deaths and why), and celebrates the strength of two parents, especially the mother.

Amandla! Revolution in Four-Part Harmony (2002) also achieves more than one goal: it informs about and criticizes apartheid, the system of brutal, sometimes lethal racial segregation and discrimination formerly enforced in South Africa. The film also celebrates the music, spirit, vivacity, community, persistence, dignity, and eventual triumph of (mostly black) South Africans who opposed apartheid. A final example of a documentary film that does more than one thing is *Murderball* (2005, Figure 8.3).

WHAT STEPS MIGHT BE TAKEN TO CONSTRUCT DOCUMENTARIES?

State of Fear: The Truth about Terrorism (2005) covers the political history of Peru from 1970 to 2004. *State of Fear* details the rise of the Shining Path, a Maoist-inspired guerrilla movement, and its use of intimidation and violence, initially against the rural Peruvian indigenous people. The film also

FIGURE 8.3 Multiple achievements of a documentary film
Murderball (2005) is an 88-minute documentary about quad (quadriplegic) rugby ("quad rugby" is unofficially called *murderball*) and those who play it. The film informs, entertains, and celebrates.

The film informs about its two main subjects: quadriplegics (including some of the commonplace misunderstandings about their injuries and eventual capabilities) and quad rugby (how someone trains for it and how to play it). To help convey its information, the film includes interviews and demonstrations of how to play a game in which the participants are strapped-in warriors wearing no body armor or helmets and who ram one another's armored wheelchairs and often overturn them. The end credits even include the Web site address for more information about the sport.

In part, *Murderball* entertains by including three human-interest stories. One focuses on the bearded Mark Zupan in training and in action (seen here with the ball on his lap) and on his relationships with his best friend and with his girlfriend. Another main story is about Joe Soares, both as an American quad rugby player who was cut from the U.S. team and became coach of the rival Canadian team and as the father of a young son who is nonathletic but bright and musically gifted. The third human-interest story is about Keith Cavill, a young athletic man whose neck was broken in a motocross accident. The film also entertains with individual and team conflict, humor, and touching situations. And it entertains by its filmmaking style, including a lot of fast pacing, rapid actions (even some speeded-up action), many point-of-view shots of the ferocious action, and occasional animation.

Finally, *Murderball* celebrates the men's rehabilitation from a major accident or childhood disease, their athleticism, team camaraderie, individual charisma, sexual successes, and the rewards of focus and persistence. *Publicity still. A&E Indie Films; MTV Films and others*

covers the heavy-handed, counterproductive military reaction of the Peruvian government; the rise to power of President Alberto Fujimori; and the police work that led to the capture of the guerrilla leader, former philosophy professor Abimael Guzmán. Finally, the film shows the power grab by Fujimori and his political ally Vladimiro Montesinos; the overthrow and exile of Fujimori; and the imprisonment of Montesinos. The film begins and concludes with some information about the Peruvian Truth and Reconciliation Commission and clips of the founding of a corresponding museum, created so that future generations might know about the mistakes of the past and thus avoid a repetition of them.

With so many subjects and so long a period to cover, how did the filmmakers fill so broad a canvas? They had many decisions to make and much work to do, including deciding what sources to incorporate, securing the necessary sources and in some cases rights to use the sources (including the music), and deciding in what order to present them (the film's **structure**). *State of Fear* includes numerous photographs, many of them of faces of Peruvians (see Plate 42 in Chapter 13). The film also has occasional informative

structure: The arrangement of all the parts of a text.

title cards, such as "Spreading Violence." In addition, the film presents many TV and movie clips, some of them mostly black-and-white re-creations of past actions, such as the abduction of a young woman before she can attend the first day of university classes (seen nearly 67 minutes into the film). From time to time, the film uses narration. Also included at several points are clips showing a teacher explaining some of Peru's recent history to a roomful of boys. At various places, the film shows Peruvians who lived during the hard times revisiting the tragic locations many years later. The filmmakers incorporate plentiful excerpts from interviews with a variety of people affected by the historical events, including the chief detective whose men eventually captured the terrorist leader Guzmán; some supporters of Guzmán and some of his opponents; and supporters of President Fujimori and later opponents of him and his rule. The film also uses commentary and background information that supplies context from two experts: one of the truth commissioners, who had been a former professor at the University of Ayacucho, where Guzmán had also taught, and a journalist. *State of Fear* illustrates that the steps used to construct a documentary may be many and widely various.

As the following sections indicate, subjects, sources, structure, and filmmaking techniques are all major considerations in constructing a documentary.

Selecting Subjects

Documentary films can be about any subject—for example, human behavior (including human creativity or any aspect of history), animal behavior, plant life, or any other aspect of science. When the subject is human behavior, documentarians nearly always use ordinary people, not actors. *Hoop Dreams*, for example, features two real Chicago inner-city youths and their families. All the people in the film were people being themselves; no actors were creating representations of them for the film. Only rarely do documentaries use actors. Charlie Sheen plays a judge in Emile De Antonio's *In the King of Prussia* (1983); actors reenact some minor roles in *The Thin Blue Line*; and actors play all the roles in the many re-created scenes of *Thirty-Two Short Films about Glenn Gould* (1993).

The subject of a documentary film usually is seen on location, not in a studio or specially constructed **setting**. In the late 1950s, location shooting became common with the development of lighter and more mobile cameras and sound recording equipment. Recent years have seen the development of digital equipment that is even more portable and versatile and produces much better-quality images and sounds, and many or even most documentaries are now shot on location with a lightweight digital video camera. Today it is possible for one or two people to go practically anywhere and film and record sound unobtrusively. If the opportunity for a theatrical release arises later, the video can be transferred to 35 mm film, as

setting: The place where the events of a narrative occur.

has been done for *Buena Vista Social Club*, *The Original Kings of Comedy* (2000), *Startup.com* (2001), *Spellbound* (2002), *Fahrenheit 9/11*, *Super Size Me* (2004), *Sicko*, and many other documentary films.

Occasionally a documentary film is not filmed entirely on location. In an interview, Les Blank told me that his "Gap-Toothed Women" (1987) was shot largely within his own studio instead of in the homes or workplaces of his subjects. Other exceptions: Errol Morris shot parts of *The Thin Blue Line* in New York City, not Texas, where the entire film is set, and he filmed the interviews for *A Brief History of Time* (1992) and *Fast, Cheap & Out of Control* in a studio.

Capturing the Friedmans (2003) illustrates that one subject of a documentary film can be the limitations of memory. The film is about the Friedman family—a father, a mother, and three sons—torn by charges that the father and youngest son sexually abused many young boys. The film presents interviews with a wide range of people, including all members of the family except the middle son (who declined to be interviewed), detectives, lawyers, the judge involved in the case, an author who had earlier written about the case, the father's brother, various people who might have been victims, and a few parents. Different people remember things differently, and nearly everyone is contradicted by something someone else says. Occasionally an interviewee contradicts himself or herself. And at various times, it seems possible that various interviewees are in denial or do not remember certain events because they are simply too painful to dredge up. At the end of the film, the viewer may have questions about the extent of the guilt and the fairness of the investigation, convictions, and sentences. Fascinating, yes. But what happened? What is the truth? In interviews, the film's director, Andrew Jarecki, who did exhaustive research on his subject, has said that he will leave it to viewers to decide for themselves. As he said, "Our memories evolve over time to suit our needs and . . . you can't trust a memory to be just this static thing you can trust" (Jarecki). What, then, of the many documentaries that rely so heavily on the memories of so many interviewees?

Occasionally, one subject of a documentary is its maker or the relationship between the maker and the film's human subject. An example is *Stevie* (2002), which is mainly about a young man who had been born out of wedlock, beaten by his mother, given up by her after she remarried, and eventually placed in various juvenile centers and foster homes, in some of which he was beaten and raped. The adult Stevie is understandably emotionally guarded. He is also given to substance abuse and to outbursts of anger and violence and is eventually tried and sentenced for sexually abusing an 8-year-old female cousin. Also prominent in the film is its primary maker, Steve James, who years earlier had served as a Big Brother while Stevie was a youth but moved away and did not stay in touch with Stevie as promised. Ten years after their last contact, James visited Stevie (as the camera films the encounter) and gradually became involved in his troubled adult life. James sometimes wondered aloud off-camera about his proper role in Stevie's life. This and other documentary films raise ethical questions about their making. To what extent should the filmmaker become involved with the subject? Is it right for the filmmaker to influence the subject's life? Should the filmmaker's fundamental allegiance be to the welfare of the subject or the good of the film?

We can see the relevance of the last question—To what extent should the filmmaker become involved with the subject?—not only for *Stevie* but also for *Apocalypse Now* if we listen to part of Francis Coppola's audio commentary on the DVD for the documentary *Hearts of Darkness: A Filmmaker's Apocalypse*. The documentary shows how stressful it had been for Coppola to be plagued by various problems and delays while filming *Apocalypse Now* on location in the Philippines. *Hearts of Darkness* also includes some of the documentary footage that Coppola's wife Eleanor shot of the troubled production. Beginning 30¼ minutes into the audio commentary on the DVD for *Hearts of Darkness*, Francis Coppola says,

> I was really on the spot and really scared and didn't have many people to talk to about this or to gain some sort of solace. I would come home at night and to my wife and I would look at her and say, "Oh, Eleanor, this movie is going to be the worst movie in history. It's going to be terrible. I'm going to get an F. It's a failure." And she would say to me, "Oh, would you wait a second. Just wait one second 'til I get the camera and then say it again." (Coppola)

Shortly after this commentary, Eleanor explains her justification for giving preference to filming or audio tape recording Coppola's anguish in order to capture his "creative process."

Documentaries made before the arrival of portable equipment often featured a strong-voiced, supposedly impartial male **narrator**, and they seem to involve no significant interaction between the filmmakers and their human subjects. But as we just saw with *Stevie*, the interaction of filmmaker and subject may be important. A documentary may even reveal that the filmmaker has become romantically attracted to a subject in the film. During the filming of Judy Irving's *The Wild Parrots of Telegraph Hill* (2003), Irving became attracted to Mark Bittner, the man who tended the wild parrots, and right before the beginning of the film's end credits she declares, "Mark and I became a pair." Probably not coincidentally, the film ends up being as much about him as about those colorful parrots. (Sometime after the film was finished, they married.)

The Maysles Brothers' cult documentary *Grey Gardens* (1975) also entails significant interaction between filmmakers and subjects. The film focuses on an elderly eccentric mother and her 56-year-old eccentric daughter who have been living alone for years in a messy, decaying twenty-eight-room mansion. From time to time, the daughter flirts with the two male filmmakers, dresses somewhat provocatively, and makes sure they notice her. Is she hoping that in the finished film the filmmakers will feature

narrator: A character, a person, or an unidentifiable voice in a film that provides commentary about subjects in the film or outside it, or both.

her more prominently than they do the mother? Is she trying to show her mother that she can still be appealing to men? Is she testing if her powers of flirtation still work? Or is she truly attracted to the filmmakers? It's difficult to know her motives. It could be a combination of two or more of these or other reasons, but nonetheless the daughter's interactions with the filmmakers (the mother's too) sometimes affect the content of the behavior filmed and later included in the finished film. In 2006, 91 minutes of **outtakes** were released as *The Beales of Grey Gardens*. In that film, the filmmakers' interactions with the two main subjects are more apparent than in the original film (more conversations, more questions), and the grown daughter is even more flirtatious with the two filmmakers—for example, often calling them "Darling" and confiding to them that she cannot decide which of them she is more attracted to.

outtake: A take (version of a shot) or a shot not included in a film's final version.

Finding and Using Sources

Once the filmmakers have settled on a subject—and occasionally that may not happen until filming or sometimes even editing is under way—they must locate and use supporting sources. A documentary film may be drawn from any combination of sources as long as the representation is primarily factual or informative. In creating a documentary film, filmmakers may film new material, staged or not. In representing subjects, they may try to capture the looks and sounds of the original as closely as possible, or they may choose to stylize the representation—for example, with soft lighting or different colors. They may use existing footage exclusively, incorporate existing footage into footage they shot, or use exclusively the new footage they shot. As we see below, they also may use other sources for information—including fragments of radio broadcasts, audio recordings in any of their permutations, still photographs, paintings, signs, and maps. They often add narration, interviews, or title cards—or a combination of two or all three. They may add **sound effects** or music—or both. Typically, documentary filmmakers do a lot of filming, which the availability of digital cameras makes easier and more economical than ever before. And typically, due to the large amount of footage they shoot, documentarians spend a lot of time selecting their shots and arranging them into some sort of unified whole. The possible sources and combinations of sources are endless, for, as this book repeatedly says, human creativity knows no bounds.

sound effect: In film, a sound other than spoken words or music.

Two of the most frequently used types of sources are artifacts (objects that people have shaped or made) and informative language. Artifacts used to make documentaries include other films (such as newsreels), clips from TV shows, photographs, and objects a person has made or owned. Sometimes only one type of artifact or a few types of artifacts are used in a documentary film. *The Atomic Cafe* (1982)—which is about the arrival of nuclear weapons and some of the U.S. government's subsequent responses—consists entirely of excerpts from commercial and government media.

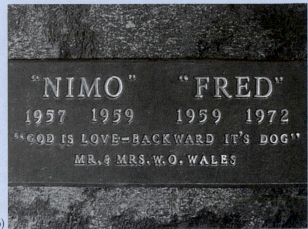

a)

b)

FIGURE 8.4 **Informative language in a documentary film**
Informative language used in documentary films may appear in a wide variety of forms. (a) Often, documentarians use subtitles to convey information, as here and in many other places in "A Great Day in Harlem" (1994) to identify various jazz musicians. (b) In a pet cemetery, informative language is visible on a plaque mounted on a boulder to honor departed dogs in Errol Morris's first film, *Gates of Heaven* (1978). (a) *Jean Bach and others; Home Vision HVE Entertainment DVD.* (b) *Gates of Heaven; MGM Home Entertainment DVD*

Emile De Antonio's *Point of Order* (1963) is a 97-minute **compilation film** made mostly from 188 hours of TV footage of the 1954 Army-McCarthy hearings.

compilation film: A film made by editing together clips from other films.

Often a documentary film includes informative language: narration (or title cards or subtitles), interviews, signs, even headstones, or a combination of sources (Figure 8.4). The words of songs may function as narration or commentary on the film's subjects, as they do throughout Les Blank's "Chulas Fronteras" (1976), a film about Chicano experiences and the centrality of music in Chicano lives. Until the early 1960s, documentary films relied heavily on all-knowing narrators, in part because the equipment then available made it cumbersome to film and to record synchronous sound on location. Most recent documentary films use interviews much more often than narration or use interviews alone, in part because of the availability of more portable filmmaking equipment and in part because of the widespread belief that no one person or narrator can do justice to a subject's complexity. Some films, such as those by Frederick Wiseman, use neither narration nor interviews. And some—such as *The Wonderful, Horrible Life of Leni Riefenstahl* (1993) and the *Up* series of documentaries (Figure 8.5)—use both.

Artifacts and informative language help persuade viewers of the accuracy of a film's representations. They may be incorporated into a film in countless creative ways. Approximately 103¾ minutes into the third part

Jackie, Sue and Lynn as seen in 49 UP, a film by Michael Apted. A First Run Features release.

FIGURE 8.5 The *Up* series of documentary films
Beginning in 1964 with a diverse group of 7-year-old British subjects, and resuming every seven years since then, director Michael Apted has made a series of documentary films about the lives of the same group of British citizens (at least with those willing to continue from film to film). This publicity still shows three subjects and images from three earlier stages of their lives. *Granada Television; First Run Features*

of Ken Burns's *Baseball* (1994), we see first a photograph of the exterior of a building, presumably where a grand jury is meeting, and later a photograph of a baseball player's face looking toward the camera. As we see these photographs, we hear a gavel banging, **ambient sounds** of people inside a room, and the voices of two actors reenacting a prosecutor's questions about the throwing of the 1919 World Series and Chicago White Sox player "Shoeless" Joe Jackson's responses to them. After the offscreen re-created testimony has finished, we are allowed about 4 seconds to continue to scrutinize the photograph of Joe Jackson. Other documentaries that include artifacts and informative language are represented in Figures 8.6 and 8.7.

As with fictional films, one possible though rare source for a documentary is an earlier documentary film. Jill Godmilow's "What Farocki Taught" (1998) is a close remake of Harun Farocki's 1969 German documentary entitled "Inextinguishable Fire," which is about Dow Chemical's development of napalm B during the war in Vietnam. The remake, which is in color and in English, re-creates the original black-and-white film shot for shot, often superimposing shots from the original (complete with subtitles) with newly staged sections. "What Farocki Taught" challenges spectators to question conventional approaches to documentary while enabling a version of Farocki's film to receive the American screening it was denied on release.

FIGURE 8.6 Artifacts and language in a documentary film
"The Match That Started My Fire" (1991) by Cathy Cook includes supporting artifacts (including existing film clips) and informative language (off-camera accounts by women). In the shot represented here, artifact is combined with informative language: a woman twirls around and around as a woman's voice recounts how as a girl she sometimes wore a certain type of skirt to school and spun around and around for her pleasure and the boys'. *Photo by Cathy Cook, dancer: Heidi Heistad; Women Make Movies, New York; Film-Makers' Cooperative, New York*

FIGURE 8.7 Multiple sources in a documentary film
Carmen Miranda: Bananas Is My Business (1994) is a film directed by a Brazilian woman about one of her compatriots, Carmen Miranda, who was first a popular singer and movie star in Brazil and later a star in American musical movies and TV. The film shows Miranda initially closely identified with her Brazilian roots but eventually alienated from them by her transforming experiences with American media, which presented her progressively as an exotic, a stereotype, and a self-parody and a subject of parody by others. She was torn between two cultures; demoralized by depression, drugs, and an abusive marriage; and dead by 1955 at age 46.

To convey a broad range of information and perspectives, the film uses a wide range of sources. Artifacts shown include a Carmen Miranda paper doll, a Miranda puppet, small Miranda models, a self-portrait painting, many photos, and calendar pages for different days rapidly floating toward and past the camera. Other artifacts used to convey information and perspectives include reenactments of Miranda's death by a heart attack and of one of the documentary director's dreams, clips from movies including Miranda, clips that parody her, an excerpt from a movie trailer, home movies, and clips from a travelogue about Brazil, newsreels, and TV shows. Informative language used includes newspaper headlines, program notes, Miranda's handwriting, narration (by the director and others), interviews, an excerpt from a song, and a fragment of a radio broadcast to the people of Brazil. Amassing so many sources and such a wide range of them and editing the film were massive endeavors. *Publicity still. Channel Four Films, Riofilmes; Women Make Movies, New York*

A documentary film may also be a **sequel** to an earlier documentary. An example is "Pets or Meat: The Return to Flint" (1993)—Michael Moore's follow-up to his satirical documentary *Roger & Me* (1989)—which shows what happened to some of the people featured in the earlier film and even more sharply satirizes its subjects. Another sequel to a documentary is *Best Man* (1998); this follow-up to the award-winning documentary *Best Boy* (1979) shows how the gentle, mentally impaired subject of the earlier film is faring nearly twenty years later. A more recent documentary sequel is Agnès Varda's *The Gleaners and I: Two Years Later* (2002), which is a follow-up to her *The Gleaners and I* (2000). But as far as documentary sequels go, the British *Up* series of documentaries that are largely about the same group of people and appear every seven years—*7 Up* (1964), *14 Up, 21 Up, 28 Up, 35 Up, 42 Up*, and *49 Up* (2005)—was originally in a class by itself (see Figure 8.5).

As is illustrated by the audio commentaries of Francis Coppola and Eleanor Coppola on the DVD release of *Hearts of Darkness*, a DVD's audio commentary may serve as another source for a documentary. In their commentaries, which were recorded separately, both Coppolas explain why parts of *Hearts of Darkness* remain embarrassing for Francis and why he believes that the film misrepresents certain situations. Hearing their comments can serve as another source for the film experience, one that supplies an additional dimension or added complexity. If the viewer can hear only a little of the original soundtrack while listening to a DVD audio commentary, the result may be akin to a remake (such is the case with the *Hearts of Darkness* DVD). If the viewer can hear much of an original soundtrack while listening to the audio commentary on a DVD, the result may be akin to a later edition of a **text**, though sometimes on such DVDs, the two audio sources will compete for the viewer's attention.

text: Something that people produce or modify to communicate meaning.

Structuring the Parts into a Nonnarrative or a Narrative Whole

Most documentary films tell no **narrative** (a representation of a series of unified events situated in one or more settings). These **nonnarrative documentaries** include most scientific films, many TV documentaries on social conditions, industrial films (which present information about a company or industry), training films, promotional films, and many TV advertisements. Most nonnarrative documentary films present various types of information organized into categories, or they make an argument.

An example of a nonnarrative documentary film that presents a variety of information is *Fast, Cheap & Out of Control*, which is about four thoughtful and articulate men who discuss their nontraditional occupations (Figure 8.8). A very different nonnarrative documentary, which also conveys a wealth of information, is Jonas Mekas's *As I Was Moving Ahead Occasionally I Saw Brief Glimpses of Beauty* (2001), which consists of more than 4 hours of edited home movies divided into 12 chapters arranged in no discernible order within the chapters or between them. The film is nonnarrative because it is impossible to mentally reconstruct all its many fragmented subjects and events into a whole. As Mekas narrates early in the film, he was not sure where the pieces of his life went, so he edited intuitively (Figure 8.9).

Other nonnarrative documentary films make an argument, as in the 4-minute "Television: The Drug of the Nation" (1992). The phrase "Television, the drug of the nation, breeding ignorance and feeding radiation" is heard repeatedly in the film. The rap narrator also claims that commercial TV is the reason so few Americans read books and the reason most Americans think "Central America means Kansas." The narrator adds, "A child watches fifteen hundred murders [on TV] before he's 12 years old, and then we wonder why we created a Jason generation." The film's chaotic but mesmerizing visuals suggest that TV is dizzying, fragmented, highly manipulative, addictive, and dangerous to our health. "Television: The Drug of the Nation" conveys information but not a story; it mainly makes the argument that (commercial) TV is detrimental to American life.

To advance an argument, a nonnarrative documentary film may use editing to praise or criticize; it may **cut** from one shot to the next to criticize. This technique is used in *Hearts and Minds*, a 1974 film about U.S. military involvement in Vietnam. About 61 minutes into the film, an enraged

cut (verb): To change from one shot to the following shot seemingly instantaneously.

FIGURE 8.8 A nonnarrative documentary film with multiple subjects
Fast, Cheap & Out of Control (1997) alternates among four main subjects: four men and the unusual occupations that they pursue. (a) One man does topiary gardening that features plants shaped like large animals. (b) Another man tames wild animals, especially lions and tigers. (c) A third man has a passion for studying mole-rats. (d) The fourth and final subject is a scientist who supervises the construction of robots shaped approximately like huge insects. Here, near the film's ending, the fourth man has explained with some feeling how

a)

b)

c)

d)

humans may eventually be superseded by their silicone creations. The film presents information about its four major subjects and ideas related to each of them yet implies meanings transcending its parts. Critic Richard Corliss wrote that the film "is a funny, thrilling tribute to people's urge to find play and profundity in the work they do." Karen Jaehne has written, "In the final sequence, we witness the lion tamer retiring and passing his baton to a kinder, gentler tamer who sticks her head in the lion's mouth. Then footage from *Darkest Africa* shows the lost city collapsing, a volcano spewing, and our hero [Clyde] Beatty scrambling for his life, before we return to the brave new world of a robot on lunar terrain, as the circus elephants depart. We see a storm looming over Green Animals, and George the gardener with his shears in his hand holding an umbrella against the raging elements. This bleak conclusion reminds us of the evanescence of human existence: not much survives. Creativity is our only consolation" (46). As commentator Peter Applebome sees it, "Mr. Morris's films . . . are about . . . epistemology—the nature of knowledge: what things are and what they seem to be, how people know what they think they know, and do they really know it or just think they know it?" All of this and more is conveyed in a nonnarrative structure. *American Playhouse, Fourth Floor Pictures; Sony Pictures Classics DVD*

high school football coach shouts at his players and hits some of them. The players are then seen in a football game, and an injured player is shown in pain. Next, President Johnson (whom viewers may equate with the out-of-control coach) declares that the United States will win (the war in Vietnam). The following footage shows some of the chaos and destruction of a massive surprise counterattack by North Vietnamese fighters against U.S. and South Vietnamese forces, which abruptly casts into doubt when and how the war in Vietnam will finally end. Elsewhere the film again uses editing to suggest guilt by association. At the conclusion of the film, 107 ¼ minutes in, a shot of countless freshly dug, empty Vietnamese graves accompanied by sounds of moaning and crying is followed by shots in the

FIGURE 8.9 A nonnarrative documentary of edited home movies

As I Was Moving Ahead Occasionally I Saw Brief Glimpses of Beauty (2001)—which is made up of thousands of shots, many of them superimposed—includes as its subjects the beauty and joy of children, nature, animals (especially cats), the seasons, New York City, and friends. In addition, the filmmaker narrates occasional observations about his subjects. Some of the film's techniques—portable, sometimes shaky camera; zoom shots; swish pans; superimpositions; fast cutting with many shots in only a vague context; fast motion; out-of-focus images; and overexposed and underexposed images—help suggest the whirlwind abundance of life's everyday and sometimes beautiful or joyous experiences. The film also suggests the difficulty of arranging memories into a meaningful whole and the inevitability of living in our own constructed worlds that nonetheless seem real to us. *Jonas Mekas; Anthology Film Archives*

United States of various patriotic parades and demonstrations, including marching soldiers, a flag-waving spectator, marching boys in military uniform, and a formation of police riding motorcycles. The suggestion is that pain and suffering in a foreign country are caused by a regimented, patriotic, and militaristic American society.

Only a small percentage of documentary films present a narrative or story. Narrative documentary films show true or largely true narratives.

Like a fictional film, a narrative documentary features someone with a goal or goals. In *The Farmer's Wife* (1999), a farmer and his wife work extremely hard to try to save their farm and their marriage. In *Brother's Keeper* (1992), the main person filmed is a man who has been accused of suffocating a brother suffering from ill health, and who wants to avoid being convicted (Figure 8.10). Another narrative documentary that focuses on a person trying to achieve a goal is *Lost in La Mancha* (2002), which shows film director Terry Gilliam trying and failing to complete filming of *The Man Who Killed Don Quixote*.

Like fictional films, narrative documentaries represent events chronologically or nonchronologically. An example of a nonchronological narrative is *Grizzly Man* (2005)—German filmmaker Werner Herzog's documentary about a young American self-named Timothy Treadwell. The film shows a little about Treadwell's childhood and a little about his troubles with drink and drugs as a youth. The film also shows a lot about him during his last thirteen years: summers spent studying Alaskan foxes and grizzly bears and trying to befriend them and the rest of the years spent promoting understanding and appreciation of Alaskan bears. The film's story also includes details of his last summer in Alaska, his death and the death of his girlfriend there, and Herzog's later investigation into Treadwell's life by means of video footage that Treadwell had shot and by means of interviews with Treadwell's parents, friends, a former friend and lover, an airplane pilot, the coroner, and wildlife specialists. That is the story's **fabula**, more or less. The film, however, has a nonchronological structure, beginning with Treadwell in Alaska, revealing the deaths of Treadwell and his girlfriend about 9½ minutes into the film, cutting repeatedly between before his death and after it, and ending at an indefinite time with Treadwell walking by a river, followed by two bears. By the end of the film, attentive viewers have no trouble constructing the fabula. And like all nonchronological structures, the structure of *Grizzly Man* allows Herzog greater control over when to reveal what: when to set up telling juxtapositions (for example, between Treadwell's views of nature and the opposing views of others), what note to begin the film with, and how to end the film appropriately and memorably.

Like fictional films, a narrative documentary film may employ a highly original structure. Piles of crushed new electric cars sit at a remote, inaccessible site in the Arizona desert. Meanwhile, many of the former leasers of those cars miss them

DELBERT WARD

FIGURE 8.10 A narrative documentary
Seen here a little more than 5 minutes into the narrative documentary *Brother's Keeper* (1992) is the main subject. As in most stories that have one character (in fiction) or one person (in documentary), the main person in *Brother's Keeper* has a goal but has trouble reaching it. Delbert Ward wants to avoid conviction for the smothering death of one of his ill brothers, but impediments include Delbert's signed confession, damaging testimony given by another brother, and a prosecution tactic discovered before the trial. *Courtesy of Creative Thinking International, New York City*

acutely. They miss the ease of using the cars; they miss how perfectly they suited their in-city driving needs and how quiet and pollution-free they were. Some of them liked nearly everything about the cars and were tearful and angry as they were hauled away by truckers working for GM. But the former electric car drivers could not renew the lease on them and could not buy them, so the cars were hauled away to the remote site to be destroyed and forgotten. How did such an outcome come about? It is a mystery. It may have been a crime. The 2006 documentary *Who Killed the Electric Car?* explores that mystery (Figure 8.11).

In investigating who committed the crime, the filmmakers bring a variety of witnesses before the camera: previous leasers, car enthusiasts, celebrities such as Tom Hanks and Mel Gibson, auto engineers, state legislators, the former head of the California Air Resources Board, and representatives for the automakers. Some of the witnesses are spokespeople for the suspects; others are sharply critical of GM's decision to discontinue the car. We film viewers hear what the witnesses have to say about the subject. Later, title cards announce various suspects. Near the film's end, more title cards declare who is "guilty": the U.S. government, Big Oil, car manufacturers, and others. Some of the suspects are declared not guilty. (The film also includes a coda: in spite of the film's evidence, several of the witnesses assert their optimism for a better energy future.) The film's structure suggests a quasi-legal investigation of a crime and a declaration about who is guilty and who is innocent. The film illustrates yet another option open to documentary filmmakers with imagination.

Narrative documentaries are never simply factual stories. Consider *Burden of Dreams* (1982), a film by Les Blank, which shows some of what happened during the filming of Werner Herzog's fictional movie *Fitzcarraldo* (1982). Viewers can easily figure out the order of events in *Burden of Dreams* and see how they are connected. The scenes are even arranged chronologically, from November 1979 to November 1981. The film concentrates on the people making *Fitzcarraldo*, although occasionally the main story is interrupted so that various details of the Amazon jungle (such as the size, speed, and dexterity of ants) and the lives of the natives of the region can be briefly explained (Figure 8.12). The narrative is also punctuated with frequent interviews, especially with Herzog. *Burden of Dreams* doesn't lack unity, but like most narratives, whether fictional or factual, it includes more than a story.

Like nonnarrative documentary films, narrative documentary films may use editing to criticize or praise a person or idea. Consider the opening of *Triumph of the Will* (1935). Leni Riefenstahl made the film to document and celebrate a huge Nazi party conference. It opens with aerial shots of clouds, church spires and the tops of other buildings, an airplane flying above a city, the shadow of the airplane speeding over the ground of the city below, and troops marching in formation. On the ground, many shots of excited crowds alternate with the plane landing and pulling to a stop, followed by the emergence of Adolf Hitler and Joseph Goebbels, the Nazi minister of propaganda. In the next sequence, shots alternate between the large and excited crowds on the sides of the streets and Hitler standing in a moving car and saluting with a stiff arm. Thus in the editing of the film's opening

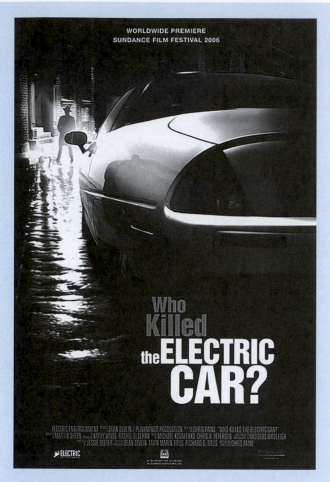

FIGURE 8.11 A documentary film as mystery
As both the title of the documentary film *Who Killed the Electric Car?* (2006) and the imagery of this poster, which is reminiscent of film noir, suggest, what happened to the electric car was a crime. This untraditional film is structured as an investigation of the possible culprits and to some extent the motivations for the crime, and it concludes with various "indictments." *Poster. Pliny-minor, Electric Entertainment*

scenes, Hitler is associated with power, speed, grace, and the adoration of the masses.

Many narrative documentary films have only one **plotline**, but like fictional films they may have two or more. *Hoop Dreams* shows the stories of two inner-city young men who dream of playing in the National Basketball Association. The film represents parts of their lives from their days in junior high to the beginning of college. Although the two stories occasionally intersect (the two commuted to the same high school for a while, and their paths cross occasionally after one of them goes to a different school), basically this narrative documentary alternates between their two stories. "The Heck with Hollywood!" (1991) alternates three stories about filmmakers who are trying to market their films outside the Hollywood network: a young man, a young woman, and three young men. Most of *Pumping Iron* (1976) consists of five plotlines (each about a bodybuilder): the background and training of two bodybuilders and their competition for the 1975 Mr. Universe title and the background, training, and competition of three men, including Arnold Schwarzenegger, for the 1975 Overall Mr. Olympia title.

Occasionally it is difficult to categorize a documentary film as nonnarrative or narrative. This is the case with one of the first feature-length documentaries, *Nanook of the North* (1922, restored 1976; Figure 8.13). There is little clear-cut unity to the film's sections (many could be switched without

FIGURE 8.12 A secondary subject in a narrative documentary film
Problems in filming Werner Herzog's movie *Fitzcarraldo* (1982) are the primary subject of Les Blank's narrative documentary *Burden of Dreams* (1982). One of the secondary subjects in Blank's film is the lifestyles of some Amazon Indians, such as those seen here almost 45 3/4 minutes into the film, including how they bathe, wash clothes, weave, prepare food, and play games. *Flower Films, El Cerrito, California; Criterion DVD*

FIGURE 8.13 Nonnarrative or narrative documentary?
Nanook of the North (1922, restored 1976), an early documentary film, reveals important aspects of Inuit life, especially getting food and surviving a harsh environment. Through the film's various parts, viewers learn how Nanook, a Canadian Inuit, and his family live. The film shows, for example, spearing fish, using a kayak, trading, hunting walrus, traveling, building an igloo, hunting seal, and preparing for a storm. Seen here, about 45 minutes into the restored version, Nanook is positioning a block of packed snow on the outside of an igloo he is building so the light will reflect off the block and through the clear ice block. The film's emphasis seems to be as much on presenting different types of information in some detail, as here, as on telling a story. *Revillon Frères; Criterion DVD*

consequences for viewers), yet the Inuits' lives are presented more or less chronologically (from a summer to a winter). Although the film's skimpy story is loosely structured and the film presents information as much as it shows a story, many critics think of *Nanook* as a narrative. Then, too, a documentary may even consist of two basic components, one narrative and one not (Figure 8.14)

Whether making narrative or nonnarrative documentaries, documentarians may pick and choose from among a huge variety of techniques.

Using a Variety of Filmmaking Techniques

Many different filmmaking techniques are used to make nearly all documentaries. In recent years, usually an unobtrusive handheld camera is used to film the subjects in action and to record the accompanying sounds. Often, the filmmakers film interviews and then use fragments from them. But the chosen techniques may be much less mainstream. *Woodstock* (1970) uses the superimposition of two shots (Figure 8.15a) and variations of **split screen** (Figure 8.15b). *The Thin Blue Line* uses some extreme **high-angle** shots, **slow motion**, lighting and color that are dramatic rather than strictly

a)   b)

FIGURE 8.14 Documentary that is both nonnarrative and narrative
Ross McElwee's *Sherman's March: A Meditation on the Possibility of Romantic Love in the South during an Era of Nuclear Weapons Proliferation* (1986) has two main intercut parts. One is a nonnarrative about Sherman's march to the sea and about the northern U.S. Civil War general William Tecumseh Sherman himself (a). The other is a narrative about the filmmaker, including his deadpan narration detailing his anxieties, and about more than a half dozen young southern women, most of whom initially interest him romantically. One such woman (b), a former flame, is now a lawyer who is emotionally involved with another man. *Ross McElwee; First Run Features DVD*

functional (note the warm-colored light on and behind the prisoner being interviewed approximately 20²/₃ minutes into the film), and imaginary and repeated re-creations filmed years after the actions depicted (Figure 8.16). *The Thin Blue Line* also uses **parallel editing**, unexpected **cutaway shots**, movie clips—some only obliquely related to the subject at hand—and a striking score by Philip Glass. As Errol Morris acknowledged, his film style is the polar opposite of Frederick Wiseman's (Bates 17). Yet both styles strike audiences as credible.

The first and last moving images of Harvey Milk in *The Times of Harvey Milk* (1984) are in slow motion, which represents the murdered member of the San Francisco Board of Supervisors as graceful yet drained of his usual charisma and vitality. Allie Light's *Dialogues with Madwomen* (1994), which is about the experiences and perspectives of seven northern California women who have suffered from mental illness, consists largely of alternating interviews with the women. During each interview, we see brief clips related to what the speaker is describing. Sometimes these cutaway shots reenact what is being described—for example, children rummaging through trash cans in search of food. Such cutaways are sometimes redundant and too literal to evoke emotional truth. More often, however, the cutaways are **symbolic** and evocative. For example, at one point as we viewers hear a woman explaining what a tyrant her father was, we see a man in a nondescript setting gesturing as if directing traffic and walking forward in slow motion. This cutaway is made even more unsettling because it is the **negative** of a black-and-white shot and the man's face looks light, indistinct, and inscrutable. (For an example of a negative image and a positive print of the same image, see Plates 43–44 in Chapter 13.)

Like fictional and experimental films, documentary films may be **self-reflexive**. Brief sections of Ross McElwee's *Time Indefinite* (1993) include a darkened screen or the tail **leader** (after the **reel** of film in the camera had presumably run out) or occasional humorous, deliberately wobbly hand-held shots. One of the earliest (experimental) documentaries is replete with

a)

b)

FIGURE 8.15 Simultaneous multiple images
(a) At times, *Woodstock* (1970) uses superimpositions of two shots, as here with two views of guitarist Jimi Hendrix almost 84 minutes into side B of the Director's Cut DVD. (b) The film also uses split screen extensively, as here where viewers see two views of singer Janis Joplin nearly 69 minutes into side B of the Director's Cut DVD. The filmmakers also use split screen to show action and simultaneous reactions; to show actions and someone commenting on them; and to show different actions occurring simultaneously. In *Woodstock*, the superimpositions and the extensive use of two or sometimes three simultaneous images on the split screen suggest that although the film runs nearly 4 hours, the events were too widespread, long-lasting, and significant to be conveyed by merely one image at a time, even large wide-screen images. *A Wadleigh-Maurice, Ltd., Production; Warner Home Video DVD, "The Director's Cut"*

self-reflexive: Characteristic of a text—such as a play, novel, or film—that refers to or comments on itself as a text.

leader: The clear or opaque piece of film that begins and concludes a reel of film.

FIGURE 8.16 Re-created scene in *The Thin Blue Line* (1988)
Here and elsewhere, the film uses re-creations to show different people's versions of the same event: the killing of a Dallas police officer. Visible on the left side of this photograph are a movie camera, tripod, and camera operator's ear. As director Errol Morris pointed out in a TV interview, it is up to viewers to decide which version of the murder is most probable. *Publicity still. Third Floor Productions, American Playhouse, and Channel 4; BFI*

self-reflexive details: Dziga Vertov's Soviet-era *Man with a Movie Camera* (1929). The film includes many shots showing the major components of both filmmaking and film exhibition (Figure 8.17). A more recent example of a self-reflexive documentary is *Decasia* (2001), which is about processing **nitrate** motion-picture film and much more so about its eventual decay (Figure 8.18).

Documentarians can use modern techniques to increase the appeal of films whose sources are not very appealing to today's audiences. Such is the case with *Chisholm '72: Unbought & Unbossed* (2004). The film's subject is U.S. Congressperson Shirley Chisholm, the first female African American to make, as she said, a "serious" run for the U.S. presidency (in 1972). The main sources of *Chisholm '72* are 1960s and 1970s predigital, fuzzy, black-and-white TV and videotape clips accompanied by monophonic sound and contemporary interviews, which look and sound fine. How to make the film's representation of its subject more engaging to twenty-first-century audiences? A stereo soundtrack of a variety of music helps. So does the use of split screen. The film's director, "[Shola] Lynch and her editors . . . [employ] a series of retro, split-screen sequences for contrast and colour, and a few of Chisholm's archival speeches [such as at the 1972 Democratic convention] benefit from the multi-angle approach" (Hasan). For contemporary audiences, contemporary filmmaking techniques can make older source material more appealing and involving.

HOW DOES FILMMAKING TECHNOLOGY AFFECT THE DOCUMENTARY FILMS MADE?

As in fictional filmmaking, filmmaking technology influences the techniques used in documentary filmmaking and the results achieved. Before the 1960s, the visual and sound recording equipment used to make documentary films was heavy and not very portable, especially when the camera was mounted on a tripod (see Figures 8.2 and 8.17). With such equipment, there was less opportunity to film at difficult locations and generally fewer moving-camera shots. The finished film tended to use a polished narration, not the interviews favored in later periods.

In the late 1950s and early 1960s, development of 16 mm **fast film**, handheld 16 mm cameras with a zoom lens, and portable sound packs gave

fast film (stock): Film stock that requires relatively little light for capturing images.

FIGURE 8.17 Self-reflexiveness in a documentary
This frame is from Dziga Vertov's experimental documentary *Man with a Movie Camera* (made largely in 1928 in the Soviet Union and first shown in January 1929). Here three images are combined to show (1) a crowd, (2) the camera operator (panning from left to right) with his camera, and (3) in the background the same camera and tripod but with no camera operator. The composite shot suggests that three components are at play: the equipment, the person operating the equipment, and the subject being filmed (the crowd). Here (just a few minutes from the end of the film) and from time to time elsewhere in the film, viewers see various aspects of filming, film editing, and film exhibition: camera, lenses, tripod, camera operator, editing table and editor, theater, audience, orchestra, projector, and a (silent) film being projected. To a degree probably unprecedented in documentary film, *Man with a Movie Camera* is self-reflexive. *VUFKU; Image Entertainment DVD*

FIGURE 8.18 Film itself as a subject of a documentary film
Decasia (2001) is a compilation film consisting almost entirely of excerpts from decaying black-and-white nitrate films and a relentless musical score. "I wasn't just looking for instances of decayed film," filmmaker Bill Morrison recalled of his two-year excavation. "Rather, I was seeking out instances of decay set against a narrative backdrop, for example, of valiant struggle, or thwarted love, or birth, or submersion, or rescue, or one of the other themes I was trying to interweave. And never complete decay: I was always seeking out instances where the image was still putting up a struggle, fighting off the inexorability of its demise but not yet having succumbed. And things could get very frustrating. Sometimes I'd come upon instances of spectacular decay but the underlying image was of no particular interest. Worse was when there was a great evocative image but no decay" (qtd. in Weschler).

Here, in a shot that begins a little more than 20 minutes into the film, can be seen part of an early amusement park ride that consists of open-air compartments that hold passengers as they circle the center of the ride in the background. It seems the ride is not only entertaining its passengers as they travel in circles but also disintegrating and disappearing, along with its human occupants.

On one level, the film is about all those films made before the early 1950s and their inevitable losing battle against decay, distortion, and demise. *Decasia* shows the many ways nitrate footage can decay: It can blister, blotch, buckle, smear, and spot. When projected, it may flicker between light and darkness, clarity and obscurity. It may show decay in only one part of the frame or obliterate everything and appear as only swirling abstract images. On another level, critics have detected other implied meanings in the film. Some see *Decasia* as an ongoing but losing battle between life/form/clarity and death/chaos/obscurity. One critic sees it as "a cinematic ghost story. Spectral figures emerge from a mist caused by deterioration of the unstable nitrate film, but given that the images were captured, in some cases, nearly 100 years ago, there's an eerie certainty that the people we see are long dead. It's like watching phantoms from the beginning of film history" (Ide). *From* Decasia, *directed by Bill Morrison, courtesy of Hypnotic Pictures; distributed on DVD by Plexifilm, New York; original source material: Ritchie Trains, Fox Movietone Newsreel outtake, archived at the University of South Carolina Newsfilm Library*

filmmakers much greater mobility and flexibility (Figure 8.19). In the United States, filmmakers using portable equipment developed **direct cinema**, a type of documentary filmmaking in which the film is shot on location with minimal planning. The aim of such films is not so much to prove a point but to explore a subject. An exchange between an interviewer for the film journal *Cineaste* and the filmmaker Frederick Wiseman, who is one of the main practitioners of direct cinema, highlights that purpose:

> CINEASTE: And your film [*Welfare*, 1975] doesn't generalize, at all. Nor does it attempt to suggest any possible solutions or answers. That stance characterizes all of your films.
>
> WISEMAN: That's right. I don't know the answers. I'm interested in the complexities and ambiguities of our experience. (Lucia 9)

long take: A shot of long duration.

Makers of direct cinema attempt to win their subjects' trust and to minimize interference with their lives; consequently, they often use the **long take** and the zoom lens so they may film people from any distance without the camera distracting them.

An example of direct cinema is Michael Wadleigh's *Woodstock*, which shows action on and off stage at a huge open-air concert in upstate New York. This film and others of direct cinema often have technical imperfections: the camera operator sometimes does not refocus on a new subject as quickly as movie viewers are used to seeing. The camera work might occasionally be wobbly; sometimes the dialogue is indistinct; and at times the images

FIGURE 8.19 Increased portability of filmmaking equipment
To film the onstage and offstage action of a three-day outdoor concert attended by an estimated 400,000 people, one or two cameras would have been inadequate. By the time of the Woodstock concert in 1969, documentary filmmakers could use portable 16 mm cameras and lightweight, largely unobtrusive magnetic tape recorders. In this photograph can be seen two of the many cameras (left and extreme left) used in making the documentary *Woodstock* (1970). Some of the cameras were propped on the stage itself; some were mounted on tripods; others were handheld. *Publicity still. A Wadleigh-Maurice, Ltd., Production*

might be too dark or too light. To some viewers these imperfections only strengthen the film's credibility. They can imagine that the film is not a slick, manipulated representation but more nearly a representation of actions as they happened. Nonetheless, as we saw with *Belfast, Maine*, direct cinema entails its own, perhaps less obvious, manipulations. For instance, the filmmakers choose what to film, how to film it, and what shots to include and in what context.

At about the same time as direct cinema emerged, and using the same type of equipment, a similar type of documentary filmmaking, **cinéma vérité**, developed in France. During filming, however, French filmmakers were likely to ask questions of their subjects and talk with them, as in the later cinéma vérité film *Divorce Iranian Style* (1998, Figure 8.20).

Since the late 1990s, documentarians' much wider use of digital video has made possible much longer **takes**, fewer interruptions while filming, and greater portability and thus greater access to subjects. The smaller, more portable equipment may also make the filming less noticeable and intrusive. Perhaps most significantly, because digital equipment is relatively inexpensive, it has opened up documentary filmmaking to many who previously could not afford to make documentaries.

FIGURE 8.20 Documentarians as observers and participants Although *Divorce Iranian Style* (1998) is mostly cinéma vérité, occasional narration is used to fill gaps in the information that viewers need to follow the situations, including occasional questions from the filmmakers to their subjects. Late in the documentary, the filmmakers are unwittingly and briefly transformed from observers and recorders to participants when the divorce court judge turns to the filmmakers and asks if they saw the woman depicted here tear the judge's court order as her husband alleged. After the filmmakers reply that they did not, the judge rescinds his order that the woman be held in detention for a day, although she is still under order to turn over custody of her child, shown here, to her previous husband. *Publicity still. Twentieth Century Vixen; Women Make Movies, New York*

Like fictional filmmakers, documentarians have countless options when it comes to subjects, sources, structure, and techniques, and thus enormous influence over the films they create. All documentary films purport to be factual, not imaginary. Unless viewers lose faith in the credibility of the filmmakers or know of contradictory information from other sources, they accept such films as credible representations of their subjects.

An original extensive 1998 interview with documentary filmmaker Errol Morris can be found on the Web site for this book at <bedfordstmartins .com/phillips-film>.

CLOSE-UP: *HEARTS OF DARKNESS: A FILMMAKER'S APOCALYPSE* AS A NARRATIVE DOCUMENTARY FILM

Hearts of Darkness: A Filmmaker's Apocalypse is a 96-minute narrative documentary written and directed by Fax Bahr with George Hickenlooper. The 1991 film shows some of the background and planning for the making of *Apocalypse Now* (1979) and many of the problems director Francis Coppola and his crew faced as they filmed his fictional Vietnam War epic in the Philippines.

In many ways, *Hearts of Darkness* shows a classic story of one man facing tests of both character and nature as he tries to realize his vision. The film is like **classical Hollywood cinema** in its focus on an individual with goals, a succession of problems that the individual faces in trying to reach them, clear cause-and-effect relationships, **closure**, and unobtrusive filmmaking techniques. *Hearts of Darkness* is also an example of an **independent film** made outside the Hollywood system. It was made on a low budget for the Showtime cable network and was later shown in theaters. For a limited time it was available on videotape, then was out of print, and eventually became available on DVD in 2007.

NARRATIVE COMPONENTS

Hearts of Darkness begins at the Cannes Film Festival in May 1979; soon flashes back to the large, mostly chronological, middle section; then returns briefly to the 1979 Cannes Film Festival and events after it. The film's structure can be represented as B, A, C, although the huge middle section is not always arranged chronologically.

Francis Coppola is the main person in the story of *Hearts of Darkness*, and his goal is transparent: to finish filming an effective story within a reasonable time and at an endurable cost. In attempting to achieve his goal, he is beset with problem after problem—after problem.

Hearts of Darkness shows the three types of conflict possible in a narrative: people versus people, people versus nature, and conflict within a person. The cast was one major source of conflict between people or at least a cause of delays and difficulties. After Coppola replaced Harvey Keitel with Martin Sheen, many scenes had to be reshot. Later, Sheen's heart attack created additional delays and expense. Like many U.S. soldiers late in the Vietnam War, some actors in *Apocalypse Now*, most conspicuously Dennis Hopper and Sam Bottoms, consumed drugs copiously, and Hopper was slow to learn his lines. Marlon Brando's being unprepared and being slow to get into his role caused a major oblique conflict as well.

Coppola was also forced to struggle with nature when a typhoon hit the Philippines and halted production for two months. The American technology that Coppola brought to the Philippines was no match for the storm, which destroyed sets and disrupted the production. Both Sheen and Coppola suffered from conflict within themselves: Sheen during filming of the hotel room scene and Coppola from time to time as he despaired about being able to finish and finish well the Herculean task involving himself and many others.

Hearts of Darkness has yet other narrative components. Like most successful stories, its beginning intrigues the audience, in this case by emphasizing that the production was plagued with problems. In the film's opening shots, at a Cannes Film Festival news conference, Coppola says,

> My film is not about Vietnam. It *is* Vietnam. It's what it was really like. It was crazy. And the way we made it was very much like the way the Americans were in

a)

b)

FIGURE 8.21 **Editing that comments on a subject indirectly**
(a) Filipino boys have been playing with a toy sailboat seen here immediately after it topples over.
(b) The next shot is of Coppola talking about building projects inevitably going over budget. The juxtaposition of images suggests that Coppola is like a boy with a toy that is not entirely under control and ends up in an accident. The juxtapositioning of the two shots is sly but expressive. *American Zoetrope; Paramount DVD*

Vietnam. We were in the jungle. There were too many of us. We had access to too much money, too much equipment, and little by little we went insane.

The film continues by supplying additional background, including information about Coppola's despair about being able to conclude filming *Apocalypse Now* successfully. The large middle section presents problems for Coppola and his company that were vexing to them but are of interest to the viewers. The ending of this narrative documentary has closure, a sense of wholeness and completion, implying that eventually the obstacles were overcome and the film became a commercial and critical success.

Like some other narrative documentary films, such as *Hoop Dreams*, *Hearts of Darkness* has two plotlines: Coppola facing major problems while filming and, in far less detail, Coppola facing personal problems (stress, collapse, depression, and suicidal impulses).

Using a structure not uncommon in narrative documentaries, *Hearts of Darkness* presents its tale out of order. The film's middle section is a huge **flashback** that itself is not arranged entirely chronologically. And like nearly all narratives, *Hearts of Darkness* is often vague about when certain actions occurred and how much time it took for some of them to transpire. In common with the treatment of time in nearly all narrative films, the film's **story time** (approximately 4 years) far exceeds its running time (96 minutes). Finally, like nearly all documentaries, the dominant style of *Hearts of Darkness* is **realism**: representation in a text that is widely believed to render its subjects accurately.

DOCUMENTARY ASPECTS

Documentaries are mediated reality and involve the selection and arrangement of information. Like the construction of many other documentaries, the making of *Hearts of Darkness* entailed an enormous amount of selecting and arranging. When the makers of *Hearts of Darkness* were selecting excerpts from earlier texts—such as clips from *Apocalypse Now* and from Eleanor Coppola's footage of the filming of *Apocalypse Now*—they were presenting a mediated reality based on earlier mediated realities.

Hearts of Darkness illustrates yet other recurrent features of the documentary film. It uses real people being themselves. The excerpts from Eleanor Coppola's footage show people doing what they do in their work and in their spare time,

a)   b)

FIGURE 8.22 **Interviewee in late 1970s and more than a decade later**
(a) Dennis Hopper being interviewed during the making of *Apocalypse Now*. (b) The next shot is of Hopper being interviewed during the making of *Hearts of Darkness*. *American Zoetrope; Paramount DVD*

not (presumably) acting or posing for her camera. Like so many other documentaries, *Hearts of Darkness* was filmed on location where the subjects live and work—in this case, mostly in the Philippines.

As has been explained, various documentary films—such as those by Frederick Wiseman and those of Errol Morris—use quite different filmmaking techniques. Sometimes documentarians use a wide variety of techniques within the same film. As a few examples illustrate, *Hearts of Darkness* uses a fairly wide range of techniques. A little more than 37 1/2 minutes into the film, the film cuts from Filipino boys to Coppola himself to suggest a point (Figure 8.21). Editing also shows how much a person has changed when the film occasionally juxtaposes shots of an actor then and now (Figure 8.22). Another particularly expressive example of filmmaking occurs when the camera moves in on a photograph of Coppola and on one of his darkened eyes; after a **fade-out** and **fade-in**, the camera moves back, and viewers see a different photo of Coppola holding a pistol to his head (Figure 8.23).

Hearts of Darkness: A Filmmaker's Apocalypse illustrates some of the possibilities of both narratives and documentaries. In showing the trials and eventual triumph of an individual and his associates, the film informs and entertains. It also shows how unpredictable, conplicated, and difficult the

creative process can become. Like other narrative documentaries, *Hearts of Darkness* also gives viewers the opportunity to ponder the unexpected, sometimes far-reaching consequences of actual decisions and actions.

FIGURE 8.23 **Techniques suggesting darkness and despair**
Here, nearly 86 1/2 minutes into *Hearts of Darkness*, a black-and-white photograph shows Coppola with darkened eyes and a face seemingly drained of its usual vitality. In the documentary, this image is paired with excerpts from audio recordings of Coppola despairing about ever finishing the film successfully. The result: Coppola seems desperate and even suicidal. However, in her audio commentary on the DVD for *Hearts of Darkness*, Eleanor Coppola says she thinks the photo is merely another example of the many gags the filmmakers indulged in while on location and has been taken out of context. *American Zoetrope; Paramount DVD*

SUMMARY

Although live-action fictional films have been by far the most popular films in the history of world cinema, there are other major types of films, including the documentary film.

What Are Documentary Films?

- A documentary film or video is a filmed (and usually edited) representation of actual (not imaginary) subjects.

- Documentary films are not reality and are never completely objective and "accurate." They always mediate between reality and the viewer.

- A documentary is a representation by one group of filmmakers. Other filmmakers working on the same subject would inevitably fashion a different representation.

What Might Documentaries Do?

- Documentaries may inform, entertain, criticize (perhaps with the intention of motivating the viewers to action), and celebrate.

- All documentaries inform. Nearly all entertain; otherwise, they will fail to hold the audience's attention. Many documentaries criticize or celebrate their subjects.

- Many documentaries have more than one of those four major results. *Justifiable Homicide*, for example, informs, entertains, criticizes, and celebrates.

What Steps Might Be Taken to Construct Documentaries?

- In making a documentary, filmmakers select the subject or subjects, locate and select from a huge variety of possible sources, structure the material into a nonnarrative or narrative, and use various filmmaking techniques, possibly a huge range of them.

- A documentary may be about almost any actual or real subject such as human behavior, animal behavior, plant life, or any other aspect of science.

- Documentary films usually include supporting artifacts—such as photographs or film clips—and informative language, such as narration or interviews, or both.

- Most documentary films present no narrative or story. The information in many nonnarrative documentary films is organized into groups or categories.

■ Narrative documentary films present stories that are largely factual, but like fictional films they are never simply a succession of related events. For example, they may linger on settings from time to time or interrupt the narrative for interviews.

■ As *Woodstock* and *The Thin Blue Line* illustrate, documentarians may use an enormous variety of film techniques.

How Does Filmmaking Technology Affect the Documentary Films Made?

■ Before the 1960s, the visual and sound recording equipment used to make documentary films was heavy and not very portable, and documentarians had few opportunities to film and record sound at difficult locations and to make moving-camera shots.

■ In the late 1950s and early 1960s, development of 16 mm fast film, handheld 16 mm cameras with a zoom lens, and portable sound packs gave filmmakers much greater mobility and flexibility, and filmmakers in the United States and France, for example, began making documentary films that were shot on location with minimal planning.

■ Since the late 1990s, documentarians' much wider use of digital video has made possible much longer takes, fewer interruptions while filming, and greater portability and thus greater access to subjects. The smaller, more portable equipment may also make the filming less intrusive. Because digital equipment is relatively inexpensive, it has opened up documentary filmmaking to many who previously could not afford to make documentaries.

Major Terms about Documentary Films

Below, numbers in italics refer to the pages where the terms are explained. All terms are defined in more detail in the Illustrated Glossary beginning on p. 667.

cinéma vérité *391*
compilation film *377*
direct cinema *390*
documentary film *364*

mediated reality *364*
narrative documentary film *382*
nonnarrative documentary film *380*

QUESTIONS ABOUT DOCUMENTARY FILMS

The following questions are intended to help viewers understand a documentary film, which is one of the major alternatives to live-action fictional films. Not all the questions are appropriate for every film. In thinking out, discussing, and writing responses to the questions most appropriate for the film being examined, be careful to stick with the issues the questions raise, to answer all parts of the questions, to explain the reasons for your answers, and to give specific examples from the film.

1. In what ways is the film a mediation on reality?

2. A documentary may inform, entertain, criticize (and sometimes motivate viewers to take certain actions), or celebrate. Which of these does the film do? Why do you say so? If editing is used to criticize or praise a subject, give a detailed example.

3. What is the film's major subject(s)?

4. What are the different types of sources used to represent the film's subject(s)?

5. Is the film a nonnarrative or narrative? Explain why you say so.

6. What major filmmaking techniques are used? To what effect?

WORKS CITED

Applebome, Peter. "A Taste for the Eccentric, Marginal, and Dangerous." *New York Times on the Web* 26 Dec. 1999.

Apted, Michael. Interview. *The Bob Edwards Show*. XM Satellite Radio. 22 Feb. 2007.

Bates, Peter. "Truth Not Guaranteed: An Interview with Errol Morris." *Cineaste* 17.1 (1989): 16–17.

Berardinelli, James. "*Winged Migration*: A Film Review." *ReelViews* online.

Blank, Les (independent filmmaker). Telephone interview. Apr. 1995.

Coppola, Francis. Audio commentary. *Hearts of Darkness: A Filmmaker's Apocalypse*. Paramount DVD, 2007.

Corliss, Richard. "Take This Job and Love It." *Time* 27 Oct. 1997: 111.

Gardner, Robert. "Chronicles of the Human Experience: *Dead Birds*." *Nonfiction Film Theory and Criticism*. Ed. Richard Meran Barsam. New York: Dutton, 1976. 342–48.

Hasan, Mark R. Rev. of DVD of *Chisholm '72: Unbought & Unbossed*. KQEK.com.

Ide, Wendy. "Decasia." [London] *Times Online* 2 Oct. 2003.

Jaehne, Karen. Rev. of *Fast, Cheap & Out of Control*. *Film Quarterly* 52.3 (Spring 1999): 43–47.

Jarecki, Andrew. Interview. *Fresh Air*. Nat'l. Public Radio. 24 June 2003.

Lucia, Cynthia. "Revisiting *High School*: An Interview with Frederick Wiseman." *Cineaste* 20.4 (Oct. 1994): 5–11.

Nichols, Bill. *Introduction to Documentary*. Bloomington: Indiana UP, 2001.

Weschler, Lawrence. "Sublime Decay." *New York Times* 22 Dec. 2002, late ed.: sec. 6: 44.

FOR FURTHER READING

Bruzzi, Stella. *New Documentary: A Critical Introduction*. London: Routledge, 2000. Provides a comprehensive account of the last two decades of documentary filmmaking in the United States, Great Britain, and Europe. Also explores how issues of gender identity, queer theory, performance, "race," and spectatorship are important to an understanding of contemporary documentary.

Collecting Visible Evidence. Ed. Jane M. Gaines and Michael Renov. Minneapolis: U of Minnesota P, 1999. Sixteen essays by various film scholars for the advanced introductory student.

Documenting the Documentary: Close Readings of Film and Video. Ed. Barry Keith Grant and Jeannette Sloniowski. Detroit: Wayne State UP, 1998. Essays by twenty-seven film scholars; each essay is focused on one or two major films.

Ellis, Jack C., and Betsy A. McLane. *A New History of Documentary Film*. New York: Continuum, 2005. Focuses mainly on the history of U.S., U.K., and Canadian documentaries. Each chapter concludes with a list of key documentaries for the chapter's period or genre. Appendixes list all the winners of the Academy Award for Best Documentary and the winners of the Grierson Award.

Five Films by Frederick Wiseman: Titicut Follies, High School, Welfare, High School II, Public Housing. Transcribed and edited by Barry Keith Grant. Berkeley: U of Calif. P, 2006. Transcription of each film's soundtrack, including spoken words, music, and some of the ambient sound, plus notes about the editing and camera work. Also includes photographs, a bibliography, and a filmography.

Rothman, William. *Documentary Film Classics*. Cambridge: Cambridge UP, 1997. Detailed analyses, supported with many frame enlargements, of some major documentary films, such as *Nanook of the North*, *Chronicle of a Summer*, and *Don't Look Back*.

CHAPTER 9

Experimental, Hybrid, and Animated Films

T HE PREVIOUS CHAPTER DISCUSSES **documentary films**, one major alternative to the live-action fictional film. This chapter considers three additional alternatives: **experimental**, **hybrid**, and **animated** films.

EXPERIMENTAL FILMS

> The experience [of studying experimental films] provides us with the opportunity (an opportunity much of our training has taught us to resist) to come to a clearer, more complete understanding of what the cinematic experience actually can be, and what—for all the pleasure and inspiration it may give us—the conventional movie experience is *not*. (MacDonald 2)

Scott MacDonald is a scholar of the experimental film; he and other scholars believe, as I do, that studying experimental films broadens and deepens one's understanding of the film medium. As experimental filmmaker and **film theorist** Edward Small demonstrates in his book *Direct Theory: Experimental Film/Video as Major Genre*, restricting one's study to fictional films limits one's understanding of the film medium.

In this section, we consider these four questions: What are experimental films? What are sources and subjects for experimental films? What **film techniques** might be used to make them? What are some of the types of experimental films? But first, to get an idea of what an experimental film might be, let's examine one in some detail.

Although no one film can be representative of such a large and diverse group of films, "Refraction" (2004), a digital video installation by the Dutch artist Aernout Mik, has many typical experimental qualities. Its subject, the aftermath of an accident, has appeared in many **narratives**, or stories, including countless movies. But in "Refraction," the artist steadfastly refuses to supply viewers with enough information to construct a coherent narrative.

Terms in **boldface** are defined in the Illustrated Glossary beginning on page 667.

hybrid film: A film that has characteristics of two or all three film categories: fictional, documentary, or experimental.

film theorist: A person who formulates a general explanation of the film medium or part of the medium.

film(making) technique: Any aspect of filmmaking, such as the use of sets, lighting, sound effects, music, or editing.

aspect ratio: The proportion of the width to the height of the image on a TV or movie screen or on individual frames of film.

event: In a narrative or story, either an action by a character or person or a happening (a change brought about by a force other than a person or character, such as a lightning strike).

The film, which has a **running time** of about 30 minutes, runs continuously in a loop with no beginning and no ending and with no opening or closing credits. It is shown on three side-by-side rear-projection screens mounted inside two temporary white walls that are joined at a slight angle. Two of the screens are on one wall, and the contiguous third screen is at a slight angle from the other wall. The composite wide film images, which nearly reach the museum floor, have an **aspect ratio** (or screen shape) of about 4:1. In the installation I saw in Chicago, viewers who wanted to could walk behind the walls and see the three video projectors on the floor and the projected images reversed, so, for example, what was seen originally on the right side of the composite **frame** was then seen on the left. The video's **events** take place at a rural highway crash site and the adjacent area.[1] The action consists mainly of lots of people seemingly engaged in various aspects of rescue and, even more so, of investigation after a large bus has crashed (Figure 9.1).

---

[1]The exhibition catalogue for the video installation, *Aernout Mik: Refraction*, includes seventeen large color photos representing parts of the film (see p. 433).

FIGURE 9.1 Antithesis of classical Hollywood cinema
Aernout Mik's digital video installation "Refraction" (2004), which is shown in a loop and has no clear beginning or ending, shows some of what happens after a bus has presumably crashed and split in two. This publicity still illustrates only about one-third of the width of the image. At various points in the film, viewers see military, fire, and rescue personnel, medical workers, and police. Later we see some of the drivers of that long line of vehicles, seen here in the background, held up as a consequence of the "accident." Elsewhere in the film, a flock of shepherd-less sheep and goats that no one at the crash site seems to pay any attention to crosses one side of the rescue area. More than once we see hogs snorting and wallowing in mud. Officials seem to be searching the nearby surrounding area. What we never see are blood or injured or dead victims, though we see two or three survivors who seem to have suffered no trauma. Throughout the film, the camera moves nearly constantly, pausing only ever so briefly, never giving viewers a chance to examine any of the many details. *Aernout Mik. New Museum of Contemporary Art, New York; Museum of Contemporary Art, Chicago; Hammer Museum, Los Angeles*

As is usual, we try to make sense of the film as we watch it—for example, by figuring out what its story is. What happened? A bus accident. Why? Impossible to say. Post–9/11 viewers of "Refraction" may suspect that terrorists or bioterrorists are to blame. Perhaps. But would terrorists bother with a mere bus out in the countryside? There is no central character or group of characters. There is no sound at all to offer viewers clues. There are no **close-ups** of faces, **reaction shots**, or meaningful **cuts** from one **shot** to another. The film is fluid and unobtrusive, not only in camera movement but also in transitions from shot to shot.

What **meanings** might viewers construct? Maybe the film suggests that major operations in modern life are only elaborate, slow-moving, mysterious busywork by individuals who work without emotion and largely in their own world, even as their actions thwart others from achieving their goals (in this case, traveling away from the town or city that we can see in the far background). The film lacks the unity, focus, and clarity that a story can bring to a succession of events, and the causes and consequences of the silent moving show before us remain mysterious.

Generally speaking, American audiences and the Dutch filmmaker have different outlooks. Countless students of American life have observed that the United States can be a land of possibilities for hard working or lucky individuals. Many popular American movies celebrate this **ideology** of individuality—the belief that one person can achieve much and be important in the scheme of things (see Chapter 11). The installation by Aernout Mik, however, suggests no such meaning, showing instead a group whose actions seem unclear, repetitive, and unending and whose achievements are by no means certain, meaningful, or celebrated.

What Are Experimental Films?

The enormous variety of films labeled "experimental" makes *experimental film* difficult to define. At one time or another, films that I consider experimental have been referred to as "avant-garde," "underground," "personal," or "independent." All these labels reveal something of the nature of such films while also hinting at the inadequacy of any one term. Whenever you encounter the term experimental film in this book, think of films that explore the possibilities of the film medium, may be ahead of their times, are out of the mainstream, rely heavily on self-expression, and remain largely or entirely free of the limitations placed on commercial movies.

Experimental films always reject the **conventions** of the most popular (mainstream) films and explore the film medium—for example, the filmmakers may scratch or paint the film itself. Often a major impulse of experimental filmmakers is to rebel against what movies are and what they stand for. Experimental filmmaker, teacher, and author Stan Brakhage argues: "Everything we have been taught about art and the world itself separates us from a profound, true vision of the world. We are straitjacketed

shot (noun): An uninterrupted strip of exposed motion-picture film or videotape that represents a subject during an uninterrupted segment of time.

meaning: An observation or a general statement about a subject, such as a film.

ideology: The fundamental beliefs and values of a society or social group.

convention: A subject or technique that makers of texts and audiences accept as natural or typical in certain contexts.

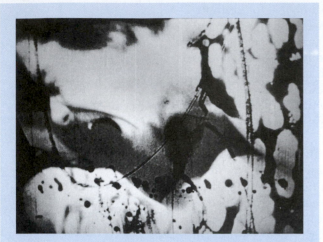

FIGURE 9.2 Experimental film defying sexual mores
"Fuses" (1964–1967) shows filmmaker Carolee Schneemann and her lover enjoying each other sexually in ways unimaginable in commercial movies of the time. As film scholar Wheeler Winston Dixon has written, "this film . . . celebrates the beauty of the female and male body without shame or censorship, with a freedom at once casual and (to some viewers) terrifying" (141). The film momentarily obscures the brief but explicit views of lovemaking by using various techniques: markings on the film stock because it has been baked or scratched, out-of-focus shots, superimpositions, unexpected camera angles, fast cutting, and darkness and ambiguity. *Anthology Film Archives*

by myriad conventions that prevent us from really seeing our world. So it is with the filmmakers" (qtd. in Peterson 4).

Conventional movies reflect the prevailing, usually unexamined, beliefs of a society—its ideology—such as the U.S. belief that one individual can influence the outcome of major developments and that hard work leads to success. In contrast, experimental films tend to question the dominant ideology, including political assumptions and sexual mores. Various experimental U.S. films of the 1960s—for example, Kenneth Anger's "Scorpio Rising" (1963), Barbara Rubin's "Christmas on Earth" (1963), Andy Warhol's "Couch" (made in 1964 but unreleased), and Carolee Schneemann's "Fuses" (1964–1967)—are occasionally sexually explicit (Figure 9.2). Today, this may seem like no big deal, but in the 1960s United States—the production code remained more or less in effect until 1968—it very much was.

Experimental films contrast with movies in other ways. Many are made by one person or a few people; commercial movies are the products of large groups of specialists. Experimental films can be made on a low budget with a video camera or computer (or both); commercial movies typically require large budgets and are made with the latest equipment. Because experimental filmmakers may not seek input from others or face time or budget constraints, there is a danger that viewers may find the result self-indulgent, overly long, and boring. The makers of commercial movies typically try to avoid those very features.

Experimental films frustrate the expectations of viewers brought up on **classical Hollywood cinema** and often aim to startle, shock, or perplex the viewer. For example, in its dreamlike association of scenes, "Un chien andalou" (1928) has no coherent story (Figure 9.3). The film's director, Luis Buñuel, later wrote that "Un chien andalou" "has no intention of attracting nor pleasing the spectator; indeed, on the contrary, it attacks him, to the degree that he belongs to a society with which **surrealism** is at war" (30).

Experimental films rarely show a story.[2] Even if an experimental film initially seems to show a story, such as Michael Snow's 45-minute film

surrealism: In 1920s and 1930s, a movement in European art, drama, literature, and film in which an attempt was made to portray the workings of the subconscious mind as manifested in dreams.

---

[2] In the following paragraphs, I have used some of the phrases that Edward Small uses in his book *Direct Theory: Experimental Film/Video as Major Genre*, but I have added, combined, and renamed characteristics and supplied my own examples.

"Wavelength" (1967), viewers eventually realize that it does not. "Wavelength" has only four brief actions: (1) At the beginning of the film, two men carry in a bookcase accompanied by a woman who indicates where to leave it. The men set the bookcase down, and all three leave. (2) Later, two women enter the room and go to the far side, where one turns on a radio that plays part of a song and the other closes a window. Soon one woman leaves, and the other woman turns off the radio and leaves. (3) After a variety of breaking sounds and footsteps are heard offscreen, a man slowly walks into the room and collapses. (4) Later a woman enters the frame, looks toward where the man had fallen, goes to the phone, and calls someone. The woman says that she thinks the man is dead, asks what to do, and asks the person on the other end of the phone to come over. She hangs up the phone and leaves. Those limited actions are glimpsed during a seemingly continuous 45-minute zoom shot, from wide angle to close-up of a photograph of waves on the back wall, but like nearly all actions in experimental films, they do not add up to a coherent story. "The long journey across the loft . . . deliver[s] the audience to the absolute nemesis of the conventional cinema: to a still photograph viewed in silence for several minutes" (MacDonald 36). At first, "Meshes of the Afternoon" (1943) also seems as if it is going to be a story—we see the same character in consecutive scenes—but narrative continuity soon breaks down (Figure 9.4).

FIGURE 9.3 **Lack of coherence in an experimental film** Throughout "Un chien andalou" (1928), directed by Luis Buñuel, the film rejects narrative conventions and often surprises or shocks viewers. For example, at the end of the film, a shot of the main couple walking along a beach is followed by the title card "In the Spring," which is followed by a brief shot of the couple as seen here, buried in sand and presumably dead. To the end, the film rejects coherent narrative. *Luis Buñuel; Les grands films classiques; Transflux Films DVD*

Two other experimental films that are the antithesis of traditional narrative motion pictures are *Blue* (1993)—which was directed by Derek Jarman and is not to be confused with another film of the same title directed by Krzysztof Kieslowski of Poland—and Andy Warhol's *Empire* (1964). *Blue*, Jarman's last film, shows not moving pictures conveying a story but 76 minutes of unvarying solid blue light. The soundtrack of the film does not help convey a story or a group of related stories. Instead, it uses fragments of **narration** (both prosaic and poetic) and other voices, sound effects, and music to reveal some of Jarman's thoughts, observations, memories, and feelings as his eyesight is failing, his body is wasting away, and he is dying of AIDS.[3]

narration: Commentary in a film about a subject in the film or about some other subject, usually by someone offscreen.

---

[3]For the text of *Blue*, see Derek Jarman, *Blue: Text of a Film* (Woodstock, NY: Overlook Press, 1994). For the CD of the film's complete soundtrack (along with a printed transcript), hear *Blue: A Film by Derek Jarman*, Mute/Elektra Nonesuch 79337-2, perhaps while staring at a blue flat surface, such as a blue wall.

FIGURE 9.4 **Lack of narrative in an experimental film**
Alexander Hammid and Maya Deren's "Meshes of the Afternoon" (1943) focuses on one character and various events but lacks narrative continuity and coherence. These ten frames illustrate five consecutive but discontinuous shots. First shot (a–c): The woman (Deren herself) looks down and off-frame; the camera pans left and viewers see what she was seeing: a knife and then herself sleeping. Second shot (d): Now near a window, she looks down, perhaps at herself sleeping. Third shot (e–f): Outside and below, a woman—whom viewers had seen earlier dressed in black and with a mirror instead of a face—rushes away, carrying a large plastic flower. Later in the shot, Deren runs after her (here she is seen at the top of the frame). Fourth shot (g–h): The mysterious woman is in the distant background walking rapidly, rounding a corner, and going out of sight. Deren is running toward the mysterious woman but is even farther behind her than she was toward the end of the previous shot; Deren stops and walks off to the left of the frame. Fifth shot (i–j): Deren is again seen at the window; later in the shot she takes a key from her mouth. Like "Un chien andalou" (see Figure 9.3), "Meshes" seems dreamlike and ambiguously symbolic. *Maya Deren; Film-Makers' Cooperative, New York*

Warhol's *Empire* is also far from being a narrative film. It consists of eight seemingly uninterrupted hours of a view of the Empire State Building from the same camera position and comes close to being only static images, especially in the short term. The film is the antithesis of traditional films. It has no human subject, no perceptible variation in its subject, little noticeable movement from moment to moment, and no variation in filmmaking techniques. Furthermore, the **pace** is *so* slow that the film gives viewers extremely little information during its very lengthy duration, except that outdoor lighting changes gradually over time, which is something everyone already knows.

> **pace:** The rate of speed at which the film's subjects (such as events in a narrative film or information in a documentary film) are revealed.

Experimental films also often draw attention to themselves as films or to the film medium itself. As we have seen, both fictional and documentary films may also be **self-reflexive**, but experimental films are even more likely to be so. For example, they may show the camera filming part of what will be included in the final version of the film or include a film's opening **leader**. They may show the parts of a projector as it is projecting a film. They may make motion-picture film itself the main subject of a film, as Owen Land did in "Film in which there appear sprocket holes, edge lettering, dirt particles, etc." (1965–66).

> **self-reflexive:** Characteristic of a text—such as a play, novel, or film—that refers to or comments on itself as a text.

> **leader:** The clear or opaque piece of film that begins and concludes a reel of film.

What Are Sources and Subjects for Experimental Films?

Experimental filmmakers have seemingly unlimited reservoirs of sources at their disposal. Sometimes, they explore the creative possibilities of new technology that they can access. For example, experimental filmmakers have explored the expressive possibilities of the **anamorphic lens**. As computer graphics evolved, experimental filmmakers began to experiment with them. Once video became less cumbersome and less costly (and **film stock** and developing film became more expensive), artists and experimental filmmakers increasingly investigated video's creative possibilities. And after computer-editing programs became more affordable, experimental filmmakers explored their creative potential.

> **anamorphic lens:** A lens that squeezes an image onto a film frame in the camera. On a projector, another anamorphic lens returns the image to its original wider shape.

Other experimental filmmakers take a variety of **footage**—TV ads and old movie footage, for example—and reedit it to create **compilation films** that surprise, entertain, and often "take a critical stance toward the culture that supplies their imagery" (Peterson 11). Bruce Conner's first film, a 12-minute work entitled "A Movie" (1958), includes disparate footage from "cowboy and Indian" and submarine adventure movies, newsreels, documentaries, so-called girlie movies (which feature nude or scantily dressed young women posing for the camera), various types of leader including black leader, and **title cards** (Figure 9.5).

> **compilation film:** A film made by editing together clips from other films.

"A Movie" is the antithesis of classical Hollywood cinema. It "is a series of middles and connections, a film without a beginning, with titles and credits broken up and interspersed in the middle; rather than an ending, there is a respite—the film runs down, exhausted" (Mellencamp 192).

> **title card:** A card or thin sheet of clear plastic on which is written or printed information included in a film.

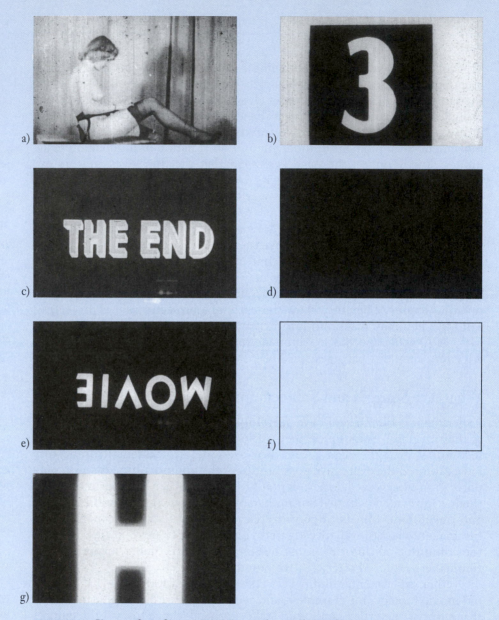

FIGURE 9.5 **Sixteen shots from an experimental compilation film**

Early in Bruce Conner's "A Movie" (1958) occur the following seven brief consecutive shots:
(a) woman taking off a nylon stocking; (b) frame from the leader that normally appears at the
beginning of a reel of film but is used here by Conner after his film is under way; (c) the first
but not the last time the title card "The End" appears; (d) some black frames; (e) part of the
film's title but here upside down; (f) one of four clear frames, which when projected results in
a split second of bright white light; (g) an "H," which will be followed by "E," "A," and "D,"
letters that are also included in the leader that is attached to the beginning of a reel of film.

The film immediately shows that it will differ from classical Hollywood movies in many
fundamental ways. No story is begun, let alone developed. In fact, it is difficult to see how the
shots are related. Some of the apparatus of cinema—especially the leader—is shown rather than

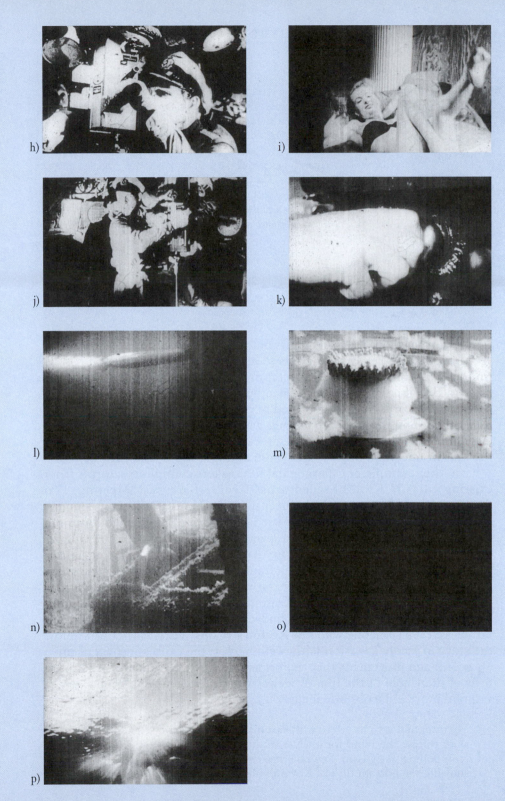

h)

i)

j)

k)

l)

m)

n)

o)

p)

hidden from viewers as it normally would be. Some images are inverted. Parts of the film are blank, either black or white. And parts of the film are placed out of order. For example, "The End" title card appears early in the film, but not at the conclusion.

Later in "A Movie" occur the following six shots: (h) a submarine officer looking into a periscope; (i) a woman dressed in a bikini posing for the camera; (j) the officer giving an order; (k) a hand pushing a mechanism forward; (l) a torpedo being fired from a submarine; and (m) a nuclear explosion. Here the editing creates sexually playful or ominous results: the suggestion that the submarine's phallic-shaped projectile fired at the sexy woman results in a huge explosion.

The film ends with the following three shots: (n) a scuba diver descending into an opening in a sunken ship; (o) some black frames; and (p) the surface of the water seen from below with shimmering sunlight on the surface. During these concluding shots, the music swells to a resolution, though the corresponding visuals convey no sense of unity or completion. There is not even a "The End" title card.

As these images illustrate, "A Movie" lacks continuity and conveys no narrative. In fact, except for its violence and sex, occasional shots of exotic locales (East Asia and Africa), fast cutting, and jaunty music, "A Movie" has little in common with the usual entertaining feature films commonly referred to as "movies." The title of Conner's film is tinged with irony. *Bruce Conner; Anthology Film Archives*

407

FIGURE 9.6 **Compiling excerpts from existing films to create a new film** In "Meeting Two Queens" (1991), shots from the movies of Greta Garbo (left) and Marlene Dietrich (right) are combined to suggest that the two stars interact and eventually become lovers. The film is organized into a dozen or so silent film–style vignettes (a few include music), and each is preceded by a title card indicating the location or situation. Sample vignette titles are "The library," "The telephone," "The dialogue" (in which superimpositions and a split screen make it appear that the two actors interact), and "The alcove" (in which the editing makes it appear that the two stars face each other and begin to undress). *Cecilia Barriga; Women Make Movies, New York*

In its incorporation of leader and its untraditional placement of title cards, "A Movie" is self-reflexive: it refers to its own status as a film. And it continuously thwarts audience expectations. "The End" title card appears early in the film and more than once but not at the end of the film. The opening title cards also are repeated at various points in the film. And the film has rousing music to accompany many images of accidents and disasters (auto, motorcycle, and plane crashes; sinking ships; a dirigible on fire; the mushroom cloud of an atomic blast; falling bridges; and the like).

Another example of experimental filmmakers compiling excerpts from existing films is Chilean video artist Cecilia Barriga's "Meeting Two Queens" (aka "Meeting of Two Queens," 1991, Figure 9.6).

Experimental filmmakers may use not only excerpts from various existing films but also whole films, especially films no longer protected by copyright law, and modify them. In "Keaton's Cops" (1991), Ken Jacobs shows only the bottom fifth of each frame of Buster Keaton's classic silent film "Cops" (1922). In Jacobs's version we can see a subject in its entirety only rarely—for example, when Keaton falls down. Throughout the film, viewers see many feet (and horses' hooves) but not facial expressions. Nevertheless, even someone who saw Keaton's "Cops" years earlier can follow the story in Jacobs's version fairly well. Such is the expressiveness of **mise en scène** and movement that the partial view evokes much of what happens in the whole of the film. A viewer who has never seen "Cops" might respond more as Jacobs intended:

mise en scène: An image's setting, subjects, and composition (the arrangement of setting and subjects within the frame).

My intention is to interfere with narrative coherence and sense. To deny it, so as to release the mind for a while from story and the structuring of incident (compelling as it is in Keaton's masterly development). My filming, only showing the bottom fifth of Keaton's black-and-white screen-world, limits us to the periphery of story. Moves us, from the easy **reading** of an illustrated **text**, towards active seeing. Reduced information means we now must struggle to identify objects and places and, in particular, spaces. A broad tonal area remains flat, clings to the screen, until impacted upon by a recognizable object: Keaton smashes into it, and so it's a wall, diagonal to the screen . . . or a foot steps on it or a wheel rolls across it and it's a road! We become conscious of a painterly screen alive with many shapes in many tones, at the same time that we notice objects and activities (Keaton sets his comedy in some actual street traffic) normally kept from mind by the moviestar-centered moviestory.

Experimental filmmakers may use entire films in many other creative ways. For "Intolerance (Abridged)" (1971), Stan Lawder took D. W. Griffith's *Intolerance* (1916), which runs over 2 hours, copied every twenty-sixth frame twice, and used only those frames in the finished film, thus reducing that film's running time by a factor of thirteen. During a screening, most of the title cards are unreadable, but so expressive are the film's images that much of its story, **structure**, mise en scène, editing, and camera work flash through the onrush of images. Much more recently, R. Luke DuBois developed a digital process to compress feature films into a minute or so. Yes, most of it is a blur, but some individual images are distinct. DuBois used that technique to create *Academy* (2006), a 76-minute film in which each movie that has won the Academy Award for Best Picture is compressed into a minute.

At an opposite extreme, a film's running time may be much increased, as in Scottish video artist Douglas Gordon's transformation of Alfred Hitchcock's *Psycho* (1960) into Gordon's *24 Hour Psycho* (1993). The new film consists of *Psycho* projected onto a large screen suspended from a ceiling but shown not at the usual 24 frames per second but at 2 frames per second. As a consequence, the film's running time of nearly 2 hours is stretched to 24 hours. During such a showing, viewers typically see no movement. Any movement that is fairly rapid in a regular showing of *Psycho* is slow and jerky in *24 Hour Psycho*. At such a slow speed, all sense of pace is lost. Also, the showing of *24 Hour Psycho* unavoidably eliminates all sound. Gordon's simple manipulation of the film transforms *Psycho* into an exceedingly long series of large, silent, still photographs.

The loss of pace and sound eliminates the film's suspense, as when viewers see a vague shadow on the other side of the shower curtain before the famous attack begins 47 minutes into the film. The 12 seconds before the attacker pulls the shower curtain aside last almost 2 1/2 minutes in *24 Hour Psycho*. During *24 Hour Psycho*, viewers are unable to get caught up in the narrative: in the characters, their actions, and the consequences of their actions. Viewers also are denied the satisfaction of experiencing the entire film. Where could one see the complete *24 Hour Psycho*? Certainly not during a museum's normal hours. One could approximate the experience by using a DVD remote to advance the film one frame every half second. But

reading: An interpretation of a text or part of one.

structure: The arrangement of all the parts of a text.

cinematography: Motion-picture photography.

imagine doing that for nearly 24 hours! Anyway, Gordon's film is meant to be experienced as a fragment on a large screen in a museum room. On the other hand, the exceedingly slow speed of *24 Hour Psycho* gives viewers plenty of time to study each frame's **cinematography** and to some extent mise en scène. (The fragment of the 2005 presentation I saw at the Milwaukee Art Museum was not in the original 1.85:1 aspect ratio, as in Figure 5.9a on p. 233, but in approximately 1.33:1.) Gordon's *24 Hour Psycho* also gives viewers lots of time to ponder what is gained and lost when a film is projected at an exceedingly slow speed and without its soundtrack. Another way to put it: *24 Hour Psycho* allows viewers to ponder what the soundtrack and normal projection speed contribute to the film experience.

Other sources for experimental films include subjects usually avoided in narrative. One such subject is the possible combinations of abstract forms and music, as in Norman McLaren and Evelyn Lambart's "Begone Dull Care" (1949, Figure 9.7). Another subject for experimental films is the scope and limitations of mental activities, as in "(nostalgia)" (1971, Figure 9.8).

Yet another nonnarrative subject for an experimental film is human perception and cognition, as in J. J. Murphy's "Print Generation" (1974). The film consists of 3,002 shots: fifty generations of sixty shots plus two title cards. A generation is a copy, so the second generation of a shot is not quite as distinct as the first, and the third generation is a copy of a copy and

FIGURE 9.7 Exploring ways to combine shifting abstract forms and music
Here, the acclaimed Canadian filmmaker Norman McLaren paints on clear 35 mm film in making part of "Begone Dull Care" (1949), a 7 1/2-minute abstract film with a soundtrack played by a jazz trio. "After the score was recorded, McLaren and Evelyn Lambart began working on the visual material. . . . They painted long strips of film jointly and separately, then they would view the freshly painted strips (after drying) through a Moviola [editing/viewing machine] with the music. Many times they would paint five or six variations for one section of music, then select the one which went best with the music" (Richard 70). *Norman McLaren and Evelyn Lambart; National Film Board of Canada*

FIGURE 9.8 **The limits of memory and other subjects**
Hollis Frampton's experimental film "(nostalgia)" (1971) begins with (a) the title card and the simultaneous narration: "These are recollections of a dozen still photographs I made several years ago." Each of the following shots shows (b) a bird's-eye view of a photograph and (c) the photograph slowly catching fire on top of a hot plate and completely combusting as a narrator gives background and brief commentary about the *next* photograph viewers will see. After the narration accompanying each photo ends, in one to two minutes of silence we see (d) ashes slowly twisting on the hot plate. The film's last shot includes narration for a photo we viewers never get to see (even at the film's beginning) about which the narrator concludes, "What I believe I

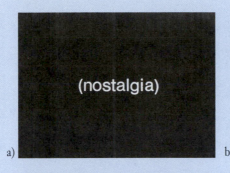 a)

 b)

 c)

 d)

see recorded in that speck of film fills me with such fear, such utter dread and loathing, that I think I shall never dare to make another photograph. Here it is. Look at it. Do you see what I see?" Then the image goes black. The film is constructed to prevent viewers from experiencing synchronized image and sound throughout and suggests the difficulty of linking memory to the appropriate image, the transitory quality of images, and the impossibility of capturing and holding on to the past. *Hollis Frampton; Film-Makers' Cooperative, New York*

is even less clear. Before the fiftieth generation of a shot, its content is unrecognizable. (The same thing happens with a photocopy machine if you make a copy, then a copy of the copy, and so forth for a total of fifty generations.) The film begins with the forty-ninth generation of each of sixty shots; these images are a series of abstract patterns of indistinct lights against a reddish background, such as in Figure 9.9a. Gradually viewers figure out that the film is made up of many brief full-color shots of the same duration (1 second each) and can discern more and more of the subjects of other shots until, near the middle of the film, almost all of the subjects are recognizable (Figure 9.9b–h). However, it's impossible to see much of a connection between the sixty shots, so by near the film's middle viewers conclude that the sixty shots do not constitute a story.

After the title card "Print Generation/(A-WIND)/JJ Murphy/©1973–74," the images begin to return gradually to the abstract patterns seen at the film's beginning. The film ends with the fiftieth generation of each shot and a second title card: "Print Generation/(B-WIND)/JJ Murphy/

FIGURE 9.9 Perception and cognition as subjects
Eight spaced frame enlargements from different generations of the same 1-second shot illustrate the gradual increased resolution of an image during the first half of J. J. Murphy's "Print Generation" (1974). *J. J. Murphy; Film-Makers' Cooperative, New York*

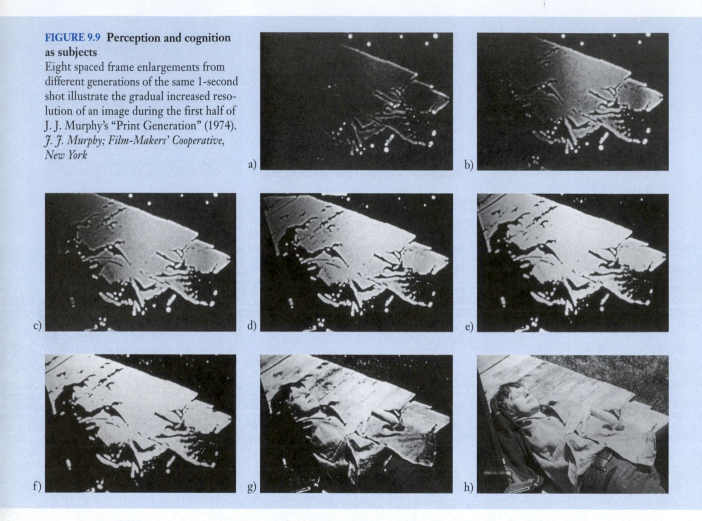

©1973–74." Overall as the film progresses from abstract patterns to recognizable subjects and back to abstract patterns, an opposite action is happening on the soundtrack: sounds of ocean waves gradually become unrecognizable, then, after the middle title card, again gradually become recognizable.

In experiencing "Print Generation," viewers watch, listen, and think as they try to perceive the film's subjects, see a unity to the shots, and make some meaning from the film's 3,002 shots. On one level, the film is about the changes that occur to images as more and more generations are made from them: beneath recognizable film images are increasingly abstract patterns, and underneath a full-color film image is less and less color until only red remains (the bottom layer of color **emulsion**). "Print Generation" is also about the limitations of perception, visual and auditory, and

emulsion: A clear gelatin substance containing a thin layer of the tiny light-sensitive particles (grains) that make up a photographic image.

cognition: as more and more distortion is introduced into the **representation** of the subjects, viewers are limited as to what they can perceive and understand. On the most general level, the film shows that signs of life emerge from chaos and just as quickly return to chaos. Murphy could have structured the film so that it began with recognizable subjects that gradually decompose and later regenerate into the original images. Such a structure would have suggested a different, more upbeat meaning: life may decompose into unrecognizable parts and just as quickly regenerate itself and end up whole and knowable.

representation: A likeness of a subject created in a text.

What Film Techniques Might Be Used to Make Experimental Films?

Experimental filmmakers tend to explore film techniques. They may superimpose a readable text over a moving image, present parts of the film upside down (see Figure 9.5e), or use double or triple exposure. Experimental filmmakers may scratch, paint, dye, or bake a strip of exposed and processed film. An entire film may be made without a camera: the film consists of images scratched or painted directly onto film or leader plus perhaps a soundtrack (see Figure 9.7). For part of an untitled black-and-white film made by George Kuchar and his college film class, Kuchar gave each student actor "white eyebrows, lipstick, etc., on a face that was painted black." Then the footage of the black-faced actors was processed and the processed **negative** was included with the rest of the finished film. Kuchar later wrote, "It all worked out OK except that their teeth appeared black whenever they smiled. This made for a rather horrifying and funny effect as we were shooting glamour shots of the rather attractive cast." In "Pas de deux" (aka "Duo," 1968), Norman McLaren uses two dancers dressed in white against a black background and on a black floor, opposing bright light from each side of the frame, and frequent flowing multiple images made with an **optical printer**. In a dance in **slow motion**, the film shows the isolation, courtship, and tentative union of male and female with novelty, grace, and feeling (Figure 9.10).

As a traditional film, video, or DVD is made, the camera, film or videotape, lenses, and so on are used in fundamentally conventional ways. For example, the camera is used to film consecutive frames, not every other one or every third one. When a conventional film,

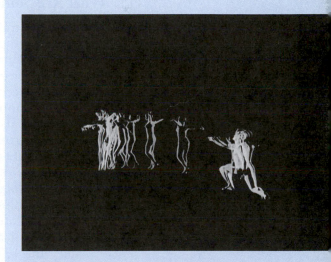

FIGURE 9.10 Untraditional filmmaking techniques, traditional subject
Using an optical printer to make multiple images of one or both of the dancers in the 13-plus-minute black-and-white "Pas de deux" (1968), Norman McLaren combines music with the expressiveness of human movement during a dance of male and female courtship. Here, nearly 11 1/4 minutes into the film, the male reaches toward the female. A few moments later, they both gradually and temporarily appear as single images again—as they do at the end of the film. *National Film Board of Canada; Image Entertainment DVD*

video, or DVD is shown, its components—film–projector–screen, video-tape–video player–monitor, or DVD–DVD player–monitor/screen—also tend to be used in the usual ways. For example, traditionally the same lens is used throughout a film showing. Many experimental films, though, change one or more of the basic components of making and exhibiting a film, video, or DVD. A film is normally projected onto a flat, white, reflective, rectangular screen or wall, but it need not be. During the opening night of the 1996 Los Angeles exhibition on the relationship of film and art since 1945, a film was projected onto a woman's bare chest, and throughout the exhibition different films were projected onto objects such as a bucket of milk and a spinning fan. In another part of the exhibit, a video projector suspended above an unmade bed projected a video image of a reclining man onto the bed. Table 9.1 lists basic components of film apparatus and some conventional and unconventional ways in which filmmakers may use them.

What Are Some of the Types of Experimental Films?

Experimental films have been categorized in different ways by different scholars. Sometimes they are divided into "representational" and "abstract." In representational experimental films, the subjects are recognizable as people and real objects, as in "Un chien andalou" (see Figure 9.3). In **abstract films**, the subjects are unrecognizable, as in "Begone Dull Care" (see Figure 9.7). In a more sophisticated classification, film theorist James Peterson divides American experimental films since World War II into three "open and flexible grouping[s]": poetic, minimal, and assemblage (especially compilations of footage) (10). Edward Small divides experimental film and video into five categories: European avant-garde, American avant-garde, American underground, expanded cinema, and minimalist-structuralist (81). So boundless is human imagination, however, that two or three or five categories often prove inadequate, and many experimental films elude clear-cut classification.

abstract film: An experimental film whose subjects are shapes and perhaps sounds that do not represent the real world.

Since the 1970s, some films, videos, or DVDs have been combined with other visual objects and arts and shown in museums, usually museums of modern or contemporary art. Such ensemble artworks are called **installation art**. An example is Jeff Wall's "Eviction Struggle" (1988), which combines a fluorescent-lit transparency (about 13 1/2 feet wide and 7 1/2 feet tall) on one side of a gallery wall with nine close-up or **medium close-up** video excerpts of the same struggle and reactions to it on the other side of the wall (Figure 9.11). One version of the installation *Bordering on Fiction: Chantal Akerman's "D'Est"* (1995) consisted of a showing of *D'Est* (*From the East*, 1993), which is Akerman's feature-length documentary, in one museum room; video clips from it on twenty-four monitors in the next room; and in a third room a single video monitor and the filmmaker's recorded voice from yet another source reading a passage in Hebrew from the Bible and a

installation art: An art exhibit or ensemble integrating various objects or arts, such as video images, photographs, furniture, and recorded voices.

TABLE 9.1

Film Apparatus and the Experimental Film: A Few of the Visual Possibilities*

APPARATUS	TRADITIONAL USES	EXPERIMENTAL USES
PRODUCTION		
▪ CAMERA	Filming at the same speed within each shot	Using distorting camera lens(es)
		Filming at variable speeds
		Filming, cranking back, and filming again to produce multiple exposures
▪ FILM	Recording consecutive fragments of space, time, or, most often, both on consecutive frames	Recording mostly clear frames, perhaps resulting in a strobe effect
		Painting
		Scratching
▪ EDITING	Coordinating multiple shots, usually through continuity editing in narrative films	Rejecting editing by making a film consisting of one shot
		Avoiding continuity
		Making a compilation film, a film made up of clips from other films
EXHIBITION		
▪ PROJECTOR	Running at an unvarying speed of 24 or 25 frames per second for modern sound film	Projecting the images upside down, backward, or both
	Using no distorting projector lens(es) other than possibly anamorphic	Causing multiple images, superimposed images, or both through multiple versions
		Projecting through some intervening substance, such as a full fish tank
▪ FINISHED FILM	Depicting consecutive fragments of time, action, or both	Depicting discontinuous fragments of time, action, or both
▪ SCREEN	Using a flat or concave, white, reflective, rectangular, uniform surface for projected film	Using a person's body or an inanimate object, such as a shirt or milk jug, for projected film
▪ THEATER	Allowing audience members to be in full sight of other audience members	Shutting off audience members from each other by erecting panels between seats

*A comparable table could be made for video production and exhibition.

a)

b)

FIGURE 9.11 **Installation art: photography and video**
Jeff Wall's installation "Eviction Struggle," made in British Columbia in 1988, has two sides. (a) On one side of an art gallery wall is a large still photograph showing two officers struggling with a man (to the right of the car parked at an angle to the sidewalk), a woman rushing from the direction of a house toward them, and various other people in the neighborhood watching the conflict. (b) The other side of "Eviction Struggle" consists of nine 19-inch video monitors showing brief close-up and medium close-up clips enacting some of the situations seen in the huge photograph. The three monitors on the left and the two monitors on the right side of the wall show people looking at the struggle. The four central monitors show, from left to right, an officer, the struggling man, another officer, and a woman running toward the men. By looking at the large image and then at the nine video monitors (or vice versa), viewers can compare the expressiveness of the photograph's mise en scène with the expressiveness of video clips of the same subject. The nine monitors also allow viewers to function as editors in that they select the order, duration, and repetition, if any, of the clips seen. The installation gives viewers the opportunity to compare and contrast two different representations of the same subject and to consider the expressiveness and limitations of still photography and video. *Collection: Ydessa Hendeles Art Foundation, Toronto*

selection from her own writings about the film. "Viewed in its entirety, *Bordering on Fiction: Chantal Akerman's 'D'Est'* engages in a deconstructive tour of the production process, working back from the completed feature film to the individual shot segments of which it is constructed and, in the end, back to language itself" (*Bordering* 9).

One of the biggest problems facing the student of experimental films is getting to see them, especially if one does not live near a museum of modern or contemporary art or near a large city offering a wide range of film show-ings. Video stores rarely carry them. (For that matter, some experimental filmmakers do not allow their films to be transferred to videotape or DVD.) Cable channels are of limited help, although the Sundance Channel and the Independent Film Channel sometimes show them. Some libraries have a few of the classic titles or may be able to get them for you through interlibrary loan. Some university film series show them from time to time. For videos and DVDs, Facets Multimedia in Chicago has some titles or collections of short experimental films. The DVD series of award-winning short films called "Short" (Short 1, Short 2, and so forth) includes some experimental films. Searches on the Web will help you locate some of the classic short experimental films, such as "Un chien andalou." *By Brakhage: An Anthology* (2003) is a two-DVD set that includes twenty-six Stan Brakhage films, and the DVDs for the two-volume set *The Films of Kenneth Anger* (2007) together contain ten of Anger's most important short films. On the Web, Flicker in-cludes information about a wide array of experimental films and filmmakers and many useful links. As Flicker's home page asserts, "Here you will find films and videos that transgress the boundaries of the traditional viewing experience, challenge notions of physical perception, and provide cutting edge alternatives to the media information technocracy."

HYBRID FILMS

Most films are clearly one of the three major film types: fictional, documen-tary, or experimental. Viewers watching any of the *Lord of the Rings*–related films, for example, never think of them as anything other than fiction. View-ers of *Hoop Dreams*—which is about two actual Chicago inner-city youths hoping to one day play in the National Basketball Association—see the film strictly as a documentary. "Un chien andalou" is unmistakably an experi-mental film. Some films, however, are difficult to categorize. A film with characteristics of two or all three of the major film types is a hybrid film.

Combinations of experimental and documentary appear from time to time in **independent films** from various nations. Two examples are *Man with the Movie Camera* (1929; see Figure 8.17 on p. 389) and *Decasia* (2001; see Figure 8.18, also on p. 389). Another experimental documentary is Andy Warhol's *Sleep* (1963), which shows only a man sleeping for nearly 5 1/2 hours. *Sleep* is a documentary film—it shows its subject factually—yet it is so unconventional as to be experimental (so long, so uneventful, so unvaried, so unengaging).

"You Take Care Now" (1989) by Canadian Ann Marie Fleming is an experimental **narrative documentary**. The film uses a blank screen, a wobbly camera that causes blurred images, repeated close-ups of a live bird's head surrounded by animated lines and patterns, the head of a man jumping up into the frame briefly and repeatedly (the camera is aimed

independent film: Film made mainly or entirely without support or input from the dom-inant, established film industry.

narrative documentary: A film or video representation of an actual (not imaginary) narrative or story.

above his head), an **extreme close-up** of a man's mouth as he presumably shouts curses as viewers hear a dog barking, snow on a TV screen, an out-of-focus night shot, and many other techniques to help convey the disorientation and physical and psychological pain of being raped and on another occasion being hit by one car and run over by another. The film's female **narrator** recounts two brief, presumably factual stories and provides whatever context and continuity the film has; the visuals show little of the stories and instead create or reinforce moods.

Experimental documentaries are also made by the Iranian American filmmaker Shirin Neshat. In "Turbulent" (1998), two black-and-white videos are projected on opposite sides of a room as viewers sit against either of the two remaining walls (Figure 9.12). In one of the videos, "a veiled woman waits by a microphone before an empty auditorium. In the other, a bearded man dressed in a white shirt and dark pants, like the men who fill the audience before him, sings a classical Persian song . . . about divine love. . . . When the man has finished, the woman begins. Her wordless song . . . is a primal emotional language, poised uncertainly between love and lament, bliss and pain. The camera swirls around her as her face contorts with the rhythmic, guttural cries emerging from her body" (Camhi 151). The film reinforces the idea that the man and woman reside in different worlds by three means: (1) There are many differences between the man and woman, including the ways they are dressed, their audience (or lack of one), the subjects of their songs, and the manner of their singing. (2) She is filmed with a moving, exploratory camera and he with a stationary one. (3) Finally, they are seen on opposite walls and in no way interact with each other.

It is possible, though extremely rare, for parts of a film to be fictional and other parts of the same film to be documentary. Such a rare combination is found in Su Friedrich's *Hide and Seek* (1996), which **cross-cuts** between (1) a short fictional film set in the 1960s about a 12-year-old girl beginning

narrator: A character, a person, or an unidentifiable voice in a film that provides commentary about subjects in the film or outside it, or both.

cross-cut: In editing, to alternate between events occurring at different settings and often presumably at the same time.

a)

FIGURE 9.12(a) Hybrid film: experimental and documentary
During a showing of "Turbulent" (1998), footage of a man singing a traditional song presumably in contemporary Iran is shown on one wall of a room as on the opposite wall the woman seen on p. 419 waits. *Shirin Neshat, "Turbulent," Video Still, © 1998 Shirin Neshat, Courtesy Barbara Gladstone*

puberty and more attracted to girls than to boys, (2a) documentary interviews of adult lesbians recounting some of their childhood feelings and experiences, and (2b) various documentary artifacts, such as photographs of lesbians when they were young girls, clips from movies, and archival footage from home movies and educational films, including the kinds of sex education films used in schools at that time.

A film may look and sound like a documentary but in fact be fictional. Such films have been given different names: mock documentaries (or mock docs or mockumentaries), fake documentaries, and pseudodocumentaries. All such films are mock or fake in the sense that they are imitative or counterfeit. But such a variety of films cannot accurately be labeled by one name, so I am calling one group ***mock documentaries*** and the even smaller group of fictional films that pass as documentaries ***fake documentaries***.

As is explained in Chapter 5, mock documentaries, such as *This Is Spinal Tap* (1984), are **parodies** of documentary films (see Figure 5.17 on p. 239). Another example of a mock documentary is Sacha Baron Cohen's *Borat: Cultural Learnings of America for Make Benefit Glorious Nation of Kazakhstan* (2006). That film looks and sounds as if it could be a Kazakhstan TV documentary that shows some aspects of Borat Sagdiyev's life in Kazakhstan, then highlights of his eventful trip to New York and across the "U.S. and A.," and finally and briefly his situation after his return to his home country. Viewers are meant to catch on to the joke early in the film and realize that the film is actually a parody. If viewers have not learned beforehand that *Borat* is an amusing put-on or do not figure that out during the film, they can learn from the end credits that the film has screenwriters. Four of them are credited, including Sacha Baron Cohen (who plays the character of Borat in the film). The surest giveaway that a film is not a documentary is writers' credits in the film's credits. Documentaries have no "writers," whereas fictional narratives always have at least one.

parody (noun): An amusing imitation of a text, part of a text, or group of texts, often to satirize or to playfully poke fun.

FIGURE 9.12(b) **Hybrid film: experimental and documentary**
During a showing of "Turbulent" (1998), after the man seen on p. 418 finishes singing a traditional Iranian song and waits, footage of an Iranian woman singing an untraditional song is seen on the opposite wall. *Shirin Neshat, "Turbulent," Video Still, © 1998 Shirin Neshat, Courtesy Barbara Gladstone*

b)

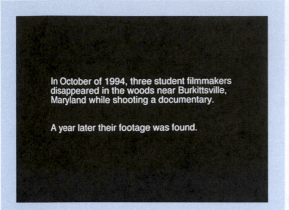

In October of 1994, three student filmmakers disappeared in the woods near Burkittsville, Maryland while shooting a documentary.

A year later their footage was found.

FIGURE 9.13 A narrative fake documentary Title cards—such as the one seen here at the beginning of *The Blair Witch Project* (1999)—are often used in documentaries to convey factual information. *Blair Witch* has other characteristics of many documentaries, such as shaky, handheld camera shots and interviews. As many viewers watch the film, they are convinced it is a documentary. In fact, *The Blair Witch Project* is not a documentary but the product of the imaginations and work of some film students at the University of Central Florida. *Haxan Entertainment; Artisan Entertainment DVD*

At first, mock documentary films seem to be factual to the viewer, in part because they follow many of the conventions of documentary filmmaking—for example, by using interviews, subtitles, and handheld camera shots. But the mock documentary does not mean to trick viewers into permanently believing that the film's subjects are actual people. Instead, by the use of extreme exaggeration, preposterous coincidence, and other means, the mock documentary clues viewers that it is a (good-natured) parody of documentaries and thus an extended joke to be enjoyed beginning just as soon as the viewer catches on.

Other, very rare hybrids also look and sound like documentaries but are not parodies; they are instead earnest imitations of documentaries that are meant to sustain the viewers' belief in their factuality. An example of these fake documentaries is *The Blair Witch Project* (1999, Figure 9.13). A fake documentary does not necessarily show a narrative or story, as is illustrated by *Slacker* (1990, Figure 9.14). Viewers beware. One of the lessons of the fake documentary: skillful filmmakers can use documentary techniques to mislead viewers into believing a representation is essentially factual when it is not.

Peter Watkins's "The War Game" (1965), which shows the horrifying consequences of a nuclear attack on Britain, is another film that looks and sounds like a documentary. The concluding credits identify it as "this documentary film." The film won an Academy Award for Best Documentary. Yet unlike other documentaries, it does not record or reenact what *happened* but instead enacts what *could* happen. A number of times in the film, the narrator reminds viewers that what is being seen has not happened but could. For example, a little more than 33 minutes into the film, the narrator says, "Everything that you are now seeing happened in Germany after the heavy bombing in the last war. It would almost certainly have to happen in Britain after a nuclear war." The film also has some of the major components of a fictional film: a writer, entirely enacted actions, and actors. "The War Game" is not a documentary in the usual sense. It is not exactly a **docudrama**, either, because its representations are all fictional and it has a narrator reminding us that the actions haven't happened but could. The film is certainly not a mock documentary. And it is not a nonnarrative fake documentary in all the same ways *Slacker* is. Though the film blends fictional and documentary, it is difficult to categorize.

Films, especially independent films, may also combine elements of fiction and the experimental. *The Cabinet of Dr. Caligari* (1919) is a fictional

docudrama: A film that re-creates and dramatizes occurrences from history.

FIGURE 9.14 A nonnarrative fake documentary

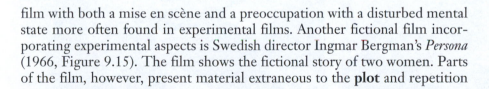

While watching *Slacker* (1990), the viewer might initially think that the film is a documentary made by a highly mobile camera crew that recorded a few subjects briefly (often a one-sided conversation or monologue), picked up a new small group of people and followed them, and repeated this pattern throughout the film. But after a certain point, when it becomes clear that the film has no coherent narrative, the viewer might conclude that the film is a nonnarrative documentary. Then, as the film unspools even further, the viewer might start to suspect that the film is not a documentary after all (for one thing, some episodes seem too contrived and not entirely credible). The concluding credits cite a "writer" (the same person as the producer and director) and someone in charge of casting. *Slacker* is a nonnarrative fake documentary.

The character on the left, identified in the closing credits as "Been on the moon since the 50s," has attached himself to the young man on the right and soon begins spouting a stream of mostly unorthodox theories. He claims, for example, that the United States first got to the moon in the 1950s by using antigravity technology stolen from the Nazis after World War II and that "we've been on Mars since '62." This episode begins 13 3/4 minutes into the film and runs for a little more than 5 minutes. As in the film's other episodes, the one represented here looks and sounds like part of a narrative documentary. The film's episodes, however, are only loosely related (people out of the mainstream, the same 24 hours or so, and the same city). Richard Linklater—the film's producer, writer, and director—has not created a story but re-created a society of mostly youthful outsiders, eccentrics, and loners in Austin, Texas, at the end of the 1980s. *Detour Filmproduction; Criterion DVD*

film with both a mise en scène and a preoccupation with a disturbed mental state more often found in experimental films. Another fictional film incorporating experimental aspects is Swedish director Ingmar Bergman's *Persona* (1966, Figure 9.15). The film shows the fictional story of two women. Parts of the film, however, present material extraneous to the **plot** and repetition

plot: The structure or arrangement of a narrative's events.

FIGURE 9.15 Hybrid film: experimental and fictional
The two main characters of *Persona* (1966) are a nurse, Alma (left), and her patient, Elisabeth (right), a famous actor who suddenly has become mute and withdrawn. As this publicity still suggests, at times the two characters seem to change roles. At other times, as when a shot shows the halves of the two faces seemingly fused into one, they seem to blend into one another. In these and many other ways, *Persona* blends a fictional story and experimental filmmaking. *Svensk Filmindustri; The Museum of Modern Art/Film Stills Archive*

rarely found in a fictional film: self-reflexive shots of motion-picture cameras, projectors, and 35 mm film that do not fit into the plot; accusations by Alma as we see Elisabeth; and the same accusations by Elisabeth as we see Alma. *Persona* also includes a lengthy shot that begins badly out of focus and soon comes into focus.

An occasional hybrid exhibits characteristics of all three major film types. *David Holzman's Diary* (1968), for example, initially seems to be a narrative documentary with experimental aspects such as self-reflexive shots of the equipment used during filming and editing, shots of the dark screen accompanied by narration, a galloping succession of shots supposedly representing one frame from each shot of an evening's worth of TV, and a shot looking down on the top of "David Holzman's" head (Figure 9.16). But the end credits reveal that the film was scripted and acted and is

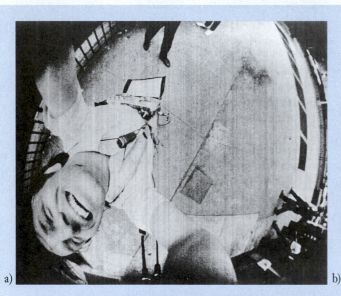

a)   b)

FIGURE 9.16 A hybrid with fictional, documentary, and experimental components
(a) This view through a fisheye lens showing the main character seemingly dangling above sidewalks occurs about 47 3/4 minutes into *David Holzman's Diary* (1968). In this frame, the title character is about to reach up and turn off the camera. This and other shots are characteristic of experimental films; in fact, it's hard to see how this shot fits into the story of this hybrid film. (b) This frame enlargement from 58 1/4 minutes into the film illustrates the film's occasional self-reflexiveness by showing most of the apparatus used to make the film: from left to right, the main character's portable reel-to-reel audio tape recorder, rewinds and 16 mm reels, and a 16 mm editor/viewer, and above them and reflected in the mirror, a tripod holding a 16 mm camera. Elsewhere in the film, viewers see shots of the zoom lens presumably used in filming *David Holzman's Diary* and the portable tape recorder and the accompanying microphone. *Paradigm; The Museum of Modern Art/Film Stills Archive*

not factual, and the viewer realizes that the film is fictional with documentary and experimental components.

Critics and scholars sometimes disagree about how to classify a film. Some film specialists see *Female Trouble* (1974) and other early films directed by John Waters as experimental fiction, whereas others believe that they are fictional films done in a particular style—**black comedy** (see Figure 6.25 on p. 294). Such disagreements signal judgment calls and, sometimes, different uses of terminology. Also, informed and thoughtful people will inevitably categorize some films differently. The result of filmmakers' imaginations and creativity often eludes clear-cut classification by critics and scholars.

black comedy: A narrative style that shows the humorous possibilities of warfare, death, illness, and other subjects often considered off-limits to comedy.

ANIMATION

Beginning with films made in 2001, the Academy of Motion Picture Arts and Sciences added the category "Best Animated Feature Film" to its list of Oscars. Some of the biggest moneymakers of recent years, particularly *The Lion King* (1994), *Finding Nemo* (2003), and *Happy Feet* (2006), are animated. Big-name actors such as Peter O'Toole, Julia Roberts, Billy Crystal, Mike Myers, Eddie Murphy, and Cameron Diaz are willing or even eager to do the voices for animated features. Especially since Robin Williams did the voice for the genie in *Aladdin* (1992), many feature-length animated films include parodies and **allusions** that adult viewers enjoy (see Figure 5.13 on p. 236). In addition, the scripts for *Toy Story* (1995), *Antz* (1998), *Finding Nemo*, and others are so carefully written, revised, and polished that the stories delight both children and adults. Japanese animation (anime) has grown in popularity and can now be seen occasionally in American theaters and often on DVD (see Plates 34–37 in Chapter 13); it has also strongly influenced video games. Films such as *Natural Born Killers* (1994), *Run Lola Run* (1998), *Amélie* (2001), *Hedwig and the Angry Inch* (2001), *Frida* (2002), *Bowling for Columbine* (2002), *Kill Bill: Vol. 1* (2003), *The SpongeBob SquarePants Movie* (2004), and *Enchanted* (2007) combine animation with **live action**. Film festivals are inundated with submissions for the animated film categories. Ever since the success of *The Simpsons* in 1989, more and more animated television shows have been running on cable networks. *The Simpsons*, *SpongeBob SquarePants*, *King of the Hill*, *Beavis and Butt-head*, and others are all hits. The Cartoon Network has been on the air since 1992, and one of its late-night animated shows has sometimes beat Jay Leno and David Letterman in the ratings. Popular animated TV shows, such as *The Simpsons*, *South Park*, *SpongeBob SquarePants*, and Nickelodeon's *Rugrats*, have been adapted into movies. Like the *Star Wars*, James Bond, Austin Powers, and other movie franchises, some animated movies have commercial tie-ins, such as toys, video games, and fast foods. Short animated films, many of them parodies, are commonplace on the Web. Animation is studied in various types of college

allusion: A reference in a text to a person, an event, or another text.

live action: Behavior by living (not animated) people or some other creatures.

a)

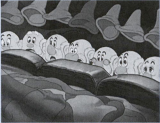

b)

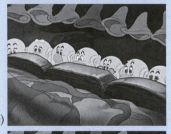

c)

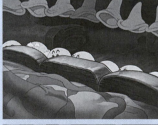

d)

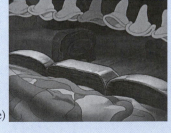

e)

FIGURE 9.17 Animation of flat (two-dimensional) subjects
Animation is usually used to create the illusion of smooth, continuous movement, as it is throughout Disney's classic *Snow White and the Seven Dwarfs* (1937). Note that in the five contiguous frames seen here, which appear 36 minutes into the film, there are only minor differences between the frames. In animation of this type, sometimes it is difficult to detect any changes in two neighboring frames (in addition, in some animation the same frame is printed twice throughout the film). To detect differences between two frames, one might have to compare two frames that are separated by several other frames. *Walt Disney Productions; Disney DVD Platinum Edition*

courses, including in many introduction to film courses, and many articles and books are being published on the subject. In short, in recent years, increasing numbers of animated films are being made, seen, enjoyed, and studied.

Animation is not a type of film (as are fictional, documentary, and experimental films) or a combination of types of films (as is the hybrid film). Rather, it is a technique for making a film or part of one. It is also an alternative to live-action films. Animation is used in fictional films, documentary films (though extended use of animation in documentaries is rare), and experimental films. Occasionally—as in *Mary Poppins* (1964), *Jurassic Park* (1993), *Stuart Little* (1999), and *Enchanted*—animation is combined with live action, thereby joining imaginary worlds with more familiar ones.

To "animate" means to bring to life. Both flat (two-dimensional) and plastic (three-dimensional) subjects may be animated. A frequent source of animation is a series of drawings (Figure 9.17). Other flat subjects that may be animated include paintings,[4] photographs, paper cutouts with hinged and movable body parts, computer graphics images, and drawings, scratchings, or paint applied directly on the film itself (see Figure 9.7). Plastic objects that may be animated include people in rigid poses, clay, and plasticine, a synthetic material used as a substitute for clay (see Plates 45–46 in Chapter 13).

In **stop-motion cinematography**, a two-dimensional or three-dimensional subject, such as a drawing or a puppet, is filmed for a frame or two; then usually something in the image is changed, one or two more frames are filmed, and so on (see Figure 9.17 and Plates 45–46). Stop-motion cinematography is normally used to show continuous movement, and the process is time-consuming and costly. It also may

---

[4]Experimental animator Robert Breer paints on individual 4-by-6-inch cards. After he has completed a number of consecutive cards, he flips through them to see how that section will look and move. Next, he redoes some cards and then perhaps omits some cards, adds to the stack of cards, and rearranges the cards. Once he is happy with the results, he photographs each finished frame.

FIGURE 9.18 Pixilation
These five consecutive frames from Canadian Norman McLaren's experimental fictional film "Neighbours" (1952) illustrate pixilation, which is animation that shows three-dimensional subjects moving continuously or discontinuously, in ways impossible in the real world. Here, a little more than 2½ minutes into the film, the two competing neighbors appear to circle each other clockwise while they are above the ground (note how much space they cover in 5 frames or only about one-fifth of a second). *National Film Board of Canada; Image Entertainment DVD*

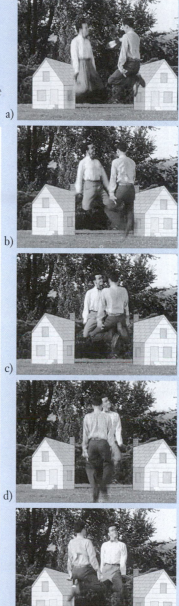

be used to show other types of movement. Bill Plympton, for example, creates only six different drawings for a second of film because he prefers to create moving images that twitch and wiggle, not move with a close approximation of life's fluidity. Sometimes the choice to create noncontinuous animation is not aesthetic but economic. Some traditional animators, including more than an occasional student animator, may use only six or so frames per second because time or budget, or both, are severely limited.

Pixilation is animation that shows three-dimensional subjects moving discontinuously or continuously in ways impossible to show in live action. Examples of pixilation from Norman McLaren's "Neighbours" (1952) are a picket fence rapidly installing itself one picket at a time and two men circling each other while all the time they are in the air above the ground (Figure 9.18). Pixilation may be achieved in two ways. The animators may use stop-motion cinematography (the picket fence installing itself one picket at a time). Less often, animators film a series of shots containing movement, such as of men jumping up into the air, select a frame from each of those shots, copy those selected frames, and then project the results (Figure 9.18). Pixilated movement is now also possible with computer animation. Pixilation may be used for various purposes. "One is to manipulate time, as in 'Neighbours' (the quick building of the fence). Another . . . is to create a caricature by altering the tempo of human action, in other words, by creating . . . exaggerated movements to distort human behavior, as in . . . 'Neighbours' (the violence emphasized in the fight scene)" (Richard 37).

Animation is not always created by photographing a series of images or objects. One may animate without a camera. One way is to scratch or paint onto the individual frames of film, or, as Stan Brakhage and others have done, to affix small objects to the film stock and copy the film (Figure 9.19). Increasingly, animation is done with computers. In some computer-assisted animation, penciled drawings are scanned into the computer. Next, the computer is used to choose and assign colors to areas of the image, ink and paint the images, set the characters against a background, add "camera movements," match the image to the soundtrack, and transfer the finished product to either

FIGURE 9.19 Film made without a camera
To make "Mothlight" (1963), a 4-minute silent film, Stan Brakhage pasted pieces of moth wings, grass, seeds, leaves, and flowers on clear 16 mm film, then copied the results. *Courtesy of Stan Brakhage*

composition: The arrangement of settings, lighting, and subjects within the frame.

morphing: The alteration of a film image by degrees by using sophisticated computer software and multiple advanced computers.

film, videotape, or DVD. It is now also possible to do the animation completely within the computer and eventually transfer the results to film. And it is possible to combine noncomputer animation with computer animation while making a film.

The Web has become a major source for producing and viewing short animation, in part because of the availability of an easy-to-use software program called Flash animation. Some of this animation is interactive— for example, the user can manipulate the mouse to change the direction of an animated character or control the story's pace. Much Web-based animation is clearly drawn and the sound is appropriate. But the animation is without fluid movement, the skin tones are flat and unvaried, and the faces are restricted to a narrow range of expression. Like the movie **serials** that used to be shown in weekly installments in neighborhood movie theaters, some animated stories on the Web are divided into episodes of a few minutes, each episode except the last ending in a dangerous or unresolved situation for the main character. Again, like some of the old serials, some Web series feature a (male or female) superhero triumphing over a series of dangers. In spite of its technical limitations, the Web is proving to be a place for animators to develop their skills and perhaps attract attention and funding for more ambitious projects.

An animated film may be as accomplished in its visuals, soundtrack, and narrative as live-action fictional films. "T.R.A.N.S.I.T." (1997) exemplifies how complex, sophisticated, subtle, and engaging a short animated film can be (see feature on p. 427). Although only 12 minutes long, the film shows the complicated story of a love triangle, an attempted murder, and two murders. The film's seven **sequences** are arranged in reverse chronological order, so viewers need to be particularly attentive to the film's plot to figure out the chronological arrangement of the events—the **fabula**. Viewers are rewarded with each repeat viewing of this carefully made film as the characterization and plot and the subtleties in the filmmaking (such as the symbolism of the strawberries, selective use of red, and the appropriateness and expressiveness of the music) become more evident.

Animation can allow viewers to see and experience from a new perspective. In "The Fly" (1980), we see the countryside and the inside of a large country home entirely from the point of view of a fly. We see, hear, and to some extent experience the flying and stopping, flying and stopping. Near the end, we also hear footsteps and the sounds of a person swatting at the fly and finally see through a blur a collection of mounted insects as the fly's life and the film end together.

Compared with live-action filming, animation has many advantages. It provides filmmakers greater control of mise en scène: they control all aspects of **settings**, subjects, and **composition**. Perhaps especially significant are the wider range of movements possible (as with pixilation) and the **morphing** of subjects possible in animation. As many scenes in animated

"T.R.A.N.S.I.T." (1997): A Description

a. Live action. Suitcase presumably floating. Opening title card superimposed. Travel labels on suitcase. Last label shown (in French): "SS L'AMERIQUE DU SUD."

1. Ship in ocean. Hold of ship: men stoking furnace. On deck: rich passengers passing their time. Newspaper headline: "Oil Tycoon Murdered in Egypt. Wall Street in Turmoil." Oscar (we learn his name at the end of the film) comes onto the deck. One arm is in a sling; his head is bandaged. He carries the heavy leather suitcase seen at beginning of the film (see Plate 47 in Chapter 13). All activities on deck stop momentarily. Oscar walks across a shuffleboard game in progress. From the back of the ship he throws the suitcase overboard. It floats away from the ship. Lap dissolve to the suitcase covered with travel labels.

2. Orient Express train. Night. Map: Venezia (Venice) → Verona → Milano. Emily (we learn her name at the end of the film) opens a train window and a suitcase with travel labels. She takes a red cloth from the suitcase and tosses it (and the gun inside it) out the window into water below. Oscar, with a bandaged head, is on a plane within sight of the train. The plane passes the train. Oscar is waiting at Paris train station. Train arrives. He gets on, enters a compartment, seems to kill Emily, then sits with his head in his hands.

3. Venice. Large luxurious hotel. Emily and Oscar in bed. She has a black eye and a bruised mouth (see Plate 48 in Chapter 13). She gets up, gets a gun, and shoots at Oscar twice. Emily leaves hotel as a Charlie Chaplin movie being shown outside is finishing. Carrying the suitcase, she gets into a gondola. Oscar, bloodied, staggers out onto the balcony of the hotel room.

4. Egypt. Desert near pyramids. Guide, Emily, and a tycoon. Emily ignores guide's gesture to help her down off her camel and instead accepts the tycoon's help. The guide is enraged. Tycoon starts to kiss Emily. Guide stabs tycoon with a knife and is revealed to be Oscar. He slaps Emily in the face. Using his own garment, Oscar covers up the tycoon. Emily has a black eye.

5. St. Tropez (France). Emily and Oscar picnic. She feeds him a strawberry and eats one herself. The juice bleeds down her chin. They kiss. Nearby a sports car is parked.

6. Baden Baden (Germany) resort. Men's steam room. Tycoon getting a massage. In casino, Oscar wins at roulette. Emily stands near tycoon and smiles in Oscar's direction. In Oscar's hotel room, Emily and Oscar are partially undressed (see Plate 49 in Chapter 13). She rubs fresh strawberries on his body and indicates her sexual availability. At dawn, she returns to the room where the tycoon is sleeping, kisses him lightly, and slips into her bed.

7. Emily and the tycoon drive through the Dutch countryside. Amsterdam street: suitcase falls out of the back of the car (same car as in sequence 5). Oscar picks it up and hands it to Emily. She kisses a card advertising the Amsterdam Hotel (where presumably the couple will be staying) and gives it to Oscar. He's a handsome though unshaven butcher in a bloody apron and has a pregnant wife and two small children (see Plate 50 in Chapter 13).

b. Live action with animated effects. The suitcase full of travel labels floating in the ocean and superimposed title cards about Emily Buckingham Parker, who was last seen boarding the Orient Express in Venice in 1928. A shark swims nearby, then the suitcase sinks abruptly and a faint red (Emily's blood) briefly stains the sea. Title cards tell about Oscar Bleek's later successful new life in Argentina.

Plot = a, 1–7, b
Fabula = 7, 6, 5, 4, 3, 2, 1, a, b

movies demonstrate—the death of Bambi's mother in *Bambi* (1942), the terror of the evil witch in *Sleeping Beauty* (1959), the death of Mufasa in *The Lion King*, and the reunion of father and son in *Finding Nemo*—animation can also call forth strong emotional responses from both children and adults. Perhaps because animation is seen as less threatening or less serious than live-action films and other texts, it can get away with being raunchier, more subversive, sharper in its social critiques, or even politically incorrect—or all four—as is illustrated by parts of *Pink Floyd The Wall* (1982), *The Simpsons* and other animated TV shows, *South Park: Bigger, Longer and Uncut* (1999), *Team America: World Police* (2004), and *The Simpsons Movie* (2007). See Figure 9.20.

Animation can create characters that are as memorable as people are. For years throughout the world, Mickey Mouse was as popular as any movie star. (Perhaps as computer animation grows more and more powerful and subtle, animated stars will come to rival flesh-and-blood stars and even partially displace them.) No wonder animation so animates animators: they can play **designer**, casting director, director, and editor; they can show entire stories from otherwise impossible points of view; they can create life, set it in motion, act out whatever they wish, and decide the precise moment when life fades out or the image cuts to black.

designer: The person responsible for the appearance of much of what is photographed in a movie, including locations, costumes, and hairstyles.

a)

b)

FIGURE 9.20 Leeway granted an animated film
In *Pink Floyd The Wall* (1982), the main character, Pink, has learned that his wife is having an affair. In the next scene, as so often in this film, viewers see what Pink is imagining: the interaction of a male flower and a female one. At first, about 37 1/4 minutes into the film, Pink's imagination conjures up visions of erotic interplay (a). But soon, and only briefly, the images turn violent (b). Gerald Scarfe's animation conveys a brief nonverbal story of mutual attraction quickly devolving into the female attempting to emasculate the male. This version of the story is from Pink's disturbed point of view and reflects his cauldron of emotions, such as anger, vulnerability, and fear. Could a live-action representation of his feelings have conveyed as much, done so as quickly, and been included in the finished film? Very unlikely. *Alan Marshall; MGM DVD*

CLOSE-UP: "UN CHIEN ANDALOU" (1928) AS AN EXPERIMENTAL FILM

With the 17-minute film "Un chien andalou," director Luis Buñuel and to a lesser extent artist Salvador Dalí made the most famous experimental film in the history of Western cinema.

Unlike traditional movies, many individual shots of "Un chien andalou" contain puzzling mise en scène. Perhaps the most perplexing and most famous/notorious shots are the following: A young man has been sexually aroused and fondled a young woman, but then she runs away from him in the room and threatens to hit him with a tennis racket. Next, inexplicably, the man seems to think it will be a good idea to pull on two ropes that now lie on the floor, though neither he nor the viewer knows what they are attached to. Excerpts from the script give some sense of the burden he is about to shoulder:

> The man slings the ropes over his shoulders [about 8 minutes into the film] and, making a tremendous effort, begins pulling a mysterious cargo towards the young woman. . . . Visible on each rope near his shoulders are a cork mat and a melon. Seen from behind, the full load is now visible. On two huge grand pianos lie the carcasses of two donkeys, badly ripped and decaying. . . . Close-up of a donkey's head hanging down over the keyboard of one of the pianos. The eye which is visible has been gouged out. . . . Two priests are lying . . . [on their backs] and allowing themselves to be pulled along [by the ropes]; they . . . look completely relaxed. (Buñuel 108–9)

How is the viewer to make much sense of such bizarre actions and all the disparate subjects that the young man pulls as he tries to reach the young woman?

As was illustrated in Chapter 3, "Un chien andalou" also contains many examples of surprising, sometimes even shocking combinations of shots. Early in the film, wispy clouds floating past the moon are followed by a shot of a straight razor supposedly slicing through a docile woman's eye (see Figure 3.15 on p. 131). The film ends with a shot of a couple walking romantically on the beach to the accompaniment of tango music, followed by a shot of the film's final title card, "In the Spring," and finally by a shot of the man and the woman buried up to their chests in sand, immobile and presumably dead (see Figure 9.3). As so often in this untraditional film, shots encourage certain expectations that are then thwarted: here, by the film's startling final image of immobility, barrenness, decay, and death.

It is not just that the film surprises or shocks by its editing. Like dreams, which "Un chien andalou" closely resembles, one film image may follow another in ways that defy the laws of science and our sense of time and space. From the time that the first man (played by Buñuel himself) sharpens a straight razor to the time that he supposedly cuts the woman's eye, he has changed shirts. Most filmmakers take pains to avoid such inconsistencies, but they abound in "Un chien andalou." Almost 6 minutes into the 1960 version (the version with music approved by Buñuel), a young woman (in his script, Buñuel refers to her as an androgynous person) stands in the street with her arms upraised, and the striped box she had been holding is on the ground nearby. In the next shot (a **jump cut**), she is hugging the box to her chest, and a split second later a car that had been hurtling toward her presumably hits her. Given the speed of the approaching car and its distance from the woman, not enough time has elapsed for her to have picked up the box. As the script describes it, in the ropes-corks-melons-donkeys-priests-pianos shots, the two priests are initially shown "lying back and allowing themselves to be pulled along; they . . . look completely relaxed" (109). A few seconds later, the priests "look terrified" (109). Besides the change in mood between the two shots, there is also a change of actors: the man on the left in the first shot is on the right in the second shot; the man on the right in the first shot is played by a different man in the second shot. Here's a final example of the film's defiance of the laws of time and space: when a man throws pieces of clothing out a window, it is nighttime inside the room and daytime outside.

"Un chien andalou" is not a fictional film: it is not a narrative that shows mostly or entirely imaginary events selected and arranged in some sort of unified, meaningful order. "Un chien andalou" is not a documentary: a film or video representation of actual (not imaginary) subjects. In its puzzling mise en scène, surprising juxtapositions of shots, and perplexing dreamlike representation of space and time, "Un chien andalou" is an experimental film that consistently rejects traditional movies and the coherence of a story; puzzles, surprises, shocks, and provokes viewers; and defies interpretation.

Work Cited

Buñuel, Luis. *"L'age d'or" and "Un chien andalou": Films by Luis Buñuel*. Trans. Marianne Alexandre. New York: Simon, 1968.

SUMMARY

Along with documentary films (discussed in Chapter 8), experimental films and hybrid films are alternatives to live-action fictional films. Animation is not a type of film but a filmmaking technique that can be used in any type of film.

Experimental Films

- Because experimental films are so various, no one term—*experimental, underground, avant-garde, personal,* or *independent*—adequately captures their complexity and variety.

- Unlike commercial movies, experimental films often radically reject the conventions of earlier films and explore the possibilities of the film medium.

- Unlike commercial movies, experimental films tend to rebel against a society's ideology (the underlying social and political beliefs of a society or social group).

- Experimental filmmakers may work alone and tend to be largely free of censorship.

- Experimental filmmakers may explore the uses of recent technological advances in communications (such as personal computers and the Web), explore uses of computer graphics, manipulate existing films or parts of them in a changed form, or explore subjects rarely explored in fictional films, such as the limits of memory.

- Experimental films are usually highly visual (and not very verbal) and often self-reflexive.

- Experimental filmmakers often explore film techniques. They may, for example, superimpose a readable text over a moving image, present parts of the film upside down, or use double or triple exposure.

- Often experimental filmmakers change one or more components of film-making or film exhibition—for example, by scratching, painting, or dyeing the film or by projecting a film onto a hanging shirt.

- Experimental films may be divided into two or more categories. Because of their individuality and enormous variety, however, experimental films are difficult to classify.

- Installation art, which is usually displayed in museums of modern or contemporary art, often incorporates film, video, or DVD into an ensemble or environment of arts and objects.

Hybrid Films

- Although most films are exclusively fictional, documentary, or experimental, some films are hybrids: they share characteristics of two or all three of the major film types. For example, *The Cabinet of Dr. Caligari*, though mainly fictional, also has characteristics of experimental films, and "The War Game" combines elements of documentary and fiction.

Animation

- Animation is a technique that may be used in making any type of film. It may "bring to life" flat or plastic subjects, and it may be done with or without a computer.

- Compared with live action, animation has many advantages. For example, animators have total control over the mise en scène. They can also show movements from place to place that are not possible outside movie theaters and the morphing of subjects into new subjects.

- Perhaps because animation is seen as less threatening or less serious than live-action films and other texts, its makers have fewer restrictions than creators of other kinds of texts and can more easily get away with being raunchier, more subversive, sharper in their social critiques, or even politically incorrect—or all of the above.

Major Terms about Experimental, Hybrid, and Animated Films

Below, numbers in italics refer to the pages where the terms are explained. All terms are defined in more detail in the Illustrated Glossary beginning on p. 667.

abstract film *414*

animation *424*

compilation film *405*

experimental film *401*

fake documentary *420*

hybrid film *417*

installation art *414*

mock documentary *419*

stop-motion cinematography *424*

surrealism *402*

QUESTIONS ABOUT EXPERIMENTAL, HYBRID, AND ANIMATED FILMS

The following questions are intended to help viewers understand experimental, hybrid, and animated films. Not all the questions are appropriate for every film. In thinking out, discussing, and writing responses to the questions most appropriate for the film being examined, be careful to stick with the issues the questions raise, to answer all parts of the questions, to explain the reasons for your answers, and to give specific examples from the film.

1. Is the film an alternative to live-action fictional films and documentaries? If so, explain why you think it is.
2. a. If the film is experimental, in what ways is it unlike classical Hollywood cinema?
   b. What are the types of sources used (such as earlier films)?
   c. In what ways does the film surprise or frustrate you, or both?
3. If the film is a hybrid, what major types of films are combined?
4. a. If the film or part of it is animation, are the movements smooth and continuous or jumpy and discontinuous? Is the type of movement shown appropriate to the subject or mood? If so, explain.
   b. What does the animation make possible that would be extremely difficult or impossible to achieve with live action?

WORKS CITED

Bordering on Fiction: Chantal Akerman's "D'Est." Minneapolis: Walker Art Center, 1995.

Breer, Robert. Showing and lecture. "Breer on Breer: The Films of Robert Breer." Walker Art Center, Minneapolis. 25 Feb. 2000.

Buñuel, Luis. "Notes on the Making of 'Un Chien Andalou.'" *Art in Cinema*. Ed. Frank Stauffacher. 1947. New York: Arno, 1968. 29–30.

Camhi, Leslie. "Lifting the Veil." *ARTnews* 99.2 (Feb. 2000): 148–51.

Dixon, Wheeler Winston. *The Exploding Eye: A Re-Visionary History of 1960s American Experimental Cinema*. Albany: State U of New York P, 1997.

Jacobs, Ken (independent filmmaker). Letter to the author. Jan. 1998.

Kuchar, George (independent filmmaker and author). Letter to the author. Jan. 1998.

MacDonald, Scott. *Avant-Garde Film: Motion Studies*. New York: Cambridge UP, 1993.

Mellencamp, Patricia. *Indiscretions: Avant-Garde Film, Video, and Feminism*. Bloomington: Indiana UP, 1990.

Peterson, James. *Dreams of Chaos, Visions of Order: Understanding the American Avant-Garde Cinema*. Detroit: Wayne State UP, 1994.

Richard, Valliere T. *Norman McLaren, Manipulator of Movement: The National Film Board Years, 1947–1967*. Newark: U of Delaware P, 1982.

Small, Edward S. *Direct Theory: Experimental Film/Video as Major Genre*. Carbondale: Southern Illinois UP, 1994.

FOR FURTHER READING

Aernout Mik: Refraction. Ed. Dan Cameron, Andrea Inselmann, and Lisa Phillips. New York: New Museum of Contemporary Art, 2005. Includes two essays and color photographs of parts of the installation.

Bendazzi, Giannalberto. *Cartoons: One Hundred Years of Cinema Animation*. Bloomington: Indiana UP, 1994. A comprehensive and detailed history and critique of film animation. Includes ninety-five color plates and comprehensive indexes of names and titles.

Canyon Cinema Film/Video Catalog No. 8. San Francisco: Canyon Cinema, 2000. Descriptions of available films and videos. Especially valuable for information on experimental films and videos.

Clements, Jonathan, and Helen McCarthy. *The Anime Encyclopedia: A Guide to Japanese Animation since 1917*. Berkeley: Stone Bridge P, 2001. More than two thousand short entries that describe and evaluate anime films—including *Astro Boy*, *Princess Mononoke*, *Akira*, *Giant Robo*, *Pokémon*, and *Sailor Moon*—plus entries on directors, writers, animators, composers, and studios.

Experimental Cinema: The Film Reader. Ed. Wheeler Winston Dixon and Gwendolyn Audrey Foster. New York: Routledge, 2002. Four parts: "Origins of the American Avant-Garde Cinema, 1920–1959," "The 1960s Experimental Explosion," "Structuralism in the 1970s," and "Alternative Cinemas, 1980–2000."

Film-Makers' Cooperative Catalogue No. 7 and *Film-Makers' Cooperative Catalogue No. 7 Supplement*. New York: Film-Makers' Cooperative, 1989, 1993. Descriptions of films and videos available through the co-op, arranged alphabetically by filmmaker. Especially valuable for information on experimental films.

MacDonald, Scott. *A Critical Cinema: Interviews with Independent Filmmakers*. 5 vols. Berkeley: U of California P, 1988–2006. Each volume includes an overview for each interviewee, interviews with experimental filmmakers, film/videographies, bibliographies, and an index.

———. *Screen Writings: Scripts and Texts by Independent Filmmakers*. Berkeley: U of California P, 1995. Includes introduction and a script for or a partial description of a wide variety of experimental films. Also includes nearly a hundred stills, most of them frame enlargements; distribution sources; and a bibliography.

O'Pray, Michael. *Avant-Garde Film: Forms, Themes, and Passions*. London: Wallflower P, 2003. A 144-page introduction and history for the student.

Rees, A. L. *A History of Experimental Film and Video*. London: British Film Institute, 1999. A history of avant-garde film and video ranging from Cézanne and Dada, via Cocteau, Brakhage, and Le Grice, to the new wave of British video artists in the 1990s.

Wells, Paul. *Understanding Animation*. New York: Routledge, 1998. Includes history and theory. Discusses such issues as representations of race and gender, "Disneyesque hyper-realism," and animation and audience research.

Part Four
UNDERSTANDING FILMS

T HUS FAR, WE HAVE EXPLORED the impact of various filmmaking techniques; the sources, components, and types of fictional films; and alternatives to live-action fictional films. Part Four considers some of the ways a film can be understood. In Chapter 10, we examine how recognizing a film's contexts helps us understand the film more completely. The process of filmmaking is influenced by where and how a film is made, as well as by where the film will be seen and by whom. All these factors influence filmmakers and their films and in turn viewers' understanding. Sometimes which version of a film we see also influences our understanding. Chapter 11 considers some of the ways viewers think about a film. The chapter examines our expectations about and interactions with a film and explores the types of meanings we find in films or make from them. Chapter 11 concludes with a consideration of the ways in which our previous knowledge of a film, our background, and our analytical approaches influence the way we analyze a film.

◄ A successful film more or less lives up to viewers' expectations and captures and holds their interest. During a showing, viewers often formulate hypotheses about what might happen next or about why something happened, and then they modify them as the film progresses. During and after the showing, viewers often formulate and reformulate meanings, what the film suggests or says about its subjects. The early stages of the whole process — the viewing, engagement, and interactions between film and viewers — are evident in this image from a scene in *The Accidental Tourist* (1988). *Publicity still. Warner Bros.*

Links to a variety of sources, including supplementary readings and short films, are available for each chapter on the Web site for this book at <bedfordstmartins.com/phillips-film>.

CHAPTER 10

Understanding Films through Contexts

CONTEXT IS WHAT PEOPLE USE to make sense of new information. An unfamiliar word can make sense in a sentence. An unfamiliar place can have meaning on a map. An isolated event can be significant in the context of history. Context turns information into knowledge. It's the difference between a warehouse and a museum. (Herz 1999)

We have all heard people complain about being misunderstood because their statements were "taken out of context." Statements examined in context are much less likely to be misunderstood. As this chapter illustrates, information about (1) the conditions that preceded and coexisted with the making of a film, (2) the version of the film that is being shown, and (3) the conditions in which the film is viewed helps viewers understand the film more completely.

There are so many possible contexts for a film that it would take a sizable book to begin to explore them. The first part of this chapter—the contexts of a film's making—introduces five contexts: social and political attitudes, censorship, artistic **conventions**, financial constraints, and filmmaking technology. The second part of the chapter—the version of the film that is seen—surveys different versions of a film that may be available. The third part of the chapter—the setting in which a film is seen—describes how the intended viewing environment and audience can influence filmmakers, the films they make, and in turn viewers' understanding of films.

Terms in **boldface** are defined in the Illustrated Glossary beginning on page 667.

convention: A subject or technique that makers of texts and audiences accept as natural or typical in certain contexts.

THE CONTEXTS OF A FILM'S MAKING

A film does not begin when the houselights dim and the projector sends forth dancing lights through the darkness or when we turn on the TV and pop a disc into the DVD player. What has happened before a film was made and sometimes what is going on while the film is being made influence how the finished film begins, how it all unwinds, and eventually how viewers understand it.

Let's consider three examples of how knowledge of the contexts of a film's making can help the viewer understand the film. Before you are shown a 1920s Soviet film in a course or a film series, someone may stand before the audience and explain the political climate in the Soviet Union at the time the film was made. As a result, when you watch the film, you understand why it focuses not on one individual or a few individuals but on large groups. And you understand why the film clearly favors one large group (the proletariat, or working people). Imagine that before you see *Fatal Attraction*, you learn that shortly before the film appeared in 1987, the AIDS epidemic had led to mass media warnings about the dangers of unprotected sex. You also learn that in the 1980s, growing numbers of American men felt threatened by successful, financially independent, career-minded, sexually active single women—or at least were uneasy about them. When you see *Fatal Attraction*, you notice that the film shows horrible consequences after a married man has unprotected sex with a single career woman, and you notice that the movie's career woman is shown unsympathetically. You can then understand how *Fatal Attraction* can be understood in part as a product of its place and time: the United States in the 1970s and 1980s. Finally, imagine that you see *The World of Apu*, a 1958 film from India, and think it curious that the young married couple never kiss, though they are clearly in love. Later you learn that censorship regulations for Indian films of that time prohibited kissing, so the couple's affection had to be conveyed by other means (Figure 10.1). In these three situations and countless others, knowing something about when and under what conditions a film was made helps you understand the film.

Filmmakers and sometimes film exhibitors often consider how much of a film's context their audiences are likely to know. Most filmmakers assume that audiences know something about the context of the film's story. If audiences may not, filmmakers often include background information in the film itself. **Title cards** give tidbits of historical information throughout *Schindler's List* (1993). The opening two title cards in the German film *Das Boot*, or *The Boat* (1981, 1997), inform viewers that "the battle for control of the Atlantic is turning against the Germans" as the story begins in the autumn of 1941 and that of the 40,000 German sailors

FIGURE 10.1 Showing affection in a 1950s film from India
Kissing was not allowed in films from India in the 1950s, so filmmakers had to convey loving or romantic feelings in other ways. Almost 56 minutes into *The World of Apu* (1958), Apu's new wife rests her chin on his shoulder with tenderness and a natural, unforced intimacy. Elsewhere in the scene she also gives him loving looks. Without seeing them kiss and embrace, viewers can still see how much in love they are. *Satyajit Ray Productions; Columbia TriStar Home Entertainment DVD*

who "served on U-boats during World War II, 30,000 never returned." Television channels that focus on old movies, such as Turner Classic Movies, also usually include a brief introduction to each film explaining at least a little of the film's contexts.

Once viewers understand that social and political attitudes influence how filmmakers represent political, religious, and sexual subjects, viewers are less likely to misjudge how a film represents those three subjects. Viewers who know when and where a film was made and under what conditions are also more likely to notice when filmmakers follow conventions and when they depart from them. They are more likely to understand how the film's budget precluded certain options and how the available filmmaking technology and the audio and visual presentations of competing media and electronic entertainments may have influenced the film.

Social and Political Attitudes

There are always limits to what filmmakers can show. Various forces restrict the choice of subjects and then the scope, depth, and manner in which subjects are shown. Two such powerful influences on how **texts** represent their subjects are social and political attitudes. For many years, various film scholars have studied the **representation** of recurring subjects in movies—such as **gender** roles, sexual orientation, social class, ethnic group, race, religion, and national identity. They do so to increase understanding of what those representations reveal about the filmmakers' beliefs and values and those of the society in which they work. Consequently, as some of the entries in the "For Further Reading" section of this chapter suggest, there are many books on cinematic representations of Native Americans, African Americans, Asians and Asian Americans, Arabs, women, lesbians, gays, and many other recurrent subjects. Studies of representation may focus on subjects in mainstream cinema or in **independent films** and **experimental films**, where representations are likely to be less traditional and more individualistic.

REPRESENTATIONS OF HOMOSEXUALITY IN FILM

GAY MEN Social attitudes here strongly influenced whether, when, and how homosexuality has been represented in film. From the birth of cinema in the 1890s until 1934, when the U.S. production code was revised and began to be more stringently enforced, gay male characters in U.S. movies were nearly always represented as laughable or pathetic. After the revised production code placed restrictions on filmmakers (see the feature on pp. 462–64), from 1934 into the 1960s homosexual characters were seldom identified openly in movies. In *The Maltese Falcon* (1941), for example, although several characters are homosexual, the film, unlike the source novel, does not make their homosexuality explicit (Figure 10.2).

representation: A likeness of a subject created in a text.

gender: A person's sexual identity as indicated by clothing, makeup, hairstyle, conversational style, body language, and various other signals.

independent film: Film made mainly or entirely without support or input from the dominant, established film industry.

experimental film: A film that rejects the conventions of mainstream movies and explores the possibilities of the film medium.

FIGURE 10.2 A 1940s movie that hints at a character's homosexuality
The explicit representation or mention of homosexuality was forbidden by the U.S. production code, but filmmakers sometimes found ways to suggest homosexuality, as here 24 minutes and 25 seconds into *The Maltese Falcon* (1941) where the character's homosexuality is suggested by showing the umbrella handle near his mouth. *Warner Bros.– First National; Warner Home Video DVD*

stereotype: A commonplace, simplified, and in some ways inaccurate likeness of a subject created in a text.

As attitudes in Western societies have changed, so have representations of gays in films. In his book *The Celluloid Closet: Homosexuality in the Movies*, Vito Russo says that the first positive images of gays in commercial cinema appear in two 1961 British movies, *A Taste of Honey* and *Victim* (126–33). In *A Taste of Honey*, a sensitive homosexual friend cares for the main character, an unwed pregnant teenager. In *Victim*, a British movie star, Dirk Bogarde, plays a man who passionately admits to his desire for another man.

After the U.S. film industry abandoned the production code and instituted a rating system in 1968, more adult subjects, including homosexuality, began to appear on movie screens. *The Boys in the Band* (1970) was the first widely distributed U.S. movie featuring gays. The cast consists of eight gay or bisexual male characters and one heterosexual character who may have tried homosexuality while in college. Probably because the film and the source play are products of the 1960s and their audiences included many heterosexuals, the film does a lot of explaining. For example, it explains how a married man could finally realize that he was more gay than straight. The film also shows that gay people wrestle with the same issues as straight people. One male couple, for example, quarrels about fidelity: one partner wants the right to have an occasional fling, whereas his lover wants them both to be monogamous. Although the film was initially seen as groundbreaking, somewhat after the beginning of the gay liberation movement in the late 1960s many gays began to disavow it as **stereotypical** and dated. They also criticized it for too often showing the gay characters as catty, venomously witty, self-involved, self-loathing, and alcohol and drug dependent. In recent years, however, some critics have seen the film as a largely accurate representation of American gay life in the pre-gay-liberation times of enforced secrecy and repression.

Even after the ratings system was instituted, more than a few movies represented gay characters as mostly miserable, depressed, suicidal, dangerous, or laughable. In *La cage aux folles* (1978), its sequels, and its remake as *The Birdcage* (1996), gay characters have pivotal roles, though they and the situations they end up in are stereotypical, amusing, and nonthreatening to heterosexual audiences.

Since the 1990s, films with credible gay characters have become commonplace in the United States and other cinemas, and even societies that have attempted mightily to repress homosexuality, such as Castro's Cuba, have permitted an occasional film sympathetic to gays (Figure 10.3). By the 1990s, times and social attitudes had changed in the United States—

FIGURE 10.3 Stereotypical yet complex and sympathetic gay male character
The Cuban film *Strawberry and Chocolate* (1993) can be seen as mainly the story of a growing friendship in spite of the two men's many differences. The main character, Diego (left), is a gay photographer who is religious and critical of Cuban governmental policies. The other main character, David (right), is a heterosexual, initially virginal university student from an impoverished village background who is not religious and basically supports the Castro government. Gradually, Diego teaches David a greater awareness of the power of the arts and increases David's tolerance toward those who have been labeled as different. The film devotes much time to Diego's homosexuality, though since the film is a product of 1990s Cuba, no homosexual contact is shown. Often the actor playing Diego plays the part broadly and amusingly, with a full range of belongings, dress, tastes, gestures, and manners thought typical of gays. But because of some details in the script and the often nuanced performance of the main actor, Diego can be subtle, amusing, engaging, complicated, and sympathetic. Furthermore, he is articulate, intelligent, talented, and brave in speaking out for more tolerance and artistic diversity in Cuba, yet proudly Cuban as well. *Cuban Institute of the Arts and Film Industry (ICAIC), Miramax Films, and others; Miramax Home Entertainment DVD*

considerably. U.S. audiences largely embraced the U.K. film *The Crying Game* (1992), which features an Irish Republican Army volunteer and a transgenderist hairdresser and questions whether sexual and gender preferences are the only major considerations in a close relationship. As further evidence of the increased acceptance of gay subjects by U.S. audiences, consider the 6-hour, two-part HBO award-winning miniseries/movie that has met with wide acclaim, *Angels in America* (2003). The film includes two very conservative attorneys: one who is immersed in politics, obsessed with his status and power, but closeted and dying of AIDS and the other a young Mormon who is struggling against his own homosexuality and is stuck in a sexless marriage to a drug-consuming Mormon woman. *Angels in America* also features a young gay couple, one partner afflicted with AIDS and the other struggling with the question of leaving his sick lover or sticking with him. The fifth major male character is a black gay nurse, intelligent, articulate, and nurturing but also cynical and sometimes bitter. All five of the film's main male characters are gay, and their situations and personalities are wide-ranging, complex, and credible (Figure 10.4). *Brokeback Mountain* (2005), which is a universal love story whose two leads are male, was another critical and popular success. In that film, Ennis Del Mar (Heath Ledger) and Jack Twist (Jake Gyllenhaal) fight a decades-long battle between their "domestic lives" that include wives and children and their "wilderness lives," which include lush scenery and their passionate love for each other. Both men, though particularly Ennis, fear coming out

FIGURE 10.4 Contemporary representations of gay characters Seen here, just 3 minutes short of the 3-hour running time of the second part of *Angels in America* (2003), are three of the film's five main male characters. The character on the right has AIDS and was largely abandoned by his male partner (on the left of the frame). The man seen here smiling at the Meryl Streep character is a nurse who may be good at heart but is no sentimentalist. The representations of all five of the film's gay characters are complex and credible. *Avenue Pictures Productions; HBO Video DVD*

in the sixties through the eighties because, as the source story and film (and U.S. history) all show, doing so could be extremely dangerous.

The **documentary** *The Celluloid Closet* (1995), which is based on Vito Russo's book of the same title, shows and explains many representations of closeted and "coded" gays and lesbians throughout the history of film in the Western world.

Lesbians Cinematic representations of lesbians have been similar to those of gays: initially, oblique representations or insulting stereotypical representations and viewer rejection and scorn. However, in time, societal attitudes changed and the movies changed as audiences increasingly accepted truer-to-life representations of same-sex relationships. The histories of gay cinema and lesbian cinema are similar except for perhaps one major difference. Because many male viewers are titillated by scenes of women being physically intimate and because men largely control so much of the production and exhibition of movies, at most stages in the history of movies, audiences have accepted representations of lesbian sex more readily than representations of gay behavior. An example of the greater flexibility females had and have in transgressing gender and sexual orientation roles can be seen in a well-known scene in the 1930 U.S. movie *Morocco* (Figure 10.5). Nowadays, such movie behavior would not shock most U.S. viewers. In the 1930s, it did, at least a little, because it hints at one woman's sexual attraction to another and suggests that Amy is probably bisexual. In 1930, could there have been a comparable scene in a mainstream movie with a man dressed as a woman kissing another man? Even quickly and seen from a distance? No way.

For a combination of reasons—including the widespread social attitudes of the time and concern about a film's rating and box office appeal—a film may be shy about including characters who are openly gay or lesbian. Such a film is *Fried Green Tomatoes* (1991), which focuses on a close rela-

FIGURE 10.5 Transgressing gender and sexual orientation roles
Approximately 16 minutes into *Morocco* (1930), the Marlene Dietrich character (a singer named Mademoiselle Amy Jolly), dressed as a man and smoking a cigarette, comes onstage before a cabaret audience that immediately jeers her and boos. She begins singing, is offered a glass of champagne, climbs over a thigh-high wooden railing as a man might, drinks the champagne, and asks for and receives the flower in a young woman's hair. Up to this point, Amy's eyes have been repeatedly coming back to the woman—at least five times. Once, she appears to check out how the woman looks from head to foot. Then Amy bends over and quickly kisses the woman on the lips. The cabaret audience laughs and applauds. *Paramount Pictures; Universal Studios Home Video DVD*

tionship of two female characters in early-twentieth-century rural Alabama: Idgie and Ruth, who run a café together and raise Ruth's child together. Some viewers think their relationship is never physically intimate. Others think it is and criticize the filmmakers for their timidity. (Those who know the popular source novel, *Fried Green Tomatoes at the Whistle Stop Cafe*, by Fannie Flagg—an out lesbian writer—are probably more likely to interpret the film characters as lesbian.) Yet other viewers applaud the film's daring for its time: the film received an award from the Gay & Lesbian Alliance Against Defamation (GLAAD) as the year's best **feature film** with lesbian content. Some think the film succeeded in having it both ways. It earned a PG-13 rating and thus could be seen by a broad audience, many members of which probably see the two women as simply very close friends. But many viewers detect a lesbian subtext or hidden subject (Figure 10.6).

In many of the more recent U.S. movies, the representation of lesbianism is more overt than in earlier periods, especially if the budgets are small and those who raise the funds to make the movies do not have to worry about attracting a large audience. Such was the case with *The Incredibly True Adventure of Two Girls in Love* (1995, Figure 10.7). The girls' lesbianism is not hinted at or ambiguous. It is overt. The film also shows two additional lesbian couples but does not explore the class and racial

FIGURE 10.6 Two women, one ambiguous relationship
No. This is not an image from a horror film. It's a food fight, and the two young women are having fun. *Fried Green Tomatoes* (1991) devotes much of its total time to the story of two females who develop a very close, virtually lifelong friendship and who love each other. Beginning about 62½ minutes into the DVD's commentary, the director says, "This scene [represented here] was a very, very important scene to me. . . . Cause in a way it's a love scene. I mean it's the closest we have to a love scene in the movie" (Avnet). *Universal Pictures, Fried Green Tomatoes Productions, and others; Universal Home Video Collector's Edition DVD*

FIGURE 10.7 Lesbianism as an explicit movie subject
The Incredibly True Adventure of Two Girls in Love (1995), which was made quickly on a very small budget, is mainly the story of two senior high school girls. Evie (on the left) gets to travel internationally, finds school easy, has a big vocabulary, and reads poetry. She lives with her mother in a large, luxurious house and drives her own Range Rover. Randy could scarcely be more different. She is bored with school and not doing well in it, works after school in a gas station, and lives in a crowded home in a working-class neighborhood with three adult lesbians, including an aunt. Evie is straight; Randy is lesbian. Evie is femme, and Randy is butch. Oh, and though little mention is made of it, Evie is African American and Randy is not. Opposites attract and humorous complications escalate as Evie and Randy draw closer and become lovers. The film's last image is of the two girls facing each other and caressing as in the background family, friends, and others all speak at the same time, and the two girls and the audience can hear no one distinctly. *Smash Pictures, Fine Line Features; New Line Home Entertainment DVD*

issues it touches on. "The film includes a mature lesbian couple [in the home where Randy lives] as well as a glimpse of two old women lovers in a motel. . . . The film maintains its light tone by glossing over the difficulties of the many issues it raises. . . . The potential conflicts of race and class are touched on only gently. Evie worries that Randy's aunt Rebecca has a problem with her being black; Randy suggests instead it might be a problem with people who can afford to go to Paris" (Michel).

Kissing Jessica Stein (2002) is another fairly low-budget movie that also openly explores the subject of a straight woman trying out a same-sex relationship, but the movie features a woman about a decade older than the two leads in *The Incredibly True Adventure of Two Girls in Love*. Early in *Kissing Jessica Stein*, Jessica answers a personal ad after years of failed dates with a variety of disappointing men, including one who is so intent on splitting the restaurant bill equally that he factors in the current market prices of the vegetables! Later, Jessica begins a friendship that turns into a sexual relationship with a bisexual woman, behavior she hides from her family, coworkers, and even, we are told, her therapist (because "it's personal"). After many complications, the two women move in together but soon realize they might be better off as friends than lovers. By the end of the film, Jessica's former partner has begun an affair with another woman, and Jessica seems to be drifting back to a man who was once her college boyfriend and later and for most of the movie's story her supervisor at a newspaper.

The Incredibly True Adventure of Two Girls in Love, *Kissing Jessica Stein*, and other films of recent years can now be overt about female relationships.

The two films explore the conflicting values, the turbulent emotions, and some of the challenges of finding a sexual identity and forming close relationships. They are also credible and especially relevant in diverse societies.

REPRESENTATIONS OF GENDER IN FILM

What does it mean to "act like a man" or "act like a woman" in any given culture? If you can define a society's dominant male or female roles, you've discovered that culture's gender roles, often so rigidly held that deviation from them can be dangerous or even deadly.

Gender can be distinguished from both *sex*, a person's biological or physical characteristics (male, female, or intersexed—historically called "hermaphrodites"), and *sexual orientation* (straight, lesbian or gay, bisexual, or questioning). Gender is a social construction influenced by biological sex, upbringing, social class, time and place, and perhaps other factors. As feminist writer Simone de Beauvoir wrote, "One is not born a woman, but becomes one" (267). Those interested in gender issues have explored the different ways that gender, sex, and sexual orientation may interface in one person.

Gender subjects include the *androgyne* (a person who creates an ambiguous gender presentation by adopting characteristics of both genders) and the *cross-dresser* (aka *transvestite*, a person, either hetero- or homosexual, who enjoys occasionally wearing clothes identified with the opposite gender). Gender issues are also paramount in the case of the *transgenderist* (a person who lives either part-time or full-time as a gender opposite to his or her anatomical sex and who may opt for sex-reassignment surgery to biologically become the opposite sex).

Gender is such a large and complex subject that in the very limited space that can be devoted to it here no systematic treatment is possible. Instead, we focus on only two recurrent subjects. According to the movies, what are some reasons men sometimes dress or act as women, and what are some reasons women may dress or act as men?

WHY MIGHT MOVIE MEN WANT TO BECOME MOVIE WOMEN? Most cross-dressers tend to be heterosexual men who dress temporarily as women for the pleasure of it. But in some movies, straight men behave as women or dress as women for reasons other than their own pleasure. Often, movies show men dressed as women because the filmmakers want to entertain audiences and make them laugh. Ever since nearly the beginning of cinema, gender roles have been a (usually humorous) subject in movies. Mainly for laughs, many male actors dressed in women's clothing and acted (more or less, mostly less) as people of the time thought women dressed and acted (Figure 10.8). In Charlie Chaplin's "A Woman," as in many later films, including the one discussed in the next paragraph, male characters also dress as women to escape detection by someone else in the story.

a)

b)

FIGURE 10.8 Switching gender roles for laughs Male characters dressed as women appeared early in the movies. Here in Charlie Chaplin's "A Woman" (1915), the traditional Chaplin character—seen on the left in (a)—dresses as a woman to escape detection by the angry father of the young woman Charlie had become attracted to. Problems ensue. The father, who seems to be distracted by every creature in a skirt except his wife, is immediately attracted to Charlie as a female—seen on the right in (b). So is a man the father brought home with him. The film's story is farcical and thus has unlikely plot developments, exaggerated characters, and abundant slapstick. One implication of the story: randy straight men may be easily fooled by traditional indicators of gender—clothing, hairstyle, hairless faces, makeup, and gestures. But like other early short films, "A Woman" does not explore gender issues but instead mines them for laughs. *Essanay Films; Delta Entertainment DVD*

Sometimes the results of male characters dressing and acting as women were not only humorous but also illuminating about men and gender roles (Figure 10.9). As the story in *Some Like It Hot* (1959) turns out, Jerry/Daphne (Jack Lemmon, on the right in Figure 10.9a–b) is more flexible in gender roles and more willing to pass as a female. Soon he is more appreciative of being a "female" and is enjoying the attention of a persistent straight male. Joe/Josephine [Tony Curtis] is initially revealed as a love-'em-and-leave-'em male seducer who eventually comes to a better understanding of what women may have to endure, including unwanted attention from randy men and casual seduction and abandonment by males such as Joe himself. By the end of the film, Joe is not so cynical, selfish, and exploitative. He confesses his lies to the Marilyn Monroe character, and presumably the two will have a future together.

Other films show different reasons for male characters dressing as females. For instance, *Tootsie* (1982) and *Mrs. Doubtfire* (1993) are successful comedies in which the male leads dress as women to get a job. Dustin Hoffman as Michael Dorsey has little success as an actor until he becomes the middle-aged Dorothy Michaels (see Figure 1.19 on p. 26). The Robin Williams character is so desperate to spend time with his children that he transforms himself into Mrs. Euphegenia Doubtfire, a kind and elderly nanny, so that his estranged wife will hire him as their children's live-in caretaker and housekeeper.

A film may show that a man may want to dress and act as a woman and finally be a woman because he feels he is a woman stuck in a man's body.

a) b)

FIGURE 10.9 **Gender roles played for laughs—and explored** *Some Like It Hot* (1959) is set in the U.S. Prohibition era of 1920 to 1933 and stars Marilyn Monroe, Jack Lemmon, and Tony Curtis. Near the beginning of the story, the two main male characters witness a Chicago gangland massacre and then escape from the murderers by dressing as females in an all-women band that travels to Florida. *Publicity stills. Ashton Productions and Mirisch Corporation*

That's the situation in the HBO movie *Normal* (2003), which focuses on the relationship of farm-machinery factory foreman Roy and his wife Irma. Shortly after celebrating their twenty-fifth anniversary, Roy tells Irma and their minister that for years he has been struggling with his strong feelings that he is actually a woman in the wrong body. The rest of the story shows Roy's gradual transformation into a transgenderist, which creates complications for him with the men at his workplace and the members of his church. The story also shows the confusion and anguish that result, particularly for Roy himself, Irma, and their grown son. (Their tomboy daughter quickly decides that her dad's intended transformation is "cool.")

WHY MIGHT MOVIE WOMEN WANT TO BECOME MOVIE MEN? Movies in which a female character dresses or acts as a male are not usually basically humorous. More often, for example, the female character feels strongly that she is a male in the wrong body and wants to pass as a male or be transformed into one, or she seeks protection from harm from males by passing as a male, or she tries to pass as a male to benefit economically.

Boys Don't Cry (1999), which is a fictional film closely based on actual events, is about a 1990s Nebraska biological female (Teena Brandon) who felt compelled to change genders by dressing and acting as a straight male (Brandon Teena) (Figure 10.10).

Another film in which the main female character dresses and acts as a man is the **revisionist** western *The Ballad of Little Jo* (1993; see Figure 7.9 on p. 317). But unlike in *Boys Don't Cry*, in *The Ballad of Little Jo* the main

revisionist: A novel or revised interpretation or representation of a subject.

FIGURE 10.10 Gender switch because of compelling feelings
Here, almost 2 minutes into *Boys Don't Cry* (1999), Brandon is
checking out his new haircut and new clothes. At first, Brandon is
more successful socially than Teena had been, being accepted into a
new (dysfunctional) extended family that includes the beautiful Lana
and the unstable John, who is a former convict obsessed with Lana.
Brandon is also successful in winning the love of Lana and retaining
it even after she learns that Brandon is anatomically female. But in-
surmountable problems multiply for Brandon, including numerous
past and present run-ins with the law, a web of lies that hurt or infu-
riate others, John's jealousy about Brandon's success with Lana, and
prejudice against Brandon's transgender choice and new identity. *A
Killer Films/Hart-Sharp Entertainment Production and Independent Film
Channel; 20th Century Fox Home Entertainment DVD*

celluloid: Movie, as in "celluloid heroes."

character does not feel she is trapped in the
wrong body. Instead, she needs protection
from various males in a dangerous patriarchal
society, so she inflicts a scar on herself, dresses
as a man, and learns to live like one. As film
critic Philip French has observed, "There is
a long tradition in Western drama of women
cross-dressing to make their way in a patriarchal society"—a tradition that began at least
as early as some of Shakespeare's plays.

In films from a non-Western society, a
female may also dress as a male to get by in a
male-dominated society that imposes strict
limitations on females. She may try to pass as
a male, for example, for economic reasons,
though, as the Afghan film *Osama* (2003)
shows, doing so brings with it great personal
danger (Figure 10.11). (For definitions of sex-
and gender-related terms and explanations of
the concepts, see Alan McKee's entry "Gender" on pp. 190–94 of the *Critical Dictionary
of Film and Television Theory*.)

REPRESENTATIONS OF AFRICAN AMERICANS IN FILM

For years, film scholars have studied **celluloid** representations of various races and
ethnic groups. Race and ethnicity are complex subjects. Indeed there is
disagreement about what constitutes a human "race" or even if what the
term has generally come to stand for has any validity. Scientists who have
studied the subject have concluded that "race" cannot be defined by people's exterior features, such as skin color, or by genetics (for example,
the DNA of two African Americans may differ more than the DNA of
an African American and a Norwegian). The modern species of humans
cannot be divided into subspecies. For many historians, "race" is most
usefully understood as an evolving social construct or way of thinking that
people develop to categorize large masses of people, usually with the
implication that one race is superior to other races. Early European settlers
in what has become the United States, for example, used racial categori-
zation to help justify their belief that they were superior to such groups
as Native Americans, African slaves, Mexicans, and the Chinese ("Race:
The Power of an Illusion"). There is space here to discuss the cinematic
representation of various groups of people only briefly, so the following
discussion is restricted to a few observations about U.S. movies that

FIGURE 10.11 Female dressed as male for economic reasons The Taliban, a Sunni Islamist movement, ruled much of Afghanistan from 1996 to 2001. It was extremely dangerous for women to ignore the strict Taliban guidelines that forbade them from working outside the home, from being outside the home without wearing a burka (seen here), and from being on the street without a male relative as an escort.

Osama is a 2003 Afghan film set in the Taliban-controlled capital city of Kabul and made shortly after the Taliban lost power over much of Afghanistan. The film shows the story of a 12-year-old girl who lives with her mother and grandmother. The three women have no surviving male family members and little income, especially after the Taliban close the hospital where the mother and daughter work. In hopes that she can find the girl employment, the mother cuts her daughter's hair short and dresses her as a boy. Here, almost 21 1/2 minutes into the film, the girl is seen on a sidewalk with her mother. This is the first time she has been outside as a boy, and she is frightened and is breathing hard. The film shows a society with inflexible gender roles, the difficulty of appropriating the detailed ways of the opposite gender, and some consequences of the strict controls of female behavior in such a society. The film also shows why women sometimes transgress gender roles, the dangers of doing so, and the severe penalties if they are caught. *Barmak Film and others; MGM Home Entertainment DVD*

include Africans or African Americans and movies that include Latin Americans or Latinos.

In U.S. films of the early twentieth century, the parts of Africans and African Americans (and Native Americans) were usually acted by European Americans, who often wore crude makeup. In keeping with widespread beliefs in European American society of the time, African Americans were usually represented as simpleminded and faithful slaves or servants or as lazy, corrupt, or lecherous. All these stereotypes are displayed in the classic 1915 American movie *The Birth of a Nation* (Figure 10.12). During the following decades, these negative stereotypes endured in U.S. movies. They were also perpetuated in minstrel shows: live variety shows of songs, dances, jokes, and skits, usually performed by white actors in blackface (for some vivid examples of minstrel shows, see the discussion of Spike Lee's 2000 film *Bamboozled* on pp. 290–92). And these stereotypes were also kept alive in various stereotypical objects, including bric-a-brac (also prominent in *Bamboozled*) and lawn ornaments with exaggerated features.

Studies show that in earlier eras, as now, American blacks were avid moviegoers. After *The Birth of a Nation* and until the late 1940s, some low-budget films were made by American blacks, most notably Oscar Micheaux, who were frustrated because they could rarely see recognizable let alone positive images of themselves on the big screens. Most of these films were shown in (mainly big-city) movie theaters catering to black audiences or

FIGURE 10.12 Stereotypical representation of the black male as a danger to white females
D. W. Griffith's *The Birth of a Nation* (1915) helped perpetuate negative images of black Americans, especially African American males. Seen here is the film's most notorious example: Gus, a freed slave who becomes enamored of a young white woman and chases her to the edge of a cliff. She chooses to jump to her death rather than submit to him. Like many other black characters in *The Birth of a Nation*, Gus was played by a white person in blackface. In this shot, which appears nearly 2 hours and 16 minutes into the Kino Video DVD version of the film, one can see imperfections in the makeup over the actor's right eye and below the right side of his lower lip. As scholar Michele Faith Wallace has written, "Gus is so transparently a Caucasian done up in blackface as to appear clownish to anybody not in the grip of the 'Confederate myth'" (89). *D. W. Griffith Corp., Epoch Producing Corp.; Kino Video DVD*

realism: Representation that is widely believed to render its subjects faithfully.

event: In a narrative or story, either an action by a character or person or a happening (a change brought about by a force other than a person or character, such as a lightning strike).

late at night in theaters that catered to white audiences during the earlier, more popular hours.

From the beginning of U.S. cinema until recent years, mainstream movies rarely showed African American life in a **realistic** way. An exception is the independent film *Nothing But a Man* (1964), which shows an African American man in the 1960s South trying to decide whether to assume responsibility for a boy who may be his son, attempting to relate to an aloof alcoholic father, and marrying outside his social class (a preacher's daughter who teaches grade school). The film also shows how the man struggles to endure his white coworkers' demeaning treatment and his efforts outside work to cope with pervasive prejudice against African American men (Figure 10.13). Another film representing blacks in nonstereotypical ways is Charles Burnett's low-budget black-and-white *Killer of Sheep* (1977). The film is set in the Los Angeles ghetto of Watts and shows completely credible everyday events in the lives of a slaughterhouse worker who sleeps poorly, seems to have lost his amorous interest in his wife, and never fully smiles; his often tired or quietly frustrated devoted wife; their two children; and some friends. Also, in the foreground or background of much of the film are a gaggle of children who often giggle as they push, kick, or wrestle and who make do with what is at hand, such as rock throwing and plywood sheets used as shields. In this poor neighborhood, there is an occasional beat-up bicycle but no toys and nothing to use in sports. Two more films that show African American life in credible stories are Spike Lee's *She's Gotta Have It* (1986), which is about an attractive independent woman and her three competing lovers, and his *Do the Right Thing* (1989), which is set in a recognizable city neighborhood and shows believable characters and **events** (see Figures 1.46 and 1.56 on p. 47 and p. 53).

Sweet Sweetback's Baadasssss Song (1971)—which was "dedicated to all the Brothers and Sisters who had enough of the Man" and is considered to be the first of the so-called **blaxploitation** movies—focuses on police brutality against the Los Angeles African American community and exalts the sexual potency and the resilience of an African American male. The film spoke to black frustration, determination, and pride and proved wildly popular with black audiences. Other blaxploitation movies were *Shaft* (the original, 1971 version) and perhaps two hundred more films made during the following few years for, (largely) by, and about American blacks. Often these movies show American blacks caught up in inner-city crime, as do many later U.S. movies featuring African American characters, such as *Boyz N the Hood* (1991), *New Jack City* (1991), and *American Gangster* (2007).

For various reasons—probably including the gradual acceptance of more and more American blacks into the mainstream—in recent years, a wider range of black people (in documentaries such as Marlon T. Riggs's 1995 film *Black is . . . Black ain't*) and credible black (mostly male) characters (in fictional films) have been seen more often on the big screen.

FIGURE 10.13 **Credible, not stereotypical, representation of African American lives**
Nothing But a Man (1964), which is set in 1960s Alabama but was filmed in New Jersey, shows the story of a black man who marries, has trouble holding on to jobs without being hassled by white men demanding subservience, and eventually takes out his frustrations on his loving, supportive wife. Critics and historians have praised the film for its credible yet sympathetic and understanding representation of the two main characters, seen here during a scene of crisis almost 77 3/4 minutes into the film. *DuArt, Nothing But a Man Company; New Video DVD*

REPRESENTATIONS OF LATIN AMERICANS AND LATINOS IN FILM

Various film scholars—such as Rosa Linda Fregoso, Charles Ramírez Berg, and Chon Noriega—and the documentary film *The Bronze Screen: 100 Years of the Latino Image in Hollywood* (2002) have explored the representations of Latin Americans and Latinos in American movies.[1] A brief history of the representation of Latinos in U.S. films reveals similarities to the history of the representation of African Americans in U.S. movies.

---

[1]*Latin American* usually designates a citizen of the Spanish Caribbean, Mexico, or a country in Central or South America. *Latino* signifies people of Latin American descent—such as Puerto Ricans, Mexicans, Guatemalans, and Peruvians—living in the United States. And *Chicano*, as Charles Ramírez Berg explains, "is a term made popular by the Mexican American civil rights movement in the 1960s and 1970s; as an ethnic self-identifying label, it implied pride as well as activism and oppositional politics. . . . Our children, however, tend to prefer the term 'Mexican American'" (6).

Early celluloid Latinos and Latin Americans were usually minor roles or negative role models. In the earliest U.S. movies, for example, the Mexican man was, as the writers of *The Bronze Screen* term him, "Hollywood's First Bad Guy." In countless westerns, Mexican American and Mexican males have been portrayed (sometimes by European American actors) as crude, ignorant, lazy, and vicious (Figure 10.14). To advance their acting careers, some Latinas—such as Dolores Del Rio, Rita Hayworth (see Figure 7.15 on p. 322), and Raquel Welch—dyed their hair a lighter color. Others—including Rita Hayworth, who was originally named Margarita Cansino—changed their names. Countless minor Latino and Latin American roles and even some major ones were mainly stereotypes, such as the hot-blooded Latin male lover, the immoral woman, the lazy and ignorant Mexican, and the "greaser" (an insulting term for a Latin American, especially a lower-class Mexican). The reasons for these pervasive simplified and mostly demeaning cinematic representations may be partially understood in historical context: "In the United States, especially in the Southwest, Manifest Destiny meant taking land from Mexico, displacing Mexican landowners, subjugating . . . Texans, New Mexicans, and Californians of Mexican heritage . . ., and exploiting them as cheap and expendable labor. In order to rationalize the expansionist goals . . ., Latinos [and Latin Americans] . . . needed to be shown as lesser beings. Movie stereotyping of Latinos [and Latin Americans], therefore, has been and continues to be part of an American imperialistic discourse about who should rule the hemisphere" (Berg 4–5).

As is the case with representations of African Americans in movies, in recent years a wider range of believable Latino and Latin American characters have been appearing in movies, though this is more true of males than females. More films about Latinos, such as *Real Women Have Curves* (2002), are being made by Latinos. And now a number of the most promi-

FIGURE 10.14 Stereotypical representation of Mexicans in a U.S. movie
Much of the story of *The Wild Bunch* (1969) is set in Mexico, which the film sometimes represents stereotypically: both the worry-free village of nurture, comfort, and pleasure and the army camp with its abundance of women who are nearly all beautiful, young, and available. At other times, the film represents Mexico as stereotypically hellish: the army men of all ranks are crass and cruel. For example, as a form of celebration for the soldiers, their girlfriends, and boys, the man seen here almost 122 1/4 minutes into the Director's Cut DVD has been dragged facedown in the dust on a rope pulled by a car as the men and women drink whiskey, smile, and laugh. *Warner Bros./Seven Arts; Warner Home Video DVD*

nent stars—such as Salma Hayek, Jennifer Lopez, Antonio Banderas, and Benicio del Toro—are Latino/a. Nonetheless, from time to time, studies point out that the percentages of Latinos in mainstream movies and TV are still disproportionately low.

Film history reveals the same progression of events for the representations of African Americans and Latinos. Initially, both groups were represented in celluloid by others. The result: (mostly negative) stereotypes and belittlement. Whether consciously intended or not, those films imply that the status quo should continue. Later, as African Americans and Latinos gained access to the means of production and distribution and made the representations themselves, viewers saw fewer stereotypes, more positive images of the minority, more variety of characters, more complex characters, and more celebration of the minority group. Sometimes, as with many blaxploitation movies, viewers also saw increased criticism of those in power. Remember the story of *Sweet Sweetback's Baadasssss Song* and its dedication: "to all the Brothers and Sisters who had enough of the Man."

As we have seen, where and when a film was made (and by whom) strongly influences whether gays, lesbians, African Americans, and Latinos and Latin Americans are included at all and, if they are, how they are represented. As studies by film scholars cited in "For Further Reading" at the end of this chapter demonstrate, the same is true of representations in mainstream movies of other minority groups, such as American Indians, Asians and Asian Americans, and Arabs and Arab Americans.

So far, we have examined how the social attitudes of a time and place affect the making of individual films. Knowing about those attitudes also can help us understand how representations of a recurrent story change depending on the time and place where the films were made. Some stories resonate with certain audiences and get made and remade and remade— but always differently. Consider British and U.S. celluloid Tarzans. In those films, characters, story, and concerns vary according to the social attitudes of the time and place of their making (Figure 10.15).

It is not just social attitudes that influence the making of films. Often, political attitudes of the time and place where the films were made affect what subjects are chosen and how they are represented. Consider the situation in the United States shortly after the end of World War II, with the Soviet Union's rise in power and the beginning of the cold war. With heavy media coverage of those political developments, many Americans began to worry about Communist infiltration of American institutions. As part of its activities, in 1947 the House Committee on Un-American Activities (HUAC, as the committee was often imprecisely called) held hearings in Hollywood to investigate Communist infiltration of the film industry. Some filmmakers—either from the conviction that the committee's actions infringed on their constitutional rights or because they had

FIGURE 10.15 **Different societies, different Tarzans**

(a) Edgar Rice Burroughs's novel *Tarzan of the Apes* (1912) was first adapted, in most of its essentials, into an American film of the same title six years after publication. The first Tarzan movie is set in what for 1918 American audiences must have been exotic locales and features plenty of action, including attacks by wild animals. *Tarzan of the Apes* stars a boy playing Tarzan at a youthful age and the portly Elmo Lincoln as the strong but not particularly grace-ful adult Tarzan, who never swings through trees—perhaps for fear of cracking tree branches. Typical of the film's racial insensitivity is the title card stating that before Jane, Tarzan had never seen a woman, although earlier in the film viewers saw him looking at African women. The film consistently shows that Tarzan is much more at home with apes than with native Africans and reflects the fear and distrust so many European Americans of the time felt about people with dark skin. (b) *Tarzan: The Ape Man* (1932) stars former Olympic swimming champion Johnny Weissmuller and Maureen O'Sullivan. This *Tarzan* gives no explanation of how Tarzan happened to be living in the jungle with wild animals. The film can be seen as Depression-era escapist fare featuring exotic locales, lots of action, numerous condescending stereotypes of Africa and Africans, a love triangle of two men pursuing the same woman, a crowd-pleasing resolution, and little interest in such issues as race, colonialism, and identity. (c) *Greystoke: The Legend of Tarzan, Lord of the Apes* (1984) was an international though largely British production. The story alternates between western Africa and Scotland, as it focuses on the loneliness and loss of being caught between two worlds and two families: "lord of the apes" and earl of Greystoke. The film also shows the artifice and shortcomings of civilized society, and "civilized" man's exploitation of the African environment and callous treatment of its wild-life. As Kenneth M. Cameron writes, the film was "heavily weighted . . . toward environmental concern—the Green Party version of Tarzan—. . . [and] examined the great apes, particularly, in far more detail and with far more sympathy than other Tarzan pictures" (166). (d) Disney's *Tarzan* (1999) is curiously void of Africans and, as so many Disney films do, exalts the glories of nature and the worth of an outsider. Here a handsome, athletic Tarzan moves through trees as youths do when they surf or skateboard. Like the 1984 *Greystoke*, Disney's *Tarzan* also shows "civilized" men's cruelty and their callous and exploitative treatment of animals. The film also deals with such subjects as the outsider, family, assimilation, and identity—issues generally of more concern to the late twentieth century than to early in the century when Tarzan came to light. Unlike *Greystoke* but in keeping with the Disney tradition, the film is often amusing and concludes with romantic love triumphant. (a–c) *Publicity stills.* (a) *National Film Corp. of America; The Museum of Modern Art/Film Stills Archive.* (b) *MGM.* (c) *Warner Bros. and others.* (d) *Walt Disney Pictures and others; Walt Disney Home Video DVD*

been Communist Party members (or both)—refused to cooperate with the committee. Ten filmmakers, mostly screenwriters, dubbed the "Holly-wood Ten," were eventually sentenced to prison for contempt of Congress. In 1951, HUAC held a second round of hearings on Communist influence in Hollywood, and more than three hundred Hollywood filmmakers either confessed to past membership in the Communist Party or were accused by witnesses of having been members. Until well into the 1960s, most of

a)

b)

c)

d)

those people were blacklisted and could not find work in the American film industry.

The atmosphere of fear and distrust caused enormous upheaval in the industry. Some filmmakers found other work; some moved abroad to find film work; others worked in the American film industry under assumed names. Freedom of expression was curtailed for all who worked in the U.S. film industry at the time, not just for those who were accused of being

Communists. Filmmakers shied away from controversial projects, especially those with political subjects or political implications. However, according to some commentators, some of the films indirectly criticized the political climate of the time. For example, some observers saw parallels between those who refused to cooperate with HUAC and the town marshal in the western *High Noon* (1952); both acted on their principles and refused to give in to intimidating forces. *The Invasion of the Body Snatchers* (1956) shows the gradual, unobtrusive invasion of alien life forms that take on the appearance of people but not their emotions and then replace the people. To some critics, the film was symptomatic of a spreading menace to society and the passivity of the era.

In every period, political climate influences the choice and representation of subjects. Another example is seen during the cold war period, from the late 1940s to the 1980s. Such American movies as *Red Dawn* (1984), which shows Soviets and Cubans invading a small Colorado town, and *Rambo: First Blood Part II* (1985) depict Soviets as untrustworthy and treacherous. *Rocky IV* (1985) also reflects the political mood of the time through two boxing matches between representatives of the Soviet Union and the United States, and it is unsurprising which political system the movie champions (Figure 10.16). *Rocky IV* and other cold war–era movies exalt Americans and encourage nationalism while denigrating Soviets and the Soviet system. In contrast, since the breakup of the Soviet Union in 1991 and the increased cooperation between Russia and the United States, few anti-Russian American movies have been forthcoming.

Censorship

Censorship is closely related to societal attitudes and political climate. From the beginning of cinema, some people have been concerned about the possible harm inflicted on *others* who see certain behavior, especially sex and violence, or who are exposed to certain ideas, particularly religious and political ones. Different societies express these concerns in different ways.

Some societies forbid the making of certain films. Iranian movies, most of which are funded by the government, forbid criticism of the Iranian Islamic government and all religions. In Iranian films women must be shown in headscarf and long coat. Forbidden are **close-ups** of women, makeup, kissing, handholding, and eye contact between men and women. To ensure compliance with these and other guidelines, the government imposes multiple stages of censorship, beginning with approval of the script.

In Vietnam, a censor is always present during filming, as one was during the filming of *Three Seasons* (1999). If the censor sees or hears anything questionable, the filmmakers must make changes on the spot or come to an agreement with the official. In China, filmmakers are not supposed to make sexy films, films that criticize the government explicitly or implicitly,

close-up: An image in which the subject fills most of the frame and little of the surroundings is shown.

FIGURE 10.16 The cold war in a boxing ring

Rocky IV (1985) culminates in a boxing match between Rocky and his Goliath Soviet opponent, Ivan Drago. It's not giving away a surprise ending to reveal that Rocky prevails. He does so for a combination of reasons. In no small part, Rocky wins because *Rocky IV* is an American movie made during the cold war. Rocky's victory is also a victory for the old ways of doing things. Before the fight, the film has a long sequence that cross-cuts between Rocky and Drago's different training routines. Here, a little more than 62 minutes into the film, appears this match cut between Rocky lifting an old-style two-wheel cart with three people in it and Drago doing a similar lift. Throughout the sequence, Rocky trains in nature with nature's objects (rocks, mountains, snow, logs) and simple country tools (sled, ax, block and tackle, rope, yoke, cart, and saw). By contrast, Drago uses all the most advanced computerized exercise equipment and is injected with drugs. Rocky is advised by a trainer with years of experience with professional boxing. Drago is trained by a cadre of state-employed scientists and a trainer with no professional experience in boxing. Other factors contribute to Rocky's victory. For example, he keeps getting back up and going at Drago, and he is not burdened by arrogance. By the twelfth round, if you can believe it, even the initially hostile Soviet crowd begins chanting "Rocky!" "Rocky!" "Rocky!" Before the final round, a Soviet official berates Drago, who announces that he fights to win—for himself. Drago is then alone and on the doorstep of defeat. *Rocky IV* gave 1985 U.S. movie audiences the thrill and satisfaction of a cold war victory reminiscent of a 1980 Winter Olympics ice hockey game in which the underdog U.S. team composed of amateur and collegiate players defeated the heavily favored Soviet team and went on to win the gold medal. *Chartoff-Winkler Productions, MGM, and United Artists; MGM Home Entertainment DVD*

a)

b)

or depressing films with sad endings. Filmmakers who shoot their film without first getting the script approved and a permit face the likelihood of stiff fines and exclusion from the large Chinese market. *Xiu Xiu: The Sent Down Girl* (1998), which Joan Chen filmed on the sly in a remote western Chinese province, is a film suffering this fate, as is the more widely seen *Farewell My Concubine* (1993). Chinese control over movies is far reaching. *Postman* (1995)—not to be confused with the Italian film *Il Postino* (*The Postman*) of the same year or with Kevin Costner's *The Postman* (1997)—touches on adultery, prostitution, homosexuality, and drug use. Even before its completion, its director was banned from making further films.

Sometimes government authorities may halt a production. Soviet filmmaker Sergei Eisenstein was forced both to abandon *Bezhin Meadow* in 1937 and to repudiate it publicly. Eisenstein ran into trouble with *Bezhin Meadow* and most of his later films because he did not follow the general

style: The way that subjects are represented in a text, such as a film.

guidelines of **socialist realism.** This Soviet doctrine and **style**, which was in force from the mid-1930s to the 1980s (until the Gorbachev era), decreed that all creative works—including music, artworks, and films—must promote socialism, communism, and thus the proletariat, or working people. Soviet creative works were also not to imply approval of Western ideas and lifestyles or even ambivalence toward them. Under socialist realism, creative works were supposed to be "realistic" (actually an idealized representation of the working class) and readily accessible to mass audiences. Styles judged innovative, arty, or western European were taboo. Works judged to fall short of the standards of socialist realism were labeled "decadent," "bourgeois," "capitalistic," or "formalist," and at times in the 1930s and 1940s the Soviet dictator Stalin himself made that judgment. At a minimum their makers were publicly rebuked; some met other, more painful fates. For fifty years, socialist realism severely restricted the subjects and styles of Soviet artists, not just such filmmakers as Eisenstein and Lev Kuleshov but also the composers Dmitri Shostakovich and Sergei Prokofiev, writer Isaac Babel, theater director Vsevolod Meyerhold, and many others.

In the United States, early films were sometimes censored by state or city boards (Figure 10.17). By the early 1930s, many American viewers found many popular American movies offensive. Many but by no means all. Whereas some viewers seemed especially upset by violence, others swarmed to such popular gangster films as *Little Caesar* (1930), *The Public Enemy* (1931), and *Scarface* (1932). Similarly, films featuring unrepentant, sexually assertive women, such as the different characters played by Mae West, were offensive to some audiences but popular with others (Figure 10.18). Of West's impact, scholar Ramona Curry writes, "Unlike most other Hollywood movies of the 1930s, West's films do not suggest that morality or questions of taste dictate female sexual behavior. Instead, West's films and star image present female sexual allure as a commodity that women themselves can control and benefit from. . . . West's movie image exposed contradictions in the well-established American capitalist practice of simultaneously exploiting and repressing female sexuality as a commodity under men's control" (28). Some of the films of the time tested the limits of audience tolerance. In *Baby Face* (1933), Barbara Stanwyck plays an attractive young woman who learns to use her physical and psychological assets with a succession of men in order to advance her career and amass a collection of jewelry and fancy clothes.

producer: A person in charge of the business and administrative aspects of making a film.

Rather than face government interference, in 1930 American film **producers** and distributors set up a written production code, a self-regulatory system of acceptable speech and behavior in films (see the feature on pp. 462–64). In 1934, the code was revised and from then on more strenuously enforced. Until 1968, all movies to be shown in U.S. movie theaters were supposed to be submitted first to the Production Code Administration for a seal of approval. The code restricted the explicit or positive representation of vast areas of human experience—such as illegal drugs, illicit sex, scenes

a)

b)

FIGURE 10.17 **Early, local censorship**
(a) A 1-minute or so 1896 American film, "Fatima, Muscle Dancer" (aka "Fatima's Dance"), shows a woman's dance that includes twirling, shimmying, and bumping. A Web commentator called Venus observes, "Whether or not her dancing is racy must surely be in the eye of the beholder. The unrestrained motions of shoulders, breasts, hips, and abdomen are in direct contravention of Victorian notions of feminine decorum, modesty, and restraint. Fatima's spins cause her skirt to fly up so that we see her lower legs and the bottoms of her knickers. However, she makes no lewd gestures or expressions, only smiling slightly." According to Venus, this style of dancing was known as "coochee coochee dance," "oriental dance," or the "muscle dance." (b) Some exhibitors showed a censored version of the film with scratched emulsion concealing some of her body but not much obscuring the suggestiveness of her movements. *Edison; The Museum of Modern Art; Kino International DVD*

FIGURE 10.18 **Mae West's movie sexuality**
In *She Done Him Wrong* (1933)—which includes a youthful Cary Grant (seen here)—West wears an abundance of diamond jewelry and her usual variety of revealing, glamorous clothes. As in so many of her films, she plays a single woman who is quick-witted, resourceful, confident, attractive to men, and nearly always fully in control of situations with them. Although she is skimpy with her affection and usually turns away from the men's attempted embraces and kisses, she often looks at men directly (not obliquely), wears tight and revealing clothing, and sings suggestively as she gently sways her hips. Even today, Mae West characters are sometimes still quoted for their well-timed witty sayings. Two examples from *She Done Him Wrong*: "When women go wrong, men go right after them" and "I wasn't always rich. . . . There was a time I didn't know where my next husband was coming from." By today's standards, the Mae West characters in her early 1930s movies are campy and mildly suggestive—not carnal, and certainly not as one Hearst newspaper editorial of the time proclaimed a "menace to . . . the American Family." To many 1930s U.S. viewers wanting family fare, she was sexual, assertive, unrepentant, and shocking, and her movies have been blamed as partially responsible for stricter enforcement of the production code. *Paramount Pictures; Universal Studios Home Entertainment DVD*

Excerpts from *The Production Code of the Motion Picture Producers and Directors of America, Inc., 1930–1934*

PREAMBLE

Motion picture producers recognize the high trust and confidence which have been placed in them by the people of the world and which have made motion pictures a universal form of entertainment.

They recognize their responsibility to the public because of this trust and because entertainment and art are important influences in the life of a nation.

Hence, though regarding motion pictures primarily as entertainment without any explicit purpose of teaching or propaganda, they know that the motion picture within its own field of entertainment may be directly responsible for spiritual or moral progress, for higher types of social life, and for much correct thinking. . . .

On their part, they ask from the public and from public leaders a sympathetic understanding of their purposes and problems and a spirit of co-operation that will allow them the freedom and opportunity necessary to bring the motion picture to a still higher level of wholesome entertainment for all the people.

GENERAL PRINCIPLES

1. No picture shall be produced which will lower the moral standards of those who see it. Hence the sympathy of the audience shall never be thrown to the side of crime, wrong-doing, evil, or sin.
2. Correct standards of life, subject only to the requirements of drama and entertainment, shall be presented. . . .

   I. CRIMES AGAINST THE LAW

   These shall never be presented in such a way as to throw sympathy with the crime as against law and justice or to inspire others with a desire for imitation.

   1. Murder
      a) The technique of murder must be presented in a way that will not inspire imitation.
      b) Brutal killings are not to be presented in detail.
      c) Revenge in modern times shall not be justified. . . .

   II. SEX

   The sanctity of the institution of marriage and the home shall be upheld. Pictures shall not infer that low forms of sex relationship are the accepted or common thing.

   1. Adultery and illicit sex, sometimes necessary plot material, must not be explicitly treated or justified, or presented attractively.
   2. Scenes of passion
      a) These should not be introduced except where they are definitely essential to the plot.
      b) Excessive and lustful kissing, lustful embraces, suggestive postures and gestures are not to be shown.
      c) In general, passion should be treated in such manner as not to stimulate the lower and baser emotions.
   3. Seduction or rape
      a) These should never be more than suggested, and then only when essential for the plot. They must never be shown by explicit method.
      b) They are never the proper subject for comedy.

Note: Approximately 40 percent of the Code is excerpted here.

462

4. Sex perversion or any inference to it is forbidden. . . .

6. Miscegenation (sex relationship between the white and black races) is forbidden. . . .

III. VULGARITY

The treatment of low, disgusting, unpleasant, though not necessarily evil, subjects should be guided always by the dictates of good taste and a proper regard for the sensibilities of the audience.

IV. OBSCENITY

Obscenity in word, gesture, reference, song, joke, or by suggestion . . . is forbidden.

V. PROFANITY

Pointed profanity and every other profane or vulgar expression, however used, is forbidden.

No approval by the Production Code Administration shall be given to the use of words and phrases in motion pictures including, but not limited to, the following:

. . . broad (applied to a woman); . . . God, Lord, Jesus, Christ (unless used reverently); . . . fanny; fairy (in a vulgar sense); finger (the); . . . hot (applied to a woman); . . . louse; lousy; . . . nerts; nuts (except when meaning crazy); pansy; . . . slut (applied to a woman); S.O.B.; son-of-a; tart; . . . traveling salesman and farmer's daughter jokes; whore; damn. . . .

The Production Code Administration may take cognizance of the fact that the following words and phrases are obviously offensive to the patrons of motion pictures in the United States and more particularly to the patrons of motion pictures in foreign countries: Chink, Dago, Frog, Greaser, Hunkie, Kike, Nigger, Spig, Wop, Yid. . . .

VIII. RELIGION

1. No film or episode may throw ridicule on any religious faith.

2. Ministers of religion in their character as ministers of religion should not be used as comic characters or as villains. . . .

REASONS SUPPORTING PREAMBLE OF CODE

. . . The moral importance of entertainment is something which has been universally recognized. It enters intimately into the lives of men and women and affects them closely; it occupies their minds and affections during leisure hours; and ultimately touches the whole of their lives. A man may be judged by his standard of entertainment as easily as by the standard of his work. . . .

3.D. The latitude given to film material cannot, in consequence, be as wide as the latitude given to book material. In addition:

a) A book describes; a film vividly presents. One presents on a cold page; the other by apparently living people.

b) A book reaches the mind through words merely; a film reaches the eyes and ears through the reproduction of actual events.

c) The reaction of a reader to a book depends largely on the keenness of the reader's imagination; the reaction to a film depends on the vividness of presentation.

Hence many things which might be described or presented in a book could not possibly be presented in a film. . . .

F. Everything possible in a play is not possible in a film:

a) Because of the larger audience of the film, and its consequential mixed character. Psychologically, the larger the audience, the lower the moral mass resistance to suggestion.

b) Because through light, enlargement of character, presentation, scenic emphasis, etc., the screen story is brought closer to the audience than the play.

c) The enthusiasm for and interest in the film actors and actresses, developed beyond anything of the sort in history, makes the audience largely sympathetic toward the characters they portray and the stories in which they figure. Hence the audience is more ready to con-fuse actor and actress and the characters they portray, and it is most receptive of the emotions and ideals presented by their favorite stars.

G. Small communities, remote from sophistication and from the hardening process which often takes place in the ethical and moral standards of groups in larger cities, are easily and readily reached by any sort of film. . . .

In general, the mobility, popularity, accessibility, emotional appeal, vividness, straightforward presentation of fact in the film make for more intimate contact with a larger audience and for greater emotional appeal.

Hence the larger moral responsibilities of the motion pictures.

of passion, prostitution, miscegenation, childbirth, and obscene and profane speech (Figure 10.19). From 1934 to 1968, to earn the seal of approval American films had to be suitable for audiences of all ages, including young children. They had to be essentially what are now G-rated movies. Some of the differences between films made before and after the code was enforced are evident in stills for *Gold Diggers of 1933* and *Gold Diggers of 1937* (Figure 10.20).

Enforcement of the code often undermined a story's plausibility or logic, sometimes even resulting in incoherence. *The Big Sleep* (1946) is confusing because it omits nearly all references to the sex and drugs so prominent in the source novel by Raymond Chandler. As critic Frank Krutnik shows, enforcement of the code in a romantic scene involving the two main characters in *Out of the Past* (1947) created confusion:

The couple run through the rain to the beach-house, laughing like carefree young lovers. When they arrive there, Kathie dries his hair, and Jeff does the same for her. He kisses her on the back of the neck and then [about 27 minutes into the film] tosses away the towel, which knocks the lamp over. When the light goes out, there is a swirl of music, and the camera then **tracks** towards the door, which blows open in the wind. There is then a **cut** to the outside, with the camera continuing its forward-tracking. This leading away from the scene, together with the reprisal of the film's love-theme and the dousing of

track (verb): To film while the camera is being moved around.

464

the light, suggests that Jeff and Kathie are making love. However, the film cuts back to the inside of the beach-house: Jeff closes the door, and Kathie takes a record off the gramophone. There is a marked, seemingly post-coital change in their attitudes. However, although the slow forward-tracking of the camera has implied that intercourse takes place, the cut back to the inside, and the continuity of Jeff shutting the door after it has blown open, suggest that there has been no time-lapse. Sex is thus both firmly suggested and disavowed. (246)

Following the code also resulted in more than one implausible ending, such as in *Detour* (1945). That film was initially refused a seal of approval because it ended with the main character, who had inadvertently killed someone, free and walking along a road. To gain a seal, a short scene was appended: the police drive up, stop, pick up the man, and drive off, as he narrates, "Someday a car will stop to pick me up that I never thumbed. Yes. Fate or some mysterious force can put the finger on you or me for no good reason at all." In this case, the not so "mysterious force" was the production code.

If restrictions are imposed on creative people, some will find ways to work around them. Since the code explicitly forbade movie representations of much of human sexual behavior, for example, during the code era scriptwriters and directors found ways to hint at sexual subject matter without incurring the censor's rebuke. Perhaps starting with Mae West, double entendres—words or phrases with two meanings, one of them usually sexual—became popular in movies. In *Some Like It Hot*, when one of the men posing as female musicians is strongly attracted to the Marilyn Monroe character and she joins him in his upper bunk on a train and they start to share a bottle of whiskey, he says suggestively, "This may even turn out to be a surprise party." His probable meaning: he may surprise her by later revealing that he is a virile straight man. Her likely understanding: he has an innocent surprise in store for her. There were additional creative but unobtrusive ways filmmakers working

FIGURE 10.19 **A visualization of production code–era cinematic no-nos**
Paramount Studio's Whitey Schafer photographed this staged situation in 1940 to illustrate subjects forbidden by the production code: a police officer killed, a gun pointing at someone, an automatic machine gun, the inside of a woman's thigh, lacey lingerie, a partially exposed breast, narcotics (the syringe on the table), alcoholic drinks, and gambling (note the clever prominence of the deadly ace of spades in the lower right-hand corner). *A. L. (Whitey) Schafer; Courtesy of The Academy of Motion Picture Arts and Sciences*

FIGURE 10.20 Pre-1934 movies and post-1934 movies (a) From the "Pettin' in the Park" musical number in *Gold Diggers of 1933* (1933). After the production code was applied to all movies from 1934 until the 1960s, such glimpses of sexuality were forbidden in U.S. movies. (b) A few years after the production code was fully in effect, *Gold Diggers of 1937* (1936) represents men and women as innocent (dressed in white), childlike (small in comparison to the chairs), and unerotic (covered up and sitting, not partially uncovered and lying down as in the 1933 film). The language of *Gold Diggers of 1937* is also less suggestive than that of *Gold Diggers of 1933*, and in the later film, words such as *pettin'* or *petting* are never heard. *Publicity stills.* (a) *Warner Bros.* (b) *Warner Bros.–First National Pictures*

a)

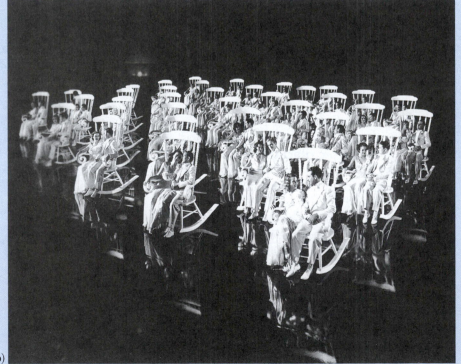

b)

in the production code era could suggest forbidden subjects, as is illustrated in another example from *Some Like It Hot* (Figure 10.21).

As more and more films were released without a seal in the 1950s and 1960s, it became harder and harder to enforce the code. As film historian and scholar Robert Sklar explains:

> The tendency in motion-picture production and exhibition had always been to get away with as much risqué and socially disreputable behavior as the vigilance of censors would allow and economic necessity dictated. For nearly two decades after 1934, the Production Code Administration had maintained stringent control over Hollywood productions, and rising box-office figures through 1946 seemed to confirm that clean family entertainment was the road to prosperity. But as families found their clean entertainment on the TV screen, there was a natural impulse in the movie trade to revert to shock and titillation. (294)

In 1953, the American film *The Moon Is Blue* was refused a seal because it treated seduction and adultery comically, and its distributor, United Artists, resigned from the producers' association and released the film on its own without a seal. Later in the 1950s and in the 1960s, such European films as the French *And God Created Woman* (1956) and the Swedish *The Silence* (1963) were more candid sexually than American films and were shown without a seal of approval in art theaters in large U.S. cities (Figure 10.22).

FIGURE 10.21 Suggesting sexual arousal during the U.S. production code era
A little more than 83½ minutes into Billy Wilder's *Some Like It Hot* (1959), a reclining man posing as unresponsive to women reveals otherwise when the Marilyn Monroe character kisses him and immediately one of his legs stiffly, suggestively, but only briefly and rather unobtrusively, rises from the couch. *Ashton Productions, Mirisch Productions; MGM Home Entertainment DVD*

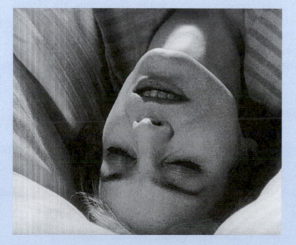

FIGURE 10.22 Sexual frankness in 1950s and 1960s European films
Some European films of the 1950s and 1960s were more candid in their representations of sexuality than American films of the time and were shown without the production code seal of approval in mostly big-city American theaters. Here, about 20 minutes into Ingmar Bergman's *The Silence* (1963), one of the two main characters is seen reacting as she masturbates, an act that is clearly suggested. Elsewhere, the other main character sees a woman and man having sexual intercourse in the back of a variety theater. In both instances, the representations of sexuality would have been inconceivable in mainstream American movies of the time because of the force of the production code. The inclusion of such scenes made these European films more appealing to many American viewers and distributors and probably contributed to the abandonment a few years later of the U.S. production code and adoption of a ratings system that permitted more adult films for adult U.S. audiences. *Svensk Filmindustri; Criterion DVD*

Finally in 1968, the U.S. production code was replaced with a rating system loosely modeled on the British rating system. The American ratings have been modified several times since then. (For an explanation of the current American ratings, see Figure 10.23.) Studios that belong to the Motion Picture Association of America are required to submit finished films for a rating. Independent film companies, which operate outside Hollywood control, are not. Advertisements and theaters are to display the rating so viewers will know what to expect, and theaters are supposed to exclude certain age groups from films with certain ratings. Although the industry and the public generally approve of the system, it is a source of persistent problems and persistent complaints. Many filmmakers complain about the rating assigned their film and a lack of clear, consistent guidelines. The ratings board continues to tend to be much harsher on films with sexual content than on films with violence. And the NC-17 rating, which was intended to remove the pornographic stigma from frank but serious representations of sexual subjects, has not had that result. Films released with the NC-17 rating are shut out of many theaters, Blockbuster and Wal-Mart stores, and many advertising venues and thus lose significant amounts of revenue. Films so rated are often released by the distributor without a rating. Filmmakers who appeal the rating to the appeals board, which is made up mostly of film industry bigwigs, are allowed to cite no precedents in arguing their case and are never told what specific aspects of their film might be changed or cut to achieve a more favorable rating.[2] Because of dissatisfaction with the rating system, from time to time alternatives to it emerge.[3] In spite of all the imperfections in the rating system, some critics argue that the system is useful:

> Mostly, filmmakers complain that they must work against muddled or moving boundaries. And parents' groups grouse about "ratings creep," a perceived tendency for a category like PG-13 to permit ever more violence, sex, and profanity over the years to reach impressionable youth. Yet it was Mr. [Jack] Valenti's genius to have devised an apparatus [in 1968] that is not bound by precedent, changes its definitions at will and, ultimately, serves the motion picture industry by becoming, at any given moment, as permissive or restrictive as the prevailing climate seems to demand. . . . Indeed, for nearly 40 years, Mr. Valenti's raters have largely kept politicians and busybodies out of the film business, even if that meant playing somewhat unpredictable busybodies themselves. They haven't always been fair, and not entirely pleasant to deal with. But in the end, theirs was no mean achievement. (Cieply)

---

[2]The documentary *This Film Is Not Yet Rated* (2006)—which has nothing good to say about the MPAA ratings board and the appeals board—exposes the ratings board's inconsistencies, arbitrariness, and secretiveness.

[3]For years, an agency of the United States Catholic Conference has provided brief movie reviews, the USCC's classification, and the Motion Picture Association of America rating of each film, an archive of USCC movie reviews, and other types of film information.

What Everyone Should Know About The Movie Rating System.

GENERAL AUDIENCES

G

G | GENERAL AUDIENCES
All Ages Admitted

Nothing that would offend parents for viewing by children.

PARENTAL GUIDANCE SUGGESTED

PG

PG | PARENTAL GUIDANCE SUGGESTED
SOME MATERIAL MAY NOT BE SUITABLE FOR CHILDREN

Parents urged to give "parental guidance." May contain some material parents might not like for their young children.

PARENTS STRONGLY CAUTIONED

PG-13

PG-13 | PARENTS STRONGLY CAUTIONED
Some Material May Be Inappropriate for Children Under 13

Parents are urged to be cautious. Some material may be inappropriate for pre-teenagers.

RESTRICTED

R

R | RESTRICTED
UNDER 17 REQUIRES ACCOMPANYING
PARENT OR ADULT GUARDIAN

Contains some adult material. Parents are urged to learn more about the film before taking their young children with them.

NO CHILDREN UNDER 17 ADMITTED

NC-17

NC-17 | NO CHILDREN
UNDER 17
ADMITTED

Patently adult. Children are not admitted.

FIGURE 10.23 The current U.S. movie rating classifications Before the latest change in the ratings system in 1990, both sexually explicit films and serious films unable to win an R rating were given an X, which meant that many theaters would not show them, many newspapers would not advertise them, and many video stores would not carry them. The NC-17 rating was devised for films that are made primarily to present their subjects with candor and not to stimulate sexual arousal. Since the inception of the NC-17 rating, the Motion Picture Association of America no longer assigns films an X rating. Few sexually explicit films were ever submitted for a rating anyway. © *Motion Picture Association of America, Encino, Calif.*

Knowing something about the restrictions on filmmakers, film distributors, and film exhibitors helps viewers understand and judge films more accurately and fairly. Such knowledge may help one understand, for example, why *Detour* stumbles to its conclusion and why two films that share the same general subject and are only a few years apart are so different (see Figure 10.20).

Artistic Conventions

Subject: Things You Learn at the Movies

- It does not matter if you are heavily outnumbered in a fight involving martial arts. Your enemies will wait patiently to attack you one by one and will dance around in a threatening manner until you have knocked out their predecessors.
- Once applied, lipstick will never rub off—even while scuba diving.
- In war it is impossible to die unless you make the mistake of showing someone a picture of your sweetheart back home.
- A man will show no pain while taking the most ferocious beating but will wince when a woman tries to clean his wounds.
- If staying in a haunted house, women should investigate any strange noises alone and while wearing their most revealing underwear.
- If you decide to start dancing in the street, everyone you meet will know all the steps.

(from an uncredited list circulated widely on the Internet)

film(making) technique: Any aspect of filmmaking, such as the use of sets, lighting, sound effects, music, or editing.

In films and other texts, a convention is a subject or **filmmaking technique** that makers of texts and audiences have grown to accept as natural or typical in certain contexts. Different types of movies have their own conventions. Countless martial-arts movies and numerous Hong Kong action movies feature behavior that to the novice viewer may seem odd. *Crouching Tiger, Hidden Dragon* (2000) includes impossible airborne acrobatics—including flying through the air and effortlessly bounding from the ground up to a rooftop. In John Woo's *The Killer* (1989) the many bad guys won't die unless their gunshot wounds are numerous, even if the shots are from close range. The aggressive hordes can also appear oddly considerate by not attacking in unison and thereby overwhelming the beleaguered hero(es). Sometimes it seems as if they simply bide their time **offscreen** until it is their turn to rush forward and get slaughtered. In **Bollywood** movies, it is a convention that musical numbers are included frequently and sometimes in places that surprise viewers who have not seen a lot of Bollywood movies. In *The Legend of Bhagat Singh* (2002), for example, "The action simply stops for a few minutes as the characters burst into song, tablas and sitars throb on the soundtrack. . . . The political-historical nature of *Bhagat Singh* forces the filmmakers to curtail some of the more extreme tendencies of the Bollywood musical, but there are still plenty of startling moments: jailed hunger strikers [near death] breaking into song . . . and the hero and his two closest comrades smiling broadly and singing lustily of the glory of self-sacrifice

Bollywood: Extremely popular Hindi-language movies made in India.

as they march to the gallows" (Kehr). Filmgoers raised on Bollywood films probably pay no attention to these conventions, but an audience unfamiliar with singing jailed hunger strikers and men walking briskly and with a swagger as they sing cheerfully about their impending hangings may find these interludes surprising or perplexing.

Music in movies from the Western world has its own conventions. For example, as yet another cowboy dressed in black enters yet another saloon, the music changes from a major to a minor key, but audiences in the West don't notice the shift because they've heard it in so many other westerns (Figure 10.24). Approximately 80½ minutes into the musical *Dreamgirls* (2006), Effie (Jennifer Hudson) begins singing "I Am Changing." At first she is accompanied only by a man playing a piano, but soon and initially unobtrusively more instruments—such as strings, drum, and occasional trumpets—can be heard playing along. Some viewers are so caught up in the song that they do not notice the augmented accompaniment, even though no one visible in the scene is playing music except that piano player. He's an excellent player but not so good he can create the sound of a small orchestra! There is more. Before Effie finishes singing, it's evening sometime later and the place is packed with appreciative listeners. As she continues singing, viewers can glimpse not only that piano player but also a drummer and two electric guitar players who may be just faking it. We viewers can still hear many unseen violins blended into the mix. It is a movie convention that a scene includes music from both a source in the scene and a source not in the scene.

Most movies are permeated with conventions. Consider dialogue:

> Does anyone believe that when police show up at a bank heist, the criminals say coolly, "We got company"? And has a real police detective ever said to a reticent witness, "You and I are going downtown for a little chat"? At no point in my life has anyone used these words with me: "I hope so, Todd. I hope so." In fact, I hardly ever hear anyone use my name at all in conversation. It would sound peculiar, yet in movies it happens all the time, and it sounds perfectly natural. Movie dialogue obeys its own customs. We accept it according to the terms of the cinema, not of reality. (Berliner 3)

Some conventions endure for decades. Examples are showdowns and shoot-outs in westerns, telephone conversations in which one speaker is shown but both are heard, and pistols belching smoke or flaming like a blowtorch when fired (Figure 3.21a, Figure 5.14a, Figure 10.25, and Plates 1 and 38). If used too often or for too long, conventions may become boring or in other ways ineffective, as has happened with tremolo stringed instruments used to accompany suspenseful movie moments. Conventions may also fall out of favor but later be rediscovered. An example is the reintroduction of various techniques, such as **iris shots**, **iris-in** shots, and **iris-out** shots, by

FIGURE 10.24 A musical convention in movies

iris shot: A shot in which part of the frame is masked or obscured, often leaving the remaining image in a circular or oval shape.

French new wave (cinema): A film movement consisting of a loose grouping of untraditional movies made in France in the late 1950s and early 1960s.

the directors of **French new wave** films (see Figure 7.30c on p. 339). Another example is the reintroduction by *Star Wars* (1977) of **wipes**—a transition in which it appears that one image pushes off the preceding image as it replaces it (see Figure 3.9 on p. 125). Yet other conventions—such as the introduction of **flashbacks** by a brief undulation of the image—simply disappear for long stretches of film history (and may be revived).

Iconoclastic filmmakers often draw attention to filmmaking conventions by flouting them. Mel Brooks is one such filmmaker. In *High Anxiety* (1977), for example, the camera moves toward French doors through which viewers can see people sitting at a formal dinner. The camera moves forward and forward until it loudly shatters a glass pane, and the dinner party stares at it; after a brief pause, the camera begins to retreat. In the last scene of the same film, the camera pulls back from its subjects rapidly, and viewers hear a camera operator warn, "We're going too fast. We're going to hit the wall." Almost instantaneously they do, noisily, and make a gaping hole in it. As the camera continues to retreat, the other man says, "Never mind. Keep moving back. Maybe no one will notice." Gliding exploratory camera work is a conventional technique most viewers take for granted. But most viewers have probably neither seen a camera operator have an accident nor considered when, how, and why camera movement is used.

A film may also be unconventional in its subjects. In the conventional western **genre**, for example, the protagonist is a European American male, and his antagonists are American Indians, Mexicans, or European American male outlaws. In American westerns since the 1950s, the protagonist may be female (*The Ballad of Little Jo*, 1993, and *Bad Girls*, 1994), African American (*Posse*, 1993), or European American and Mexican outlaws (*The Wild Bunch*, 1969). On the other side, the antagonists may be European American males, as throughout Jim Jarmusch's *Dead Man* (1995). The antagonist may be a law enforcement officer (*Unforgiven*, 1992, and *Posse*). European American outlaw antagonists may even be supported by the inaction of the townspeople (*High Noon*).

genre: A group of fictional films that share enough similarities that both filmmakers and audiences recognize the films as members of the same group.

Some breaks with convention—such as having an actor step out of character to speak directly to the audience, which is used throughout *High Fidelity* (2000)—never much catch on with other filmmakers. Other breaks with convention seem odd initially but are imitated by other filmmakers and eventually become conventions themselves. One example is the use of **slow motion** to represent violence. When *Bonnie and Clyde* (1967) used slow motion in a violent scene, many viewers commented on its use and found it distracting. But soon other movies followed the practice. It became widespread and, through repetition, came to seem natural to many viewers.

lap dissolve: A transition between shots in which one shot begins to fade out as the next shot fades in, overlapping the first shot before replacing it.

Unconventional filmmakers help us see that conventions do not have inevitable and unchanging meanings or significance. For instance, a **lap dissolve**—in which one image fades out as the next image fades in, momentarily overlaps it, and replaces it—does not have to mean "now the **setting** changes," though it usually does in films of recent decades. In films before that, lap dissolves are occasionally used within a scene (see Figure 3.8 on p. 124). Filmmaking practices take on widely understood meanings or associations through repeated use in similar contexts. For instance, if enough filmmakers use lap dissolves to suggest that the action now shifts to another setting, viewers learn that new meaning (similarly, we all learn the meanings of most words we know by hearing or reading them in context, not by hearing, reading, or memorizing definitions).

When we examine **filmic** conventions, we start to see how widespread, expressive, and influential they are. Conventions influence how a film is made and in turn how viewers understand the film. Conventions are something like teachers and clergy: they strongly influence succeeding generations though most people take them for granted most of the time.

filmic: Characteristic of the film medium or appropriate to it, such as parallel editing.

Financial Constraints

> Lot of times just your schedule, your budget determines how you're going to do things. (Altman)

The budget for a film influences the choice of equipment to be used, personnel employed, settings, time that can be devoted to making the film, and promotion and distribution. Consider the situation of Terry Zwigoff, the director of the documentary *Crumb* (1994), whose lack of money as he made the film restricted what he could film and influenced how he filmed it: "I just didn't have any film to use. It was horrible. I'd be in this situation with great stuff happening, and I'd have to allot myself two rolls of film instead of ten. And it was also what forced me to prompt and to stage and to manipulate a lot of things—you just couldn't wait for them to happen naturally with that kind of budget" (Katz 38).

Big feature films are terrifically expensive to make and market. A movie with stars, **special effects**, lots of action filmed at foreign **locations**, and widespread advertising requires a budget of perhaps more than $100 million.[4] To attract enough viewers to earn back the expenses in making and marketing the film and to make a profit, such a movie has to draw in huge audiences. In other words, once a big-budget deal is fashioned—for example, for *300* (2006) or *Beowulf* (2007)—or the making of the film proves much more costly than it was budgeted for—as with *Titanic* (1997)—the filmmakers are under a lot of pressure to deliver a movie with some proven

---

[4]Two sources on the breakdown of movie expenses are found in Art Linson, "The $75 Million Difference," *New York Times Magazine* 16 Nov. 1997: 88, 89, and "Bills, Bills, Bills" in *The Los Angeles Calendar* (*online*) 20 Dec. 1998. The *L.A. Times* article lists "the typical costs associated with producing a major Hollywood studio movie," including "Sound equipment: $1,800 a week," "Ferrari Daytona: $850 to $1,000 a day," "Rattlesnake: $400 a day," and "50-caliber machine-gun blanks: $3 each."

popular characteristics. Features that have remained popular over the years include chases, fights, explosions, spectacular sights, romantic or sexual attraction and interaction, at least one youthful heartthrob, captivating music, and a happy ending. Filmmakers responsible for making a movie with a big budget are also under pressure to avoid generally unpopular subjects, such as religion, and unconventional styles, such as **magic realism**.

magic realism: A style in which occasional wildly improbable or impossible events occur in an otherwise realistic story.

In financial terms, many movies are not just movies. They are mines for other products to be marketed by other components of the media conglomerate that includes the company that made or distributed the movie in the first place. Consider *Austin Powers: The Spy Who Shagged Me* (1999), which is distributed in the United States by New Line Cinema, which had been taken over by Ted Turner, who in turn agreed to a merger with Time Warner. The Austin Powers movies, in other words, are now the property of Time Warner. As one commentator explained shortly before the film's initial release,

> Within weeks, Warner Brothers retail stores and Spenser Gifts stores across the country will roll out a plethora of merchandise from snazzy nightshirts to the Austin Powers Swedish Penis Enlarger ("the perfect gift for Dad on Father's Day!"). TBS and TNT, two cable networks owned by Time Warner, will feature wall-to-wall promotion of the movie. *Entertainment Weekly*, the glossy magazine owned by Time Warner, is set to have an Austin Powers cover.
>
> Warner Records will release the soundtrack album, which includes a single, "Beautiful Stranger," by Madonna, whose label, Maverick Records, is also a Warner subsidiary. And by now, Warner Books has probably delivered to stores the first of its no doubt multiple printings of *The Austin Powers Encyclopedia*.
>
> There's more. The home video, due out in the fall [of 1999], will be sold by Time Warner's sales force; early next year there will be an animated series by HBO, a Time Warner subsidiary. . . .
>
> There may also be a theme park tie-in with Six Flags Great Adventure, which was sold recently by Time Warner but retains a licensing agreement with the company. (Hass)

For other films, finances are not such a small cage. For an independent film without stars or with stars willing to accept a small part or to work for a much-reduced payment, no special effects, and no distant locations, the budget will be far less. "Digital video has [also] dramatically lowered the barriers to feature film-making. For aspiring filmmakers who don't have $200,000 to shoot on 35 mm, or $50,000 for 16 mm, it's an affordable alternative. Instead of spending years searching for financing, filmmakers can devote their time to improving the script, rehearsing the actors and shooting the best possible movie. When their film is finished, they can decide if it is good enough to launch their careers. If not, they can make another feature for a few thousand dollars, learning from their mistakes. . . . DV is shifting power from financiers to film-makers, who no longer need their money, permission, or approval" (Broderick 7). With a smaller budget, the return need not be huge to cover all the expenses and turn a profit. Independent filmmakers—such as John Sayles, Jim Jarmusch, and Julie Dash—are freer to fashion a film more to their liking, such as one with a controversial or offbeat subject or perhaps an ending that lacks **closure** or a happy fate for characters that viewers identify with. As one director indicated, a low budget can have yet other advantages: "I've always found that not having a lot of money was a tremendous source of strength. It forces you back onto your wits, your intelligence, your imagination and gives you a sort of defiance, which is very invigorating" (Stephen Frears, qtd. in Burlingame). However, as illustrated in *Plan 9 from Outer Space* (1959), budgets may be so restricted as to cause curious results (Figure 10.25).

closure: A sense of coherence and completion at the end of a narrative.

Today, the budget for a **short film** or video can be so small that many filmmakers can afford to shoot and **edit** until they get nearly the results they want. Because makers of short films do not require a large audience, they have enormous freedom to express themselves on film. And on the Internet and through **microcinema** or **kino** screenings, they can reach audiences with similar interests because there is "a certain hunger, particularly in younger people, for films that aren't formulaic, that express something more personal, honest, or quirky than what you could see at the local cineplex or even at an independent film festival like Sundance" (Shuster).

microcinema: A program of untraditional short videos that may be shown on the Internet or in a casual atmosphere or that may be purchased on DVD.

kino: An informal group that meets periodically to show short films shot and edited digitally.

Filmmaking Technology

Although new technology makes possible effects that were previously impossible, advances in filmmaking technology are not without their costs

FIGURE 10.25 Low budget, curious results
The budget for Ed Wood's *Plan 9 from Outer Space* (1959) was minimal. When actor Bela Lugosi died early in the filming, another actor was brought in to take over the part. Rather than reshoot Lugosi's scenes, Wood had the new actor cover his face, presumably so no one would notice Lugosi's absence! As seen here almost 15 1/2 minutes into the film, the results are laughable. At least the situation made possible an intriguing claim for the film's DVD case: "almost starring BELA LUGOSI." *Reynolds Pictures, Inc.; Image Entertainment DVD*

and sometimes limitations. In the late 1920s, films began to be made with sound synchronized with the image, but because the microphones picked up the camera noise during filming, the cameras were placed in sound-proof rooms and camera movement in dialogue scenes largely came to a halt (Figure 10.26). Such films tended to be unmoving and overwhelmed by dialogue.[5]

New technology can also affect the types of movies that get made. In the late 1920s, for example, the introduction of **film stock** that contained a soundtrack along one edge made possible new types of films but ended other types:

> Sound . . . made possible a bringing together into one unit elements of **vaudeville** with filmed images which previously had been two disparate entertainment forms in silent cinema spectacles. In the case of Hollywood this produced a new genre—the musical. However, it also put an end to other generic types, such as the gestural, slapstick comedy associated with Chaplin and Keaton. Conversely, it created a new type of comedy: the fast repartee comedy with snappy dialogue (as with the Marx Brothers and W. C. Fields) and screwball comedy—usually based on the "battle between the sexes." (Hayward 333)

From time to time, competition from other media spurs the movie industry to develop technology that makes movies more appealing to consumers. For example, the growing popularity of small-screen black-and-white television in the United States in the late 1940s and the fall of movie box office

film stock: Unexposed and unprocessed motion-picture film.

vaudeville: A type of live U.S. theatrical show that consisted of various short acts and was the most popular form of entertainment in the United States early in the twentieth century.

Vitaphone: Early motion-picture sound system consisting of a movie camera synchronized to a phonograph recorder and a movie projector synchronized with the phonograph recording.

---

[5] *Singin' in the Rain*—a 1952 American musical whose story is set in the late 1920s—includes fairly accurate, humorous scenes demonstrating some of the problems encountered in filming early sound films while recording the sound (beginning about 51⅓ minutes into the film) and keeping the (presumably) **Vitaphone** records in sync with the projected images (beginning 58¼ minutes into the film).

FIGURE 10.26 The coming of sound
In the early months of sound films, in the late 1920s, the camera was entombed in a small soundproof room so the microphones on the set would not pick up the sounds of a running movie camera. Seen here are director Alfred Hitchcock on the set of the first British sound film, *Blackmail* (1929), the star of the movie, and behind the glass, the camera operator and camera. Such an arrangement ended the mobility of the camera during shots. The chalked message below the window reads "Please keep away from front of CAMERA." *British International Pictures; British Film Institute Stills, Posters and Designs*

revenues prompted the film industry to counter with greater use of color films and various other new technologies. One of the most spectacular was the **Cinerama** process introduced in 1952, which showed movies by using three projectors and seven-**track** stereo sound (Figure 10.27a). Because of the onrushing images on both sides of the curved Cinerama screen, the system proved most effective for action **shots**, such as of **point-of-view shots** of roller-coaster rides or running the rapids, but during quieter moments, viewers were sometimes aware of the three side-by-side images demarcated by two somewhat fuzzy lines (not shown in the scale model shown in Figure 10.27a). Then, too, close-ups were out of the question because no one wanted to see parts of someone's face simultaneously in more than one of the three projected images. For these and other reasons, Cinerama had a life span of only a few years and then mainly only in large cities. Because of the growing popularity of TV, the film industry tried to lure customers into theaters with a few 3-D movies such as *Bwana Devil* (1952), with lions and spears seemingly hurtling toward the audience, and Hitchcock's *Dial M for Murder* (1954), a suspenseful movie about a man plotting his wife's murder (Figure 10.27b). By the end of the 1950s, Hollywood was presenting large

shot (noun): An uninterrupted strip of exposed motion-picture film or videotape that represents a subject during an uninterrupted segment of time.

FIGURE 10.27 Competing with the popular new medium, TV During the 1950s, moviemakers and movie exhibitors introduced new technologies in filmmaking and film exhibition to try to lure customers away from their new and small but captivating black-and-white TV sets. Three of the technologies of the 1950s and 1960s are illustrated here. (a) Cinerama (a scale model) was a wide-screen format created by the use of three cameras during filming and three projectors during screenings. (b) 3-D movies required viewers to wear simple, lightweight special glasses provided by the theater. A few such American movies were made and marketed between 1952 and 1954. (c) Huge and super wide-screen images along with superior sound were the era's most successful and enduring technological answer to TV. When shown in the theaters, *Ben-Hur* (1959), seen here, had an aspect ratio of 2.75:1, meaning the image's width was nearly three times greater than its height. (a–b) *The Museum of Modern Art/Film Stills Archive.* (c) *MGM; Warner Home Video DVD*

and occasionally the widest of **wide-screen** images ever shown commercially in the United States (Ultra-Panavision 70), as in the critical and popular success, *Ben-Hur* (1959, Figure 10.27c).

Ever since the 1990s, computers have been used to create effects with a verisimilitude previously impossible in **live-action** films. For example, computers can be used to change moving parts of images. For **morphing**, the transformation of one shape into another, sophisticated software can make something seem to become something else. In *Terminator 2: Judgment Day* (1991), for example, a cyborg transforms itself from a pool of shiny liquid into its usual appearance as a man and at another time from its usual appearance into what looks like a police officer (see Figure 2.58 on p. 102).

live action: Behavior by living (not animated) people or some other creatures.

Computers have many other uses for filmmakers. Digital manipulation can be used to eliminate part of a subject, such as part of a character's legs in *Forrest Gump* (1994). Computers were also used to combine images to show Forrest Gump meeting and mingling with Presidents Nixon and Kennedy and to show characters interacting with President Clinton in *Contact* (1997).[6] With computers, people can be placed in any setting, whether in an actual location or on a **set** constructed of building materials or of photographs stored in a computer. In *Contact*, for instance, computers were used to move images of President Clinton from one place to another. Perhaps most impressively of all, computers can be used to create **virtual realities**—computer-generated worlds with changing imaginary environments and virtual people who can interact and change shape (be morphed) as in *The Lawnmower Man* (1992; see Plate 51 in Chapter 13). Virtual realities and other filmmaking effects possible only with computers were also used even more extensively in *The Matrix* and its successors (1999; see Figure 7.25 on p. 333).

set: A constructed setting, indoors or outdoors, where action is filmed.

The coming of high-definition video (HDV) has also had a major impact on the ways movies can be filmed and shown. With celluloid, the length of a shot was limited by the amount of film the camera could hold, and for 35 mm film that usually meant 10 to 15 minutes, depending on the speed of filming. With videotape, a single shot can last hours. Because of improvements in the quality of HD video images, it is possible to film on HDV, do any editing digitally, then transfer the results to 35 mm film for theatrical showings. That process was used to make *Time Code* (2000), which consists of four shots, each 97 minutes long and seen simultaneously

---

[6]"Through the Eyes of Forrest Gump" (1994), a documentary/promotional film, shows how the shot of Forrest meeting President Kennedy was a composite of altered **footage** of the president meeting with a football team in the White House and a shot of Forrest shaking hands with the air against a blue background. The film also explains how computers were used in the scenes of Lieutenant Dan without his legs, Forrest's championship Ping-Pong match, and that floating feather.

on a quadrant of the same movie screen (see Figure 6.18 on p. 279). *Russian Ark* (2002), which was also shot on HDV and runs 96 minutes, consists of a single shot made with a highly mobile digital camera, just outside and mostly inside the vast Hermitage Museum in St. Petersburg, Russia. In these and other films, HDV allows filmmakers to experiment with lengthy shots and to edit less often or not at all.

It is not just visuals that have changed with the times. More recently, in the face of competition from cable and satellite, DVDs, and CDs, filmmakers and theaters have countered yet again with superior multitrack digital sound systems: DTS (Digital Theater Sound), SDDS (Sony Dynamic Digital Sound), and DDS (Dolby Digital Sound) (see Figure 4.3 on p. 161).

THE VERSION OF THE FILM THAT IS SEEN[7]

Often, changes made after a film is released are of little consequence to viewer understanding of the film. However, sometimes changes made after a film was originally released are significant.

The images in the original copies of the 1919 German movie *The Cabinet of Dr. Caligari* were crystal clear because the movie was filmed and projected on **nitrate** stock. The movie was not in color, but each scene was **tinted** (see Plate 52 in Chapter 13). A live orchestra played a score especially selected for the film and coordinated with it, excerpts from some of the most avant-garde composers of the day. The man who compiled and adapted the music for the U.S. premiere of *Caligari* later wrote:

> In the phantasmagorical scheme of *Dr. Caligari* people move and live in a world out of joint. The cracked country is dotted with grotesque houses, skinny twisted trees, enormously steep and rutted pathways. . . . The key principle of this sprawling architecture and wild terrain is, [sic] distortion. With that steadily in mind . . . [the conductor and I] built up the score. We went to Schönberg, Debussy, Stravinsky, Prokofieff [sic], Richard Strauss for thematic material. We assembled our themes, assigned characteristic ideas to the principals of the play, and then proceeded to distort the music. The music had, as it were, to be made eligible for citizenship in a nightmare country. (S. L. Rothafel, qtd. in Rogers 359)

Today, few people have a chance to see *The Cabinet of Dr. Caligari* in a 35 mm tinted print accompanied by a live orchestra. Instead, many see a videotape or DVD, perhaps one based on a mediocre 16 mm print (in the United States, the film is in the public domain and is widely available in various qualities). Such a version contains the same shots as the original,

nitrate: Film stock used until the early 1950s that could produce high-quality images but was subject to decomposition and combustion.

tinting: The process of dyeing motion-picture film with a color.

---

[7]Adapted from Chapter 11 of William H. Phillips, *Analyzing Films: A Practical Guide.*

but it is a copy of a copy of a copy, and so on, and has an overall fuzziness and a lot of contrast: black and white and not many shades of gray. In such a version it is hard to see some details. Most videotape versions and even some DVD versions have no tinting. Many versions have no music or maybe only a piano score. Compared with the original version of the film, most of these more recent versions are harder for viewers to get caught up in. They have the same title as that earlier film shown on a large screen and accompanied by a special live orchestra score, but they are not the same film. Different version, different viewer responses.

For anyone who wants to see films as they were originally meant to be seen, DVDs can be a wonder and a blessing. For viewers who care about completeness and visual and auditory quality, some companies expend much effort and expense to present the best-quality DVD versions. Currently in the United States that means DVDs by Criterion, and to a lesser extent Kino, and perhaps other conscientious companies. But DVDs have not solved all the problems with film versions. The original DVD releases of *Lawrence of Arabia*, the films of Stanley Kubrick, *Casablanca* (1942), *Unforgiven*, and many others did not do justice to the original film versions, and those titles and many others have been re-released in improved DVD versions. Other substandard DVDs remain on the market. And some films have been available only in a substandard DVD version or in VHS—or available only in a substandard DVD version *and* in VHS.

Frequently, multiple versions, perhaps quite different versions, of a title exist, especially of older films. In significant ways, the film you are seeing or studying may not be the film your readers or listeners saw, and a film you read about may not be exactly the film you see. The version of the film that viewers see today may differ from the original film in many ways. Differences are likely to be most significant in the shape of the projected image, **resolution** and brightness, color, sound, translations in foreign films, and length.

resolution: The degree of detail visible in an image.

Shape of the Projected Image

reel: A metal or plastic spool to hold motion-picture film.

Inside the can of the first **reel** of the French film *Grand Illusion* (1937) was found the following letter from the director to the projectionist:

Dear Sir,
    This appeal is from one technician to another. You're going to show my *Grand Illusion*.
    This film is still in good shape despite its age: twenty-two years. But it still has a few characteristics that were in style in 1936. One of these is that it is designed for an **aspect ratio** of 1.33 × 1. I have composed each image to fill up this surface and leave no empty space. I have arranged details both at the top and the bottom of the **frame**. By projecting my film on a screen of enlarged dimensions, you would risk eliminating these details that I feel are important and also cutting off part of the heads of the actors, which seems to me unaesthetic.

aspect ratio: The proportion of the width to the height of the image on a TV or movie screen or on individual frames of film.

I ask you to help me to present my work under the best conditions—that is to say, on a screen with dimensions that will suit it.

Thanks in advance.

Regards,
Jean Renoir[8]

Renoir was concerned that the projectionist would use a wide-screen **aperture plate** that would give his film a wide, modern look by **cropping** some of the top and bottom of the image.

If the filmmakers' original **compositions** are changed significantly, the relationships between characters and setting may be distorted, and whole characters may not be visible in some shots. Although showings of pre-1950s films with a wide-screen aperture plate do occur, a more frequent problem is wide-screen films shown in less than their original widths (see Figure 1.31d on p. 38). When the sides of an image are cropped, the results can be misleading. Late in the Italian film *(The) Red Desert* (1964), for example, the characters are scattered across the wide frame and facing in different directions. If less than the original aspect ratio is used, the viewer loses a sense of distances between characters, and the sense of estrangement and rootlessness is decreased. Indeed, some of the characters are cut right out of the picture. In some films, characters may be diminished by a nose, an ear, or another body part. Film versions that crop the sides of the image also decrease the expanse of a locale, whether it is a meadow or outer space.

Resolution and Brightness

The version that viewers see may differ from the theatrical release print in its resolution (or sharpness) and its brightness. The film image's sharpness and brightness depend on the type of film stock, the projection light, the speed and focus of the lens(es) through which light is projected to the screen, and the reflective qualities of the screen. For videotape and DVD showings, the sharpness and brightness of the images depend on the quality of the videotape, videotape player, and monitor or screens, or the quality of the DVD, DVD player, and monitor or screen.

Consider what happens to resolution and brightness when *Citizen Kane* (1941) and *Psycho* (1960) are shown on videotape on a television set or monitor. The 35 mm release prints of those two films have sharp, bright images. But when they are shown on an analog TV or monitor, the results are **grainy** (because video images have less definition than film images). The lighting is without subtle shades of gray, and in shadowed areas details tend to get lost because TV has less range of tones than film. Thus, many details in night scenes are especially difficult to see. As a consequence, many analog television viewers are likely to miss details such as the whiskey bottle

aperture plate: In a motion-picture projector, the rectangular opening that helps determine the size and shape of light sent from the projector to the screen.

composition: The arrangement of settings, lighting, and subjects within the frame.

grainy: Having graininess or rough visual texture in an image.

---

[8]Jean Renoir, *La Grande Illusion: Decoupage integrale* (Paris: Edition du seuil/Avant-scene, 1971), 6. This letter was translated and brought to my attention by Fred Simeral.

Kane finds in Susan's bookcase in Xanadu after she leaves him (109 ½ minutes into the film).

Details may also be missed in some 16 mm prints that are copies of copies of copies and so forth of the original because those later versions have **high contrast** and **graininess**. They blur detail. We can see this loss of resolution and brightness if we compare two versions of the same image: one from a 16 mm print many, many generations removed from the source material and one from a high-quality DVD (Figure 10.28).

high contrast: A photographic image with few gradations between the image's darkest and lightest parts.

graininess: Rough visual texture in an image.

Color

Unfortunately, when we study film color, we cannot be certain we are seeing the shades and intensities that the filmmakers intended. Several factors determine the color quality of the film versions we see. Prints of color films, including those for theatrical release, may vary in quality because most are mass-produced. Eastman color films, especially those made for many years after 1949, usually turn reddish with age. In these instances, the moods and meanings that the color originally conveyed are altered.

With the aid of computers, some black-and-white films on videotape have been colorized: years after the films were made, the blacks, whites, and grays are replaced with colors. Even in the best of circumstances, color

a)   b)

FIGURE 10.28 Resolution and brightness in two versions of the same shot
Versions may vary considerably from one to another, especially in older films, as in the example here from the classic German film *M* (1931). Frame (a) is from a 16 mm print many generations removed from the original 35 mm print. Frame (b) is from a restored DVD. The many differences in resolution (the degree of detail visible in an image) and brightness are obvious. (a) *Nero Films; unknown 16 mm source.* (b) *Nero Films; Criterion DVD*

film is an approximation of the color we see in life, and colorized images are only **desaturated** approximations of color film. Furthermore, the colorized colors are chosen not by directors, **designers**, or costumers but by video technicians whose judgment in choosing colors is often questionable, especially for films made many years earlier and perhaps in a different culture. They may choose a color that draws undue attention to an unimportant part of the image or that underplays the importance of its subject. For people who tend to dislike black-and-white films, colorization has appeal. But to film scholars, film teachers, and filmmakers, perhaps especially directors, the process is offensive. Director John Huston, after watching 7 minutes of the colorized version of his own *The Maltese Falcon* (1941)—he could stand no more—said, "It's not color any more than pouring tablespoons of sugar water over a roast constitutes flavoring."

desaturated color: Drained, subdued color approaching a neutral gray.

designer: The person responsible for the appearance of much of what is photographed in a movie, including locations, costumes, and hairstyles.

Sound

Nearly all the earliest projected films were shown with some kind of musical accompaniment to cover the noises of the projectors and audience and to support continuity and mood. Before the adoption of the soundtrack along the film's edge in the late 1920s, exhibitors often chose the music and sound effects and supervised their presentations (see Figure 4.1 on p. 159). But discovering the original music and sound effects or even the kind of original music and sound effects is nearly always impossible for early films. Another limitation: some re-released films and videos include distracting, inappropriate music and sound effects. Some of Charlie Chaplin's early short films have suffered this fate.

There is also a danger that the soundtrack inadequately re-creates the original multitrack soundtrack. Even if one sees and hears a multitrack DVD, without a home theater or at least a multispeaker system, much of the original soundtrack may go unheard, and the contribution of the sound to the overall film experience is lessened.

Translations

For foreign films, many people prefer **dubbed** prints to subtitles, but dubbing presents problems. The major drawback of dubbed prints—in which the voices of the original foreign performers are replaced by the voices of native performers speaking translated dialogue—is that spoken translated words can never be totally synchronized with the lip movements of the actor speaking the original foreign language. Another disadvantage is that spoken words can be dropped, added, or mistranslated by the distributors. In some dubbed prints, the entire soundtrack is redone, and many of the effects from the original spoken words, sound effects, and music are lost. But in other dubbed prints, only the spoken words are changed; the effects and music tracks are the same as in the original.

dub: To replace sounds in a film's soundtrack after the film has been shot.

Nearly all filmgoers are aware of the problems with subtitles in foreign-language films, especially in older films. Often, dialogue goes untranslated; but prints with a complete and accurate translation could be costly to make, and for many films a complete set of subtitles could distract the audience from the film's visuals and even interfere with the showing of the story. There may be additional limitations with subtitles. Sometimes the translations are inaccurate. Sometimes they include distracting errors in spelling, punctuation, or syntax. Parts of the subtitles may be unreadable, especially in versions with white subtitles.

Length

The length or duration of the version of the film is often a major consideration in analyzing a film.

Many DVDs feature the director's cut of a film. Almost always, such a version is longer than the theatrical release and perhaps an improvement. But perhaps not.

Criterion, Kino International, and other DVD companies release reconstructed or restored versions of some important older films. The 2002 Kino Video restored authorized edition of *Metropolis* (1926) was reconstructed in Germany from footage from different prints. At 124 minutes, the restored Kino digital version is a third longer than a 93-minute version (the film is available in many different lengths and with different musical soundtracks). Someone writing about this restored version is seeing a different film than someone writing about one of the much shorter versions.

A film may be shortened after its original release. Films of one culture are often shocking or unsettling to people of a different culture, especially in sexual and political matters; thus, many films shown in a foreign country have been cut. To hold down production costs and increase the chances that a film will be widely seen, producers and studios sometimes intervene to shorten a film. In some cases, though—the classic American silent film *Greed* (1925) is a glaring example—much of the original film is lost. When this happens, whether or not the original would be judged superior by current standards is unknowable.[9]

THE SETTING IN WHICH A FILM IS SEEN

It is March 1921 and you are approaching the Capitol Theater in Manhattan, a **movie palace** that has seating for more than five thousand viewers.

movie palace: A large opulent type of movie theater built in the United States and Europe between the mid-1910s and the 1930s.

---

[9]Usually **cutting continuity scripts**, which describe a finished film, fail to discuss the source or reliability of the film version described. For example, the Simon and Schuster script of the German film *M* says nothing about the film's different versions, and the introductory page of Theodore Huff's 1961 shot analysis of *The Birth of a Nation* says that it is "based on a 16 mm print of the original 12-reel version, circa 1939" but gives no explanation of the relationship of the print described to the original 1915 versions.

This is no ordinary theater. It's larger and more ornate than any theater you have ever attended. In the lobby and in the theater itself, you see evidence of wealth and exoticism everywhere. It looks something like what we see inside a later, somewhat smaller movie palace (see Figure 10.30b). The U.S. premiere of the German movie *The Cabinet of Dr. Caligari* is about to take place. You and the rest of the audience sit in cushioned seats as comfortable as those found in an upscale Broadway theater or opera house. The houselights dim. A beam of bright light emerges from behind and high overhead and instantly fills the huge screen as a live orchestra plays a score especially commissioned for this showing (see Plate 52 in Chapter 13).

Now imagine another showing of *The Cabinet of Dr. Caligari.* You are sitting in a classroom, seeing *Caligari* on videotape, a 16 mm film print, or a DVD based on a 16 mm print. You do not notice if the film has music or not. The setting is nothing special. It is certainly no picture palace. There is more light in the room than there would be in a movie theater. The seats are not very comfortable, and from time to time outside noises intrude into your awareness. You recall your professor saying that where a film is seen can affect viewers' involvement and thus understanding.

In this section, we focus on some of the main viewing environments since the birth of cinema, and we consider how they have indirectly influenced filmmakers and the films they made.

Nickelodeons

During the second decade of motion pictures (from about 1905 to 1915), most movies were seen in **nickelodeons** (the word means five-cent theaters). Their interiors tended to be plain and functional, not very decorative or even comfortable (Figure 10.29). The audiences consisted of perhaps a hundred or two, initially mostly recent immigrants and working-class viewers, many with only a shaky command of English. Nearly always, some form of musical accompaniment was provided, at least a piano or a piano and drums. More than a few nickelodeons provided "lecturers" to explain the films as they ran.[10]

Going to a nickelodeon was a modest experience easily accessible to the masses. Given the multiethnic and mostly uneducated U.S. audiences of the time, the limitations of the technology, and the nickelodeons' spartan accommodations, early filmmakers made short and mostly intellectually undemanding films that they hoped would be entertaining and popular. As nickelodeons grew popular, they quickly became part of the neighborhood

[10]During the silent era in Japan, film showings usually included live music and a *benshi*, a man or occasionally a woman who stood to the side of the movie screen and supplied an introduction to the film, explanation and commentary, and sometimes the voices of the various characters as they appeared on the screen.

a)

b)

c)

FIGURE 10.29 **Setting in which a film was seen: nickelodeons**
Nickelodeons were small storefront movie theaters popular in the United States from roughly 1905 to 1915. It is estimated that by 1910 there were already ten thousand of them, and most towns and urban neighborhoods had at least one. They were inexpensive to attend, accessible (though initially perhaps thought not very respectable), yet small and modest in environment and presentation. In the early years, their programs of short films lasted from 20 to 30 minutes. (a) The Cascade Theatre in New Castle, Pennsylvania, purchased by the Warner family in 1903. Sam Warner, seen on the left, sang to the audience during reel changes and intermissions, as was the usual practice in nickelodeons. He was one of the four brothers who later founded Warner Brothers Pictures. The small signs visible in this photograph include the information that the shows were "Refined Entertainment for ladies, gentlemen, and children," which assured would-be patrons that *this* theater was respectable. Other signs indicate that the pictures were changed twice a week, admission was always a nickel, and performances were continuous. (b) An unidentified 1913 nickelodeon with mostly male audience members, a male uniformed usher, unpadded wooden chairs, a framed white sheet serving as the screen, and probably no ventilation. Swanky it was not. (c) A sample slide projected onto a nickelodeon screen. Before trailers with moving images were developed in 1915 or so, projected slides also were used to announce the names of future movies that would be shown. (a) *The Museum of Modern Art/Film Stills Archive.* (b) *Unidentified U.S. trade magazine; Courtesy Bison Archives, Hollywood, California.* (c) *Unknown source*

scenery. Eileen Bowser's account of Indianapolis nickelodeons in 1908 is illustrative of the situation:

> There were twenty-one nickelodeons and three ten-cent theaters in 1908, only three years after the first nickelodeon had appeared there. Each nickelodeon in this city gave a show consisting of one reel of film, which might contain two or three different subjects, and an illustrated song, with the show taking

twenty to twenty-five minutes—"except when there is a crowd waiting, then it is speeded up to 15 to 17 minutes." The shows in Indianapolis were open from nine in the morning till eleven at night, which allowed about twenty to thirty shows each day. If you could afford ten cents, you could go to one of the three high-class theaters and get an evening of three or four reels of pictures with live entertainment consisting of illustrated songs, vaudeville acts, and slide lectures lasting from one to one-and-a-half hours. By 1911, the number had increased to seventy-six motion-picture theaters alone, not including regular theaters that changed over to movies during the summer. However, only fifteen of the movie houses remained downtown in 1911, because of the high rents. (6)

Movie Palaces

As moviegoing grew as a business in the United States and elsewhere, beginning around 1914 and continuing into the early 1930s, movie palaces were erected in various American cities, mostly in downtowns: "The greatest of silent picture palaces was unquestionably the Roxy in New York, the 6,214 seat 'cathedral of the motion picture.'. . . Patrons who were not intimidated by a trip under the massive, five-story tall rotunda faced a squadron of ushers drilled by a retired Marine Corps captain. The statuary, the carpeting, the mural decorations, all worked together to create an effect of overwhelming grandeur, but the frame had grown far more important than any picture" (Koszarski 23, 25). Also adding to the experience was a large pipe organ (often a Wurlitzer) used to accompany the films and fill the interludes.

Movie palaces cost more to attend than nickelodeons, attracted wealthier customers, and showed longer and more involved programs (including vaudeville acts). Such an environment encouraged moviegoers to think of movies and their venues as bigger than life, for the images and sounds were bigger and more involving than ever. The opulent and often exotic settings reflected by theater names such as the Egyptian, the Chinese, the Aztec, Loew's Paradise, and the Kings also nurtured the feeling that moviegoing offered an escape into a new world, a world of soft lights and live music throughout the theater and huge moving images up on the screen. Such theaters could function as an opiate against the unreliable world outside. Venue, in short, could strongly affect viewer anticipation and response. Note the order in which the Brooklyn Paramount Theatre of 1928 touted what it had to offer: "beauty, comfort, luxury, and entertainment" (Figure 10.30a). More than at any other time in movie history, the place where movies were shown was more exciting, more special than the movies themselves.

For a better understanding of what going to a movie palace in 1920s America involved, look again at Figure 10.30 (for the Brooklyn Paramount), then read a sample program for the largest U.S. movie palace, the Roxy Theatre (pp. 490–91), and after that, look at a sample film that was first shown in a different New York movie palace in 1921 (see Plate 52 in Chapter 13). (Unfortunately, photos of a movie palace, the program for a

a)

b)

FIGURE 10.30 Setting in which a film was seen: movie palaces
(a) The Brooklyn Paramount Theatre was eleven stories high. Inside were forty-one hundred plush upholstered seats for patrons on the main floor and the five levels above it. When this movie palace opened on Flatbush Avenue in Brooklyn late in 1928, it was the second-largest theater in New York City. Part of the sign on the side of the building says "Brooklyn Paramount Theatre, the last word in beauty, comfort, luxury, and entertainment." (b) The stage setting was huge, exotic, and ornate, and heavy decorated curtains opened up to a bright, shimmering world as the movie began. Ticket prices ranged from approximately 25 cents to $1.25 depending on when patrons went and where they sat. For years, the theater was used to show either movies or various live shows, such as rock-and-roll stage shows. It was last used to show a movie in 1962. Like most of the ornate American movie palaces built in the 1910s, 1920s, and 1930s, it did not survive intact. Eventually, parts of the Paramount were incorporated into a building that is part of Long Island University. From 1963 to 2005, the L.I.U. basketball team played on a gym floor that covered the original stage and orchestra seating and under the auditorium's much-admired blue recessed dome. *Sic transit gloria mundi.* (a–b) *The Museum of Modern Art/Film Stills Archive*

film shown there, and a frame from that film are unavailable, but the photos of outside and inside one movie palace plus the program provided for another movie palace and a color plate for a movie first shown in yet another movie palace will convey something of what it must have been like to experience a movie in a movie palace.)

IMAX Theaters

Some of the specialness of a movie palace showing was recaptured in the 1970s by the Canadian **IMAX** (short for "image maximization") system for filming and showing motion pictures. Like movie palaces, IMAX theaters seem special partly because they are generally available only in or near large cities. Like movie palaces, IMAX theaters provide the biggest images of their era and sometimes the most enveloping sound available, especially in **IMAX Dome** theaters (Figure 10.31). Some IMAX theaters also provide the most satisfying 3-D experience yet achieved. Unlike the movie palaces, however, IMAX theaters in name and decor are plain and functional. The IMAX screen can be up to approximately eight stories high and a hundred or so feet wide. For 3-D IMAX, viewers wear special glasses, and a subject in the extreme foreground can appear to be in the viewer's face or to move to the side of the viewer's head. The sense of three-dimensionality is so convincing that it's hard not to duck—or at least flinch—as objects seem to hurtle toward the audience or as the camera skims over the top of terrain. While viewing "Alaska: Spirit of the Wild" (1997) and other IMAX films in three dimensions, viewers may feel queasy while seemingly looking down as an airplane flies over a vast territory. With no noticeable distortion to most viewers, the accompanying multitrack digital sound system can vibrate the viewers' feet, armrests, and seats.

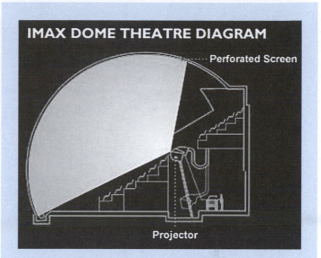

FIGURE 10.31 Setting in which a film may be seen: an IMAX Dome theatre
The screen in an IMAX Dome theatre is concave, which helps make watching a movie there perhaps the world's most immersive movie experience. Even more so than in the usual IMAX theater, the image extends beyond viewers' peripheral vision, side to side and top to bottom. While watching a film in such a theater, viewers looking straight ahead see only the image and are caught up in it. Such theaters also include a powerful surround sound system. *Courtesy of IMAX Corporation*

Although IMAX films have proven effective for short documentaries, it is not yet certain how amenable the system is to the *making* of feature-length **narrative** films. IMAX cameras are noisy, heavy, bulky, and hard to move around quickly and fluidly (no **Steadicam** shots here!), so IMAX films do not have as much camera movement as many theatrical movies. Gigantic close-ups of faces can look grotesque or at least strange. Occasionally, a film not made with IMAX cameras is converted to IMAX and re-released in IMAX theaters. Examples are *Apollo 13* (2002 in IMAX), *The Lion King: IMAX* (2002), *The Matrix Reloaded: The IMAX Experience* (2003), *300: The IMAX Experience* (2007), and *Beowulf* (2007), which has been digitally converted into IMAX 3-D and remastered. Even the re-releases that have undergone special digital remastering (DMR) suffer in spots from increased graininess. Some computer animated shots are less credible because the images from 35 mm have been blown up to fill the much larger IMAX frames (see Figure 2.2b and d on p. 63) and then those IMAX frames are projected to fill the huge IMAX screen. Then, too, some viewers believe that watching a feature film on an IMAX screen is a bit of an eyestrain. How widespread IMAX

narrative: A representation of unified events (happenings and actions) situated in one or more settings.

Steadicam: A lightweight and portable mount for holding a movie camera (and usually a monitor) that provides for relatively steady camera movements during moving handheld shots.

FIRE NOTICE—Look around NOW and choose the nearest Exit to your seat. In case of fire, walk (not run) to THAT Exit. Do not try to beat your neighbor to the street.—JOHN J. DORMAN, Fire Commissioner.

50th Street and 7th Avenue
Telephone, Circle 6000

Personal Direction of S. L. Rothafel, "Roxy"
Under Whose Supervision the Programs Are
Conceived, Staged and Lighted

PROGRAM

Week Beginning Friday, Oct. 4th, 1929
De Luxe Performances Approximately at 2:00; 4:00;
7:30 and 9:30—Midnight Performance Nightly

1. THE ROXY ORGAN (Kimball)

   Organists: Lew White and C. A. J. Parmentier

2. THE ROXY SYMPHONY ORCHESTRA

   Conductors: Erno Rapee, Joseph Littau
   Associate Conductor: Mischa Violin
   Concertmaster: Josef Stopak

   LINCKIANA
   Paul Lincke's most famous melodies in a
   special arrangement by Maurice Baron

3. LA DAME AUX CAMELLIAS

   Patricia Bowman
   Roxy Ballet Corps
   Russell E. Markert's Thirty-Two Roxyettes

4. "RACHEM"   Mana-Zucca

   Viola Philo
   J. Parker Coombs
   Roxy Chorus
   Roxy Ballet Corps
   (Costumes by Montedoro)

   The presentation of this number is coincident with the observance
   of Rosh Hashannah, the Jewish New Year. It represents the plea
   for divine mercy which is invoked during this religious holiday.

5. **FOX MOVIETONE & HEARST METROTONE NEWSREEL**

News of the World with Sound Reproduction

6. **PROLOGUE—"SALUTE"**

Russell E. Markert's Thirty-Two Roxyettes
Roxy Ballet Corps
Roxy Chorus
(Middy outfits by courtesy of "Man 'o War")

7.   WILLIAM FOX Presents

"SALUTE"

All Talking Fox Movietone

Story by Tristram Tupper and John Stone
Dialogues by James Kevin McGuinness

Directed by John Ford

THE CAST

CADET JOHN RANDALL	George O'Brien
MIDSHIPMAN PAUL RANDALL	William Janney
MIDSHIPMAN ALBERT EDWARD PRICE	Frank Albertson
NANCY WAYNE	Helen Chandler
MARION WILSON	Joyce Compton
MAJ.-GEN. SOMERS, U.S.A.	Clifford Dempsey
REAR-ADMIRAL RANDALL, U.S.N.	Lumsden Hare
SMOKE SCREEN	Stepin Fetchit
NAVY COACH	David Butler
CADET	Rex Bell
MIDSHIPMAN	John Breeden

For Coming Attractions See Next Page

PROGRAM SUBJECT TO CHANGE WITHOUT NOTICE

TOE SLIPPERS by CAPEZIO
The STEINWAY is the official piano of the Roxy Theatre
A DUO ART piano on the main floor of the Grand Rotunda
The LYON AND HEALY HARP is used in the Roxy Symphony Orchestra
Percussion Instruments in the Roxy Orchestra from LANDAY BROS.
Scenery designed by CLARK ROBINSON; executed by JOSEPH TEICHNER Studios
Wigs by SHINDHELM   Rugs by CASTELLI BROS.   Costumes by EAVES

S. L. Rothafel invites you to have a cup of delicious BEECH-NUT Coffee. Served
in the Grand Lounge Room from 2 to 10 P.M. including Sundays

FIGURE 10.32 Context in which a film may be seen: a home theater
Seen here is part of a home theater, a room dedicated exclusively to showing VHS and DVD movies, with no windows, black walls, velvet curtains on both sides of the screen to absorb sound, acoustic tile ceiling, furniture with cloth covers and carpet to absorb sound, 5.1 speaker system for surround sound, a ceiling-mounted digital projector (glimpsed in the upper right corner), and a 100-inch screen (diagonally measured). This theater also has "stadium seating" for eight. (In this photo, the image on the screen largely is washed out because of the camera flash needed to illuminate the theater.)

theaters become will be determined, as are all technological developments, by economic imperatives: to what extent filmgoers are willing to pay for an expensive product.

Home Viewing

Many people now see more movies at home than in theaters. According to a widely circulated 2006 report about American viewing preferences, more than half of the viewers prefer home viewing over seeing a movie at a theater. Since home viewing equipment can be relatively low priced and access to some form of the films and to refreshments much less expensive than in movie theaters, home viewing—ranging from a large TV in the family room to a complete dedicated home theater—has vastly expanded the number of viewers (Figure 10.32). Viewers typically respond differently to a film seen at home than they do to one seen in a movie theater. A home presentation has many well-known advantages over a theatrical showing—control over speed of presentation, continuity of presentation, replay, volume, tone, color, contrast—but it has many potential shortcomings as well. Unless home viewers have an excellent home theater, they may miss a visual or audio subtlety because it is difficult or impossible to discern (see, for example, Figure 3.14 on p. 130). Then, too, viewers are often more distracted and less caught up in the images and sounds at home than they are in a movie theater.

Although many predicted a major drop in movie attendance with the growth of home videotape, movies via cable or satellite, DVDs, home theaters, and the Internet, theater attendance remains robust. It is likely to stay so because movie theaters can always provide technology and an environment that no home can match. Many new movie theaters have huge screens and stadium seating. In such theaters, viewers can see the entire screen regardless of who sits in front of them; in the best theaters, seats can be as large and comfortable as first-class seats on an airplane, and your neighbors' elbows cannot jab your ribs. The sound can also be superior to any home system. Some of these theaters have seen attendance jump 300 percent. As of this writing, digital projection—with its ability to project large, sharp, unfaded, unscratched, and unwavering images—seems likely to gain in use in theaters. In short, movies shown in up-to-date theaters are superior in image, sound, and perhaps comfort to movies shown at home.

Many contexts for films are included in this book's chronology for 1895 to 2008, which includes columns on major world events, the arts, mass media, and films and videos (pp. 607–66).

Now that we have explored some of the factors that influence the making of films, the film version seen, and the exhibition and viewing of films, we turn our attention in the next chapter to how viewers interact with the films themselves, including the meanings they find in them.

CLOSE-UP: HOMOSEXUALITY IN *THE MALTESE FALCON*: THE NOVEL, THE PRODUCTION CODE, AND THE 1941 MOVIE

In the excerpts we examine here, which appear early in the novel and in the 1941 movie, Effie—the secretary who works in the detective office of Sam Spade and his partner—enters Spade's office. See Table 10.1.

As we can see implied by the excerpts from the novel and film, in both fiction and film, gays were represented stereotypically. When we study the historical contexts of the time in which *The Maltese Falcon* film appeared (1941) and learn about the widespread beliefs and values of the time (in part, as implied by the production code), we can better understand the film's restraint in representing the characters' homosexuality. We also can see that

---

TABLE 10.1

Homosexuality in *The Maltese Falcon*: The Novel, the Production Code, and the 1941 Movie

LATE IN CHAPTER 4 OF THE NOVEL	THE PRODUCTION CODE AND THE SCRIPT	THE 1941 MOVIE
The girl returned with an engraved card—*Mr. Joel Cairo*. "This guy is queer," she said. "In with him, then, darling," said Spade. Mr. Joel Cairo was a small-boned dark man of medium height. His hair was black and smooth and very glossy. His features were Levantine [characteristic of countries of the eastern Mediterranean]. A square-cut ruby, its sides paralleled by four baguette diamonds, gleamed against the deep green of his cravat. His black coat, cut tight to narrow shoulders, flared a little over slightly plump hips. His trousers fitted his round legs more snugly than was the current fashion. The uppers of his patent-leather shoes were hidden by fawn spats. He held a black derby hat in	The production code is not specific about homosexuality, but the public of the time overwhelmingly disapproved of it, and enforcers of the production code always disapproved of it. Presumably those enforcing the code thought that the following two principles applied to homosexuality: *General Principles . . .* 2. Correct standards of life . . . shall be presented. . . . II. 4. Sex perversion or any inference to it is forbidden. The script that Warner Bros. submitted for approval has not been published, but historian Rudy Behlmer has researched the matter and reports, "As was the custom, the temporary script was sent automatically for approval to the	Approximately 23¼ minutes into the movie, Spade is talking on the phone as Effie enters his office carrying something in her hand before her. She hands Spade a business card. Spade finishes his call and hangs up. He takes the card from Effie, detects a fragrance, and smells the card. Effie says, "Gardenia," as she raises her eyebrows slightly. Spade replies, "Quick, darling, in with him!" Effie walks to the office door, opens it and says, "Will you come in, Mr. Cairo?" Cairo walks into the room. He has dark, curly hair and is dressed in a dark suit and wears a bow tie. In one hand he carries an expensive umbrella with a straight handle, white gloves, and a dark hat.

494

the filmmakers found ways to get around the strictures of the code by subtly suggesting Cairo's homosexuality: for example, the way he dresses, his scented calling card, and, most of all, the inclusion of that umbrella, which is not referred to in the comparable scene in the book. The umbrella's handle can be seen as a phallic symbol that Cairo gently handles and more than once nearly touches with his lips. We can also see that the production code was more restrictive than laws covering the publication and circulation of books because, as the production code states, it was believed that films had the potential to affect behavior more so than did books (see "Reasons Supporting Preamble of Code," section 3.D, on p. 463).

Works Cited

Behlmer, Rudy. *America's Favorite Movies: Behind the Scenes*. New York: Ungar, 1982.

Hammett, Dashiell. *The Maltese Falcon*. 1930. New York: Vintage, 1992.

LATE IN CHAPTER 4 OF THE NOVEL

a chamois-gloved hand and came towards Spade with short, mincing, bobbing steps. The fragrance of *chypre* came with him.

Spade inclined his head at his visitor and then at a chair, saying: "Sit down, Mr. Cairo."

Cairo bowed elaborately over his hat, said, "I thank you," in a high-pitched thin voice and sat down. He sat down primly, crossing his ankles, placing his hat on his knees, and began to draw off his yellow gloves.

Spade rocked back in his chair and asked: "Now what can I do for you, Mr. Cairo?"

THE PRODUCTION CODE AND THE SCRIPT

Production Code Administration, the film industry's self-regulatory body. Joseph I. Breen wrote back to Jack L. Warner that while the basic story was acceptable under the code, there were certain objectionable details. . . . Regarding the character subsequently played by Peter Lorre, the letter stated that 'we cannot approve the characterization of Cairo as a pansy as indicated by the lavender perfume, high-pitched voice, and other accouterments'" (136–37).

THE 1941 MOVIE

Spade says, "Will you sit down, Mr. Cairo?" . . .

Approximately 25 seconds later Mr. Cairo looks at his umbrella and turns it over in his hands as he talks with Spade. In two later shots, Cairo's lips almost touch the tip of the umbrella handle (see Figure 10.2 on p. 442).

SUMMARY

This chapter first introduces five types of contexts that influence a film's making. The second part of the chapter considers the possible importance of different versions of the same film. The last part of the chapter illustrates how the settings in which the film is seen (theater and audience) can influence filmmakers, the films they make, and viewers' understanding of the films.

The Contexts of a Film's Making

Filmmakers are subject to many influences, such as social and political attitudes, censorship, artistic conventions, financial constraints, and filmmaking technology. Viewers who know about these and other contexts can understand a film more completely.

SOCIAL AND POLITICAL ATTITUDES

- Social attitudes influence how filmmakers represent a subject. For example, before the late 1960s, American movies generally represented gays and lesbians not at all, only indirectly, or stereotypically.

- As studies of the representations of gays, lesbians, gender, African Americans, Latinos and Latin Americans, and other subjects all demonstrate, representations reflect the beliefs and values of the times, and as those beliefs and values change, so do the representations.

- As is illustrated by some Tarzan movies, other subjects, such as certain popular stories, change as social concerns and political attitudes do.

- The political climate strongly affects how much freedom of expression filmmakers have and what political outlooks are likely to be explained or implied in their films.

CENSORSHIP

- Censorship (written or implied) strongly influences the content of films.

- In the United States from 1934 into the 1960s, most films were in effect censored by an agency set up by film producers and distributors to ensure that movies were suitable for viewers of all ages.

- Often governments worldwide ban or censor a film as it is being made or after it is completed.

- In many societies a rating system is devised that allows for a wide latitude of subjects and treatments but restricts some films to certain age groups.

ARTISTIC CONVENTIONS

- Filmic conventions are representations or techniques that both film-makers and audiences have grown to accept as natural or typical in certain contexts.

- Filmmakers may follow conventional practices. Or they may reject them, as in many westerns made since the 1950s.

- Film conventions may fall out of favor, and unconventional representations or techniques may catch on and become conventional.

- Filmmaking conventions do not have inevitable and fixed meanings; usage, which varies over time, establishes their meanings.

FINANCIAL CONSTRAINTS

- Since the amount of money available to filmmakers helps determine equipment, personnel available, settings, time to film, and distribution, financing is a crucial influence on the making of films.

- Generally, the greater the finances needed to make and promote a film, the greater are the pressures to make a movie with such popular characteristics as chases, fights, explosions and other spectacular sights, romance or sex, heartthrobs, and a happy ending.

- In general, the smaller the budget, the greater is the control that filmmakers have over their work, and the more individualistic it is likely to be.

FILMMAKING TECHNOLOGY

- New filmmaking technology—such as the development of advanced computer software—influences the types of films that are made.

- Advances in the technology of competing mass media and electronic entertainments, such as television and video games, may influence the techniques filmmakers use, settings, and actions presented as well as the type of film exhibition used.

- Computers are now used to achieve effects previously impossible in live-action films, such as to change moving parts of the image, eliminate parts of a subject, combine images, place subjects in new settings, and even create a virtual reality.

The Version of the Film That Is Seen

Sometimes the changes between the film as originally shown and as later viewed are significant, especially changes in the following:

- **Shape of the projected image** If altered drastically, the original compositions and corresponding meanings and moods are changed significantly.

- **Resolution and brightness** If the image is blurred and dulled, significant details cannot be seen.

- **Color** The color may be unlike the original color. It may even have changed so much that it is distracting. The moods that the color was meant to create or support may be distorted or lost.

- **Sound** Sound effects and music for "silent" films are often omitted or if supplied may be inappropriate and distracting. The original multitrack soundtrack cannot be heard in later monophonic versions or on many home or classroom systems.

- **Translations** Dubbing and subtitles may be incomplete or inaccurate. Subtitles may contain distracting errors in spelling, punctuation, or syntax or sometimes be unreadable.

- **Length** New material may have been included, as in nearly all director's cut DVDs. Or, not all of the original footage may have been included.

The Setting in Which a Film Is Seen

- The size, design, comfort, and accessibility of the viewing environment along with the types of audiences attending the showings can affect the types of movies that are made and in turn how viewers respond to them.

Major Terms about Understanding Films through Contexts

Below, numbers in italics refer to the pages where the terms are explained. All terms are defined in more detail in the Illustrated Glossary beginning on p. 667.

blaxploitation *453*	gender *447*	movie palace *487*
Cinerama *477*	IMAX *488*	nickelodeon *485*
convention *470*	kino *475*	representation *441*
dubbed print *483*	microcinema *475*	socialist realism *460*

QUESTIONS ABOUT UNDERSTANDING FILMS THROUGH CONTEXTS

The following questions are intended to help viewers understand films through their contexts. Not all the questions are appropriate for every film.

In thinking out, discussing, and writing responses to the questions most appropriate for the film being examined, be careful to stick with the issues the questions raise, to answer all parts of the questions, to explain the reasons for your answers, and to give specific examples from the film.

1. How are sexual orientation or gender issues or both represented in the film? In what ways is that representation influenced by the place and time that the film was made?

2. What does the film convey to you about a group it represents, such as Native Americans, Latinos, or Arabs? In what ways is that representation influenced by the place and time that the film was made?

3. When and where was the film made? Did the political climate of the time and place preclude or restrict certain subjects or treatments in the film?

4. What censorship regulations were in place during the making of the film? In what ways do those regulations limit the film's content or treatment or both?

5. Does the film follow filmic conventions, or is it unconventional in its techniques or content?

6. Is the film a big-budget film aimed at large audiences, a more modestly budgeted independent film, an inexpensive documentary or experimental film, or some other type of film? In what ways did the film's budget affect the outcome of the film?

7. How does the film technology available when the film was made affect how the film turned out?

8. Did the version of the film you saw differ significantly from the original showings in any of the following: shape of the projected image, resolution and brightness, color, soundtrack, dubbing or translations of subtitles, and length? If so, how do those differences affect your experience of seeing the film?

9. What was the setting in which the film was originally shown? How did the setting affect the making of the film and its presentation?

WORKS CITED

Altman, Robert. Audio commentary. *The Player* (DVD). New Line Home Video, 1997.

Avnet, Jon. "Feature Commentary." *Fried Green Tomatoes Collector's Edition*. Universal Home Video DVD, 1998.

Beauvoir, Simone de. *The Second Sex*. 1949. New York: Bantam, 1965.

Berg, Charles Ramírez. *Latino Images in Film: Stereotypes, Subversion, Resistance*. Austin: U of Texas P, 2002.

Berliner, Todd. "Hollywood Movie Dialogue and the 'Real Realism' of John Cassavetes." *Film Quarterly* 52.3 (Spring 1999): 2–16.

Bowser, Eileen. *The Transformation of Cinema, 1907–1915*. New York: Scribner, 1990.

Broderick, Peter. "DIY = DVC." *Mediawatch '99*. Supp. to *Sight & Sound* 9.3 (Mar. 1999): 6–9.

Burlingame, Jon. "Only What Grabs Him." *Los Angeles Times* 23 Sept. 2001: F6.

Cameron, Kenneth M. *Africa on Film: Beyond Black and White*. New York: Continuum, 1994.

Cieply, Michael. "The Ratings System, Built to Endure." *New York Times on the Web* 28 Apr. 2007.

Curry, Ramona. *Too Much of a Good Thing: Mae West as Cultural Icon*. Minneapolis: U of Minnesota P, 1996.

French, Philip. Rev. of "*Osama*." *The Observer* (online). 15 Feb. 2004.

Hass, Nancy. "It's Synergy, Baby. Groovy! Yeah!" *New York Times on the Web* 2 May 1999.

Hayward, Susan. *Cinema Studies: The Key Concepts*. 2nd ed. London: Routledge, 2000.

Herz, J. C. "What Is Art? That Can Mostly Depend on the Context." *New York Times on the Web* 11 Mar. 1999.

Huff, Theodore. *A Shot Analysis of D. W. Griffith's* The Birth of a Nation. New York: Museum of Modern Art, Film Library, 1961.

Katz, Susan Bullington. "A Conversation with Terry Zwigoff." *The Journal* [Writers Guild of America, West] Feb. 1996: 36–40.

Kehr, Dave. "Gandhi Is Eclipsed by Another Indian Hero." *New York Times on the Web* 10 June 2002.

Koszarski, Richard. *An Evening's Entertainment: The Age of the Silent Feature Picture, 1915–1928*. New York: Scribner, 1990.

Krutnik, Frank. *In a Lonely Street: Film Noir, Genre, Masculinity*. London: Routledge, 1991.

M: A Film by Fritz Lang. English translation and description of action by Nicholas Garnham. New York: Simon, 1968.

Michel, Frann. Rev. of *The Incredibly True Adventure of Two Girls in Love*. *Cineaste* 21.4 (Fall 1995): 46ff.

"Race: The Power of an Illusion." Three videotape episodes produced by California Newsreel, 2003.

Rogers, Bernard. "Comes Stravinsky to the Film Theater." *Musical America* 33.25 (16 Apr. 1921): 5. Reprinted in George C. Pratt, *Spellbound in Darkness: A History of the Silent Film* (Greenwich, CT: New York Graphic Society, 1966).

Russo, Vito. *The Celluloid Closet: Homosexuality in the Movies*. Rev. ed. New York: Harper, 1987.

Shuster, Robert. "A No-Budget Production." *Los Angeles Times* 2 Sept. 2001: F8.

Sklar, Robert. *Movie-Made America: A Cultural History of American Movies*. Rev. and updated. New York: Random, 1994.

Venus. "Fatima's Coochee-Coochee Dance (1896)" (online).

Wallace, Michele Faith. "The Good Lynching and *The Birth of a Nation*: Discourses and Aesthetics of Jim Crow." *Cinema Journal* 43.1 (Fall 2003): 85–104.

FOR FURTHER READING

Chicanos/Latinos in the Movies: A Bibliography of Materials in the UC Berkeley Library (online). Information organized into four parts: reference sources, books/videos, journal and newspaper articles, and articles and books on individual films. Some of the entries are annotated.

Entertaining America: Jews, Movies, and Broadcasting. Ed. J. Hoberman and Jeffrey Shandler. Princeton: Princeton UP, 2003. About prominent Jews in U.S. entertainment and the changing representations of Jews in American movies, radio, and TV—for example, in the multiple movie versions of *The Jazz Singer*.

The Ethnic Eye: Latino Media Arts. Ed. Chon A. Noriega and Ana M. López. Minneapolis: U of Minnesota P, 1996. Examines the range of Latino media arts, from independent feature production to documentary to experimental video. The essays explore the work of Chicano, Puerto Rican, Cuban American, and Latino film and video artists.

History of the American Cinema. 10 vols. Ed. Charles Harpole. New York: Scribner, 1990–2003. The University of California Press publishes paperback editions of these volumes.

Balio, Tino. *Grand Design: Hollywood as a Modern Business Enterprise, 1930–1939*.

Bowser, Eileen. *The Transformation of Cinema, 1907–1915*.

Cook, David A. *Lost Illusions: American Cinema in the Shadow of Watergate and Vietnam, 1970–1979*.

Crafton, Donald C. *The Talkies: American Cinema's Transition to Sound, 1926–1931*.

Koszarski, Richard. *An Evening's Entertainment: The Age of the Silent Feature Picture, 1915–1928*.

Lev, Peter. *The Fifties: Transforming the Screen, 1950–1959*.

Monaco, Paul. *The Sixties, 1960–1969*.

Musser, Charles. *The Emergence of Cinema: The American Screen to 1907*.

Prince, Stephen. *A New Pot of Gold: Hollywood under the Electronic Rainbow, 1980–1989*.

Schatz, Thomas. *Boom and Bust: The American Cinema in the 1940s*.

Hollywood's Indian: The Portrayal of the Native American in Film. Expanded ed. Ed. Peter C. Rollins and John E. O'Connor. Lexington: UP of Kentucky, 2003. Essays exploring the changing representations of Native Americans in American movies.

Screening Asian Americans. Ed. Peter X. Feng. New Brunswick, NJ: Rutgers UP, 2002. Explores Asian American cinematic representations historically and socially. Includes consideration of Asian American documentary, experimental, and fictional films and a wide range of ethnicities.

Semmerling, Tim Jon. *"Evil" Arabs in American Popular Film: Orientalist Fear*. Austin: U of Texas P, 2006. By examining such films as *The Exorcist*, *Black Sunday*, *Three Kings*, *Rules of Engagement*, and *South Park: Bigger, Longer & Uncut*, Semmerling argues that those and other films portray Arabs as threatening to subvert American "truths" and mythic tales and that the insecurity this engenders causes Americans to project evil character and intentions on Arab peoples, landscapes, and cultures.

Shaheen, Jack. *Reel Bad Arabs: How Hollywood Vilifies a People*. New York: Olive Branch P, 2001. An account of the persistent and prolonged vilification of Arab peoples in mainstream Western movies. The book shows how the image of the "dirty Arab" has reemerged over the last thirty years, even as other groups have more or less successfully fought to eliminate the use of racist stereotypes.

Singer, Beverly R. *Wiping the War Paint off the Lens: Native American Film and Video*. Minneapolis: U of Minnesota P, 2001. Traces the history of Native Americans' experiences as subjects, actors, and creators since the 1970s and develops a critical framework for approaching Native work. The book's approach is both cultural and personal and provides both historical views and close textual readings.

CHAPTER 11

Thinking about Films

W E VIEWERS RESPOND TO FILMS in many complex ways. We respond to a film's sensuousness, and we may respond to what we perceive as its beauty or ugliness. For example, we may savor a sunrise that is irrelevant to the **narrative** or story but seems beautiful and life affirming to us. We respond emotionally to films, sometimes powerfully. Many of us, for instance, become anxious when a movie character we identify with is threatened by a development in the story, and many of us cry more often in movie theaters than we do outside them. We also respond to films cognitively, by thinking about them — for example, we may think about a film and generalize about what it implies.

This chapter focuses on two of the major ways we viewers think about films. First, as we see a film, we interact with it by revising our expectations, responding to clues set forth, guessing, and readjusting our hypotheses about what might happen or why something has happened. Then, as we watch a film and usually even more so after we have seen the film, we formulate and perhaps reformulate some of the film's **meanings**. The chapter concludes by considering three influences on how we think about a film: our prior knowledge of the film or of a subject in the film, our backgrounds, and the **critical approaches** we use when analyzing the film.

Terms in **boldface** are defined in the Illustrated Glossary beginning on page 667.

meaning: An observation or a general statement about a subject, such as a film.

critical approach: Related ideas about how to interpret texts.

VIEWERS' EXPECTATIONS AND INTERACTIONS

When I first showed *Smoke Signals* in Spokane to a largely Indian audience, we had to reshow it immediately because everyone had been talking so much and laughing so much. But when I showed it at the Nantucket Film Festival [in Massachusetts], it was very quiet during the showing. There was some laughter, but I don't think they saw the humor in it. There was certainly none of the raucous laughter of Indian groups watching the film.   — Sherman Alexie

All minority audiences watch movies with hope. They hope they will see what they want to see. That's why nobody really sees the same movie.
                                                                     —Arthur Laurents

Viewers' Expectations

Viewers who are told that they are going to see a film entitled "Bambi Meets Godzilla" (1969) begin to formulate expectations about the film. Some laugh at the mere mention of the title. Some years ago when I asked students to write down their expectations for the film based on its title, some guessed that they were about to see a romance. One wrote, "I expect a beautiful woman to be meeting some big, rugged guy." Others hypothesized a David and Goliath story: "Bambi is smarter than Godzilla and outwits him in the end." One student expected "a giant lizard chasing a baby deer around Tokyo." Various others expected Godzilla to fight Bambi: "I expect a gruesome tale of violence and blood sport between two very different adversaries." Godzilla has a history of violence whereas Bambi does not, so right away viewers are surprised by the matchup. If viewers know something about film history, they might assume that "Bambi Meets Godzilla" is about two types of filmmaking: Disney's high-budget color animation and the low-budget, black-and-white Japanese action films of the 1950s and 1960s. Before a film begins, we viewers begin formulating expectations and hypotheses about the plot or other developments in the film, often based on only a title (Figure 11.1).

Early in the movie, Godzilla's foot abruptly flattens Bambi as the sound shifts from flute and string music to a loud discordant chord that gradually starts fading out. Next, "the end" is **superimposed** and erased backward quickly one letter at a time as if the filmmakers had made a mistake and rushed to insert *the end* before it was time, and we realize that the film has not met our usual expectation that a film show at least some of its story *after* the opening credits. Guess what? The film is still not over. There is yet another credit: "We gratefully acknowledge the city of Tokyo for their help in obtaining Godzilla for this film." While Godzilla's foot remains unmoving on the film's hapless costar, its toenails extend straight out and then go limp and hang downward again—another unexpected and puzzling development in the "plot." Has Godzilla experienced excitement followed by release? Is Godzilla merely twitchy, stretching, or tired? Viewers cannot know the cause of the toenail movement or its significance. Finally, the image and chord fade out together as this 90-second film ends.

The film's title and opening image create certain expectations, but viewers are quickly surprised and amused. Few viewers will correctly anticipate the resulting developments: the timing and manner of Bambi's demise and the mysterious reaction of Godzilla's toenails. Nor are viewers likely to expect the prominence of the

FIGURE 11.1 Nurturing viewers' expectations If viewers know nothing about a film they are about to see, they may begin to formulate their initial expectations based on only the title and opening credits. As "Bambi Meets Godzilla" (1969) begins, soothing music accompanies the animation of Bambi's grazing. Nothing happens for a while except that from time to time Bambi stops grazing to look upward as more and more opening credits roll by. We viewers soon notice that Marv Newland did all the work on the film. *Marv Newland; Spike and Mike's Classic Festival of Animation; Slingshot Entertainment DVD*

credits and their whimsy. The minimal story (Bambi eats; Bambi meets Godzilla; Godzilla remains standing and unmoving except for some toe-nails) happens behind the credits. Rarely have credits and a filmmaker's ego (so knowingly and amusingly) been used to compete with story.

Because human creativity is boundless, films may elicit in viewers count-less expectations and interactions. For example, a film may repeat itself in an endless loop, thwarting viewers' expectations of a completed narrative. Canadian Rodney Graham's "Vexation Island" (1997) is set on a small tropi-cal island with a prominent coconut palm tree, green vegetation, a pristine beach, and aqua blue water. A buccaneer with a small wooden keg under his neck lies on his back near a large coconut palm tree, seemingly asleep, though he seems to have a wound on his forehead. Nearby are a parrot and another small wooden keg (see Plate 53 in Chapter 13). After the parrot squawks, the man slowly opens his eyes and stands up. While standing, he looks around briefly, spots the coconut palm tree, goes to it, and starts to shake its trunk. A coconut comes loose, falls, and hits him on the forehead, and he falls backward. He ends up in the same position he was in near the film's beginning, passed out and with one of those small wooden kegs under his neck. In the last **shot**, the coconut rolls to the edge of the water where a wave carries it **offscreen**. The film then begins again and repeats itself indefinitely.

Because of the film's **wide-screen** images, high-quality color, sharp **resolution**, sound, **setting** (tropical island with a prominent coconut palm), and subject (a lone man), viewers may initially expect yet another castaway movie. Soon, they may infer—from the seemingly isolated tropical island, those small wooden kegs, and the bruise on the man's forehead—that the man is shipwrecked. But by the end of this 9-minute wordless film, viewers realize that the man is likely the victim not of a shipwreck but of a world that continuously frustrates his desires and lacks progression. Like Sisyphus—the character from Greek legend who was doomed to endlessly push a boulder up a hill only to watch it roll back down, follow it, and push it up again—he seems doomed to relive a repetitive, uneventful, and thwarted existence. Viewers may realize that the film also frustrates their desire for a story with development and resolution. After all, viewers tend to expect a story to begin, develop, and end.

Normally, before we see a film, we know something about it. Usually we know its title, and that alone may conjure up visions of what is to come. Remember "Bambi Meets Godzilla," and consider a film called *Tarzan*. Most viewers have seen at least one **celluloid** Tarzan story or read a Tarzan story and thus would expect a tale about a man brought up in the wild and isolated from Western civilization until some of its emissaries intrude into his world (see Figure 10.15 on pp. 456–57). If the movie we are to see has popular actors, we may know something about at least one of them. We may know something about the director and something about the types of films he or she tends to direct. We may have heard or seen a review or

shot (noun): An uninterrupted strip of exposed motion-picture film or videotape that represents a subject during an uninterrupted segment of time.

resolution: The degree of detail visible in an image.

celluloid: Movie, as in "celluloid heroes."

talked with a friend who's seen the film. We might even know the **genre** of the film that we are to see, such as western, musical, science fiction, horror, or detective. If so, we will expect the film to conform to at least the basics of the genre. For example, if we are going to see a western, we expect to see a lawful man, usually of European descent, challenged by lawless European American men, Mexicans, or Native Americans. Normally, too, genres set parameters to a narrative: what is possible, what is not. Thus, if we know we are going to see a western, we do not expect alien invaders 60 minutes into the film, nor do we at any time expect the woman who works in the saloon to dance the salsa or merengue.

trailer: A brief compilation film to advertise a movie or video release.

Our expectations may be shaped by other factors. The film's rating may lead us to expect sex and violence. Or we may have seen a **trailer**, visited the film's site on the Internet, read Internet reviews of a test screening, seen the film promoted on TV, or seen toy spin-offs or other product tie-ins, all of which created expectations—sometimes misleading ones. Consider a poster for *High Sierra* (1941) and one for *The Maltese Falcon* (1941, Figure 11.2). The poster for *The Maltese Falcon* is misleading but probably

a)

b)

FIGURE 11.2 Publicity shaping (largely false) expectations
In 1941, Humphrey Bogart, who was then an emerging movie star, appeared in two movies. (a) In the first, *High Sierra*, he plays a criminal who is by turns cynical and kind. (b) In the second, *The Maltese Falcon*, he plays a principled private detective. If viewers who had seen *High Sierra* saw this poster for *The Maltese Falcon*, they might expect to see Bogart reprise his role as a criminal because he looks like the character he played in the earlier movie. His haircut and graying hair are the same as in *High Sierra*. He holds the same type of large handgun that he used in *High Sierra* and in posters and stills for it. In addition, he wears the same type of shirt, though in this instance without the tie he sometimes wears in *High Sierra* and in some related movie stills. Because Bogart holds a smoking gun in the poster for *The Maltese Falcon*, we might expect him to fire a gun in that film (he does not). And in *The Maltese Falcon* we might expect Mary Astor to look as she does in the poster and to sport a fancy hairdo and wear glamorous, revealing evening clothes. Wrong again. The two images illustrate how publicity may convey the wrong sense of what the film experience will be: Bogart is in both films, yes, but as a different character in very different stories. *Warner Bros.–First National*

did not hurt the film at the box office, although advertising that creates fundamentally false expectations can hurt a film's chances for success. Advertising for a movie that is released shortly after an immensely popular film but features the same star in a very different role can be especially chancy (Figure 11.3). Usually, though, the advertising for a film creates more or less reasonable expectations, as was the case with a famous poster for the Swedish film *Persona* suggesting a mystery about the film's dual subjects (1966, Figure 11.4).

From all these and other sources, we enter the theater, approach the video store rental counter, or add a movie title to our queue at Netflix with expectations: to be amused, amazed, mystified, inspired, aroused, frightened, or something else. Once the film begins, its music or visuals or both start to influence our expectations. Theatrical and DVD showings of *Ben-Hur* (1959), *West Side Story* (1961), and *Lawrence of Arabia* (1962, 1989), for example, begin with a part of a painting, design, or blank screen and an overture of the film's music, thereby giving a sampling of the music and moods to come. Much more often, music and moving images are used in tandem near the film's beginning. Consider the opening seconds of the superhero action movie *Spawn* (1997). First we see and hear a fiery explosion and briefly hear a (church?) bell ring faintly in the background. Sounds of wind and a chorus holding long notes are heard as we see a fiery round tunnel (seen later in the film as a gateway to hell). Then the **narrator** intones, "The battle between heaven and hell has waged eternal, their armies

narrator: A character, a person, or an unidentifiable voice in a film that provides commentary about subjects in the film or outside it, or both.

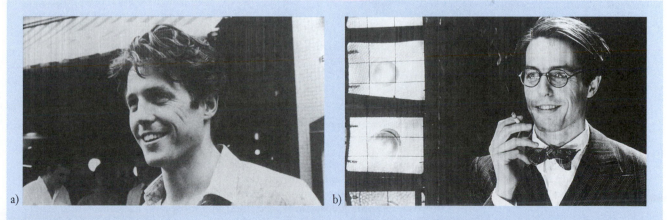

a) b)

FIGURE 11.3 Publicity, expectations, and viewers' responses
(a) In *Four Weddings and a Funeral* (1994), Hugh Grant plays a boyish, reserved, charming, yet nervous and bumbling heterosexual. (b) In *An Awfully Big Adventure* (1995), Grant plays a sarcastic gay director of a local theatrical company with whom an impressionable 16-year-old girl becomes infatuated. Before the film was publicized, its director warned that if *An Awfully Big Adventure* were marketed as the new film from the star and director of *Four Weddings and a Funeral*, "they'll kill it stone dead. . . . All the effort this time should go to altering expectations" (Maslin 11). *Publicity stills.* (a) *Channel Four Films and others.* (b) *BBC and others*

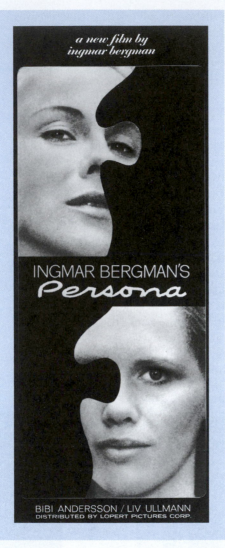

FIGURE 11.4 Publicity fostering appropriate expectations
This poster for Ingmar Bergman's *Persona* (1966) fosters appropriate viewer expectations and does so almost exclusively by its visuals. The poster's subject is two women seen close up but not seen in their entirety. If joined together, the two images would show not two complete faces but part of the first face overlapping the second and part of the second overlapping the first. *Persona* is about two women who are as closely associated as the parts of a puzzle. The film is concerned with the women's psychology and uses many close-ups of faces, and both that subject and that technique are characteristic of many Bergman films. In short, the poster suggests that *Persona* is a Bergman film about women—this one about two incomplete women who are parts of a puzzle that do not fit together naturally. *Svensk Filmindustri*

text: Something that people produce or modify to communicate meaning.

fueled by souls harvested on earth." Shortly after the beginning of the **narration**, a flying white dove is seen against the fiery background; then a bright white, round shape like the sun is seen behind the fire. Even without the narrator's **exposition**, the film immediately encourages us to anticipate the central conflict of the story: fire and destruction versus light and peace.

Viewers' Interactions with a Film during a Film Showing

As a narrative film progresses, we viewers also interact with it as readers interact with a written fictional **text**:

> The literary text may be conceived of as a dynamic system of gaps. A reader who wishes . . . to . . . reconstruct . . . the fictive world and action [that a fictional text] projects is necessarily compelled to pose and answer, throughout the reading-process, such questions as, What is happening or has happened, and why? What is the connection between this **event** and the previous ones? What is the motivation of this or that character? To what extent does the logic of cause and effect correspond to that of everyday life?

and so on. Most of the answers to these questions, however, are not provided explicitly, fully, and authoritatively (let alone immediately) by the text but must be worked out by the reader himself on the basis of the implicit guidance it affords. . . . Some [gaps] can . . . be filled in almost automatically, while others require conscious and laborious consideration; some can be filled in fully and definitely, others only partially and tentatively; some by a single [hypothesis], others by several (different, conflicting, or even mutually exclusive) hypotheses. (Sternberg 50)

Similarly, throughout a narrative film, we viewers ask and try to answer a series of questions and fill in the gaps with our own inferences and hypotheses about causes and consequences, about what caused something to happen, and about what happened because of earlier events. Without the attentive eyes and ears and thinking minds of the viewing audience, the film is incomplete—mere changing images and sounds. Viewers are not simply receptacles of a cascade of audio and visual information but collaborators and players with a wondrous, elaborate mechanism.

If the film is to hold our attention, it must quickly arouse our interest and renew that interest from time to time. In narrative films, story developments encourage us to consider causes and consequences. We will get involved and be satisfied or frustrated in part by how well the film lives up to our changing expectations. We like to be manipulated, up to a point. People who enjoy horror films, for example, want to feel the tiny hairs on the back of their necks tingle—or at least they don't mind if they do. But viewers normally also crave variety, surprise, suspense, and some mental challenges. By the film's ending, they like to think that they understand the causes and more or less anticipated the major consequences, or at least can now see how the film's developments followed from earlier events. Viewers also tend to like unity and meaning in it all. There is much to experience in one viewing; later viewings of the same film usually reveal additional complexities, subtleties, meanings, and perhaps ambiguities. In analyzing a film, many viewers find it useful to consider issues relating to expectations and interactions, including consistency, plausibility, predictability, surprise, and suspense.

Occasionally, viewers get a chance to interact with a film in a new and unexpected way. A good example was the initial theatrical showings of William Castle's tongue-in-cheek *The Tingler* (1959). The story concerns a physician who experiments on himself and others to try to learn how fear can be life threatening and screams lifesaving. The tingler is a creature that grows along the spine when someone is terrorized. If the person does not scream, the creature grows so large and powerful that the person dies (I'm not making this up). The tingler looks like the offspring of a chubby long lobster and a monster centipede and has pincers on the front end powerful enough to choke a person to death. From time to time during the original showings, some viewers *felt* tingling sensations (from their movie seats, which had been prewired with an electrical buzzer). Late in *The Tingler*, the creature has escaped into a movie theater. At this point, the movie screen in the movie goes dark, and the film's physician/scientist announces to the audience that a tingler is loose in the theater and that they should scream to save their lives. They promptly do so and thus incapacitate the uninvited creepy, crawling creature.

Interacting with cult films is a much more communal experience than the usual film showing is. The most popular of these cult favorites are *The Rocky Horror Picture Show* (1975) in the United States and elsewhere and *The Sound of Music* (1965), which was first shown in the sing-along mode in the United Kingdom and later on tour as *Sing-a-Long Sound of Music* in Canada, the United States, Australia, and other countries. Audiences know these cult films thoroughly and sing their songs at full volume in the theater.

During these showings, the films themselves create no surprises, but the film audiences do: for instance, audience members volunteer supplementary **sound effects**, wisecracks, and cheers, hisses, boos, and other sounds. During *The Rocky Horror Picture Show* they may also throw objects toward the screen or squirt water pistols.[1] A more recent example, *Hedwig and the Angry Inch* (2001; see Figure 7.20c on p. 327), has drawn similarly devoted participatory fans.

Digital filmmaking for theaters and the Internet makes possible yet other alternatives to the usual viewer interactions with a film. *Time Code* (2000), which consists of four simultaneous uninterrupted **plotlines** shown on the quadrants of the movie screen (see Figure 6.18 on p. 279), requires viewers to decide which story line to interact with and for how long. And Internet films such as Amy Talkington's 4-minute "The New Arrival" (2000) allow viewers to use the computer mouse to pan left or right around a 360-degree **filmic** world with potential action or significant details in every direction. In these and other films that are made possible by developments in technology, the viewer has choices about where to interact with the story and for how long.

plotline: A series of related events, generally involving only a few characters or people, that can function as an independent story.

filmic: Characteristic of the film medium or appropriate to it, such as parallel editing.

TYPES OF MEANINGS FOUND OR FORMULATED

> They watch moving shadows in dark caves together. Human females enjoy stories about one person dying slowly. The males prefer stories of many people dying quickly. (extraterrestrial narrator in *The Mating Habits of the Earthbound Human*, 1999)

We think about a film while we watch it; we think about it afterward. Often we discuss a film with others. Sometimes we read what others think about a film. Often we generalize about a film or about an aspect of it. We may say, for example, that one film glorifies violence and that another shows that wrongdoers end up punished. In this book, such observations or general statements about a subject such as a film or an aspect of a film are meanings.

Identifying a subject is not the same as explaining a meaning. A subject can be identified in a single word or a short phrase. For example, one of

---

[1] Some DVD versions of *The Rocky Horror Picture Show* include an option that allows viewers to periodically see a theatrical audience's reactions to a showing of *Rocky Horror* and another option that allows DVD viewers to *hear* an audience's reactions during a showing.

The film's Web site includes a variety of information, including a Prop List of what to bring to a showing and when to use it (for example, rice, newspapers, water pistols, rubber gloves, noisemakers, toasts, toilet paper, and a bell).

For a vivid account of *Sing-a-Long Sound of Music* showings in London, including sample wisecracks, see Kevin Murphy's *A Year at the Movies: One Man's Filmgoing Odyssey* (69–70).

the subjects of the western *Unforgiven* (1992) is "killing." In contrast, at least one sentence is necessary to express a meaning. One of the meanings of *Unforgiven* is "Killing a man may be difficult for a person to do."

In a fictional film, meanings are usually viewers' generalizations about subjects such as the characters' situations, personalities, ideas, and behavior. In a **documentary film**, meanings tend to be generalizations about the factual subjects represented in the film (for an example, see Figure 8.8 on p. 381). In an **experimental film**, meanings are typically generalizations that viewers make about film **conventions**, the experimental film's untraditional **representation** of its subjects, or the properties of the film medium itself (for example, see Figure 9.5 on pp. 406–7).

representation: A likeness of a subject created in a text.

Some viewers assume that to understand a film's meaning they need to find out what the makers of the film intended. Not really. Occasionally, creators of a text—novelists, playwrights, painters, filmmakers, or whatever—have persuasive insights about their own work. Much more often, though, they provide limited or no help in explaining their work's meanings. Because the creators of a text are so caught up in the creation of it, they are in a poor position to see its meanings: they are too close to the trees to discern where the various paths in the forest might lead. Often a text suggests meanings to audiences or readers that the creators were unaware of. Then, too, many artists are more intuitive than analytical. They may not be particularly skillful at or interested in analyzing and explaining anyone's text, let alone their own. Still others say that it is up to the audience or reader to decide what their creation implies about its subjects. Yet other artists, such as director Alfred Hitchcock, are evasive, playful, or misleading when they talk about the meanings of their films.

Meaning may be divided into four types: explicit, implicit, universal, and symptomatic.[2]

Explicit Meanings

Explicit meanings are general observations included in a text about one or more of its subjects. In silent films, they may be conveyed by a subtitle or a **title card**. A sound film may use these forms of language and many other forms, such as narration, dialogue, or monologue.

title card: A card or thin sheet of clear plastic on which is written or printed information included in a film.

In silent films, explicit meanings are commonplace. A title card of the American classic *Greed* (1925) reads: "First . . . chance had brought them face to face; now . . . mysterious instincts, as ungovernable as the winds of the heavens, were knitting their lives together." Another explicit meaning is found in a title card early in another classic American film, *Sunrise* (1927):

---

[2]For the terms *explicit meaning*, *implicit meaning*, and *symptomatic meaning*, I am indebted to David Bordwell's *Making Meaning: Inference and Rhetoric in the Interpretation of Cinema*.

For wherever the sun rises and sets . . .
in the city's turmoil
or
under the open sky on the farm,
life is much the same:
sometimes bitter, sometimes sweet.

Yet another explicit meaning in a film from the silent era occurs several times in the 2002 Kino Video DVD restored authorized edition of the German film *Metropolis* (1926). At the end of the film, for example, appears this translated title card: "Without the heart there can be no understanding between the hands and the mind."

Explicit meanings are probably less common in fictional sound films than in fictional silent films, but they are by no means rare. In *Unforgiven*, the Clint Eastwood character, William Munny, occasionally generalizes about one of the film's subjects, such as violence and killing. Approximately 108 $^2/_3$ minutes into the film, for example, he says, "It's a hell of a thing killing a man. You take away all he's got and all he's ever gonna have." Nearly 9 $^1/_2$ minutes into *Babe: Pig in the City* (1998), Babe (a pig who is a famous award-winning sheep herder) and Mrs. Esme Cordelia Hoggett are leaving the farm to go to the big city to try to raise money and save the farm from the creditors. As they leave, the narrator explains a characterization of the rest of the story and an assertion of a central meaning: "What follows is an account of their calamitous adventures and how a kind and steady heart can mend a sorry world." In narrative films, explicit meanings are generally not crucial to the plot. Munny's general statement and the generalization by the narrator in *Babe: Pig in the City* could have been omitted without affecting the stories. But if an explicit meaning is short and well phrased, it may be memorable, as when Uncle Ben tells Peter Parker 35 $^3/_4$ minutes into *Spider-Man* (2002), "With great power comes great responsibility."

A film's title may also reveal an explicit meaning, as in *Fatal Attraction* (1987): an attraction between two people may have deadly consequences. A title may also misrepresent a story, understate a meaning, or hint at **irony**. Mike Leigh's *Life Is Sweet* (1990)—about a husband and wife and their two very different grown twin daughters and three male friends—shows both sweetness and considerable emotional pain. The film could more accurately be characterized as bittersweet.

Like film directors' explanations of the meanings of their own films, an explicit meaning is not necessarily comprehensive or persuasive. It is certainly not the final word on any subject. A number of critics have commented that the final words of the 1940 film version of *The Grapes of Wrath* convey the film's main meaning. As the film approaches its conclusion, Ma Joad says, ". . . Rich fellas come up and they die, and their kids ain't no good and they die out, but we keep a comin'. We're the people that live. They can't wipe us out. They can't lick us. We'll go on forever, Pa, 'cause we're the people." OK. This speech conveys an important point about the film. But the film *shows* much more. It shows, for example, the strengths and conflicts in an extended family and how a family can be pulled apart when economic conditions are tough, employers exploit the workers, and the authorities do little to protect them.

A film's recitation of its subjects may not be reliable either. A little more than 3½ minutes into the documentary *Tupac Resurrection* (2003), Tupac's voice announces, "This is my story. A story about ambition, violence, redemption, and love." As viewers watch the film, they may not remember all four of those announced subjects. They may notice that important subjects were left off the film's opening list. One subject that is excluded: the challenges of growing up poor, African American, and without a male role model. Another of the film's subjects is the stress of being a celebrity at a young age.

A film's declarations about its meanings or subjects are often incomplete. In *The Grapes of Wrath*, *Tupac Resurrection*, and elsewhere, viewers should note the text's explicit meanings and stated subjects, but they should never take them as the complete and final word.

A fictional or experimental film may explain its meanings unnecessarily. If so, viewers may be annoyed that they have not been allowed to discover the meanings for themselves. Viewers may even feel a little insulted because the filmmakers did not trust them to figure out the meanings. General observations are commonplace, however, in documentary films, usually made by a narrator, interviews, subtitles, title cards, or a combination of two or more of these verbal options.

Implicit Meanings

An **implicit meaning** is a generalization that a person makes about a film or other text or about a subject in a text. In this section, we consider how viewers can create implicit meanings by generalizing about **filmmaking techniques**, narratives or stories, and symbols.

MEANINGS AFFECTED BY FILMMAKING TECHNIQUES

As is explained and illustrated throughout the first four chapters, the arrangement of subjects within the **frame** (**composition**), the lenses, lighting, camera distances and angles, sound mix, and many other aspects of filmmaking may all affect what meanings audiences detect. Consider a shot from Gus Van Sant's *Elephant* (2003; see Plate 54 in Chapter 13). To some extent, the lengthy **tracking** shots let viewers experience the school as the film's characters do: large, spread out, with plain, hard surfaces, large

film(making) technique: Any aspect of filmmaking, such as the use of sets, lighting, sound effects, music, or editing.

frame (noun): A separate, individual image on a strip of motion-picture film.

pockets of darkness or emptiness (or both), and characters on their own and in their own worlds. The settings and the moving camera work are good examples of filmmaking technique creating meaning: in a large modern high school, students may experience isolation and alienation.

How different the mood and meaning would be if this nearly 3-minute shot were much shorter and were part of a larger **scene** showing the subject often stopping to chat with other students. How different the meanings would be if the shot were brightly illuminated and in sharp focus throughout the image and with lots of other students around all the time. How different if viewers saw the subject from different camera distances and angles—for example, a **close-up** of his face from a **low angle**. Or how changed the results would be if viewers saw mainly shots of the subject's face and shots of the faces of other students. All those different ways of filming and **editing** the material would convey moods and meanings unlike those suggested by the shot represented in Plate 54.

As is explained and illustrated in Chapter 3, superimposition and **fast cutting** can also create meanings, as in the 42-second **montage** of Susan's opera career that begins almost 94 2/3 minutes into *Citizen Kane* (1941). The montage conveys an enormous amount of information, including the consequences of a man forcing a woman to do what she is ill equipped and reluctant to do.

For descriptions of the opera montage in *Citizen Kane*, see the Web site for this book at <bedfordstmartins.com/phillips-film>.

Sounds that are selected, modified, and combined can also create or change meaning. During the 1987 Academy Awards ceremony, a clip from *The Sound of Music* showed Julie Andrews running through a meadow as viewers heard not the original music but sounds of an airplane engine and machine-gun fire. Because of the sounds, viewers incorrectly (and humorously) inferred that she was under attack. In *What's Up, Tiger Lily?* (1966), Woody Allen took a Japanese movie and redubbed it. With the new soundtrack, the cast of characters now includes Phil Moscowitz, a type of James Bond character, Wing Fat, and the sisters Terri and Suki Yaki, and the action centers on rivals trying to acquire a famous egg salad recipe. Overlapping dialogue—as in some films directed by Orson Welles and some directed by Robert Altman—suggests how people may talk *at* but not entirely *to* or *with* each other. Scenes with this use of sound suggest that people may be together physically but isolated emotionally or spiritually.

Meaning in films, then, is always created or modified by the techniques of cinema, though it is important to remember that the significance of a technique can depend on the place and time the film was made. As we saw in Chapter 3, for example, years ago, filmmakers tended to use **lap dissolves** to delete insignificant action and time within a scene, but more

scene: A section of a narrative that gives the impression of continuous action taking place in continuous time and space.

montage: A series of brief shots used to represent a condensation of subjects and time.

lap dissolve: A transition between shots in which one shot begins to fade out as the next shot fades in, overlapping the first shot before replacing it.

recently, lap dissolves nearly always signify that the action is changing to a different setting or a later time or both.

NARRATIVE MEANINGS

Viewers also detect implicit meanings in fictional or documentary narratives. Sometimes they notice general qualities of settings, such as the beauty but danger of nature in *Never Cry Wolf* (1983), a thoughtful adventure film set in rural Alaska. In *Never Cry Wolf*, *Lawrence of Arabia*, *McCabe and Mrs. Miller* (1971), *Deliverance* (1972), *The Matrix*, and many other films, setting affects how events unfold and helps reveal character and meaning. Settings are often used to reveal a character's personality or situation and to compare and contrast characters. One character's residence, for example, may be very different from another's, as in *Fight Club* (1999, Figure 11.5).

More often, viewers detect significance in human behavior, which is the fundamental subject of narratives. In Miranda July's *Me and You and Everyone We Know* (2005), no character or narrator explains what any of the film's actions might suggest. Instead, the carefully selected scenes make it possible for viewers to infer certain kinds of meanings. The film has a variety of characters—young and old, young and even younger—largely in failed,

FIGURE 11.5 Residences symbolizing different situations and different personalities
In *Fight Club* (1999), the Edward Norton character's condo "on the fifteenth floor of a filing cabinet for widows and young professionals" is full of furnishings in desaturated colors, clean, uncluttered, modern, and very consumerist. The Norton character narrates, "Like so many others, I had become a slave to the Ikea nesting instinct." (a) Here, approximately 5 1/4 minutes into the film, part of his condo is seen with labeling from a catalog superimposed. (b) In contrast, the Brad Pitt character's residence, part of which is seen here nearly 47 minutes into the film, is a dark, old, abandoned house without anything beyond the basics, often without even the basics. The Pitt character narrates, "The stairs were ready to collapse. . . . Nothing worked. Turning on one light meant another light in the house went out. . . . Every time it rained, we had to kill the power. . . . Rain trickled down through the plaster and the light fixtures. . . . Everywhere were rusted nails to snag your elbow on." *Art Linson Productions, Fox 2000 Pictures, and others; 20th Century Fox Home Entertainment DVD*

FIGURE 11.6 Meaning implied by actions and mise en scène
No one in *Me and You and Everyone We Know* (2005) explains the significance of the film's actions. It is up to viewers to figure out the film's meanings. In a wordless scene almost 80 minutes into the film, we viewers see the outcome of the shoe sales clerk's younger son's intimate Internet exchanges with an anonymous female. Here, he has touched her hair briefly then pulled his hand away. She kisses him gently and briefly. Soon after that, she leaves, walking into the background and exiting the frame on the right, leaving the boy briefly alone. He is alone in loose framing, and she is returning to what viewers have figured out is an isolated life. *FilmFour; IFC Films; Sony Pictures Home Entertainment DVD*

failing, or incomplete relationships. There is a lot of longing in the film but little connection, touching, and human warmth. One of the two major characters is a female performance artist seeking to get her work accepted by a local art museum and to establish a relationship with the second major character, a shoe sales clerk whose wife is leaving him and their two young sons. The man is awkward and largely ineffectual with his sons (out of touch), and they in turn seem to live mostly joyless lives. The boys spend a lot of time at the computer and seem to have no friends. Other would-be connections in the movie also fail to come to fruition. For example, the sexual flirtation of two early teen girls with a man who's a loner ends with him hiding in his apartment when the girls seem to call his bluff and come knocking on his door. Time and again, the film shows scenes of isolation and loneliness, a condition of incompletion or of being out of touch (Figure 11.6).

Viewers also find meanings in narratives about creatures with human qualities, such as extraterrestrials wanting to go home, toys in the *Toy Story* movies, animals in *Charlotte's Web* (2006), and mermen and mermaids. Consider *The Little Mermaid* (1989). Someone who has repeatedly enjoyed its story may think that it has no implications or implicit meanings. But it does. To begin with, *The Little Mermaid* shows that a female teen may be forgetful, playful, passionate, irresponsible, impetuous, headstrong, and prone to lapses in judgment. She is also living in an adult body (Figure 11.7). The story of a 16-year-old female (Ariel) in rebellion against her stern ruling father and fiercely infatuated with an attractive young adult male has other implications. The film shows that a very young woman may abandon family and friends (and in this story undergo a transformation into a new species). She may do so to go off with a young man, even though she might be exchanging one dominating handsome man for a younger, less intimidating one. It is possible to interpret *The Little Mermaid* as being about a female teenager's strong desires for freedom to roam and explore and then for union with an attractive member of the opposite sex, even if it means she must abandon family, friends, and kind. Many critics have been intrigued by the film's implications and written about them. Professor Susan White, for example, declares that such stories of sacrifice and loss resonate with "girls' increasing awareness that growing up will make specific, often frightening, demands on them. . . . [Such stories] also echo the triumph the growing child experiences in her mastery of her body, and in the more challenging area of embracing loss as a means of being recognized and approved. Stories like Disney's *The Little Mermaid* also serve, of course, to disguise the extent of damage that these losses will incur, and to promise that male ardor will be more fulfilling than anything else could possibly be" (191). Another of the movie's implications is that although rebellion may cause a family storm, the storm will subside, and family ties will endure. The movie concludes with the father finally seeming to understand Ariel's situation and with her saying, "I love you, Daddy."

AMBIGUITY

Some stories are told in such a way that they are open to more than one plausible interpretation of their meanings. They are ambiguous. An example is from a master of **ambiguity**, British playwright and scriptwriter Harold Pinter. In the film version of *Betrayal* (1983), Jerry, a friend of a husband and wife who are having a party, confronts the wife in her own bedroom. After his passionate declaration of love, the wife calmly replies, "My husband is at the other side of that door." Does she mean, "I'm not interested, and my husband may overhear you, and there could be trouble," or "I could be interested, but this is a poor time and place," or something else? We cannot be certain. When the husband learns that his wife has been having an affair with Jerry, he tells her that he has always rather liked Jerry better than her and says that maybe he should have had an affair with Jerry himself. Does the husband mean it, or does he say it to strike out at his wife, or both? In the source play and in the film version of *Betrayal*, and in many other contemporary texts, some meanings remain uncertain or unknowable.

Ambiguity may result from the withholding of information, as in the first **sequence** of the western *The Searchers* (1956). The film begins at the remote Texas home of Aaron and Martha Edwards and their three children, where Aaron's brother Ethan shows up unexpectedly. The first word of the film is Aaron's and it is a question: as a distant horseback rider approaches the house, Aaron turns toward his wife and asks, "Ethan?" It is the first of many questions in the film's opening sequence, many of which will go unanswered. In a later scene, Ethan's nephew learns that the Civil War has been over for

FIGURE 11.7 Youthful feminine beauty in *The Little Mermaid* (1989)
The film's representation of feminine beauty is much like that of the popular culture of the time including commercial advertising: slimness yet curviness (here accentuated by low-slung "scales" and a tiny waist); large eyes (highlighted by eye makeup); full, deep red lips; white teeth; voluminous, cascading hair; and developed breasts. From the waist up, Ariel looks like the fantasy of a 12-year-old heterosexual boy. *Walt Disney Pictures; Disney DVD*

three years and asks Ethan "why didn't you come home before now?" Martha intercedes and sends the boy off to bed. Shortly after that, Aaron tells Ethan that, even before the war, he could see that Ethan wanted to give up on settling in that remote, barren area, and he asks Ethan why he hadn't left as others had. Martha again tries to intercede, but Ethan counters with his own question to Aaron. Shortly afterward, Aaron indirectly questions Ethan about the new, unmarked gold coins that Ethan has given Aaron, and Ethan responds with a question of his own, "so?" The next morning, Rev. Capt. Clayton arrives to swear in men to accompany him and others to go investigate a cattle rustling. Clayton has occasion to ask Ethan if he is wanted for a crime, and before he can respond, guess who intercedes? Martha says, "Coffee, Ethan," allowing him to evade Clayton's question.

Maybe Martha knows or senses there are troubles in Ethan's background. Maybe she just feels protective of him because, as alert viewers can see, she has tender feelings for him (as he does for her). At any rate, Ethan has arrived trailing an air of mystery, and Martha prefers that his background be left unexplained. It seems Ethan prefers it that way, too. So do the filmmakers. Why didn't Ethan clear out even before the Civil War? Was it because of his attraction to or relationship with Martha? What was the nature of their relationship? And what has this man been doing since the end of the Civil War? Are those new, unmarked gold coins from a robbery? Is Ethan wanted for some crime? The questions posed are important—after all, Ethan proves to be the film's central character—but tantalizing information is withheld and viewers are left in the dark.

Sometimes an ambiguity may be peripheral to a narrative's main concerns. An example is three brief references to the young girl's father in Jane Campion's *The Piano* (1993). The first time, the girl tells two women and her mute mother that her father was a German composer, but her mother is annoyed with that comment and quickly quiets her. Later, when the mother is not around, one of the two women asks the girl where her parents got married; the girl responds with a tale about the wedding ceremony, sees the disbelieving look on her listener's face, admits the story is a lie, and names a location where her parents got married. She then goes on to claim that her father was killed by lightning (as we see a brief animated drawing of a man catching fire and burning up) and that, simultaneously, her mother was struck dumb. In a later scene, the mother nods to her daughter in agreement that the girl's father was a teacher, and in reply to the girl's question about why her parents didn't marry, her mother signs, "He became frightened and stopped listening."

What's to be made of all this? Probably the father was a teacher who would not marry the mother. Beyond that, the truth is even less certain. Perhaps the mother doesn't want the girl talking about the father (less chance of a slipup about the girl's illegitimacy). Perhaps when the girl is asked about her father, she is afraid of revealing that her father never married her mother, so she tends to lie about him or to kill him off in her accounts so she won't have to talk about him anymore (or perhaps because she is angry at him for not marrying her mother). All the information about the father is presented so fleetingly and indirectly that his status is ambiguous, but audiences will probably not be troubled by the ambiguity, especially because the issue is touched on only briefly and is peripheral to the story's main concerns.

In other narratives, ambiguity is widespread. In the French film *Caché* (2005), a married couple, Georges and Anne, begins receiving anonymous and somewhat threatening videotapes, postcards, drawings, and telephone calls. About 20 minutes into the film, viewers learn that the couple's 12-year-old son has received a similar postcard addressed to him at his school. A videotape has been sent to Georges's boss. Childish, threatening black-and-white images with a large splash of red emanating from a human mouth accompany most of the videotapes and postcards. The images are usually of a human head, but one is of a crudely rendered rooster with a large splash of red crossing its neck (almost $27\frac{1}{2}$ minutes into the film).

The film has a very complicated **structure**, and only in bits and pieces can viewers learn the background of the story. When Georges was only 6 years old, his parents employed as farmhands an Algerian couple with a young son named Majid. After Majid's parents disappeared during a 1961 Algerian protest in Paris in which the police beat and killed many Algerians, Georges's parents planned to adopt Majid. The young Georges, however, did not want to share his parents and his privileges and told lies. He told his mother that Majid coughed up blood (so she would think the boy had TB?). (A mysterious brief shot of the young Majid with blood around his mouth is glimpsed at 13:24 into the film, and a somewhat longer but still mysterious shot of him at the same location, presumably coughing up blood, is seen at 20:28.) After telling Majid that Georges's father wanted him to kill the cranky rooster, Georges told his parents that Majid killed the rooster to scare him. Eventually, Georges's parents banished Majid from their estate and lives, though viewers never learn their exact reason(s).

After the adult Majid appears, about 47 minutes into the film, he seems the likely source of the anonymous communications. Later, it appears possible that Majid's son is making the videotapes on his father's behalf. Viewers never learn which of the two made the videotapes and which one sent them, or if they collaborated in doing one or the other. Beginning a little more than 38 minutes into the film, Georges dreams about the young Majid chopping off the rooster's head, approaching the young Georges, and seeming to strike at him with the hatchet. Now that Majid had come back into Georges's life, might Georges's disturbing dream suggest that he feels guilty about his past treatment of Majid, or is fearful of him, or both? The film has even more ambiguity. The couple's 12-year-old son comes to believe that his mother is having an affair with a close family friend, but given the evidence, viewers cannot know one way or the other.

The film ends with more ambiguity (Figure 11.8).

structure: The arrangement of all the parts of a text.

FIGURE 11.8 Ambiguity to the end
The last shot of *Caché* (2005), which is French for "hidden," runs nearly 2 minutes before the end credits begin to roll up and over the image. During that time, the camera remains unmoving and far back from the action. The scene shows parents and schoolmates greeting and in some cases chatting with the children emerging from the school. Earlier in the shot, there are many more characters than are seen here approximately 45 seconds into it. Throughout this shot, viewers can see no face clearly and can hear no distinct dialogue.

What is to be made of the film's ending? With so much going on in the shot and nothing privileged by the way the shot has been made, many viewers do not notice the two characters seen here facing each other on the left foreground of the frame. They are sons of two of the film's most important characters and are holding a brief conversation. It seems the taller boy is doing most of the talking—and from what has transpired earlier in the film, viewers know he has important information he could be telling the other boy. But viewers cannot know what the older son is telling the younger son. The film's ending is in keeping with so much else in the film: with issues of interest to viewers not being disclosed or being open to more than one interpretation. Many aspects of *Caché* are ambiguous or *hidden* from view. *Les Films du Losange and others; Sony Pictures Home Entertainment DVD*

reading: An interpretation of a text or part of one.

In *Caché*, the consequences of lying to a spouse, of trying to repress memories of painful but life-changing experiences, and of living with guilt are all implied. The film also alludes to the 1961 Parisian police massacre of unarmed Algerian demonstrators; the whole film could be **read** as being symptomatic of French attempts to repress memories of evil treatment of Algerians. But aspects of the film's characterization and plot remain unknowable or uncertain.

In *Betrayal*, *The Searchers*, *The Piano*, *Caché*, and many other films and other texts of recent years, key information is unclear or missing altogether.

REALISM AND FANTASY   Some stories seem to be realistic or true to life. Others seem mostly true to fantasy or daydreams. Many others fit in somewhere between those two extremes. The situation may be represented as in Figure 11.9.

FIGURE 11.9 The realism-fantasy continuum
The terms *realism* and *fantasy* have many different meanings. As used here, *realism* "is not a direct or

REALISM ◄─ ─► FANTASY
"The String Bean"   Stand by Me   Double Jeopardy   Lord of the Rings
(1962)   (1986; Figure 11.10)   (1999; Figure 11.11)   films

simple reproduction of reality . . . but a system of conventions producing a lifelike illusion of some 'real' world outside the text" (Baldick 184). *Fantasy* can be defined as a fictional text featuring major impossibilities. Probably most fictional films, especially popular commercial movies such as *Stand by Me* and *Double Jeopardy*, have characteristics of both extremes.

Like other film stories, "The String Bean" (1962), which is described on p. 257, shows a realistic story. The settings are believable. Every event represented in the story could have happened: an old woman who lives alone works at sewing purses and enjoys nurturing a bean plant. Movies of the **film movement** known as **Italian neorealism**, such as *The Bicycle Thief* and *Umberto D.* (pp. 334–37), also convey the lifelike illusion of an actual world outside the text.

In contrast, many other movies are mainly **fantasies**: they include settings, subjects, or events that are not possible. Examples are the *Star Wars* movies, the *Lord of the Rings* movies, and *Beowulf* (2007).

Many movies fall somewhere between the two extremes and have elements of both **realism** and fantasy. These films include settings that audiences usually have no trouble believing in and initial situations that seem possible. By the end of the film, however, viewers realize that some of the events and perhaps the resolution of the main characters' problems are more wish fulfillment than plausible outcomes. These movies may *look* true to life, but some of their events are not. They often attract audiences by incorporating enjoyable and reassuring fantasies in a mostly "realistic" story. An example is *Stand by Me* (1986), which is popular with many teens and young adults (Figure 11.10). All the movie's settings look authentic enough, and so do many of the main characters' actions, such as their bickering, insulting, and bonding. But as in so many movies, more dangerous and exciting events are packed into a short **story time** than most of us ever experience during a comparable time outside movie theaters (Figure 11.10b). It's also improbable that one of the young boys has to point a gun at the older gang's leader to persuade the gang to leave the boys alone—this from characters from a small town in 1959! Then, too, sometimes the boy who tends to act as the leader (on the left in Figure 11.10c) also acts like a surrogate father, displaying wisdom and compassion well beyond his years. Considered individually, most of the film's events are believable. However, the movie has so many events showing the dangers of adult males and the safety and reassurance of a small gang of young boys in so brief a story time that its story and the meanings implied are not completely credible.

film movement: A group of films sharing innovative styles or subjects that emerges from a country or region over a period of a few years.

story time: The amount of time represented in a film's story.

a)

b)

c)

FIGURE 11.10 Realism and fantasy in the same film
Stand by Me (1986) is about four boys who are unhappy at home
and are united in part by the indifference or hostility of adults.
(a) The boys are happy to go off on an adventure together in part
because adults consistently mistreat them. One boy's father, we
are told, held the boy's ear "to a stove and almost burned it off."
Another boy's father gets drunk and beats his son. A third father,
grieving over an older son whom he favored, alternates between
indifference and criticism of his surviving son. We learn nothing
about the father of the fourth boy—on the left in (a)—but by
implication perhaps he has been ineffective, too, because his son
is insecure and awkward and the target of much laughter. Other
adults disappoint the youths. Even a female teacher betrayed one of the boys. After he stole
milk money and turned it over to her, she used the money to buy a new skirt and allowed the
boy to suffer expulsion and a blotted reputation. (b) As in many popular movies, many dangers
are packed unrealistically into the film's brief story time. For example, the boys are threatened
by an onrushing train (presumably driven by yet another mean male adult), which has plenty of
time to brake but doesn't and nearly runs down two of the boys on a bridge high above water.
(c) This frame shows one of the three instances in the movie where a boy cries in front of at
least one of the other boys and is comforted by a mate—perhaps not an entirely credible situation given the age of the boys and the peer pressure they are under. *Columbia Pictures and others;
Columbia Tristar DVD*

Another example of a popular movie that seems realistic *while* you
watch it is *Double Jeopardy* (1999), which focuses on a woman who proves
to have extraordinary strength in more than one sense. The film is in the
tradition of Hitchcockian thrillers of a wronged person trying to set things
right before the law catches up and intervenes, and it has a high fantasy
quotient (Figure 11.11).

Often—both abroad and in the United States—films show male charac-
ters reenacting popular male fantasies in worlds that seem mostly true to life.
Several films directed by Alfred Hitchcock—such as *The 39 Steps* (1935),
Saboteur (1942), and *North by Northwest* (1959)—show the predicaments of a

FIGURE 11.11 Even more fantasy blended with realism
Double Jeopardy (1999) is a thriller about Libby, the Ashley Judd character. She is falsely imprisoned for murdering her husband, who has framed her for his supposed murder and disappeared with their young son and another woman. After six years in prison, Libby—seen here a little more than 93 1/2 minutes into the film in a final meeting with that errant husband—shows poise, intelligence, resourcefulness, and athletic skill and grace. Some of the movie's scenes are rendered as more fantasy than realism. For example, when Libby and her parole officer are trapped in a car that has run off a

ferry and is submerged and sinking, Libby takes the man's gun, swims to the surface, struggles with the parole officer who surfaces near her, hits him in the head with his gun, then swims to shore and escapes. Much later, when she regains consciousness while imprisoned in a coffin, she uses a lighter and that same gun to shoot off the coffin's locks and escape. Although the movie received mostly middling to poor reviews, it was popular with many viewers, especially women, and during its first two weeks, it grossed nearly $50 million at the U.S. box office. *Paramount Pictures and others; Paramount Home Video DVD*

man falsely accused of wrongdoing. Not to worry very much. He is re-sourceful, brave, and appealing to women and eventually clears himself by helping bring the guilty ones to justice. In *North by Northwest*, the main character is wrongly identified as a U.S. cold war agent and spends most of the story trying to elude both U.S. police and foreign agents. He not only succeeds (with a major assist from the director of U.S. agents) but also wins the love of the beautiful U.S. double agent. Through it all, he remains cool, collected, quick-witted, and amusing. After ducking into a train compartment to elude two pursuing police officers, for example, he tells the beautiful U.S. agent by way of explanation, "seven parking tickets."

The Bourne Identity enacts similar popular male fantasies by showing a main character who displays resourcefulness, bravery, and poise as he works his way out of his initial predicament. At the beginning of the film, the Matt Damon character does not know who he is or why dangerous U.S. and European agents pursue him. While attempting to avoid authorities, find safety, and clear up matters, Bourne hooks up with a good-looking woman who is attracted to him and willing to try to help him. The physical and mental powers and sexual allure of the individual male constitute one of the most recurrent meanings in recent popular American movies. The **producers** of action movies, including the James Bond movies, have raked in truckloads of money by showing countless boys and men what they enjoy imagining themselves doing: dispatching tough guys and attracting an assortment of ravishing available women.

Countless movies show characters being romantically desirable (Figure 11.12). Countless movies show characters having sexual appeal (Figure 11.13).

producer: A person in charge of the business and administrative aspects of making a film.

a)

b)

FIGURE 11.12 Female characters as romantically desirable
(a) In this scene, which appears a little more than an hour into the second half of *Gone with the Wind* (1939), Rhett Butler (played by Clark Gable) is proposing marriage to Scarlett O'Hara (played by Vivien Leigh). For years, American women viewers voted Clark Gable the most appealing of all male movie stars; he was the George Clooney of an earlier era. (b) In the French new wave classic *Jules and Jim* (1961), two men who are best friends are in love with the same woman, and she determines the nature of her relationships with them and with other men. As in many movies, a woman attracts the romantic attentions of more than one male and has power over them. (a) *Metro-Goldwyn-Mayer; Selznick International; Warner Home Video DVD.* (b) *Publicity still. Films du Carrosse and S.E.D.I.F.*

Movies may also blend realism with fantasy by playing on viewers' fears and nightmares. Because many people distrust technology (applied science) and the people who create and monitor it, movies such as *2001: A Space Odyssey* (1968), *Westworld* (1973), and *Jurassic Park* (1993) and its **sequels** show technology or scientists failing to coax, trick, or force the genie back into the bottle and nonscientists ultimately triumphing. Other movies show everyone failing to right the wrongs that people and technology have brought forth. *The Forbin Project* (1969, aka *Colossus: The Forbin Project*) cautions that if humans put complete trust in technology, it can become a Frankenstein monster that eventually dominates its creator. The *Matrix* trilogy carries the threat of supercomputers even further. In these movies, computers with artificial intelligence have created a new race of machines that use a form of fusion and human bodies that are grown and harvested as fuel to run the matrix, which is "a computer-generated dream world, built to keep . . . [humans] under control." As different technologies (such as biotechnology and bioterrorism, in recent years) capture public awareness, their possible harmful consequences become film subjects, such as the rage virus plague of *28 Days Later* (2003). Presentations of technology and technologists (a person who uses scientific knowledge to solve practical problems) need not always be so grim. The animated *Wallace & Gromit: The Curse of the Were-Rabbit* (2005) **satirizes** a zany inventor. But that film is light of touch, and the invention unleashes a monster Were-Rabbit who turns out to be a version of the inventor himself!

Fantasy films or parts of films show life as audiences wish it to be or fear it might be or might become. These films are not so much mirrors of life outside theaters as curved fun-house mirrors that briefly entertain us, often by showing us characters and situations that we can identify with and that make us feel positive or negative emotions.

a)

b)

FIGURE 11.13 Commonplace female and male sexual fantasies
(a) As in many movies, in *Splendor* (1999), one woman attracts two very different men at the same time; but unlike in most movies, she loves both of them and makes love to both of them, at first separately but soon together. Not entirely plausibly, this romantic comedy represents some of the possible problems and rewards of a long-term sexual and domestic threesome. (b) In many films, TV shows, and advertisements, images of two or more women attracted to one man are commonplace, as in this poster for the 1963 British movie *Tom Jones*. Note that four of the women look up to Tom Jones (and everything else in the image is below his head, hands, and arms), four have their mouths open, and all five of these bosomy women are touching one of his legs or a hip. The woman below the man and on her back with her left hand near his crotch could be looking at it. Many viewers enjoy such images and the suggestion that one man can have so much appeal and power: he is encircled by attractive, adoring women. In the image, he is happy, and his virility is suggested by the vaguely drawn open shirt, that sword near his left hip, and his left knee touching the inside of an exposed knee of one of his admirers. *Publicity stills.* (a) *Desperate Pictures and others; British Film Institute Stills, Posters and Designs.* (b) *Woodfall Film Productions; British Film Institute Stills, Posters and Designs*

SYMBOLIC MEANINGS

A **symbol** is anything perceptible that has significance or meaning beyond its usual meaning or function. Every society has certain universally accepted symbols: each society invests certain sounds and sights with widely understood meanings. In many societies, for example, a red traffic light symbolizes that people approaching it should stop. Painters, writers, filmmakers, and others who make imaginative texts may also create symbols (not always consciously). Depending on contexts, a sound, word (including a name), color, or representation of an object, action, or person may function as a symbol. Viewers (or readers) do not perceive a symbol as merely performing its usual functions; they see it as also suggesting meaning.

In *The Godfather* (1972), *The Godfather Part II* (1974), and *The Godfather Part III* (1990), doors or doorways do not always function simply as connections between rooms: they sometimes function as symbols. At the end of *The Godfather*—for example—when the door to Michael's new office is closed and excludes Michael's wife Kay from looking into Michael's office, the door symbolizes how criminal activities must be carried on out of sight (see Figure 6.14b on p. 272). Nearly 186 minutes into *The Godfather Part II*, Michael finds Kay, who is now estranged from him, sneaking a visit to their two children at the Corleone estate. After a tense, wordless, face-to-face confrontation of about 30 seconds—which many viewers may find to be an enormous amount of silence in a film with dialogue—Michael shuts the door in Kay's uncertain, then pained face. About 122 ½ minutes into *The Godfather Part III*, it seems that Kay is about to be reconciled with Michael, and they are holding hands. A man knocks on and opens twin doors leading into the room. In the background a woman is weeping. The man backs into the other room as Michael approaches him and asks what's wrong. The man tells Michael that a long-term associate has been shot. As Michael and the man talk, Kay moves sideways to see Michael and the man better, bends slightly sideways, and moves forward to see and hear more clearly. Still with his back to Kay, Michael has put his hand on the man's arm, thereby evidently indicating to him to move sideways; they do so, in effect making it harder for Kay to see and hear. We hear Kay's voice saying, "It never ends." After watching for a few more moments, she turns and walks out of the frame. There will be no reconciliation after all. In all three movies, the door or doorway symbolizes the barrier that has come between Michael and his wife and reinforces an important meaning of the *Godfather* films: involvement in crime precludes spousal intimacy and trust.

The *Godfather* movies are rich in symbols. Another one appears in *The Godfather* at the beginning and again at the ending of the scene where Luca Brasi (Vito's faithful henchman) is strangled to death and the camera looks into the bar through a glass window with two fish etched on it (41²/₃ and 43¹/₂ minutes into the film). Later, dead fish wrapped in Brasi's bulletproof vest are delivered to the Corleone compound, and a character explains that it is a Sicilian message that Luca "sleeps with the fishes" (is dead). At that point, viewers may remember the etched fish seen briefly in the foreground as Luca was strangled, and realize that the fish function as a symbol, not just a decorative component of the **mise en scène**.

A symbol also may be conveyed by the mise en scène of a carefully selected shot (Figure 11.14).

mise en scène: An image's setting, subjects, and composition (the arrangement of setting and subjects within the frame).

FIGURE 11.14 Symbolic mise en scène in two films

(a) Most of the action in the German film *Good Bye Lenin!* (2003) takes place around the time of the reunification of East Germany and West Germany in 1990, a time when Soviet control of East Germany ended and Western interests, including U.S. commercial interests, moved in. This image is from a shot occurring about 21 minutes into the film and lasting only 8 or so seconds. In the background can be glimpsed the changing of the guard at the New Guardhouse (Neue Wachel), a memorial in the former East Berlin. In the foreground, the shot shows this car followed in quick succession by large trucks with "Coca-Cola" painted on their sides. The second truck is pulling the body of an additional truck, so the shot gives viewers a glimpse of the car seen here and the equivalent of three large Coca-Cola trucks. The shot shows the changing of the guard in two senses. As the watch in front of the national memorial in the background is being transferred from East German to West German soldiers, so the brand names of the East German socialist economy are being replaced by the symbols of Western capitalism, which in this shot are characterized by their speed, size, and gaudiness (the car seen here). The shot is so brief and the action so rapid that the car seen here appears as a blur in the finished film; such an image fits in nicely with the shot's symbolism: capitalist commercial interests are moving into the reunited Germany so rapidly that they appear as a blur.

(b) The Mexican film *Herod's Law* (1999), which is set in 1949 Mexico, begins with the last day of life of a corrupt village mayor. The film's first shot shows him firing a pistol in what we viewers soon infer is his office (later in the scene we see he has shot someone). The man then opens a large book, the "Political Constitution of the United States of Mexico," which contains not pages but money. He hurriedly grabs the *dinero* and stuffs it into a small bag. Only a few minutes later, he is dead, killed by one of his disgruntled constituents. In this frame, the transformed book of the constitution, the hidden money, and the recently fired gun symbolize the replacement of law and order with greed, graft, and gunplay. The mayor's replacement, the main character of the movie, soon proves to have been cut from much the same cloth. As we see a little more than 109 minutes into the film, he, too, has cut out the pages of a large book (of Mexican laws) to create space to hide money that he extracted from the villagers under his jurisdiction. (a) *WDR and others; Sony Pictures Classics DVD.* (b) *Bandidos Films, Instituto Mexicano de Cinematografía, and others; 20th Century Fox Home Entertainment DVD*

Like a story, a symbol may be ambiguous and have two or more plausible interpretations. In *The Squid and the Whale* (2005)—which is about a husband and wife who are divorcing and the effects of their split-up on their two young sons—the phrase "the squid and the whale" is the title. It is also discussed briefly and represented visually:

1. *The Squid and the Whale*, the film's title, appears both at the beginning of the film *and* at the ending.

2. About 61 minutes into the film, a school counselor asks the older son Walt to tell him a "nice memory," and Walt tells him how as a boy he and his mother went to New York's American Museum of Natural History, where he was frightened by the diorama of a whale and a giant squid locked in mortal combat. He also says that his mother's description of the diorama that evening lessened the fear.

3. At the end of the film, Walt goes on his own to the same museum and looks at the diorama again (Figure 11.15).

Before and during the parents' separation, Walt had been siding with his father. By the end of the film, however, he has become disillusioned with him and finally rebels against his manipulations, abandons him in the hospital, and runs to the natural history museum, where he looks at the squid and whale diorama without fear. It's possible to read the squid and whale as a symbol of the boy's growing maturity: he goes to the museum alone and on his own initiative; he no longer needs a parent to comfort him as he confronts a childhood fear. It is also possible to read the symbol as the boy's unconscious attempt to get back to a special time he had with his mother; by the end of the film, he moves literally and symbolically away from his father to a special place he had shared with his mother. Finally, some viewers have interpreted the squid and whale as a symbol for the two parents in combat. If so, Walt's looking at them without fear may suggest his growing resignation to a combative situation over which he has no control.

Symbols also may be used in other types of films, including documentaries. In *The Agronomist* (2003), the film's main subject is Jean Dominique, a Haitian agronomist who became an independent radio station owner, journalist, and political activist who reported on Haitian politics. At one point, he speaks briefly about his involvement in a film club and its showing of an antifascist film that upset Haitian authorities. Then he says, "And the police react very badly," and he makes some faces (Figure 11.16). As in so many other texts, the symbol here is suggestive, and different viewers may interpret its significance somewhat differently. In the documentary *Theremin: An Electronic Odyssey* (1995), a **freeze frame** and **fade-out** are used to symbolize that someone may have died. Viewers learn that Leon Theremin (the inventor of the electronic musical instrument called the Theremin) was kidnapped in the United States by KGB agents

FIGURE 11.15 A symbol that may have more than one plausible interpretation
This is a frame from the third shot from the end of *The Squid and the Whale* (2005). The elder son of a divorcing couple has finally rebelled against his controlling father and run off to visit a special exhibition at Manhattan's American Museum of Natural History. There he confronts a diorama that troubled him as a child: a battle to the death between a whale and a giant squid. *Destination Films and others; Sony Pictures Home Entertainment DVD*

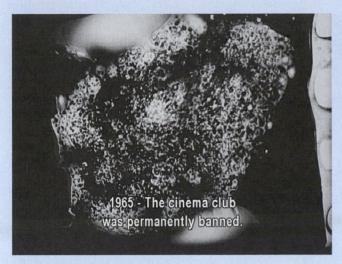

1965 - The cinema club was permanently banned.

FIGURE 11.16 A symbol used in a documentary film
About 20½ minutes into *The Agronomist* (2003) appears a shot of a piece of movie film stuck in a projector and starting to melt because of the heat of the projector lamp (notice the distorted sprocket holes on the right side of this image). Nearly simultaneously, the subtitle seen here is superimposed on the dissolving film. Instead of the image of the disintegrating film, director Jonathan Demme could have suggested his point in any number of ways. For example, he could have lingered on the previous shot of the man's face. Or he could have cut to something else, such as an abandoned building, a dark and cloudy sky, a black frame viewed in silence, or, less imaginatively, a program or poster with a notice of cancellation on it. But he chose to cut to a piece of film being destroyed by intense heat, suggesting that whatever the police did was destructive. The police action is not described or re-created, but from the image of disintegration and distortion, viewers know that the antifascist film was perceived as threatening to the status quo and was not just "banned" but destroyed. The image Demme included is not of exclusion from an event but of destruction of the means of presenting it. *HBO/Cinemax Documentary; New Line Home Entertainment DVD*

and spirited back to the Soviet Union and that investigations failed to turn up any leads. Some of his American friends feared he was dead. Then, about 28½ minutes into the film, we see a shot of Theremin as a young man with a young woman. In extreme **slow motion** they advance toward the camera; she moves off-frame to the left, and he remains on the extreme right side of the frame and is now seen in freeze frame. The shot concludes with a slow fade-out.

Objects functioning as symbols are often shown more than once, are frequently placed in prominent positions, are seen in important parts of the film, or are used under a combination of these conditions. Because so few viewers of *The Godfather* are likely to know the significance of the Sicilian message about sleeping with fish, that symbol is explained. However, if we examine how symbols are used in films and in other texts, we will notice that like other vehicles of meaning they usually go unexplained and are subject to different interpretations.

For the essay "The Significance of 'Rosebud'" in *Citizen Kane*, see the Close-Up by Don Reed on p. 542.

Universal Meanings and Symptomatic Meanings

A universal meaning is an explicit or implicit meaning that could be found in the texts of many societies. For example, many texts from different societies state or imply that "crime does not pay." Another universal meaning—seen

FIGURE 11.17 Triumph of individualism as symptomatic of many Western societies

Like so many popular movies from Western societies, *Gladiator* (2000) extols the potential power of an individual, even in the face of tremendous adversity. Such movies excite large audiences and reassure them that one person can make a difference. Such a belief is a deeply ingrained component of American ideology. Seen here is actor Russell Crowe as Maximus, a general reduced to a gladiator trying to get his own personal vengeance and to set right the wrongs of the Roman power structure. *DreamWorks, Universal, and Scott Free Productions; DreamWorks Home Entertainment DVD*

in almost all narratives—is that people make decisions and take actions expecting one result but getting a different one.

By contrast, a film's meanings may be symptomatic of a society or group. As we saw in the previous chapter, where and when a film is made influences filmmakers and their work. It is not surprising, then, that a film's meanings, whether explicit or implicit, may be symptomatic of the society or group from which the film emerged. A **symptomatic meaning** is thus an explicit or implicit generalization that is characteristic of the beliefs or concerns of a society (or group) that nurtured the text.

Films of the United States and other Western countries often emphasize the individual. Like so many popular movies, *Gladiator* (2000) demonstrates the extraordinary power of a dedicated, hardworking individual (Figure 11.17). The main character, Maximus—a Roman general—escapes execution, survives as a slave, and excels as a gladiator. Even in the one scene that best shows the value of group effort—the combat in which the gladiators coordinate their efforts and together defeat the opposing forces—one person (Maximus) organizes and rallies the others. Near the end of the story, Maximus has the loyalty and help of others, but once again it is up to *one* man to make all the difference. And that man is Maximus. Although chained up, imprisoned, and unfairly wounded by Commodus before their battle, Maximus kills Commodus in the final showdown.

Other films are symptomatic of other, very different societies. In addition to showing the story of two teenage boys and their sexually charged road trip with a young married woman, the Mexican film *Y Tu Mamá También* (2001) repeatedly shows both the advantages enjoyed by the wealthy and powerful and the disadvantages endured by the poor and powerless in present-day Mexico. The film's wealthy and powerful include the president of Mexico and his Harvard-trained secretary of state. The wealthy and powerful elite also include that official's son, Tenoch—who lives in guarded luxury and will be going to the university to study economics (as his father did)—and, to a lesser extent, Luisa, a Spaniard who has married an academic writer. In contrast, the poor and powerless Mexicans face major disadvantages. They have to guard against being exploited by the rich (years earlier Tenoch's father had been linked to a scandal involving selling contaminated food to the poor). About 7¼ minutes into the film, viewers learn that a bricklayer who had moved to Mexico City to find work avoided using a poorly located pedestrian crosswalk because using it would have required him to walk an extra two miles to work. As a consequence, he tried to cross elsewhere and was killed by a speeding bus. His body went unidentified and unclaimed in the city morgue for four days. Approximately 80½ minutes into the film, viewers learn that a fisherman and his family will be forced out of their home in a nature preserve so an exclusive hotel can be built there and that the fisherman will end up working as a janitor at the same hotel.

A film may be symptomatic of a nation's ideals, as the following examples from two Japanese films illustrate. In *The Seven Samurai* (1954), the samurai's defense of the farmers and their village depends on coordinated, unified action; thus, when the individualistic Toshiro Mifune character goes off on his own and captures one of the brigands' rifles, the samurai leader reprimands him. The idea that in unity there is strength is suggested a number of times in the film and is deeply symptomatic of Japanese society. The same film also illustrates more than once how modesty is valued in an individual (especially in the master swordsman and in the samurai leader) and how elders are held in high esteem (especially the village elder).

A film could even reflect a society's conflicting feelings about a subject. *Shall We Dance?*—a 1996 Japanese film—was enormously popular in its home country. It was also a critical success there, capturing thirteen of the Japanese equivalents of the Academy Awards. Probably part of the film's appeal to the Japanese is that many of its characters exhibit the mixed feelings the Japanese populace has toward Western lifestyles and values (Figure 11.18).

On the one hand, many Japanese cling to the values of the past, as is made clear by nearly all of the opening narration of the film version shown in the United States:

> In Japan, ballroom dance is regarded with much suspicion. In a country where married couples don't go out arm in arm, much less say "I love you" out loud, intuitive understanding is everything. The idea that a husband and wife should embrace and dance in front of others is beyond embarrassing. However, to go out dancing with someone else would be misunderstood and prove more shameful. Nonetheless, even for Japanese people, there is a secret wonder about the joys that dance can bring.

In *Shall We Dance?*, the Japanese office worker and his exuberant, disguised coworker hide their unusual extracurricular activity from their fellow workers to avoid their disapproval. The main character feels compelled to hide his dance lessons from even his wife. According to the film's director, Masayuki Suo, "Until recently, [dance] classes remained off-limits to people under 18" (Johnston 7).

On the other hand, *Shall We Dance?* shows the Japanese "secret wonder" about popular Western culture. The influences of British and American

a)

b)

FIGURE 11.18 **Japanese and Western influences**
Shall We Dance? (1996) shows the story of a modern-day office worker in Tokyo who takes up ballroom dancing, a somewhat disreputable activity in the eyes of many Japanese when the film was made. (a) Some scenes of the movie show behavior accepted as part of Japanese culture since the end of World War II—for example, office workers on their way home after a tiring day's work. (b) The movie also includes Western behavior not yet widely considered acceptable and Japanese in the mid-1990s, such as ballroom dancing lessons and competitions. As a whole, the movie is symptomatic of the changing face of Japanese society and the resistance to accept (yet fascination with) Western behavior. *Nippon Television Network Corp. (NTV) and others; Miramax; Miramax Home Entertainment DVD*

cultures are especially strong. Part of the film is set in Blackpool, England, and while witnessing the Blackpool competition as a child, one of the dance instructors in *Shall We Dance?* had been inspired to become a dancer. American popular culture is also an influence on the Japanese film. "Shall We Dance?" is not only the film's title but also the last line of the film's dialogue (in English) and the name of the famous waltz that is heard several times in the film, including at its conclusion. That popular waltz (and song) derives from the Rodgers and Hammerstein Broadway musical *The King and I* (1951) and a U.S. film adaptation, *The King and I* (1956), both of which are in part about differences between East and West. The film version of *The King and I* also inspired one of the dance instructors in *Shall We Dance?* to become a dancer.

With its characters' widespread adherence to traditional values yet attraction to popular Western culture, *Shall We Dance?* is symptomatic of 1996 Japanese society. The film is so in tune with its people and times that it attracted large audiences and in turn greatly spurred the growth of dance class enrollments and the acceptance of ballroom dancing in Japan.

A story may also be symptomatic of the concerns and beliefs of a specific group and thus be remade with variations over the decades. Consider how since the first showings of *The Jazz Singer* in 1927 various *Jazz Singer* movies and TV shows have resonated with different generations of American Jews. The story shows a young man, the son of Jewish immigrants, torn between the wishes of his father, a cantor (someone who sings hymns in

Jewish services), and his own drive to succeed as a singer in the secular world. J. Hoberman and Jeffrey Shandler—who were the curators of the exhibition "Entertaining America: Jews, Movies, and Broadcasting" and the authors of a book with the same title—propose that *The Jazz Singer* is the "'key' Jewish narrative in twentieth-century American Jewish culture. They suggest that it symbolized the archetypal clashes between sacred and secular, tradition and modernity, ghettoization and assimilation, minority and mass culture and that it compellingly addressed a generation seeking identity in a world not of its fathers" (Glueck).[3]

INFLUENCES ON THE WAYS WE THINK ABOUT FILMS

Many factors may influence our thinking about a film. Three are discussed here: our prior knowledge of the film or of a subject in the film, our backgrounds, and our use of critical approaches.

Prior Knowledge of the Film or a Subject in the Film

Prior knowledge of a film or of a film's subject may influence how we later think about the film. We may have already seen many films of the same genre. Perhaps over the years we have seen many science fiction films, so when we see a new sci-fi film or a film that combines science fiction with one or more other genres, such as *Blade Runner* (1982, 1992, and 2007) and *The Matrix* (1999), we compare and contrast it to sci-fi films we have already seen. Or before seeing a film, or perhaps before *and* after a film viewing, we might read something about the film. We might read reviews that influence our way of thinking about the film. We may have read the source novel and thus think about the film in ways that would not occur to someone who had not read the novel.

Previous reading may allow us to better understand a film in its historical and perhaps political contexts—contexts that the filmmaker excluded from the film. *The Motorcycle Diaries* (2004) focuses on one character, the Argentine Ernesto/Che Guevara. But there's little in the film about the historical and political contexts of the time and place: 1950s South America. The movie makes no mention of Juan Perón, who was then the charismatic yet fiercely and oppressively antidemocratic president of Argentina. There are no hints of the causes of the Bolivian tin workers' strike glimpsed in the

---

[3]For evidence of the many, varied representations of *The Jazz Singer* in twentieth-century American culture, see J. Hoberman's "The Jazz Singer: A Chronology" (Hoberman and Shandler 84–92).

film and no mention that Bolivia was then on the verge of revolution. Rather, as in most popular Hollywood films, the emphasis is on personal relationships and the power and importance of the individual—in *The Motorcycle Diaries* the growing awareness of a charismatic, increasingly focused individual. The film's focus is on Ernesto Guevara becoming politicized but not yet political, on Ernesto beginning his trip toward becoming the revolutionary Che. *The Motorcycle Diaries* shows events, mostly from 1952, in the life of a man who would play a major role in the early years of Castro's Cuba but who in 1967 would lie dead in a Bolivian jungle, shot repeatedly by government troops. Similarly, *Frida* (2002), which is about the life and work of the Mexican artist Frida Kahlo, omits much of the historical and political contexts of the main subjects, including the two main characters' communist beliefs, and dwells instead on personal relationships, sexuality, the creative imagination, and the sensuous pleasures of music and art. Perhaps the makers of *The Motorcycle Diaries* and *Frida* deemphasized those contexts for fear they would lose funding to make the films or a chance to market them widely. For a movie to be popular and attract large audiences—especially in the huge U.S. market—it may deemphasize politics and focus more on individual success or other popular, reassuring beliefs. But the viewer who happens to have read about the background of the two film stories will see these films not merely as explorations of character but also as part of the larger scheme of things.

Yet other prior reading may influence the ways viewers think about a film. Viewers might read the cutting continuity script for a film before or, more likely, after they have seen the film. The **cutting continuity script** is a description of a finished film. It indicates each setting, describes major events, and includes any dialogue. It may also include descriptions of camera distances, camera angles, camera movements, transitions between scenes, and indications of where music is heard. A few cutting continuity scripts even number each shot and indicate how long it is.

Here is an excerpt (shot numbers and shot lengths are omitted) from a cutting continuity script for two consecutive scenes from *Citizen Kane*. ("EXT" stands for **exterior**, a scene filmed outside; "CU" stands for close-up; "MS" for **medium shot**.)

medium shot: A shot in which the subject and surroundings are given nearly equal prominence.

EXT. HOUSE CU—mother holding Charles—snow falling—music playing—she talks [to her husband]

MOTHER

. . . he's going to be brought up where you can't get at him.

Camera moves down to Charles's face as he stares up to left.

Lap Dissolve

EXT. HOUSE MS—sled in snow—snow falling—train whistle heard—music playing

Lap Dissolve

(*The Citizen Kane Book*, 333–34)

Reading a cutting continuity script can help us understand and appreciate a film. A cutting continuity script usually provides a more complete, accurate, and legible translation for a foreign language film than is given in the film's subtitles. The script can also refresh the viewer's memory of the film and reveal details and patterns not noticed while watching it. Perhaps reading the description of the two scenes from *Citizen Kane* makes the reader more aware of the emotional costs to young Charles of being forced to leave his home: he is deprived of his mother's love and protection and of the joys of play (the sled that readers of the script had earlier read about Charles enjoying). Reading the descriptions of the two scenes might also make the reader more appreciative of the filmmakers' skill, economy, and subtlety in suggesting feelings of loss and melancholy.[4]

Viewers' Backgrounds

Often individuals interpret texts in different ways because of their different backgrounds. Let's consider three examples of how age and experience, political beliefs, and sexual orientation might influence interpretations of films.

Did you and one of your parents ever see a film together, discuss it afterward, then decide that you had not seen the same film? Differences in age and experiences can lead us to focus on different subjects in a film or to interpret their significance differently. Maybe one person is moved by the loss of love and life while watching *Titanic* (1997), whereas a person from a navy family is deeply moved by a different aspect of the film: the captain losing his ship. Scenes from *Barbershop* (2002) resulted in various interpretations, depending in part on the viewer's age and experiences. Rev. Jesse Jackson and Rev. Al Sharpton were deeply offended by some scenes (Figure 11.19). Later, Jackson and Sharpton "demanded an apology and called on MGM to remove the scenes from future releases" ("*Barbershop*"). Months later, Rosa Parks refused to attend the NAACP Image Awards because it was being hosted by Cedric the Entertainer. In contrast, most younger viewers took the film's controversial dialogue in stride. According to Professor Todd Boyd, "The younger generation has always been 'instructed to pay appropriate homage' to the civil rights movement. . . . But 'they've created their own icons.'" Boyd continues, "I would suggest Tupac . . . and Biggie . . . are

---

[4]Some commercial publishers (in the United States and foreign countries, especially France) publish film scripts. Some U.S. university presses publish them, too, sometimes with an editor's introduction, notes on changes between different versions of the script, interviews, and film reviews and commentaries. Film scripts show up on the Web. Occasionally, they are included on DVDs. Some bookstores with large collections of film books (and some Web sources) sell unbound, unpublished scripts, mostly from recent years. Regardless of the source, often there is no indication whether the script is a **screenplay**, **shooting script**, or cutting continuity script.

screenplay: The earliest version of a script, a script written before filming begins.

shooting script: The version of the script that filmmakers use during filming.

FIGURE 11.19 Interpretations influenced by age and experiences of viewer
In a scene that begins 54 1/2 minutes into *Barbershop* (2002), the barber played by Cedric the Entertainer belittles the contribution to the U.S. civil rights movement made by Rosa Parks. (Parks was most famous as an African American who in 1955 refused to give up her seat to a white man on a city bus in Montgomery, Alabama. The incident, for which she was arrested and convicted for disorderly conduct, is widely considered the spark that set off the modern civil rights movement.) Perhaps the barber belittles Parks's contribution to be contrary to the previous speaker who praised some 1960s civil rights champions. Perhaps he does so to playfully taunt his listeners. Or perhaps he speaks out of ignorance. It is up to each viewer to decide what motivates the barber to voice his unorthodox view. *MGM; MGM Home Entertainment DVD*

maybe more important to the hip-hop generation than Rosa Parks and Martin Luther King" ("*Barbershop*").

Viewers' political beliefs may also influence how they interpret a film. When *Titanic* was first screened, many American viewers and reviewers focused on the film's special effects and its psychological aspects, particularly its initial celebration of human achievement and its later scenes of courtship, love, sacrifice, and loss. The movie was enormously popular in China, too—but for different reasons. Because the Chinese government's political philosophy praises the efforts of the working class, the Chinese focused more on the film's social classes and particularly admired Jack (the Leonardo DiCaprio character) as a noble working-class man. At the time of the film's release in China, the Chinese premier praised *Titanic* for promoting "the correct class viewpoint because the hero Jack is a lower class figure" (Hessler).

Some film scholars have studied how viewers' sexual orientation may influence their interpretations of certain films. Elizabeth Ellsworth studied critics' reactions to *Personal Best* (1982), which is about two female athletes, played by Mariel Hemingway and Patrice Donnelly, competing for spots on the 1980 Olympics track team. The two become friends, then lovers who room together for three years, and then ex-lovers. Ellsworth studied mainstream reviews and lesbian feminist reviews of the film. From the latter, she concludes,

> Most lesbian feminist reviewers ignored large sections of narrative material focusing on heterosexual romance, making no reference to their existence or conventionally obvious implications for the film's preferred heterosexual "meaning." Some redefined "main characters" and "supporting characters" in order to elevate Patrice Donnelly as the film's star despite the publicity's promotion of Mariel Hemingway as star and the relative length of screen time each character occupied. Lesbian feminist reviewers consistently referred to Patrice

Donnelly's performance as convincingly "lesbian" and pleasurable to identify with, reinterpreting Donnelly as the appropriate "object of desire" against the pressbook's [promotional material's] and dominant media reviews' contextualization of Mariel Hemingway as appropriate object of heterosexual desire. (193)

In their interpretations of the film, however, lesbian feminist reviewers go only so far: they "stopped short of rearranging the film's chronological order, severing or rearranging cause-effect relationships in the narrative, and changing who does what in the narrative" (195).[5]

Critical Approaches

As film gained in popularity and status throughout the twentieth century, people with different backgrounds and ways of thinking developed different critical approaches, which are related ideas on how to interpret texts. To help explain and analyze an individual film or group of films, a viewer might use concepts from one critical approach or different concepts from various critical approaches. For example, a viewer with knowledge of Marxist theory (and Soviet **ideology**) could point out that Eisenstein's film (*Battleship*) *Potemkin* (1925) extols the masses in their struggles with the ruling class. Thus, the ship's officers are represented as cruel and indifferent to the sailors' plight (Figure 11.20). Like the ship's officers, the ship's priest also

ideology: The fundamental beliefs and values of a society or social group.

---

[5]Ellsworth provides a list of the sources for the lesbian feminist reviews in footnote 4 on p. 196 of *Issues in Feminist Film Criticism*. For further illustrations of how sexual orientation may affect viewer thinking about a film, including interpretations of meanings, see the documentary films *The Celluloid Closet* (1996) and "Jodie: An Icon" (1998) and the book *Flaming Classics: Queering the Film Canon* by Alexander Doty, which is described in the "For Further Reading" section at the end of this chapter.

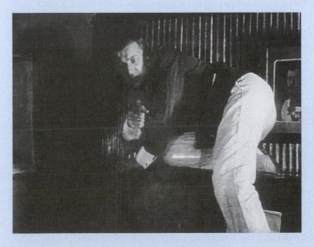

FIGURE 11.20 Film interpreted as Marxist story
Eisenstein's (*Battleship*) *Potemkin* (1925) is set during the 1905 uprisings in Russia. Sailors on the *Potemkin* are so mistreated by their officers that they eventually revolt. Seen here is a Russian naval officer atop a western European piano (a Schroder) firing a pistol at the rebelling sailors. In the background can be glimpsed a photograph of the reigning tsar, a reminder that the naval officer is part of the tsarist power structure oppressing the workers. *Goskino; Image Entertainment DVD*

indirectly supports the oppressive status quo. A Marxist critical approach also helps one understand why *Potemkin* has no individual heroes—because the film celebrates the masses, not the individual.

Many types of critical approaches have been used to interpret films. Formalist criticism, neoformalist criticism, and cognitive film theory all focus on the text and viewers' responses to qualities the viewers perceive in it. Other approaches focus more on the relationship between the text and the world beyond it. Such contextual approaches include Marxist criticism, psychoanalytic criticism, feminist criticism, genre criticism, cultural studies, reception theory (which examines how historical conditions affect how groups interpret texts at different times and in different places), queer theory, and auteur theory.

Let us briefly consider a critical approach that is very limited in its scope but has been more widely used than any other: **auteur theory**, the belief that some filmmakers, usually directors, function as the dominant creators of films and that the auteur's films embody recurrent structures, techniques, and meanings (*auteur* is a French word meaning "author" or "creator"). Let's look at an example of auteur theory applied to film analysis. By analyzing the films directed by Howard Hawks, critic Robin Wood helps his readers understand aspects of one film in the context of other Hawksian movies. Of the main female character in the western *Rio Bravo* (1959), Wood writes,

> Feathers is the product of the union of her basic "type"—the saloon girl—and the Hawks woman, sturdy and independent yet sensitive and vulnerable, the equal of any man yet not in the least masculine. The tension between background (convention) and foreground (actual character) is nowhere more evident. We are very far here from the brash "entertainer" with a heart of gold who dies (more often than not) stopping a bullet intended for the hero. Angie Dickinson's marvelous performance gives us the perfect embodiment of the Hawksian woman, intelligent, resilient, and responsive. There is a continual sense of a woman who really grasps what is important to her. One is struck by the . . . beauty of a living individual responding spontaneously to every situation from a secure centre of self. It is not so much a matter of characterisation as the communication of a life-quality (a much rarer thing). What one most loves about Hawks, finally, is the aliveness of so many of his people. (42)

All applications of critical approaches have their advantages and limitations. The auteur approach works best with directors who exercise strong creative control, such as Hawks, Stanley Kubrick, Alfred Hitchcock, Ingmar Bergman, Federico Fellini, and Gus Van Sant. For some films—such as *Gone with the Wind* (1939) and *The Wizard of Oz* (1939)—it is difficult to assign an auteur because so many people were involved in the productions in major ways. Many movies—especially most American **studio era** movies of the 1930s, 1940s, and 1950s and most animated feature films—are more the product of a studio or production company than

studio (era): The period of U.S. film history from the 1920s to the 1950s during which large studios used a factory-style system to make movies.

of any individual. During the big studio era from the 1920s to the 1950s, Warner Bros. movies were often about current social problems, such as organized urban crime during the Prohibition era, and were presented in a way that viewers thought of as true to life. MGM movies tended to be lighter, both literally and figuratively, and include the upbeat, big-budget musicals. In recent years, the auteur theory for interpreting films has lost some of its popularity because critics and scholars have decided that the qualities shared by films of the same auteur are not the only aspects to be considered in interpreting films. Those qualities are also not always clearly only the auteur's contributions (see "Credit Where Credit Is Due" on pp. 5–6). Then, too, since the birth of the auteur theory, **film theorists** have come to emphasize contexts other than additional films directed by the same person. Many film theorists now stress the types of contexts discussed in Chapter 10—for example, social attitudes, political climate, and changes in filmmaking or media technology—as factors shaping a film's subjects and **style** and downplay the contributions of individual filmmakers.[6]

> **film theorist:** A person who formulates a general explanation of the film medium or part of the medium.

Because critics have different sorts of knowledge of a film's subjects, different backgrounds, and different ways of interpreting texts, a text is subject to many different readings. Let's consider just one example. Many people in many times and places have written about *The Wizard of Oz* (see Plates 29–30 in Chapter 2) and have come up with a wide variety of readings. Some place the film within its historical and economic context and point out that Miss Gulch is from a rich family and is a cruel "witch" both in Kansas and in Oz, an aspect of the film that may be seen as a criticism of rich people during the depths of the American Depression. Compared with critics using other critical tools, a feminist critic might be more likely to stress that in *Oz* the real power is in the women—the witches and Dorothy—and that the men are weak and ineffectual. One student of yoga takes a third, very different approach to analyzing the film: "Looked at symbolically, Dorothy's search has all the elements of a classic yogic journey: the yearning, the quest, the obstacles along the way, the help available for sincere seekers and, finally, discovering the knowledge within to find the way home" (Dhaliwal 51). Many other readings have been advanced. In a wide-ranging ten-page article, novelist and essayist Salman

> **style:** The way that subjects are represented in a text, such as a film.

---

[6]For more information about auteur theory and other critical approaches used in some film journals and some film courses, see J. Dudley Andrew's *The Major Film Theories: An Introduction*; Tim Bywater and Thomas Sobchack's *An Introduction to Film Criticism: Major Critical Approaches to Narrative Film*; Marshall Cohen and Leo Braudy's *Film Theory and Criticism: Introductory Readings*, 6th ed.; Bill Nichols, ed., *Movies and Methods*, vols. 1–2; R. Barton Palmer's *Introduction to the Cinematic Text: Methods and Approaches*; Robert Lapsley and Michael Westlake's *Film Theory: An Introduction*, 2nd ed.; Robert Stam's *Film Theory: An Introduction*; John Hill and Pamela Church Gibson's *Film Studies: Critical Approaches*; and Patrick Phillips's *Understanding Film Texts: Meaning and Experience*.

Rushdie draws on his experiences as a child in India and as a parent to argue that

> . . . "The Wizard of Oz" is a film whose driving force is the inadequacy of adults, even of good adults; a film that shows us how the weakness of grownups forces children to take control of their own destinies, and so, ironically, grow up themselves. (93)

Rushdie concludes his article,

> In the place from which I began [India], after all, I watched the film from the child's—Dorothy's—point of view. I experienced, with her, the frustration of being brushed aside by Uncle Henry and Auntie Em, busy with their dull grownup counting. Like all adults, they couldn't focus on what was really important: namely, the threat to Toto. I ran away with her and then ran back. Even the shock of discovering that the Wizard was a humbug was a shock I felt as a child, a shock to the child's faith in adults. Perhaps, too, I felt something deeper, something I couldn't then articulate; perhaps some half-formed suspicion about grownups was being confirmed.
>
> Now, as I look at the movie again, I have become the fallible adult. Now I am a member of the tribe of imperfect parents who cannot listen to their children's voices. I, who no longer have a father, have become a father instead. Now it is my fate to be unable to satisfy the longings of a child. And this is the last and most terrible lesson of the film: that there is one final, unexpected rite of passage. In the end, ceasing to be children, we all become magicians without magic, exposed conjurers, with only our simple humanity to get us through.
>
> We are the humbugs now. (103)

 For examples of different viewers' thoughts about one film, see Close-Up: Thinking about *The Truman Show* on pp. 543–45.

In diverse societies, it's impossible to find a consensus on the meanings of a text. Meanings differ from group to group even during the same period and in the same general place. This view is confirmed by scholar Barbara Klinger's study of the changing critical reception to films directed by Douglas Sirk—such as *Magnificent Obsession* (1954), *All That Heaven Allows* (1955), *Written on the Wind* (1957), *Tarnished Angels* (1958), and *Imitation of Life* (1959). Academic critics of the same time and culture, for example, are likely to see many of the same or similar meanings, whereas review journalists of the same era are likely to see other meanings. Different **interpretive communities**—groups of people with common interests and a broadly shared outlook who tend to generate similar meanings from a text—also tend to make different meanings from the same text. In addition, meanings differ from time to time within the same group. Klinger, for example, found that more recent reviewers interpret Sirk's movies quite differently than did the reviewers in the 1950s. After examining films directed by Sirk and reactions to them over a nearly forty-year period by various groups, Professor Klinger concludes: "There has been nothing stable about the meaning of his melodramas; they have been subject at every cultural turn to the particular *use* to which various institutions and social circumstances put them. In this process, meaning itself becomes something we cannot determine 'once and for all' but a volatile, essentially *cultural* phenomenon that shifts with the winds of time" (159). There is also much diversity of meanings on the individual level. Even two students with similar backgrounds and similar outlooks who are living at the same time and place may very well formulate dissimilar meanings. And the same person experiencing the same text years later—whether *King Kong* or Shakespeare's *King Lear*—usually makes additional meanings or different ones, or both.

Although there are always varying interpretations of the same film, not all interpretations are based on relevant textual details or are persuasively argued. For all films, a wide range of plausible meanings is possible, but some meanings are indefensible. If a viewer does not think carefully about the interpretation and support an explanation of it with examples from the film, the meanings advanced may be nothing more than unsubstantiated opinions. In short, what is most illuminating and persuasive to readers and listeners are reasoned and supported arguments, not mere statements of beliefs, no matter how forcefully made.

Developing meanings and explaining them to others are deep-rooted human needs. In developing meanings, we clarify our own understanding. Interpretations of meaning may reveal our knowledge of a film's subjects, our backgrounds, and the critical approaches we favor. Interpretations may also disclose or suggest the historical time and place in which we live; or they may be symptomatic of a time and place. Understanding meanings and how they are derived can help us realize when a film tries to manipulate us unduly—as in propagandistic films—or when a film demeans a gender choice, ethnic group, religion, nation, or some other entity. Perhaps especially in societies where citizens need to be informed, critical of orthodoxy, and tolerant of the diversity of people, ideas, and lifestyles, we viewers benefit from training in discovering and questioning meanings in films and other texts.

CLOSE-UP: THE SIGNIFICANCE OF "ROSEBUD" (STUDENT ESSAY)

by Don Reed

A delicate crystal globe rests in the massive hand of Charles Foster Kane. Inside the globe a tiny house is lost in an eternal blizzard. We see Kane's lips move. We hear him utter a single word: "Rosebud." The sphere slips from his grasp and falls to the floor. As it shatters, Charles Foster Kane—millionaire, newspaperman, builder of castles—dies, and the secret of Rosebud dies with him.

Who or what was Rosebud? What could be so important that it would occupy the final thoughts of one of the world's most important and powerful men? These are central questions in *Citizen Kane*. The audience learns, in the final scenes, that Rosebud was the name of the sled Kane played with as a boy in Colorado. However, by accident or design, the significance of Rosebud was never directly explained in the film.

We can find many possible explanations for the significance of Rosebud. The simplest explanation would attribute it to the random mutterings of a dying mind. Rosebud may also represent the simplicity of Kane's childhood or his lost childhood innocence. However, because of the events occurring in Kane's life at the three times Rosebud appears or is mentioned, I think that the best explanation is that Rosebud represents Kane's helplessness at the hands of fate when he is unable to control the most significant losses in his life: his removal from his family, his wife Susan's departure, and his own death.

The audience sees the sled, Rosebud, for the first time when young Kane is faced with the prospect of being taken from his home and family. He uses the sled as a weapon in an attempt to dissuade Mr. Thatcher, the banker, from taking him away. However, Kane's mother, a power far stronger than Kane's boyhood fury, has already made the decision, and he is helpless to prevent the events that will lead him to so much sorrow.

The other times Rosebud is mentioned, the sled is not actually present. At these times the spirit of Rosebud, the sense of irretrievable loss at the hands of fate, is represented by the glass paperweight. The tiny house surrounded by artificial snow is like the boarding house scene re-created in miniature.

The second time we encounter "Rosebud" is when Kane's selfishness has finally driven his second wife Susan away. Kane attacks her room in a manner similar to his attack upon Thatcher. When he encounters the paperweight, his violence stops and his anger subsides into resignation. The scene from his childhood has apparently reminded him of the earlier instance, and he may realize that he is just as powerless to stop Susan from leaving as he was in stopping his mother from sending him away.

With his dying breath Kane once more speaks the word "Rosebud." He is faced, for the final time, with a situation over which his money and influence give him no control. This time, however, Kane does not fight. Perhaps he now sees the futility of fighting. More likely, he has simply lost the strength and will to fight.

Rosebud appears once more, in the final scene of the film. Overlooked by the reporters, the sled is thrown into an incinerator by a worker simply doing his job. The sight of the small wooden sled burning creates the most powerful image of the entire film. This scene says to me that no man, no matter how rich or powerful, can avoid his fate. And that, I think, is why Rosebud touches us so deeply.

CLOSE-UP: THINKING ABOUT *THE TRUMAN SHOW* (1998)

The Truman Show is about Truman Burbank, a young man who is unaware that he has lived his entire life on a gigantic television soundstage as the subject of a long-running, enormously popular TV show. As the story unfolds, Truman begins to question his life and rebel. The passages below demonstrate some of the different types of thinking about the film.

EXPECTATIONS AND INTERACTIONS

The film starts out with a burst of information, running the delicious risk of disorienting us by providing more data than we can quite absorb. Its first shot is a tight close-up of a man in a beret who looks directly at the camera and goes to the heart of the matter. "We've become bored with watching actors giving us phony emotions. We're tired of pyrotechnics and special effects. While the world he inhabits is in some respects counterfeit, there is nothing faked about Truman. No script, no cue cards. It isn't always Shakespeare, but it's genuine. It's a life."

The speaker is Christof (Ed Harris), later described as the "televisionary" who created *The Truman Show. . . .*

. . . The film is savvy enough to dole out the ramifications and specifics of Truman's situation in artfully spaced doses. Only in bits and pieces do we find out the true dimension of what has been done to Truman, how it has all been managed. —Kenneth Turan

EXPLICIT MEANINGS

There are only a few explicit meanings. Christof explains that "we accept the reality of the world with which we're presented," and he explains several explicit meanings near the end of the film, as when he says to Truman, "You were real. That's what made you so good to watch." —William H. Phillips

IMPLICIT MEANINGS
Filmmaking Techniques

From the outset there's something strange about the place: The squeaky-clean tract houses could have been designed by Disney [see Plate 55 in Chapter 13], the sunsets are so beautiful they're weird, and the town's inhabitants seem larger than life, as if they are characters, even caricatures.

Seahaven is a surreal version of America as America wishes it once was: paradise without the serpent.
—Richard Rayner

Film noir . . . fifty years later . . . looks mannered, and we find no realism worthy of our trust. Every depiction of us needs to be ironic, cool, untouched by conviction or belief. . . . And as we looked for an image that embodied our detachment, our disaffection, we found it in the high-key, undifferentiated gloss of television—a look for those who have given up on the Holy Ghost of believing what they see.

Half a century after the ascendancy of film noir, a new genre may be emerging. Call it film blanc, film lumiere, film fluorescent, film flash, or film deadpan. I like the latter two because they convey the instantaneous oneness of a kind of photography that bombs us with light just to get a picture. It's the kind of light that exists, like climate, on most TV sets and shows: a one-dimensional lighting scheme without depth, shaping, or character; a flood of light that lets you film without having to pause; a light that, with only a little heightening, seems surreal, mad, glaring, and unsettling.

The Truman Show is bathed in such light. What makes this so intriguing is the way it plays off our dependence on and loathing of TV—as if TV had become the base level of visible existence.
—David Thomson

Narrative Meanings

The Truman Show is a crowd pleaser that caters to our horror of totalitarianism, our love of personal freedom, our belief—justified or deluded—that knowledge is a powerful tool and that access to information is a God-given right. I'm not sure if the movie is more disturbing because Truman is a prisoner or because he has been lied to. —Barbara Shulgasser

Pic trades in issues of personal liberty vs. authoritarian control, safe happiness vs. the excitement of chaos, manufactured emotions, the penetration of media to the point where privacy vanishes, and the fascination of fabricated images over plain sight.

—Todd McCarthy

We're asked to believe that it took Truman 30 years to realize he was being watched—that he hadn't noticed in all that time that everyone else in his life was performing, colluding to protect his innocence.

It's an outrageous conceit, but once we've surrendered disbelief (and what great fable doesn't require such a leap?), *The Truman Show* has a lot to say about the way we live—about voyeurism and lockstep consumerism, about media surveillance and lack of privacy.

—Edward Guthmann

The captive of TV isn't Truman, it's the audience. Us. And our love of that captivity, the gobbling of shows—fictional drama or news or sports or politics, but always shows—engulfs us. We used to go to theaters and films; now . . . TV comes to our homes, entwines us. . . . The shows don't have to be dramatic. . . . They need only be shows, life outside transmitted to the TV screen inside.

—Stanley Kauffmann

Truman is living the universal fantasy, in a disease-, disaster-, war- and stress-free environment whose minute-to-minute geniality is beamed on Prozac waves into homes around the world, calming the poor, the elderly, the lonely, and the working classes with images of a life running its course in paradise.

—Jack Matthews

Its premise is a legitimate one: the shock and violent internal crisis undergone by an individual beginning to see his world for the first time, *really* see it, really see *through* it. A smiling face might suddenly suggest hidden malice, a cozy street complacency, and even suffocation. This is not paranoia, but the beginning of knowledge.

—David Walsh

Symbols

In a deft, ironic touch, even Truman Burbank's name simultaneously evokes both reality (true-man) and unreality (Burbank, Calif., of course, home to many a TV and movie studio).

—Michael O'Sullivan

In his power and special position, Christof [see Plate 56 in Chapter 13], as his name suggests, is somewhat Christ-like. In other ways, Christof is a god who restricts his subject's free will, nearly kills him, and finally implores him to continue in his role. Christof also symbolizes a strong-willed TV director-writer with an increasingly unpredictable subject, father figure to a rebellious son, and tyrant whose police force helps keep the subject ignorant and in line.

—William H. Phillips

UNIVERSAL OR SYMPTOMATIC MEANINGS

Would anyone care to guess how many TV shows routinely violate the privacy of ordinary people—often by invitation? Add up the day-time talk tabloids, then factor in all the cops-in-action shows, the seemingly endless supply of the world's funniest home videos. What does this tell us about ourselves, and how we choose to spend our time?

At a certain level, this is the central question in . . . *The Truman Show*.

—Stephan Magcosta

The accelerating blurring of news and entertainment, of real and simulated violence, of authentic history and landscape with screen and theme-park fictionalizations: they're all part of Truman's all too eerily familiar world. So is the passivity of an audience that, as Bill Gates has promised, will someday never have to leave its armchairs.

—Frank Rich

WORKS CITED

Guthmann, Edward. "Remote Control Jim Carrey Is a Born TV Star in *The Truman Show*." *San Francisco Chronicle* 5 June 1998: C1.

Kauffmann, Stanley. "Caught in the Act." *New Republic* 29 June 1998: 22.

Magcosta, Stephan. "Must-See TV: *The Truman Show*." 18 July 1998 (no longer available online).

Matthews, Jack. "He Doesn't Know His World's a Stage." 18 July 1998 (no longer available online).

McCarthy, Todd. "The Truman Show." 18 July 1998 (online).

O'Sullivan, Michael. "*Truman:* A Surreally Big Show." *Washington Post* 5 June 1998, Weekend: N58.

Rayner, Richard. "The Truman Show." *Harper's Bazaar* June 1998: 92.

Rich, Frank. "Prime Time Live." *New York Times* 23 May 1998, nat'l. ed.: A25.

Shulgasser, Barbara. "Carrey Rings True in *The Truman Show.*" *San Francisco Examiner* 5 June 1998 (online).

Thomson, David. "The Truman Show." *Esquire* May 1998: 46.

Turan, Kenneth. "His Show of Shows." *Los Angeles Times* 5 June 1998, Calendar: F1.

Walsh, David. "*The Truman Show:* Further Signs of Life in Hollywood." *World Socialist Web Site* 15 June 1998. 27 May 2001 (online).

SUMMARY

This chapter considers some of the ways viewers think about films. As viewers see a film, they interact with it by revising their expectations, responding to clues set forth, guessing about causes or consequences, and readjusting their hypotheses about what might happen or why something happened. As viewers see a film and usually even more so after they have seen the film, they may consider the film's explicit meanings and formulate and sometimes reformulate implicit or implied meanings. Certain explicit and implicit meanings are found in texts from many societies (universal); other meanings may be symptomatic of the society that nurtured the film's creation. Many factors may influence how viewers think about films, including viewers' previous knowledge of the film or of a subject in the film, their backgrounds, and critical approaches they use in analyzing the film.

Viewers' Expectations and Interactions

- Before viewers see a film, they have certain expectations based perhaps on the film's title, the stars, the director, the film's rating, some advertising, a Web site, or a review, all of which create expectations—sometimes misleading ones.

- As viewers watch a film, they interact with it, revising their expectations, responding to clues set forth, guessing, readjusting their hypotheses about what might happen or why something happened, and consequently experiencing puzzlement or clarity and feeling excitement and pleasure, disappointment, boredom, or some other response.

Types of Meanings Found or Formulated

In this book, *meaning* refers to a generalization about a subject.

EXPLICIT MEANINGS

- Explicit meanings are generalizations included in a text about one or more of its subjects. They are present more often in documentary films than in fictional films or experimental films.

- Fictional films that include more than a few explicit meanings are sometimes thought of as flawed in Western societies because modern audiences in the West generally expect movies to suggest, not tell or explain, their meanings.

- An explicit meaning is not necessarily comprehensive or persuasive, and it is not the definitive word on any of the film's subjects.

IMPLICIT MEANINGS

- An implicit meaning is a generalization that a person makes about a text (such as a film) or a subject in a text.

- As Part One of this book shows, a film's mise en scène, cinematography, editing, and sound can suggest or reinforce meanings.

- Narrative itself is a major source of implicit meanings because viewers often infer some general implications of a story. For example, popular movies often present improbable but reassuring stories that show people overcoming overwhelming adversity and achieving their goals. In formulating implicit meanings in a nonnarrative documentary film, viewers generalize about the film's representation of its factual subjects.

- A narrative or some aspect of it may be ambiguous or unknowable: it is open to two or more plausible interpretations perhaps because it provides conflicting information or withholds significant information.

- Filmmakers and other makers of texts may create symbols: anything perceptible that has significance beyond its usual meaning or function. Usually symbols go unexplained in a film, and viewers interpret them variously, although not all interpretations are equally persuasive.

UNIVERSAL MEANINGS AND SYMPTOMATIC MEANINGS

- A universal meaning is an explicit or implicit meaning in a text that could be found in the texts of many societies. For example, many texts in many societies state or imply that "crime does not pay."

- Knowledge of the society where a film was made helps viewers discover symptomatic meanings: generalizations about a text or part of a text that are characteristic of the society that nurtured the film. For example, popular American movies are permeated with the symptomatic meaning that dedicated, industrious individuals can influence the outcome of important events. This meaning, which is stated or implied in so many American movies, is symptomatic of much of American society but not of certain other nations, such as Japan and China.

Influences on the Ways We Think about Films

- Many factors may influence the meanings a person perceives in a text. Viewers' knowledge of the film or of a subject in the film may influence their thinking about the film. The meanings people find in a text also are influenced by their backgrounds, such as their political views and sexual orientation. And the critical approaches that viewers use when analyzing texts will influence their thinking about a film.

- Meanings reflect the time and place where a viewer lives and perhaps the interpretive community to which the viewer belongs. Not all interpretations are well thought out or persuasive.

Major Terms about Thinking about Films

Below, numbers in italics refer to the pages where the terms are explained. All terms are defined in more detail in the Illustrated Glossary beginning on p. 667.

ambiguity *517*
auteur theory *538*
critical approach *537*
cutting continuity script *534*
explicit meaning *511*
film theorist *539*
ideology *537*
implicit meaning *513*

interpretive community *540*
reading (def. 3) *520*
representation *511*
symbol *525*
symptomatic meaning *530*
trailer *506*
universal meaning *529*

QUESTIONS ABOUT THINKING ABOUT FILMS

The following questions are intended to help viewers understand ways they respond to films. Not all the questions are appropriate for every film. In thinking out, discussing, and writing responses to the questions most appropriate for the film being examined, be careful to stick with the issues the questions raise, to answer all parts of the questions, to explain the reasons for your answers, and to give specific examples from the film.

1. What were your expectations before the film began? What were the sources of your expectations? What developments in the film required

you to readjust your expectations and hypotheses about the plot or some other aspect of the film as you watched the film?

2. Does the film include any explicit meanings? If so, what are they? Are they necessary, or could viewers have figured out those meanings on their own?

3. Where do filmmaking techniques suggest or reinforce implicit meanings?

4. What implicit meanings does the narrative itself suggest?

5. Is any aspect of the film ambiguous or unknowable? If so, explain.

6. What fantasies does the film embody? Does the film blend elements of realism and fantasy? If so, explain.

7. Does the film have any symbols? What meaning(s) do they suggest? Why do you say so?

8. If the film has universal meanings, what are they?

9. If you know the conditions that were prevalent at the time and place the film was made, do you detect any symptomatic meanings in the film? If so, explain.

10. How might knowledge of a source for the film influence your thinking about the film? How might your knowledge of a subject *in* the film influence how you think about the film?

11. How might a person's sexual orientation, political persuasion, or nationality influence that person's interpretation of the film? Please explain in some detail.

12. What critical approach(es) might be used to analyze the film?

WORKS CITED

Alexie, Sherman (author and scriptwriter of *Smoke Signals*). Telephone interview. 13 June 2000.

Baldick, Chris. *The Concise Oxford Dictionary of Literary Terms*. New York: Oxford UP, 1990.

"*Barbershop* Controversy Boils Over." *Associated Press* 28 Sept. 2002.

Bordwell, David. *Making Meaning: Inference and Rhetoric in the Interpretation of Cinema*. Cambridge: Harvard UP, 1989.

The Citizen Kane Book: Raising Kane, by Pauline Kael, The Shooting Script, by Herman J. Mankiewicz and Orson Welles, and the Cutting Continuity of the Completed Film. Boston: Little, Brown, 1971.

Dhaliwal, Hardeep. "The Wizard of Om." *Ascent* 23 (Fall 2004): 46–51.

Ellsworth, Elizabeth. "Illicit Pleasures: Feminist Spectators and *Personal Best*." *Wide Angle* 8.2 (1986): 45–56. Reprinted in *Issues in Feminist Film Criticism*. Ed. Patricia Erens. Bloomington: Indiana UP, 1990. 183–96.

Glueck, Grace. "How Jews Shaped Show Business, and Vice Versa." *New York Times on the Web* 28 Feb. 2003, late ed., final: E44.

Hessler, Peter. Interview. *Fresh Air*. Nat'l. Public Radio. 5 Feb. 2001.

Hoberman, J., and Jeffrey Shandler, eds. *Entertaining America: Jews, Movies, and Broadcasting*. Princeton: Princeton UP, 2003.

Johnston, Sheila. "Interview: Masayuki Suo." *The Observer* (England) 10 May 1998: 7+.

Klinger, Barbara. *Melodrama and Meaning: History, Culture, and the Films of Douglas Sirk*. Bloomington: Indiana UP, 1994.

Laurents, Arthur (screenwriter). "Interview." *The Celluloid Closet*. Columbia TriStar DVD, 2001.

Maslin, Janet. "Is It Unexpected? Is It Strange? It's Here." *New York Times* 28 Jan. 1995, nat'l. ed.: 11.

Murphy, Kevin. *A Year at the Movies: One Man's Filmgoing Odyssey*. New York: Harper, 2002.

Rushdie, Salman. "Out of Kansas." *The New Yorker*. 11 May 1992: 93–103.

Sternberg, Meir. *Expositional Modes and Temporal Ordering in Fiction*. Baltimore: Johns Hopkins UP, 1978.

White, Susan. "Split Skins: Female Agency and Bodily Mutilation in *The Little Mermaid*." *Film Theory Goes to the Movies*. Ed. Jim Collins, Hilary Radner, and Ava Preacher Collins. New York: Routledge, 1993. 182–95.

Wood, Robin. *Howard Hawks*. Garden City, NY: Doubleday, 1968.

FOR FURTHER READING

Although film theory helps us understand the film medium, some writings are frustrating for students to read because of their involved sentence structure and the writers' heavy use of jargon. The books listed here, however, should prove accessible to many beginning film students.

Andrew, J. Dudley. *The Major Film Theories: An Introduction*. New York: Oxford UP, 1976. Includes an explanation of what film theory entails and a discussion of major film theories: early theorists, realist film theory, and contemporary French film theory.

Approaches to Popular Film. Ed. Joanne Hollows and Mark Jancovich. Manchester, Eng.: Manchester UP, 1995. Eight essays on different critical approaches for doing film analyses.

BFI Film Classics and *BFI Modern Classics*. London: BFI. Two series of short books published by the British Film Institute, each devoted to one film and written by a film critic, film scholar, or novelist. Sample *BFI Film Classics* titles examine *Belle de Jour*, *Blackmail*, *Bonnie and Clyde*, *The Blue Angel*, *Pather Panchali*, and *Vertigo*. Sample titles in the *BFI Modern Classics* series are *Blade Runner*, *Blue Velvet*, *L.A. Confidential*, *Eyes Wide Shut*, *Do the Right Thing*, *Trainspotting*, *Independence Day*, and *Amores Perros*.

Bywater, Tim, and Thomas Sobchack. *Introduction to Film Criticism: Major Critical Approaches to Narrative Film.* New York: Longman, 1989. Includes discussions of major ways to analyze films; sample student papers; a chronology of film reviewing, criticism, and theory; and a glossary.

Cambridge Film Handbooks. Ed. Andrew Horton. Cambridge: Cambridge UP. A series of books, each focused on one film from a variety of theoretical, critical, and contextual perspectives and consisting of essays by film scholars and critics, a filmography, and a bibliography. Sample titles are *Bonnie and Clyde*, *Persona*, *The Wild Bunch*, *The Discreet Charm of the Bourgeoisie*, *Sherlock Jr.*, *Tokyo Story*, *Do the Right Thing*, the *Godfather* trilogy, and *Fargo*.

Carson, Diane, Linda Dittmar, and Janice R. Welsch, eds. *Multiple Voices in Feminist Film Criticism.* Minneapolis: U of Minnesota P, 1994. A collection of mostly theoretical essays, most for the advanced student.

Close Viewings: An Anthology of New Film Criticism. Ed. Peter Lehman. Tallahassee: Florida State UP, 1990. Part 1 emphasizes formal analysis; Part 2, cultural analysis; Part 3, an essay, applies many forms of criticism to one film, *The Searchers*.

Critical Dictionary of Film and Television Theory. Ed. Roberta Pearson and Philip Simpson. New York: Routledge, 2001. Includes over 400 entries ranging from 500 to 3,000 words each. Sample entries are for *continuity editing*, *film noir*, *mise en scène*, *narrative*, and *western*. Also included are suggestions for further reading, cross-references, and an index.

Doty, Alexander. *Flaming Classics: Queering the Film Canon.* New York: Routledge, 2000. The author argues against the assumption that only explicitly gay films are subject to gay readings and examines six classic films—including *The Cabinet of Dr. Caligari*, *The Wizard of Oz*, and the original *Psycho*—for their gay potential.

The Film Cultures Reader. Ed. Graeme Turner. New York: Routledge, 2002. Focuses on film as a social and cultural practice and on the relationship between cinema and popular culture. Six thematic sections: "Understanding Film," "Technologies," "Industries," "Meanings and Pleasures," "Identities," and "Audiences and Consumption."

Greenberg, Harvey Roy. *Screen Memories: Hollywood Cinema on the Psychoanalytic Couch.* New York: Columbia UP, 1993. Film criticism from a psychoanalytic perspective.

Lane, Christina. *Feminist Hollywood: From* Born in Flames *to* Point Break. Detroit: Wayne State UP, 2000. Includes original interviews with women directors and close analyses of their films.

Litch, Mary. *Philosophy through Film.* New York: Routledge, 2002. Nine chapters organized into four parts: "Knowledge and Truth," "Minds, Bodies, and Persons," "Ethics and Moral Responsibility," and "Philosophy, Religion, and the Meaning of Life."

Lyden, John C. *Film as Religion: Myths, Morals, and Rituals.* New York: New York UP, 2003. Part 1 explains generally and Part 2 demonstrates specifically how film can convey beliefs and values and have ritual power to provide emotional catharsis.

Miles, Margaret R. *Seeing and Believing: Religion and Values in the Movies.* Boston: Beacon, 1996. Examines what popular films of the 1980s and 1990s say and suggest about religion and values. Essays are divided into two groups: "Religion in Popular Film" and "Race, Gender, Sexuality, and Class in Popular Film."

The Political Companion to American Film. Ed. Gary Crowdus. Chicago: Lake View, 1994. Includes essays on filmmakers, genres, racial and ethnic representations, and social characterizations (such as of politicians). Many essays discuss the implicit and symptomatic political meanings (broadly defined) of specific films. Includes a short bibliography after most of the essays.

Salt, Barry. *Film Style and Technology: History and Analysis*. 2nd ed. London: Starword, 1992. Both a critique of much of current film theory and a history of film technology and analysis of its impact on film style.

Sprengnether, Madelon. *Crying at the Movies: A Film Memoir*. Saint Paul, MN: Graywolf, 2002. In each chapter, the author describes a film, her emotional reactions to it, the parallels to her life, and the understanding of herself that she gained.

Tan, Ed S. *Emotion and the Structure of Narrative Film: Film as an Emotion Machine*. Mahwah, NJ: Erlbaum, 1996. A theoretical study of a largely neglected subject with emphasis on the traditional feature film. Sample chapter titles: "The Psychological Functions of Film Viewing," "Thematic Structures and Interest," and "Character Structures, Empathy, and Interest."

Trosman, Harry. *Contemporary Psychoanalysis and Masterworks of Art and Film*. New York: New York UP, 1996. Demonstrates how classical and contemporary psychoanalytic thought can be used to enrich one's understanding and appreciation of paintings and of films such as *Citizen Kane*, *Vertigo*, and *8 1/2*.

Part Five

WRITING ABOUT FILMS

T ALKING ABOUT A FILM WITH OTHERS can help us work out our own interpretation. Reading reviews and blogs may also help us understand a film. But the surest way to clarify and deepen our understanding and appreciation of a film is to write (and rewrite) about it. Writing poses one of the greatest challenges to the human mind — but has the potential to produce one of life's greatest rewards. Writing is time-consuming and often enough frustrating. But even in our high-tech age, writing remains indispensable for understanding a subject, remembering it, and conveying that understanding to others with some precision and permanence — or, at least, with less imprecision and impermanence. Hence the subject of Part Five: "Writing about Films." Chapter 12 provides class-tested tips on reading and writing about films. Chapter 13 presents a sample description and analysis of an entire film, *The Player*. The chapter

◀ *The Player* (1992) begins with a famous opening shot that runs more than eight minutes. Here, the camera looks into the office of the main character, Griffin Mill (right) as he hears a scriptwriter's pitch or brief summary of a proposed film. In watching the opening of this film and writing about it, you probably will notice details that viewers often take for granted, and you likely will notice some general characteristics. In this example, writing and rewriting are more likely to make you realize that the opening introduces most of the film's major characters and reveals the nature of Mill's job and the two threats to his well-being. Writing about this opening might also help you notice the wealth and status of those involved in studio moviemaking and the rapid pace of footsteps and words during a studio workday. Writing and rewriting about this part of *The Player* or about any film or any aspect of a film can help you sort out your thoughts and deepen your understanding and appreciation. Write carefully and your readers will be informed and pleased, too. *Avenue Pictures Productions; New Line Home Video DVD* illustrates what is possible when students of the film medium apply the terms, information, and concepts explained in this book to a single film.

Links to a variety of sources, including supplementary readings and short films, are available for each chapter on the Web site for this book at <bedfordstmartins.com/phillips-film>.

CHAPTER 12

Reading and Writing about Films

Having taught various writing courses during my career as a university professor — composition, business writing, and introductory creative writing (short stories and short scripts) — and having done some writing myself, I am more convinced than ever about the accuracy of the saying that reading and writing are like breathing out and breathing in. They are part of the same process: someone who writes well is invariably a good reader, and someone who reads and reads well is nearly always a good writer. Conversely, those who have read little or who read inefficiently — or both — write papers that perplex and frustrate their readers. The relationship of reading and writing may be visualized this way:

$$\text{Reading} \longleftrightarrow \text{Writing.}$$

Experienced teachers will tell you that they can read a page or two of a student's writing and know whether the student is a good reader or not.

This chapter is very much about writing about films, but necessarily it also says something about reading efficiently and about another closely related topic: writing definitions. The chapter concludes with two sample student film essays (for others, see pp. 105–7, 184–85, 247–48, 352–53, and 542) and with an annotated bibliography for the beginning film student.

READING TIPS

Different types of readings make different demands on readers. For example, for most of us, reading an e-mail from a friend is a simple and straightforward activity, but making sense of a contract that will affect our emotional and financial well-being for years to come requires closer reading. For each important reading task, follow the advice of reading specialists and preread, read, then reread. Don't simply pick up the material, read it, then set it aside. And don't just trust your memory and hope for the best.

Preread

Prereading consists of all the steps you take before reading the selection for the first time. These steps may take 5 to 10 minutes, but they will help you get much more out of the reading the first time you read it and usually will prove to be an exceptionally good investment of your valuable time:

- Consider the significance of the title.
- If there is a table of contents, examine it to see how what you are reading fits into the text as a whole.
- Read the first paragraph (and perhaps the second) and the last paragraph to see if you can discover the main point and the conclusion.
- Examine the headings and subheadings (to find out the major topics).
- Read the summary or abstract (if one is included).
- Read the study questions (if any are included).

Read

To discover the assignment's main points, the structure of the assignment, and the supporting points, during the first reading it is crucial that you read without long interruptions. As you read,

- mark (underline) important passages or take *brief* notes on a sheet of paper,
- write *brief* comments and questions in the margins or on a sheet of paper,
- draw lines between related or contrasted points,
- circle key words, and
- mark words you don't understand thus far, perhaps with a hyphen (-) or an asterisk (*) in the margin.

Your goals during the first reading should be to

- read the selection without any long interruptions,
- figure out for whom the author is writing,
- discover the purpose(s) of the writing,
- identify the structure of the piece, and
- grasp the main points.

Reread

Rereading helps readers understand and remember the material in ways that simply reading and quickly reviewing cannot.

- Reread passages that you don't fully understand, or reread the entire selection.

- Make certain you understand the structure of the selection: its main points and their arrangement. If a chapter has three major headings (or has no headings but clearly has three major parts), what are they? How do they support the purpose(s) of the entire selection? Why are the three topics presented in the order in which they appear?

- Sometimes you can figure out the meaning of an unknown word if you encounter it at several places in the reading. But if that is not possible, use a dictionary and write the definitions in the margins.

- Study all the passages that you marked. Study your marginal notes, and rewrite and expand them as necessary.

- Study the summary (if one is included), or write and rewrite your own summary of the selection, or outline the selection, or write a list of sentences summarizing the main points.

- Read any study questions and try to answer them, preferably in writing.

You probably have run across most of those tips before. If you're not already using them, why aren't you?

WRITING DEFINITIONS

Understanding definitions—and knowing how to write them—can help you both read and write with greater skill. Knowing the meanings of the terms used in political science, calculus, music, or any other subject helps one understand the subject more completely. Writing and rewriting the entries in the glossary for this book helped me understand the material much more completely than if I had never written (and rewritten and rewritten) the glossary.

To write a definition, begin by indicating the category that the object or idea being defined belongs to. After that, indicate what differentiates the term from other members of the same category. We'll apply this strategy to the term *lap dissolve*:

> **lap dissolve**: A transition between shots in which one shot begins to fade out as the next shot fades in, overlapping the first shot before replacing it.

A lap dissolve is a transition between shots, but it is not the only such transition. Wipes, fade-outs, and fade-ins also are transitions between shots. The definition must indicate what distinguishes a lap dissolve from all other transitions between shots. (The difference is that in a lap dissolve one shot begins to fade out as the next shot fades in, overlapping the first shot before replacing it.)

To write a definition, the first step you need to take is to assign the term to the correct category. Compare "a lap dissolve is a transition between shots" with "a lap dissolve is used to. . . ." The former identifies the correct category; the latter does not. How the lap dissolve is used is not the issue right now. The issue is what a lap dissolve *is*.

Do not begin a definition in any of these four ways, either:

1. _____ is when _____ .

2. _____ is where _____ .

3. This is when _____ .

4. This is where _____ .

If the designation of the category is missing, as it is in those four items, or if it is incorrect, the definition is doomed to be wrong. A definition of *Steadicam* that began "A camera. . . ." would be incorrect no matter how you finished the definition. (A Steadicam is a device or mount for holding a camera as the camera operator moves around making shots that are largely free of bouncy movements.)

In every definition, be sure that the category is the same part of speech as the word that you are defining. Be sure to define a noun as a noun and a verb as a verb. For example, do not define the noun *composition* as "to arrange settings, lighting, and subjects within the frame." Your definition of *composition* should begin, "the arrangement of settings. . . ." Similarly, your definition of the verb *mix* should begin with a verb form (an infinitive): "to select sounds. . . ."

After you place the term in the correct category, the next step is to indicate how the term differs from other members of that category. Do not attempt to define a term with only a synonym. For example, writing that an *evaluation* is "an appraisal" would not be helpful to readers with only a fuzzy notion of what *appraisal* means. After you indicate the category and describe what distinguishes the term being defined from other members of the same category, then you might want to include a synonym.

Usually, you do not need to memorize the definitions that you encounter in a textbook. But you do need to understand with some precision what the defined terms mean. If you have trouble getting the hang of definition-writing, practice writing definitions of terms you already know well. For example, here is a possible definition of *automobile:* "a motorized land vehicle that is typically used to convey one person or a few people between locations." Choose your category and distinguishing characteristic carefully, so there are no exceptions to your definition. Supposedly, the ancient Greek philosopher Plato defined *man* as a "featherless biped"—until a rival philosopher brought forth a plucked chicken.

If you have trouble remembering some definitions, you might try making vocabulary cards. On one side of a card or small sheet of paper, write the term and, if it has a difficult or unusual pronunciation, include the pronunciation as well. On the other side of the card or paper, write the following: (1) the definition and (2) two or three sentences that include the term, preferably sentences from the printed source where the term appears. Reviewing the cards at various times for short sessions works well for most students.

WRITING ABOUT FILMS

No one ever has been able to give the exact measure of his needs, his concepts, or his sorrows. The human tongue is like a cracked cauldron on which we beat out tunes to set a bear dancing when we would make the stars weep with our melodies. (Flaubert 138)

To try to capture in speech the richness and nuances of human experience and thought can be frustrating. It is no easy task to capture them in writing, either, but writing can bring us closer to that goal than speech can. For understanding and communicating about something as complicated as our responses to a film, writing is indispensable.

Nearly everyone knows about the agony of committing words to paper. After all, the writer's job is to create clear and convincing prose that someone else can read without interruption, rereading, or puzzlement—often a stranger, someone who knows nothing about the writer. It is no wonder that effective writing requires much thinking and concentration and tends to be time-consuming.

Most writers find they work most efficiently if they keep their work sessions short and alternate periods of work with rest or some other very different activity, such as physical exercise. They also know there's little time to implement this strategy in the last few days before an assignment is due. Nearly all successful writers divide their work into steps because they know that most writing is too complicated to do well in one sitting or even two.

For convenience, I divide writing into three stages: prewriting, writing (the first complete draft), and rewriting. I say "for convenience" because writing is rarely a 1–2–3 process. It defies formulas and predictions. Some writers may outline their main points (prewrite), write a first draft, then realize the structure is wrong, reorganize their outline, and redo the draft before moving on to rewriting. Other writers develop an effective structure by writing draft after draft (for most writers this is a time-consuming way to discover a useful structure).

A few people can write well by composing and rewriting one page or paragraph or sentence at a laborious time (these people are sometimes called "bleeders"). Probably fewer still compose and revise in their heads, then write and revise slightly. If one of those two approaches works for you, fine; but they probably won't work, and you will find it more useful to divide and conquer your work.

Dividing your work into manageable steps and using the strategies that I explain here will improve your chances of writing well but do not guarantee good writing. Extensive practice in writing (and reading) and much work and persistence are also required.

Prewriting

Here is one of my favorite ways of getting some of my responses to a film into writing. As I view the film, I jot down a few notes. After the viewing, I sometimes write a brief description and always write some observations (analysis). Next I reread and revise what I have written so far. The next day I rewrite my notes, select the main points, and arrange them in a brief outline.

Those are the stages I sometimes go through before I write a first draft. They take time, but they help me gather my thoughts and arrange them. I'm not saying the first draft is then easy for me. Often it is not. But because of the prewriting, the first draft is always less difficult.

Before you begin a first draft, consider the following questions:

- Who are my readers?
- What needs to be explained?
- What does not need to be explained?
- How do I want my readers to react to what I write?

Then try one or more of these strategies:

1. Write and rewrite a thesis statement: a sentence or a few concise sentences that summarize the main and unifying idea of the planned essay and, ideally, explain the major parts and their arrangement.
2. Make an outline.
3. Write a "discovery" draft.

THESIS STATEMENT   A thesis statement early in an essay—often at the end of the first paragraph or the beginning of the second—helps both writer and readers. Notice how the following thesis statement, which appears at the end of the first paragraph of a student essay (p. 247), reveals the purpose and organization of the essay it helps introduce:

> However, despite its reputation for faithfulness, a careful analysis reveals that the film [*The Dead*] is unlike Joyce's novella in three major ways. First, the adaptation expands the scope of the original narrative by adding new scenes. Second, the adaptation deletes important contextual elements from its literary

source. Finally, the adaptation modifies significant dramatic elements in the literary source.

Occasionally you can formulate a thesis statement before making an outline or writing a first draft. Sometimes the thesis statement is so well thought out and detailed that you can write a first draft without first making an outline. Often, however, the thesis emerges more clearly as you work on an outline or a first or second draft. It usually takes time and effort to figure out what you are trying to say, and often you may start out to make one point and end up saying something else. For your essay to be unified and forceful, though, the thesis eventually must step forward and introduce itself or be implied in the introduction and explained in the essay itself. Few students can create a focused, clear, and persuasive essay without stating the thesis; without it, the writer and the readers tend to get lost in a thicket of words before emerging bewildered from page 2.

OUTLINE Outlines are useful for most writers most of the time, especially in writing long essays and books or in writing about a new subject. Sometimes a short outline leads to a more detailed one that turns out to be a partial first draft. Some successful writers, however, never use outlines. Instead they think out the major points and their arrangement, jot notes, or write draft after draft.

DISCOVERY DRAFT Some writers start to organize their material by rapidly writing a draft without pausing to consider spelling and word choices. Then they look at what they have written and perhaps underline the useful parts, perhaps rearrange the draft's major points. Sometimes they toss out that draft and immediately write another one rapidly. This is how some writers get something on paper and start to discover what they have to say.

In outlines and early drafts, leave wide margins on all four sides of your text and double-space. Leave room to improve.

Writing

While writing a first draft, most writers find it best to focus on organization (what are the major topics, and in what order should they be presented?) and on examples (how can I illustrate my points to readers who do not know the subject well, who may misunderstand, or who may disagree with me?). While writing the first draft, don't get sidetracked by spelling, punctuation, or even sentence structure. Like a sculptor, rough out the paragraphs; later, do the finishing work on sentences and words. While you are writing the first draft, fussing over spelling or word choice, pausing to check a punctuation mark, or looking up a word or passage can halt your momentum and perhaps lead to writer's block: the inability to write anything.

In the first draft, try to see that your main points are arranged in a significant order and that they are explained and illustrated. Do not try to rewrite while you write the first draft. Studies of writers show that few can write and rewrite well at the same time.

Rewriting and Rewriting: Some Strategies

What is written without effort is in general read without pleasure.
             —Samuel Johnson

I never write five words but I correct seven. —attributed to Dorothy Parker

There are days when the result is so bad that no fewer than five revisions are required. In contrast, when I'm greatly inspired, only four revisions are needed.   —John Kenneth Galbraith

As you rewrite and rewrite, remember these three indispensable guidelines:

First, studies show that few readers will remember more than five major points in a speech or an essay.

Second, your goal should be to communicate, not to impress. Writers who try to impress readers often stumble and look silly, waste readers' time, and puzzle them. Consider, for example, this sentence: "Another major meaning of Orson Welles's film *Citizen Kane* is that Charles Foster Kane has an abiding and persistent hunger to be loved by others" (25 words). The writer misuses one word (*abiding*) and tries too hard to impress, with wordiness, passive voice, and formal words. In contrast, the writer of the following sentence, one of my former students, was more concerned with communicating: "The third trait to note about Kane is his need for love" (12 words). That sentence is short, is easy to understand, yet says much the same as its longer counterpart. Indeed, this second sentence is more specific: it indicates that the *third* point is next.

Third, if you focus on only one major point in each paragraph and explain it fully, with detailed examples, you will be understood, probably even appreciated. If you jump from generalization to unrelated generalization, especially within the same paragraph, you will not be understood by your unfortunate readers.

Because it is difficult to spot errors in our own writing (we are better at spotting errors in what others write), we writers need to reread our drafts many times and in different ways. Unfortunately, many writers, especially inexperienced ones, reread their drafts once—maybe twice if they want to be thorough!—and they seldom spot what to improve, so they make only a few minor changes, such as in spelling and the use of commas. One or more of the following strategies may help you see more clearly what you have actully written so that you can rewrite and improve it.

1. After you finish the first or second draft, see if each paragraph explains one important point. Choose a paragraph at random, and read it at least twice (once aloud, once silently). Underline the topic sentence or main point of the paragraph. (You may want to use a felt-tip pen so you can quickly spot each topic sentence later.) If a topic sentence is vague or misleading, rewrite it so it explains the main point of the paragraph. If the main point of the paragraph is not stated or clearly implied, write a topic sentence for that paragraph. If you have more than one important point in a paragraph, eliminate unimportant points and develop the main point, or explain each important point in its own paragraph.

    Next, select a different paragraph at random, and once again read it at least twice—once aloud and once silently. See that it has one major point that is fully and clearly explained. Proceed in this way until you have an underlined topic sentence for each paragraph. (Study your paragraphs out of order so that you can sneak up on what you wrote and more likely see each paragraph for what it is.)

    Now that you have underlined the topic sentence of each paragraph, underline the main idea of the essay (the thesis statement) with a double line; then read only the thesis statement and each topic sentence. If any topic sentences do not support the thesis or if the major points do not progress clearly, delete, add, or rearrange; then rewrite.

2. a. Reread your essay aloud at different speeds (rapidly one time, slowly the next). For many writers, reading a draft aloud—one time slowly, the next time rapidly—is the best way to spot weaknesses. They hear weaknesses they could not see.

    b. Read your essay aloud at different times (for instance, once after completing the first draft; once after taking a break; once more the next day).

    c. Reread your essay while looking for an aspect of your writing that has often given you trouble—for instance, reread your draft once for complicated, unclear sentences and at another time reread it for wordiness. If you tend to write incomplete sentences, reread your draft from the end of the essay to the beginning, a sentence at a time.

    d. Ask someone to read the draft aloud but without interruptions or commentary, perhaps as you close your eyes and listen (not recommended after lunch or late in the evening).

3. Another way to see what you have indeed written in each sentence is to read each sentence out of order. Pick up the latest draft; choose a sentence at random; read it twice (once aloud, once silently); then, if necessary, revise it. After you are finished with the sentence, place a check mark at the beginning of it. Repeat the process for every other sentence (out of order). You may be surprised how many weaknesses you can spot and eliminate by using this method.

4. Are any sentences still not right? You've thought about them. You've read them aloud. You've put them aside. But you still frown as you read them. Imagine that you are with a friend, and say aloud what you mean; then write what you just said. Chances are you'll be much closer to writing what you meant all along.

5. Reread your essay and underline or circle every general word; then consider replacing generalities with details from the film. Words like *good*, *great*, *wonderful*, *nice*, *interesting*, and *terrible* can be replaced by specific references to the film. "Vera Miles was great in *The Searchers*" neither communicates much nor convinces a reader who thought she was so-so. Instead, write a paragraph that includes examples from the film. Consider the following: "Vera Miles's Laurie is a complicated character. For example, she is not all patience and sweetness. In the scene where Martin is about to leave for the last time to rescue Debbie, Miles shows vehement and convincing frustration, wrinkling her brow and biting off her words." Although this second description is scarcely a full account of Vera Miles's performance, it is better than the original vague sentence.

   As you are examining your word choices (or diction), you may want to use a thesaurus to find more appropriate or more varied words for some of your sentences. A thesaurus can be helpful, but if used in the wrong way, it can be harmful. It can be helpful if you use it to remind yourself of a word you know well but cannot think of at the moment. It also can be helpful if you use it and a dictionary for words you do not know well. It can be harmful, however, if you simply pluck words off a list in a thesaurus because the words are different or "sound" somehow better. Using just any word in a list of approximate synonyms often results in inappropriate, even laughable, results.

   While you are checking word choices, make sure that when you describe action in a film, you use present-tense verbs. Here is an example from a student essay on *Citizen Kane* from later in this chapter: "Emily, on the other hand, is much more reserved and somber, as if something important is on her mind."

Getting Feedback

Research on writing has confirmed that feedback from others can help writers. However, if you do not follow certain procedures, getting feedback can be of little use and can even be counterproductive.

Find at least one good reader: someone who can read and explain accurately what the material actually says. If you ask someone who is not a good reader to give feedback on what you have written, the results could be disastrous. Show the assignment to your readers, and ask them to read your paper carefully (and at least twice) and tell you (1) what they understand from it and (2) where the paper is unclear or incomplete, or both. Do not tell your readers beforehand what you intended to convey; let your writing speak for itself.

If your readers *evaluate* your writing as excellent, dreadful, or whatever, disregard their evaluations. Your classmates and outside readers are in a weak position to evaluate (or grade) your work: they do not know well the course work out of which the assignment emerged, and they lack training, experience, and perspective to *grade* college-level writing (so do you). If you ignore this advice and accept the evaluation of your writing by others who are unqualified, you may end up frustrated and perhaps in an unnecessary confrontation with your instructor.

Finally, take others' feedback, and rewrite your paper to make it fulfill the assignment more successfully. Do not let readers rewrite for you. And do not let them dictate wording, either. You alone must rewrite (and rewrite) the parts that need improving.

Of course, any rewriting you do or do not do will be your responsibility. For example, if none of your readers notices an important omission from your paper, do not blame them. *You* failed to include the material. You're responsible.

If misused, feedback can hurt your writing. However, if you get a skillful reader and follow these guidelines, the reader's feedback can help you see the weaknesses in your writing and make it possible for you to improve your writing, often considerably. That is why most good writers have at least one good reader to read their drafts and respond to them.

Before you run off that last draft, be sure to consult reference sources, especially a college (not small paperback) dictionary. Some of the dictionaries online are very helpful. For example, you might want to look up words that you rarely use to make sure that you are indeed using them correctly. Remember that computer spelling checkers sometimes miss errors (for instance, if you write *it's* when you mean *its*). Remember, too, that computer "grammar checkers" often miss errors and, worse yet, are often just plain wrong.

Many ineffective writers spend most of their time mired in the first draft, flailing largely helplessly and becoming demoralized. In contrast, effective writers tend to prewrite, divide the task into different work sessions, and spend much more time on rewriting than on writing the first draft.

Few writers do all the steps I suggest, and writers generally do not follow the same steps and same order of steps for every writing task. People are different, and writing is usually complicated. Let me repeat, too, that using the writing strategies I suggest will only improve your chances of writing well. Until you have extensive previous practice in reading critically and writing carefully, you will be limited in how well you can write, no matter what strategies you use. Similarly, even if you know the rules of a sport and follow them when you play it, you cannot play well unless you have worked hard and long at developing your skills. (Skillful coaches help, too.)

To write well about film requires much previous practice in reading and writing, practical strategies (such as some of those discussed above), and patience and persistence. Writing well about anything you care about or enjoy, though, is well worth all the effort, for in writing and rewriting you think and learn, and you can communicate to others with greater precision and permanence than you can any other way. When you write about a film or the film medium, you are unlikely to "make the stars weep" with your melodies, but by writing with care you can somtimes capture some of the magic.

The best writers have the satisfaction of knowing that people of distant times and places may learn from and enjoy their writing. What scientist/teacher/writer Carl Sagan said about ancient books applies as well to all writings that are preserved and read:

> One glance at . . . [a book] and you're inside the mind of another person, maybe somebody dead for thousands of years. Across the millennia an author is speaking clearly and silently inside your head, directly to you. Writing is perhaps the greatest of human inventions, binding together people who never knew each other, citizens of distant epochs. Books break the shackles of time. . . . If information were passed on merely by word of mouth, how little we should know of our own past. How slow would be our progress. Everything would depend on what we had been told, on how accurate the account. Ancient learning might be revered, but in successive retellings it would become muddled and then lost. Books permit us to voyage through time, to tap the wisdom of our ancestors.

Two Sample Student Essays

The following essay was written in response to this assignment:

1. Choose one of the following films: *Princess Mononoke, Citizen Kane, The Godfather Part II, Hamlet* (2000), *This is Spinal Tap, Y tu mamá también, Run Lola Run, High Noon,* or *The Bicycle Thief.* View the entire film.

2. Select a complete scene consisting of at least a few shots but not more than twenty; view the scene repeatedly, and make a table that includes the shot number, brief description of the major action of each shot, and all the camera distance(s) and angle(s). Next, write a 750-word analysis on three to five major points about the expressiveness of camera distances and angles in the scene: what do they contribute to the scene? Before beginning your description and analysis, review Chapter 2, especially the sample student essay by Bret Lampman (pp. 105–7).

3. At the beginning of your paper, please indicate the title of the film. Early in your analysis, indicate the time into the film where the excerpt described and analyzed can be located.

The Expressiveness of Camera Distances

and Angles in *Citizen Kane*

by Beth Marie Beebout

GOVERNOR CAMPAIGN SPEECH SCENE

Shot	Camera Distance	Angle	Shot Description
1	Long shot	Slight high	The camera is focused on an enormous campaign banner with Kane's picture in background and tilts down to reveal Kane giving his campaign speech.
2	Extreme long shot	Eye level	A very long shot shows the crowd of people gathered to see Kane. The camera moves in a bit closer.
3	Long shot to medium shot	Low	Both the campaign banner and Kane are included in this shot. The camera moves in to a medium shot, but the low angle keeps the Kane banner included in the frame, so Kane's enormous face on the poster is just left of Kane giving his speech.
4	Medium close-up	Eye level	Kane's son and wife watching the speech.
5	Long shot	Low	The camera is back on Kane giving his speech; this time with the Kane banner to the right.

6	Medium shot	Eye level	Kane makes a joke, and the camera is at the perfect distance to show the people behind him applaud, as well as Kane's pleased reaction.
7	Medium close-up	Slight high	Another shot of Kane's son and wife. The son waves to Kane.
8	Medium shot	Eye level	Kane waves back, still amid audience applause, and continues his speech.
9	Medium shot	Slight low	Jed Leland and a bunch of unidentified men obscured in shadows seem to approve of Kane's speech.
10	Medium shot	Eye level	Kane becomes more animated in giving his speech and steps out from behind his podium.
11	Medium shot	Eye level	A shot of Mr. Bernstein among a group of men applauding Kane.
12	Medium close-up	Eye level	Kane's son asks his mother if Kane is governor yet.
13	Medium shot	Slight high	Kane makes another joke. The shot shows his and the audience's positive reactions.
14	Medium shot	Slight high	Leland and the men around him laugh and applaud Kane's joke.
15	Long shot to medium shot	Slight high	Kane continues his speech, but now the camera is above him and slowly moves to a medium shot. Kane makes a bold statement about his presumed victory over opponent Jim W. Gettys, and the crowd behind him jumps up applauding.
16	Medium shot	Slight high	Gettys watches from above as the crowd mills around Kane in congratulations. He slowly puts on his hat and exits.
17	Medium shot	Eye level	Kane shakes hands and greets important-looking audience members as he steps off his platform and is swarmed by the press.

Citizen Kane is a very visually expressive movie. Even without sound, viewers get a good sense of who Charles Foster Kane is, from his rise to power as a multimillionaire newspaper tycoon with a promising political career to his fall from grace and loss of credibility. One way of conveying Kane's importance in twentieth-century America is the use of camera distances and angles to elicit certain viewer responses. This is most apparent in the scene roughly 59 minutes into the movie, when Charles Foster Kane is campaigning for the New York governorship. He gives his campaign speech in a hall packed with thousands of people, all of whom seem very enthusiastic about what Kane has to say. Camera distances and angles are used in this scene to show multiple actions or reactions in a single shot, to suggest Kane's sense of power, to reveal emotions (or a lack thereof), and possibly to foreshadow later events.

During Kane's speech, a number of long and medium shots are used, to show not only Kane giving his speech, but the crowd surrounding him and how they react. The second shot of the scene is especially interesting: an extreme long shot of Kane speaking on a stage with a gigantic campaign poster of himself in the background. On all sides of him are what appears to be thousands of people, all listening attentively to Kane's every word. This shot reveals the sheer volume of the crowd and gives viewers a sense of the power and influence Kane had in New York. Long and medium shots are used later in the scene but not to show how large the crowd is. Instead, they are used to show Kane giving his speech in the foreground, and the audience's positive response in the background. During this scene, what Kane says is not as important as how he says it and how his audience reacts. These shots are an expressive way to show both. As Kane delivers his speech with confidence and charisma, viewers can see the audience behind him loving every bit of it.

The crowd is not the only subject used to convey a sense of Kane's power. His larger-than-life status is reinforced by low-angle shots of him giving the speech. This technique makes the viewer feel as if Kane commands a lot of power and authority. He seems to tower over all opposition and conveys the sense that he can make anything he wants happen. Kane looks so self-assured that it's hard to imagine that anyone would ever challenge him. A second effect of the low-angle shot is to include the enormous campaign poster in the frame in shots 3 and 5. During these shots, viewers see Kane in the foreground delivering his speech alongside a massive picture of his face to either his left or right. Ordinary people don't deliver speeches in front of portraits of themselves that are nearly three times larger than they are. No others are visible in these shots, making Kane look a bit egocentric but reinforcing the idea of his unlimited power.

In the entire scene, the camera never gets closer to Kane than a medium shot. Viewers are not allowed to see Kane displaying any emotion toward what he's saying, other than looking utterly pleased with himself, which makes him seem too powerful or important to be affected by petty human emotion. In fact, the only close-ups used in the entire scene are of Kane's wife, Emily, and their son, who are watching from the audience. His son seems eager and excited about the entire process, waving to his father and asking Emily whether Kane is governor yet. Emily, on the other hand, is much more reserved and somber, as if something important is on her mind. We find out later that this is because she has presumably just been informed by Kane's political opponent, Jim W. Gettys, that Kane is seeing another woman.

During this scene, camera angles change from predominantly low shots of Kane to eye-level shots and eventually to high shots. By the end of the scene, no low shots are used to show Kane. This makes Kane's presence seem to diminish and slowly makes him look less and less powerful. This is significant, because Kane's campaign speech is really the turning point of the movie. Up to this point, Kane is one of the most powerful men in the world: a multimillionaire newspaper tycoon who always gets his way, is set to win this election, and may eventually become the nation's president. After Kane gives this speech, however, his life begins to unravel. His affair is exposed, and he is defeated in the election. The rest of the film deals with his struggle to regain his influence and prestige, not only with the American public but in his personal life as well, each time looking more and more ineffective. Despite his best efforts, everything falls apart. The use of low-angled shots to high-angled shots in this scene may foreshadow events later in the film.

Clearly, there is a lot more going on in this scene than just Kane's words and actions, although it may take repeated viewings to catch everything. Camera distances and angles are especially expressive in this scene for showing multiple actions or reactions in a single shot, suggesting Kane's sense of power, revealing emotions (or a lack thereof), and foreshadowing events.

The following essay was written in response to this assignment:

Choose either *The Seven Samurai, Apocalypse Now, Jules and Jim,* or *Local Hero.* Write a 750-to-1,000-word essay on three or four major implicit meanings. Be sure to select only a few major implicit meanings, to arrange them in a significant order, and to explain and illustrate each one carefully.

In discussing meanings in a narrative, it helps to follow three procedures. First, say that a narrative shows or suggests its implicit meanings—not says them—because meanings are usually shown by the narrative, not stated directly (as explicit meanings). Second, describe each implicit meaning in at least one complete sentence; then write at least one paragraph to explain and illustrate the point. You cannot explain an implicit meaning in a word or phrase (chances are, you will identify only a subject). Third, in your first sentence about an implicit meaning, try to avoid characters' names. If you use them, you may get sidetracked from meanings to the specific characters' personalities.

Three Major Meanings of *Jules and Jim*
by Cherie L. Miranda

Jules and Jim (France, 1961) deals primarily with the relationships of its three main characters. The relationship of Jules and Jim, the strongest in the film, is a selfless friendship. In contrast, Catherine's relations to both Jules and Jim are unorthodox. Vacillating between the two friends, Catherine constantly wants the man she does not currently possess. Moreover, when she feels that she is losing control of one of her lovers, Catherine becomes desperate, even dangerous. However, the unconventional three-way relationship shared by Jules, Jim, and Catherine shows that the established morality is most appropriate and desirable.

Through the relationship of Jules and Jim, this film reveals that friendship can transcend love. Unlike any of Catherine's relationships, the friendship of Jules and Jim is selfless. In his autobiographical sketch of his friendship with Jules, Jim writes, "Each chose only the best things for the other." Though both are in love with Catherine, Jules and Jim remain the best of friends. Jules is aware of the intimacy between Jim and Catherine, but his feelings for Jim do not change. Conversely, Jim, though planning to marry Catherine at one point, always retains strong feelings of friendship for Jules. For example, when Jules and Catherine return to Paris near the end of the film, Jules and Jim are inadvertently reunited. Though Jim's affair with Catherine was very painful for all of them, the two men are happy to see each other and still seem to share an exceptional rapport. In the scene following the reunion of Jules and Jim, the two men share a gesture of their ongoing friendship: Jim, convinced that Jules's hat is improper in Paris, replaces it with his own. At the cremation of Jim and Catherine, Jules feels relief as well as loss because he had grown tired of the chaos Catherine had brought into his life (Insdorf 33). After Jules ponders his friendship with Jim, however, the narrator states that "the relationship of Jules and Jim had no equivalence in love."

Jules and Jim also demonstrates that people sometimes have the desire to control and possess others, a desire which can result in pain, even tragedy. This aspect of the film is embodied in Catherine's affairs with Jules and Jim—"She controls her relationship with the two men from the very beginning" (Petrie 181). However, her need for control is most evident in her involvement with Jim. Catherine seems to prefer Jim, but she wants to defy traditional morality and keep both Jules and Jim as lovers. Her seduction of Jules is an attempt to establish this situation. The narrator notes that because of Jim's jealousy, Catherine "did not repeat the experiment." Most important, when she feels she is losing control over Jim—even if she has previously renounced him—Catherine again wants him. For example, when the two plan to separate, Catherine tells Jim, "I don't love you and will never love anyone." But almost immediately after Jim's arrival in Paris, Catherine writes to him and tells him to come quickly because she is pregnant. When Jim writes back with indifference, Catherine responds with a letter that begins, "I love you, Jim." Furthermore, Catherine does not threaten Jim's life until she finds out that he is definitely leaving her so that he can marry and have children with Gilberte. In all likelihood, Catherine subsequently kills Jim because he is the man she cannot possess. Indeed, Catherine designates Jules, the man who would not leave her, a spectator rather than a participant in her suicide/murder. She makes certain that she and Jim are the only victims.

Though an untraditional film, *Jules and Jim* indirectly advocates conventional morality. Because of their three-way relationship, Catherine, Jules, and Jim are thrust inexorably "into a pattern of hurting, humiliating, and finally destroying one another" (Petrie 158). Jules has always been tormented by Catherine's disloyalty, but he would rather tolerate her infidelity with Jim than suffer the even greater pain of losing her altogether. As mentioned above, Jim becomes jealous of Catherine's relations with Jules and is consequently torn between his feelings for her and his feelings for Jules—the narrator states, "In vain did Jim tell himself that he had no right to be jealous." Similarly, Catherine is hurt by Jim's infidelity, though she causes him pain through unfaithfulness as well. Though not a member of the threesome, Gilberte is inevitably hurt by the confused, vacillating relationship of Jules, Jim, and Catherine. Toward the end of the film, Jim appears to have accepted Gilberte and renounced Catherine. However, the viewer is left with the impression that this interminable, cyclical relationship would have continued indefinitely if the film had not ended with the deaths of Jim and Catherine.

As demonstrated above, *Jules and Jim* is concerned with human relationships. Though love is a recurring motif throughout the film, the camaraderie of the two men suggests that friendship can be more lasting and powerful. Through Catherine, the film also shows that the desire to possess another human being can be destructive and painful both to oneself and to others. As mentioned in class, *Jules and Jim* is often criticized as an immoral film, but it actually supports traditional morality. Much of the pain caused by this untraditional, three-way relationship could have been avoided if conventional morality had been observed.

Works Cited

Insdorf, Annette. *François Truffaut*. Boston: Twayne, 1978.

Petrie, Graham. *The Cinema of François Truffaut*. New York: Barnes, 1970.

For additional sample student essays, see the Close-Up sections near the end of Chapters 2, 4, 5, 7, and 11.

For an example of an essay that is much more comprehensive than the ones included in this chapter and the short essays at the ends of some of the book's chapters, see the next chapter for a sample description and analysis of *The Player*.

ANNOTATED BIBLIOGRAPHY FOR THE INTRODUCTORY FILM STUDENT

BOOKS

Enser's Filmed Books and Plays: A List of Books and Plays from Which Films Have Been Made, 1928–2001. 6th ed. Ed. Ellen Baskin. Burlington, VT: Ashgate, 2002. The main part of the book is an index arranged alphabetically by film titles, with brief information on each film and the name of the author of the source fiction or play. Also includes author and change-of-title indexes and information on made-for-TV movies and classic British television series.

Film Review Annual. 1981–2001. Ed. Jerome S. Ozer. Englewood, NJ: Film Review, 1982–. Reprints complete reviews of the feature films released in the United States during the previous year. Includes full credits, many different indexes, listings of major film awards.

Halliwell's Who's Who in the Movies. 4th ed. Ed. John Walker. New York: Harper, 2006. More than 13,000 entries on scriptwriters, actors, directors, and others. According to Mary Ellen Quinn, "Appendixes house material such as entries for 'Movie Remakes, Series, Themes and Genres'; a glossary of technical and critical terms; a somewhat random and not consistently up-to-date survey of national cinemas; and lists of award winners."

The International Dictionary of Films and Filmmakers. 4th ed. 4 vols. Ed. Tom and Sara Pendergast. Chicago: St. James, 2000. Critical essays, bibliographies, and filmographies. Vol. 1: *Films*; vol. 2: *Directors*; vol. 3: *Actors and Actresses*; vol. 4: *Writers and Production Artists* (including cinematographers, producers, editors, and designers).

Katz, Ephraim. *The Film Encyclopedia*. 5th ed. Rev. Fred Klein and Ronald Dean Nolen. New York: Collins, 2005. A comprehensive one-volume encyclopedia of world cinema. More than 7,000 entries on individual scriptwriters, producers, directors, and many others; studios and production companies; movements or styles of filmmaking; national cinemas; filmmaking personnel; and jargon and technical terms. For each person discussed, a selected list of films she or he worked on is also supplied.

Leff, Leonard J. *Film Plots: Scene-by-Scene Narrative Outlines for Feature Film Study*. 2 vols. Ann Arbor: Pierian. Vol. 1: scene-by-scene descriptions of 67 films often studied or written about (1983); vol. 2: descriptions of 50 more feature films (1988).

Leonard Maltin's Movie and Video Guide. New York: Signet. Published annually. Brief description and evaluation of thousands of feature films, theatrical and made-for-TV. Indicates which titles have been released on videotape, which on laser disc, and which on DVD. For films made in a wide-screen process, an indication of which process was used. Also an indication of black-and-white titles available in a "computer-colored version."

Magill's Cinema Annual. Farmington Hills, MI: St. James. Published annually beginning in 1982. For major films of the previous year and occasional older films, includes credits, synopsis of the narrative, essay review, bibliography of reviews, and eight indexes.

Sadoul, Georges. *Dictionary of Films*. Trans., ed., and updated Peter Morris. Berkeley: U of California P, 1972. Brief essays on approximately 1,300 films.

Slide, Anthony. *The New Historical Dictionary of the American Film Industry*. Lanham, MD: Scarecrow, 1998. More than 750 entries on film studios, production companies, distributors, technical innovations, film series (such as *The Thin Man*), industry terms, organizations, and other subjects (such as nickelodeons).

The St. James Women Filmmakers Encyclopedia: Women on the Other Side of the Camera. Ed. Amy L. Unterburger. Detroit: Visible Ink, 1999. More than 200 entries—each of which includes a short biography, filmography, and analysis—on female filmmakers, mainstream and independent, from around the world.

Thomson, David. *The New Biographical Dictionary of Film*. Expanded and updated. New York: Knopf, 2004. More than 1,300 essays, ranging in length from one paragraph to several thousand words, arranged alphabetically, on filmmakers and key figures from film history. Many entries include a selective listing of films the person worked on.

The Video Source Book. Detroit: Gale. Published annually. Comprehensive information on programs available on videotape, laser videodisc, and DVD. Includes six indexes: alternate title, subject, credits, awards, special formats, and program distributors.

Welch, Jeffrey Egan. *Literature and Film: An Annotated Bibliography, 1900–1977*. New York: Garland, 1981.

———. *Literature and Film: An Annotated Bibliography, 1978–1988*. New York: Garland, 1993. Both volumes list and annotate books and articles published in North America and Great Britain having to do with the relation between literature and films.

The Women's Companion to International Film. Ed. Annette Kuhn and Susannah Radstone. Berkeley: U of California P, 1994. Approximately 600 alphabetized entries, many including filmographies or bibliographies or both. Also includes an index of films directed, written, or produced by women.

Indexes for Periodicals

Film Literature Index. Albany: Film and Television Documentation Center. Published since 1973. Indexes articles in more than 300 international film and nonfilm periodicals. Entries are arranged alphabetically by author and subject (including film titles) and indicate the presence of filmography, credits, biography, and interviews.

Humanities Index. New York: Wilson. Published since 1974. At the end of each volume is a section on book reviews.

International Index to Film Periodicals. "The main database, the International Index to Film Periodicals contains over 400,000 article citations from more than 330 periodicals. It offers in-depth coverage of the world's foremost academic and popular film journals. Each entry consists of a full bibliographic description, an abstract, and comprehensive headings (biographical names, film titles, and general subjects)."

Readers' Guide to Periodical Literature. From 1910 to March 1977, film reviews are listed under "Moving Picture Plays"; after March 1977, film reviews are listed under "Motion Picture Reviews." Since March 1976 (vol. 36), book review citations are listed at the end of each volume.

Journals and Magazines

Because film journals and magazines often change their coverage, place of publication, frequency of publication, even their names or subtitles, some of the following information may no longer be accurate. For links, go to the appropriate section on the Web site for this book at <bedfordstmartins .com/phillips-film>.

American Cinematographer. Includes in-depth articles on the cinematography used in making particular movies, interviews with major cinematographers, and ads for such equipment as cranes, Steadicams, and cameras.

Camera Obscura. Focuses on feminist perspectives on film, TV, and visual media. Each issue may include debates, essays, interviews, and summary pieces.

CineAction. Film criticism in terms of race, gender, sexual orientation, and politics. Published in Toronto since 1984.

Cineaste. Provides coverage of the art and politics of world cinema. Includes film reviews, book reviews, and interviews.

Cinema Journal. Published in cooperation with the Society for Cinema and Media Studies, a professional association made up largely of college and university film teachers. Includes essays on a wide variety of subjects from diverse methodological perspectives.

Documentary. Published by the International Documentary Association. Articles and departments, including information on premieres, funding, and festivals.

DOX. An international film magazine dedicated to the documentary. Includes reviews of new films and information about festivals, markets, funding bodies, and broadcasters.

Film & History: An Interdisciplinary Journal of Film and Television Studies. Articles, film reviews, and book reviews. Published since 1970.

Film Comment. Published by the Film Society of Lincoln Center (New York). Articles, interviews, and book and film reviews.

Film Criticism. Articles, interviews, festival reports, and book reviews. Published at Allegheny College.

Film History: An International Journal. Each issue focuses on "the historical development of the motion picture and the social, technological, and economic context in which this has occurred."

Filmmaker: The Magazine of Independent Film. Published by the Independent Feature Project mostly for filmmakers, directors, producers, cinematographers, writers, and editors.

Film Quarterly. Interviews, discussions of film theory and film history, and reviews of films, videos, and books. Published since 1958 by the University of California Press.

Films in Review. The oldest film publication in the United States. Many short film reviews, longer articles on filmmakers, and obituaries. Published in print until 1997; since then, available only on the Web.

The Independent. Formerly known as *The Independent Film & Video Monthly.* Published by the Foundation for Independent Video and Film (FIVF). Includes profiles of filmmakers, producers, and distributors; festival listings; information on new technology; coverage of political trends and legislation affecting independents; and reports from film festivals and markets.

Journal of Film and Video. Published by the University Film and Video Association, which consists mostly of filmmakers and university film teachers. Earlier known under the title *Journal of the University Film and Video Association.*

Journal of Popular Film and Television (formerly *Journal of Popular Film*). Articles on stars, directors, producers, studios, networks, genres, series, and other topics. Also includes interviews, filmographies, bibliographies, and book reviews.

Journal of Religion and Film. Publishes articles, brief reviews of recently released films especially as they relate to religions and religious themes, and occasional book reviews.

Jump Cut: A Review of Contemporary Media. Published irregularly since 1974. Recent perspectives on film, television, video, and related media and cultural analysis. *Jump Cut* "is a nonsectarian left and feminist publication, open to a variety of left interpretations and to criticism which may not be explicitly left but which contributes to the development of a vigorous political media criticism." Past issues are available online.

Literature Film Quarterly. "Articles on individual movies, on different cinematic adaptations of a single literary work, on a director's style of adaptation, on theories of film adaptation, on the 'cinematic' qualities of authors or works, on the reciprocal influences between film and literature, on authors' attitudes toward film and film adaptations, on the role of the screenwriter, and on teaching of film." Also includes interviews, film reviews, and book reviews.

Monthly Film Bulletin. Detailed credits, a brief description of the film's content, and a review are included for feature films and short films, contemporary and "retrospective." International coverage. Published from 1934 to April 1991. In May 1991, *Monthly Film Bulletin* was incorporated into *Sight & Sound* (listed below).

MovieMaker: The Art and Business of Making Movies. Focuses on independent films and independent filmmakers.

New Review of Film and Television Studies. Publishes articles about the results of "current research making a central contribution to film and television studies."

Quarterly Review of Film and Video. Articles on film production, history, theory, reception, and criticism, including the widest possible range of approaches and subjects plus book reviews and interviews.

Sight & Sound. Published by the British Film Institute. Articles, interviews, book reviews, and a review for each film released in the United Kingdom, each preceded by credits and a brief description of the film's content.

Variety. A U.S. trade publication on the entertainment industry, including film reviews and many other types of related information. Available in daily and weekly versions.

The Velvet Light Trap: A Critical Journal of Film and Television. Critical essays, especially on American film.

Wide Angle. Usually each issue stresses a single topic. Also includes interviews with filmmakers and book reviews.

Other online sources for the beginning film student can be found via links on the Web site for this book at <bedfordstmartins.com/phillips-film>.

WORKS CITED

Flaubert, Gustave. *Madame Bovary.* Trans. Paul de Man. New York: Norton, 1965.

Sagan, Carl. "The Persistence of Memory." Program 11. *Cosmos.* PBS. The wording is from the television program, not the book based on the series.

CHAPTER 13

A Sample Description and Analysis: *The Player*

T HIS BOOK OFTEN BREAKS FILMS DOWN into elements and addresses them one at a time — for example, one chapter on cinematography and much of one chapter on meanings. When a film is shown, the cinematography and all the other elements function simultaneously and, ideally, complement one another. This chapter applies many of the book's concepts to a single film and serves as a partial summary and review of the book. If read before the rest of the book, the chapter may serve as a useful introduction to the book. The goal of the chapter is to help you appreciate ways to use some of the book's concepts in your own film analyses and in your explorations of the film medium. Like any analysis of a film, this one cannot address every aspect of this book or of the film being analyzed. Likewise, no single film can exemplify every aspect of cinema; the medium is far too wide-ranging for any film to serve that function.

The film analyzed here, *The Player*, came out in 1992 and was written by Michael Tolkin and directed by Robert Altman (1925–2006). This film was selected because it is often used in introductory film courses; is readily available on videotape, laser disc, and DVD; is fun to watch; and exemplifies many aspects of interest to filmmakers, film critics, film scholars, film professors, and film students. Also, *The Player* is a movie about the Hollywood movie industry, filled with references to earlier films and observations about the industry.[1]

DESCRIPTION

If you have not seen *The Player* recently or will not be seeing it, please read the following description at least twice.

---

[1]Vicki Whitaker of Aztec, New Mexico, assisted me with much of this chapter during preparation for the first edition.

The Player is set in modern Hollywood and focuses on a film studio executive named Griffin Mill whose job it is to listen to and approve brief summaries of stories to be made into movies. Griffin processes hundreds of pitches a week, but the studio can produce only twelve movies a year.

Viewers quickly learn three aspects of Griffin's situation: an unidentified screenwriter is threatening Griffin; rumor has it that an executive at a rival studio named Larry Levy will be brought in to take over Griffin's position; and Griffin is involved romantically with a subordinate, a story editor named Bonnie Sherow.

After some hasty searching through office records, Griffin decides that the writer who has been threatening him is named David Kahane. That night, Griffin telephones Kahane from outside Kahane's house. He sees Kahane's girlfriend, an artist named June Gudmundsdottir, answer the phone and is attracted to her (Plate 58). (The color plates discussed in this chapter follow p. 582.) June tells Griffin that Kahane went to a movie. Later Griffin finds Kahane at the movie theater and afterward has drinks with him (Plate 59). The two men end up in a parking lot, tempers flare, and Griffin kills Kahane and then makes it look as if the motive for the murder was robbery.

The next day, Griffin returns to his job and finds that Larry Levy has come to work at the studio (Plate 62). Later, Griffin learns that the writer who had been threatening him is still alive. Griffin attends Kahane's funeral and soon begins to pursue Kahane's girlfriend romantically.

Because Griffin is a suspect in Kahane's murder, the police come to Griffin's office and interview him. After two men pitch Griffin their story for *Habeas Corpus*—a grim narrative likely to be a huge flop if ever produced—Griffin "allows" Levy to take over championing the story in the hope that the movie will fail and Levy will be discredited.

The police summon Griffin to the police station, where Detective Avery's questions and methods fluster him. Later, Griffin and June slip off to a desert hideaway where at the conclusion of a romantic evening they become lovers. The next day, Griffin is called in for a police lineup, but the only eyewitness selects a police detective from among the possible suspects.

A year later, the finished film of *Habeas Corpus* includes stars and a preposterous happy ending after all. After a screening at the studio, Bonnie Sherow complains to the director that he "sold it out. . . . What about truth? What about the reality?" and Levy fires her. Griffin is now in charge of the studio, and he and Levy are on good working terms. When Bonnie tries to make an emotional appeal to Griffin, he walks past her without looking at her and says she "will land on her feet."

In the final sequence, Griffin is cruising to his home in a Rolls-Royce convertible while listening to a pitch on his car phone. The caller obliquely identifies himself as the writer who had been threatening Griffin and proposes a story about a movie executive who gets away with murder—

in fact, the story of the movie that viewers have just seen. Griffin's main concern, expressed to the caller, is that the movie executive gets away with the murder and lives happily ever after married to the dead writer's girlfriend. The writer assures him that an OK to make the film will guarantee that outcome, and Griffin agrees to make the movie. The writer proposes that the film be called *The Player*. Griffin arrives home and is greeted warmly by June, who is visibly pregnant.

ANALYSIS

Mise en Scène

In *The Player*, the mise en scène shows selected aspects of contemporary Hollywood and lets viewers mingle with the powerful and enjoy the trappings of wealth.

SETTINGS

The Player begins in an office interior; then the camera tracks up and back to give an overview of a movie lot in contemporary sunny southern California. The weather is warm and mostly sunny; the parking lot is tidy and features an expensive car; the limited landscaping is well manicured. All players are nattily attired and perfectly coiffed. At once the setting suggests wealth (the clothes, the car), power (the studio itself), and surface orderliness. The lengthy opening shot also introduces nearly all the main characters (Table 13.1).

Griffin Mill's office is crammed with movie posters for *King Kong* (1933), *The Blue Angel* (1930), and six movies dealing with crime, especially murder: *Prison Shadows* (1936), *Hollywood Story* (1951), *Laura* (1944), *Prison Break* (1938, Plate 57), *Murder in the Big House* (1942, Plate 57), and *M* (the 1951 remake). The posters in Mill's office associate Mill with movies about murder. By contrast, the office of the studio head has a poster for *Casablanca* (1942), whose subject is not crime but romance, patriotism, and sacrifice.

Cars are used especially expressively. During most of the film, Mill drives a black Range Rover—a status symbol for moneyed Angelenos and a vehicle that can comfortably accommodate actor Tim Robbins's 6-foot 5-inch frame. The studio head, Joel Levison, drives a black Mercedes, and Mill's rumored rival, Larry Levy, drives a black Mercedes convertible. The cars suggest that Levy has the same tastes as the studio head and is a major player. In the film's last scenes, when Mill is now the studio head, he drives a black Rolls-Royce convertible, an obvious symbol of his promotion.

The cars, car phones, car faxes, and clothing so expensive that the cost of a single suit would support a family in a barrio for a month—these are symbols of power within the industry.

TABLE 13.1

The Opening Shot of *The Player* (a little more than 8 minutes long)

SCENE NUMBER AND ACTION

1. A young woman in Joel Levison's office takes a brief call from Larry Levy and hangs up. Another woman scolds her before sending her hurrying off for the day's trade papers.

2. Griffin drives his Range Rover into a parking space and is immediately accosted by Adam Simon, who begins pitching a story for a possible movie. Griffin tells him to run the idea by Bonnie Sherow.

3. A man in a suit and another man who makes (mail) deliveries on a bicycle each briefly describe a memorable lengthy movie tracking shot.

4. From outside Griffin's office, we see Mill arrive in his office where a man in a cap (actor Buck Henry) is waiting for him and soon begins making a pitch for *The Graduate Part Two*. Mill asks his assistant to ask studio security how Adam Simon got on the lot.

5. Adam Simon and Bonnie Sherow emerge from the same building; he is pitching his story to her. The delivery man on a bike has had an accident. Bonnie tries to help him. On the pavement, a postcard has a message on its front: "Your Hollywood is Dead."

6. A man in a Porsche convertible briefly flirts with a young woman and asks where Joel Levison's office is. We learn that Levison is the studio head.

7. Another man is giving a studio tour to a group of Japanese.

8. Very briefly, Adam Simon is glimpsed talking with Bonnie, who can barely be heard telling him to write down something and send it to her office.

9. Immediately after the young woman of scene 1 arrives back at the office and gives the papers to the other secretary, Joel Levison arrives in a large Mercedes and gets out.

10. Two men and a woman emerge from the building and talk about rumored upcoming changes at the studio, including the possibility that Griffin will be replaced.

11. In his office, Griffin gets a call from studio security; he questions why security is so lax; and then he turns his attention to two women, who make a story pitch almost simultaneously. One says, "It's *Out of Africa* meets *Pretty Woman*."

12. The delivery man of scenes 3 and 5 mistakenly thinks that a man looking for Griffin Mill is the director Martin Scorsese (he's actually writer and director Alan Rudolph).

13. The man in the suit from scene 3 and the man who made the pitch for *The Graduate Part Two* discuss editing and tracking shots in movies.

14. While crossing the parking lot, Bonnie scolds her assistant for meeting with a writer, in this case Alan Rudolph.

15. In Mill's office, Alan Rudolph makes a movie pitch to Griffin. Mill's assistant gives him some mail, on top of which is the postcard glimpsed in scene 5. On the other side, the postcard reads, "I hate your guts asshole!" Mill turns around to look out his office window.

PLATE 33 **TV as source and subject for a film**
In this scene from *Natural Born Killers* (1994), represented by this image almost 57 ¼ minutes into the director's cut DVD, the main male character is finally caught and shot by police officers outside a "Drug Zone" store, who then give him a savage beating as a TV crew films. During the episode, this is the extent of the TV reporter's commentary: "Mickey's quite virile." "He has a very large gun." "He's now rendered impotent." The film's frequent music, garish saturated colors that bathe entire scenes, fast cutting, occasional discontinuity, images from the couple's minds within scenes of the couple, and frequent use of Dutch angles (as here) all contribute to the hallucinatory or nightmarish quality of the film, which at times looks and sounds like a music video. *Regency, Warner Bros.; Trimark Pictures DVD*

Plate 34

Plate 35

PLATES 34–37 **Opposing forces in a fictional film**
Hayao Miyazaki's anime (Japanese animated film) *Princess Mononoke* (1997) has a long, complicated story, but as in many fictional tales, two forces war with each other: those who seek to protect nature and those who seek to convert it for industrial uses. On the one side is Princess Mononoke or San, who has been raised by wolf gods and lives with them (Plate 34). She is allied with wild animals and (Plate 35) forest spirits to defend the natural environment. On the other side of the central

conflict is Lady Eboshi (Plate 36), her ironworkers, and her soldiers, who all intend to industrialize nature. Jigo (on the right in Plate 37) is another threat to nature: he and his men intend to take the great forest spirit's head (Plate 35) back to the emperor, who believes it will gain him immortality. One major character belongs to neither warring group: Ashitaka (on the left in Plate 37), a brave young man who tries to mediate between the warring factions. *Studio Ghibli and others; Miramax Home Entertainment DVD*

Plate 36

Plate 37

PLATE 38 The earliest known western
"The Great Train Robbery" (1903) was sometimes shown in hand-painted versions. Like all films of the time, the movie was filmed in black and white, but parts of some shots were hand-painted. Here, during the final showdown and shoot-out, the posse in the background is shooting beyond those poor horses at three remaining outlaws in the foreground. The people doing the painting may have thought that handguns either discharge colored smoke or should so they would appear more dramatic. *Edison; Museum of Modern Art; Kino International DVD*

PLATE 39 Multiple functions of a musical number
In a well-known dance number that begins approximately 41¼ minutes into *Seven Brides for Seven Brothers* (1954) and lasts for over 6 minutes, six country brothers (on the right) compete with six male small town rivals for the acceptance of six eligible young women. The musical number contributes to the film's story in a number of ways. For one thing, the dance number demon-

strates that country men who have been tutored by a woman (their new sister-in-law) in hygiene, manners, courtship, and dancing can be attractive to women and can more than hold their own in a competition with more urban male rivals. The musical number also demonstrates the country men's greater vitality and athleticism. (In fact, all the dancers were ballet dancers but were not supposed to look as if they were dancing ballet.) And the musical number shows that though the young women enjoy dancing with both types of men, they prefer the country men: the high-energy competition ends with the women in their arms. *MGM; Warner Home Video DVD*

PLATE 40 Combining genres in only part of a film
"Girl Hunt: A Murder Mystery in Jazz," which is a stylish jazz-and-dance number that begins about 95½ minutes into the musical *The Band Wagon* (1953) and runs 11½ minutes, combines elements of film noir with the musical. The number begins at night in a city, which is later revealed to be New York, where the detective played by Fred Astaire is soon trying to solve a murder. During his investigation, he finds himself in the underworld nightspot seen here where all the men carry guns and resent his presence. The other two major characters of "Girl Hunt" are danced by Cyd Charisse, here as a brunette dressed in bright shiny red and playing the femme fatale and elsewhere as a blonde dressed in white and "playing" the innocent in need of help. *Arthur Freed; Loew's Incorporated; MGM; Warner Home Video DVD*

Plates 38–40

PLATE 41 Documentary as a source for information

In a 7-minute documentary "A Girl like Me" (2005), which was made by a high school student, the filmmaker interviewed a number of Harlem 4- or 5-year-olds (mostly girls). She asked the children to choose between two dolls (see right), and fifteen out of the twenty-one children chose the white doll. The film provides information, but it also raises questions for many viewers. Why do the black children prefer the white doll? How do the children learn their values? *Kiri Davis; various sources on the Web*

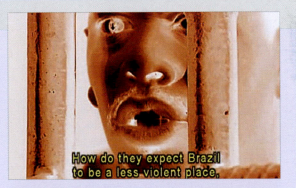

PLATE 42 Two of many sources for a documentary

Like many documentaries, *State of Fear: The Truth about Terrorism* (2005) uses many sources, including shots of people superimposed on footage of action (or on photos that fill the frame in the background). Here, in a brief shot 72 seconds into the film, we see a largely unmoving Peruvian woman superimposed on a riot in an unidentified Peruvian city in 2004. These two sources—footage from the past and a shot of this person in the then present—suggest that behind her and the 13 others whose images follow hers in quick succession is a history of unrest, specifically a country's 20-year war with an internal terrorist group, Shining Path, and the attendant political unrest and massive upheaval. *Paco de Onis; Skylight Pictures*

Plate 43

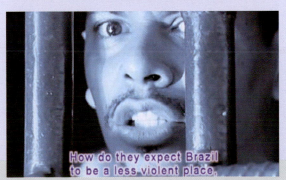

PLATES 43–44 Negative image in a film and a positive print of it not in the film

Approximately 83½ minutes into the Brazilian documentary *Bus 174* (2002), someone opens a door and viewers see in negative image part of a room and then a superimposed title card that reads "Any jail in Rio, 2002." Viewers then see the jail's crowded conditions, still shown in negative images, and hear such inmate complaints as the following: "where there's room for five, they put eleven"; "check out how we sleep in here, on top of each other"; "they brought us here beating us up on the way"; "they give us rotten food"; "we don't get any medical assistance"; and "some are in here illegally." Soon afterward, viewers see the negative image of the prisoner in Plate 43. The inmate asks, "How do they expect the prisoner to be rehabilitated? How do they expect Brazil to be a less violent place, treating the prisoners the way they do?" The negative images in this section of the film render the place and people as distorted, even spooky and unsettling images of themselves. When the prisoner is seen as a positive image, in Plate 44, he looks very different. This positive print does not appear in the film but is included here to illustrate how different negative and positive images can be. *Zazen Produções; Hart Sharp Video DVD*

Plate 44

Plate 45

PLATES 45–46 **Animation of plastic (three-dimensional) subjects**
Seen in Plate 45 is an adjustment being made to a pliable Plasticine model before the filming of one frame for *Wallace & Gromit: The Curse of the Were-Rabbit* (2005). Plate 46 shows approximately how the frame looks at about 34½ minutes into the finished film. The finished film consists of over 115,000 frames. Plate 45: "Behind the Scenes of 'The Curse of the Were-Rabbit'" on *Wallace & Gromit: The Curse of the Were-Rabbit*. Plate 46: *Wallace & Gromit: The Curse of the Were-Rabbit; Aardman; DreamWorks DVD*

Plate 46

Plate 47

PLATES 47–48 **Complex and sophisticated short animated film**
"T.R.A.N.S.I.T." (1997) is a 12-minute nonchronological animated film composed of seven sequences, each made by a different animation team. (See p. 427 for a description.) Plate 47: Early in the film but late in the fabula, an injured man (we learn later in the film he is named Oscar) appears on the deck of a luxury ocean liner. Plate 48: In a Venetian hotel room, Emily and the sleeping Oscar, who had slapped her. *Piet Kroon; Short 4: Seduction (DVD)*

Plate 48

Plate 49

Plate 50

PLATES 49–50 Complex and sophisticated short animated film (continued)
Plate 49: Earlier still in the fabula of "T.R.A.N.S.I.T.," in a casino at Baden Baden, Germany, Oscar has won large stakes at roulette, and later Emily is about to go to bed with him. Plate 50: The earliest sequence in the fabula: moments before, Oscar has met Emily, and the story and its tragic consequences all begin. *Piet Kroon; Short 4: Seduction (DVD)*

PLATE 51 Computers used to represent virtual reality in movies
For *The Lawnmower Man* (1992), the filmmakers used computers to create scenes of virtual reality, a computer-generated artificial world complete with changing imaginary environment and virtual people who interact with their environment and each other. About halfway through *The Lawnmower Man*, a man and a woman in an advanced laboratory don virtual-reality headgear then seem to experience themselves and each other as virtual people who change shape. Here the cybercouple inadvertently demonstrate the unifying powers of mutual attraction. *Lane Pringle Productions and others; New Line Home Entertainment DVD*

PLATE 52 Film seen in a movie palace
When *The Cabinet of Dr. Caligari* (1919) had its 1921 U.S. premiere at the Capitol Theater, a New York movie palace, the images looked something like this: the angular expressionistic sets, including window and walls, were clearly visible as they were intended to be. This frame also illustrates how different scenes were tinted a particular color, here a shade of amber. *Decla-Bioscop; Restored Authorized Edition, Kino Video DVD*

Appearance nurturing viewers' expectations

"Vexation Island" (1997), which was shot on 35 mm film, has the color, resolution, and wide-screen format we expect to see when we go to a movie. Those qualities, along with the film's setting and subject, encourage viewers to initially expect a Hollywood-style adventure movie, perhaps something like *Cast Away* (2000) set in an earlier era. *Rodney Graham, Vexation Island 1997; Courtesy Rodney Graham and 303 Gallery, New York*

Mise en scène and cinematography creating meaning

Gus Van Sant's *Elephant* (2003) uses many lengthy tracking shots, as here, usually from behind high school students walking to or, more often, in the school. The backgrounds of these shots are usually partially out of focus because they were filmed with a long lens. Here, almost 12 minutes into the film and 43 seconds into a shot that lasts nearly 3 minutes, viewers see a student as he walks through parts of the school, briefly stopping to greet his girlfriend before the two of them walk to the school office. *HBO Films; HBO Video DVD*

Setting in *The Truman Show* (1998)

Truman Burbank lives out his life in the picture-perfect town of Seahaven, a gigantic soundstage that is incredibly clean, orderly, and light. *Scott Rudin Productions and Paramount Pictures; Paramount Pictures DVD*

Symbolic name in *The Truman Show* (1998)

Christof (on the right), whose name rings of *Christ*, is the god of Truman's world. From his command center inside a large fake moon that overlooks the huge TV soundstage that serves as Truman's hometown, Christof oversees his creation and commands the sun to rise and set and the sea to churn and calm. *Scott Rudin Productions and Paramount Pictures; Paramount Pictures DVD*

PLATE 57 Symbolic setting
Most of the many movie posters in Mill's office in *The Player* (1992) are for films involving crime and punishment, an appropriate backdrop for a man who has committed murder and hopes to evade punishment. *Avenue Pictures Productions; New Line Home Video DVD*

PLATE 58 Colors associated with two characters
From outside the writer's house and looking in, Mill sees a luminous vision in the night, an artist who dresses mainly in whites and here briefly sucks on an ice cube. Her studio, a little of which is seen here, is dominated by whites and blues. In contrast, Mill is in the dark and wearing a brown suit. *Avenue Pictures Productions; New Line Home Video DVD*

PLATE 59 Reds for a tense scene
Reds dominate the scene of Mill and Kahane in a karaoke bar. The setting includes red objects and red lighting. The writer wears a red shirt, and his forehead is reddish; the saké jar sits on a red napkin; and the overhead red light hits Mill's forehead and hands. The reds seem appropriate to the mood of rising anger and possible violence. *Avenue Pictures Productions; New Line Home Video DVD*

PLATE 60 Soft light contributing to a romantic mood
About 101 minutes into *The Player*, Mill and June are beginning an evening of dining, dancing, and romance. The soft, even lighting on her face and hair enhances her attractiveness and contributes to the scene's mellow, romantic mood. *Avenue Pictures Productions; New Line Home Video DVD*

Plate 61

PLATES 61–62 **Editing to suggest a point**

About 39 2/3 minutes into *The Player*, the image of the murdered writer's body is seen (Plate 61) as viewers become aware that the accompanying soundtrack has changed from music and an off-screen barking dog to conversation about allowing test audiences to choose the ending of a movie. Within seconds, the discussion assumes a normal volume as viewers see people sitting around a conference table (Plate 62). Soon Larry Levy says that the studio should make movies without using writers. The film cuts from a scene of a studio executive murdering a writer to a scene of another studio executive (Levy, second on the right) proposing to eliminate writers from the filmmaking process. The juxtaposition of the two shots suggests the studio's low regard for writers. *Avenue Pictures Productions; New Line Home Video DVD*

Plate 62

Plate 63

PLATES 63–64 **Sound and image manipulations within a shot**

Part of a 78-second shot in *The Player* shifts viewers' attention from the foreground (Plate 63) to the background (Plate 64). The effect is achieved by raising the volume of the dialogue of the two subjects in the background, then fading out the dialogue of the two subjects in the foreground, and then zooming in on the background subjects as they continue to talk. The result is a smooth, unobtrusive redirection of viewers' attention from the two subjects in the foreground to the two subjects in the background. *Avenue Pictures Productions; New Line Home Video DVD*

Plate 64

SUBJECTS

Except for the writer who is murdered, his girlfriend, and the police, all the main characters are involved in making studio movies. Of them, the central character is Griffin Mill. Because viewers see him in nearly every scene and in a variety of situations that are difficult for him, both professionally and personally, viewers get to know Mill fairly well, though we never get to know his thoughts directly. He is a complex character: calculating, manipulative, guarded, professionally successful, vulnerable to rage and violence, adept at surviving—and lucky to survive his encounter with the law.

Even to a casual viewer, *The Player* includes an extraordinary number of cameos, mainly of famous actors but also of directors, a Los Angeles film critic, and others. As is typical of cameo performances, none affects the plot in any significant way. One could argue that the sixty-five cameos are part of the densely populated decor, part of the setting rather than subjects in their own right. The cameos also add an element of surprise—whom will viewers notice next?—though there is a danger that the cameos could distract viewers from the story. There are so many cameos, some of them inconspicuous, that attentive viewers may notice even more of them on later re-viewings.

COMPOSITION

According to the DVD case, Altman specified a 1.77:1 aspect ratio. That makes it a wide-screen film but not as wide as it might have been—for example, an anamorphic version with a 2.4:1 aspect ratio. Rarely does *The Player* show subjects isolated from each other on opposite sides of the wide frame. Occasionally something significant is going on in both the foreground and the background simultaneously, as briefly in the opening shot where a man in a Porsche convertible (an investor's son) flirts with a woman as a group of Japanese are being given a studio tour behind them.

Much more typically, the film uses a moving camera or zoom lens to follow a few characters for a while then pick up new characters and follow them. The mobile camera and many characters moving rapidly within the frame, and in and out of it, make for frequent changes in composition and a sense of exploration and perhaps energy or restlessness.

MISE EN SCÈNE AND THE WORLD OUTSIDE THE FILM

The most obvious product placement is the Range Rover (p. 684). It appears in many scenes and is photographed from a variety of distances and angles. Its logo (on both the front and the back of the vehicle) is legible at least four places in the film. Probably the Range Rover is so prominent because the film's producers and the vehicle maker struck a mutually advantageous deal. Among the people and businesses singled out for "Special Thanks" in the end credits is "Range Rover of North America" (see the appendix, "How to Read Film Credits," for the closing credits for *The Player* on p. 700).

Cinematography

Aside from the opening shot (described on p. 582), the cinematography by Jean Lepine tends to be unobtrusive. It supports the story and helps make the movie easy to follow and pleasurable to watch. Viewers with training in film studies, however, are likely to notice some of the techniques that influence viewers' responses to the film.

COLOR

The film uses expressive color at various points. One instance occurs after dark when Griffin Mill drives to David Kahane's house. Mill drives up to a distinctly lit house whose windows glow with an unusual icy, crystalline bluish white light. Unbeknownst to the woman inside, June Gudmundsdottir, Mill watches her as she speaks to him on the phone while working at a canvas surrounded by a clutter of art paraphernalia—all in a variety of blues, whites, and silvers (Plate 58). She claims to have no particular interest in movies as she ranges languidly around in the liquid, shimmering bluish light, which emphasizes the icy environment. (Later Kahane will refer to her as the "ice queen.") Throughout the film, Gudmundsdottir is associated with white. She wears white shoes, a white dress, and a white hat and a light blue scarf to Kahane's funeral. At the end of the film, she wears a white maternity dress speckled with many small flowers. Because she has been shown as a disengaged entity—in fact, to be restrained and unemotional—we can understand this radical departure from traditional colors. Mill, in contrast, dresses in different colors. Initially he wears an off-white suit, but he wears darker and darker suits as the film progresses until finally, in the last sequence, he is wearing black.

Another particularly expressive use of color occurs the night Mill kills Kahane. Reds are used to light the karaoke bar where they drink together (Plate 59). When Mill leaves the bar, a splash of red neon light colors his footsteps out the door. Just before Kahane mockingly asks to borrow Mill's cell phone, another red flash originates from behind the camera and is directed onto the back wall. Seconds later, it again flashes against the wall as Kahane makes his imaginary phone call. Eventually, red dominates the scene and is reflected by the shallow pool of water in which Mill kills Kahane (Plate 61). As is often the case in imaginative texts, the red in this scene underscores violence and the loss of blood and life.

LIGHTING

The Player is not a dark film. It begins in the outdoor morning light and concludes in sunny afternoon light. Night scenes are without deep atmospheric shadows, and viewers can still see the subjects distinctly. As might be expected, the light is especially soft during the night scene of romance between Mill and Gudmundsdottir at the desert resort (Plate 60). There are also numerous interior daytime scenes, many with light shadows from the open venetian blinds. All the daytime interiors are well illuminated. To accomplish a soft texture in the daytime interiors, cinematographer Jean Lepine used filters that create the feeling of naturally diffused light. Many filters are also used throughout the daytime shots to dampen the glare. The film's lighting supports its moods: mostly brightly lit day scenes that have minimal glare and some night scenes for murder, attempted assault with a snake, romance, and sex.

THE CAMERA

The camera is rarely positioned close to the subjects. When the subject is a talking individual, she or he is usually seen in a medium shot or a medium close-up. One exception is when viewers briefly see Mill's face in close-up as he holds Kahane's head under the puddle of water. Another notable exception is when Mill is with Detective Avery in the Pasadena police station. Avery is twirling a tampon and asking difficult questions; her assistant is stalking a fly and swatting it; and the three police personnel are laughing at Mill's desperate responses. Mill's bewildered, frightened reactions are seen in close-up and extreme close-up.

Lepine and Altman often use deep focus to capture group scenes that simultaneously portray the private interactions of famous people (without invading their conversations) and the "busyness" of the larger view. *The Player* also includes deep-focus shots during which the audience is made privy to activities and conversations in the foreground and background (Plate 63). On the other hand, when it suits the purposes of the scene, many shots of individuals and small groups are taken with a long lens so the background is out of focus and the viewer's attention can remain on the human subject(s) in the foreground.

The film also relies heavily on eye-level camera placements; viewers get to see players at an interactive level. Here, as in other films, the film-makers play to the belief that viewers have a right both to explore the world of people who wield enormous power and to be on an equal footing with them (Plates 63–64).

As in other Altman films, many moving, exploratory camera shots are used throughout, as in the film's famous 8-minute opening shot (see Table 13.1). The many shots of moving, fast-talking actors filmed by a moving camera or zoom lens (or both) contribute to the sense that people in the movie industry are an energetic group wrapped up in their work but not each other. Often scenes are filmed so that one character is walking away as another character walks alongside or behind, talking at rather than talking to each other—all the while without making eye contact.

Editing

The Player is a suspenseful, satirical film in which the main character confronts several problems simultaneously. The editing by Geraldine Peroni unifies the elements of Mill's story and moves the story along at a pace that entertains audiences and keeps them involved.[2]

CONTINUITY EDITING

Continuity editing is used throughout *The Player*. An example of effective continuity editing is six consecutive scenes in which Mill tracks down a writer, meets him, and kills him:

1. *Tracking the writer.* Mill looks through the office datebooks and at data on a computer, decides that Kahane is the threatening writer, and gets Kahane's address and phone number.
2. *Calling Kahane's house.* Mill parks near a house and talks with the woman inside the house on his cell phone while he stands outside.
3. *The Rialto movie theater.* Mill sees the end of *The Bicycle Thief.*
4. *The theater lobby.* Mill talks with Kahane.
5. *The karaoke bar.* Mill and Kahane drink together and talk some more.
6. *Confrontation and murder.* Mill and Kahane confront each other in a parking lot; Mill murders Kahane.

In this nearly 16 1/2-minute sequence, which is made up of six scenes, the film represents approximately 2 hours of story time. Viewers can easily follow the action, and the content and pace of the sequence seem appropriate.

Another example of editing used to support continuity occurs a little more than 71 minutes into the film, when a match cut juxtaposes the dead snake Mill kills with the thick curvy line that June draws with blue chalk.

IMAGE ON IMAGE AND IMAGE AFTER IMAGE

The film includes no lap dissolves or superimpositions. The only transitions between scenes other than cuts are two fade-out, fade-ins that are used near the end of the film: one before and the other after the title card "One Year Later."

Among the most expressive cuts in the film is the transition from the murdered writer to movie studio employees (Plates 61–62). Also expressive is the cut from the lovemaking scene to the mud bath (nearly 106 minutes

---

[2]Geraldine Peroni is listed as the editor in the film's opening credits, in various printed sources, and on the laser disc jacket, the DVD cover, and the videotape box, but the concluding credits list Maysie Hoy as editor and many secondary sources list both people as coeditors.

into the film). In the throes of passion, Griffin Mill confesses his responsibility for David Kahane's death, but Gudmundsdottir does not want to hear such talk. There is a natural lack of clarity in this erotic exchange as the lovers are more concentrated on their physical arousal than on what is being said. Regardless of Gudmundsdottir's ardor, a murky element sullies their liaison. In fact, morally they are up to their necks in hot muck. And that is what viewers can sense in the cut from the lovemaking scene to the mud bath scene where the lovers are immersed separately, do not touch, and make no eye contact.

At least two sets of reaction shots warrant discussion. The first, which occurs a little more than 10 minutes into the film, concerns the scene in which Reggie Goldman, a banker's son, is trying to exercise his leverage in his pursuit of various attractive female actors. The scene includes multiple reaction shots of the amused and knowing Joel Levison, Walter Stuckel, and Griffin Mill.

The second set of particularly expressive reaction shots occurs approximately 93 minutes into the film, during the scene at the Pasadena police station where Mill has been summoned to review mug shots. Detective Avery nonchalantly unwraps a tampon and begins to twirl it while asking Mill whether he had gone out with Gudmundsdottir the night before. Avery wants to know how long Mill has known her and whether he has had sex with her. Mill becomes confused and incensed and says he won't answer that question without a lawyer present; then he contends in effect that his rights are being ignored. The camera cuts to Avery, who laughs in reaction to Mill's defensive behavior. Her laughter bubbles over as Detective De-Longpre and two others join in. Close-up and extreme close-up reaction shots of Mill accompanied by raucous background laughter complete the scene.

The film begins with the rare situation of one shot showing multiple scenes (see Table 13.1). However, as in most scenes in movies, most of the scenes in *The Player* consist of multiple shots. Consider the scene in which Mill talks to Gudmundsdottir on his cell phone. The scene runs 225 seconds and consists of 26 shots. This scene needs to be long enough to reveal something of Gudmundsdottir's character and allure and to make credible Mill's infatuation with her even though he is preoccupied with locating the threatening writer and dealing with him. The scene also needs to be visually varied and interesting. And it is. The moving subject (Mill) and the moving camera suggest Mill's restlessness and his curiosity about this luminous vision; he wants to view her continually and from various distances and angles. Likewise, Gudmundsdottir is usually in motion. It is not only the subjects' movements and the camera movement that inject vitality into the scene. The editing—as well as the varied camera distances and angles it makes possible—also contributes visual variety while excising uneventful time. Although the editing is not fast, its average shot length of 8.65 seconds is brisk enough to impart some energy to the scene.

Sometimes editing helps vary the pace within scenes. Consider the scene where Mill drives off from the St. James's Club,[3] receives a fax, uncovers a present on the floor of the Range Rover, and reacts to the snake. The first 45 seconds of the scene have an average shot length of 4.5 seconds. The last 54 seconds of the scene, after Mill discovers the rattler, have an even shorter average shot length of 2.7 seconds, with some shots lasting only a second or two. Given the danger to Mill (a crash, snakebites, or both), the fast cutting reinforces his panicky reaction after he uncovers the snake.

Sound

Sound in *The Player* contributes to the varied moods. For example, in many scenes in which the characters display nervousness and tension, the music is jangling and edgy, not melodic. The few scenes featuring soothing music and relaxed conversation, such as when Mill and Gudmundsdottir dance at the desert hideaway, offer viewers (and Mill) a welcome break from the tension.

SPOKEN WORDS

Overlapping dialogue (a common experience in everyday life and in most Altman films) is used in group scenes to make some word and phrase recognition possible yet allow other snippets of language to function as ambient sound. In their rush, characters speak without being entirely heard, and the cacophonous mixture of voices suggests that the attempt to be heard may be in vain. In such an environment, communication can be incomplete, fragmentary, and stressful.

The commentary on the laser disc version (but not the DVD) points out that for the scene of Larry Levy's first executive meeting, which occurs almost $39\frac{1}{2}$ minutes into the film, each actor wore a separately wired microphone (Plate 62). Such an arrangement allowed the sound editor to raise and lower the volume or shift the focus of dialogue interaction to replicate the flow of sound energy among participants in a high-level business meeting. Because the objective is so well achieved, viewers are more likely to feel like participants in that meeting. A shot that begins a little more than $21\frac{1}{2}$ minutes into the film redirects viewer attention by a coordinated effort of sound and image. Small concealed mics were placed on two actors in the foreground and two actors in the background, and a zoom lens was used for the shot (Plates 63–64). The shot illustrates two techniques Altman explored the use of in various films: the moving camera or zoom lens to redirect viewer attention and multiple sources of dialogue used in untraditional ways.

---

[3]The punctuation is as it appears on the postcard Mill receives while sitting poolside at the club and talking with the two men eagerly pitching the story for *Habeas Corpus*.

Spoken words are altered for effect when Griffin Mill cries out "Keep it to yourself" during his rage that results in Kahane's murder, and the sound seems amplified by an echo chamber. It seems loud enough to get the attention of anyone in the vicinity but does not; however, the distortion helps convey Mill's rage.

Although film is not generally a medium in which spoken words dominate, *The Player* involves a protagonist who is a professional listener in a busy but never loud environment. Thus, it is appropriate that in many scenes conversations dominate and surround him.

MUSIC

As in many movies, the soundtrack consists of previously recorded music and music composed specifically for the film, in this case by Thomas Newman. A major musical theme by Newman is introduced in the opening shot; it does not have a recognizable melody but is strongly rhythmical. What it does have is a certain feeling, busy and visceral yet at the same time light, shimmering, and chiming. As in most movies, including *The Player*, whenever dialogue is important, the music fades out to make room for it.

When Mill seats himself by the outdoor pool of the St. James's Club, the music includes a jazzy saxophone reminiscent of film noir. Background sirens and the sounds of a flying helicopter are blended in to enhance the feeling of a "big city at night." As Mill is driving home from the St. James's Club and discovers that a rattlesnake has been planted in his car, the music understandably becomes chaotic. It has an accelerated rhythm when Mill uncovers the snake; then it is dominated by loud, rapid bongo drums, horns, and a recurrent sibilant rattling sound.

Music is also a vital component of the lovemaking scene. Visually, there is simply the incontrovertible suggestion of lovemaking created by the screen filled with two glistening heads arranged horizontally and facing each other, kissing, moaning, breathing heavily, and speaking intimately. The music takes on complex rhythms while combining rapid chimes, a bongo drum, a snare drum, and various electronic sounds that together enhance the eroticism and suggest orgasm, then fade out. The music helps make the scene erotic.

In *The Player*, the music underpins, focuses, and helps blend the various film ingredients. Its power is achieved not through identifiable or memorable melodies but through its versatility and the appropriate feelings the music conjures up or supports.

SOUND EFFECTS AND SILENCE

Sound effects are limited in *The Player* because spoken words and music play prominent roles, and the film does not showcase violence or action (traditional subjects requiring extensive sound effects). Where sound effects are used—as with the faint, distant offscreen barking dog after Kahane's murder—their presence melds so effectively with what is being shown that viewers are unlikely to notice them and are not meant to.

Silence is used briefly after David Kahane is murdered to emphasize that he is dead. Other than that, there are conventional split-second slivers of silence to differentiate scenes. Skillful sound editing allows these brief silences to be used as a subtle form of punctuation. Otherwise the silences might become awkward transitions inadvertently left unfilled.

In some scenes, two major types of sound help establish the setting. For example, a little more than 90 minutes into the film, as Mill arrives at the Pasadena police station, both spoken words and sound effects reveal the strident setting. Two suspects being hauled toward a hallway scream defiantly at the arresting officers, and a siren wails in the background.

SOUND TRANSITIONS

As in many movies, music is used to connect scenes, as between the end of the opening shot and the next scene, in Mill's secretary's office. Music is used again to connect the ending of that scene to the beginning of the following scene, where Mill and his secretary are outside walking and talking.

Spoken words, conversations particularly, are also used to ease the transitions between scenes. Twice an actor's name is mentioned, such as Anjelica Huston, and the next shot is of the actor named. An intriguing transition occurs immediately after Mill leaves Kahane for dead. The camera focuses on the murder scene, which is momentarily silent, but viewers' attention is soon diverted by a conversation that is fading in. Briefly, viewers are curious about two places at once: the red pool of water where the body lies and the conversation that is slowly fading in (Plates 61–62).

Sources for Fictional Films

Michael Tolkin's novel *The Player* was first published in 1988. Tolkin also wrote the screen adaptation and acted the part of one of the two Schecter brothers, writers who are with Mill when Bonnie Sherow comes to his office to ask him if he is involved with someone new.

NOVEL AND FILM

In their characters and plots, the novel and film have much in common. Both focus on a 30-something Hollywood studio executive, Griffin Mill, whose job it is to listen to and pass judgment on pitches for movies. In both novel and film, Mill is romantically involved with Bonnie Sherow. In both, he seeks out a writer he thinks is sending him threatening postcards, finds him at a screening of *The Bicycle Thief*, has drinks with him, and later that night kills him. At the writer's funeral, Mill meets the writer's girlfriend, June, who soon becomes Mill's love interest. In both novel and film, both the studio head of security and the Pasadena police treat Mill as a suspect, but he is not identified in a police lineup and ends up with a job promotion and the love of the murdered writer's girlfriend.

Although the source novel and the film are fundamentally the same, many changes were made in converting the novel to a script and then a film because the filmmakers chose to add, delete, or change details. In both novel and film, Mill continually hides his feelings from others and usually reins in his emotions, although at the conclusion of Chapter 14, when he fears arrest is imminent, he cries. Film critic Michael Wilmington points out that unlike the novel, the film surrounds the central character with a large and varied group: "Tolkin's novel was chilly, spare, and lean: It zeroed right into Griffin's skull. Altman, predictably, has enriched the milieu and built up a huge community around the cipher at the center."

Because of other decisions made by the filmmakers, the novel and film differ in yet other ways. In the book, the screenwriter does not pitch his script called *Habeas Corpus* as an independent film with unknown actors and a tragic ending. In the film, he does. In the novel (and the script), Mill and June go to a Mexican seaside resort for a weekend vacation. Given the limited budget for making *The Player*, the filmmakers shifted the vacation from Mexico or a Mexico look-alike to a desert hideaway. In the novel, because of Mill's reluctance, Mill and June do not entirely consummate their relationship until the epilogue, which takes place six months later and implies that Mill and June are married, though with no clue that she is pregnant. In the film, Mill and June consummate their relationship at the conclusion of the romantic evening at the desert hideaway resort, and at the end of the story, one year later, Mill and June are living together. Though it is unclear if they are married, she is clearly pregnant. In the novel, Mill agrees to move to a different type of position with a different company before the head of the studio is ousted. Near the end of the film, Mill has mysteriously displaced the studio head. In the book's epilogue, the anonymous postcard writer quits scriptwriting, moves out of state, and sends Mill a letter of apology and $1,000 cash to pay for the car windows the writer had shot out while stalking Mill. In the film, he calls Mill and indirectly threatens to blackmail him.

The filmmakers also decided to change the female characters. In the book, June is an art director for Wells Fargo banks, and readers get to know her somewhat better than viewers get to know the cinematic June, though in both her attraction to Mill is more contrived than credible. Police detective Susan Avery is also a different character in the novel: for example, sometimes she is attracted to Mill and is impressed by his position and power. According to Altman, Whoopi Goldberg devised much of the tampon-twirling scene where she questions Mill in her office, and the film Avery, as Goldberg can be, is more confident, ironic, and forceful than the book's Avery. In the book, Bonnie Sherow works for a different studio and is less prominent than in the film. But because Cynthia Stevenson is a charming, skilled actor, the filmmakers gave the film Sherow more prominence and presented her in a more sympathetic light. The casting of Goldberg and Stevenson are examples of how casting influences characterization, a situation not uncommon in films, particularly Altman's, which tend to be more collaborative and improvisatory in their making than most films.

Some changes were made in converting the novel to a film because of different strengths of each medium. The most striking difference between the novel and the film is that the novel is driven by Mill's frequent thoughts and the film by dialogue, action, and expressive images. In the novel, readers have frequent access to Mill's thoughts and feelings. While on a vacation with June in Mexico, for example, Mill thinks: "He had made too many mistakes. He had lied to too many people. When the first card arrived, no, when the third card arrived, the card with the death threat, he should have gone straight to Walter Stuckel [head of studio security], straight to Levison [head of the studio], and showed it to them. He should have asked for help. He shouldn't have worried about the cards' effect on his job. And now it was too late to show the cards to anyone" (Tolkin 168). In the book, Mill is preoccupied with events that led up to the murder and with ways to avoid getting caught for his crime. Mill also thinks about the complex and unstable world of the movie industry. Throughout the book, Mill worries about how he appears to others. Since the film presents the characters' personalities through action and dialogue, we never learn what Mill ruminates about, and the celluloid Mill is far less reflective than the conjecture-obsessed creation in the book.

SCRIPT AND FILM

The differences between the script and the film are similar to the differences between the novel and the film. In general, the film is more biting and satirical, and less emotional, than the script and certainly than the novel. For example, at Kahane's funeral the script calls for Kahane's brother to deliver the following eulogy:

54   INT. CHAPEL—DAY

We hear Kahane's brother over a p.a. system. Mill takes a black yarmulke from a basket and puts it on.

BROTHER: Einstein said that God doesn't play dice. I'd like to say that we could console ourselves with the thought that in God's plan, David Kahane's death is necessary for the universe to unfold its majestic design . . .

He [Mill] opens the door to the chapel.

55   INT. CHAPEL—DAY

The coffin. About thirty mourners. The brother, 25, continues.

BROTHER: . . . but I can't say that, because David always laughed at mindless faith. Someone in the night killed him, and that person will have to bear his guilt, and he'll never know what he took from David's friends and family.

Griffin takes a seat in the back row. A few people in the front row turn to see who has come in. June looks at Griffin. She says something to the man sitting next to her, who turns around to see the last man who saw Kahane alive.

BROTHER: My brother died after seeing a movie, which I guess is sort of fitting. I hope you don't take this the wrong way, but he really loved movies, and I'm glad he didn't die on his way in, you know, before he saw it. That would have hurt me a lot more and this hurts a lot.

The pressure is too much for Griffin. He goes outside. We hear the Kaddish from inside.

56   EXT. HILLSIDE MEMORIAL—DAY

Mourners shovel earth onto the casket in the open grave. Finished. People walk away. (Tolkin script 44)

About 47½ minutes into the film, a fellow writer delivers Kahane's eulogy:

> The Hollywood system did not murder David Kahane. Not the ninety-eight-million-dollar movie, not the twelve-million-dollar actor, not even the million-dollar deal that David Kahane never landed. No, the most that we can pin on Hollywood is assault with intent to kill because society is responsible for this particular murder. And it is to society that we must look if we are to have any justice for that crime. Because someone in the night killed David Kahane and that person will have to bear the guilt. And, if David were here right now, I know in my heart that he would have said, "Cut the shit, Phil. What did you learn from all of this? Did you learn anything from this?" I'd say, "Yeah, David, I've learned a lot. We here will, uh, take it from here and the next time we sell a script for a million dollars, the next time we nail some shit-bag producer to the wall we'll say 'That's another one for David Kahane.'" . . . David was working on something the day he died. I'd like to share it with you. "Blackness. A mangy dog barks. Garbage can lids are lifted as derelicts in the street hunt for food, buzzing as a cheap alarm clock goes off. INT—FLOP HOUSE ROOM—EARLY MORNING. A tracking shot moves through the grimy room. Light streams in through holes in the yellowing window shades. Moths dance in the beams of light. Track down along the floor. The frayed rug. Stop on an old shoe. It's empty." It's as far as he got. That's the last thing he wrote. So long Dave. Fade-out. Thank you.

In the script, the funeral is Jewish, and the eulogy is given by a grieving member of Kahane's family. In the film, the funeral is secular; the eulogy is given by an angry fellow writer; and there is no sign of Kahane's family. In the script, the eulogy and the mourners at the open grave show the devastating impact Kahane's death has had on his family. In the film, the eulogy is more about anger than grief.

The film's eulogy is longer than the one in the script and is supplemented by visual information. Thus, viewers can allow the droning speech to become background noise because they sense the visual information is more important. During the speech, viewers see Griffin Mill arrive silently in his black Range Rover; he approaches the gathering gingerly; he stands differentiated by his clothing (an expensive suit). June Gudmundsdottir, dressed in white, glances back to him. We also see Detective DeLongpre (who has not yet been identified) approach the mourners and stand at the other side of a broad monument next to a tree. Up to this point the audience has been teased with this character. He is curious-looking, suspicious perhaps, and viewers may be wondering whether he is the postcard writer.

The scene illustrates the point that, typically, films are much more expressive visually than is indicated by the script. This combination of sounds and moving images is unique to the film and video media, and the differences between the script and the film allow us to see and hear how the filmmakers have capitalized on this distinctive capability.

OTHER FILMS

Films are called intertextual when they evoke or use other films and other forms of human expression. And *The Player* does this throughout. It is, after all, a movie whose main subjects are moviemakers and the early stages of making movies. Intertextuality in *The Player* runs from the lengthy opening shot and its inclusion of discussions of similar lengthy shots in other films, to the screening of *Habeas Corpus*, a parody of popular movies with serious subjects but distracting stars and last-minute rescues. In between, there are all those movie posters on the walls of Mill's and Levison's offices; the sixty-five cameos, most by famous movie actors but including the film's scriptwriter; the "one of us" allusion to the ending of *Freaks* (1932); the clips from the ending of *The Bicycle Thief*; and all the talk about other films and other filmmakers. *The Player* draws on a wealth of detail not merely from a novel and script but also from other films and a long tradition of moviemaking.

Components of Fictional Films

Like all narrative films, *The Player* consists of selected and structured events presented over time.

STRUCTURE

The Player has two parts: five or six days of selected events; then, one year later, selected events from the day of the screening of the studio's latest offering, *Habeas Corpus*. The two parts are bridged by a title card informing viewers that the following action occurs one year later.

In the first and far lengthier part, viewers meet Griffin Mill and learn of his twin problems (the anonymous threatening writer and the rumor that Levy is being groomed for Mill's job) and of his goals (retaining power at work and winning the love of a beautiful artist). To eliminate the first source of anxiety, Mill seeks out a man he believes is the threatening writer and ends up killing him. Thus, an action designed to help Mill eliminate one of his two major problems thrusts him into an arena where he lacks knowledge or leverage. A misstep or bad luck will unravel his career and plunge him into a legal abyss. He survives his brush with the law only by luck. At about this time, the Levy problem is also solved. Mill is not ousted from the studio; the studio head is. Interwoven with Mill's studio-related problems are scenes of his love life, first with Sherow, for whom he displays no ardor, then with Gudmundsdottir.

By a year later, Mill has assumed the helm of the studio; *Habeas Corpus* has been reworked beyond recognition; the former rival has become an ally; and Mill resumes his life with an even greater degree of power and prosperity than before. Mill approves a story pitch that describes the movie we've just seen. The story promises to be circular. In the last scene, viewers see that Mill and the pregnant June are in love, living together, and seemingly safe.

TIME

The story of *The Player* is conveyed chronologically. There are no flashbacks or flash-forwards. The first part of the story—from the introduction of Mill and his problems and his goals to his winning of Gudmundsdottir and getting away with murder—transpires over five or six days. As in most other films, *The Player* is usually vague about how much time elapses between scenes. If one notes when day scenes give way to night scenes, the first part of the story consumes at least five and a half days. The overall story time is approximately one week plus one year; the film's running time is 124 minutes. As usual in fictional films, the events of *The Player* are highly selective. There is nothing unconventional or even challenging about the film's handling of structure and time, except for the final twist that the anonymous writer's proposed story is the one viewers have just seen.

Types of Fictional Films

The Player is both classical Hollywood cinema and independent film. It has enough qualities of classical Hollywood cinema, such as some famous performers and a happy ending, to help ensure its commercial success. The film has enough qualities of the independent film, such as satire, to win laudatory reviews and various awards and nominations beyond a few Academy Awards nominations, including Cannes Film Festival awards, National Society of Film Critics' best film award, Independent Spirit award for best film, Golden Globe awards and nominations, and British Academy Awards nominations.

CLASSICAL HOLLYWOOD CINEMA

The Player exemplifies all the major features of classical Hollywood cinema: the story is set entirely in a present, external world and is largely seen from outside the action, although point-of-view shots are sometimes included. *The Player* focuses on a character that has an initial goal: to survive in his position of wealth and power. In trying to attain his goal, Griffin Mill confronts two major problems: the anonymous threatening writer and an executive perhaps being groomed for Mill's job. Early in the film, Mill develops a second goal: to win June Gudmundsdottir. The film has closure: the plot has no "loose ends" or unresolved issues, other than the identity of the threatening writer (though he may be the eulogizer at Kahane's funeral; see p. 593). Mill reaches his goals: he gets free of the two threats to his success, gets away with murder, gets promoted, and settles down with the beautiful artist. Like so many popular Hollywood movies, *The Player* shows a male succeeding both professionally and personally. By the end of the film, what happens and why are unambiguous. Finally, the film uses continuity editing and, except for the opening shot, other unobtrusive filmmaking techniques.

American Independent Films

The Player also exhibits characteristics of the American independent film. Besides having a lower budget than typical Hollywood products and freedom from studio creative control, *The Player* has other earmarks of an independent film. Its content has limited appeal, not because it is particularly controversial but because it requires a certain level of awareness of the film industry; more essentially, *The Player* is a complex and subtle satire that rewards attentive viewing. Finally, its plot is by no means formulaic. For example, the main character gets away with murder, which would be inconceivable before the production code was abandoned in 1968. The story is surprising and unpredictable, and, like most independent films, *The Player* fits into no genre. The VHS videotape box categorizes *The Player* as a "thriller," and the DVD cover characterizes the film as a "celebrity-studded thriller of murderous obsession." Well, somewhat. The movie is not exactly an example of the mystery genre either: for one thing, much of the story is not devoted to the mystery of *who* is threatening Mill. The possible Levy threat and Mill's romances with Sherow and Gudmundsdottir also take up much of the plot.

The movies made by the studio that Mill works for are classical Hollywood cinema of the most commercial stripe. As he explains to Gudmundsdottir approximately 103 minutes into the film, the films his studio makes need "suspense, laughter, violence, hope, heart, nudity, sex, happy endings . . . mainly happy endings." As initially proposed, *Habeas Corpus*, the movie within the movie, is to become an independent film: no stars, mostly true-to-life events, issues outside the mainstream, and a credible unhappy ending. As made by Mill's studio, *Habeas Corpus* is an exaggerated example of crowd-pleasing classical Hollywood cinema, with stars, improbable action, and a happy ending.

Understanding *The Player* through Contexts

Any text is a product of its time and culture. Viewers who know about some contexts of *The Player* can understand the film more completely than those who know only the film.

SOCIETY AND POLITICS

Historically, Los Angeles fought for recognition amid aspersions that it was "sleepy," too much a part of the West to be considered a challenge to the East's position as the bastion of intellectual, financial, and social validity. The values that emerged and eventually grew to define Los Angeles are directly related to the emergence and eventual ascension to power of the movie industry. As a theatrical reviewer for the *Los Angeles Times* wrote in 1999, L.A. is "a city built on deception." The irony that Los Angeles has little to define itself other than its image is not lost on Angelenos. In fact, there is an air of pride rather than apology surrounding the statement. After all, it is a mesmerizing image.

    The Player is L.A. on L.A. In this movie Los Angeles, unfiltered water is to be avoided, even though Los Angeles water has long been rated among the best-tasting and safest of all large American cities. Business contacts are generated at AA meetings, and Range Rovers may be equipped with fax machines. Success requires that people recognize one another but remain unencumbered by relationships or obligations. These elements help re-create something of the Los Angeles of the late 1980s and early 1990s.

CENSORSHIP

The Player was made free of Hollywood studio control; thus the director, writer, and actors enjoyed a wide range of freedom to present the subjects as they saw fit, including gently satirizing Hollywood studio filmmaking. The film is rated R—presumably for its partial nudity; a sex scene of heavy breathing and two sweaty, bobbing heads; vulgar language; and one scene of violent murder. The rating allowed its makers to roam a broad field. The film does not attract audiences because of its sex and violence. In truth, there is little. Its concerns and appeal lie elsewhere—with Hollywood-style deal making and people who make movies and the pleasures of seeing them mocked genially.

ARTISTIC CONVENTIONS

The Player follows certain filmmaking conventions, except for the film's virtuoso opening shot, which is described in Table 13.1. For instance, everyone, from principal characters to the studio mail carrier, is attractive. Some Angelenos would argue that that is true to life. It is, however, more an adherence to what viewers expect in movies (convention) than what is true of the gene pool in Los Angeles. All the "players" are white males. Women are portrayed as competent in a tough, competitive atmosphere, but they are not "players." The most sympathetic of them, Bonnie, gets fired and loses her footing. (That is not only adherence to film convention; it is part of the environment that must be shown if the story is to be credible.) The main female character, June, is represented as a beacon in the night dressed in white whose radiance allows her to stand out even among the Beautiful People.

FINANCIAL CONSTRAINTS

By 1991, director Robert Altman had been relatively successful both at the box office and in the reviewers' columns, but in the years before he made *The Player* he had not had a recent popular or critical success. He also had the reputation of being a Hollywood outsider. With its satiric story of Hollywood studio moviemaking, lack of big stars in big roles, and a low quotient of sex and violence, *The Player* had almost no chance of attracting big audiences. So how did the film get funding? Keeping the satire amusing and good-natured (what Altman himself calls "tame" in the DVD commentary) probably helped. Although the concluding credits list a stunt coordinator, special effects, and set medic, the film has no costly special effects or dangerous action scenes, such as a car crash described in the source novel. Instead of filming in Mexico, as the novel indicated, some scenes were filmed at a desert resort during the off-season. Certainly, the relatively modest budget of approximately $8 million and the willingness of many actors, some of them stars, to be involved in an Altman film at minimal rates also helped make possible the funding and the making of the film.

Thinking about *The Player*

The Player has multiple and unexpected story developments—especially the murderer getting away with it. It also has many possible meanings. Only a few examples are developed here, but others are likely to occur to anyone who has seen the film and thought about it.

EXPECTATIONS AND INTERACTIONS

Early in *The Player*, viewers read the title card "A Robert Altman Film." Those who have seen other Altman films—such as *M*A*S*H* (1970), *McCabe and Mrs. Miller* (1971), *The Long Goodbye* (1973), *Nashville* (1975), *A Wedding* (1978), *Short Cuts* (1993), *Gosford Park* (2001), and *A Prairie Home Companion* (2006)—will have certain expectations: satire; surprises; some complexity in characterizations, plot, or meanings; and a potential for a viewing experience that will linger in the mind after they leave the theater.[4] ▶

A film entitled *The Player* may pique a viewer's curiosity to see which meaning(s) of the word will apply. By denotation, *player* has at least seven meanings about different types of people, including a person who engages in illegal activity. By connotation, the word can evoke shades of artifice, sleight of hand, and imposture. It may also suggest an elevated level of skill and competition.

In the opening shot, viewers discover immediately that they must process visual and verbal information at a demanding pace. We are going to get an insider's simultaneous, multichanneled view of Hollywood film-makers at work. By reputation we know it to be a treacherous, illusory environment set in luxurious surroundings. By the film's conclusion, we understand that Griffin Mill is a player. Larry Levy is a player. Bonnie is not. Levison was a player—then suddenly and inexplicably was not. The director of *Habeas Corpus* has been converted into one.

TYPES OF MEANING

There are only a few explicit meanings in *The Player*. Probably the most noteworthy one is Griffin's explanation to June about what makes for a successful Hollywood movie, especially a happy ending. Generally, fictional films invite viewers to construct their own sense of the characters' attributes and motivations and the film's meanings. Otherwise, it would be like playing cards with all hands dealt faceup.

The Player is rich in implicit meanings. The film's portrayal of film industry personnel confirms the industry's reputation: Hollywood threatens constancy in human relationships. *The Player* shows only one lasting alliance, and that one (between Griffin and June) has the potential for survival only because she is outside the movie industry (she does not even go to movies).

In *The Player* actors and talk of them are plentiful, and, of course, writers are prominent, appearing in the initial scenes and often thereafter. The film exposes the low esteem in which writers are held. We see this most clearly when Larry Levy proposes doing away with them (expensive and unnecessary appendages) and suggests that the executives can create their own story lines from things as mundane as current newspaper headlines. Levy's next idea is to advocate production of *Habeas Corpus*, complete with unknown actors and unhappy ending. As pitched, beginning with the title, it is hard to imagine a less promising story for a commercial film. So after Levy's two false starts, what is his fate? Evidently when Griffin assumes

---

[4]Many Altman films, including his final one, *A Prairie Home Companion*, also have a large community of characters—such as guests at a wedding; residents, employees, and guests at a British estate; participants in a complex radio show broadcast; and many who are part of the Hollywood movie industry. Shortly after Altman's death, a new award was named in his honor: the Robert Altman Award for the best film ensemble cast and direction in an independent film. See p. 344.

control of the studio, Levy gets promoted to Griffin's old job. Continuity of the usual product is ensured.

When Bonnie cries at the end of *The Player*, she violates a cardinal principle of the filmmaking industry: at work, emotions must be kept under control. Near the film's end, Griffin breezes past her without so much as a backward glance and says that she "will land on her feet." In contrast to Bonnie's emotional reactions, recall Griffin's largely nonplussed demeanor when the studio's security chief questions him regarding Kahane's death. Remember Griffin's controlled response to each postcard. At one point he dismisses his secretary's suggestion that he involve studio security to help track down the threatening writer. Griffin knows he must not show fear if he is to remain a player, especially at this time when he believes that his job is in jeopardy.

Satire is the representation of an individual or a group that indirectly exposes and perhaps ridicules thinking or behavior for being foolish, evil, or stupid or for exhibiting some other shortcoming. *The Player* is wide-ranging in its satiric targets. Writers are satirized for being desperate and for wavering when they sense Mill's reluctance. Directors are satirized for selling out the integrity of a story for the sake of commercial success. Studio executives are shown as concerned more with profits than with creating quality products. Of course, the product of all these studio personnel—the studio movie—is parodied and satirized by the distracting presence of stars and the preposterous happy ending of *Habeas Corpus*.

Meaning is also suggested by symbols—for example, the main character's name. Hollywood is a griffin mill: a manufacturer of fabled creations. The product includes any number of chimerical masterpieces. But it likewise includes monstrosities. *Mill* has additional relevant meanings, including an institution or a business that makes a profit by turning out product without regard to quality, as in "diploma mill," a school that turns out graduates without regard to standards.

The Player is symptomatic of much of life in late-twentieth-century America in its representation of the competition within and between companies, the use of consumer technology (such as cars, fax machines, and cell phones) in people's work, and the immersion in work at the expense of personal connections.

As the "Postscript to Part One" illustrates (pp. 193–99), filmmakers decide how subtly to use techniques. Sometimes the expressive aspects of the settings—such as the movie posters—are seen only fleetingly. Another example of subtlety occurs nearly 25 minutes into the film as viewers glimpse a book in a desk drawer as Mill begins his search for leads about the threatening writer. For less than a second, viewers have a chance to read the title of the book, *They Made Me a Criminal*, which is also the title of a 1939 movie. In an interview with Geoff Andrew, Altman implies that the postcard writer is the eulogizer at Kahane's funeral (187), and in the

Criterion laser disc version of *The Player* (but not on the DVD), Tolkin says that the actor who plays the eulogizer was used for the telephone voice of the blackmailing writer at the film's end. Both characters use the phrase "some shit-bag producer." That detail is too subtle for nearly all viewers to notice: the two speeches are brief, far apart, and the second is heard only as a telephone voice. Occasionally, though, significant details may be emphasized a little much, as when the camera lingers on a movie poster or moves in on a photograph of the cinematic master of mystery, murder, and suspense—director Alfred Hitchcock (1:03:37 into the film). Alert viewers have already understood the point about the poster and will glimpse the Hitchcock photo in the background on their own.

Although *The Player* adheres to the basics of its source novel and screenplay, the film typifies Robert Altman's film work and could be a candidate for the auteurist approach.[5] Like many Altman films, *The Player* relies heavily on satire without ever becoming venomous, and it is sometimes sprawling in number of characters and intricacies of plot. And like other Altman films, there is a heavy reliance on the moving camera, the zoom lens, and overlapping dialogue. Other viewers will see these and other meanings. Here is a sample:

EXPECTATIONS AND INTERACTIONS

"There's a chill at the center of *The Player*. Altman gets us rooting for Griffin by subtle degrees—first, because his job is threatened; later, because he's in love and in trouble. But the movie needles us by degrees, too, by gradually exposing Griffin's corruption. If we're cheering Griffin on even though he's a cad (and worse), that makes us somehow accomplices in his perfidy. And, in the end, when he prevails while the nice but decidedly less glamorous folk around him tumble, Altman slathers on the triumphant music and sunshine in a way that may make us squirm. He's not letting anyone off the hook—not even the audience. After all, we're part of the system, too. We're the ones clamoring for '*Ghost* meets *The Manchurian Candidate*'; we're the ones drooling over Bruce [Willis] and Arnold [Schwarzenegger] and Julia [Roberts] and Mel [Gibson]. No one leaves *The Player* with a clear conscience" (Schiff 143).

EXPLICIT MEANINGS A few commentators quoted the film's most prominent explicit meaning, Mill's explanation to June about the ingredients of a successful Hollywood movie: "suspense, laughter, violence, hope, heart, nudity, sex, happy endings . . . mainly happy endings."

---

[5]For an example of an auteurist reading of various films directed by Robert Altman, including *The Player*, see Richard Combs, "Robert Altman: Death and the Maidens," *Sight & Sound* 17:2 (Feb. 2007): 14–17.

IMPLICIT MEANINGS Nearly always, *The Player* shows and suggests its meanings rather than states them, and as commentator Stephen Schiff observes, "Altman demonstrates all this [implicit meaning] without getting windy about it" (138).

"*The Player* is about how the industry crushes the originality out of anyone who participates in it—any Player, be he writer, director, or production chief. And that's because the Hollywood system makes it impossible to view the world afresh, to derive inspiration or even information from it" (Schiff 138).

"*The Player* . . . satirizes Hollywood mores and mannerisms, but, at the same time, never truly disturbs its audience and can easily be enjoyed, absorbed, and promoted by the industry itself" (Quart).

"The film should captivate anyone with a taste for bold cinematics, unpredictable storytelling, and pitch-black humor aimed at the worthiest of targets: a self-involved and self-congratulatory industry that often gives lip-service to art while worshipping the bottom line" (Sterritt 14).

SYMPTOMATIC MEANINGS "*The Player* does capture L.A. and today's Hollywood with chilling exactness. It's more than the way the details are right, things like the cars, the houses, the restaurants, even the mineral water. . . . Tolkin and Altman are also hip to the mind set of a completely self-absorbed, not to say amoral, business awash in frenzied round-the-clock schmoozing" (Turan).

In a 1992 interview with Geoff Andrew, Altman said that *The Player* is "*of* Hollywood, but it's not really just *about* Hollywood. Hollywood is a metaphor for our society, which is based on greed—take, take, take, and don't give anything back to the system; lie and cheat. So though the film is about the stupidity of Hollywood, it's also about the moral problems of our society at large" (185).

As with all films, viewers' interactions with the film and the meanings they formulate depend in part on their backgrounds and ways of thinking.

WORKS CITED

Altman, Robert. Audio commentary. *The Player* (DVD), N4032. New Line Home Video, 1997.

Andrew, Geoff. "The Player King." Interview with Robert Altman. *Time Out* no. 1137 (3 June 1992): 18–20. Reprinted in *Robert Altman Interviews*. Ed. David Sterritt. Jackson: UP of Mississippi, 2000. 182–87.

The Player. Screenplay by Michael Tolkin. Dir. Robert Altman. Fine Line Features, 1992. (The film's end credits are reprinted on pp. 696–701 of this book.)

The Player. Laser disc. Criterion Collection, 1993.

The Player. DVD. New Line Home Video, 1997.

Quart, Leonard, and Alissa Quart. Rev. of *The Player*. *Cineaste* 19.2–3 (1992): 60 ff.

Schiff, Stephen. "Auteur! Auteur!" *Vanity Fair* 55.4 (April 1992): 136–43.

Sterritt, David. "A Movie That Pokes Fun at Movies." *Christian Science Monitor* 10 Apr. 1992: 14.

Tolkin, Michael. *The Player: A Novel*. New York: Atlantic Monthly, 1988.

———. *The Player*. Script, 20 Apr. 1989, first draft. Hollywood: Script City, [1993?]. Photocopy. 124 leaves.

Turan, Kenneth. Rev. of *The Player*. *Los Angeles Times* 10 Apr. 1992, Calendar: 1 ff.

Wilmington, Michael. "*The Player* Marks Altman's Return to Hollywood." *Los Angeles Times* 29 Sept. 1991, home ed.: Calendar: 23+.

APPENDICES

Links to a variety of sources, including supplementary readings and short films, are available for the chronology and the glossary on the Web site for this book at <bedfordstmartins.com/phillips-film>.

A Chronology:
Film in Context (1895–2008)

Some film history books stress the artistic achievements of films that scholars regard as significant or representative; they are mainly aesthetic histories. Industrial histories help readers understand films as products of an industry. Some histories focus on film as one of the arts. Social histories emphasize how a society influences what films are made (a topic discussed in Chapter 10). Sociological history focuses on how films influence viewers. There are many other types of histories of film as well, although increasingly historians blend various approaches within the same written accounts because attempting to study films on their own (out of context) makes for incomplete and misleading history. Film scholar Dana Polan argues that films "are what they are because of the meanings given them by surrounding situations. A history of films is a history of films in history" (54).

Scholars who think about historiography—how to study history—have concluded that there is no one history, only various histories. Thus, the title *A History of Film* suggests that Jack Ellis and Virginia Wright Wexman's book is *an* interpretation of the history of cinema. There are other approaches, too. Douglas Gomery's *Movie History: A Survey* interweaves aesthetics, technology, economics, and sociology, as do the authors in the History of the American Cinema series, under the general editorship of Professor Charles Harpole. Geoffrey Nowell-Smith coordinated the work of some international film scholars to create *The Oxford History of World Cinema*, which encompasses not just films but "the audience, the industry, and the people who work in it . . . and the mechanisms of regulation and control which determine which films audiences are encouraged to see and which they are not" (xix).

The following year-by-year chronology supplies information about (1) world events that have affected the lives of many people and often have been the subjects of films; (2) the arts, including works that were sources for films or were derived from films; (3) developments in the mass media; and (4) critically acclaimed films and videos, innovative films, and films and videos about filmmakers or films. Although the chronology is long and complicated, it is woefully incomplete. Unavoidably, everyone who has studied history will have quarrels with parts of it.

Nevertheless, the chronology can be useful in a number of ways. You can read down an entire column to get a sense of the order and occasionally the connections between related events (for example, how conditions in Germany after World War I fostered the Nazis' rise to power). Or you can read across all four columns for any given year to get a sense of what happened in a particular year.

You also can use the chronology to place a film in other contexts. Suppose you are studying *Casablanca*, which was first shown in November 1942. The chronology will inform you what was happening before and during 1942. You will notice, for example, that Europe plunged into World War II in September 1939 but the United States remained (officially) neutral for over two years (until the Japanese attacked Pearl Harbor in December 1941). On one level, *Casablanca* calls for Americans to put aside any inclination to isolationism and rally behind a traditional ally, France, which at the time of the film's release was under Nazi occupation. Once you consider when *Casablanca* was made, you can better understand its fervor in denouncing the Nazis, extolling the Free French, and criticizing the French government in Vichy that cooperated with the occupying Germans. The chronology can help you understand not only the times when a film was made but also the times in which a film is set. For example, the information about events leading up to World War II can help you better understand *Saving Private Ryan* (1998).

The chronology reveals that plays often are made into films, and vice versa, and that films often interface with other arts (such as novels) and other media (especially TV). Also, the chronology repeatedly illustrates an underlying message of this book: films draw from the infinite, fascinating permutations of individual and group behavior and reflect them.

The year given for a film is the year it was first shown. Sometimes sources disagree about an original release date. Whenever I became aware of such discrepancies, I tried to consult at least one additional authoritative source, but some inaccuracies may remain. When the title of a film in printed sources differs from the title in the film itself (as, for example, *M*A*S*H* and *MASH*), I use the title in the opening credits of a video or DVD version of the original film (for example, *MASH*). Some films do not fit neatly into one of the three categories of films used in this book (fictional, documentary, and experimental), but to save space in the "Films and Videos" columns I list fictional films first and then label most other films as *documentary* or *experimental*.

Two notes about film titles: (1) The titles of films that are less than 60 minutes long are enclosed in quotation marks. Titles of longer films appear in italics. (2) Parentheses around part of a film's title indicate that the film is sometimes known by its short title (without the words in parentheses). For example, the entry (*The Life and Times of*) *Rosie the Riveter* means that documentary film is sometimes known as *The Life and Times of Rosie the Riveter* and sometimes as *Rosie the Riveter.*

This chronology is intended as a limited beginning. Other more complete, coherent, and authoritative accounts are included in the list of sources following the chronology.

	World Events	Arts	Mass Media	Films and Videos
1895	Cuba fights for independence from Spain First U.S. automobiles for sale on a regular basis W. C. Roentgen discovers X-rays Invention of diesel engine *Studies in Hysteria*, Sigmund Freud (book)	*The Red Badge of Courage*, Stephen Crane (fiction) *The Time Machine*, H. G. Wells (fiction) *The Importance of Being Earnest*, Oscar Wilde (play)	Lumière Brothers invent a portable motion-picture camera/projector to film short films and to show them publicly First U.S. demonstration of a motion picture shown on a screen, New York City Guglielmo Marconi sends and receives a radio signal	Lumière Brothers' first (and very brief) film, "Workers Leaving the Lumière Factory," is perhaps also the first documentary film Other Lumière films: "The Arrival of a Train at the Station" and "Feeding (the) Baby" "The Execution of Mary, Queen of Scots," Edison's company
1896	Olympic Games of ancient Greece reestablished Anti-imperialist violence in Africa: Ethiopian warriors defeat Italian soldiers; tribal rebellion erupts in Rhodesia Gold rush in Alaska First glider flight	First major U.S. photography exhibition *Uncle Vanya*, Anton Chekhov (play) *Pont Boieldi in a Drizzle*, Camille Pissarro (painting)	Georges Méliès begins making short films in France Some U.S. vaudeville theaters include short films in their programs Some newspapers give synopses of film programs but little criticism of them Some films are hand-painted with colors	"The Kiss," Edison "The Vanishing Lady," Georges Méliès "The Fairy in the Cabbage Patch," first film by the first female film director, Alice Guy-Blaché
1897	Discovery of the electron U.S. annexes Hawaii	*Dracula*, Bram Stoker (fiction)	Fire kills 140 people at a charity film showing in Paris	Fitzsimmons-Corbett boxing match filmed and shown in theaters
1898	Spanish-American War; Spain cedes Cuba, Puerto Rico, Guam, and Philippines to U.S.	*The Turn of the Screw*, Henry James (fiction) *The War of the Worlds*, Wells (fiction) "J'accuse," Émile Zola (letter)	First photograph taken with artificial light William Randolph Hearst epitomizes the ethics of "yellow journalism" with his comment: "You furnish the pictures, I'll furnish the war."	"Tearing Down the Spanish Flag" (a staged documentary and perhaps the first propaganda film) "Express Train on a Railway Cutting," Cecil Hepworth (documentary)

	World Events	Arts	Mass Media	Films and Videos
1899	Aspirin first marketed, as a prescribed drug U.S. goes to war with insurgents in Philippines	*McTeague*, Frank Norris (fiction) "Maple Leaf Rag," Scott Joplin (ragtime music)	First magnetic recording of sound Marconi sends a wireless signal across the English Channel	"The Dreyfus Affair," Méliès (a film that re-creates a political scandal) "Cinderella," Méliès
1900	Boxer Rebellion in China, mainly against foreigners *The Interpretation of Dreams*, Freud (book) Max Planck proposes quantum theory of energy Anarchist assassinates King Humbert I of Italy Russia annexes Manchuria	*The Wonderful Wizard of Oz*, L. Frank Baum (fiction) *Sister Carrie*, Theodore Dreiser (fiction)	At about this time, Edison uses artificial light in his rooftop film studio in New York City Lumière Brothers use a 70-×-53-foot translucent screen at Paris World's Fair so 25,000 people on both sides of the screen can see short films George Eastman introduces the cheap, popular portable Kodak camera	"One Man Band," Méliès (the filmmaker himself plays the six band members and the conductor)
1901	Edward VII succeeds Queen Victoria of England Nobel Prizes first awarded Anarchist assassinates president McKinley Australian Commonwealth established	*Three Sisters*, Chekhov (play)	Marconi sends a radio signal from Wales to Newfoundland by tapping out "S" in Morse code Electric typewriter invented	"Queen Victoria's Funeral" (documentary)
1902 (cont'd on next page)	Boer War in South Africa ends Riots rage in southern Russia Aswan Dam finished in Egypt	*The Virginian*, Owen Wister (fiction) *Heart of Darkness*, Joseph Conrad (fiction)	First English film studio built in Ealing, near London Pathé builds film studio in France	"A Trip to the Moon," Méliès "Coronation of Edward VII," Méliès (documentary re-creation)

	World Events	Arts	Mass Media	Films and Videos
1902 (cont'd)		*The Wings of the Dove*, James (fiction)	First phonograph recording by the singer Enrico Caruso	
1903	Ford Motor Company founded and begins new assembly-line system of automobile construction Wright brothers fly airplane	*Call of the Wild*, Jack London (fiction) *Man and Superman*, (George) Bernard Shaw (play) Isadora Duncan pioneers modern dance (1903–08)	Edwin S. Porter uses matte shots in "The Great Train Robbery" First radio message from U.S. to Britain	"The Great Train Robbery," "Life of an American Fireman," and "Uncle Tom's Cabin," all by Edwin S. Porter "La damnation de Faust," Méliès
1904	Theodore Roosevelt elected U.S. president Russo-Japanese War Roosevelt Corollary to Monroe Doctrine asserts U.S. policing rights in Latin America	*Peter Pan*, J. M. Barrie (play) *The Cherry Orchard*, Chekhov (play)	A few nickelodeons—small storefront movie theaters showing programs of short films—open in U.S. Comic books, disk phonographs, and telephone answering machines are invented	"An Impossible Voyage," Méliès
1905	Police crush demonstration in St. Petersburg; general strike in Russia Russian sailors mutiny on battleship *Potemkin* Albert Einstein proposes theory of relativity	*The House of Mirth*, Edith Wharton (fiction) *Major Barbara*, Shaw (play) Fauvism and expressionism (art movements)	Pittsburgh theater is first to show films exclusively and regularly	"Rescued by Rover," Hepworth
1906	Britain launches first large battleship, *Dreadnought*	*The Jungle*, Upton Sinclair (fiction)	Nearly 1,000 nickelodeons in the U.S.	"Dream of a Rarebit Fiend," Porter

	World Events	Arts	Mass Media	Films and Videos
1906 (cont'd)	British Labour Party formed In India, Mahatma Gandhi begins campaign of nonviolent protest	*Portrait of Gertrude Stein*, Pablo Picasso (painting)	Movies are usually one reel (13–16 minutes) Victrola (record player) first marketed	*The Story of the Kelly Gang*, Charles Tait (regarded as the first feature-length film)
1907	First completely synthetic plastic developed Ross Harrison grows human cells outside the body First blood test for syphilis	*The Playboy of the Western World*, John Millington Synge (play) Picasso's first cubist painting	Chicago creates its first film censorship board	"Ben Hur," Sidney Olcott
1908	Ford begins manufacturing the Model T Middle East oil boom begins in Persia	*A Room with a View*, E. M. Forster (fiction) Ashcan school of American realism (painting)	From 1908 to 1913, D. W. Griffith directs or supervises hundreds of short films at Biograph film production company	"The Adventures of Dollie," D. W. Griffith "The Last Days of Pompeii," Luigi Maggi
1909	Half of U.S. population lives on farms or in small towns Congress passes U.S. copyright law	The Italian book *Futurist Manifesto* exalts the beauty and dynamism of machines	At about this time, 35 mm becomes standard film gauge throughout the world	"A Corner in Wheat" and "The Lonely Villa," Griffith
1910	Mexican civil war begins Portuguese monarchy ends after uprisings in Lisbon African American boxer Jack Johnson defeats white boxer Jim Jeffries, and race riots erupt throughout U.S.	*Howards End*, Forster (fiction) *The Dream*, Henri Rousseau (painting)	10,000 nickelodeons throughout U.S. Film credits begin to identify U.S. actors First U.S. motion-picture newsreel exhibited Max Linder (France) writes, supervises, and performs in short comic movies	"A Child of the Ghetto," Griffith

	World Events	Arts	Mass Media	Films and Videos
1911	Mexican civil war ends First air flight across U.S. Indianapolis 500-mile auto race first held	*Ethan Frome*, Wharton (fiction) *I and My Village*, Marc Chagall (painting)	Standard aspect ratio (4:3) widely used in film showings	"The Battle" and "The Lonedale Operator," Griffith
1912	Revolution in China and abdication of the last Chinese emperor *Titanic* hits iceberg and sinks on maiden voyage; more than 1,500 die 2,000 Turks killed by soldiers of the Balkan alliance	*Death in Venice*, Thomas Mann (fiction) *Tarzan of the Apes*, Edgar Rice Burroughs (fiction)	About 5 million see American movies daily Most American films now made in Los Angeles, not on East Coast U.S. Universal Studios founded Wireless communication used when the sinking *Titanic* signals for help	"The Musketeers of Pig Alley," Griffith "Keystone Kops," Mack Sennett (series of short comic films) *Quo Vadis?*, Enrico Guazzoni (popular spectacle) "Queen Elizabeth" ("Les amours de la reine Élisabeth"), Louis Mercanton and Henri Desfontaines
1913	Niels Bohr publishes his model of atomic structure Pancho Villa leads rebellion in northern Mexico; president of Mexico deposed and killed in coup	First showing of avant-garde European art in U.S. *Nude Descending a Staircase*, Marcel Duchamp (painting) *The Rite of Spring* (ballet with music by Igor Stravinsky)	Olga Wohlbruck becomes first German female filmmaker	*Judith of Bethulia*, Griffith "The Student of Prague," Stellan Rye and Paul Wagener
1914	World War I begins in Europe (1914–18) Panama Canal opens Term *birth control* coined	*Dubliners*, James Joyce (short stories, including "The Dead")	In U.S., feature films become the norm Strand Theater, perhaps the first movie palace, opens in New York City	"Gertie the Dinosaur," Winsor McCay (series of short animated films) *Cabiria*, Giovanni Pastrone

	World Events	**Arts**	**Mass Media**	**Films and Videos**
1915	Germans use poison gas on western front German submarine sinks British liner *Lusitania*; approximately 1,200 die	*Of Human Bondage*, Somerset Maugham (fiction) *The Metamorphosis*, Franz Kafka (fiction) New Orleans jazz popular in U.S.	First long-distance phone service between New York and San Francisco	*The Birth of a Nation*, Griffith *The Cheat*, Cecil B. De Mille "The Tramp," Charles Chaplin *Les vampires*, Louis Feuillade (10-part serial, 1915–16)
1916	Germans use poison gas in Battle of Verdun, which lasts from Feb. to Dec. Pancho Villa's forces cross U.S. border and kill 14 Irish insurrection on Easter Day ("Bloody Sunday")	*A Portrait of the Artist as a Young Man*, Joyce (fiction) Dada (art and literary movement) founded in Zurich	Camera crane used to film parts of *Intolerance* *The Art of the Moving Picture* by Vachel Lindsay and *The Photoplay: A Psychological Study* by Hugo Münsterberg are early books on film theory Chaplin achieves worldwide fame and makes his most esteemed short films at Mutual Film Corp. (1916–17)	*Intolerance*, Griffith *Civilization*, Thomas Ince "The Pawn Shop," "The Vagabond," and "The Rink," Chaplin *Her Defiance*, Cleo Madison
1917	Puerto Ricans granted U.S. citizenship by act of Congress Revolution in Russia; provisional government formed; Romanov tsar abdicates U.S. enters World War I In Russia, Bolsheviks seize power; later V. I. Lenin becomes chief commissar	Symphony 1 ("Classical"), Sergei Prokofiev	UFA (major German film studio) formed Technicolor Corporation founded; experimentation with color film continues First jazz phonograph recordings	"The Immigrant" and "Easy Street," Chaplin

	World Events	Arts	Mass Media	Films and Videos
1918	World War I ends Romanov royal family executed in Russia World influenza epidemic kills 20 million	*The Magnificent Ambersons*, Booth Tarkington (fiction)	Warner Brothers Pictures incorporated by Harry, Albert, and Jack Warner During World War I, U.S. film industry drastically increased its share of the world market	"Shoulder Arms," Chaplin "The Sinking of the Lusitania," McCay (animation) *Carmen*, Ernst Lubitsch
1919	Civil war in Russia League of Nations founded Versailles peace treaty formally ends World War I	*Winesburg, Ohio: A Group of Tales of Ohio Small Town Life*, Sherwood Anderson (fiction) *Ten Days That Shook the World*, John Reed (nonfiction) Jazz arrives in Europe	United Artists (distribution company) formed by Chaplin, Griffith, Mary Pickford, and Douglas Fairbanks RCA founded	*Broken Blossoms*, Griffith *Blind Husbands*, Erich von Stroheim *The Homesteader*, Oscar Micheaux (first feature film about U.S. blacks written and directed by an African American) *The Cabinet of Dr. Caligari*, Robert Wiene *J'accuse*, Abel Gance (the "Griffith of Europe") *South: Ernest Shackleton and the Endurance Expedition*, Frank Hurley (documentary)
1920	Gandhi leads India's struggle for independence from Britain U.S. women get the vote by constitutional amendment Russian civil war ends U.S. prohibition amendment makes manufacturing or consuming alcohol illegal	*Main Street*, Sinclair Lewis (fiction) *The Age of Innocence*, Wharton (fiction)	Lev Kuleshov founds workshop in Moscow and begins experimenting with editing U.S. films popular throughout much of the world KDKA in Pittsburgh offers regularly scheduled radio programs	*Way Down East*, Griffith *The Golem*, Paul Wegener and Henrik Galeen

	World Events	Arts	Mass Media	Films and Videos
1921	Adolf Hitler's storm troopers in Germany and Fascist blackshirts in Italy terrorize political opponents Irish Free State (excluding Northern Ireland) established	*Six Characters in Search of an Author,* Luigi Pirandello (play) *The Dream,* Max Beckmann (painting)	British Broadcasting Corp. (BBC) begins U.S. president Warren G. Harding makes first presidential radio address	*The Kid,* Chaplin's first feature *Orphans of the Storm,* Griffith *Destiny,* Fritz Lang "Rhythmus 21," Hans Richter (experimental)
1922	Benito Mussolini forms Fascist government in Italy U.S.S.R. formed by various Soviet republics Fuad I begins rule of Egypt Insulin isolated and used to treat diabetes King Tutankhamen's tomb discovered in Egypt	*Ulysses,* Joyce (fiction) "The Waste Land," T. S. Eliot (poem) Beginnings of surrealism (art and literary movement) *Twittering Machine,* Paul Klee (watercolor and pen and ink)	New York Philharmonic radio concert	*Foolish Wives,* von Stroheim *Nosferatu(, A Symphony of Horror),* F. W. Murnau *La roue,* Gance *Nanook of the North,* Robert Flaherty (documentary) *Witchcraft through the Ages,* Benjamin Christensen (hybrid) *Kino-Pravda,* Dziga Vertov (creatively edited newsreels, 1922–25)
1923	Hitler's coup attempt fails Former Mexican revolutionary Pancho Villa ambushed and assassinated Earthquake in Japan kills 800,000	*St. Joan,* Shaw (play) "Stopping by Woods on a Snowy Evening," Robert Frost (poem)	Kodak produces first 16 mm movie film (black-and-white) Vladimir Zworykin develops television camera tube *Time* magazine begins	*Safety Last,* Sam Taylor and Fred Newmeyer (starring Harold Lloyd) *Our Hospitality,* Buster Keaton and Jack Blystone *The Ten Commandments,* De Mille "Retour à la raison," Man Ray (experimental)
1924 (cont'd on next page)	Lenin dies; succession struggle begins in U.S.S.R. American Indians granted full U.S. citizenship by act of Congress	*A Passage to India,* Forster (fiction) *Juno and the Paycock,* Sean O'Casey (play)	MGM film studio formed 1.25 million radios in use in U.S. Introduction of Moviola editing machine *Little Orphan Annie* comic strip begins	*Greed,* von Stroheim *The Last Laugh,* Murnau *Die Nibelungen (Die Nibelungen: Siegfrieds Tod),* Lang *Waxworks (Das Wachsfigurenkabinett),* Leo Birinsky and Paul Leni

	World Events	Arts	Mass Media	Films and Videos
1924 (cont'd)	First winter Olympics, in France Ottoman dynasty ends 600-year rule; modern country of Turkey formed	"Surrealist Manifesto," André Breton (essay) *Rhapsody in Blue*, George Gershwin (music)	Leica portable still camera invented in Germany	*(The Story of) Gösta Berling*, Mauritz Stiller *Strike*, Sergei Eisenstein "Entr'acte," René Clair (experimental) "Le ballet mécanique," Fernand Léger (experimental)
1925	John Scopes tried for teaching evolution in violation of Tennessee statute Hitler publishes part of *Mein Kampf* (*My Struggle*) French build Maginot Line for defense against invasion	*The Great Gatsby*, F. Scott Fitzgerald (fiction) *The Trial*, Kafka (posthumous fiction) *Ralph 124C 41+*, Hugo Gernsback (science fiction) Art deco movement begins	Cinematographer Karl Struss uses colored makeup and color filters to depict the healing of lepers *Grand Ole Opry* radio show begins (eventually becomes longest continuously running radio show in U.S.)	*The Gold Rush*, Chaplin *Ben-Hur*(*: A Tale of the Christ*), Fred Niblo *Body and Soul*, Micheaux (film debut of singer and actor Paul Robeson) *The Joyless Street*, G. W. Pabst *Variety*, E. A. Dupont *(Battleship) Potemkin*, Eisenstein
1926	New York–London telephone service begins Rocket launched by R. H. Goddard (U.S.) Hirohito becomes emperor of Japan Chiang Kai-shek takes control of Chinese government	*The Sun Also Rises*, Ernest Hemingway (fiction) *Orphée*, Jean Cocteau (play) Harlem Renaissance begins	*Don Juan* made with Vitaphone: film plus synchronized music from disks *The Black Pirate*: one of the first films to use the two-color Technicolor process	*The General*, Keaton *Mother*, V. I. Pudovkin *Faust*, Murnau
1927	Charles Lindbergh flies solo nonstop from New York to Paris German economy collapses Physicist Walter Heisenberg introduces his uncertainty principle	*To the Lighthouse*, Virginia Woolf (fiction) *Show Boat*, Jerome Kern and Oscar Hammerstein (musical)	Warner Bros. releases *The Jazz Singer* using Vitaphone sound system *Napoléon* (Gance) includes triptych: wide-screen image made up of three standard images	*Underworld*, Josef von Sternberg (early gangster film) *Metropolis*, Lang *Sunrise*, Murnau *Napoléon* [*Bonaparte*], Gance *The Italian Straw Hat*, Clair *Bed and Sofa*, Abram Room

	World Events	Arts	Mass Media	Films and Videos
1927 (cont'd)	Chinese government crushes Mao Zedong's Autumn Harvest Uprising	*Bird in Space*, Constantin Brancusi (sculpture) *Manhattan Bridge*, Edward Hopper (painting)	"To Build a Fire," experimental fiction by Claude Autant-Lara, first film to use anamorphic lenses developed by Henri Chrétien AM radio band created Sales of radio sets increase dramatically in U.S.	*Berlin, Symphony of a Great City*, Walther Ruttmann (experimental documentary)
1928	German dirigible Graf Zeppelin makes first transatlantic crossing Penicillin, first antibiotic, discovered *The Oxford English Dictionary* published	*Lady Chatterley's Lover*, D. H. Lawrence (fiction) *Orlando*, Woolf (fiction) *The Front Page*, Ben Hecht and Charles MacArthur (play) *Greta Garbo*, Edward Steichen (photograph) *Three-Penny Opera*, Kurt Weill and Bertolt Brecht (musical)	First all-talking film, *The Lights of New York*, uses Vitaphone sound system Feature films released on two rival sound-on-film systems, Movietone and Photophone Kodak introduces 16 mm color movie film First scheduled TV broadcast, in Schenectady, N.Y.	*The Circus*, Chaplin *The Crowd*, King Vidor *The Wind*, Victor Sjöström "Steamboat Willie," Walt Disney (first Mickey Mouse film released) *October*, aka *Ten Days That Shook the World*, Eisenstein *The Passion of Joan of Arc*, Carl Theodor Dreyer "Un chien andalou," Luis Buñuel (experimental) "The Seashell and the Clergyman," Germaine Dulac (experimental)
1929 (cont'd on next page)	U.S. stock prices plunge U.S. and European economic crisis begins Josef Stalin becomes absolute ruler of U.S.S.R.	*A Farewell to Arms*, Hemingway (fiction) *All Quiet on the Western Front*, Erich Maria Remarque (fiction) "A Room of One's Own," Woolf (essay)	Sound film projector speed standardized in U.S. at 24 frames per second Postdubbing (adding sound after filming) first used First Academy Awards ceremony held, for films for 1927–28	*Applause*, Rouben Mamoulian *Hallelujah!*, Vidor (first sound feature with all-black cast) "Big Business," James W. Horne and Leo McCarey (starring Stan Laurel and Oliver Hardy) *Blackmail*, Alfred Hitchcock (first British sound film)

	World Events	Arts	Mass Media	Films and Videos
1929 (cont'd)		Museum of Modern Art opens in New York City	*Amos 'n' Andy* radio show debuts and quickly proves popular *Buck Rogers in the 25th Century* (sci-fi comic strip)	*Pandora's Box*, Pabst "Drifters," John Grierson (documentary) *Man with a Movie Camera*, Vertov (experimental documentary)
1930	Stalin orders collectivization of Soviet farms Major Indian cities in turmoil after arrest of Gandhi and his followers for civil disobedience against British rule	*The Maltese Falcon*, Dashiell Hammett (fiction) *Composition in Red, Yellow and Blue*, Piet Mondrian (painting)	U.S. production code for certifying movies instituted but loosely enforced Rear projection developed Worldwide, approximately 250 million people attend movies weekly 12 million U.S. homes have radios	*All Quiet on the Western Front*, Lewis Milestone *The Blue Angel*, Josef von Sternberg "The Blood of a Poet," Jean Cocteau (experimental)
1931	Cyclotron invented by Ernest Lawrence Big Bang theory is formulated U.S. unemployment reaches 16 percent, and over 800 banks close Japan occupies Manchuria	*The Persistence of Memory*, Salvador Dalí (painting) "The Star Spangled Banner" becomes U.S. national anthem	*Dick Tracy* comic strip begins *Mädchen in Uniform*, by Leontine Sagan, early film with a lesbian character and all-female cast	*City Lights* (includes sound effects and music but no spoken words), Chaplin *Frankenstein*, James Whale *Dracula*, Tod Browning *The Public Enemy*, William Wellman *M* (*M — Eine Stadt sucht einen Mörder*), Lang
1932	First nuclear reaction U.S. unemployment: 24 percent Franklin D. Roosevelt elected U.S. president Neutron, a subatomic particle, is discovered	*Brave New World*, Aldous Huxley (fiction) *Mobiles*, Alexander Calder (mobile sculptures)	First international film festival: Venice Film Festival Technicolor three-color process first used, in a Disney cartoon: "Flowers and Trees" Radio City Music Hall, a huge, opulent movie palace, opens in NYC	*Scarface*, Howard Hawks *I Am a Fugitive from a Chain Gang*, Mervyn LeRoy *Trouble in Paradise*, Lubitsch *Dr. Jekyll and Mr. Hyde*, Mamoulian *À nous la liberté* (*Freedom for Us*), Clair

	World Events	Arts	Mass Media	Films and Videos
1932 (cont'd)				*Boudu Saved from Drowning* (*Boudu sauvé des eaux*), Jean Renoir
1933	Hitler appointed German chancellor Revolution in Spain spreads to southern Spain Nazis erect first concentration camp and begin persecution of Jews in Germany First round-the-world airplane flight, by Wiley Post Prohibition ends in U.S.	*Shape of Things to Come*, Wells (fiction) *Blood Wedding*, Federico García Lorca (play) *Man at the Crossroads*, Diego Rivera (temporary fresco for Rockefeller Center)	British Film Institute founded Nazis control German film industry World's first drive-in movie theater, in Camden, N.J. President Roosevelt uses radio for "fireside chats" to the nation *The Lone Ranger* radio program debuts	*King Kong*, Ernest Schoedsack and Merian C. Cooper *Duck Soup*, McCarey (starring Marx Bros.) *Gold Diggers of 1933*, LeRoy (with choreography by Busby Berkeley) "Lot in Sodom," James Watson and Melville Webber (experimental) "Zero for Conduct," Jean Vigo (experimental)
1934	Radar developed Stalin begins purge of Soviet Communist Party U.S. bank robbers Bonnie Parker and Clyde Barrow killed in police ambush	*The Postman Always Rings Twice*, James M. Cain (fiction) *The Children's Hour*, Lillian Hellman (play)	Production Code Administration seal of approval required for U.S. public film showings (1934–68)	*It Happened One Night*, Frank Capra *The Thin Man*, W. S. Van Dyke (first in a series of comedy/mystery films) *L'Atalante*, Vigo *Man of Aran*, Flaherty (documentary) "Composition in Blue," Oskar Fischinger (experimental)
1935 (cont'd on next page)	Germany begins massive military buildup Dust storms plague nearly half of U.S. Italy invades Ethiopia Persia becomes modern state of Iran Nuremberg Laws codify German anti-Semitism	*The Treasure of the Sierra Madre*, B. Traven (fiction) *Porgy and Bess*, Gershwin (opera) Popular songs: all five Irving Berlin songs from the film *Top Hat*, including "Cheek to Cheek"	Museum of Modern Art Film Library opens First three-color Technicolor feature film: *Becky Sharp*, directed by Mamoulian	*Mutiny on the Bounty*, Frank Lloyd *The Informer*, John Ford *Top Hat*, Mark Sandrich (starring Fred Astaire and Ginger Rogers) *The 39 Steps*, Hitchcock *Toni*, Renoir

	World Events	Arts	Mass Media	Films and Videos
1935 (cont'd)			"The March of Time" newsreel series appears monthly in the nation's theaters, until 1951 Approximately 22 million U.S. homes have radios	*Triumph of the Will*, Leni Riefenstahl (Nazi-sponsored propaganda/documentary)
1936	Spanish civil war (1936–39) Mussolini and Hitler agree to be allies Jawaharlal Nehru becomes president of Indian National Congress First Volkswagen ("people's car") built	Frank Lloyd Wright's Kaufmann House, Pennsylvania (architecture) "A Fine Romance" (popular song from the movie *Swing Time*)	La Cinémathèque Française (France's film archive) founded *Life* magazine begins	*Modern Times*, Chaplin *Swing Time*, George Stevens *Sabotage*, Hitchcock *Fury*, Lang "A Day in the Country," Renoir "The Plow That Broke the Plains," Pare Lorentz (documentary) *Olympia*, Riefenstahl (documentary)
1937	Stalin's purges result in millions of deaths and imprisonments in slave labor camps (1937–38) German warplanes bomb Guernica, Spain, killing hundreds, mostly civilians Japan invades China Italy withdraws from League of Nations	*Of Mice and Men*, John Steinbeck (fiction) *The Hobbit*, J. R. R. Tolkien (fiction) *The Cradle Will Rock*, Marc Blitzstein (opera) *Guernica*, Picasso (mural depicting results of German aerial bombardment in Spain)	Henri Chrétien links two cameras with an anamorphic lens to produce an image 200 feet wide by 33 feet high for a Paris exhibition Burning and crash of dirigible *Hindenburg* in New Jersey is broadcast live on transcontinental radio	*A Star Is Born*, Wellman *Snow White and the Seven Dwarfs* (first Disney animated feature) *Grand Illusion*, Renoir
1938	Germany annexes Austria	*Our Town*, Thornton Wilder (play)	Orson Welles's radio broadcast of *The War of the Worlds* causes panic nationwide on Halloween	*Bringing Up Baby*, Hawks *The Lady Vanishes*, Hitchcock *Alexander Nevsky*, Eisenstein

	World Events	Arts	Mass Media	Films and Videos
1938 (cont'd)	U.S. House Committee on Un-American Activities (HUAC) formed U.S. and Germany sever diplomatic relations	*Les parents terribles*, Cocteau (play) *Recumbent Figure*, Henry Moore (stone sculpture)	Superman first appears, in *Action Comics*	
1939	Spanish civil war ends with Francisco Franco's forces victorious Pan-American Airlines begins scheduled flights between U.S. and Europe World War II begins when Germany invades Poland Ho Chi Minh creates Viet Minh Party, which opposes French colonialism in Indochina	*The Big Sleep*, Raymond Chandler (fiction) *The Grapes of Wrath*, Steinbeck (fiction) *Alexander Nevsky*, Prokofiev (cantata based on his film score) "Over the Rainbow" (popular song from the movie *The Wizard of Oz*)	Hollywood studios produce 400 movies National Film Board of Canada founded RCA demonstrates television at New York World's Fair First FM station begins operation, Alpine, N.J. Batman first appears, in *Detective Comics*	*The Wizard of Oz*, Victor Fleming *Stagecoach*, Ford *Gone with the Wind*, Fleming (last of several directors to work on the film) *Mr. Smith Goes to Washington*, Capra *The Rules of the Game*, Renoir
1940	Winston Churchill becomes British prime minister German army enters Paris Germans begin all-night air raids on London France divided into occupied northern zone and collaborative Vichy southern zone	*Farewell, My Lovely*, Chandler (fiction) *The Ox-Bow Incident*, Walter van Tilburg Clark (fiction) "When You Wish upon a Star" (popular song from the Disney movie *Pinocchio*)	28 1/2 million American homes have radios Edward R. Murrow's radio broadcasts from London during German air raids Republican and Democratic National Conventions broadcast on radio First American TV network broadcast	*The Grapes of Wrath*, Ford *The Great Dictator*, Chaplin *His Girl Friday*, Hawks *The Bank Dick*, Eddie Cline (starring W. C. Fields) *The Great McGinty*, first film directed by Preston Sturges *Dance, Girl, Dance*, Dorothy Arzner *Fantasia* and *Pinocchio* (Disney animated features) *Jud Süss*, Veidt Harlan (influential Nazi anti-Semitic film)

	World Events	Arts	Mass Media	Films and Videos
1941	First jet airplane flies German armies invade Greece and Yugoslavia Germany begins invasion of U.S.S.R. Japan bombs Pearl Harbor U.S. and Britain declare war on Japan Germany and Italy declare war on U.S.	*What Makes Sammy Run?*, Budd Schulberg (fiction) *Moonrise, Hernandez, New Mexico*, Ansel Adams (photograph)	NBC and CBS granted commercial TV licenses	*Citizen Kane*, first film directed by Orson Welles *The Maltese Falcon*, first film directed by John Huston *Sullivan's Travels*, Sturges "Target for Tonight," Harry Watt (documentary)
1942	Germany begins killing Jews in gas chambers Japan invades Philippines Heavy German air raids on London Fungus destroys Indian rice crops; 1.6 million die in famine	*The Stranger*, Albert Camus (fiction) *Nighthawks*, Hopper (painting)	In U.S., radio is the main source of information about the war	*Casablanca*, Michael Curtiz *The Magnificent Ambersons*, Welles *To Be or Not to Be*, Lubitsch *Ossessione*, Luchino Visconti "The Battle of Midway," Ford (documentary) "Why We Fight," produced by Capra (series of seven wartime documentaries, 1942–45)
1943	Allied forces land in Sicily Mussolini dismissed as Italian premier Italy surrenders to Allies and declares war on Germany German forces fail to take Stalingrad after yearlong siege	*Oklahoma!*, Richard Rodgers and Oscar Hammerstein (musical)	*Perry Mason* radio series begins with Raymond Burr; later a TV series	*Shadow of a Doubt*, Hitchcock *The Ox-Bow Incident*, Wellman "Report from the Aleutians," Huston (documentary) *Fires Were Started*, Humphrey Jennings (documentary) "Meshes of the Afternoon," Maya Deren and Alexander Hammid (experimental)
1944	Allies land in northern France (D-Day) Germany launches V-2 rockets at Britain	*The Glass Menagerie*, Tennessee Williams (play)	First general-purpose computer built, at Harvard University, funded in part by IBM	*Hail the Conquering Hero* and *The Miracle of Morgan's Creek*, Sturges

	World Events	Arts	Mass Media	Films and Videos
1944 (cont'd)	Forces under command of U.S. general Douglas MacArthur recapture Philippines Roosevelt elected U.S. president for unprecedented fourth term			*Double Indemnity*, Billy Wilder *Murder, My Sweet*, Edward Dmytryk *Laura*, Otto Preminger *Henry V*, Laurence Olivier "Memphis Belle," William Wyler (documentary)
1945	Roosevelt dies unexpectedly UN charter signed in San Francisco War ends in Europe; 35 million killed, 6 million of them Jews U.S. drops two atomic bombs on Japan, and Japan surrenders Independent republic of Vietnam formed Nuremberg trials of Nazi war criminals begin	*Animal Farm*, George Orwell (fiction) *Carousel*, Rodgers and Hammerstein (musical) Beginnings of abstract expressionism (art movement)	*Meet the Press*, radio show 5,000 American homes have a TV set *Ebony*, first African American glossy magazine, begins	*The Lost Weekend*, Wilder *Detour*, Edgar G. Ulmer *Open City* (aka *Rome, Open City*), Roberto Rossellini *Brief Encounter*, David Lean *Ivan the Terrible, Part I*, Eisenstein *Children of Paradise*, Marcel Carné (made in France during German occupation) "The Battle of San Pietro," Huston (documentary)
1946	Cold war begins between U.S.S.R. and its allies and U.S. and its allies Juan Perón elected president of Argentina Philippine independence from U.S., July 4 Nuremberg trials end French women get the vote France recognizes independence of Vietnam	*Zorba, the Greek*, Nikos Kazantzakis (fiction) *All the King's Men*, Robert Penn Warren (fiction) *Annie Get Your Gun*, Irving Berlin (musical)	Each week about 90 million Americans go to the movies, a record Cannes (France) Film Festival founded Sony Corporation founded in Japan	*My Darling Clementine*, Ford *The Killers*, Robert Siodmak *The Best Years of Our Lives*, Wyler *It's a Wonderful Life*, Capra *Beauty and the Beast*, Cocteau *Great Expectations*, Lean *Shoeshine*, Vittorio de Sica "Let There Be Light," Huston (documentary not released until many years later)
1947 (cont'd on next page)	India gains independence from Britain	*A Streetcar Named Desire*, Williams (play)	↓	*Out of the Past* (aka *Build My Gallows High*), Jacques Tourner

	World Events	Arts	Mass Media	Films and Videos
1947 (cont'd)	Pakistan, partitioned off from India, gains independence Jackie Robinson becomes first African American to play major league baseball U.S. jet plane flies faster than sound U.S. Central Intelligence Agency (CIA) founded	Actor's Studio, which teaches Method acting, founded in New York	House Committee on Un-American Activities (HUAC) investigates possible Communist influence in Hollywood British Film Academy formed Regular TV news broadcasts begin in U.S. Zoom lens developed, at first for use in TV	*Crossfire*, Dmytryk *Monsieur Verdoux*, Chaplin *Odd Man Out*, Carol Reed "Fireworks," Kenneth Anger (experimental) "Motion Painting No. 1," Fischinger (experimental)
1948	Gandhi assassinated in India U.S. Congress passes Marshall Plan: economic assistance for rebuilding Europe Israel proclaimed a country Apartheid becomes governmental policy of South Africa U.S.S.R. blocks all traffic between Berlin and the West; Western countries begin to airlift supplies into Berlin North Korea proclaims independence from Republic of Korea	*The Naked and the Dead*, Norman Mailer (fiction) *Cry, The Beloved Country*, Alan Paton (fiction) *The Loved One*, Evelyn Waugh ("black comedy" fiction) *Christina's World*, Andrew Wyeth (painting) *City Square*, Alberto Giacometti (bronze sculpture)	Drive-in theaters increase in popularity Hollywood Ten found guilty of contempt of Congress In "Paramount case," U.S. Supreme Court rules that major Hollywood studios' control of production, distribution, and exhibition violates antitrust laws TV becoming a threat to the film industry Long-playing phonograph record introduced Transistor developed 135 million paperback books sold in U.S. during the year	*The Treasure of the Sierra Madre*, Huston *The Naked City*, Jules Dassin *Force of Evil*, Abraham Polonsky *The Lady from Shanghai*, Welles *Fort Apache*, Ford *The Red Shoes*, Michael Powell *Oliver Twist*, Lean *The Fallen Idol*, Reed *The Bicycle Thief* (aka *Bicycle Thieves*), De Sica *Les parents terribles*, Cocteau (film version of his own play of the same title)
1949	North Atlantic Treaty Organization (NATO) created, a collective defense alliance initially of 12 nations	*1984*, Orwell (fiction) *Death of a Salesman*, Arthur Miller (play)	1 million TV sets in U.S. *The Lone Ranger*, the first western TV series 45 rpm record introduced	*Gun Crazy* (aka *Deadly Is the Female*), Joseph H. Lewis *Pinky*, Elia Kazan *All the King's Men*, Robert Rossen

	World Events	Arts	Mass Media	Films and Videos
1949 (cont'd)	Berlin airlift ends U.S.S.R. tests its first atomic bomb Chinese Communists come to power; Nationalists flee to Formosa, later called Taiwan Republic of India formed	*South Pacific*, Rodgers and Hammerstein (musical) Zither music from the film *The Third Man* is popular		*The Third Man*, Reed *Kind Hearts and Coronets*, Robert Hamer *Late Spring*, Yasujiro Ozu *The Quiet One*, Sidney Meyers (documentary) "Begone Dull Care," Norman McLaren (experimental)
1950	U.S. senator Joseph McCarthy claims U.S. State Department is full of Communists North Korea invades South Korea; Korean War begins Birth control pill developed	*The Third Man*, Graham Greene (fiction published after the film) *Guys and Dolls*, Abe Burrows and Frank Loesser (musical)	Live TV comedy show *Your Show of Shows* with Sid Caesar and Imogene Coca begins and runs until 1954 *The Jack Benny Show* (TV) begins *Peanuts* comic strip begins	*Sunset Boulevard*, Wilder *Night and the City*, Dassin *Asphalt Jungle*, Huston *All about Eve*, Joseph L. Mankiewicz *Rashomon*, Akira Kurosawa *Los olvidados* (literally *The Forgotten Ones*, but sometimes known as *The Young and the Damned*), Buñuel *Diary of a Country Priest*, Robert Bresson
1951	Japanese women get the vote Organization of American States (OAS), an organization of Western Hemisphere countries, founded Chinese Communists occupy Tibet Libya becomes an independent state with UN help	*The Caine Mutiny*, Herman Wouk (fiction) *From Here to Eternity*, James Jones (fiction) *Catcher in the Rye*, J. D. Salinger (fiction) *The King and I*, Rodgers and Hammerstein (musical)	Second congressional committee hearing on possible Communist influence in Hollywood (1951–52) Flammable nitrate-base film, used for most 35 mm movies, replaced with cellulose acetate safety base *Cahiers du cinéma* (*Movie Notebooks*), a French film magazine, first published Color TV introduced in U.S. TV shows *I Love Lucy* and *Today* begin	*The African Queen*, Huston *A Streetcar Named Desire*, Kazan *Strangers on a Train*, Hitchcock *The Lavender Hill Mob*, Charles Crichton *Forbidden Games*, René Clément

	World Events	Arts	Mass Media	Films and Videos
1952	Juan Batista seizes power in Cuba Coup in Egypt deposes king and leads to establishment of Egyptian Republic Puerto Rico becomes a U.S. commonwealth U.S. explodes first hydrogen bomb (General) Dwight D. Eisenhower elected U.S. president	*Invisible Man*, Ralph Ellison (fiction) *The Old Man and the Sea*, Hemingway (fiction) *Waiting for Godot*, Samuel Beckett (play) "Do Not Forsake Me," from the film *High Noon* (popular song)	A three-projector version of Cinerama is introduced with the feature-length travelogue *This Is Cinerama* *Bwana Devil* starts a brief flurry of 3-D movies Eastman Color film, easier to process and cheaper than Technicolor, is introduced and results in increased use of color in Hollywood films Handheld transistor radios marketed in U.S. *Mad* magazine debuts	*High Noon*, Fred Zinnemann *Singin' in the Rain*, Gene Kelly and Stanley Donen *Limelight*, Chaplin (with Buster Keaton playing a major role) *Umberto D.*, De Sica *Ikiru* (*To Live*), Kurosawa "Neighbours," McLaren (experimental fictional film)
1953	Stalin dies Announcement that DNA's double-helix structure can be deciphered Elizabeth II of Great Britain crowned Korean War ends First humans scale Mt. Everest	*Fahrenheit 451*, Ray Bradbury (fiction) *Picnic*, William Inge (play) *The Crucible*, Miller (play) *Apples*, Georges Braque (painting)	U.S. theaters begin to show anamorphic wide-screen movies Academy Awards ceremony first telecast *The Moon Is Blue* released without a Motion Picture Association of America seal President Eisenhower's inauguration is broadcast live on TV *Playboy* magazine begins	*Shane*, Stevens *The Band Wagon*, Vincent Minnelli *Rififi*, Dassin *Mr. Hulot's Holiday*, Jacques Tati *I Vitelloni* (aka *The Young and the Passionate*), Federico Fellini *Ugetsu* (*Monogatari*), Kenji Mizoguchi *Tokyo Story*, Ozu *Gate of Hell*, Teinosuke Kinugasa *Peter Pan* (Disney animated feature) "Duck Amuck" (animation with "Voice Characterizations" by Mel Blanc), Chuck Jones

	World Events	Arts	Mass Media	Films and Videos
1954	Polio vaccine discovered U.S. Supreme Court rules school segregation unconstitutional French defeated in Vietnam; Vietnam divided into North and South Senator Joseph McCarthy discredited and censured by U.S. Senate	*Invasion of the Body Snatchers*, Jack Finney (fiction) *Lord of the Flies*, William Golding (fiction) First volume of *The Lord of the Rings*, J. R. R. Tolkien (fiction)	*White Christmas* filmed in VistaVision, a nonanamorphic widescreen system Approximately half of American homes have TV Army-McCarthy hearings carried live on TV First U.S. TV color telecast, Rose Bowl parade *The Tonight Show* (with Steve Allen) debuts on TV	*On the Waterfront*, Kazan *Rear Window*, Hitchcock *A Star Is Born* (with Judy Garland), George Cukor *Salt of the Earth*, Herbert J. Biberman *La Strada*, Fellini *The Seven Samurai*, Kurosawa *Late Chrysanthemums*, Mikio Naruse *Godzilla*, Inoshiro Honda (science fiction action)
1955	Civil war between North and South Vietnam begins East European countries sign Warsaw Pact Blacks boycott segregated city buses in Montgomery, Ala. Coup overthrows Perón regime in Argentina McDonald's and Kentucky Fried Chicken start first fast-food franchises	*Lolita*, Vladimir Nabokov (fiction) *The Diary of Anne Frank*, Albert Hackett and Frances Goodrich (play) *The Family of Man*, Steichen (photographic exhibit)	Filming from helicopters becomes more practicable Todd-AO (a nonanamorphic widescreen) process used in film version of *Oklahoma!* Disneyland opens in California Highest-rated TV show (1955–56): *The $64,000 Question* (quiz show) *Alfred Hitchcock Presents*, TV show (1955–62)	*Rebel without a Cause*, Nicholas Ray *Night of the Hunter*, Charles Laughton *Smiles of a Summer Night*, Ingmar Bergman *Lola Montes*, Max Ophüls *Pather Panchali* (aka *Song of the Little Road*), Satyajit Ray (first of three films featuring the character Apu) "Night and Fog" ("Nuit et brouillard"), Alain Resnais (documentary)
1956 (cont'd on next page)	Soviets crush revolt in Hungary Israel invades Sinai Peninsula Fidel Castro leads revolution in Cuba (1956–59)	*Long Day's Journey into Night*, Eugene O'Neill (posthumous play) *Look Back in Anger*, John Osborne (play)	Elvis Presley appears on *The Ed Sullivan Show* (TV) TV westerns popular Singer Nat King Cole becomes first African American to host a network TV show	*The Searchers*, Ford *The Killing*, Stanley Kubrick *The Seventh Seal*, Bergman *A Man Escaped*, Bresson "The Red Balloon," Albert Lamorisse

	World Events	Arts	Mass Media	Films and Videos
1956 (cont'd)	Britain, Israel, and France invade Egypt over Egypt's nationalization of Suez Canal	*My Fair Lady*, Alan Jay Lerner and Frederick Loewe (musical)	*The Huntley-Brinkley Report*, a TV news program, debuts	
1957	Martin Luther King, Jr., and others found Southern Christian Leadership Conference President Eisenhower sends troops to help desegregate University of Arkansas Soviets launch Sputnik, first satellite to circle Earth	*Doctor Zhivago*, Boris Pasternak (fiction) *On the Road*, Jack Kerouac (fiction) *The Cat in the Hat*, Dr. Seuss (fiction) *West Side Story*, Leonard Bernstein and Arthur Laurents (musical)	*Raintree County*, first film released in Ultra-Panavision 70 *Perry Mason* begins nine-season run on TV *American Bandstand* (with Dick Clark) first airs on national TV Motown Records is founded and popularizes the music style that bears the company's name	*Paths of Glory*, Kubrick *A Face in the Crowd*, Kazan *The Sweet Smell of Success*, Alexander Mackendrick *Wild Strawberries*, Bergman *Throne of Blood* (based on Shakespeare's *Macbeth*), Kurosawa "Two Men and a Wardrobe," Roman Polanski (experimental) "What's Opera, Doc?" Chuck Jones (animation) "A Chairy Tale," McLaren and Claude Jutra (experimental)
1958	European Common Market formed First successful launch of a U.S. satellite U.S. troops sent to intervene in Lebanon's civil war General Charles de Gaulle becomes president of France's Fifth Republic	*Things Fall Apart*, Chinua Achebe (fiction) *The Birthday Party*, Harold Pinter (play) *A Raisin in the Sun*, Lorraine Hansberry (play) *Numbers in Color*, Jasper Johns (painting)	More than 4,000 U.S. drive-in movie screens in operation Stereophonic LPs and phonographs come into use Most popular TV show (1958–59): the western *Gunsmoke*	*Touch of Evil*, Welles *Vertigo*, Hitchcock *Ashes and Diamonds*, Andrzej Wajda *Ivan the Terrible, Part II*, Eisenstein (completed in 1946) *Room at the Top*, Jack Clayton *The World of Apu*, Satyajit Ray "A Movie," Bruce Conner (experimental)
1959	Castro becomes premier of Cuba after successful revolution against President Batista	*The Tin Drum*, Günter Grass (fiction)	TV quiz show scandal *The Twilight Zone*, TV show, begins	*Ben-Hur*, Wyler *North by Northwest*, Hitchcock *Some Like It Hot*, Wilder

	World Events	Arts	Mass Media	Films and Videos
1959 (cont'd)	Yasir Arafat and others found Palestine Liberation Organization (PLO) Russia launches two monkeys into space Chinese suppress uprising in Tibet	*Naked Lunch*, William Burroughs (fiction) "Happenings," multimedia events, first staged *Kind of Blue*, Miles Davis (jazz album)	*Adventures in Good Music*, classical music radio program by Karl Haas, begins on a Detroit station Microchip invented	*Imitation of Life*, Douglas Sirk *The 400 Blows*, François Truffaut's first feature *Breathless*, Jean-Luc Godard's first feature *Hiroshima, mon amour*, Resnais's first feature *Look Back in Anger*, Tony Richardson *Floating Weeds*, Ozu "Window Water Baby Moving," Stan Brakhage (experimental)
1960	U.S. Food and Drug Administration (FDA) approves use of birth control pill Nigeria becomes independent nation Laser invented South African government bans major anti-apartheid groups after protests turn violent Organization of Petroleum Exporting Countries (OPEC) formed Wave of decolonization as France and Belgium give up African territories First Xerox photocopier U.S. senator John F. Kennedy elected president	*To Kill a Mockingbird*, Harper Lee (fiction) *Camelot*, Lerner and Loewe (musical) Minimalist style in painting, sculpture, and music *Coltrane Plays the Blues* and *My Favorite Things* (albums by John Coltrane) Fluxus movement begins in New York and Germany (multimedia arts)	*Echo 1*, the first communications satellite, launched First TV debate between presidential candidates (Kennedy and Nixon) *Harvest of Shame*, TV documentary film on migrant farmworkers, Edward R. Murrow, commentator Approximately 100 million TVs in Europe and U.S. The twist dance craze influences songs, books, movies, and TV shows	*Psycho*, Hitchcock *Shadows*, John Cassavetes's first film as director *Saturday Night and Sunday Morning*, Karel Reisz *The Entertainer*, Richardson *L'avventura*, Michelangelo Antonioni *La Dolce Vita* (aka *The Sweet Life*), Fellini *Shoot the Piano Player*, Truffaut *Cruel Story of Youth*, Nagisa Oshima *Primary*, (Robert) Drew Associates (documentary)
1961 (cont'd on next page)	U.S. establishes Peace Corps U.S.S.R. begins manned space flights	*Catch-22*, Joseph Heller (fiction)	First live TV coverage of a U.S. presidential news conference	*West Side Story*, Robert Wise *Jules and Jim*, Truffaut

	World Events	Arts	Mass Media	Films and Videos
1961 (cont'd)	U.S.-sponsored Bay of Pigs invasion of Cuba fails Communists build Berlin Wall to deter East Germans from fleeing to the West Patrice Lumumba, first prime minister elected in Congo, is assassinated	*The Moviegoer*, Walker Percy (fiction) Comic-strip and comic-frame paintings, Roy Lichtenstein	*The Dick Van Dyke Show* begins on TV and runs five years	*Last Year at Marienbad*, Resnais (experimental fiction) *Viridiana*, Buñuel *Chronicle of a Summer*, Jean Rouch and Edgar Morin (documentary) "Prelude: Dog Star Man," Brakhage (experimental)
1962	John Glenn is first American to orbit Earth in a spacecraft Algeria wins independence from France U.S. and U.S.S.R. in tense confrontation over Soviet missiles in Cuba UN troops enter Congo to control civil war *Mariner 2* spacecraft sends back first close-up photos of another planet, Venus	*A Clockwork Orange*, Anthony Burgess (fiction) *The Death of Artemio Cruz*, Carlos Fuentes (fiction) *One Flew over the Cuckoo's Nest*, Ken Kesey (fiction) *The Thin Red Line*, Jones (fiction) *Who's Afraid of Virginia Woolf?*, Edward Albee (play)	*The Alfred Hitchcock Hour*, TV show, airs from 1962 to 1965 Johnny Carson becomes host of NBC's late-night TV talk show, *The Tonight Show*, and remains host until 1992 Walter Cronkite becomes anchor (until 1981) of *CBS Evening News* Telstar satellite (for TV and telephone relays) launched Most popular TV show (1962–64): *The Beverly Hillbillies*	*The Man Who Shot Liberty Valance*, Ford *Dr. No*, Terence Young (first James Bond movie) *Lawrence of Arabia*, Lean *The Loneliness of the Long Distance Runner*, Richardson *Vivre sa vie* (*My Life to Live*), Godard *Knife in the Water*, Polanski "An Occurrence at Owl Creek Bridge" ("La Rivière du hibou"), Robert Enrico (experimental fiction) "La jetée," Chris Marker (experimental fiction) "Cosmic Ray," Conner (experimental)
1963	Alabama civil rights march results in beatings of blacks, arrest of Martin Luther King, Jr., and the sending of federal troops	*The Feminine Mystique*, Betty Friedan (nonfiction) *Cinema*, George Segal (life-size sculpture)	New York Film Festival established "Movietone News" last presented in U.S. movie theaters First movie multiplex built, in Kansas City	*The Birds*, Hitchcock *Tom Jones*, Richardson *Billy Liar*, John Schlesinger *Dr. Strangelove: Or, How I Learned to Stop Worrying and Love the Bomb*, Kubrick *Lord of the Flies*, Peter Brook *8 1/2*, Fellini

	World Events	Arts	Mass Media	Films and Videos
1963 (cont'd)	Four black girls killed in bombing of church in Birmingham, Ala. President Kennedy assassinated; Vice President Lyndon Johnson becomes president By year's end, U.S. has sent economic aid and 16,000 "advisers" to South Vietnam Kenya gains independence from British rule	*Mona Lisa*, Andy Warhol (painting)	TV now the major news source for most Americans TV networks expand evening news programs from 15 to 30 minutes Martin Luther King, Jr.'s "I have a dream" speech in Washington, D.C., is televised Unprecedented four-day TV coverage of President Kennedy's assassination and burial Abraham Zapruder's 26-second, 8 mm amateur film is only moving-picture record of Kennedy assassination Audio cassettes used to play back music	*The Leopard* (*Il Gattopardo*), Visconti *Dead Birds*, Robert Gardner (documentary) *7 Up*, Michael Apted (first in documentary series tracing lives of same small group of British citizens in seven-year increments) *Sleep*, Andy Warhol (experimental documentary) "Scorpio Rising," Anger (experimental) "Mothlight," Brakhage (experimental) "Christmas on Earth," Barbara Rubin (experimental)
1964 (cont'd on next page)	Martin Luther King, Jr., wins Nobel Peace Prize Zambia (formerly Rhodesia) becomes independent nation Following an attack on U.S. warships, Congress passes Gulf of Tonkin Resolution, which justifies U.S. military buildup in Vietnam Nelson Mandela sentenced to life in prison in South Africa	*The Woman in the Dunes*, Kobo Abé (fiction) *Little Big Man*, Thomas Berger (fiction) *Fiddler on the Roof*, Jerry Bock and Sheldon Harnick (musical) *Jackie*, Andy Warhol (painting of Jacqueline Kennedy) First Moog (electronic) synthesizer	Sports telecasts begin to use videotaped instant replay Beatles' first American TV appearance, on *The Ed Sullivan Show* *Understanding Media: The Extensions of Man*, Marshall McLuhan (book)	*Nothing but a Man*, Michael Roemer *A Hard Day's Night*, Richard Lester *The Gospel according to St. Matthew*, Pier Paolo Pasolini *Woman in the Dunes*, Hiroshi Teshigahara *A Married Woman*, Godard *(The) Red Desert*, Antonioni *Point of Order*, Emile De Antonio (documentary on 1954 Army-McCarthy hearings)

	World Events	Arts	Mass Media	Films and Videos
1964 (cont'd)	Civil Rights Act becomes law in U.S. Premier Nikita Khrushchev ousted in U.S.S.R.			*A Stravinsky Portrait*, Richard Leacock (documentary) "Fuses," Carolee Schneemann (experimental, 1964–67) *Dog Star Man*, Brakhage (experimental, 1961–64)
1965	Malcolm X, a Black Muslim leader, murdered in New York City In U.S., growing demonstrations against U.S. involvement in Vietnam U.S. deploys Marines to Dominican Republic	*The Autobiography of Malcolm X*, Alex Haley (nonfiction) Luis Valdez founds Teatro Campesino in California *Campbell's Soup Can*, Andy Warhol (painting)	Super-8 film introduced TV expands coverage of Vietnam War Eight-track tape player introduced	*The Pawnbroker*, Sidney Lumet *Pierrot le fou*, Godard *Juliet of the Spirits*, Fellini *The Shop on Main Street*, Jan Kadár and Elmar Klos "The Dot and the Line," Chuck Jones and Maurice Noble (animation) "The War Game," Peter Watkins (a BBC TV fictional-documentary hybrid) *To Die in Madrid*, Frédéric Rossif (documentary) "The Sins of the Fleshpoids," Mike Kuchar (experimental)
1966	Cultural Revolution—led by Mao Zedong—begins in China (ends in 1971), resulting in terrorism, purges, destroyed artworks, and restructuring of the education system Black Panther Party founded in Oakland, Calif. National Organization for Women (NOW) formed	*The Last Picture Show*, Larry McMurtry (fiction) *Valley of the Dolls*, Jacqueline Susan (fiction) *In Cold Blood*, Truman Capote (nonfiction) *Cabaret*, John Kander and Fred Ebb (musical)	Color TV becomes popular in U.S. *Star Trek* begins three-season run on TV *Mission Impossible*, TV adventure series, first airs and runs until 1973 William F. Buckley, Jr.'s *Firing Line* TV interview show first airs; runs until 2000	*Who's Afraid of Virginia Woolf?*, first film directed by Mike Nichols *Seconds*, John Frankenheimer *Blowup*, Antonioni *Persona*, Bergman *Closely Watched Trains*, Jiri Menzel *The Battle of Algiers*, Gillo Pontecorvo *La guerre est finie*, Resnais *Black Girl*, Ousmane Sembène

	World Events	Arts	Mass Media	Films and Videos
1966 (cont'd)	By year's end, 389,000 U.S. troops in Vietnam France withdraws its troops from NATO Indira Gandhi becomes prime minister of India	*Sweet Charity*, Cy Coleman, Dorothy Fields, and Neil Simon (musical based on Fellini's film *The Nights of Cabiria*) *Witness to Our Time*, Alfred Eisenstaedt (photographs) *The State Hospital*, Edward Kienholz (mixed media)	*Amos 'n' Andy* reruns dropped from TV because of protests against program's racial stereotypes *Sixteen in Webster Groves*, TV documentary "How the Grinch Stole Christmas," animation by Chuck Jones, first shown on TV	*The Chelsea Girls*, Warhol (experimental) *No. 4 (Bottoms)*, Yoko Ono (experimental documentary, 1966–67) "Film in Which There Appear Sprocket Holes, Edge Lettering, Dirt Particles, Etc.," George Landow (aka Owen Land) (experimental) "The Flicker," Tony Conrad (experimental) "Lapis," James Whitney (experimental)
1967	Six-Day War between Arab nations and Israel results in Israeli victory and brings Judaea, Samaria, Gaza, Sinai Peninsula, and Golan Heights under Israel's control Thurgood Marshall becomes first African American U.S. Supreme Court justice First human heart transplant, in South Africa By year's end, more than 500,000 U.S. troops in Vietnam Five-year military dictatorship in Greece begins	*One Hundred Years of Solitude*, Gabriel García Márquez (fiction) *Rosencrantz and Guildenstern Are Dead*, Tom Stoppard (play) *The Great White Hope*, Howard Sackler (play) *Hair*, Gerome Ragni and Jim Rado (rock musical) First major rock festival, Monterey, Calif.	American Film Institute founded *Rolling Stone* magazine begins *Ironsides*, TV series, with Raymond Burr (1967–75) *The Carol Burnett Show*, TV show (1967–79)	*Bonnie and Clyde*, Arthur Penn *The Graduate*, Nichols *In Cold Blood*, Richard Brooks *Weekend*, Godard *Playtime* (aka *Play Time*), Tati *Belle de jour*, Buñuel *Accident*, Joseph Losey *Don't Look Back*, D. A. Pennebaker (documentary about Bob Dylan during some time in England) *Portrait of Jason*, Shirley Clarke (documentary) *Titicut Follies*, first documentary by Frederick Wiseman "Quixote," Bruce Baillie (revised version; experimental documentary) "Wavelength," Michael Snow (experimental)
1968 (cont'd on next page)	Surprise Tet offensive demoralizes U.S. and South Vietnamese forces	*2001: A Space Odyssey*, Arthur C. Clarke (fiction)	Recent Czech film movement ended by Soviet invasion of Czechoslovakia	*Faces*, Cassavetes *Night of the Living Dead*, first film by George Romero

	World Events	Arts	Mass Media	Films and Videos
1968 (cont'd)	Martin Luther King, Jr., assassinated U.S senator Robert Kennedy assassinated Soviet army invades Czechoslovakia and ends liberal Czech policies Riots and police brutality outside Democratic National Convention in Chicago Richard M. Nixon elected U.S. president	*Black Rain*, Masuji Ibuse (fiction) *I Never Sang for My Father*, Robert Anderson (play)	Motion Picture Association of America institutes four-part audience rating system for films *60 Minutes*, TV magazine news show, begins *Rowan and Martin's Laugh-In* on TV features very short satiric pieces (1968–73)	*2001: A Space Odyssey*, Kubrick *Once upon a Time in the West*, Sergio Leone *Shame*, Bergman *Memories of Underdevelopment* (*Memorias del subdesarrollo*), Tomás Gutiérrez Alea *David Holzman's Diary*, Jim McBride (fake documentary) *High School*, Wiseman (documentary) "Pas de deux," McLaren (experimental)
1969	Arafat becomes head of PLO U.S. astronauts land on moon for the first time and return Woodstock (N.Y.) music festival draws 500,000 Large U.S. demonstrations against Vietnam War continue Massacre of villagers in My Lai (Vietnam) by U.S. soldiers revealed American Gay Liberation movement begins with the Stonewall Inn riot in New York City	*Fat City*, Leonard Gardner (fiction) *The Godfather*, Mario Puzo (best-selling U.S. novel of the 1970s) *Portnoy's Complaint*, Philip Roth (fiction) *Slaughterhouse-Five*, Kurt Vonnegut, Jr. (fiction)	Live TV broadcast from moon captures the world's attention PBS begins broadcasting TV programs, including *Sesame Street*, which uses techniques of TV commercials to teach children basic language skills Most popular TV show (1969–70): *Rowan and Martin's Laugh-In*	*Midnight Cowboy*, Schlesinger *Medium Cool*, Haskell Wexler *The Wild Bunch*, Sam Peckinpah *I Am Joaquin*, Luis Valdez (possibly the first film written, produced, and directed by Latinos in the United States) *My Night at Maud's*, Eric Rohmer *If . . .*, Lindsay Anderson *Boy*, Oshima *Army of Shadows*, Jean-Pierre Melville *Monterey Pop*, Pennebaker (early rock documentary) *Salesman*, Albert and David Maysles (documentary) *In the Year of the Pig*, De Antonio (documentary) *Tom, Tom, The Piper's Son*, Ken Jacobs (experimental) "Back and Forth," Snow (experimental)

	World Events	Arts	Mass Media	Films and Videos
1970	U.S. Supreme Court allows school busing to achieve integration U.S. and South Vietnamese troops enter Cambodia At Kent State University, Ohio National Guard members shoot at demonstrating students and kill four Student demonstrations against Vietnam War close hundreds of U.S. colleges and universities Muammar al-Qaddafi comes to power in Libya Coup leaves Cambodia under oppressive military dictatorship	*Deliverance*, James Dickey (fiction) *Spiral Jetty*, Robert Smithson (1,500-foot jetty, Great Salt Lake, Utah)	Rapid growth of film studies in U.S. colleges and universities IMAX ("image maximum"), extremely large-screen film format, introduced at World's Fair National Public Radio (NPR) begins broadcasting *The Phil Donahue Show* is first seen nationally on TV and runs until 1996 About 231 million TV sets used throughout the world *The Mary Tyler Moore Show* (TV sitcom) begins *Doonesbury* (satirical) comic strip begins	*MASH*, Robert Altman *Patton*, Franklin Schaffner *The Great White Hope*, Martin Ritt *The Wild Child*, Truffaut *Even Dwarfs Started Small*, Werner Herzog *Woodstock*, Michael Wadleigh (documentary) *The Sorrow and the Pity*, Marcel Ophüls (documentary) *Gimme Shelter*, Maysles Brothers (documentary) *Zorns Lemma*, Hollis Frampton (experimental) "Remedial Reading Comprehension," George Landow (aka Owen Land) (experimental) "Runs Good," Pat O'Neill (experimental) "Serene Velocity," Ernie Gehr (experimental)
1971	Saddam Hussein seizes power in Iraq Pakistan attacks India but is defeated in two-week war Bangladesh established as independent nation Failed coup attempt in China	*Maurice*, Forster (posthumous fiction) *Being There*, Jerzy (N.) Kosinski (fiction) *. . . And the Earth Did Not Devour Him*, Tomás Rivera (fiction)	Movie theater receipts are down sharply *Ms. Magazine* founded to promote the women's movement Ban on TV cigarette advertising goes into effect *Masterpiece Theatre* begins on PBS, with Alistair Cooke as host Top U.S. TV show (1971–76): *All in the Family*, with Carroll O'Connor as Archie Bunker	*McCabe and Mrs. Miller*, Altman *The Last Picture Show*, Peter Bogdanovich *Sweet Sweetback's Baad-asssss Song*, Melvin Van Peebles *A Clockwork Orange*, Kubrick *Get Carter*, Mike Hodges *Claire's Knee*, Rohmer *Walkabout*, Nicolas Roeg *The Conformist*, Bernardo Bertolucci "(nostalgia)," Frampton (experimental) "Kiri," Sakumi Hagiwara (experimental)

	World Events	Arts	Mass Media	Films and Videos
1972	White House announces last U.S. ground combat units have left Vietnam Britain assumes direct control of Northern Ireland Men working for Republican Party caught breaking into Democratic National Headquarters in Watergate apartment building in Washington, D.C. Terrorists invade Israeli compound at Munich Olympics and kill two; later developments lead to loss of more lives	*Bless Me, Ultima*, Rudolfo A. Anaya (fiction) *Story Show*, Laurie Anderson (multimedia performance) *Grease!*, Jim Jacobs and Warren Casey (musical) Christo wraps large section of Australian coastline in plastic sheeting	*M*A*S*H* TV series, based on the movie *MASH*, begins and runs for 11 seasons Home Box Office (HBO) first available through cable TV First International Festival of Women's Films held in New York City	*The Godfather*, Francis Ford Coppola *Cabaret*, Bob Fosse *Fat City*, Huston *Deep Throat*, Gerard Damiano (first sexually explicit feature to gain U.S. national audience) *Frenzy*, Hitchcock *The Discreet Charm of the Bourgeoisie*, Buñuel *Last Tango in Paris*, Bertolucci *Aguirre, The Wrath of God*, Herzog *Cries and Whispers*, Bergman "Near the Big Chakra," Anne Severson (experimental documentary)
1973	U.S. Supreme Court, in *Roe v. Wade*, rules abortion is constitutional Vietnam cease-fire agreement signed; U.S. combat deaths: approximately 58,000 Salvador Allende, Marxist president of Chile, overthrown and reportedly commits suicide Amid scandal, Spiro T. Agnew resigns as U.S. vice president; U.S. congressman Gerald Ford succeeds him During Yom Kippur, Egyptian and Syrian forces attack Israeli-held Sinai Peninsula and Golan Heights	*Fear of Flying*, Erica Jong (fiction) *The Gulag Archipelago*, Aleksandr Solzhenitsyn (first volume of three-volume fiction) *Equus*, Peter Shaffer (play) Scott Joplin's ragtime music popular after its use in movie *The Sting*	Omnimax, huge dome screen for use with IMAX, developed U.S. Senate Watergate hearings broadcast on TV *An American Family*, 12-hour TV documentary series on PBS	*Mean Streets*, Martin Scorsese *American Graffiti*, George Lucas *The Long Goodbye*, Altman *Payday*, Daryl Duke *The Harder They Come*, Perry Henzell *Don't Look Now*, Roeg *Day for Night*, Truffaut *Fantastic Planet*, René Laloux (animated) *Spirit of the Beehive*, Victor Erice *Distant Thunder*, Satyajit Ray *Touki Bouki (The Journey of the Hyena)*, Djibril Diop Mambety "No Lies," Mitchell Block (fake documentary) "Three Transitions," Peter Campus (experimental videos)

	World Events	Arts	Mass Media	Films and Videos
1974	Nixon resigns presidency; Vice President Gerald Ford becomes president Ford pardons Nixon for possible criminal offenses committed while in office OPEC embargo causes oil shortages and serious economic problems in U.S. and elsewhere Turkish forces invade Cyprus; Greek forces mobilized to repel the invasion	*Jaws*, Peter Benchley (fiction) *Carrie*, Stephen King's first novel	*Little House on the Prairie*, TV show (1974–83) *The Rockford Files*, TV show (1974–80) *Happy Days*, TV show (1974–84) Ali-Foreman boxing match in Zaire, the "Rumble in the Jungle," is best-documented prizefight in history *Prairie Home Companion*, radio program with Garrison Keillor as host, begins Word processors hit the U.S. market	*The Godfather Part II* and *The Conversation*, Coppola *Chinatown*, Polanski *A Woman under the Influence*, Cassavetes *Ali: Fear Eats the Soul*, Rainer Werner Fassbinder *Amarcord*, Fellini *Scenes from a Marriage*, Bergman *Xala* (*Impotence*), Sembene "Antonia: A Portrait of the Woman," Jill Godmilow (documentary) "8½ × 11," James Benning (experimental fiction) *Film about a woman who . . .*, Yvonne Rainer (experimental) "Print Generation," J. J. Murphy (experimental)
1975	U.S. ends all involvement in Vietnam Soviet space probes transmit first pictures of Venus's surface Franco of Spain dies; Juan Carlos sworn in as king Khmer Rouge kill at least a million Cambodians (1975–79)	*Ragtime*, E. L. Doctorow (fiction) *Heat and Dust*, Ruth Jhabvala Prawer (fiction) *American Buffalo*, David Mamet (play) *A Chorus Line*, James Kirkwood, Nicholas Dante, and Marvin Hamlisch (musical that plays in New York 15 years)	Personal computers introduced Dolby film noise-reduction system introduced *Saturday Night Live*, TV show, debuts Sony introduces Beta home videotape format	*Nashville*, Altman *Shampoo*, Hal Ashby *One Flew over the Cuckoo's Nest*, Milos Forman *Barry Lyndon*, Kubrick *The Rocky Horror Picture Show*, Jim Sharman *Picnic at Hanging Rock*, Peter Weir *The Mystery of Kaspar Hauser*, Herzog *The Story of Adele H.*, Truffaut *The Passenger*, Antonioni *Grey Gardens*, Maysles Brothers (documentary) *Jeanne Dielman*, Chantal Akerman (experimental documentary)

	World Events	Arts	Mass Media	Films and Videos
1976	Argentine military government begins "dirty war" against dissidents; tens of thousands disappear or are murdered or both Apple Computer company founded Two U.S. spacecraft land on Mars but find no signs of life Georgia governor Jimmy Carter elected U.S. president	*The Woman Warrior,* Maxine Hong Kingston (fiction) *The Shining,* King (fiction) *The Kiss of the Spider Woman,* Manuel Puig (fiction) *Roots,* Haley (nonfiction)	Steadicam, a lightweight, portable mount for holding a movie camera, first used in making a feature film (*Bound for Glory*) Louma (lightweight, modular, 25-foot) camera crane with remote-control camera head first used in filming a feature (*The Tenant*) U.S. telecasts views from Mars worldwide *The McNeil-Lehrer* [news] *Report* begins on PBS (TV)	*Taxi Driver,* Scorsese *Network,* Lumet *All the President's Men,* Alan J. Pakula *Face to Face,* Bergman *Seven Beauties,* Lina Wertmuller *In the Realm of the Senses,* Oshima *Harlan County U.S.A.,* Barbara Kopple (documentary) *Word Is Out,* Robert Epstein and Peter Adair (documentary) "Chulas Fronteras," Les Blank (documentary) "Projection Instructions," Morgan Fisher (experimental)
1977	U.S. space probes *Voyager 1* and *Voyager 2* are launched and two years later send back data and photographs of Jupiter Indira Gandhi of India arrested on charges of corruption President Carter pardons all Vietnam War draft evaders	Pompidou Center, Richard Rogers and Renzo Piano (Paris architecture) Cindy Sherman begins her photographic series of herself in various movie poses	Eight-part TV dramatization of Alex Haley's book *Roots* a popular and critical success *The Lou Grant Show,* TV show (1977–82)	*Annie Hall,* Woody Allen *Star Wars,* Lucas *Equus,* Lumet *Close Encounters of the Third Kind,* Steven Spielberg *Killer of Sheep,* Charles Burnett *Providence,* Resnais *1900,* Bertolucci *Ceddo,* Sembene "Video Weavings," Stephen Beck (experimental video) "Turn to Your ~~Gods~~ Dogs," Richard Beveridge (experimental)
1978	In Nicaragua, Sandinista guerrilla war develops into a civil war that lasts until 1988	*Zoot Suit,* Valdez (play) *Betrayal,* Pinter (play)	120 million people see the U.S. TV movie *Holocaust* *Dallas,* TV show (1978–91)	*The Deer Hunter,* Michael Cimino *Grease,* Randal Kleiser *Girlfriends,* Claudia Weill

	World Events	Arts	Mass Media	Films and Videos
1978 (cont'd)	Vietnamese occupy Cambodia and end Khmer Rouge slaughter of Cambodians First "test-tube" baby born, in England At Jonestown, Guyana, 909 American cultists commit suicide	*Ain't Misbehavin'*, jazz musical celebrating the music of Fats Waller Soundtrack albums for the movies *Saturday Night Fever* and *Grease* are popular	Laser videodisc players and videodiscs first marketed in U.S. 98 percent of all U.S. households have at least one television set Gene Siskel and Roger Ebert appear on a weekly TV film review show	*Get Out Your Handkerchiefs*, Bertrand Blier *Autumn Sonata*, Bergman *The Marriage of Maria Braun*, Fassbinder *Gates of Heaven*, first film by Errol Morris (documentary) "Daughter Rite," Michelle Citron (hybrid)
1979	Shah of Iran forced into exile; new leader is Ayatollah Ruhollah Khomeini Nuclear disaster averted at Three Mile Island, Pennsylvania Margaret Thatcher becomes first female British prime minister Sandinistas overthrow Nicaragua's president and establish Marxist government About 100 U.S. Embassy personnel taken hostage in Tehran, Iran Smallpox declared eradicated worldwide	*Sophie's Choice*, William Styron (fiction) *The Right Stuff*, Tom Wolfe (nonfiction) Spalding Gray begins to write and perform mostly autobiographical monologues *Evita*, Andrew Lloyd Webber and Tim Rice (musical)	Sony Walkman (portable audio cassette player) introduced in U.S. *The Far Side*, comic strip by Gary Larson, begins *I Know Why the Caged Bird Sings*, TV adaptation of Maya Angelou's autobiography C-SPAN (government) and ESPN (sports) cable networks founded	*Apocalypse Now*, Coppola *All That Jazz*, Bob Fosse *Breaking Away*, Peter Yates *Breaker Morant*, Bruce Beresford *My Brilliant Career*, Gillian Armstrong *Best Boy*, Ira Wohl (documentary) "Peliculas," Patrick Clancy (experimental) "Thriller," Sally Potter (experimental) "Hearts," Barbara Buckner (experimental video) "A Portrait of Light and Heat," Bill Viola (experimental video)
1980 (cont'd on next page)	U.S.S.R. continues its invasion of Afghanistan Rhodesia gains independence and becomes the republic of Zimbabwe Lech Walesa becomes leader of Polish trade union Solidarity	*The Name of the Rose*, Umberto Eco (fiction) *Amadeus*, Shaffer (play)	*Cosmos*, TV series with scientist and educator Carl Sagan on PBS Home dish antennas to receive TV signals from satellites begin to gain in popularity Cable News Network (CNN) begins	*Raging Bull*, Scorsese *Atlantic City*, Louis Malle *Melvin and Howard*, Jonathan Demme *The Empire Strikes Back*, Irvin Kershner *The Shining*, Kubrick *Berlin Alexanderplatz*, Fassbinder (TV miniseries later shown briefly in theaters)

	World Events	Arts	Mass Media	Films and Videos
1980 (cont'd)	Iraq invades Iran, starting a war that lasts until 1988 and kills more than a million Mariel boat lift brings tens of thousands of Cubans to Florida Ronald Reagan elected U.S. president		U.S. TV networks begin to offer some captioning for hearing-impaired viewers First interactive videodisc: *How to Watch Pro Football*	*Moscow Does Not Believe in Tears*, Vladimir Menshov *Kagemusha*, Kurosawa *Model*, Wiseman (documentary) (*The Life and Times of*) *Rosie the Riveter*, Connie Field (documentary)
1981	Iran releases remaining U.S. hostages First U.S. space shuttle successfully flown Scientists first identify AIDS Sandra Day O'Connor becomes first female U.S. Supreme Court justice Egyptian soldiers assassinate Egypt's president Anwar Sadat	*Sixty Stories*, Donald Barthelme (fiction) *A Soldier's Play*, Charles Fuller (play)	Walter Cronkite retires from regular TV broadcasting *Hill Street Blues*, TV show (1981–87) Highest-rated TV show (1981–82): *Dallas* MTV, a 24-hour-a-day music video channel, begins	*Zoot Suit*, Valdez (first Chicano Hollywood film) *Gallipoli*, Weir *Pixote*, Hector Babenco *Das Boot* (*The Boat*), Wolfgang Petersen *Céleste*, Percy Adlon *Mephisto*, Istvan Szabo "Ancient of Days," Viola (experimental videos, 1979–81)
1982	Argentina invades Falkland Islands, starting a war that Britain wins Maya Lin's Vietnam Veterans' War Memorial, with 58,000 etched American names, dedicated in Washington, D.C. First permanent implant of a mechanical heart in a human	*The Color Purple*, Alice Walker (fiction) *Schindler's Ark*, Thomas Keneally (nonfiction) *Cats*, Andrew Lloyd Webber and Trevor Nunn (musical) Popular songs: "Eye of the Tiger" from the film *Rocky III* and the "Chariots of Fire" melody from the film of that title	28 million U.S. homes have cable TV *Cagney and Lacey*, TV show (1982–88) *Cheers*, TV show (1982–93) *USA Today*, newspaper available nationwide, begins publication Computer technology used to make images of settings and props for the film *Tron* Digital audio CDs first marketed	*Tootsie*, Sydney Pollack *E.T., The Extraterrestrial*, Spielberg *Blade Runner*, Ridley Scott *Fanny and Alexander*, Bergman *Night of the Shooting Stars*, Paola and Vittorio Taviani *Fitzcarraldo*, Herzog *Lola*, Fassbinder *Wend Kuuni* (*God's Gift*), Gaston Kaboré *Burden of Dreams*, Blank (documentary) "Reassemblage," Trinh T. Minh-ha (experimental documentary) "Tides," Amy Greenfield (experimental)

	World Events	Arts	Mass Media	Films and Videos
1983	President Reagan backs Contra rebels in their war with Marxist Nicaraguan government U.S. troops sent into Grenada International introduction of highly addictive and destructive drug "crack cocaine"	American Telephone and Telegraph Building in New York City designed by Philip Johnson and John Burgee and regarded as an important postmodernist structure	*The Day After*, a TV movie about nuclear war, seen by half of U.S. adults Final episode of TV show *M*A*S*H* seen by an estimated 50 million HBO begins producing feature films First civilian cellular (cell) phones hit the market	*A Christmas Story*, Bob Clark *El Norte*, Gregory Nava *Betrayal*, David Jones *Local Hero*, Bill Forsyth *Entre nous*, Diane Kurys *Eréndira*, Ruy Guerra *Koyaanisqatsi*, Godfrey Reggio (experimental documentary)
1984	Apple Macintosh computer first sold Indian army troops invade Sikh temple and kill 1,000 Sikh fundamentalists using the temple as a haven and headquarters India's prime minister Indira Gandhi assassinated Ethiopia-Eritrea war, disease, and famine kill 1 million In the worst industrial accident ever, thousands die because of a gas leak at Union Carbide plant in Bhopal, India	*The Lover*, Marguerite Duras (fiction) *Love in the Time of Cholera*, García Márquez (fiction) *The Unbearable Lightness of Being*, Milan Kundera (fiction) *The House on Mango Street*, Sandra Cisneros (fiction) Soundtrack for *Purple Rain* is huge success	PG-13 film rating begins *The Cosby Show*, TV show (1984–92) *Murder, She Wrote*, TV show (1984–96) U.S. Supreme Court rules noncommercial private home video-taping of off-the-air programs is legal Criterion (company) releases *Citizen Kane* on laser videodisc	*Stranger Than Paradise*, Jim Jarmusch *This Is Spinal Tap*, Rob Reiner *Blood Simple*, first film directed by Joel Coen *Frida*, Paul Leduc *Paris, Texas*, Wim Wenders *Yellow Earth*, Chen Kaige *The Times of Harvey Milk*, Robert Epstein (documentary) "In Heaven There Is No Beer?," Blank (documentary) *Marlene*, Maximilian Schell (documentary) "Thriller," Michael Jackson (video)
1985 (cont'd on next page)	Mikhail Gorbachev becomes general secretary of Soviet Communist Party Rock Hudson, movie star, dies of AIDS	*The Handmaid's Tale*, Margaret Atwood (fiction) *Black Robe*, Brian Moore (fiction) *Old Gringo*, Fuentes (fiction)	Home movie video revenues exceed those of theatrical revenues Sundance Film Festival founded by Robert Redford to promote independent films	*Prizzi's Honor*, Huston *The Purple Rose of Cairo*, Allen *My Life as a Dog*, Lasse Hallström *Vagabond*, Agnès Varda

	World Events	Arts	Mass Media	Films and Videos
1985 (cont'd)	Gorbachev and Reagan meet for a summit in Geneva Marxist Sandinistas gain control of Nicaragua; U.S. continues to support Contra rebels The year is marked by terrorist hijackings, bombings, kidnappings, and murder, including at airports in Rome and Vienna	*The Accidental Tourist*, Anne Tyler (fiction) *Les Liaisons Dangereuses*, Christopher Hampton (play) *Les Misérables*, Alain Boublil and Claude-Michel Schönberg (musical)	First 3-D IMAX film shown, in Japan *Desert Hearts*, first lesbian love story on film to obtain mainstream distribution First laser videodisc players and videodiscs having digital sound	*The Official Story*, Luis Puenzo *Ran*, Kurosawa *Shoah*, Claude Lanzmann (documentary) *George Stevens: A Film Maker's Journey*, George Stevens, Jr. (documentary) *The Man Who Envied Women*, Rainer (experimental) *Naked Spaces: Living Is Round*, Minh-ha (experimental documentary) "Standard Gauge," Fisher (experimental)
1986	U.S. space shuttle *Challenger* explodes shortly after lift-off, killing entire crew Haitian dictator Jean-Claude Duvalier ousted by revolution and flees the country Corazón Aquino declared winner of Philippine presidential election; President Ferdinand Marcos flees into exile Soviets orbit first long-term space station, *Mir* Nuclear accident at Chernobyl, Ukraine, pollutes Europe President Reagan admits subordinates sold weapons illegally to Iran to raise money for Nicaraguan rebels 25,000 AIDS cases diagnosed in U.S.	*Paco's Story*, Larry Heinemann (fiction) *A Summons to Memphis*, Peter Taylor (fiction) *Phantom of the Opera*, Andrew Lloyd Webber and Charles Hart (musical)	Colorization of videos of older black-and-white films is controversial *L.A. Law*, TV show (1986–94) *The Oprah Winfrey Show*, TV talk show, begins Highest-rated TV show (1986–89): *The Cosby Show* *Calvin and Hobbes*, comic strip, begins Nintendo video game system hits U.S. market	*Blue Velvet*, David Lynch *Down by Law*, Jarmusch *Platoon*, Oliver Stone *True Stories*, David Byrne *Mona Lisa*, Neil Jordan *Tampopo*, Juzo Itami *Sherman's March*, Ross McElwee (documentary) *Mother Teresa*, Ann and Jeanette Petrie (documentary) *Rate It X*, Lucy Winer and Paula De Koenigsberg (documentary) *Private Practices: The Story of a Sex Surrogate*, Kirby Dick (documentary) *Home of the Brave*, Laurie Anderson (documentary) "Street of Crocodiles," Timothy and Stephen Quay (experimental fiction)

	World Events	Arts	Mass Media	Films and Videos
1987	World population: 5 billion Iran-Contra congressional report faults President Reagan Gorbachev and Reagan sign treaty banning short- and medium-range nuclear weapons in Europe	*The Bonfire of the Vanities*, Wolfe (fiction) *Beloved*, Toni Morrison (fiction) *Fences*, August Wilson (play) *Driving Miss Daisy*, Alfred Uhry (play) Soundtrack for *Dirty Dancing* is huge hit	Home videotape rentals in U.S. continue to grow Iran-Contra congressional hearings televised live *Eyes on the Prize*, TV series on civil rights movement, shown on PBS	*The Dead*, Huston *Full Metal Jacket*, Kubrick *The Last Emperor*, Bertolucci *Red Sorghum*, Zhang Yimou *A Taxing Woman*, Itami *Yeelen* (*Brightness*), Souleymane Cissé "Damned If You Don't," Su Friedrich (experimental fiction)
1988	Soviet troops begin retreat from Afghanistan UN mediates ceasefire between Iran and Iraq; Iraq attacks rebelling Kurds Uprising by Palestinians in West Bank and Gaza Strip Crack cocaine increasingly used in U.S. cities Vice President George H.W. Bush elected U.S. president	*The Satanic Verses*, Salman Rushdie (fiction condemned by Muslim fundamentalists, who force Rushdie into hiding) *The Player*, Michael Tolkin (fiction) *The Heidi Chronicles*, Wendy Wasserstein (play) *Buster Keaton*, Jeff Koons (wood sculpture)	Morphing first used in making parts of a feature film, *Willow* *P.O.V.* series of documentary films begins on PBS *Roseanne*, TV show (1988–94) TNT cable network founded *Oxford English Dictionary* becomes available on CD-ROM Apple Macintosh with CD-ROM player can play music CDs	*The Last Temptation of Christ*, Scorsese *The Unbearable Lightness of Being*, Philip Kaufman *Dangerous Liaisons*, Stephen Frears *Little Vera*, Vasily Pichul *Saaraba* (*Utopia*), Amadou Seck *The Thin Blue Line*, Morris (documentary) *Comic Book Confidential*, Ron Mann (documentary) *Hotel Terminus: The Life and Times of Klaus Barbie*, Ophüls (documentary) *Who Framed Roger Rabbit?*, Robert Zemeckis (live action–animation)
1989 (cont'd on next page)	In Czechoslovakia, large peaceful opposition to Soviet dominance	*The Mambo Kings Play Songs of Love*, Oscar Hijuelos (fiction) *The General in His Labyrinth*, García Márquez (fiction)	U.S. National Film Registry established to recognize significant American films; the first films announced include *Citizen Kane* and *Casablanca*	*Drugstore Cowboy*, Gus Van Sant *Mystery Train*, Jarmusch *Do the Right Thing*, Spike Lee *sex, lies, and videotape*, Steven Soderbergh

	World Events	Arts	Mass Media	Films and Videos
1989 (cont'd)	Pro-democracy students occupy Tiananmen Square in Beijing; two months later, government tanks disperse them; thousands believed killed Berlin Wall torn down Playwright Václav Havel becomes president of Czechoslovakia	*The Joy Luck Club*, Amy Tan (fiction) *Remains of the Day*, Kazuo Ishiguro *When Harry Met Sally*, popular film soundtrack	Time Inc. buys Warner Communications, creating world's largest entertainment group Sony Corporation purchases Columbia Pictures (thereby securing film production, distribution, and exhibition) and promotes Columbia films in print and TV media under Sony's control Most popular TV shows (1989–90): *Roseanne* and *The Cosby Show*	*The Little Mermaid* (Disney animation) *Lawrence of Arabia*, rereleased in revised and restored version *My Left Foot*, Jim Sheridan *The Killer*, John Woo *Yaaba*, Idrissa Ouedraogo *Roger & Me*, Michael Moore (satirical documentary) "You Take Care Now," Ann Marie Fleming (experimental narrative documentary)
1990	Mandela freed from prison in South Africa Yugoslavia moving toward split-up Russian politician Boris Yeltsin resigns from Soviet Communist Party Iraq invades Kuwait; various diplomatic solutions sought Germany reunited Walesa elected Poland's president Haiti holds first democratic elections	*The Snapper*, Roddy Doyle (fiction) *Possession: A Romance*, A. S. Byatt (fiction) *Orphée*, Philip Glass (music) and Jean Cocteau (libretto and screenplay for his film of the same title) *Mo' Better Blues*, Branford Marsalis (music from film of same title)	NC-17 rating instituted; *Henry and June* first film so rated *The Civil War*, 11-hour TV documentary on PBS, directed by Ken Burns *Twin Peaks*, TV show directed by David Lynch *Billboard* announces that revenue from home video movies is twice that from theatrical box offices	*GoodFellas*, Scorsese *Reversal of Fortune*, Barbet Schroeder *To Sleep with Anger*, Burnett *The Grifters*, Frears *Life Is Sweet*, Mike Leigh *Vincent & Theo*, Altman *Ju Dou*, Zhang *Tilaï*, Ouedraogo *Finzan: A Dance for the Heroes*, Cheick Oumar Sissoko *Berkeley in the Sixties*, Mark Kitchell (documentary) *Paris Is Burning*, Jennie Livingston (documentary) *Privilege*, Rainer (experimental fiction)
1991	U.S. and its UN allies defeat Iraq in 100-hour battle and free Kuwait	*The Sweet Hereafter*, Russell Banks (fiction)	Highest-rated TV show (1990–91): *Cheers*	*Europa, Europa*, Agnieszka Holland

	World Events	Arts	Mass Media	Films and Videos
1991 (cont'd)	Rajiv Gandhi, prime minister of India, assassinated Yeltsin elected president of Russia Bosnia and Herzegovina, parts of former Yugoslavia, wage civil war Coup against Gorbachev fails, Communist rule ends in U.S.S.R., and cold war ends	*Maus II: A Survivor's Tale: And Here My Troubles Began*, Art Spiegelman (graphic novel) *Lost in Yonkers*, Simon (play)	Morphing used in parts of *Terminator 2* to show the transformation of a character into various other characters	*Raise the Red Lantern*, Zhang *Sango Malo (The Village Teacher)*, Bassek ba Kobhio *Hearts of Darkness: A Filmmaker's Apocalypse*, Fax Bahr and George Hickenlooper (documentary) "First Comes Love," Friedrich (experimental documentary)
1992	Jury in Rodney King's state trial finds police defendants not guilty; riots in Los Angeles leave 58 dead and hundreds of millions of dollars in property damage U.S.S.R. splits into 15 nations, including Russia Leader of Peruvian terrorist group The Shining Path arrested Thousands die in Muslim-Hindu conflict in India Arkansas governor Bill Clinton elected U.S. president	*All the Pretty Horses*, Cormac McCarthy (fiction) *The English Patient: A Novel*, Michael Ondaatje (fiction) *Angels in America*, Tony Kushner (two-part play) Soundtrack with Whitney Houston from *The Bodyguard* becomes best-selling soundtrack of all time	Johnny Carson retires as host of *The Tonight Show* (TV) and is replaced by Jay Leno Internet begins with the "Internet Society," a collection of 1 million linked host computers	*The Player*, Altman *Unforgiven*, Clint Eastwood *Reservoir Dogs*, Quentin Tarantino *Like Water for Chocolate*, Alfonso Arau *The Crying Game*, Jordan *Quartier Mozart*, Jean-Pierre Bekolo *Guelwaar*, Sembene *A Brief History of Time*, Morris (documentary) *Brother's Keeper*, Joe Berlinger and Bruce Sinofsky (documentary) "Women Who Made the Movies," Gwendolyn Foster and Wheeler Dixon (documentary) *Visions of Light: The Art of Cinematography*, Arnold Glassman, Todd McCarthy, and Stuart Samuels (documentary)
1993 (cont'd on next page)	Israel and PLO formally recognize each other	*The Shipping News*, E. Anne Proulx (fiction)	Last original *Cheers* episode draws record TV audience	*Schindler's List*, Spielberg *Short Cuts*, Altman *The Ballad of Little Jo*, Maggie Greenwald

	World Events	Arts	Mass Media	Films and Videos
1993 (cont'd)	Despite outside diplomatic pressures, parties in former Yugoslavia continue fighting Czechoslovakia divides into Czech Republic and Slovakia Agents of U.S. Bureau of Alcohol, Tobacco, and Firearms attempt to enter cult Branch Davidian compound in Waco, Texas; gunfights end in fatal fire	*Before Night Falls*, Reinaldo Arenas (fiction) *Jesus' Son*, Denis Johnson (fiction) *Arcadia*, Stoppard (play) *Full Moon*, Bill Irwin and David Shiner (mime) *Marilyn*, Ezra Laderman (opera about Marilyn Monroe)	*The X-Files* first airs, on Fox Network	*Orlando*, Potter *Naked*, Leigh *The Piano*, Jane Campion *Farewell My Concubine*, Chen *(Tim Burton's) The Nightmare before Christmas*, Henry Selick (animation) *Thirty-Two Short Films about Glenn Gould*, François Girard (documentary) *The Wonderful, Horrible Life of Leni Riefenstahl*, Ray Müller (documentary) *Blue*, Derek Jarman (experimental)
1994	Civil wars in Georgia (part of former U.S.S.R.), Yemen, and Rwanda Mandela elected president in first multiracial South African election People from Chechnya seek independence from Russia and begin guerrilla warfare U.S.-led occupation of Haiti leads to reinstatement of democratically elected president World Trade Center bombed in first foreign terrorist attack on U.S. soil Channel Tunnel (Chunnel) links Britain and France	*Felicia's Journey*, William Trevor (fiction) *The Ice Storm*, Rick Moody (fiction) *Trainspotting*, Irvine Welsh (fiction) *The Hour We Knew Nothing of Each Other*, Peter Handke (100-minute wordless play with sound effects) *La belle et la bête*, Cocteau's film without soundtrack but with supertitles and live music composed by Philip Glass ("an opera for ensemble and film")	Steven Spielberg, Jeffrey Katzenberg, and David Geffen form DreamWorks SKG to produce theatrical films, animation, television programs, records, and interactive media Independent Film Channel offered on some cable systems (Short) IMAX 3-D films shown in U.S. (previously shown in Japan and Europe) More than 80 percent of all U.S. households have at least one VCR Marketing films first in video and perhaps later to theaters is a small trend DirectTV, Digital TV, offers multiple channels from a satellite	*Pulp Fiction*, Tarantino *Vanya on 42nd Street*, Malle *Ed Wood*, Tim Burton *Natural Born Killers*, Stone *Exotica*, Atom Egoyan *Il Postino (The Postman)*, Michael Radford *Red*, Krzysztof Kieslowski *Burnt by the Sun*, Nikita Mikhalkov *To Live*, Zhang *Eat Drink Man Woman*, Ang Lee *The Lion King*, Disney animation *High School II*, Wiseman (documentary) *Crumb*, Terry Zwigoff (documentary) *The Troubles We've Seen*, Ophüls (documentary) *Hoop Dreams*, Steve James (documentary) *Carmen Miranda: Bananas Is My Business*, Helena Solberg (documentary)

	World Events	Arts	Mass Media	Films and Videos
1994 (cont'd)	Mexican Indian guerrillas in southern state of Chiapas demand more land and self-rule; Mexico's ruling party candidate assassinated and replaced by Ernesto Zedillo, later elected president	*The Dangerous Liaisons*, Conrad Susa and Philip Littell (opera) Soundtrack for *The Lion King* is a big hit Andy Warhol Museum opens in Pittsburgh	Megaplexing of the U.S. begins when AMC Entertainment opens a megaplex in Dallas	"A Great Day in Harlem," Jean Bach (documentary) "Cremaster 4," Matthew Barney (first of five experimental films)
1995	American astronauts dock with Russian space station *Mir* and work with cosmonauts Unrelated terrorists use gas in Japan and a bomb in Oklahoma City to kill civilians Presidents of Serbia, Bosnia, and Croatia agree to U.S.-brokered peace plan for Bosnia-Herzegovina Right-wing Israeli radical assassinates Yitzhak Rabin, Israeli prime minister	*Seven Guitars*, Wilson (play) *Rent*, Jonathan Larson (musical) *Untitled 8½-by-11-inch film-related stills*, Cindy Sherman *24 Frames per Second*, Bill T. Jones and Lyon Opera Ballet (dance homage to the Lumière Brothers, early French filmmakers)	*Toy Story* is first feature film made entirely with computer animation Percentage of Americans reading a newspaper daily continues decades-long decline Two studies show the average American continues to spend more on books each year than on recorded music or home videos Disney and Capital Cities/ABC merge and form world's largest media company *Calvin and Hobbes*, comic strip, ends	*Welcome to the Dollhouse*, Todd Solondz *A Little Princess*, Alfonso Cuarón *To Die For*, Van Sant *Richard III*, Richard Loncraine *Babe*, Chris Noonan (live action and extensive animatronics) *Hate*, Mathieu Kassovitz *Black is . . . Black ain't*, Marlon T. Riggs (documentary) *Orson Welles: The One-Man Band*, Vassili Silovic (documentary) *Theremin: An Electronic Odyssey*, Steven M. Martin (documentary) "A Cinema of Unease: A Personal Journey by Sam Neill," Sam Neill and Judy Rymer (documentary on cinema of New Zealand) "Buried Secrets," Viola (experimental video and audio)
1996 (cont'd on next page)	Yeltsin reelected president of Russia	*Angela's Ashes: A Memoir*, Frank McCourt (nonfiction)	Sundance (independent) Channel offered on some cable and satellite systems	*Fargo*, Coen Brothers *The English Patient*, Anthony Minghella

	World Events	Arts	Mass Media	Films and Videos
1996 (cont'd)	War and famine in eastern Zaire kill massive numbers of people Suicide bombings by militant Muslims kill 61 in Israel, hamper peace talks, and contribute to election defeat of Israel's ruling party Unabomber captured and convicted after 17-year U.S. bombing spree Bomb explodes during Olympics in Atlanta, Ga.	*The Tailor of Panama*, John Le Carré (fiction) *Last Orders*, Graham Swift (fiction) *In the Beauty of the Lilies*, John Updike (fiction)	*The Phil Donahue Show* (TV talk show) ends Federal Communications Commission (FCC) standards for digital TVs include wider screens and sharper pictures than those found in analog TVs 45 million people using the Internet, two-thirds of them in North America	*Trainspotting*, Danny Boyle *Secrets & Lies*, Leigh *Shall We Dance?*, Masayuki Suo *Hide and Seek*, Friedrich (fiction and documentary) *The Celluloid Closet*, Rob Epstein and Jeffrey Friedman (documentary) *A Personal Journey with Martin Scorsese through American Movies* (documentary) *The Devil Never Sleeps*, Lourdes Portillo (documentary) *Lumière and Company*, Sarah Moon (documentary of 40 films, each by a different director, each less than a minute long and shot with the Lumière Brothers' original 1895 camera) *Sergei Eisenstein: Autobiography*, Oleg Kovalov (documentary) "Trouble in the Image," O'Neill (experimental)
1997	China's top leader, Deng Xiaoping, dies Scottish embryologist announces sheep cloning Labour Party's Tony Blair becomes British prime minister and ends 18 years of Conservative rule	*Cold Mountain*, Charles Frazier (fiction) *American Pastoral*, Roth (fiction) *How I Learned to Drive*, Paula Vogel (play) *The Lion King*—a Disney musical based on the film and designed and directed by Julie Taymor—opens on Broadway	*Star Wars* revised slightly, re-released to theaters, and passes *E.T.* as highest-grossing movie in history (until *Titanic* passes it in 1998) 413 movies released in U.S., 125 more than in 1987 U.S. movie box office receipts set record Los Angeles Latino International Film Festival begins	*L.A. Confidential*, Curtis Hanson *The Ice Storm*, Ang Lee *Eve's Bayou*, Kasi Lemmons *The Apostle*, Robert Duvall *The Sweet Hereafter*, Egoyan *The Full Monty*, Peter Cattaneo *The Wings of the Dove*, Iain Softley "T.R.A.N.S.I.T.," Piet Kroon (animation) *Will It Snow for Christmas?*, Sandrine Veysset

	World Events	Arts	Mass Media	Films and Videos
1997 (cont'd)	Rebel forces capture the rest of Zaire; longtime dictator Mobutu Sese Seko flees into exile; country is renamed Democratic Republic of Congo and, later, Congo Britain returns control of Hong Kong to China, ending 156 years of British rule Unmanned *Pathfinder* lands on Mars; first mobile explorer of another planet sends data and photographs to Earth Algerian Islamic extremists continue to massacre civilians; more than 60,000 killed since 1992	Soundtrack for *Titanic* is a huge success *Film Noir*, Carly Simon (CD)	Broadcast and cable networks begin using a four-part age-based rating system for most of their programs Digital video discs (DVDs) and DVD players first marketed in U.S., but not all studios agree to market their films on them; most DVD players also play music CDs Compaq introduces the PC theater: combination of computer and large-screen TV More than 31,000 movie screens in U.S.	*Life Is Beautiful*, Roberto Benigni *The Eel*, Shohei Imamura *Taste of Cherry*, Abbas Kiarostami *Welcome Back, Mr. McDonald*, Koki Mitani *Princess Mononoke*, Hayao Miyazaki (animation) *Fast, Cheap & Out of Control*, Morris (documentary) *Public Housing*, Wiseman (documentary) *Waco: The Rules of Engagement*, William Gazecki (documentary) "2 or 3 Things but Nothing for Sure," Tina DiFeliciantonio and Jane C. Wagner (experimental documentary) "Bill Viola: Trilogy (Fire, Water, Breath)" (experimental installations)
1998 (cont'd on next page)	Ethnic Albanian majority in Kosovo demands greater autonomy from Serb-dominated Yugoslavia Ireland, Britain, and U.S. broker peace settlement for Northern Ireland, which Irish voters later accept President Suharto of Indonesia forced to step down after 32 years in power	*Cloudsplitter: A Novel*, Banks *The Hours*, Michael Cunningham (fiction) *A Beautiful Mind*, Sylvia Nasar (biography of John Forbes Nash, Jr.) *Wit*, Margaret Edson (play) *Art*, Yasmina Reza (play)	*Titanic* passes *Star Wars* as highest-grossing movie, but *Gone with the Wind* has sold more tickets *Seinfeld* TV show airs its last episode Adrian Lyne's film version of *Lolita* shown in U.S.—first on Showtime Survey reveals Internet use up (an estimated 30 to 60 million users); TV- and VCR-watching and reading are all down	*The Truman Show*, Weir *Happiness*, Solondz *Smoke Signals*, Chris Eyre *The Big Lebowski*, Coen *Touch of Evil* (1958) rereleased in a revised and restored version *Croupier*, Mike Hodges *Run Lola Run*, Tom Tykwer *Dreamlife of Angels*, Erick Zonca *Central Station*, Walter Salles *The Terrorist* (aka *Malli*), Santosh Sivan *Best Man*, Wohl (documentary sequel)

	World Events	Arts	Mass Media	Films and Videos
1998 (cont'd)	Asian economic crisis continues to worsen and to hurt world economies Terrorist bombs near U.S. embassies in Kenya and Tanzania kill 258 India and Pakistan, declared enemies, conduct independent nuclear tests U.S. and Britain bomb Iraqi targets in retaliation for Iraq's failure to cooperate with UN weapons inspections	*Elaborate Lives: The Legend of Aida*, Tim Rice and Elton John (first Disney musical not based on a film)	Ticket sales for summer movies set U.S. record Four interactive movies released on DVD allow viewers to choose plot developments Some high-definition television reception available in more than 30 U.S. cities	*Wild Man Blues*, Kopple (documentary about Woody Allen) "Everest," David Breashears, Stephen Judson, and Greg MacGillivray (documentary initially shown in IMAX theaters) *Divorce Iranian Style*, Kim Longinotto and Ziba Mir-Hosseini (documentary) *The Farm: Angola U.S.A.*, Liz Garbus, Jonathan Stack, and Wilbert Rideau (documentary) "Human Remains," Jay Rosenblatt (documentary) "Mother and Son," Alexander Sokurov (experimental)
1999	U.S. House of Representatives impeaches President Clinton but Senate acquits him In Columbine High School massacre, two students shoot and kill 12 students and a teacher before killing themselves Prince Abdullah of Jordan succeeds his father, King Hussein NATO sends ground forces into former Yugoslavia to protect ethnic Albanian majority in Kosovo, and bombs Serbia Earthquakes kill 21,000 in Turkey	*House of Sand and Fog*, Andre Dubus III (fiction) *Interpreter of Maladies*, Jhumpa Lahiri (fiction) *A Star Called Henry*, Doyle (fiction) *Close Range: Wyoming Stories*, Proulx (fiction) *Dinner with Friends*, Donald Margulies (play) *Betty's Summer Vacation*, Christopher Durang (play)	Highest summer movie revenues ever: $2.9 billion Nearly 91 percent of U.S. homes have a VCR; most have more than one Reality-based TV show *Big Brother* premieres in Europe; features 9 people living under total surveillance for 100 days *The Sopranos*, TV series, is critical and popular success Video game software sales reach $6.2 billion, $1.1 billion less than domestic movie box office revenues	*Boys Don't Cry*, Kimberly Peirce *American Beauty*, Sam Mendes *The Matrix*, Andy and Larry Wachowski *Three Kings*, David O. Russell "George Lucas in Love," Joe Nussbaum (first shown on Internet) *Titus*, Julie Taymor *Topsy-Turvy*, Leigh *Il Mio Viaggio in Italia* (*My Journey to Italy*), Scorsese (documentary about postwar Italian films) *American Movie*, Chris Smith (documentary) *Buena Vista Social Club*, Wenders (documentary)

	World Events	Arts	Mass Media	Films and Videos
1999 (cont'd)	UN declares East Timor independent of Indonesia; pro-Indonesian forces attack the new nation For the second time in a decade, Russia launches major military offensive against separatist guerrillas in Chechnya U.S. turns control of Panama Canal over to Panama Russian president Yeltsin resigns; Vladimir Putin succeeds him	*Songs and Stories from "Moby Dick,"* Laurie Anderson (stage multimedia production) Score for video reissue of 1931 *Dracula*, Philip Glass *Jazz in Film*, Terence Blanchard (CD)	DVD audio and super CD recorded audio formats become available 150 million Internet users worldwide; over half in U.S. Digital projection (using computer equipment, prisms, and liquid crystal arrays) used to show *Star Wars: Episode 1* on selected standard theatrical screens Silent American film classic *Greed* partially restored with inclusion of still photographs and premiers on Turner Classic Movies Disney's *Fantasia/2000* is first feature-length studio film prepared for IMAX	*Keeper of the Frame*, Mark McLaughlin (documentary on film preservation and restoration) *Mr. Death: The Rise and Fall of Fred A. Leuchter, Jr.*, Morris (documentary) *Belfast, Maine*, Wiseman (documentary) *Genghis Blues*, Roko Belic (documentary) *My Best Fiend: Klaus Kinski*, Herzog (documentary) *Cinéma vérité*, Peter Wintonick (documentary about cinéma vérité) "Encounter in the Third Dimension," Ben Strassen (documentary about 3-D films) "Negative Space," Christopher Petit (documentary) "Soliloquy," Shirin Neshat (film installation) "In Camera," Edward Stewart and Stephanie Smith (experimental) "Outer Space," Peter Tscherassky (experimental)
2000 (cont'd on next page)	Putin elected president of Russia Augusto Pinochet, former Chilean dictator ruled physically unfit to be extradited to Spain on charges of human rights abuses, is returned to Chile after four years of house arrest in Great Britain	*Blonde: A Novel*, Joyce Carol Oates (fiction based on Marilyn Monroe) *The Blind Assassin*, Atwood (fiction) *Persepolis 1*, Marjane Satrapi (first of a series of graphic memoirs, originally published in France)	Final original installment of *Peanuts* comic strip; thereafter past installments are reprinted Stephen King's *Riding the Bullet*, first mass-market success in e-book format *Life* magazine ceases publication (again)	*You Can Count on Me*, Kenneth Lonergan *Memento*, Christopher Nolan *Gladiator*, Scott *State and Main*, David Mamet *Shadow of the Vampire*, E. Elias Merhige *Cecil B. DeMented*, John Waters *Before Night Falls*, Julian Schnabel

	World Events	Arts	Mass Media	Films and Videos
2000 (cont'd)	Longtime Syrian president Hafez al-Assad dies; his son succeeds him Human genome, the entire genetic code for a human being, mapped in a rough draft Vicente Fox of opposition Alliance for Change wins Mexico's presidential election Yugoslav president Slobodan Milošević leaves office after domestic protests and international appeals More than a month after a close election, Texas governor George W. Bush declared U.S. president-elect Worst drought in 100 years strikes India, affecting about 130 million people	*Cats*, Webber and Nunn, longest-running Broadway production, closes after nearly 18 years *Dead Man Walking*, Jake Heggie and Terrence McNally (opera) *Nighthawks*, Lynn Rosen (play based on Edward Hopper paintings)	"Quantum Project," first major film production developed exclusively for Internet distribution "The New Arrival," first film allowing viewers to navigate around characters and props, shown at Cannes and later on the Internet "Dickson Experimental Sound Film" (approximately 1890) reunited with original, restored sound Museo Nazionale del Cinema in Turin, Italy, opens, the biggest cinema museum *Time Code*, one of first major feature films recorded entirely with digital technology More than half of U.S. households have a computer U.S. has 37,000 movie theater screens; foreign screens number about four times more Foreign cinema revenues make up 55 percent of U.S. film industry income Modest, critically acclaimed films often earn much more in video than initial theatrical release; *Boys Don't Cry*, for example, takes in $3.7 million in the theaters but $17.5 million in 10 weeks of video rentals	*Girlfight*, Karyn Kusama *George Washington*, David Gordon Green *Ratcatcher*, Lynn Ramsay *Amores perros*, Alejandro González Iñárritu *Faithless*, Liv Ullmann *Beau Travail*, Claire Denis *Murderous Maids*, Jean-Pierre Denis *Blackboards*, Samira Makhmalbaf *The Circle*, Jafar Panahi *Yi-Yi* (*A One and a Two*), Edward Yang *Battle Royale* (*Batoru rowaiaru*), Kinji Fukasaku *In the Mood for Love*, Wong Kar-wai *Crouching Tiger, Hidden Dragon*, Ang Lee *Dark Days*, Marc Singer (documentary) *Divine Trash*, Steve Yeager (documentary about filmmaker John Waters and the making of one of his movies) *Calle 54*, Fernando Trueba (documentary) "The God of Day Had Gone Down upon Him," Brakhage (experimental) *I'm the One That I Want*, Lionel Coleman (concert film with Margaret Cho) "Kyupi Kyupi I++," Kyupi Kyupi (a Japanese artists' collective) (experimental laserdisc)

	World Events	Arts	Mass Media	Films and Videos
2001 (cont'd on next page)	Democratic reformer Zoran Djindjić becomes prime minister of Serbia NATO forces collect arms from rebel forces in Macedonia, preventing civil war Mexico wins seat on UN Security Council U.S. places severe restrictions on human cloning U.S. submarine accidentally strikes and sinks a Japanese fishing boat, killing nine Terrorists highjack four airliners and crash two into the Twin Towers of the World Trade Center in New York, which collapse, and one into the Pentagon; the fourth plane crashes in Pennsylvania after passengers attempt to wrest control from the terrorists. These terrorist acts constitute the most destructive attack on U.S. soil Person or persons unknown use U.S. postal system to deliver anthrax spores to media companies and governmental centers U.S. and Great Britain go to war in Afghanistan, and ruling Taliban government is toppled	*True History of the Kelly Gang*, Peter Carey (fiction) *Proof*, David Auburn (play) San Francisco Museum of Modern Art and Whitney Museum hold first large-scale exhibitions of "digital art" *The Producers* (Mel Brooks), the Broadway musical based on Brooks's film of the same name, wins Tony for Best Musical In China, Chinese film director Zhang Yimou stages a ballet version of his film *Raise the Red Lantern* *One Man Star Wars Trilogy*, a play based on the original *Star Wars* films, written and performed by Canadian actor Charles Ross	Academy Awards include new category: Best Animated Feature Film DVD-RW (computer) drive allows users who have transferred digital footage into a computer to burn it on a DVD; with a DVD-RW drive, users can also play or record regular music and data CDs and play DVD movies *Lara Croft: Tomb Raider* (video game) Microsoft settles federal antitrust case and avoids being broken up into smaller companies XM Radio launches first digital satellite radio service nationwide, offering 100 channels of music, news, sports, and entertainment USA Patriot Act grants U.S. law enforcement agencies sweeping powers to intercept computer communications White Stripes release the album *White Blood Cells*, which includes the song "The Union Forever," the lyrics for which are almost entirely from dialogue, newsreel narration, and two songs in the 1941 movie *Citizen Kane*	*Apocalypse Now Redux*, Coppola (expanded and rereleased film) *Mulholland Drive*, Lynch *Gosford Park*, Altman *The Lord of the Rings: The Fellowship of the Ring*, Peter Jackson *Ghost World*, Zwigoff *Lantana*, Ray Lawrence *A ma soeur!*, Catherine Breillat *How I Killed My Father*, Anne Fontaine *No Man's Land*, Danis Tanovic *Kandahar*, Mohsen Makhmalbaf *La Ciénaga (The Swamp)*, Lucrecia Martel *Monsoon Wedding*, Mira Nair *Lan Yu*, Stanley Kwan *Shrek*, Andrew Adamson and Vicky Jenson (animation) *Waking Life*, Linklater (animation) *Spirited Away*, Miyazaki (animation) *Decasia*, Bill Morrison (documentary) *Startup.com*, Chris Hegedus and Jehane Noujaim (documentary) *The Endurance: Shackleton's Legendary Antarctic Expedition*, George Butler (documentary) "Shackleton's Antarctic Adventure," George Butler (IMAX documentary) *As I Was Moving Ahead Occasionally I Saw Brief Glimpses of Beauty*, Jonas Mekas (documentary)

	World Events	Arts	Mass Media	Films and Videos
2001 (cont'd)	Energy trading giant Enron declares bankruptcy amid accusations of massive financial wrongdoing			
2002	Al Qaeda leader Osama bin Laden continues to evade capture Taliban largely overthrown in Afghanistan; U.S. bombing raids continue to target Al Qaeda terrorists; Hamid Karzai elected Afghan head of state as his country attempts to rebuild UN food agency warns that more than 38 million Africans face prospect of famine Child sex abuse claims against Catholic Church make headlines Enron and WorldCom at center of corporate governance scandal; world markets slump and investor confidence plummets World leaders concerned after North Korea admits having a secret nuclear weapons program Search for life on Mars advances when *Odyssey* probe finds huge reservoirs of ice just beneath the surface	*Atonement*, Ian McEwan (fiction) *Three Junes*, Julia Glass (fiction) *Hairspray* (musical), based on John Waters's 1988 movie of the same name, opens on Broadway *Def Poetry Jam* with its hip-hop poets is a hit on Broadway	For the year, DVD sales were $8.7 billion and rental revenue was $2.9 billion More than $9 billion worth of movie tickets sold in North America for the year; actual attendance reaches levels not seen since Eisenhower was president *Spider-Man: The Movie* (video game) More than 80 percent of U.S. households subscribe to cable or satellite service A group of movie studios start Movielink, an online video-on-demand service *The X-Files*, TV series, ends	*About Schmidt*, Alexander Payne *Adaptation*, Spike Jonze *Funny Ha Ha*, Andrew Bujalski *All or Nothing*, Leigh *City of God*, Fernando Meirelles *Y tu mamá también*, Cuarón *Talk to Her*, Almodóvar *Oasis*, Chang-dong Lee *Hotel*, Mike Figgis (experimental fiction) "Baadasssss Cinema," Isaac Julien (documentary about blaxploitation films) *The Bronze Screen: 100 Years of the Latino Image in American Cinema*, Nancy De Los Santos, Alberto Domínguez, and Susan Racho (documentary) *The Kid Stays in the Picture*, Brett Morgen and Nanette Burstein (documentary about film producer Robert Evans) *Searching for Debra Winger*, Rosanna Arquette (documentary) *In the Mirror of Maya Deren*, Martina Kudlácek (documentary) *Domestic Violence*, Wiseman (documentary) *Bowling for Columbine* (satirical documentary), Moore

	World Events	Arts	Mass Media	Films and Videos
2002 (cont'd)				*Lost in La Mancha*, Terry Gilliam (documentary about attempting to make a movie that never got finished) *To Be and to Have*, Nicolas Philibert (documentary) *Bus 174 (Ônibus 174)*, José Padilha and Felipe Lacerda (documentary) *Cremaster 3*, Barney (last of a cycle of five experimental films) *Corpus Callosum*, Snow (experimental)
2003 (cont'd on next page)	North Korea continues to taunt U.S. with threats of nuclear proliferation SARS, a contagious and deadly respiratory syndrome, spreads throughout much of the world but is largely under control by year's end U.S. space shuttle *Columbia* disintegrates over Texas while attempting reentry; all seven astronauts aboard are killed	*Ten Little Indians: Stories*, Sherman Alexie (fiction) *Garbo Laughs*, Elizabeth Hay (fiction) *The Kite Runner*, Khaled Hosseini (fiction) *Anna in the Tropics*, Nilo Cruz (play) *Little Shop of Horrors*, one of off-Broadway's most enduring musicals and the source of film adaptations, opens yet again on a New York stage	Although Hispanics make up 13.5 percent of U.S. population, Hispanic characters received only 3 percent of screen time in fall 2002 programs on the six major TV networks, according to a UCLA study HBO's film adaptation of Tony Kushner's play *Angels in America* D-VHS videotape decks make it possible to record and play back high-definition material on tape Approximately 43 million U.S. households have a DVD player More and more theaters convert to digital projection, in some foreign countries more readily than in U.S.	*Mystic River*, Eastwood *Elephant*, Van Sant *Baadasssss!*, Mario Van Peebles *21 Grams*, González Iñárritu *House of Sand and Fog*, Vadim Perelman *American Splendor*, Shari Springer Berman and Robert Pulcini *The Company*, Altman *The Lord of the Rings: The Return of the King*, Jackson *Dracula: Pages from a Virgin's Diary*, Guy Maddin *28 Days Later*, Boyle *The Best of Youth*, Marco Tullio Giordana *Good Bye Lenin!*, Wolfgang Becker *Whale Rider*, Niki Caro *The Return*, Andrei Zvyagintsev *Finding Nemo*, Disney animation *The Triplets of Belleville*, Sylvain Chômet (animation)

	World Events	Arts	Mass Media	Films and Videos
2003 (cont'd)	In March and April, without UN approval, U.S., Britain, and other countries— though not France, Germany, Canada, and many others— invade Iraq but find no "weapons of mass destruction" (initially, the main justification for the invasion); occupying forces have major problems ensuring safety and stabilizing Iraq, and nearly 500 U.S. soldiers are killed by year's end; late in the year, U.S. forces capture Saddam Hussein NATO assumes control of peacekeeping force in Afghanistan Paul Martin succeeds Jean Chrétien as Canadian prime minister Scientists prove existence of dark matter, particles that do not emit or reflect light and are thought to take up most of the universe's space More than 40,000 die in Iranian earthquake	*Evil Dead: The Musical*, a Canadian production based on the 1983 film *The Evil Dead*, opens in Toronto; in 2006, it opens in New York *The Movie Album*, Barbra Streisand (CD)	*Devdas*, adaptation of a popular Indian novel, wins seven awards, including Best Picture and Best Director, at India International Film Awards Increasingly, marketers of consumer products seek to capitalize on movies that the studios unleash each summer by negotiating extensive and expensive movie tie-ins	*A Decade under the Influence*, Richard LaGravenese and Ted Demme (documentary about 1970s U.S. movies) *The Fog of War*, Morris (documentary) *This So-called Disaster*, Michael Almereyda (documentary about a rehearsal and about acting for the stage) *Capturing the Friedmans*, Andrew Jarecki (documentary) *Bukowski: Born into This*, John Dullaghan (documentary on the writer Charles Bukowski) *Amandla! A Revolution in Four-Part Harmony*, Lee Hirsch (documentary) *Spellbound*, Jeff Blitz (documentary) *Love & Diane*, Jennifer Dworkin (documentary) *Tupac: Resurrection*, Lauren Lazin (documentary) *The Agronomist*, Demme (documentary) *Decay of Fiction*, O'Neill (experimental)
2004	NASA's probe lands safely on Mars and begins sending back photos	↓	↓	*Eternal Sunshine of the Spotless Mind*, Michel Gondry *Mysterious Skin*, Gregg Araki

	World Events	Arts	Mass Media	Films and Videos
2004 (cont'd on next page)	In Madrid, 191 killed and over 1,000 injured when Islamic militant terrorist bomb blasts hit four commuter trains Photographs of American soldiers abusing prisoners at Baghdad's Abu Ghraib prison surface in the media and spark worldwide outrage In August, Olympic Games begin in Athens, Greece Government-backed Arab militia in Sudan is accused of ethnic cleansing campaign against black Africans in Darfur Hamid Karzai elected president of Afghanistan in the country's first presidential elections Scientists discover a new 3-foot-high species of human that lived in Indonesia at least 12,000 years ago President Bush wins reelection PLO leader Arafat dies Massive earthquake near Indian Ocean island of Sumatra sets off tsunamis, causing approximately 150,000 deaths in neighboring countries	*Noir*, a site-specific dance (in a New York parking garage) inspired by films noirs and with dancers dressed as thugs and molls *The Master*, Colm Toibin (fiction) *The Plot against America*, Roth (fiction) *Runaway*, Alice Munro (fiction) A musical (stage) version of *Mary Poppins* opens in London and in 2006 opens on Broadway *The History Boys*, Alan Bennett (play) *A Wedding* (opera), based on Robert Altman's 1978 film of the same name	Michael Moore causes controversy with *Fahrenheit 9/11*, which chronicles how Bush administration allegedly used events of 9/11 to support its agenda for the Iraqi war. The film wins the Palm D'or at Cannes Film Festival Mel Gibson's *The Passion of the Christ*, released in U.S. theaters in February, criticized for graphic violence and anti-Semitism VUDU service begins. From the company self-description: "The VUDU box delivers movies and television shows from major motion picture studios and numerous independent and international distributors directly to the television via a broadband Internet connection, bypassing the computer and without the need for cable or satellite TV service." Global video game industry revenue is $24.5 billion for the year; U.S. movie theatrical revenue, $9.5 billion, a record and a slight increase over 2003's figure. However, attendance for the year falls slightly	*My Summer of Love*, Pawel Pawlikowski *Red Lights* (*Feux rouges*), Cédric Kahn *Maria Full of Grace*, Joshua Marston *Duck Season* (*Temporada de patos*), Fernando Eimbcke *Only Human* (*Seres queridos*), Dominic Harari and Teresa Pelegri *Live-in Maid*, Jorge Gaggero *Head-On* (*Gegen die Wand*), Fatih Akin *Nobody Knows*, Hirokazu Koreeda *Moolaadé*, Sembene *Henri Langlois: The Phantom of the Cinémathèque*, Jacques Richard (documentary about life and career of creator of Cinémathèque Française and Musée du Cinéma) *Tell Them Who You Are*, Mark Wexler's documentary about his father, acclaimed cinematographer Haskell Wexler, and their relationship *The Cutting Edge: The Magic of Movie Editing*, Wendy Apple (documentary) *Edge Codes.com: The Art of Motion Picture Editing*, Alex Shuper (documentary) *Darwin's Nightmare*, Hubert Sauper (documentary) *Born into Brothels*, Zana Briski and Ross Kauffman (documentary)

	World Events	Arts	Mass Media	Films and Videos
2004 (cont'd)	U.S. and allies continue to fight Iraqi insurgents, and violence against U.S. troops continues to increase in Iraq		Facebook begins on the Web	*Plagues and Pleasures on the Salton Sea*, Chris Metzler and Jeff Springer (documentary)
2005	Sudan's government and southern rebels sign peace agreement to end 20-year civil war that claimed 2 million lives Assassination of former Lebanese prime minister Rafik Hariri, a nationalist who called for Syria's withdrawal from Lebanon; after weeks of protests in Lebanon, Syrian military withdraws Hard-line conservative Mahmoud Ahmadinejad wins Iran's presidential election and defiantly pursues Iran's nuclear ambitions Islamic terrorist bombings in London kill 52 and wound about 700 Irish Republican Army announces it is officially ending its violent campaign for a united Ireland President Bush signs Central American Free Trade Agreement (CAFTA), which removes trade barriers between the U.S. and six countries	*Anime Dance Theater* of New York presents a danced story in the form of an anime *Saturday*, McEwan (fiction) *The Year of Magical Thinking*, Joan Didion (nonfiction) *Black Maria: Poems Produced and Directed by Kevin Young* (book of poetry based on films noirs) *Fatal Attraction: A Greek Tragedy*, Alana McNair and Kate Wilkinson (one-act off-Broadway play based on the 1987 film) *Keystone*, Dave Douglas (jazz CD tribute to silent film comedian Roscoe "Fatty" Arbuckle)	YouTube.com begins: a site where users can share videos. The site states that on YouTube people, "can see first-hand accounts of current events, find videos about their hobbies and interests, and discover the quirky and unusual. As more people capture special moments on video, YouTube is empowering them to become the broadcasters of tomorrow." CD and digital album sales continue to decline as increasing numbers of listeners acquire music via the Internet More than 53,000 different DVD titles are available in the North American market. That number excludes imports and pornographic films, and includes TV shows, self-help videos, and music and sports videos	*Brokeback Mountain*, Ang Lee *The Three Burials of Melquiades Estrada*, Tommy Lee Jones *The Motel*, Michael Kang *Nine Lives*, Rodrigo García *Tristram Shandy: A Cock and Bull Story*, Michael Winterbottom *The Proposition*, John Hillcoat *Caché (Hidden)*, Michael Haneke *L'enfant (The Child)*, Jean-Pierre Dardenne and Luc Dardenne *Army of Shadows (L'Armée des Ombres)*, Jean-Pierre Melville (rerelease of the 1969 movie) *House of Sand*, Andrucha Waddington *The Death of Mr. Lazarescu*, Cristi Puiu *The Passenger*, Antonioni (rerelease of the 1975 film in a slightly longer version) *Paradise Now*, Hany Abu-Assad *Be with Me*, Eric Khoo *51 Birch Street*, Doug Block (documentary) *49 Up*, Apted (documentary) *After Innocence*, Jessica Sanders (documentary) *Grizzly Man*, Herzog (documentary)

	World Events	Arts	Mass Media	Films and Videos
2005 (cont'd)	Israel begins evacuating Israeli settlers from Gaza Strip, occupied by Israel for the last 38 years In August, Hurricane Katrina devastates the U.S. Gulf Coast; more than 1,000 die and millions are left homeless A 7.6 earthquake centered in Kashmir kills more than 80,000 and leaves an estimated 4 million homeless Angela Merkel becomes Germany's first female chancellor Several weeks of violent rioting begin in the impoverished French-Arab and French-African suburbs of Paris		*Batman Begins* (video game) 27,000 of 37,000 U.S. movie screens show advertising before film showings *The Colbert Report*, a satirical show, begins on Comedy Central channel Survey reveals that young men are going to fewer movies than in the past because they are busy surfing the Web, instant-messaging with friends, and playing video games	*The March of the Penguins* (*La marche de l'empereur*), Luc Jacquet *The Last Mogul*, Barry Avrich (documentary about Hollywood studio executive Lew Wasserman) *Midnight Movies: From the Margin to the Mainstream*, Stuart Samuels (documentary about six midnight movies) "My Dad Is 100 Years Old," Guy Maddin (experimental documentary in part about Italian neorealist filmmaker Roberto Rossellini) *Wallace & Gromit: The Curse of the Were-Rabbit*, Steve Box and Nick Park (animation)
2006 (cont'd on next page)	In Iraq, a coalition of Shiites and Kurds dominates the new government. Sectarian violence kills tens of thousands, and fatality rates rise throughout the year; some observers describe the situation as a civil war between Sunnis and Shiites	Disney Theatrical Productions version of *Tarzan* opens on Broadway. The show has music and lyrics by Phil Collins and is based on the original 1912 novel and the 1999 Disney film *Grey Gardens*, a musical based on the cult 1975 documentary of the same name, opens on Broadway	*Los Angeles Times* survey reveals that 54 percent of those 24 and under prefer to watch movies on a DVD at home rather than go to the local multiplex First HD DVD players and discs go on sale in U.S. *The Godfather: The Game* (video game) *X-men: The Official Game* (video game)	*Little Children*, Todd Field *The Cabinet of Dr. Caligari*, David Lee Fisher (remake of classic 1919 film with same settings but modern actors and spoken dialogue) *Babel*, Alejandro González Iñárritu *Away from Her*, Sarah Polley *Children of Men*, Cuarón *The Queen*, Frears *Ten Canoes*, Rolf de Heer and Peter Djigirr (first feature entirely in an Aboriginal language) *Days of Glory* (*Indigènes*), Rachid Bouchareb

	World Events	Arts	Mass Media	Films and Videos
2006 (cont'd)	Defying the UN Security Council, Iran's president Ahmadinejad announces that Iran has enriched uranium Conservative candidate Felipe Calderon declared winner of Mexican general election North Korea test-fires missiles over Sea of Japan and explodes a nuclear device in North Korean mountains India test-launches a missile. Two days later, more than 200 people die and hundreds more are wounded when bombs explode on commuter trains in Mumbai, India July 13–August 15: Hezbollah, a Lebanese militant group, fires rockets into Israel. Israel launches a major military attack, sending thousands of troops into Lebanon Saddam Hussein, convicted of crimes against humanity by an Iraqi court, is hanged in Baghdad	*Falling through the Earth: A Memoir,* Danielle Trussoni (nonfiction) *The Omnivore's Dilemma: A Natural History of Four Meals,* Michael Pollan (nonfiction)	Italian filmmakers make perhaps the world's first feature-length film shot with a cell phone, *New Love Meeting* *The Da Vinci Code* movie angers some Christians UCLA brain research shows problems with studying while TV is on	*Lady Chatterley (Lady Chatterley et l'homme des bois)*, Pascale Ferran *Pan's Labyrinth (El laberinto del fauno)*, Guillermo del Toro *Volver (To Return)*, Almodóvar *The Lives of Others (Das Leben der Anderen)*, Florian Henckel von Donnersmarck *12:08 East of Bucharest*, Corneliu Porumboiu *Letters from Iwo Jima*, Eastwood (in Japanese) *Dry Season (Daratt)*, Mahamat-Saleh Haroun *Paprika*, Satoshi Kon (animation) *A Scanner Darkly*, Linklater (animation) *Who Killed the Electric Car?*, Chris Paine (documentary) *(Dixie Chicks:) Shut Up and Sing*, Barbara Kopple and Cecilia Peck (documentary) *Cinematographer Style*, Jon Fauer (documentary) *Coming Attractions: The History of the Movie Trailer*, Michael J. Shapiro and Jeff Werner (documentary) *This Filthy World*, Jeff Garlin (documentary of a stand-up comedy routine delivered by filmmaker John Waters) *The War Tapes*, Deborah Scranton (documentary) *The Ground Truth*, Patricia Foulkrod (documentary) *The Heart of the Game*, Ward Serrill (documentary)

	World Events	Arts	Mass Media	Films and Videos
2007	A Virginia Tech student kills 32 before killing himself Defaults on subprime mortgages—high and adjustable–interest rate home loans for people who could not qualify for the lowest market rates—increase in alarming numbers, undermining bond investments held by mortgage companies, banks, and investment firms with money invested in mortgage-backed securities In response to massive protests, government security forces in Myanmar (formerly Burma) beat, arrest, and jail many, including Buddhist monks Scientists announce a way to reprogram human skin cells to behave like embryonic stem cells without having to make or destroy human embryos Former Pakistani prime minister Benazir Bhutto assassinated while campaigning in Pakistan	*Zeroville*, Steve Erickson (novel about a film-obsessed young man who goes to Hollywood in 1969) The last novel of the seven-volume Harry Potter series is published: *Harry Potter and the Deathly Hallows* *Tree of Smoke*, Denis Johnson (fiction) *Playing for Pizza: A Novel* (John Grisham) *I Am America (And So Can You!)*, Stephen Colbert (satire)	Netflix, the online DVD rental service, introduces a service to deliver movies and television shows directly to users' PCs, not as downloads but as streaming video Criterion releases on DVD the remastered version of *Berlin Alexanderplatz*, Rainer Werner Fassbinder's acclaimed 1980 14-episode TV series DVD sales dip for the first time since introduction of DVDs in 1997. DVD rentals hold steady. Once again, for the year, DVD sales and rentals far exceed the box office total Presidential debates on YouTube Apple iPhone is released: it surfs Web, e-mails, plays videos and iTunes, makes phone calls, and takes photos	*No Country for Old Men*, Coen Brothers *There Will Be Blood*, Paul Thomas Anderson *Juno*, Jason Reitman *Michael Clayton*, Tony Gilroy *The Savages*, Tamara Jenkins *I'm Not There*, Todd Haynes *Into the Wild*, Sean Penn *Atonement*, Joe Wright *4 Months, 3 Weeks and 2 Days*, Cristian Mungiu *The Diving Bell and the Butterfly*, Julian Schnabel *Flight of the Red Balloon*, Hsiao-hsien Hou, inspired in part by the 1956 film "The Red Balloon" *Showbusiness: The Road to Broadway*, Dori Berinstein (documentary) *Manufacturing Dissent*, Debbie Melnyk and Rick Caine (documentary about filmmaker Michael Moore) *Hollywood Chinese: The Chinese in American Film*, Arthur Dong (documentary) *Terror's Advocate*, Schroeder (documentary) *Chicago 10*, Brett Morgen (experimental documentary, about a third of it in animation) *Ratatouille*, Brad Bird and Jan Pinkava (animation) *Persepolis*, Vincent Paronnaud and Marjane Satrapi (animation)

	World Events	Arts	Mass Media	Films and Videos
2008	China cracks down on protests by monks and other Tibetan citizens In Beirut, Hezbollah (Iran-backed Shiite militia) battles supporters of Lebanon's government Cyclone kills at least 80,000 in Myanmar, and earthquakes kill more than 100,000 in western China Georgia (a former part of the Soviet Union) tries to retake one of two Georgian breakaway regions by force. Russian forces counterattack and occupy U.S. politicians agree on a 700-billion-dollar rescue plan for major troubled financial institutions World stock markets plummet Barack Obama elected U.S. president Heavily armed men cause havoc in Mumbai, India. At least 163 people die in three days of violence Iraqi parliament approves agreement with the U.S. under which foreign forces will leave the country by 2011 Israeli attacks on Hamas-run Gaza Strip kill at least 228 Palestinians and cause major property damage	*Ancient Highway*, Bret Lott (novel in part about different generations of a family drawn to L.A. and the movie worlds) *The Widows of Eastwick*, Updike (sequel to his novel *The Witches of Eastwick*) *Pictures at a Revolution: Five Movies and the Birth of the New Hollywood*, Mark Harris (nonfiction book about what five 1967 movies nominated for best picture reveal about the times and Hollywood filmmaking then) Disney's musical version of *The Little Mermaid* opens on Broadway Musical version of the 1936 source novel *Gone with the Wind* and the 1939 movie adaptation opens in London New Broadway production of *West Side Story* features some Latino characters speaking and singing in Spanish when the situations in the story warrant it	ABC News and Facebook sponsor Republican and Democratic New Hampshire presidential primary debates Short (and often satirical) videos on YouTube play a role in presidential campaign E-mails and videos, especially from the Obama campaign, play prominent role in election campaign According to U.S. Census Bureau, for every 1 million U.S. residents, there are on average 65 video rental stores, 17 movie theaters, and 1 drive-in theater Young Japanese (mostly) women write texting novels on cell phones Camcorder model records one hour of HD video and weighs only 3.3 oz. IBM supercomputer processes a quadrillion calculations per second Entertainment Software Association claims that 40 percent of video game players 18 and older are women and that the average age of gamers is 35	*Doubt*, John Patrick Shanely *The Wrestler*, Darren Aronofsky *Milk*, Van Sant *My Winnipeg*, Maddin *Slumdog Millionaire*, Boyle *Of Time and the City*, Terence Davies *Hunger*, Steve McQueen *Son of Rambow*, Garth Jennings *A Christmas Tale*, Arnaud Desplechin *The Beaches of Agnès*, Varda *The Class*, Laurent Cantet *Gomorrah*, Matteo Garrone *The Headless Woman*, Martel *Tokyo Sonata*, Kiyoshi Kurosawa *Trumbo*, Peter Askin (documentary about blacklisted Hollywood screenwriter Dalton Trumbo) *U2 3D*, Catherine Owens and Mark Pellington (documentary) *Shine a Light*, Scorsese (documentary) *Man on Wire*, James Marsh (documentary) *Up the Yangtze*, Yung Chang (documentary) *Encounters at the End of the World*, Herzog (documentary) *Wall•E*, Andrew Stanton (animation) *Moscow on the Move*—a huge public video installation on top of a Moscow building—consists of works by Russian and foreign artists and runs 24 hours a day

SOURCES

Barnouw, Erik. *Tube of Plenty: The Evolution of American Television*. 2nd ed. New York: Oxford UP, 1990.

Benét's Reader's Encyclopedia. 3rd ed. Ed. Katherine Baker Siepmann. New York: Harper, 1987.

Bohn, Thomas W., and Richard L. Stromgren. "A Film Chronology." *Light and Shadows: A History of Motion Pictures*. 3rd ed. Palo Alto: Mayfield, 1987: xiv–xlv.

Brooks, Tim, and Earle Marsh. *The Complete Directory to Prime Time Network and Cable TV Shows, 1946–Present*. 8th ed. New York: Ballantine, 2003.

Brownstone, David M., and Irene M. Franck. *Timelines of the Arts and Literature*. New York: Harper, 1994.

———. *Timelines of the Twentieth Century: A Chronology of 7,500 Key Events, Discoveries, and People That Shaped Our Century*. Boston: Little, 1996.

Chronicle of the 20th Century, North American Edition. Ed. Clifton Daniel. Liberty, MO: JL International, 1994.

Cinema: Year by Year, 1894–2005. Ed. Robyn Karney. London: DK, 2005.

Cook, David A. *A History of Narrative Film*. 4th ed. New York: Norton, 2003.

Ellis, Jack C., and Betsy A. McLane. *A New History of Documentary Film*. New York: Continuum, 2005.

Ellis, Jack C., and Virginia Wright Wexman. *A History of Film*. 5th ed. Boston: Allyn, 2002.

Gomery, Douglas. *Movie History: A Survey*. Belmont, CA: Wadsworth, 1991.

Greenspan, Karen. *The Timetables of Women's History: A Chronology of the Most Important People and Events in Women's History*. New York: Simon, 1994.

Grun, Bernard. *The Timetables of History: A Horizontal Linkage of People and Events*. 3rd ed. New York: Simon, 1991.

Hilliard, Robert L., and Michael C. Keith. *The Broadcast Century and Beyond: A Biography of American Broadcasting*. 4th ed. Boston: Focal, 2004.

Kane, Joseph Nathan. *Famous First Facts*. 6th ed. New York: Wilson, 2007.

Katz, Ephraim. *The Film Encyclopedia*. 5th ed. Rev. Fred Klein and Ronald Dean Nolen. New York: Collins, 2005.

Mast, Gerald, and Bruce F. Kawin. *A Short History of the Movies*. 9th ed. New York: Longman, 2005.

McNeil, Alex. *Total Television: The Comprehensive Guide to Programming from 1948 to the Present*. New York: Penguin, 1996.

Monaco, James. *How to Read a Film: Movies, Media, Multimedia*. 3rd ed. New York: Oxford UP, 2000.

Nowell-Smith, Geoffrey, general ed. *The Oxford History of World Cinema*. Oxford: Oxford UP, 1996.

Ochoa, George, and Melinda Corey. *The Timeline Book of the Arts*. New York: Ballantine, 1995.

Polan, Dana. "History of the American Cinema." *Film Quarterly* 45.3 (Spring 1992): 54–57.

Rood, Karen L. *American Culture after World War II*. Detroit: Gale, 1994. Pages xix–xxx consist of two timelines: works and events.

Samuelson, D. "Equipment Inventions That Have Changed the Way Films Are Made." *American Cinematographer* 75.8 (1994): 74, 76.

Sklar, Robert. *Film: An International History of the Medium*. 2nd ed. Upper Saddle River, NJ: Prentice, 2002.

Strauss, William, and Neil Howe. *Generations: The History of America's Future, 1584–2069*. New York: Morrow, 1991.

Thompson, Kristin, and David Bordwell. *Film History: An Introduction*. 2nd ed. Boston: McGraw, 2003.

Thomson, David. *The New Biographical Dictionary of Film*. Expanded and updated ed. New York: Knopf, 2006.

Winston, Brian. "Z for Zoetrope." *Sight and Sound* July 1998: 28–30.

Various issues of *Billboard*, the *Los Angeles Times*, the *New York Times*, *USA Today*, and the *World Almanac*.

On the Web

Information on the Internet Movie Database
Reviews accessed via Movie Review Query Engine
Reviews and tabulations of reviews at Metacritic.com
The History Channel
Infoplease year by year
University of Minnesota Timeline of Major Events in the History of Mass Communications
University of Minnesota Media History Project, 2000–2009
Many newspaper, magazine, and journal articles accessed via LexisNexis Academic

Illustrated Glossary

F ILMMAKERS USE MANY TERMS—for example, *frame-accurate effect*—that most film critics and scholars have little or no occasion to use. Occasionally, filmmakers, film critics, and film scholars use the same term differently, such as *sequence*, or they use different terms for the same subject, such as *deep focus* and *great depth of field*. In this glossary, I define and explain the main terms used in this book, normally with the same meanings intended by film critics and scholars, and a few widely used but often misunderstood terms such as *irony* and *satire*. A number in parentheses at the end of an entry indicates the page where that term is discussed most extensively. Page numbers in *italic* type refer to illustrations, captions, or both.

For additional terms or other explanations of the terms listed in this glossary, see the following books: Robert Atkins's *ArtSpeak: A Guide to Contemporary Ideas, Movements, and Buzzwords, 1945 to the Present*, 2nd ed. (1997); Chris Baldick's *The Concise Oxford Dictionary of Literary Terms*, 2nd ed. (2004); Frank E. Beaver's *Dictionary of Film Terms: The Aesthetic Companion to Film Analysis*, rev. ed. (1994); Steve Blandford, Barry Keith Grant, and Jim Hillier's *The Film Studies Dictionary* (2001); Susan Hayward's *Cinema Studies: The Key Concepts*, 3rd ed. (2006); Kevin Jackson's *The Language of Cinema* (1998); Ira Konigsberg's *The Complete Film Dictionary*, 2nd ed. (1997); Dave Knox's *Strike the Baby and Kill the Blonde: An Insider's Guide to Film Slang* (2005); Ross Murfin and Supryia M. Ray's *The Bedford Glossary of Critical and Literary Terms*, 2nd ed. (2003); Roberta E. Pearson and Philip Simpson's *Critical Dictionary of Film and Television Theory* (2001); and Gerald Prince's *Dictionary of Narratology*, rev. ed. (2003).

abstract film: An experimental film whose subjects are shapes and perhaps sounds that do not represent the real world (above).

allusion: A reference in a text to a person, an event, another text, or a part of a text. Unlike an homage or a parody, an allusion does not convey clear-cut admiration for or poke fun at the subject but simply refers to it.

ambient sound: Background sound that is so unobtrusive that people tend not to notice it. In a forest, for example, ambient sound may consist mainly of trees moving in the breeze and insects heard at a low volume.

ambiguity: An aspect of a text (such as a character's motivations for doing something) that is open to two or more plausible interpretations. Ambiguity can result because of the makeup of the text itself, perhaps because the writer deliberately withheld certain clarifying information or because viewers experience a confusing, truncated version of the original text. In fictional films and other imaginative texts, ambiguity is usually seen as a strength. In texts that primarily convey information or ideas, such as a documentary film or a college student's essay, ambiguity is usually seen as a distracting flaw.

anamorphic lens: A lens that squeezes a wide image onto a film frame in the camera, making everything look tall and thin (bottom, left). On a projector, an anamorphic lens expands the image, returning it to its original wide shape (bottom, right). Many movies from the 1950s to the 1980s and some since then have been filmed and projected with anamorphic lenses. See also **CinemaScope** and **spherical lens**. (82)

animation: The process of photographing or creating a series of individual images normally with visual variations from one frame to the next so that later a showing of the series of still images can give the appearance of movement. *Animate* means to give life to or to fill with life. Opposite of **live action**. See also **claymation**, **stop-motion cinematography**, and **time-lapse cinematography**. (423)

animatronic: A puppet likeness of a human, a creature, or an animal whose movements are directed by electronic, mechanical, or radio-controlled devices.

anime: Japanese word for *animation*, so the term often refers to animated movies made in Japan. In other contexts, *anime* refers to Japanese animated films derived from *manga*, which are graphic Japanese comic books that can be about any of a huge range of subjects and are aimed at all age groups.

aperture: (1) The adjustable opening in the camera lens that permits the operator to regulate how much light passes through the lens to the film. (2) The rectangular opening in a motion-picture projector that helps determine the size and shape of light sent from the projector to the screen.

aperture plate: (1) A small metal plate with a rectangular opening that is used in cameras to determine the shape and area of the light reaching the film. (2) A small

metal plate with a rectangular opening used in front of a projector's aperture or opening to help determine the shape and area of the light reaching the screen.

art director: See **designer**.

aspect ratio: The proportion of the width to the height of the image on a TV or movie screen or on the individual frames of the film. Common examples are 1.33:1 and 1.85:1 (the image is nearly twice as wide as it is high). The aspect ratio has nothing

> **1.85:1**
> The aspect ratio used for most U.S. theatrical showings since the 1960s

to do with the size or area of the image; rather it indicates the *shape* (width in proportion to height) of film images. (37)

asynchronous sound: A sound that either precedes or follows its on-screen source, such as words that are not synchronized with lip movements. (182)

auteur ("oh TOUR") theory: The belief that some filmmakers—usually directors though sometimes producers, writers, or actors—function as the dominant creators of films and that the auteur's films embody recurrent subjects, techniques, and meanings. (538)

avant-garde film: See **experimental film**.

backlight or **backlighting:** Lighting from behind the subject. If backlight is used alone or is the strongest light used, the subject's identity may be obscured. Used in combination with other lighting, backlighting may help set the image of the subject off from the background. (72)

big studio era: See **studio (era)**.

big studio system: See **studio (era)**.

bird's-eye view: A camera angle achieved when the camera films the subject from directly overhead. (*91*)

black comedy: A narrative style that shows the humorous possibilities of subjects often considered off-limits to comedy, such as warfare, murder, death, and illness. Black comedies are often satiric. Examples of films using black comedy are the original (1955) *The Ladykillers* (especially the five deaths and disposal of the five bodies that are treated comically toward the end of the film); *Kind Hearts and Coronets*; *Dr. Strangelove: Or, How I Learned to Stop Worrying and Love the Bomb*; *Life of Brian*; *Eating Raoul*; and *Thank You for Smoking*. (294)

blaxploitation (film): A U.S. film movement from 1971 to 1975 or 1976 consisting of low-budget movies usually made by African American filmmakers, with black characters, for black audiences. *Sweet Sweetback's Baadasssss Song* (1971) is regarded as the first blaxploitation film. (294)

Bollywood: Extremely popular Hindi-language movies made in India that usually feature complicated plots, large casts of mostly uncomplicated characters, frequent extravagant musical interludes, and happy endings. The word *Bollywood* was derived from a combination of *Bombay* (India) and *Hollywood*. Some use *Bollywood* affectionately, and others reject the term as derisive and condescending. (344)

boom: See **crane**.

bridge (music): Music used to link two or more scenes, typically to enhance continuity.

cameo: A brief role in a narrative entertainment—such as a TV show or film (fictional or occasionally documentary)—performed by a well-known person, usually a famous actor, whose name is often not included in the credits or publicity. A cameo actor may play one of the film's fictional characters or may play herself or himself. Cameos may also be played by famous people who are not actors or by insiders in the film community—a type of cinematic in-joke. (30)

canted framing: See **Dutch angle**.

catchlight: The light from one or more sources that is visible in the pupils of a subject's eyes. By examining the catchlight, one can discover the number and direction of some or all of the light sources (below).

cel: A thin sheet of clear plastic on which images are painted for use in making some animated films. To produce some animated films, a series of cels is superimposed on a painted background, and then each composite image is photographed.

celluloid: (1) Short for *cellulose nitrate*, film stock used until the early 1950s that could produce high-quality images but was subject to decomposition (see Figure 8.18 on p. 389) and combustion (illustrated by the projection room fire in *Cinema Paradiso*). (2) Any transparent material used as the base for motion-picture film (see the "clear base" part of Figure 2.1 on p. 62). (3) Synonym for *movie*, as in "celluloid heroes."

character actor: An actor who tends to specialize in well-defined secondary roles. Dennis Hopper, for example, is a character actor who has largely made a career of playing unstable secondary characters (right). (29)

cinéma noir: See **film noir**.

CinemaScope: A wide-screen process introduced in 1953 and made possible by filming and projecting with anamorphic lenses.

cinematic: See **filmic**.

cinematographer: The person responsible for the motion-picture photography during the making of a film. Often called *director of photography* (DP).

cinematography: Motion-picture photography, including technical and artistic concern with such matters as choice of film stock, lighting, choice and use of lenses, camera distance and angle, and camera movement. (Chapter 2)

cinéma vérité: Literally, "film truth." A type and style of documentary filmmaking developed in France during the early 1960s whose aim was to capture events as they happened. Cinéma vérité filmmakers used unobtrusive lightweight equipment to film and to record sound on location. Practitioners include Jean Rouch, Chris Marker, and Marcel Ophüls (as in his monumental *The Sorrow and the Pity*). See **direct cinema**. (391)

Cinerama: A wide-screen process involving the use of three synchronized projectors showing three contiguous images on a wide, curved screen (see Figure 10.27a on p. 477). Cinerama was first used commercially in the early 1950s and was available only in selected theaters in large cities. (477)

classical Hollywood cinema: Films that show one or more characters facing a succession of problems while trying to reach their goals and that tend to hide the manner of their making by means of unobtrusive filmmaking techniques. (308)

claymation: Stop-motion animation that uses subjects made of clay.

close-up: An image in which the subject fills most of the frame and little of the surroundings is shown. When the subject is someone's upper body, the close-up normally reveals the entire head and perhaps some of the shoulders. Filmmakers use close-ups to direct viewers' attention to texture or to a detail or, most often, to the expressions on a person's face. (*85*)

closure: A sense of coherence and completion at the end of a narrative. A story that has closure leaves its audience with no major unanswered questions about the consequences of the narrative's most significant events. (270)

compilation film: A film made by editing together clips from other films. Sometimes used in creating a documentary film—as in *Point of Order*, *As I Was Moving Ahead Occasionally I Saw Brief Glimpses of Beauty*, and *Decasia*—or in making an experimental film, as in Bruce Conner's "A Movie." (*389, 406–7*)

composition: The arrangement of settings, lighting, and subjects (such as people and objects) within the frame. (37)

continuity editing: Film editing that maintains a sense of uninterrupted time and action and continuous setting within each scene of a narrative film. (126)

contrast: In photography and cinematography, the difference between the lightest and darkest parts of an image. Low-contrast images show little difference between the intensity of the lightest part of the image and that of the darkest part. In high-contrast images, the dark parts are very dark and the light parts very light.

convention: In films and other texts, a subject or technique that makers of texts and audiences have grown to accept as natural or typical in certain contexts. For example, it is a convention that westerns include showdowns and shoot-outs, and it is a convention that audiences are often allowed to hear both sides of a telephone conversation even if they see only one of the conversationalists. The authors of *The Film Studies Dictionary* point out, "conventions function as an implied agreement between makers and consumers to accept certain artificialities." Contrast with **revisionist**. (470)

crane: A mechanical device used to move a camera through space above the ground or to position it at a place in the air (see Figure 2.51 on p. 94). A shot taken from a crane gives the camera operator many options: different distances and angles from the subject, different heights from the surface, fluid changes in distance and angle from the subject, and different speeds with which the camera moves through the air. (96)

critical approach: Related ideas about how to interpret texts. The ideas constituting a critical approach are sometimes only loosely connected and by no means agreed on by all those professing to use that approach. Examples of critical approaches are Marxist criticism, cultural studies, auteur theory, feminist criticism, viewer-response criticism, reception theory, and genre criticism.

crop: To trim or block out one or more parts of an image. For example, the publicity photo illustrating *catchlight* (p. 669) was cropped to save space and to direct viewers' attention to the most important part of the image: the actor's head.

cross-cut: In editing, to alternate between events occurring at different settings and often presumably transpiring at the same time. See **parallel editing**.

cut: *As a noun:* (1) The most common transition between shots, made by splicing or joining the end of one shot to the beginning of the following shot. When the two shots are projected, the transition from the first shot to the next appears to be instantaneous. (2) A version of an edited film, as in "director's cut," meaning the version the director intended. *As a verb:* (1) To change from one shot to the following shot seemingly instantaneously.

This transition between shots is achieved whenever the end of the first shot has been spliced to the beginning of the following shot. (2) To edit or edited, as in "They cut the movie in four months." (3) To sever film, splice film, or sever and splice film while editing. (*120*)

cutaway (shot): A shot that briefly interrupts the representation of a subject to show something else. Used in many ways, such as to reveal what a character is thinking, show reactions, maintain continuity, avoid showing sex or violence, or allow a passage of time. In *The Dead*, for example, viewers see the beginning of a dinner, a cutaway to the street outside, then the dinner table again where the guests have finished eating.

cutting continuity (script): A script that describes a finished film. Often contains detailed technical information, such as shot and scene divisions, descriptions of settings and events, dialogue, camera angles and distances, sometimes even the duration of shots and transitions between them. See **screenplay** and **shooting script**. (534)

dailies: The positive prints usually made from a day's filming (exposed negatives). The director, cinematographer, and perhaps editor usually check the dailies to see if the recently filmed shots are satisfactory and if additional takes or shots are needed.

deep focus: Photography in which subjects near the camera, those in the distant background, and those in between are all in sharp focus (above). Achieved in photography by use of a wide-angle lens, a small lens aperture, or both. In low illumination, fast lenses and fast film stock also help create deep focus. Filmmakers are likely to use the term *great depth of field* rather than *deep focus*, the term favored by film critics. Opposite of **shallow focus**. (81)

depth of field: The distances in front of the camera in which all objects are in focus.

desaturated color: Drained, subdued color approaching a neutral gray. Often used to create or enhance an effect, as throughout Werner Herzog's *Nosferatu the Vampyre* and Tim Burton's *Sleepy Hollow*. Opposite of **saturated color**. (66, Plates 6–7)

designer: The person responsible for the appearance of much of what is photographed in a movie, including locations, architecture, sets, costumes, makeup, and hairstyles.

diffuser: (1) Material such as spun glass or a silk or thin nylon stocking placed in front of or on the camera lens to soften the image's resolution. (2) Translucent material such as silk, spun glass, thin paper, or fabric placed in  front of a light source to create soft light. See also Figure 2.30 on p. 83.

digital effect: An image or a part of an image created or modified by use of computers and specially designed software. See also **optical effect**.

digital intermediate: A process available since the late 1990s in which filmmakers can transfer exposed film to digital, manipulate the colors and contrast with a computer program, and then transfer the images back to film.

direct cinema: A type and style of documentary filmmaking developed in the United States during the 1960s in which actions are recorded as they happen, without rehearsal, using a portable 16 mm camera with a zoom lens and portable magnetic sound recording equipment. Editing is minimal, and usually narration and interviews are avoided. Used by such American documentary filmmakers as Robert Drew and Richard Leacock, Albert and David Maysles, Donn Pennebaker, and Frederick Wiseman and an influence on some fictional filmmakers, such as John Cassavetes. See **cinéma vérité**. (390)

director of photography: See **cinematographer**.

dissolve: See **lap dissolve**.

docudrama: A film that re-creates and dramatizes occurrences from history, often recent history, by blending fact and fiction. The term is usually applied to TV movies that purport to be factual re-creations of newsworthy people or occurrences.

documentary (film): A film or video representation of actual (not imaginary) subjects. A documentary film may present a story (be a narrative film), or it may not. (364)

Dogme 95: Film movement begun by Danish filmmakers in 1995 when they drew up the "Vow of Chastity," a set of rules expressing their rejection of the expensive filmmaking techniques used by commercial film industries in Denmark, France, and the United States; "superficial actions," such as murders; and genre films. Instead, the focus was to be on realistic characters and settings. Although initially established in Denmark, the movement eventually spread to include directors from many countries. The most famous film from this movement is the first Dogme 95 film, Thomas Vinterberg's *The Celebration*. See also **Italian neorealism** and **French new wave (cinema)**.

Dolby sound: Trade name for a system that reduces noise on optical and magnetic soundtracks. (Figure 4.3c–d on p. 161)

dolly: *As a noun:* A wheeled platform most often used to move a motion-picture camera and its operator around while filming (below). *As a verb:* To film while the camera is mounted on a moving dolly or wheeled platform. See **track** (as a verb).

dominant cinema: See **classical Hollywood cinema**.

DP: Director of photography. See **cinematographer**.

dub: (1) To add sound after the film has been shot, sometimes to supplement sounds that were recorded during filming. (2) To replace sounds in a film's soundtrack after the film has been shot—for example, to substitute native speaking voices for the original voices of a foreign-language film.

Dutch angle: A camera angle in which the vertical and horizontal lines of the film's image appear at an angle to the vertical and horizontal lines of the film's frame. For example, in a Dutch angle shot, the vertical lines of a door frame appear slanted. Often used to suggest disorientation by the film's subjects or to disorient viewers or both (below). (89)

edit: To select and arrange the processed segments of photographed motion-picture film or videotape. Editors, often in collaboration with directors, determine the shots to include, the most effective take (version) of each shot, the arrangement and duration of shots, and transitions between them. To edit a film is sometimes called "to cut a film." (Chapter 3)

effect: See **sound effect** and **special effect**.

emulsion: A clear gelatin substance containing a thin layer of tiny light-sensitive particles (grains) that make up a photographic image. The emulsion and a clear, flexible base are the two main components of a piece of film. (*62*)

episodic plot: A story structure in which some scenes have no necessary relation to each other; many scenes could be switched without strongly affecting the overall story or audience response. Episodic plots are used in *Nashville*, *Clerks*, and occasional other films. Such stories may be unified by means other than character and action, such as setting.

establishing shot: A shot, usually a long shot or an extreme long shot, used at the beginning of a scene to show where and sometimes when the events that are to follow take place.

event: In a narrative or story, either an *action* by a character or person or a *happening* (a change brought about by a force other than a person or character). Settings, subjects, and events are the basic components of a narrative. (256)

experimental film: A film that rejects the conventions of mainstream movies and explores the possibilities of the film medium. Probably the best-known experimental film is "Un chien andalou." (399)

explicit meaning: A general observation included in a text about one or more of its subjects. In films, explicit meanings may be revealed by a narrator, a character's monologue or dialogue, a title card, a subtitle, a sign, a newspaper headline, or some other means. See **implicit meaning** and **meaning**. (511)

exposition: Information supplied within a narrative about characters (or people in a narrative documentary) and about events that supposedly transpired before the earliest event in the plot. Exposition is intended to help the audience understand the characters or people and make sense of the plot. (265)

expressionism: A style of art, literature, drama, and film used to represent not external reality in a believable way but emotions in striking, stylized ways. As Ira Konigsberg says, in film this goal "was accomplished through distorted and exaggerated settings, heavy and dramatic shadows, unnatural space in composition, oblique angles, curved or nonparallel lines, a mobile and subjective camera, unnatural costumes and makeup, and stylized acting" (126). A film that uses expressionistic settings throughout is *The Golem* (1920), as can be seen in the irregularly shaped windows in the background, the staircase in the background near the middle of the frame, the archways, and the fireplace behind the back of the seated character (top of next page).

exterior: A scene filmed outdoors or on a set that looks like the outdoors.

extreme close-up: An image that shows one subject and largely or completely excludes the background. If the subject is someone's face, only part of it is visible. (*85*)

extreme long shot: A shot in which the subject appears to be far from the camera. If a person is the subject, the entire body is visible (if not obstructed by some intervening object) but very small in the frame, and much of the surroundings is visible. Usually used only outdoors, often to establish the setting of the following action. (*84*)

eye-level angle: A camera angle that creates the effect of the audience being on the same level as the subject. (*91*)

eyeline match: A transition between shots in which the first shot shows a person or animal looking at something offscreen and the following shot presumably shows what was being looked at from the approximate angle suggested by the previous shot. (*128*)

fabula: A term used by the Russian Formalist school of literary theory and some later film theorists to mean the reconstruction of all the events of a nonchronological narrative (fictional or factual) into a chronological order. See also **plot**. (*283*)

fade-in: An effect in which the image changes by degrees from darkness (usually black) to illumination. Frequently used at the beginning of a film and sometimes at the beginning of a sequence.

fade-out: An effect in which the image changes by degrees from illumination to darkness (usually black). Sometimes used at the conclusion of a sequence and at the end of a film as a gradual exit from its world.

fade-out, fade-in: A transition between two shots in which an image changes by degrees from illumination to darkness (usually to black); then, after a pause, perhaps an extremely brief pause, the image changes from darkness to illumination (usually a new image). Sometimes used to suggest the passage of time. (*121*)

fake documentary: A fictional film that convinces viewers that it is a documentary film until they learn from the end credits or another source that it is not. An example is *The Blair Witch Project*. See **mock documentary**. (*420*)

fantasy: Representation that includes integral narrative impossibilities that makers of the text and consumers of the text accept as conventions. As the authors of *The Film Studies Dictionary* point out, fantasy may feature "imaginary creatures" (as in *The Little Mermaid*), "the alteration of natural laws" (the *Matrix* films), "alternate worlds" (the *Lord of the Rings* movies), or "superheroes" (*Iron Man*). "Fantasy films feature stories with impossibilities rather than, as in science fiction, possibilities" (91). See also **realism**.

fast cutting: Editing characterized by frequent brief shots, sometimes shots less than a second long. Most recent American action movies, music videos, and trailers have extensive fast cutting. Opposite of **slow cutting**. (*142*)

fast film (stock): Film stock that requires relatively little light for capturing images. Fast film, especially before the last decade or so, tended to produce grainy images. Opposite of **slow film (stock)**. (*64*)

fast lens: A camera lens that is efficient at transmitting light and thus transmits more light than a slow lens used in the same circumstances. Opposite of **slow lens**.

fast motion: Motion in which the action on the screen occurs much more rapidly than its real-life counterpart, as when the cowboys in early 1920s films seem to ride horses faster than any yet seen by people outside movie theaters. Achieved whenever the projector runs at a significantly faster speed than the speed at which the camera filmed—for example, when the projector runs at 24 frames per second and the camera filmed at 14 frames per second. Opposite of **slow motion**.

feature (film): A fictional film that is at least 60 minutes long.

fill light: A soft light usually coming from a source near the camera and used to fill in unlit areas of the subject or to soften any shadows or lines made by other, brighter lights. (71)

film continuity: See **cutting continuity (script)**.

filmic: Characteristic of the film medium or appropriate to it, such as parallel editing or viewing a subject from different camera distances and angles. For example, a novel or play with many short scenes or frequent shifts between two locales (similar to parallel editing in a film) may be called *filmic*.

film(making) technique: Any aspect of filmmaking, such as the use of sets, lighting, sound effects, music, or editing. How effectively techniques are used is a strong determinant of a film's content, style, and impact.

film movement: A group of films sharing innovative styles or subjects (or both) that emerge from the same country or region over a period of a few years and that are in opposition to the dominant cinema(s) of the time. Examples are Italian neorealism and blaxploitation.

film noir ("nwahr"): Literally, "black film." A type of film first made in the United States during and after World War II, characterized by frequent scenes with dark, shadowy (low-key) lighting; (usually) urban settings; characters motivated by selfishness, greed, cruelty, ambition, and lust; and characters willing to lie, frame, double-cross, and kill or have others killed. Examples are *Murder, My Sweet*; *Out of the Past*; and *Touch of Evil* (below). (319)

film stock: Unexposed and unprocessed motion-picture film. Sometimes called *raw stock*. (61)

film theorist: A person who formulates a film theory or a general explanation of the film medium or part of the medium. See also **film theory**.

film theory: A set of evolving ideas about the general characteristics of the film medium that is created for scholars, critics, and other informed spectators. As Dudley Andrew has pointed out in his *Major Film Theories*, a film theory often includes considerations of the properties of the film medium, its techniques, its forms, and its purposes and value. The concepts constituting a theory are sometimes only loosely related, evolve over time, and lack universal acceptance. Not all theorists calling themselves feminist, for example, will agree about what "feminist theory" or "feminist criticism" entails.

filter: A sheet of transparent plastic or glass either in a color or in a shade of gray attached before or sometimes behind the camera lens to change the quality of light reaching the film.

final cut: The last version of an edited film.

fine cut: A late version of an edited film, though perhaps not yet the final cut. See **rough cut**.

fisheye lens: A lens that captures nearly 180 degrees of the area before the camera and causes much curvature of the image, especially near the edges, as in a famous publicity still for *Seconds* (below). (*Seconds* itself includes a number of striking wide-angle lens shots but no fisheye lens shots.) (80)

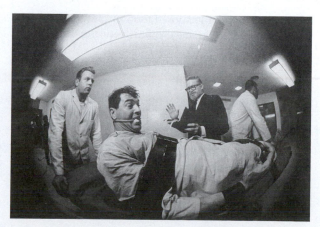

flashback: A shot or a few shots, a brief scene, or (rarely) a sequence that interrupts a narrative to show earlier events. (281)

flash-forward: A shot, scene, or sequence—though usually only a shot or two—that interrupts a narrative to show events that happen in the future. For example, *GoodFellas* begins with a few scenes that occur again late in an otherwise chronological narrative. Flash-forwards are rarely used, though examples are found in *Don't Look Now* and *The Gift*. (280)

flat lens: See **spherical lens**.

Foley artist: A sound specialist who uses various objects such as different types of floor surfaces (usually in a Foley studio) to simulate sounds and synchronize them with corresponding movie images (below). (Figure 4.5b on p. 169)

footage: A length of exposed motion-picture film (as in "They had enough footage to finish editing the film").

form: See **structure**.

form cut: See **match cut**.

found footage: Exposed motion-picture film or videotape, parts or all of which are incorporated into a later film or video.

frame: *As a noun:* (1) A separate, individual photograph on a strip of motion-picture film (see Figure 3.4 on p. 120). (2) The borders of the projected film, TV set, or monitor. *As a verb:* To position the camera so that the image is composed in a certain way, as in "She framed the shot so that the two characters would be on the opposite sides of the image."

frame enlargement: A photograph of an individual frame from a motion picture, blown up (enlarged) to reveal its details. Used in some publications, including this one, to illustrate certain features of a film or the film medium. See also **publicity still**. (Figure 2.16a on p. 75)

freeze frame: An unmoving motion-picture or video image that looks like a still photograph, which is achieved by reprinting the same frame or two repeatedly. Sometimes used at the end of a film as in *Tom Jones* and *Good-Fellas* and often used at the conclusion of TV sitcoms. Many videotape, videodisc, and DVD players also have a freeze frame or still frame option.

French new wave (cinema): A film movement made up of a loose grouping of untraditional movies made in France in the late 1950s and early 1960s. French new wave filmmakers reacted against the carefully scripted products of the French film industry, explored more current subjects, and sometimes employed untraditional filmmaking techniques. Examples of French new wave cinema are the early feature films of Truffaut (such as *The 400 Blows* and, more so, *Shoot the Piano Player*), Godard (*Breathless*), and Claude Chabrol (*Handsome Serge*). (337)

gauge: The width of a film, usually measured in millimeters, as in "The gauge of most theatrical movies is 35 mm." (62)

gender: In this book and elsewhere though not universally, a person's sexual identity as exhibited by various signals, including clothing, cosmetics, hairstyles, conversational styles, and body language. *Gender* is distinguished from *sex*, which means the biological or physical characteristics of men and women. (447)

genre ("ZHAHN ruh"): A group of *fictional* films—such as western, science fiction, horror, gangster, musical, and screwball comedy—that share enough similarities that both filmmakers and audiences recognize the films as members of the same group.

grain: One of the many tiny light-sensitive particles embedded in gelatin that is attached to a clear, flexible film base (celluloid). After the film is exposed to light and developed, a huge number of grains make up a film's finished images.

graininess: Rough visual texture, as in "that film stock produces excessive graininess." In a film, graininess results when individual particles clump together in the film emulsion. Graininess also results if a film is magnified excessively during projection, as when a 16 mm print is projected onto a large screen intended for 35 mm film showings.

grainy: Having graininess or rough visual texture. See also **graininess**.

great depth of field: See **deep focus**.

habitat of meaning: See **interpretive community**.

happening: As defined by some narrative theorists, a change brought about by a force other than a person or character. In the animated film "T.R.A.N.S.I.T.," for example, a suitcase falling off the back of a sports car results in a man meeting and becoming infatuated with an attractive woman, which in turn leads to murders (see the description of the film's plot and fabula on p. 427). Happenings and actions by characters or persons constitute events in narratives.

hard light: Light that has not been diffused (scattered) or reflected before illuminating the subject. On subjects illuminated by hard light, any shadows are sharp-edged and surface details are more noticeable than with soft light (right). Examples of hard light: midday sunlight on a clear day or unreflected and focused light from a spotlight. Opposite of **soft light**.

high angle: A view of a subject from above, created by positioning the camera above the subject. (*91*)

high contrast: A photographic image with few gradations between the darkest and lightest parts of the image. Black-and-white high-contrast photos are made up mostly of blacks and whites with few shades of gray. Opposite of **low contrast**. (*422*)

high-key lighting: A high level of illumination on the subject. With high-key lighting, the bright frontal key lighting on the subject prevents dark shadows. Often used to create or enhance a cheerful mood, as in many stage and movie musicals. Opposite of **low-key lighting**. (73)

homage (in French and in film studies, pronounced "oh MAZH"): In film studies, a tribute in a text to a person, to another text (such as a film), or to part of a text. Examples of homages in a film are the inclusion of part of an earlier film, a re-creation of parts of an earlier film, or a respectful imitation of aspects of an earlier film. An homage may also be to a specific director's films. (240)

hybrid film: A film that is not exclusively fictional, documentary, or experimental but instead shares characteristics of two or all three of the major film categories. An example is *David Holzman's Diary*, which is not a fictional, documentary, or experimental film but contains aspects of all three. (417)

ideology: In film studies, *ideology* usually means the fundamental beliefs and values of a society or social group. Often, these beliefs and values are unexamined by the group's members and are assumed to be true and not the product of the group's way of thinking. For example, part of the ideology of most citizens of the United States is the belief that individuals can influence major events in significant ways and that individualism is a positive value. This aspect of American ideology is often conveyed by popular American movies. See also **symptomatic meaning**. (537)

IMAX (short for "image maximization"): A Canadian company's system for filming and showing very large screen motion pictures. The system consists of special cameras that can accommodate 70 mm film run horizontally through the camera (see Figure 2.2d on p. 63) and large theaters with special projectors, huge screens (some as high as an eight-story building), multiple speaker clusters behind the porous screens, and a multitrack sound system (now usually digital). With the steeply raked seating and huge screen, typically the image extends beyond the viewers' peripheral vision, and viewers feel a greater sense of presence and involvement than they do at any other type of film showing. Also available in some locales is IMAX 3-D, which creates a credible 3-D movie experience for viewers wearing IMAX 3-D glasses with polarizing filters or electronic liquid-crystal shutter glasses.

IMAX Dome: A theater in which film is projected through a fisheye lens onto a huge curved screen. For the spectators, the projected images can be even more enveloping and involving than in the standard IMAX theater with its flat screen. See also **IMAX**. (*489*)

implicit meaning: A generalization that a viewer or reader makes about a text (such as a film) or a subject in a text. An implicit meaning, for example, may be a viewer's generalization about the implications of a narrative's events (such as crime doesn't pay, or a person's motives may be complicated or even unknowable). See also **meaning** and **symbol**. (513)

independent film: (1) Film made mainly or entirely without support or input from the dominant, established film industry. Sometimes called an *indie*. (2) In some publications, the phrase is used as an alternative to *experimental film*. (340, 342)

installation art: An art exhibit or ensemble, which is usually shown in a museum of modern or contemporary art, integrating various objects or arts, such as video images, photographs, furniture, and recorded voices. The installation "Eviction Struggle" (below) consists of a huge photo on one side of a gallery wall and nine video clips of different parts of the same situation on the other side of the wall. (414)

intercut: See **cross-cut**.

intercutting: See **parallel editing**.

interior: A scene filmed indoors, either in an existing building or in one constructed for filming.

interpretive community: A group of people with common interests and a broadly shared outlook who tend to generate broadly similar meanings from a text. Examples of two interpretive communities are film scholars and college students who see a lot of movies. Meanings that one interpretive community formulates tend to be similar yet differ in general from the meanings formulated by a different interpretive community. (540)

intertextuality: The relation of one text (such as a film) to another text or texts (such as a journalistic article, a play, or another film). Types of intertextuality in films include allusion, homage, parody, remake, prequel, sequel, and compilation film. (203)

intertitle (card): See **title card**.

iris-in: An effect usually functioning as a transition between shots in which the image is initially dark, then a widening opening—often a circle or an oval—reveals more and more of the next image, usually until it is fully revealed. (*127*)

iris-out: An effect usually functioning as a transition between shots in which the image is closed out as a constricting opening—usually a circle or an oval—closes down on it. Normally the iris-out ends with the image fully obliterated. (Figure 7.30c on p. 339)

iris shot: A shot in which part of the frame is masked or obscured, often leaving the remaining image in a circular or an oval shape. Although rarely used today, the iris shot was widely used in films directed by D. W. Griffith, Sergei Eisenstein, and Abel Gance and in many other early films, such as *The Cabinet of Dr. Caligari* (below).

irony: A statement, an event, or a situation involving an incongruity or a discrepancy between appearance and reality. As the authors of the second edition of *The Bedford Glossary of Critical and Literary Terms* illustrate, "A discrepancy may exist between what someone says and what he or she actually means, between what someone expects to happen and what really does happen, or between what appears to be true and what actually is true" (220). Irony can be a tool of the satirist and other makers of texts.

Italian neorealism: A film movement in Italy during and after World War II that created films that combine imaginary and actual events, are usually located in actual settings, and show ordinary and believable characters caught up in dif-ficult social and economic conditions, such as poverty and unemployment. Probably the best-known neorealist film is *The Bicycle Thief* (above) (also known as *Bicycle Thieves*). (334)

Italian westerns: See **spaghetti westerns.**

jump cut: A transition between shots that causes a jarring or even shocking shift in space, time, or action. A jump cut may be used to shorten the representation of an event or to disorient viewers, or both (below). It sometimes results unintentionally from careless editing or missing footage. Opposite of **continuity editing**. (*133*)

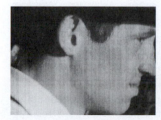

key light: (1) The main light in a shot, usually the sun or some sort of electric light. (2) The lighting instrument used to create the main and brightest light hitting the subject. (71)

kino: (1) An informal group that meets periodically, often monthly, to show short films shot and edited dig-itally. (2) A short film shot and edited digitally, often in a short time, which is later shown at a gathering of other amateur digital filmmakers and other audience members. See also **microcinema**.

lap dissolve: A transition between shots in which one shot begins to fade out as the next shot fades in, overlapping the first shot before replacing it. Usually used between scenes or sequences to suggest a change of setting or a later time or both. Also frequently known as a *dissolve*, but *lap dissolve* better conveys what happens: (over)lapping (by the second shot) and dissolving (of the first). (*123*)

leader: Clear or opaque motion-picture film of any color that usually precedes and concludes a reel of film. It is now used mainly to decrease the chances of damage to the film print during shipment. Fragments of leader have been included in some experimental films, as in Bruce Conner's "A Movie." (Figure 9.5b and g on p. 406)

letterbox format: A videotape, videodisc, and DVD format that retains the film's original theatrical widescreen aspect ratio (or a close approximation of it) by not using a portion of the top and bottom of the TV or monitor screen. (*40*)

limbo: An indistinct setting. In such a setting, the background may be all white (as in most shots in George Lucas's *THX 1138*), all black, or all the same color. Also called *limbo background* or *limbo set*. (14)

live action: Behavior by living (not animated) people or animals. Opposite of **animation**.

location: Any place other than a film studio that is used for filming. For example, the Monument Valley region in Utah and Arizona was a location for the 1939 John Ford film *Stagecoach* and other westerns, and *Schindler's List* was filmed on location in Poland, not on studio sets built to resemble parts of Poland. See **set**.

long lens: See **telephoto lens.**

long shot: A shot in which the subject may be seen in its entirety and much of its surroundings is visible. Not to be confused with **long take**. (*84*)

long take: A shot of long duration, as in the opening of *Touch of Evil*, *Halloween*, and *Boogie Nights*. The more than 8-minute opening shot of *The Player* is another example of a long take (see Table 13.1 on p. 582). Not to be confused with **long shot**.

loose framing: An image in which the main subject has ample space and does not seem hemmed in by the edges of the frame and the background. Such framing can be used to give a sense of the subject's freedom of movement or of its being lost in or engulfed by its environment (below). Opposite of **tight framing**. (*18*)

loose shot: See **loose framing**.

low angle: A view of the subject as seen from below eye level. (*92*)

low contrast: A photographic image with many gradations between the darkest and lightest parts of the image. In black-and-white film, low-contrast images have many shades of gray. Opposite of **high contrast**. (*134*)

low-key lighting: Lighting with predominant dark tones, often deep dark tones. By using little frontal fill lighting, the filmmakers can immerse parts of the image in shadows. Often used to contribute to a dramatic or mysterious effect, as in many horror films and many detective and crime films. Opposite of **high-key lighting**. See the image that illustrates *film noir* on p. 675.

magic realism: A style in which occasional wildly improbable or impossible events are included in an otherwise realistic story. For example, in *Like Water for Chocolate*, the food the film's main female character prepares causes those who eat it to feel the way she felt as she prepared it. (295)

masking: A technique used to block out part of an image (usually) temporarily. Normally used to block out extraneous details and focus viewers' attention, to elongate or widen the image, or to exclude certain details for censorship reasons. Used more often in silent films than in sound films. See the image used to illustrate *iris shot* on p. 678 and the image atop the next column.

master-scene format: A screenplay format that briefly describes scenes but does not break them down into shots. A screenplay in the master-scene format includes brief descriptions of setting and action and any dialogue but usually excludes instructions about the making of the film, such as indications about the camera setups. (208)

master shot: A shot usually made with a wide-angle lens that records an entire scene. Parts of the master shot plus other shots for the same scene may be used as the final version of the scene, or occasionally the entire master shot is used to convey the scene.

match cut: A transition between two shots in which an object or movement (or both) at the end of one shot closely resembles (or is identical to) an object or movement (or both) at the beginning of the next shot, as in the example from *Rocky IV* below. (121)

meaning: An observation or a general statement about a subject, such as a film or an aspect of a film. Meaning in texts may be explicit: a general observation in the text itself about one or more of its subjects. Or a meaning may be implicit: a generalization a viewer makes about a text or subject in the text. (510)

medium close-up: An image in which the subject fills most of the frame, though not as much as in a close-up.

When the subject is a person, the medium close-up usually reveals the head and shoulders. Like the close-up, the medium close-up is often used to direct viewers' attention to a part of something or to show facial expressions in detail. (*85*)

medium shot: A shot in which the subject and surroundings are given about equal importance. When the subject is a person, he or she is usually seen from the knees or waist up. (*84*)

Method acting: Acting in which the performer studies the background of a character in depth, immerses himself or herself in the role, and creates emotion in part by thinking of emotional situations from his or her own life that resemble those of the character. (*27*)

microcinema: A program of untraditional short videos that may be shown on the Internet or in a casual atmosphere such as a coffeehouse or that may be purchased on DVD. See also **kino**.

mise en scène ("meez ahn sen," with a nasalized second syllable): French for "staging." An image's setting, subjects (usually people or characters), and composition (the arrangement of setting and subjects within the frame). (Chapter 1)

mix: *As a verb:* To select sounds from soundtracks of music, dialogue, and sound effects; adjust their volumes; and combine them into a composite soundtrack. *As a noun:* A final composite soundtrack consisting of a blend of other soundtracks.

mock documentary: A fictional film that parodies or amusingly imitates documentary films. Because mock documentaries have characteristics of documentaries—such as interviews, handheld camera shots, and the absence of stars—viewers at first may think they are seeing a documentary but soon realize the film is an extended joke. Examples of mock documentaries are *This Is Spinal Tap*, purportedly a documentary about an aging heavy metal band, and *Fear of a Black Hat*, supposedly a documentary film about the endless problems confronted by a hip-hop group. See also **fake documentary**. (238, 419)

montage ("mon TAZH"): From the French *monter*, "to assemble." (1) A series of brief shots used to represent a condensation of subjects and time. Instead of a series of consecutive scenes, filmmakers may use a montage to convey much of the same general information and moods. *The Third Man*, for example, begins with a mon-

tage about the political and social conditions in Vienna after the end of World War II. (2) A type of editing used in some 1920s Soviet films and advocated by some Soviet film theorists. In films using this type of editing, the aim is not so much to promote the invisible continuity of a narrative favored in classical Hollywood cinema as to suggest meanings from the dynamic juxtaposition of many carefully selected details. (3) Editing, especially in European usage. (118)

morphing: The noun *morph* means "shape," and *morphing* means "changing shape." In filmmaking, morphing is the alteration of a film image by degrees through the use of sophisticated computer software and multiple advanced computers. As Kevin Jackson has written, "Thanks to morphing, the director of live-action films can now achieve the kind of wild images previously reserved for the animator" (161). Used increasingly since 1988 in TV commercials and feature films, as in *Spawn*, *X-Men*, and many others (below).

movement: See **film movement**.

movie palace: An opulent type of movie theater built in the United States and Europe between the mid-1910s and the 1930s and seating at least 1,000 and as many as 6,200 patrons. Movie palaces were usually ornately decorated in both the lobbies and the auditoria, spacious, and extremely comfortable, in part because their lengthy programs included more than a feature film. With the steep decline in movie attendance beginning in the 1950s, most movie palaces were divided into smaller auditoria, torn down, or converted to other uses, such as churches. (*488*)

narration: Commentary in a film about a subject in the film or about some other subject, usually by someone offscreen. Occasionally the narration comes from a person on-screen. Filmmakers may use narration off and on throughout a film or only occasionally. Sometimes they use it only at the film's beginning or ending, or both. Narration is sometimes used in documentary films and in TV commercials, in fictional films, and on rare occasions in experimental films.

narrative: A representation of unified events (happenings and actions) situated in one or more settings. A narrative may be fictional or factual or a blend of the two. Its events may be arranged chronologically or nonchronologically. (255)

narrative closure: See **closure**.

narrative documentary: A film or video representation of an actual (not imaginary) narrative or story. Examples are *Hearts of Darkness* (pp. 392–94), *Hoop Dreams*, and *Genghis Blues*. See also **docudrama**. (382)

narrator: A character, a person, or an unidentifiable voice in a film that provides continuous or intermittent commentary about subjects in the film or outside it, or both. As in written fiction, a narrator is not necessarily a reliable source for information.

negative: (1) Unexposed film stock that can be used to record negative images. (2) Other than reversal film—which is film stock that can be exposed and then developed to create positive images without making a negative first—film that has been exposed but not yet developed. (3) Excluding reversal film, film that has been exposed and developed. An exposed and developed negative is normally used to make (positive) prints for projection but is occasionally used in part of a finished film (as in the documentary *Bus 174*).  In color photography and cinematography, the colors of the negative image are complementary to those of the subject photographed. In black-and-white negatives, the light and dark areas are reversed (Plates 43–44).

neorealism: See **Italian neorealism**.

new wave (cinema): See **French new wave (cinema)**.

nickelodeon: Literally, "five-cents theater." A small, modest storefront converted into a theater for showing a brief program of short films (top of next column). Nickelodeons were popular in the United States from 1905 to roughly 1915 and were the successors to one-person peephole machines and the forerunners of larger and more comfortable movie theaters, the largest and most elaborate of which were sometimes called *movie palaces*. See also **movie palace**. (485)

nitrate: See **celluloid**, definition 1.

nonfiction film: See **documentary (film)**.

nonlinear editing: Editing that involves using a computer and software to select and combine digitized shots.

nonnarrative documentary: A film or video that uses no narrative or story in its representation of mainly actual (not imaginary) subjects. Examples abound, such as Frederick Wiseman's *Public Housing* and Errol Morris's *The Fog of War*, many TV commercials, and many industrial and training films. See **documentary (film)**. (380)

normal lens: A camera lens that provides the least distortion of image and movement. The normal lens—50 mm on a 35 mm camera—comes closest to approximating the perceptions of the human eye. (79)

nouvelle vague: Literally, "new wave." See **French new wave (cinema)**.

objective camera: Camera placement that allows the film viewer to see the subject approximately as an outsider would, not as someone in the film sees it. Opposite of **point-of-view shot**.

offscreen: The area beyond the frame line, which has many possible uses. For example, someone may look offscreen at someone else, a shadow may be cast into the frame by something or someone offscreen, or a sound may be heard from offscreen. See **offscreen sound**.

offscreen sound: Sound that does not derive from an on-screen source, such as an unseen dog barking or music that is not made by anyone within the frame. (180)

OMNIMAX: See **IMAX Dome**.

180-degree system: Filming and editing so that all shots in a scene are from the same side of an imaginary straight line running between the scene's major subjects. The 180-degree system helps keep relationships between subjects and between subjects and setting consistent and clear (below). See also **continuity editing**. (128)

on-screen sound: Sound that derives from an on-screen source, such as someone viewers see and hear sneezing. (180)

optical effect: A special effect made with an optical printer. Examples are lap dissolves, wipes, and freeze frames. Now, nearly all filmmakers use computers to achieve the same effects. See also **digital effect**.

optical printer: A device consisting of a movie camera and one or more movie projectors used to reproduce images or parts of images from already processed film. An optical printer can be used to make lap dissolves, wipes, and many other optical effects, though today most filmmakers achieve such effects while doing non-linear editing on a computer.

outtake: A take (version of a shot) or a shot not included in a film's final version. Occasionally some outtakes are included during the ending credits, especially if they might be amusing.

pace: The rate that the film's subjects (such as events in a narrative film or information in a documentary film) are revealed or presented. The viewer's sense of pace is subjective and is influenced by many aspects of the film, such as its editing (fast cutting or slow cutting) and the frequency with which it introduces significant subjects. (142)

panning: Filming while the movie camera is pivoted horizontally, usually while the camera is attached to a stationary base, often a tripod, or is being held by a stationary camera operator. Used frequently to show the vastness of a setting, such as a sea, a plain, a mountain range, outer space, or the inside of an immense building. The term derives from the word *panoramic* because with this movement the camera shows an extensive area. See also **swish pan** and **tilting**. (*94*)

parallel editing: Editing that alternates between two or more events, often suggesting that the events are related to each other or are occurring simultaneously. Parallel editing also may be used to represent events from different times or eras (as in D. W. Griffith's *Intolerance*). See **cross-cut**. (138)

parody: *As a noun:* An amusing imitation of human behavior or of a text, or group of texts, often to satirize or to playfully poke fun at the subjects or styles of the source. Examples of film parodies are *Rocky Horror Picture Show*, a musical parody of horror movies,  and *Spaceballs*, a parody of sci-fi movies, especially the original *Star Wars* (above). *As a verb:* To imitate a text, part of a text, or a group of texts in an amusing way. (235)

perspective: As used by painters, photographers, and cinematographers, the relative size and apparent distances between objects in a created image. (88)

pixilation: Animation that shows three-dimensional subjects (living or nonliving) moving in rapid, jerky ways that are impossible in the real world. Here are two examples from Norman McLaren's "Neighbours": a picket fence rapidly installing itself one picket at a time and two men circling each other while all the time they are above a surface (see top of next page). According to the 4th edition of *The American Heritage Dictionary*, *pixilated* means behaving as if mentally unbalanced, very eccentric; whimsical, prankish; or (as slang) intoxicated or drunk, and often the movements created by pixilation could be so characterized. See **stop-motion cinematography**. (425)

plot: The structure or arrangement of a narrative's events. (285)

plotline: A narrative or series of related events usually involving only a few characters or people and capable

of functioning on its own as a story. Short films tend to have one plotline; many feature films combine two or more. (271)

point-of-view shot: Camera placement at the approximate position of a character or person (or occasionally an animal) that gives a view similar to what that subject would see. Opposite of **objective camera**. (92)

pop art: Short for *popular art*. An art movement begun mainly in the United States and Britain in the 1950s and extending into the 1960s whose subjects were everyday objects—such as soup cans, clothespins, comic strips, graphic print ads, and celebrity images—that were represented archetypically, whimsically, or ironically or in a combination of these ways.

postproduction: All the work involved in finishing up a film or video after the filming or taping is completed, usually including editing the shots, preparing a soundtrack, and making the credits.

p.o.v. shot: See **point-of-view shot**.

preproduction: All the work involved in making a film or video before the filming or taping begins, usually including such tasks as writing the script, casting, hiring the other necessary personnel, and selecting locations or designing and building sets.

prequel: A narrative film that shows characters from a previous film at earlier stages of their lives. For example, *Butch and Sundance: The Early Days* (1979) is a prequel to *Butch Cassidy and the Sundance Kid* (1969). Opposite of **sequel**. (242)

preview (of a coming attraction): See **trailer**.

producer: A person in charge of the business and administrative aspects of making a film. The (main) producer's job typically includes acquiring rights to the script and hiring the personnel to make the film. Sometimes producers influence the filmmaking process—for example, by changing directors before or during filming or insisting on changes in the script or editing. Producers may be known under a variety of titles, such as executive producer and assistant producer; the nature of their involvement (if any) remains obscure to those outside the production.

production: (1) The making of a film or video, which typically involves three stages: preproduction (which in a large production may include planning, budgeting, scripting, designing and building sets, and casting); production (filming or taping); and postproduction (which includes editing, preparing and mixing sound, and making the credits). (2) The actual filming or taping needed to make a film. The phrase "in production" usually means that the filming or taping is under way. See also **preproduction** and **postproduction**.

production designer: See **designer**.

production still: See **publicity still**.

product placement: The practice of including in films identifiable commercial products or services, such as Coca-Cola cans or a particular airline. Makers of movies often make agreements with companies to display their products or services in exchange for money or, much more often, goods, promotion of the finished movie, or services (such as airline tickets, hotel accommodations, or use, or ownership, of certain vehicles, as below in *The Player*). See also the "Special Thanks To" section of the end credits for *The Player* on pp. 700–701. (52)

product plug: See **product placement**.

prop: Short for *property*. A movable object used as part of a setting. A prop may contribute to verisimilitude or function as a symbol, or do both. Examples of props are the oranges in *The Godfather* films and the family photo and roughed-up tennis ball seen in the first shot of the end credits of *Fatal Attraction* (below). The photograph in the image below illustrates how a prop may function as a symbol (here, of happier family times). The tennis ball is presumably the one used in the scene in which the father, the family dog, and the father's new female companion play with a tennis ball in a park, and here it functions as a reminder of that disruption of family life.

publicity still: A posed photograph taken with a still camera, usually during production, to help later publicize a film. (Figure 2.16b on p. 75)

pull focus: See **rack focus**.

rack focus: Changing the sharpness of focus *during* a shot from foreground to background or vice versa. (47)

raw stock: See **film stock**.

reaction shot: A shot, usually of a face, that shows someone or occasionally an animal presumably reacting to an event. Used frequently in films to cue viewers how to react or to intensify viewers' responses. (138)

reading: (1) A tryout in which the applicant reads aloud from a script. (2) The amount of light or sound as measured by a light meter or sound meter. (3) In film studies, an interpretation of a text or part of one, as in "Her reading of *Citizen Kane* stresses the contexts in which the film was made."

realism: Representation that is widely believed to render its subjects faithfully. In *The Concise Oxford Dictionary*

of Literary Terms, Chris Baldick defines *realism* this way: it "is not a direct or simple reproduction of reality . . . but a system of conventions producing a lifelike illusion of some 'real' world outside the text" (184). A person's sense of what realism is depends on when and where the person lives and what that person's society deems as true-to-life representations. What seems realistic in one place or time often seems unrealistic in another place or time. See also **fantasy**.

rear projection: The process of projecting (usually moving) images on a screen behind actors seen in the foreground. Often used to create the illusion of characters in a moving vehicle.

rear-screen projection: See **rear projection**.

reel: (1) A metal or plastic spool to hold film, such as the two 16 mm reels in the background of Figure 9.16b on p. 422. (2) Approximately one thousand feet of 35 mm motion-picture film stored on a reel. Because the speed of projection was not standardized before the late 1920s, early films were measured in number of reels. For example, the 1925 version of *Les Misérables* reputedly consisted of 32 reels (each reel could take from 13 to 16 minutes to project). Today, a 35 mm reel of sound film takes approximately 11 minutes to project if the film has leader attached to it or 10 minutes if it has no leader.

reflexive: See **self-reflexive**.

reflexivity: See **self-reflexive**.

representation: A likeness of a subject created in a text. A representation of an event (action or happening) is not the event itself but someone's manufactured likeness, or re-presentation (a presentation again or anew) of it in a text. As different people create texts, they unavoidably make different decisions (and have different skills), and different representations result. For example, each group of filmmakers that creates another Tarzan movie makes many decisions about how to represent the subject and ends up with a new representation of the story (see Figure 10.15 on pp. 456–57).

resolution: (1) The degree of detail visible in an image; the greater the visible detail, the higher the resolution. One could say, for example, that with the appropriate film stock, lighting, and lens, high-resolution images are possible. (2) The culmination or concluding events of a plot, as in this example: "The resolution of the narrative is implausible because it is not consistent with earlier events in the story."

restricted depth of field: See **shallow focus**.

revisionist: Referring to a new or revised interpretation or representation of a subject (such as history, a narrative, or genre). *Unforgiven* is a revisionist western, for example, in that most of the film is critical of violence and killing. Opposite of *conventional*. See **convention**. (313)

rough cut: An early version (usually the first complete or nearly complete version) of an edited film. See also **fine cut**.

running time: The time that elapses when a complete film is projected. The running time of most feature films is 80 to 120 minutes, though in recent years many features run longer than 120 minutes. See **story time**. (286)

rushes: See **dailies**.

satire: A representation of individual or group thinking or behavior that indirectly exposes the subject as flawed. Creators of texts may use satire in an attempt to amuse but also to chide or to ridicule, or they may use satire to inform and maybe to try to reform. In trying to reach these goals, satirists often resort to exaggeration, irony, and styles such as parody or black comedy. The tone of a satire may range from gentle and good-natured to scathing and bitter or somewhere in between. (289)

saturated color: Intense, vivid, or brilliant color. Opposite of **desaturated color**. (66, Plates 4, 5, 9, and 10)

scanned print: A version of a film made in the standard aspect ratio from an original anamorphic film. In making a scanned print, a technician—not the film's editor or director—decides which part of the width of the original anamorphic image to show at each moment of the film or video. (Figure 1.31d on p. 38)

scene: A section of a narrative that gives the impression of continuous action taking place in continuous time and space. Most feature films consist of many scenes—often one hundred or more—as do narrative documentary films, such as *Hearts of Darkness*, *Hoop Dreams*, and *Genghis Blues*. Most short narrative films consist of far fewer scenes. It is possible, though very rare, for a narrative to consist of a single scene. (119)

scope lens: See **anamorphic lens**.

screenplay: The earliest version of a script, a script written before filming begins. Usually a finished film varies considerably from the original screenplay. See **shooting script** and **cutting continuity (script)**.

self-reflexive: Characteristic of a text—such as a play, novel, or film—that refers to or comments on itself as a text. A self-reflexive text draws readers' or viewers' attention to itself as something constructed and thus not inevitable in its techniques, subjects, and conventions. Examples of self-reflexiveness are found in Luigi Pirandello's play *Six Characters in Search of an Author*, John Fowles's novel *The French Lieutenant's Woman*, the documentary film *Man with a Movie Camera*, and the fictional films *Tom Jones* and *High Fidelity*. In self-reflexive movies, a character may interrupt the story to seemingly look at the audience or speak directly to it (see Figure 7.32 on p. 341). Unlike films of the classical Hollywood cinema, self-reflexive films do not as often downplay the conventions and manner of their making but foreground them. Many experimental films are self-reflexive at times, as are occasional documentary films (see Figure 8.17 on p. 389). (341)

sequel: (1) A narrative that further develops at least some of the story from an earlier narrative film. An example: *The Son of Kong* (1933) is a sequel to a famous film made earlier in the same year, *King Kong* (1933). (2) Though rare, a documentary film may show more about a subject from an earlier documentary. One example: *Best Man: 'Best Boy' and All of Us Twenty Years Later* (1997) is a sequel to *Best Boy* (1979).

sequence: A series of related consecutive scenes, perceived as a major unit of a narrative film, such as the Sicilian sequence in *The Godfather*. A sequence may be analogous to a chapter in a novel or an act in a play. (120)

serial: From the 1910s until the early 1950s, a low-budget action film divided into chapters or installments, one of which was shown each week in downtown and neighborhood movie theaters (top of next page). Typically, serials feature fast-paced action, danger to the heroes, touches of tepid romance, and cheap special effects. Villains often wear bizarre costumes, and the stories are often set in exotic locales. Usually, each chapter or installment ends with an unresolved problem. For example, one or more of the main characters are placed in mortal danger or seem to be killed. Serials have strongly influenced the *Star Wars* films, the *Raiders of the Lost Ark* films, *The Lord of the Rings* trilogy, and many other action movies.

"FLAMING DEATH"

Chapter 6

THE NEW UNIVERSAL PRESENTS

FLASH GORDON CONQUERS THE UNIVERSE with LARRY "Buster" CRABBE as FLASH GORDON

set: A constructed setting where action is filmed; it can be indoors or outdoors (below). See **location**.

setting: The place where a narrative's events occur. In a film, the setting is either a set, which has been built for use in a film, or a location, which is any place other than one built for use in a movie. Setting is often used to indicate a period and to reveal or enhance the narrative's style, characters, moods, and meanings. (13)

shallow depth of field: See **shallow focus**.

shallow focus: Photography with sharp focus in only a short distance between the foreground and the background—for example, between 10 and 15 feet in front of the camera. Achieved by use of a telephoto lens, a large lens aperture, or both. Filmmakers often use the technique to deemphasize the background and focus  attention on the subject in the foreground. Sometimes shallow focus directs viewers' attention to a subject in the background of the image (see Figure 2.28b on p. 81). Filmmakers are likely to use the terms *restricted depth of field* or *shallow depth of field* rather than *shallow focus*, the term favored by film teachers and scholars. Opposite of **deep focus**. (82)

shooting script: The version of the script that filmmakers use during filming. Because many changes are usually made during filming and editing, the finished film typically varies considerably from the shooting script. See **screenplay** and **cutting continuity (script)**.

short film: Variously defined but often regarded as a film of less than 60 minutes. (258)

short lens: See **wide-angle lens**.

short subject: See **short film**.

shot: *As a noun:* An uninterrupted strip of exposed motion-picture film or videotape that represents a subject, perhaps even a blank screen, during an uninterrupted segment of time (see Figure 3.4 on p. 120). *As a verb:* Filmed, as in "They shot the movie in seven weeks."

shot/reverse shot: A filming and editing technique in which a shot of one subject seen from one camera position alternates with a shot of a second nearby subject seen from a different camera position. Most often used to show the face of the first person speaking or reacting as the camera looks from behind and to the side of the second person, followed by a shot of the second person's face (perhaps speaking, perhaps listening) as the first person is now seen from behind and to the side. The shot/reverse shot technique is normally used in conjunction with the 180-degree system and helps contribute to continuity editing, as in Figure 3.12 on p. 128. See **continuity editing**.

simulated documentary: See **fake documentary**.

slow cutting: Editing characterized by frequent shots of long duration. Most of the early films directed by Michelangelo Antonioni and *2001: A Space Odyssey*, for example, have extensive slow cutting, as does the experimental film "(nostalgia)." Opposite of **fast cutting**. (142, 143)

slow film (stock): Film stock that requires a large camera aperture or bright light for appropriate recreation of images. Slow film produces images with fine grain and sharp detail. Opposite of **fast film (stock)**. (64)

slow lens: A camera lens that is inefficient at transmitting light and thus transmits less light than a fast lens used in the same circumstances. Opposite of **fast lens**.

slow motion: Motion in which the action on the screen is slower than its real-life counterpart, as when people are seen running more slowly than is possible. Achieved whenever the projector runs at an appreciably slower speed than the speed at which the camera filmed. Opposite of **fast motion**.

socialist realism: A Soviet doctrine and style in force from the mid-1930s to the 1980s that decreed that Soviet texts, including films, must promote communism and the working class and must be "realistic" (actually, an idealized representation of the working class) so that they would be understandable to working people. After World War II, socialist realism was also enforced in the East European countries under Soviet rule. (460)

soft light or **soft lighting:** (1) Light that has been diffused or reflected before illuminating the subject. On subjects illuminated by soft light, any shadows are soft-edged, and surface details are less noticeable than with hard light (right). One source of soft light is the so-called magic hour, the time after sunset but before dark or the time of increasing light before sunrise. Another source of soft light is the light emitted through a frosted light bulb then reflected off or through a cloth lampshade. Opposite of **hard light**. (2) A type

of open-faced lamp that creates soft or diffused light. (70)

sound dissolve: A transition between two shots in which a sound begins to fade out as the next sound fades in and overlaps the first sound before replacing it. (177)

sound effect: A sound in film other than spoken words or music. Three examples of sound effects are a door slamming, a dog barking, and thunder. (166)

soundstage: A permanent enclosed area for shooting film and recording sound. A soundstage is especially useful because its controlled environment allows for filming and sound recording without unwanted sights and sounds.

Soviet montage: See **montage**, definition 2.

spaghetti (or Italian) westerns: An Italian film movement from 1964 to the mid-1970s consisting of hundreds of westerns typically filmed in Italian studios and on mostly barren locations in Italy, Spain, or Yugoslavia and predominantly starring U.S. and Italian actors. (315–16)

special effect: A shot unobtainable by live-action cinematography. Includes freeze frames, most superimpositions, and many other effects, such as simulated explosions, live action combined with a painted background, and countless computer effects, as in *Lawnmower Man* (Plate 51).

spherical lens: A lens that transmits the image to the film in the camera without squeezing or compressing the image. Movies shown in the widely used 1.85:1 aspect ratio are filmed with spherical lenses. See also **anamorphic lens**.

splice: *As a verb:* To attach the end of one piece of film to the beginning of another piece of film. *As a noun:* The connection between two shots. See Figure 3.4 on p. 120.

spoof: See **parody**.

staged documentary: See **fake documentary**.

standard aspect ratio: Until the 1950s, the usual shape of motion-picture screens throughout the world and the approximate shape of analog (predigital) TV screens. On screens with the standard aspect ratio, the ratio of the width to the height is 1.33:1 or 4:3 (below). (38)

> **1.33:1 or 4:3**
> Standard aspect ratio

Steadicam: A lightweight and portable mount for holding a movie camera (and usually a monitor) that provides for relatively steady camera movements during moving handheld shots. Especially useful for filming in rugged terrain or tight quarters. (97)

stereotype: A commonplace, simplified, and in some ways inaccurate representation (likeness of a subject created in a text). As various scholars who have studied the representations of groups in films have shown, stereotypes of groups can help perpetuate the belief that certain groups are inferior to other groups. Films and other texts may use stereotypes in many other ways—for example, to represent subjects in an exaggerated manner for the purpose of satire. See also **representation**.

still: See **publicity still**.

stock footage: Footage stored for possible duplication and use in other films. Often stock footage is of subjects and locations difficult, impossible, or costly to film anew, such as warfare or the Paris background in the flashback sequence of *Casablanca*.

stop-motion cinematography: The process of filming a two- or three-dimensional subject, stopping the camera, making some change(s) in the subject being filmed, and resuming filming, either in the same laborious manner or by filming continuously. Usually the term refers to the process of filming a subject for one frame or a few frames, stopping the camera, changing something in the mise en scène, filming one more frame or perhaps a few frames, and repeating this process many times. Most often, stop-motion cinematography is used to create animated films (see Figures 9.17–9.18 on pp. 424, 425). Stop-motion cinematography also may be used to show the disappearance of a subject or the replacement of one subject by another one. It also may be used to show

changes in a subject over a long period of time—for example, the different stages of building a barn. See also **pixilation** and **time-lapse cinematography**. (424)

story: In this book, a narrative—that is, a representation of a series of unified events situated in one or more settings. See **narrative** and **fabula**.

storyboards: A series of drawings (or occasionally photographs) of each shot of a planned film or video story, often accompanied by written dialogue, brief descriptions, or notes (below). (209)

story time: The amount of time represented in a film's narrative or story. For example, if a movie's earliest scene occurs on a Sunday and its latest scene takes place on the following Friday, then the story time is six days. The story time for a movie is nearly always much longer than its running time. See **running time**. (286)

straight cut: See **cut** (as a noun).

structure: The arrangement of the parts of a whole text. In a narrative film, structure can be thought of as the arrangement of scenes or sequences. In nonnarrative films, *structure* refers to the arrangement of a film's discernible parts. In a nonnarrative documentary film, for example, the structure might consist of the arrangement of interviews and film clips. Sometimes called *form*. (261)

studio (era): The period of U.S. film history from the 1920s to the 1950s during which large studios such as MGM, Paramount, and Warner Bros. used a factory-style system with each worker employed in a specialized department such as editing and with creative control largely concentrated in the hands of senior studio executives.

Using this system, studios mass-produced mostly genre movies that dominated film markets throughout the United States and much of the world.

studio system: See **studio (era)**.

style: The way that subjects are represented in a text, such as a film. Styles for films or parts of films include abstract, black comedy, expressionism, magic realism, parody, realism, satire, and socialist realism. Style is sometimes contrasted with subject, though many theorists argue that the two are symbiotic. (289)

subjective camera: See **point-of-view shot**.

superimposition:

Two or more images photographed or printed on top of each other. Can be achieved in the camera during filming or, more often, by using an optical printer or computer (above). At the beginning of many movies, the credits are superimposed on graphic designs or on the film's opening events. During a lap dissolve, one image is momentarily superimposed on another. Sometimes, as in several scenes in *Drugstore Cowboy*, two or more shots are superimposed to suggest a character's emotional or physical instability. The technique is used often in experimental films and sometimes in documentary films. (130)

surrealism: A movement in 1920s and 1930s European art, drama, literature, and film in which an attempt was made to portray the workings of the subconscious mind as manifested in dreams. Surrealism is characterized by an irrational, noncontextual arrangement of subjects. The surrealist movement has been especially influential on some experimental filmmakers, such as Luis Buñuel ("Un chien andalou" and *L'age d'or*) and Jean Cocteau, especially his "The Blood of a Poet." Directly or through intermediate sources, surrealism has also influenced some music videos and later experimental filmmakers.

swish pan: (1) The too-rapid horizontal pivoting of a movie camera during filming that results in blurred images. (2) The shot that results when a movie camera is pivoted too rapidly during filming and blurred footage results. A swish pan may be used as a shot or within a shot (see Figure 2.52 on p. 95). (95)

symbol: Anything perceptible that has meaning beyond its usual meaning or function. Depending on the contexts, a sound, object, person, word (including a name), color, action, or something else perceived by the senses may function as a symbol. In *Citizen Kane*, for example, many viewers believe that the glass paperweight that Kane drops at the beginning of the film and that is seen two other times is not simply an object serving its usual function (as a paperweight) but is also a symbol. (525)

symptomatic meaning: A meaning in a text that is the same as a belief of a society or social group. For example, one meaning of the classic 1954 Japanese film *The Seven Samurai* is that in unity (not individuality) there is strength, and that meaning is also a deeply held belief in traditional Japanese society. When a meaning is the same as part of a group's ideology, it can be called a *symptomatic* meaning. See **ideology** and **meaning**. (530)

take: A version of a shot. Directors often call for additional takes because of some mistake or imperfection in the original take. Different takes of each shot are usually made in shooting theatrical films. One of the major tasks of the editor is to select the most effective take of each shot that is used in the finished film.

technique: See **film(making) technique**.

telephoto lens: A

lens that makes all subjects in an image appear closer to the camera than is the case with a normal lens. With its long barrel, a telephoto lens resembles a telescope. Not to be confused with a zoom lens, which is capable of varying by degrees from telephoto range to normal, sometimes even to wide-angle range, while the camera is filming. (79)

text: Something that people produce or modify to communicate meaning. Examples are films, photographs, paintings, newspaper articles, operas, T-shirts with a message, or a piece of driftwood that has "Help!" or something else written on it.

theme: See **meaning**.

THX sound: A multispeaker sound system developed by Lucasfilm and used in selected movie theaters to increase frequency range, audience coverage, and dialogue intelligibility while decreasing low bass distortion.

tight framing: A shot in which there is little visible space around the main subjects—for example, the main subjects are near the edges of the frame, and a wall behind them is nearby. Uses for such framing include giving a sense of the subject's confinement or lack of mobility (below). Opposite of **loose framing**. (*18*)

tilting: Pivoting a movie camera vertically during filming, usually while the camera is attached to a stationary base, such as a tripod, or is being held by a stationary camera operator. Often used to gradually reveal information, as when we first see someone's shoes and then the camera tilts up to reveal the wearer. This is done memorably near the beginning of Hitchcock's *Strangers on a Train*. See also **panning**.

time-lapse cinematography: The process of filming the same subject one frame at a time, usually at regularly spaced intervals during which considerable time passes—for example, one frame every hour or one frame every 24 hours. When the processed film or the video is projected at normal speed, any change that was photographed is much accelerated, perhaps even blurred. Can be used to show quickly the changes in a long process, such as the building of a house or the budding of a flower. Time-lapse cinematography can be used for many other purposes, as in parts of the experimental documentary *Koyaanisqatsi* to suggest the hectic pace of modern urban life (top of next column). See **stop-motion cinematography**.

tinting: The process of dyeing motion-picture film with color. Sometimes used before the adoption of color film stock in the 1930s. In tinted movies, often each scene or sequence was dyed the same color. For example, blue was often used for night scenes or scenes set in the cold, and red for scenes of violence, danger, passion, or heat. (Plates 2–3)

title card: A card or thin sheet of clear plastic on which is written or printed information included in a film. Before the late 1920s, title cards were used to supply credits, exposition, dialogue, thoughts, descriptions of actions not shown, the numbered parts of a movie, and other types of information. Since the late 1920s, they have been used less often, but they are seen, for example, in some documentary films, such as *The Thin Blue Line*, *Hearts of Darkness*, and *Hoop Dreams*; in occasional experimental films; and sometimes in fictional films, as in the 1995 *Richard III* and *The Blair Witch Project* (below).

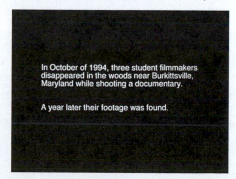

track: *As a verb:* To film while the camera is being moved around. Sometimes the camera is mounted on a cart set on tracks. Other times, the camera is handheld, and the camera operator moves or is moved about in a wheelchair, on roller skates, or by some other means. In some publications, *to track* and *to dolly* are used interchangeably. *As a noun:* A film soundtrack, a narrow band on the film that contains recorded optical, magnetic, or digital sound. (*99, 161*)

trailer: A brief compilation film shown in movie theaters, before some videotaped movies, on DVDs, on TV, and on the Web to advertise a movie or video release. Trailers are so named because originally they appeared at the end of a reel of film, not, as now, before a film showing.

treatment: A condensed written description of the content of a proposed film, often written in paragraphs and without dialogue.

underground film: See **experimental film**.

vaudeville: A type of live U.S. theatrical show consisting of a variety of short acts, such as comedy duos, slapstick comedy acts, dancers, song-and-dance acts, magicians, acrobats, jugglers, and trained animal acts. Although it is not identified as such, a vaudeville act is included in the movie *Singin' in the Rain* (below). Vaudeville was the most popular form of public entertainment in the United States during the early twentieth century, and many movie actors—such as Buster Keaton, the Marx Brothers, W. C. Fields, Ginger Rogers, and Eddie Cantor—had a background in vaudeville. In the early years of cinema, vaudeville acts often preceded a movie showing or were included between short movies, and they influenced many later movie musicals and movie comedies and later still radio and TV shows. For various reasons, vaudeville theaters disappeared as early sound movies and radio grew in popularity.

virtual reality: A three-dimensional computer-generated environment that users experience by wearing special goggles, fiber-optic gloves, and perhaps body sensors. While in virtual reality, users of the technology feel as if they are interacting with the simulated world. Images of virtual reality have been an occasional subject in movies, such as *Logan's Run*, *Lawnmower Man*, and the *Matrix* films. (Plate 51)

Vitaphone: Motion-picture sound system first used commercially in 1927 consisting of (1) a movie camera synchronized to a phonograph recorder and (2) a movie projector synchronized with the phonograph recording. (*160*)

voice-over: See **narration**.

wide-angle lens: A camera lens (significantly shorter than 50 mm on a 35 mm camera) that makes all subjects in an image appear farther from the camera and from each other than is the case with a normal lens. The wide-angle lens also renders subjects at all distances from the camera in sharp focus and captures more of the sides of the image than is possible with a normal lens, though at the cost of some distortion (below). (*79*)

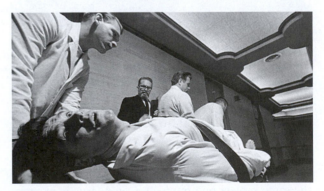

wide-screen: A film format with an aspect ratio noticeably greater than 1.33:1 (a shape wider than that of an analog or predigital TV screen). Most current films shown in U.S. commercial theaters have a wide-screen aspect ratio of 1.85:1. Wide-screen film formats have been tried since nearly the beginning of cinema but have been used in most movie theaters only since the 1950s. (*39*)

wipe: A transition between shots, usually between scenes, in which one shot appears to be pushed off the screen by the next shot. Many kinds of wipes are possible—such as a vertical line (sharp or blurred) that moves across the frame from one side to the other, seemingly "wiping away" a shot and replacing it with the next one (below). (124)

zip pan: See **swish pan**.

zoom: To use a zoom lens on a movie or video camera to cause the image of the subject to either increase in size as the area being filmed seems to decrease (zoom in) or to decrease in size as the area being filmed seems to increase (zoom out).

zoom lens: A camera lens with variable focal lengths that can be adjusted by degrees during a shot so that the size of the subject and the size of the area being filmed both change. *During* filming, the lens may assume the properties of a telephoto lens, normal lens, or wide-angle lens. Since the 1960s, the zoom lens has often been used in documentary filmmaking and in making many other films. For example, throughout nearly all of the experimental film "Wavelength," the movie camera imperceptibly zooms in on a photograph on the background wall. Instead of using a zoom lens, some cinematographers prefer to use lenses with a fixed focal length because they produce somewhat sharper images than zoom lenses do.

How to Read Film Credits

Most movies now run a list of credits at the end identifying the many people who worked on the film. Some movies use the closing credits to slip in a fleeting disclaimer about the story's sources or about material that was not a source. In recent years, closing credits have generally become longer—and longer. Perhaps the closing credits for *The Lord of the Rings: The Return of the King* (2003) set the record for length, running an eye-glazing 9½ minutes (Kennedy). So tedious have some closing credits become that some are broken up by outtakes of flubbed shots or by whimsical messages. According to veteran film critic Andrew Sarris, the closing credits for one film included the reminder that if you had left the theater "at the beginning of these credits, you'd be home by now" (Fox). Other filmmakers have included whimsical fake credits, such as "Things to Do After the Movie." At the end of John Waters's *Serial Mom* (1994), viewers can read that "No Flies Were Harmed in the Making of This Film" (Fox). And in the closing credits of *Airplane!* (1980), Mike Finnel is credited as being "GENERALLY IN CHARGE OF A LOT OF THINGS." But did you ever wonder what all the other, more serious credits mean—what, for example, a gaffer does, or a best boy, or a grip? To help you appreciate the work involved in making a movie, the closing credits from *The Player* (1992) are reprinted here along with brief explanations of the terms that a typical viewer might not know.

Parts of this book explain the roles of the filmmakers with the high-profile jobs: writers, producers, directors, actors, designers, cinematographers, editors, and composers. As in many recent films, in *The Player* these people are identified in the opening credits. (In many older films, additional filmmakers are listed in the opening credits, but that is now rarely done.) The closing credits of *The Player*, listed here, identify all the actors and many other people who are associated with the production but are not listed at the film's beginning.

A caution: Film credits do not always indicate accurately who did what. Some job titles are largely ceremonial, favors to friends, supporters, or movie executives with clout. Two films may use a different term to indicate the same type of work. Then, too, some job titles are simply vague, and others (such as *construction coordinator* and *construction foreman* and *promotion* and *publicity*) are synonymous or overlapping. All these caveats aside, most titles and descriptions accurately describe who did what. Although you cannot always know what certain producers do, you can be certain what Foley artists and dolly grips do.

CLOSING CREDITS FOR *THE PLAYER*

CAST

These actors have major roles and appear in several scenes. Except for Sydney Pollack's name, their names also appear in the opening credits.

Griffin Mill	TIM ROBBINS
June Gudmundsdottir	GRETA SCACCHI
Walter Stuckel	FRED WARD
Detective Avery	WHOOPI GOLDBERG
Larry Levy	PETER GALLAGHER
Joel Levison	BRION JAMES
Bonnie Sherow	CYNTHIA STEVENSON
David Kahane	VINCENT D'ONOFRIO
Andy Civella	DEAN STOCKWELL
Tom Oakley	RICHARD E. GRANT
Dick Mellen	SYDNEY POLLACK
Detective DeLongpre	LYLE LOVETT
Celia	DINA MERRILL
Jan	ANGELA HALL

These actors have minor roles. Most of them appear in only one scene.

Sandy	LEAH AYRES
Jimmy Chase	PAUL HEWITT
Reg Goldman	RANDALL BATINKOFF
Steve Reeves	JEREMY PIVEN
Whitney Gersh	GINA GERSHON
Frank Murphy	FRANK BARHYDT
Marty Grossman	MIKE E. KAPLAN
Gar Girard	KEVIN SCANNELL
Witness	MARGERY BOND
Detective Broom	SUSAN EMSHWILLER
Phil	BRIAN BROPHY
Eric Schecter	MICHAEL TOLKIN
Carl Schecter	STEPHEN TOLKIN
Natalie	NATALIE STRONG
Waiter	PETE KOCH
Trixie	PAMELA BOWEN
Rocco	JEFF WESTON

AS THEMSELVES

These are all of the sixty-five cameos—brief roles played by well-known people.

STEVE ALLEN	MAXINE JOHN-JAMES
RICHARD ANDERSON	SALLY KELLERMAN
RENE AUBERJONOIS	SALLY KIRKLAND
HARRY BELAFONTE	JACK LEMMON
SHARI BELAFONTE	MARLEE MATLIN
KAREN BLACK	ANDIE MacDOWELL
MICHAEL BOWEN	MALCOLM McDOWELL
GARY BUSEY	JAYNE MEADOWS
ROBERT CARRADINE	MARTIN MULL

These are all of the sixty-five cameos—brief roles played by well-known people.

CHARLES CHAMPLIN
CHER
JAMES COBURN
CATHY LEE CROSBY
JOHN CUSACK
BRAD DAVIS
PAUL DOOLEY
THEREZA ELLIS
PETER FALK
FELICIA FARR
KASIA FIGURA
LOUISE FLETCHER
DENNIS FRANZ
TERI GARR
LEEZA GIBBONS
SCOTT GLENN
JEFF GOLDBLUM
ELLIOTT GOULD
JOEL GREY
DAVID ALAN GRIER
BUCK HENRY
ANJELICA HUSTON
KATHY IRELAND
STEVE JAMES

JENNIFER NASH
NICK NOLTE
ALEXANDRA POWERS
BERT REMSEN
GUY REMSEN
PATRICIA RESNICK
BURT REYNOLDS
JACK RILEY
JULIA ROBERTS
MIMI ROGERS
ANNIE ROSS
ALAN RUDOLPH
JILL ST. JOHN
SUSAN SARANDON
ADAM SIMON
ROD STEIGER
JOAN TEWKESBURY
BRIAN TOCHI
LILY TOMLIN
ROBERT WAGNER
RAY WALSTON
BRUCE WILLIS
MARVIN YOUNG

Works closely with the producer(s) on artistic and financial matters. Unlike some "producers," the associate producer has day-to-day involvement with the making of the film.

Manages the production crew and the business arrangements for each day's shooting, such as housing, meals, transportation, and payroll.

The director's assistants; typically they keep track of scheduling, manage crowd scenes, supervise rehearsals, and prepare call sheets and production reports.

Responsible for the business and administrative aspects of making a film; assisted by the associate producer.

Associate Producer	DAVID LEVY
Unit Production Manager	TOM UDELL
First Assistant Director	ALLAN NICHOLS
Second Assistant Director	CC BARNES

Often the film editor is listed only in the opening credits. For *The Player*, the opening credits list Geraldine Peroni as the editor; thus, this listing is a puzzle. Perhaps the credit here should have read "Assistant Film Editor." Or perhaps Maysie Hoy edited only the clip from *Habeas Corpus*, the film-within-the-film in *The Player*.

Film Editor	MAYSIE HOY

Aka Production Manager. Supervises and coordinates all business and technical matters.

Production Executives	CLAUDIA LEWIS
	PAMELA HEDLEY
Production Supervisor	JIM CHESNEY

Decides how to decorate the indoor sets with furniture, props, art, and so on.

Creates the look of the film and runs the art department; ultimately responsible for all the visuals in the film, including architecture, locations, sets, decor, props, costumes, and makeup.

Art Director	JERRY FLEMING
Set Decorator	SUSAN EMSHWILLER
Leadman	PETER BORCK
Location Manager	JACK KNEY

Finds locations for shooting and negotiates for their use.

In *The Player*, one scene occurs in a karaoke bar, where videos are playing in the background. This person made those videos.

First Assistant Camera	ROBERT REED ALTMAN
Second Assistant Camera	CARY McKRYSTAL
Third Assistant Camera	CRAIG FINETTI
Karaoke Videos	LARRY "DOC" KARMAN

The camera crew; they maintain the equipment, load the film, and use a clapboard or comparable electronic device to mark the beginning of each take.

The editor's assistants; they splice the film, maintain the editing equipment, and keep records.

Assistant Editor
Second Assistant Editor
Apprentice Editor

A. MICHELLE PAGE
ALISA HALE
DYLAN TICHENOR

Supervising Sound Editor
Dialogue Editors
Sound Effects Editor
Assistant Sound Editor

MICHAEL REDBOURN
JOSEPH HOLSEN
ED LACHMANN
KEN BURTON
BILL WARD

Responsible for the final soundtrack; supervises the mixer, ADR (automated dialogue replacement) editor, dialogue editor, sound effects editor, music editor, and assistant sound editor.

Edits the music to make sure it complements the film's action and the other elements of the soundtrack.

Music Editor
Music Scoring Mixer
Orchestration By

BILL BERNSTEIN
JOHN VIGRAN
THOMAS PASATIERI

Blends and balances the tracks of the various film scores.

Arranges the score for the parts of the orchestra.

Postproduction technicians who mix vocals, sound effects, music, and silence to produce the master soundtrack.

Re-Recording Mixers

MATTHEW IADAROLA
STANLEY KASTNER
RICH GOOCH
JOHN POST
PAUL HOLTZBORN
BOB DESCHAINE
DAVID JOBE

Records sound during shooting; reports to the production sound mixer.

Recordist
Foley Artists

Foley Mixer
Foley Recordist

Sound specialists who use various objects to simulate and record sound effects while synchronizing them with their corresponding movie images.

Mixes the sound produced during shooting to get the desired combination of vocals, sound effects, and ambient sound.

Production Sound Mixer
Boom Operator
Cable Puller

JOHN PRITCHETT, C.A.S.
JOEL SHRYACK
EMILY SMITH-BAKER

Sound technician who operates the boom, a pole with a microphone at one end.

Protects the cables and wires of the sound equipment from damage and the production crew from injuries from the cables and wires.

Gaffer
Best Boy Electric
Electricians

DON MUCHOW
ANDREW DAY
ROBERT BRUCE
VAL DE SALVO
TOM McGRATH
CHRIS REDDISH
ANTHONY T. MARRA II
MICHAEL J. FAHEY
WAYNE STROUD

The head electrician, assisted by the best boy electric. Supervises the electricians, who are responsible for supplying current and lights on the set.

Manages the grips, or stagehands, who set up and move equipment and props. Assisted by the best boy grip.

Key Grip
Best Boy Grip
Dolly Grip

Moves the dolly during shooting.

Stagehands or crew workers.

Grips

KEVIN FAHEY
SCOTT "EL GATO" HOLLANDER
TIM NASH

Obtains the costumes and takes care of them during filming. Assisted by the wardrobe assistants.

Wardrobe Supervisor
Wardrobe Assistants

LYDIA TANJI
ANGELA BILLOWS
VICKI BRINKKORD
DEBORAH LARSEN
SCOTT WILLIAMS
SYDNEY COOPER

Arranges the actors' hair.

In *The Player*, the character June is an artist, and her artworks are seen in her house. This person created that art.

Runs the makeup department; applies the makeup to the actors.

Make-Up Artist
Hairdresser
June's Artwork

Oversees acquisition and maintenance of all props. ———▶ Property Master   JAMES MONROE

Assistant Property Master   JULIE HEUER

Set Dressers   MATTHEW ALTMAN

Get the set ready for filming and disassemble it after filming.

JOHN BUCKLIN

DAVID RONAN

JIM SAMSON

Swing Gang   DANIEL ROTHENBERG

MARIO PEREZ

Assistant Location Manager   PAUL BOYDSTON

Scenic Painter   JOHN BEAUVAIS

The member of the construction crew who paints the sets. ———▶ Painter   RICKY RIGGS

Construction Coordinator   LOREN CORNEY

Construction Foreman   PAT MAURER

Supervise the construction crew, who make the sets.

Build the sets, furniture, props, and camera tracks. ———▶ Carpenters   CHRIS MARNEUS

DARRYL LEE

KENNETH FUNK

THOMAS CALLOWAY

JOHN EVANS

JUSTIN KRITZER

Responsible for coordinating the visual elements of the film (other than the camera work). ———▶ Art Department Coordinator   MICHELE GUASTELLO

Production Coordinator   CYNTHIA HILL ◀———

Assistant Coordinator   BETSY CHASSE

Production Secretary   STACY COHEN

An administrator in charge of communication, correspondence, travel, accommodations, and bill paying. Assisted by the assistant coordinator and the production secretary.

Keeps track of all expenditures during production and supervises payment of salaries and bills. Assisted by the assistant accountant. ———▶ Production Accountant   KIMBERLY EDWARDS SHAPIRO

Assistant Accountant   CHERYL KURK

Avenue Financial Representative   SHERI HALFON ◀———

Additional Accounting Service   JUDY GELETKO

Post-Production Accountant   CATHERINE WEBB

Avenue Pictures was a small film production company. Its chairman at the time *The Player* was produced was Cary Brokaw, who served as executive producer of *The Player*.

Personal assistants, who help the director and producers.

Assistant to Robert Altman   JIM McLINDON

Assistants to Cary Brokaw   ROBIN HAGE

DANIELLE KNIGHT

Sandcastle 5 Productions, Inc., is a small film and TV production company closely associated with Robert Altman. ———▶

Assistant to Nick Wechsler   ALISON BALIAN

Sandcastle 5 Representative   CELIA CONVERSE

Production Assistants   ANGIE BONNER

JOHN BROWN III

SIGNE CORRIERE

STEVE DAY

KELLY HOUSEHOLDER

Run errands for the director and assist him or her in various other small ways.

Keeps a log of the details in each shot to make sure continuity is maintained from shot to shot. ———▶ Script Supervisor   CAROLE STARKES

Stunt Coordinator   GREG WALKER ◀———

Plans, arranges, and supervises the stunts.

Special Effects   JOHN HARTIGAN ◀———

The department responsible for the shots unobtainable by live-action cinematography.

Handles the animals on the set; in *The Player*, a rattlesnake appears twice. ———▶ Animal Trainer   JIM BROCKETT

Still Photographer   LOREY SEBASTIAN ◀———

Takes photographs for publicity and advertising.

Set Medic   TOM MOORE

Responsible for maintaining and operating all vehicles.

Drive the vehicles that transport equipment and personnel.

Perform odd jobs, such as getting coffee and snacks for the cast and crew.

Hires the actors who speak no lines and do not stand out as individuals.

Lab person who adjusts the color of the negative as needed, often in coordination with the cinematographer.

Designs the words that appear on the screen (such as the credits).

This organization, here a Japanese-based bank, lent the producers money to produce the film.

Publicizes the film through advertising and other publicity.

Arranges publicity events, such as interviews and appearances.

Transportation Coordinator	DEREK RASER
Transport Captain	"J. T." THAYER
Drivers	CHRISTOPHER ARMSTRONG
	RON CHESNEY
	STEVE EARLE
	DON FEENEY
	D. J. GARDINER
	GREG WILLIS
Caterer	RICK BRAININ CATERING
Craft Service	STUART McCAULEY
	ANDREA BERTY
Extras Casting	MAGIC CASTING
Location Security	ARTIS SECURITY
Negative Cutter	BOB HART
Color By	DELUXE ®
Color Timer	MICHAEL STANWICK
Titles & Opticals By	MERCER TITLE & OPTICAL
Title Design	DAN PERRI
Legal Services	SINCLAIR TENNENBAUM & Co.
	WYMAN & ISAACS
Financing Provided By	THE DAIWA BANK LTD.
Completion Bond	FILM FINANCES, INC.
Promotions Arranged By	ANDREW VARELA
Publicity By	CLEIN + WHITE INC.
Title Painting By	CHARLES BRAGG

Maintains security for scenes shot on location.

Cuts and splices the negative to make it match the final edited version of the film.

Uses an optical printer or perhaps a computer to create the words that appear on the screen.

The company responsible for drawing up the contract between the producers and the financiers that guarantees the film will be completed at a set time and within a set budget.

SPECIAL THANKS TO

PATRICK MURRAY	SUZANNE GOLDMAN	MIMI RABINOWITZ
RANDY HONAKER	TOYOKO NEZU	MORGAN ENTREKIN
LUIS ESTEVEZ	REEBOK	GEOWORKS
BASELINE	MARK EISEN	BALLY

These people or companies donated products or services or allowed the filmmakers to use certain locations. For *The Player*, companies such as Reebok, Bally, and Range Rover may have paid a fee for product placement.

GERALD GREENBACH & TWO BUNCH PALMS
BOB FLICK & ENTERTAINMENT TONIGHT
STEVE TROMBATORE & ALL PAYMENTS
RANGE ROVER OF NORTH AMERICA
MARCHON/MARCOLIN EYE WEAR
SPINNEYBECK/DESIGN AMERICA
HARRY WINSTON JEWELERS
L.A. MARATHON

These people or companies donated products or services or allowed the filmmakers to use certain locations. For *The Player*, companies such as Reebok, Bally, and Range Rover may have paid a fee for product placement.

THE LOS ANGELES COUNTY MUSEUM OF ART
JANIS DINWIDDIE
JULIE JOHNSTON
RON HAVER
THE LES HOOPER ORCHESTRA

THE BICYCLE THIEF
© RICHARD FEINER & CO., INC.

These are copyright acknowledgments, required whenever a film uses material that someone else claims copyright to.

"SNAKE" & "DRUMS OF KYOTO"
© Lia-Mann Music
Written & Performed By
KURT NEUMANN

"TEMA PARA JOBIM"
© Mulligan Publishing Co., Inc.
Music by GERRY MULLIGAN
Lyrics by JOYCE
Performed by JOYCE
MILTON NASCIMENTO
Courtesy of Estudio Pointer Ltda.
& RCA Electronica Ltda.

"PRECIOUS"
Written by LES HOOPER
© Chesford Music Publications

ENTERTAINMENT TONIGHT
Theme by
MICHAEL MARK
Published by ADDAX MUSIC CO. INC.

Re-Recording Facilities
SKYWALKER SOUND
A division of LucasArts Entertainment Company

This film recorded digitally in a THX Sound System Theatre.

RECORDED IN
ULTRA-STEREO

SOURCES

Fox, Margalit. "Where There's Life after 'The End.'" *New York Times* 29 Nov. 1998, late ed.: sec. 2: 17.
IMDb Film Glossary (Internet Movie Database Web site).
Katz, Ephraim. *The Film Encyclopedia*. 5th ed. Rev. Fred Klein and Ronald Dean Nolen. New York: Collins, 2005.
Kennedy, Randy. "Who Was That Food Stylist? Film Credits Roll On." *New York Times* 11 Jan. 2004, final ed.: sec. 1: 1.

Knox, Dave. *Strike the Baby and Kill the Blonde: An Insider's Guide to Film Slang*. New York: Three Rivers, 2005.

Konigsberg, Ira. *The Complete Film Dictionary*. 2nd ed. New York: Penguin, 1997.

Oracle ThinkQuest Education Foundation. Reference section. Glossary. Web source.

Singleton, Ralph S., and James A. Conrad. *Filmmaker's Dictionary*. 2nd ed. Hollywood: Lone Eagle, 2000.

Acknowledgments

Front Cover Photos, from top to bottom:
An Inconvenient Truth
Lagaan
Casablanca
2046
Persepolis

Back Cover Photos, from top to bottom:
The Lives of Others
No Country for Old Men
Killer of Sheep
Maria Full of Grace

All Photos: The Kobal Collection

Text Illustrations (in addition to individual captions):
Dave Blazek. "Loose Parts." First published in the *Eau Claire Leader Telegram*, 5/18/05.
    Used with permission of The Permissions Group, on behalf of TMS Reprints.
Jonik. Cartoon Arts International/CWS. Reprinted with permission.
Gary Larson. *The Far Side.* Copyright © 1992 Farworks, Inc. Used with permission of
    Creator's Syndicate.
NON SEQUITUR © 1999 Wiley Miller. Distributed by Universal Press Syndicate.
    Reprinted with permission. All rights reserved.
"The Roxy Movie Theatre Booklet." Used with permission of Photofest, Inc.

Index

P AGE NUMBERS IN **boldface** type refer to the most helpful discussion of a subject. Page numbers in *italic* type refer to the images or captions. Numbers within parentheses are usually dates of films.

Many films get made because of people and funding from various countries. For example, *Babel* (2006) was made by a Mexican director, Mexican writers, a Mexican cinematographer, and various Mexican actors, but the film stars an American male actor and an Australian female actor; the film's original music is by an Argentinean; filming took place in the four countries where the film's four plotlines take place: Japan, Morocco, Mexico, and the United States. *Babel* incorporates the following languages: English, Arabic, Spanish, Japanese, Japanese Sign Language, Berber, and French. It is impossible for the casual researcher to discover where all the funding came from. The Internet Movie Database (IMDb) identifies the film's "country" as France, USA, and Mexico. Due to these kinds of complications, judgment calls were made with regard to the "country" of certain films. A subentry for *Babel*, for instance, is included under the entry "Mexico, cinema of," but not under the entries for France or the United States.